IFIP Advances in Information and Communication Technology 455

IFIP – The International Federation for Information Processing

IFIP was founded in 1960 under the auspices of UNESCO, following the First World Computer Congress held in Paris the previous year. An umbrella organization for societies working in information processing, IFIP's aim is two-fold: to support information processing within its member countries and to encourage technology transfer to developing nations. As its mission statement clearly states,

> *IFIP's mission is to be the leading, truly international, apolitical organization which encourages and assists in the development, exploitation and application of information technology for the benefit of all people.*

IFIP is a non-profitmaking organization, run almost solely by 2500 volunteers. It operates through a number of technical committees, which organize events and publications. IFIP's events range from an international congress to local seminars, but the most important are:

- The IFIP World Computer Congress, held every second year;
- Open conferences;
- Working conferences.

The flagship event is the IFIP World Computer Congress, at which both invited and contributed papers are presented. Contributed papers are rigorously refereed and the rejection rate is high.

As with the Congress, participation in the open conferences is open to all and papers may be invited or submitted. Again, submitted papers are stringently refereed.

The working conferences are structured differently. They are usually run by a working group and attendance is small and by invitation only. Their purpose is to create an atmosphere conducive to innovation and development. Refereeing is also rigorous and papers are subjected to extensive group discussion.

Publications arising from IFIP events vary. The papers presented at the IFIP World Computer Congress and at open conferences are published as conference proceedings, while the results of the working conferences are often published as collections of selected and edited papers.

Any national society whose primary activity is about information processing may apply to become a full member of IFIP, although full membership is restricted to one society per country. Full members are entitled to vote at the annual General Assembly, National societies preferring a less committed involvement may apply for associate or corresponding membership. Associate members enjoy the same benefits as full members, but without voting rights. Corresponding members are not represented in IFIP bodies. Affiliated membership is open to non-national societies, and individual and honorary membership schemes are also offered.

More information about this series at http://www.springer.com/series/6102

Hannes Federrath · Dieter Gollmann (Eds.)

ICT Systems Security and Privacy Protection

30th IFIP TC 11 International Conference, SEC 2015
Hamburg, Germany, May 26–28, 2015
Proceedings

 Springer

Editors
Hannes Federrath
Universität Hamburg
Hamburg
Germany

Dieter Gollmann
Technische Universität Hamburg-Harburg
Hamburg
Germany

ISSN 1868-4238   ISSN 1868-422X   (electronic)
IFIP Advances in Information and Communication Technology
ISBN 978-3-319-38707-9   ISBN 978-3-319-18467-8   (eBook)
DOI 10.1007/978-3-319-18467-8

Springer Cham Heidelberg New York Dordrecht London
© IFIP International Federation for Information Processing 2015
 Softcover reprint of the hardcover 1st edition 2015

Printed on acid-free paper

Springer International Publishing AG Switzerland is part of Springer Science+Business Media
(www.springer.com)

Preface

These proceedings contain the papers presented at the 30th IFIP International Information Security and Privacy Conference (SEC 2015), hosted in Hamburg, Germany, May 26–28, 2015.

IFIP SEC conferences are the flagship events of the International Federation for Information Processing (IFIP) Technical Committee 11 on Information Security and Privacy Protection in Information Processing Systems (TC-11).

In response to the call for papers, 232 papers were submitted to the conference, of which 20 were withdrawn by the authors. Thus, 212 papers were distributed to the reviewers. These papers were evaluated on the basis of their significance, novelty, and technical quality.

Using EasyChair, each paper was reviewed by four members of the Program Committee and Additional Reviewers. The Program Committee meeting was held electronically with a discussion period of one week. Of the papers submitted, 42 full papers were accepted for presentation at the conference.

We wish to thank the 126 Program Committee members and the 180 additional reviewers for their great effort in managing the unexpected quantity and variety of the papers submitted to IFIP SEC 2015. Additionally, we thank all authors for their submissions and contributions to the conference.

We thank the University of Hamburg for hosting this conference, HITeC e.V. for their organizational support, and all people who spent their time on various organization tasks in the background and at the conference desk. A very special thank is dedicated to the Organizing Chair Dominik Herrmann.

March 2015

Hannes Federrath
Dieter Gollmann

Organization

IFIP SEC 2015 was organized by the Department of Computer Science, University of Hamburg, Germany.

General Chairs

Kai Rannenberg	Goethe-Universität Frankfurt, Germany
Steven Furnell	Plymouth University, UK

Program Chairs

Hannes Federrath	University of Hamburg, Germany
Dieter Gollmann	Technische Universität Hamburg-Harburg, Germany

Organizing Chair

Dominik Herrmann	University of Hamburg, Germany

Program Committee

Luca Allodi	University of Trento, Italy
Frederik Armknecht	University of Mannheim, Germany
Vijay Atluri	Rutgers University, USA
Matt Bishop	University of California, Davis, USA
Joan Borrell	Universitat Autònoma de Barcelona, Spain
Joppe W. Bos	NXP Semiconductors, Belgium
Christina Brzuska	Microsoft Research, UK
Rainer Böhme	University of Münster, Germany
William Caelli	International Information Security Consultants Pty Ltd, Australia
Jan Camenisch	IBM Research, Zurich, Switzerland
Iliano Cervesato	Carnegie Mellon University, USA
Eric Chan-Tin	Oklahoma State University, USA
Nathan Clarke	Plymouth University, UK
Frédéric Cuppens	Télécom Bretagne, France
Nora Cuppens-Boulahia	Télécom Bretagne, France

Sokratis Katsikas	University of Piraeus, Greece
Stefan Katzenbeisser	Technische Universität Darmstadt, Germany
Florian Kerschbaum	SAP Research, Germany
Dogan Kesdogan	University of Regensburg, Germany
Kwangjo Kim	KAIST, South Korea
Valentin Kisimov	University of National and World Economy, Bulgaria
Zbigniew Kotulski	Warsaw University of Technology, Poland
Stefan Köpsell	Technische Universität Dresden, Germany
Peter Lambert	Australian Defence Science and Technology Organisation
Christof Leng	International Computer Science Institute, USA
Luigi Logrippo	Université du Québec en Outaouais, Canada
Javier Lopez	University of Málaga, Spain
Emil Lupu	Imperial College London, UK
Heiko Mantel	Technische Universität Darmstadt, Germany
Stephen Marsh	University of Ontario Institute of Technology, Canada
Fabio Martinelli	IIT-CNR, Italy
Michael Meier	University of Bonn, Germany
Erik Moore	Regis University, USA
Martin Mulazzani	SBA Research, Austria
Yuko Murayama	Iwate Prefectural University, Japan
Vincent Naessens	Katholieke Universiteit Leuven, Belgium
Kara Nance	University of Alaska Fairbanks, USA
Eiji Okamoto	University of Tsukuba, Japan
Federica Paci	University of Trento, Italy
Jakob Illeborg Pagter	Security Lab, The Alexandra Institute Ltd, Denmark
Sebastian Pape	Technische Universität Dortmund, Germany
Malcolm Pattinson	The University of Adelaide, Australia
Philippos Peleties	USB BANK PLC, Cyprus
Günther Pernul	University of Regensburg, Germany
Gilbert Peterson	US Air Force Institute of Technology, USA
Joachim Posegga	University of Passau, Germany
Kai Rannenberg	Goethe-Universität Frankfurt, Germany
Indrajit Ray	Colorado State University, USA
Indrakshi Ray	Colorado State University, USA
Konrad Rieck	University of Göttingen, Germany
Carlos Rieder	isec ag, Luzern, Switzerland
Yves Roudier	EURECOM, France
Mark Ryan	University of Birmingham, UK
P.Y.A. Ryan	University of Luxembourg, Luxembourg
Pierangela Samarati	Università degli Studi di Milano, Italy
Thierry Sans	Carnegie Mellon University, USA

Damien Sauveron	XLIM/UMR University of Limoges, France
Ingrid Schaumüller-Bichl	University of Applied Sciences Upper Austria, Austria
Björn Scheuermann	Humboldt University of Berlin, Germany
Sebastian Schinzel	Münster University of Applied Sciences, Germany
Guido Schryen	University of Regensburg, Germany
Joerg Schwenk	Ruhr-Universität Bochum, Germany
Anne Karen Seip	Finanstilsynet, Norway
Jetzabel Serna-Olvera	Goethe-Universität Frankfurt, Germany
Abbas Shahim	University of Amsterdam, The Netherlands
Haya Shulman	Technische Universität Darmstadt, Germany
Adesina Sodiya	Federal University of Agriculture, Nigeria
Radu State	University of Luxembourg, Luxembourg
Thorsten Strufe	Technische Universität Dresden, Germany
Kerry-Lynn Thomson	Nelson Mandela Metropolitan University, South Africa
Bhavani Thuraisingham	University of Texas at Dallas, USA
Nils Ole Tippenhauer	Singapore University of Technology and Design, Singapore
Carmela Troncoso	Gradiant, Spain
Markus Tschersich	Goethe-Universität Frankfurt, Germany
Pedro Veiga	University of Lisbon, Portugal
Michael Vielhaber	Hochschule Bremerhaven, Germany
Teemupekka Virtanen	Ministry of Social Affairs and Health, Finland
Melanie Volkamer	Technische Universität Darmstadt, Germany
Rossouw Von Solms	Nelson Mandela Metropolitan University, South Africa
Jozef Vyskoc	VaF, Slovak Republic
Lingyu Wang	Concordia University, Canada
Christian Weber	Ostfalia University of Applied Sciences, Germany
Edgar Weippl	Vienna University of Technology, Austria
Steffen Wendzel	Fraunhofer FKIE, Germany
Gunnar Wenngren	Sweden
Jeff Yan	Newcastle University, UK
Zhenxin Zhan	Juniper Networks, USA
Alf Zugenmaier	Hochschule München, Germany
André Zúquete	DETI/IEETA, University of Aveiro, Portugal

Additional Reviewers

Abdali, Jamal	Arp, Daniel	Bilzhause, Arne
Ahn, Soohyun	Bal, Gökhan	Bkakria, Anis
Albarakati, Abdullah	Barrère, Martín	Blanco-Justicia, Alberto
Alcaraz, Cristina	Beck, Martin	Bottineli, Paul
Aminanto, Muhamad Erza	Belgacem, Boutheyna	Bou-Harb, Elias

Boukayoua, Fasyal
Boukoros, Spyros
Boulares, Sofiene
Budurushi, Jurlind
Buhov, Damjan
Caballero, Juan
Calviño, Aida
de La Piedra, Antonio
De Sutter, Bjorn
Denzel, Michael
Diener, Michael
Drijvers, Manu
Drogkaris, Prokopios
Engelke, Toralf
Farcasin, Michael
Fischer, Lars
Fitzsimons, Joseph
Fomichev, Mikhail
Freisleben, Bernd
Fuchs, Karl-Peter
Fuchs, Ludwig
Garcia, Fuensanta Torres
Garn, Bernhard
Gascon, Hugo
Gay, Richard
Gazeau, Ivan
Geneiatakis, Dimitris
Gerber, Christoph
Gerber, Paul
Gottschlich, Wolfram
Grewal, Gurchetan
Gruhn, Michael
Gudymenko, Ivan
Gutmann, Andreas
Hay, Brian
Heim, Stephan
Hernandez, Julio
Hils, Maximilian
Hobel, Heidi
Hu, Jinwei
Härterich, Martin
Imran Daud, Malik
Iwaya, Leonardo
Jakobsen, Thomas P.
Jakobsson, Markus
Jensen, Jonas Lindstrøm

Johansen, Christian
Jäschke, Angela
Kalloniatis, Christos
Kambourakis, Georgios
Kasem-Madani, Saffija
Katos, Vasilios
Kaur, Jaspreet
Kieseberg, Peter
Kim, Hakju
Koens, Tommy
Kokolakis, Spyros
Krasnova, Anna
Krombholz, Katharina
Kulyk, Oksana
Kunz, Michael
Kurtz, Andreas
Lackorzynski, Tim
Lancrenon, Jean
Lazrig, Ibrahim
Le, Meixing
Lemaire, Laurens
Lindemann, Jens
Liu, Jia
Liu, Joseph
Liu, Zhe
Lortz, Steffen
Lueks, Wouter
Mahalanobis, Ayan
Manzoor, Salman
Marktscheffel, Tobias
Mayer, Peter
Melissen, Matthijs
Mikhalev, Vasily
Mikkelsen, Gert Læssøe
Milutinovic, Milica
Moataz, Tarik
Morales, Roberto
Moussa, Bassam
Mulamba, Dieudonne
Muñoz-González, Luis
Müller, Tilo
Najafiborazjani, Parnian
Netter, Michael
Neumann, Stephan
Neuner, Sebastian
Nieto, Ana

Nikova, Svetla
Nishioka, Dai
Nordholt, Peter Sebastian
Nuñez, David
Octeau, Damien
Ølnes, Jon
Ordean, Mihai
Palomaki, Jussi
Perner, Matthias
Pimenidis, Lexi
Pohl, Christoph
Prigent, Nicolas
Put, Andreas
Ray, Sujoy
Reinfelder, Lena
Reiser, Hans P.
Reubold, Jan
Ribes González, Jordi
Ricci, Sara
Richthammer, Christian
Riek, Markus
Ringers, Sietse
Roman, Rodrigo
Roos, Stefanie
Roscoe, Bill
Roth, Christian
Rothstein Morris, Eric
Sabouri, Ahmad
Saito, Yoshia
Samelin, Kai
Saracino, Andrea
Schmitz, Christopher
Schöttle, Pascal
Sgandurra, Daniele
Simkin, Mark
Simos, Dimitris
Skjernaa, Berit
Skrobot, Marjan
Soria-Comas, Jordi
Starostin, Artem
Stepien, Bernard
Strizhov, Mikhail
Sänger, Johannes
Tesfay, Welderufael
Timchenko, Max
Tomandl, Andreas

Tonejc, Jernej	Wang, Ding	Yang, Shuzhe
Tzouramanis, Theodoros	Wang, Zhan	Yasasin, Emrah
Ullrich, Johanna	Weber, Alexandra	Yesuf, Ahmed Seid
Urquidi, Miguel	Weber, Michael	Yin, Xucheng
Venkatesan, Sridhar	Weishäupl, Eva	Yu, Jiangmin
Veseli, Fatbardh	Wressnegger, Christian	Yu, Jiangshan
Voelzow, Victor	Wundram, Martin	Zhang, Lei
Vossaert, Jan	Yaich, Reda	Zhang, Yuexin
Vullers, Pim	Yamaguchi, Fabian	Zimmer, Ephraim

Contents

Network Security

Security Management and Human Aspects of Security

Software Security

Applied Cryptography

Privacy

O-PSI: Delegated Private Set Intersection on Outsourced Datasets

Aydin Abadi, Sotirios Terzis, and Changyu Dong$^{(\boxtimes)}$

Department of Computer and Information Sciences,
University of Strathclyde, Glasgow, UK
{aydin.abadi,sotirios.terzis,changyu.dong}@strath.ac.uk

Abstract. Private set intersection (PSI) has a wide range of applications such as privacy-preserving data mining. With the advent of cloud computing it is now desirable to take advantage of the storage and computation capabilities of the cloud to outsource datasets and delegate PSI computation. In this paper we design O-PSI, a protocol for delegated private set intersection on outsourced datasets based on a novel point-value polynomial representation. Our protocol allows multiple clients to independently prepare and upload their private datasets to a server, and then ask the server to calculate their intersection. The protocol ensures that intersections can only be calculated with the permission of all clients and that datasets and results remain completely confidential from the server. Once datasets are outsourced, the protocol supports an unlimited number of intersections with no need to download them or prepare them again for computation. Our protocol is efficient and has computation and communication costs linear to the cardinality of the datasets. We also provide a formal security analysis of the protocol.

1 Introduction

Cloud computing allows clients with limited computation and storage capabilities to outsource their private data and at a later time, ask the cloud to perform computation on them. Delegation of data storage and computation to the cloud has become common practice for individuals and big enterprises alike [1,2]. As a result, often the need arises for clients to perform computation on their outsourced private data jointly, ideally without the need to download the data.

In this paper, we consider a particular such scenario, in which the private data take the form of sets and the computation of interest is set intersection, i.e. private set intersection (PSI).

In PSI, two parties want to find out the intersection of their sets and also want to prevent the other party from finding out anything more about their own set than the elements of the intersection. In general, PSI captures a wide range of real-world applications such as privacy preserving data mining [3], homeland security [4] and so on. For example, consider a case where a law enforcement agency has a list of suspects and wants to compare it against flight passenger lists. Here the names of the suspects should be kept hidden from the airlines

© IFIP International Federation for Information Processing 2015
H. Federrath and D. Gollmann (Eds.): SEC 2015, IFIP AICT 455, pp. 3–17, 2015.
DOI: 10.1007/978-3-319-18467-8_1

while the agency should not be able to find out about other passengers in order to protect their privacy. As another example, consider the situation where a social welfare organization wants to know whether any of its members receives income from another organization, but neither organization can reveal their list of members.

Although a number of protocols have been proposed for PSI (see section 2 for a survey), cloud computing introduces additional challenges as the private datasets are outsourced and the private set intersection is delegated to cloud servers. In addition to keeping their sets confidential, clients are also interested in preventing cloud servers from finding out anything about their sets and the intersection. In other words, clients are interested in *delegated private set intersection on outsourced data*. To allow for more flexibility it is desirable that clients should be able to engage in PSI computation with any other client of the cloud provider. However, they should remain in charge of deciding which clients are allowed to use their sets. To fully take advantage of the cloud capabilities and minimize costs, clients should not have to keep locally or download their datasets every time an intersection needs to be computed, while their involvement to the computation should be limited.

We propose O-PSI, a PSI protocol that addresses these requirements. Our protocol uses homomorphic encryption and a novel point-value polynomial representation for datasets that allows clients to independently secure their sets and outsource them to the cloud, while cloud servers are able to calculate their intersection. The protocol ensures that intersections can only be computed with the permission of the clients and that the result will remain secret from the server. The protocol also allows outsourced sets to be used an unlimited number of times securely without the need to secure them again. More interestingly, the novel set representation means that computation and communication costs are linear to the size of the sets.

The paper starts with a survey of related work in section 2, followed by a brief overview of our security model and key concepts we rely on in section 3. Section 4 presents the design of our protocol, while section 5 proves its security. Section 6 proposes extensions to support data integrity verification and multiple clients, while section 7 presents an analysis of its computation and communication complexity, and a comparison to work that is closest to our aims. Section 8 concludes the paper and identifies directions for future work.

2 Related Work

Private set intersection (PSI) was introduced in [5]. Following that [6] proposed a number of protocols supporting further set operations and multiple clients based on additive homomorphic encryption and polynomial representation of sets. More recently, several efficient protocols have been proposed. For example, [4,7] use blind signatures and hash functions to provide efficient PSI in the semi-honest and the malicious security models respectively, [8] uses Bloom filters, secret sharing and oblivious transfer to offer even more efficient protocols, and [9] extends [8] and uses hash tables and a more efficient oblivious transfer extension protocol for better efficiency. However, all these regular PSI protocols are interactive, in the sense that clients jointly compute the intersection. They are not designed with the capability to outsource any data or delegate any of the computation to a third party.

In another line of research, in [10,11] the protocols proposed for outsourced verifiable dynamic set operations, including set intersection. These protocols make use of bilinear map accumulators and authenticated hash tables (i.e. accumulator trees) to verify the correctness of operations carried out by a server on outsourced sets. However, these protocols are designed for a single client to outsource a collection of sets to a server and later to compute the intersections of its own sets. The protocols are designed to provide verifiability of computation, not data privacy. Data are outsourced in plaintext and the protocols do not work if data are encrypted.

More interestingly, a number of PSI protocols have been proposed in which clients delegate computation to a server [12–16]. A protocol proposed in [14] allows clients to outsource their sets to a server by hashing each element and adding a random value. They then delegate the computation of the intersection to the server. However, this protocol is not fully private, as it reveals to the server the cardinality of the intersection. In addition to the above issue, because of the way the sets are encoded if the intersection between the sets of client A and B is computed, followed by that between the sets of client A and C, then the server will also find out whether some elements are common in the sets of client B and C without their consent. In [16] clients also delegate the computation to a server. Clients encrypt their sets and outsource them. The server also provides a proof that allows the clients to verify the correctness of the result. However, the protocol is not fully private and suffers from the same issues described above. Another protocol that delegates computation to a server is proposed in [12]. The protocol is based on a pseudorandom permutation (PRP) of the set elements with the key for the PRP generated jointly by the clients at setup. One variant of the protocol can hide the cardinality of the intersection. However, in this variant computation is delegated to one of the clients rather than the server. The server's role is limited to re-encoding one client's set to maintain the privacy of the computation. In the protocol, clients can detect if the server provided incorrect results at the cost of replicating a number of times all elements of the sets.

In a similar line of research, a protocol proposed in [13] allows one client, say client A, to encrypt and outsource its set, and delegate computation to a server. The server can then engage in a PSI protocol on this client's behalf with another client, say client B. However, this delegation is one-off: if A wants to compute set intersection with C, then A must encrypt its set with a new key and re-delegate to the server. In addition to this protocol, in [15] two clients can delegate the PSI computation to a server. In this protocol rather than encrypting and outsourcing their sets, the clients encrypt and outsource bloom filters of their sets that are then used by the server to privately compute their intersection. However, in this case in order for the clients to get the result of the intersection they need to keep a local copy of their sets. So, this protocol does not really allow outsourcing the sets.

From the above discussion, it should be clear that none of the protocols above allows clients to fully delegate PSI computation to the server without the need to either maintain the sets locally or having to re-encode and re-upload the sets for each intersection computation, namely none support *delegated private set intersection on outsourced sets*. As a result, none of them are particularly suited for a cloud computing setting.

3 Preliminaries

3.1 Security Model

We consider a setting in which *static semi-honest* adversaries are present. In this setting, the adversary controls one of the parties and follows the protocol specification exactly. However, it may try to learn more information about the other party's input. The definitions and model are according to [17].

In a delegated PSI protocol, three parties are involved: a server P, and two clients A and B. We assume the server does not collude with A or B. As the server (or cloud provider) is often a well established IT company, it is reasonable to assume it will not collude with the clients because collusion will seriously damage its reputation and decrease its revenue. This non-colluding assumption is widely used in the literature [12, 18, 19]. The three-party protocol π computes a function that maps the inputs to some outputs. We define this function as follows: $F : \Lambda \times 2^{\mathcal{U}} \times 2^{\mathcal{U}} \to \Lambda \times \Lambda \times f_\cap$, where Λ denotes the empty string, $2^{\mathcal{U}}$ denotes the powerset of the set universe and $f_\cap$ denotes the set intersection function. For every tuple of inputs Λ, S_A and S_B belong to P, A and B respectively, the function outputs nothing to P and A, and outputs $f_\cap(S_A, S_B) = S_A \cap S_B$ to B.

In the semi-honest model, a protocol π is secure if whatever can be computed by a party in the protocol can be obtained from its input and output only. This is formalized by the simulation paradigm. We require a party's *view* in a protocol execution to be simulatable given only its input and output. The view of the party i during an execution of π on input tuple (x, y, z) is denoted by $\text{view}_i^\pi(x, y, z)$ and equals $(w, r^i, m_1^i, ..., m_t^i)$ where $w \in (x, y, z)$ is the input of i, r^i is the outcome of i's internal random coin tosses and m_j^i represents the jth message that it received.

Definition 1. *Let F be a deterministic function as defined above. We say that the protocol π securely computes F in the presence of static semi-honest adversaries if there exist probabilistic polynomial-time algorithms Sim_P, Sim_A and Sim_B that given the input and output of a party, can simulate a view that is computationally indistinguishable from the party's view in the protocol:*

$$Sim_P(\Lambda, \Lambda) \stackrel{c}{\equiv} \text{view}_P^\pi(\Lambda, S_A, S_B)$$

$$Sim_A(S_A, \Lambda) \stackrel{c}{\equiv} \text{view}_A^\pi(\Lambda, S_A, S_B)$$

$$Sim_B(S_B, f_\cap(S_A, S_B)) \stackrel{c}{\equiv} \text{view}_B^\pi(\Lambda, S_A, S_B)$$

3.2 Homomorphic Encryption

A semantically secure additively homomorphic public key encryption scheme has the following properties:

1. Given two ciphertexts $E_{pk}(a), E_{pk}(b)$, $E_{pk}(a) \cdot E_{pk}(b) = E_{pk}(a + b)$.
2. Given a ciphertext $E_{pk}(a)$ and a constant b, $E_{pk}(a)^b = E_{pk}(a \cdot b)$.

One such scheme is the Paillier public key cryptosystem [20]. It works as follows:

Key Generation: Choose two random large primes p and q according to a given security parameter, and set $N = pq$. Let u be the Carmichael value of N, i.e. $u = lcm(p - 1, q - 1)$ where lcm stands for the least common multiple. Choose a random $g \in \mathbb{Z}^*_{N^2}$, and ensure that $s = (L(g^u \bmod N^2))^{-1} \bmod N$ exists where $L(x) = \frac{(x-1)}{N}$. The public key is $pk = (N, g)$ and the secret key is $sk = (u, s)$.

Encryption: To encrypt a plaintext $m \in \mathbb{Z}_N$, pick a random value $r \in \mathbb{Z}^*_N$, and compute the ciphertext: $C = E_{pk}(m) = g^m \cdot r^N \bmod N^2$.

Decryption: To decrypt a ciphertext C, $D_{sk}(C) = L(C^u \bmod N^2) \cdot s \bmod N = m$.

3.3 Polynomial Representation of Sets

Many PSI protocols e.g. [5,6], use a polynomial representation of sets. Let R be a field, then we denote a polynomial ring as $R[x]$. The polynomial ring $R[x]$ consists of all polynomials with coefficients from R. Given a set S of size d, $|S| = d$, we can map each element in S to an element in a sufficiently large field R. Then we can represent this set as a polynomial in the polynomial ring $R[x]$. The polynomial is defined as $\rho(x) = \prod_{s_i \in S}(x - s_i)$ and has the property that every element $s_i \in S$ is a root of it.

For two sets S_A and S_B represented by polynomials ρ_A and ρ_B respectively, then $gcd(\rho_A, \rho_B)$ represents the set intersection $S_A \cap S_B$, where gcd stands for the greatest common divisor. For polynomials ρ_A and ρ_B of degree d and γ_A and γ_B that are degree d polynomials chosen uniformly at random from $R[x]$, it is proved in [6] that $\gamma_A \cdot \rho_A + \gamma_B \cdot \rho_B = \mu \cdot gcd(\rho_A, \rho_B)$ such that μ is a uniformly random polynomial. This means that if ρ_A and ρ_B are polynomials representing sets S_A and S_B, then the polynomial $\gamma_A \cdot \rho_A + \gamma_B \cdot \rho_B$ contains only information about $S_A \cap S_B$ and no information about other elements in S_A or S_B. This forms the basis of their PSI protocol in which a party obtains $\gamma_A \cdot \rho_A + \gamma_B \cdot \rho_B$ to find the set intersection but learns nothing more about elements in the other party's set.

4 O-PSI: Delegated Private Set Intersection on Outsourced Datasets

4.1 Polynomials in Point-value Form

In section 3.3 we showed that a set can be represented as a polynomial and set intersection can be computed by polynomial arithmetic. All previous PSI protocols using polynomial representation of sets, represent a polynomial as a vector of polynomial's coefficients. They represent a degree d polynomial $\rho = \sum_{i=0}^{d} a_i x^i$ as a vector $\mathbf{a} = (a_0, a_1, ..., a_d)$. This representation, while it allows the protocols to correctly compute the result, has a major disadvantage. The complexity of multiplying two polynomials of degree d in co-efficient representation is $O(d^2)$. In PSI protocols, this leads to significant computational overheads. Usually in such protocols, one polynomial needs to be encrypted and the polynomial multiplication has to be done homomorphically. Homomorphic multiplication operations are computationally expensive. Thus using a co-efficient representation means that the protocols are not scalable.

In O-PSI, we solve this problem by representing the polynomials in another well-known form, point-value. A degree d polynomial ρ can be represented as a set of n $(n > d)$ point-value pairs $\{(x_0, y_0), ..., (x_{n-1}, y_{n-1})\}$ such that all x_i are distinct and $y_i = \rho(x_i)$ for $0 \leq i \leq n-1$. If the x values are fixed, we can omit them and represent polynomials as vectors $\mathbf{y} = (y_0, y_1, ..., y_{n-1})$. A polynomial in point-value form can be translated into co-efficient form by polynomial interpolation [21]. Polynomial arithmetic in point-value representation can be done by point-wise addition or multiplication. For two degree d polynomials ρ_A and ρ_B represented in point-value form by two vectors $\mathbf{y}^{(A)}$ and $\mathbf{y}^{(B)}$, $\rho_A + \rho_B$ can be computed as $(y_1^{(A)} + y_1^{(B)}, y_2^{(A)} + y_2^{(B)}, ..., y_{n-1}^{(A)} + y_{n-1}^{(B)})$, and $\rho_A \cdot \rho_B$ can be computed as $(y_1^{(A)} \cdot y_1^{(B)}, y_2^{(A)} \cdot y_2^{(B)}, ..., y_{n-1}^{(A)} \cdot y_{n-1}^{(B)})$. Note because the product of $\rho_A \cdot \rho_B$ is a polynomial of degree $2d$, ρ_A and ρ_B must be represented by at least $2d + 1$ points to accommodate the result. The key benefit of point-value representation is that multiplication complexity is reduced to $O(d)$. This makes O-PSI much more scalable.

4.2 O-PSI Protocol

The interaction between parties in O-PSI is depicted in Fig. 1. At a high level, the protocol works as follows. Each client first outsources its set to the server. To do so, the client uploads a vector that encodes its set to the server. The vector is blinded so that the server cannot figure out the client's set, and the other client cannot figure out any element outside the intersection. If a client,

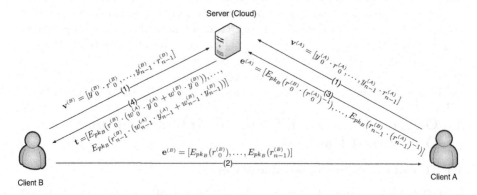

Fig. 1. Interaction between parties in O-PSI

client B, wants to compute the intersection of its own set and another client's set, say client A's set, it must obtain permission from A. If A agrees, A can compute jointly with B some encrypted values. The encrypted values will be used by the server to remove part of the blinding factors from A's data, and this then allows the set intersection to be computed. At the end of the protocol client B receives an encrypted vector which it can decrypt and use the decrypted values to interpolate a polynomial that encodes the intersection. The protocol is described below. We will explain the rationale behind the protocol design after the protocol description.

1. **Setup** Let $\mathcal{U}$ be the universe of set elements. There is a public finite field R that is big enough to encode all elements in $\mathcal{U}$ and also when an element is picked uniformly at random from R has only negligible probability of representing an element of a set. Client A has a set $S_A \subset \mathcal{U}$ and client B has a set $S_B \subset \mathcal{U}$. Without loss of generality, we let $|S_A| = |S_B| = d$. The server publishes a vector $\mathbf{x}$ containing $n = 2d + 1$ random distinct values from R. The server also publishes a pseudorandom function $f : \{0,1\}^l \times \mathbb{Z} \to R$, which maps an l-bit string to an element in R pseudorandomly.

2. **Outsource** This step is the same at both clients. Let $I \in \{A, B\}$, then the client I does the following:
   (a) Generates a Paillier key pair (pk_I, sk_I) (see section 3.2) and publishes the public key. It also chooses a random private key k_I for the pseudo-random function f. All keys are generated according to a given security parameter.
   (b) Constructs a polynomial $\tau_I = \prod_{s_i^{(I)} \in S_I} (x - s_i^{(I)})$ that represents its set S_I. Evaluates τ_I at every value in the $\mathbf{x}$ published by the server producing $\mathbf{y}^{(I)}$ such that $y_i^{(I)} = \tau_I(x_i)$ for $0 \le i \le n - 1$.
   (c) Sends $\mathbf{v}^{(I)}$ to the server, where $\forall v_i^{(I)} \in \mathbf{v}^{(I)}, v_i^{(I)} = y_i^{(I)} \cdot r_i^{(I)}$, $y_i^{(I)}$ is the ith element in $\mathbf{y}^{(I)}$, $r_i^{(I)} = f(k_I, i)$. Here, $\mathbf{v}^{(I)}$ is a blinded version of its set polynomial.

3. **Set Intersection** In this step, client B wants to know the intersection of its set and client A's set.
   (a) Client B sends a request to client A. Along with the request, client B also sends its ID and a vector $\mathbf{e}^{(B)}$, such that $e_i^{(B)} = E_{pk_B}(r_i^{(B)})$ where $r_i^{(B)} = f(k_B, i)$ for $0 \le i \le n - 1$ are the values used to blind its set polynomial.
   (b) Client A can send a **Deny** message to end the protocol here, or if it agrees to engage in the computation of the set intersection, it sends a **Permit** message to client B. It also sends a **Compute** message that contains its own and B's IDs, and a vector $\mathbf{e}^{(A)}$ to the server. The vector $\mathbf{e}^{(A)}$ is computed as follows: for $0 \le i \le n - 1$, $e_i^{(A)} = (e_i^{(B)})^{(r_i^{(A)})^{-1}} = E_{pk_B}(r_i^{(B)} \cdot (r_i^{(A)})^{-1})$ where $r_i^{(I)} = f(k_I, i)$ for $I \in \{A, B\}$ are the values from step 2c above.
   (c) After receiving the **Compute** message from A, the server extracts $\mathbf{e}^{(A)}$ and retrieves the data $\mathbf{v}^{(A)}$ and $\mathbf{v}^{(B)}$ from its storage. The server then chooses two degree d polynomials ω_I randomly from $R[x]$ and computes

two vectors $\mathbf{w}^{(I)}$ ($I \in \{A, B\}$) such that $w^{(I)}_i = \omega_I(x_i)$ for $0 \le i \le n-1$ where x_i is the ith element in the public vector $\mathbf{x}$.

(d) The server computes a result vector $\mathbf{t}$ such that for $0 \le i \le n-1$:

$$
\begin{aligned}
t_i &= (e^{(A)}_i)^{v^{(A)}_i \cdot w^{(A)}_i} \cdot E_{pk_B}(w^{(B)}_i \cdot v^{(B)}_i) \\
&= E_{pk_B}(r^{(B)}_i \cdot (r^{(A)}_i)^{-1} \cdot y^{(A)}_i \cdot r^{(A)}_i \cdot w^{(A)}_i) \cdot E_{pk_B}(w^{(B)}_i \cdot y^{(B)}_i \cdot r^{(B)}_i) \\
&= E_{pk_B}(r^{(B)}_i \cdot (w^{(A)}_i \cdot y^{(A)}_i + w^{(B)}_i \cdot y^{(B)}_i))
\end{aligned}
$$

The server sends $\mathbf{t}$ to client B.

(e) After receiving $\mathbf{t}$, client B computes a vector $\mathbf{z}$ such that for $0 \le i \le n-1$:

$$
\begin{aligned}
z_i &= D_{sk_B}(t_i) \cdot (r^{(B)}_i)^{-1} \\
&= r^{(B)}_i \cdot (w^{(A)}_i \cdot y^{(A)}_i + w^{(B)}_i \cdot y^{(B)}_i) \cdot (r^{(B)}_i)^{-1} \\
&= w^{(A)}_i \cdot y^{(A)}_i + w^{(B)}_i \cdot y^{(B)}_i
\end{aligned}
$$

It then interpolates the polynomial ζ using point-value pairs (x_i, z_i). The roots of ζ are the elements in the set intersection.

Remark 1: In the Setup step, the server needs to publish a vector $\mathbf{x}$ that has $2d + 1$ elements, because the polynomial ζ in step 3e is of degree $2d$ and at least $2d + 1$ points are needed to interpolate it. The elements in $\mathbf{x}$ are picked at random from R so that the probability of x_i being a root of a client's polynomial is negligible.

Remark 2: In step 2c, the client blinds its vector. If the client stores $\mathbf{y}$ directly on the server without blinding, then the server can use $\mathbf{y}$ and $\mathbf{x}$ to interpolate the client's polynomial, thus revealing the client's set. With blinding this is not possible unless the server knows the pseudorandom function key used by the client. The protocol blinds values by multiplication. However, multiplication cannot blind a value if the value is 0. This is why we require the probability of x_i in $\mathbf{x}$ being a root of a client's polynomial to be negligible. If x_i is a root then y_i is 0 and cannot be blinded.

Remark 3: The data values stored on the server are blinded by their owner. To compute the set intersection those blinding factors ($r^{(I)}_i$ in the protocol) must be eliminated. In step 3b, client A and B jointly compute the vector $\mathbf{e}^{(A)}$ to "switch" A's blinding factors to B's blinding factors. In step 3d, $\mathbf{e}^{(A)}$ is used to eliminate $r^{(A)}_i$ and replace it with $r^{(B)}_i$. This factor switching makes it possible later to eliminate $r^{(B)}_i$ in step 3e. The values in $\mathbf{e}^{(A)}$ are encrypted with B's public key, so the server learns nothing in this process.

Remark 4: The client's original blinded dataset remains unchanged in the server. In fact in step 3c, the server multiplies *a copy* of the client's blinded dataset by the vector $\mathbf{w}^{(I)}$.

5 Proof of Security

Now we sketch the security proof of O-PSI in the semi-honest model (see section 3.1). We conduct the security analysis for the three cases where one of the parties is corrupted.

Theorem 1. *If the homomorphic encryption scheme is semantically secure, the O-PSI protocol is secure in the presence of a semi-honest adversary.*

Proof. We will prove the theorem by considering in turn the case where each of the parties has been corrupted. In each case we invoke the simulator with the corresponding party's input and output. Our focus is in the case where party A wants to engage in the computation of the intersection. If party A does not want to proceed in the protocol, the views can be simulated in the same way up to the point where the execution stops.

Case 1: Corrupted server In this case, we show that we can construct a simulator Sim_P that can produce a computationally indistinguishable view. In the real execution, the server's view is as follows:

$$\text{view}_P^{\pi}(\Lambda, S_A, S_B) = \{\Lambda, r_P, \mathbf{v}^{(A)}, \mathbf{v}^{(B)}, \textbf{Compute}, \mathbf{e}^{(A)}, \Lambda\}$$

where r_P are the random coins of the server, $\mathbf{v}^{(A)}, \mathbf{v}^{(B)}$ are the blinded set representations of A's and B's sets, **Compute** is the command to proceed from A, and $\mathbf{e}^{(A)}$ is the encrypted vector that is used in the protocol to switch blinding factors.

To simulate the view, Sim_P does the following: it creates an empty view, then appends Λ and uniformly at random chosen coins r'_P to the view. It then randomly generates two d-element sets S'_A and S'_B. It also chooses two random keys k'_A and k'_B for a pseudorandom function f. It encodes S'_A into its polynomial representation, evaluates the polynomial with the public values $\mathbf{x}$, and blinds the evaluation results with $r_i^{(A)'} = f(k'_A, i)$ for $0 \leq i \leq n-1$. The result is $\mathbf{v}^{(A)'}$. Similarly it can generate $\mathbf{v}^{(B)'}$. Then $\mathbf{v}^{(A)'}$ and $\mathbf{v}^{(B)'}$ are appended to the view. Following that, the simulator generates the **Compute** command string with the correct format and appends it to the view. It then computes $r_i^{(B)'} \cdot (r_i^{(A)'})^{-1}$ and encrypts the results with B's public key. This produces $\mathbf{e}^{(A)'}$ that is appended to the view. Finally, the simulator appends Λ to the view and outputs the view.

We argue that the simulated view is computationally indistinguishable from the real view. In both views, the input parts are identical, the random coins are both uniformly random, and so they are indistinguishable. In the real view $\mathbf{v}^{(A)}, \mathbf{v}^{(B)}$ are blinded with the outputs of a pseudorandom function, so do the vectors in the simulated view. Since the outputs of the pseudorandom function are computationally indistinguishable, the distributions of $\mathbf{v}^{(A)}, \mathbf{v}^{(B)}, \mathbf{v}^{(A)'}, \mathbf{v}^{(B)'}$ are therefore computationally indistinguishable. If the homomorphic encryption is semantically secure, then $\mathbf{e}^{(A)}$ and $\mathbf{e}^{(A)'}$ are also computationally indistinguishable. The output parts in both views are identical. So, we conclude that the views are indistinguishable.

Case 2: Corrupted client A In the real execution, the A's view is as follows:

$$\mathsf{view}_A^\pi(\Lambda, S_A, S_B) = \{S_A, r_A, \mathbf{e}^{(B)}, \Lambda\}$$

The simulator Sim_A does the following: it creates an empty view, then appends Λ and uniformly at random chosen coins r_A' to the view. It then chooses n random values r_i and encrypts each r_i with B's public key. The result is $\mathbf{e}^{(B)'}$ and it is appended to the view. The simulator then appends Λ to the view. It is easy to see that If the homomorphic encryption is semantically secure, then $\mathbf{e}^{(B)}$ and $\mathbf{e}^{(B)'}$ are computationally indistinguishable. So, the two views are indistinguishable.

Case 3: Corrupted client B In the real execution, the B's view is as follows:

$$\mathsf{view}_B^\pi(\Lambda, S_A, S_B) = \{S_B, r_B, \mathbf{Permit}, \mathbf{t}, f_\cap(S_A, S_B)\}$$

The simulator Sim_B does the following: it creates an empty view, and appends Λ and uniformly at random chosen coins r_B' to the view. Then it generates the **Permit** command string with the correct format and appends it to the view. Following that, it creates two d-element sets S_A' and S_B' such that $S_A' \cap S_B' = f_\cap(S_A, S_B)$, converts S_A' to its polynomial representation, evaluates the polynomial using the public values $\mathbf{x}$ and obtains $\mathbf{y}^{(A)'}$. Similarly the simulator can obtain $\mathbf{y}^{(B)'}$. The simulator chooses randomly two degree d polynomials ω_A' and ω_B', evaluates them using the public values $\mathbf{x}$ and obtains $\mathbf{w}^{(A)'}$ and $\mathbf{w}^{(B)'}$. It also chooses a random key k_B' for a pseudorandom function f and computes $r_i^{(B)'} = f(k_B', i)$ for $0 \le i \le n-1$. Then the simulator computes for each i, $E_{pk_B}(r_i^{(B)'} \cdot (w_i^{(A)'} \cdot y_i^{(A)'} + w_i^{(B)'} \cdot y_i^{(B)'}))$. The result is $\mathbf{t}'$. The simulator appends $\mathbf{t}'$ to the view and then appends $f_\cap(S_A, S_B)$. It is easy to see that the distributions of $\mathbf{t}$ and $\mathbf{t}'$ are computationally indistinguishable. So, the two views are indistinguishable.

Combining the above, we conclude the protocol is secure and complete our proof.

6   Extensions

In this section we extend O-PSI to support dataset integrity verification and multiple clients. These extensions require no major modification of the protocol.

6.1   Dataset Integrity Verification

To add data integrity verification to O-PSI we can use the verification mechanism of any provable data possession protocol that does not reveal any information about the confidential data to the server. For this purpose, we can adopt the homomorphic verification tags proposed in [22]. These tags are homomorphic in the sense that given two tags T_a and T_b for elements a and b one can combine them $T_a \cdot T_b$ which is equal to the tag Tag_{a+b} of the sum $a+b$ of the two elements.

In O-PSI, client $I \in \{A, B\}$ defines a tag for each element $v'^{(I)}_i$ of the blinded dataset as: $T_{v'^{(I)}_i} = (h(k_I||i) \cdot g^{v'^{(I)}_i})^{d_I} \bmod N$, where h is a secure deterministic hash-and-encode function that maps strings uniformly to a unique cyclic subgroup of $\mathbb{Z}_N^*$, QR_N, k_I is a random value used for all elements in the set, $g = a^2, a \xleftarrow{R} \mathbb{Z}_N^*$, and $N = p'q'$ is a RSA modulus, $p' = 2p'' + 1, q' = 2q'' + 1$ and $d_I \cdot e_I = 1 \bmod p''q''$, where q'' and p'' are prime numbers. The hash value $h(k_I||i)$ binds the tag $T_{v'^{(I)}_i}$ to the value $v'^{(I)}_i$ and prevents the server from using the tag to compute a proof for a different value. Note, $v'^{(I)}_i = y'^{(I)}_i \cdot r^{(I)}_i$ is a uniformly random value. Consequently, each tag $T_{v'^{(I)}_i}$ does not leak any information about the private value $y'^{(I)}_i$ to the server. In this protocol client I, along with its blinded dataset, outsources a vector $\mathbf{tag}^{(I)}$ comprising values $T_{v'^{(I)}_i}$ ($0 \le i \le n-1$) to the server. The challenge, proof generation and verification phases of the protocol remain unchanged to those described in [22].

6.2   Multiple Clients

O-PSI can be used to compute the intersection of the outsourced datasets of multiple clients. In this case, the client interested in the intersection, client B, sends the same request (see step 3a of the protocol) to all other clients, A_j ($1 \le j \le m$). The protocol for each client A_j remains unchanged (see step 3b). For each client A_j, the server carries out step 3c, and computes the result vector $\mathbf{t}$ such that for $0 \le i \le n-1$:

$$t_i = E_{pk_B}(w^{(B)}_i \cdot v^{(B)}_i) \cdot \prod_{1 \le j \le m} (e^{(A_j)}_i)^{v^{(A_j)}_i \cdot w^{(A_j)}_i}$$

$$= E_{pk_B}(r^{(B)}_i \cdot (w^{(B)}_i \cdot y^{(B)}_i + \sum_{1 \le j \le m} w^{(A_j)}_i \cdot y^{(A_j)}_i))$$

Then the server sends $\mathbf{t}$ to client B, that carries out the final step, step 3e, unchanged. Note that in this protocol, even if $m - 1$ clients collude, none can infer the set elements of the non-corrupted client, as the random polynomials $\omega^{(A_j)}_I$, picked by the server, are unknown to the clients.

7   Evaluation

We evaluate O-PSI by comparing its properties to those provided by other protocols that delegate PSI computation to a server. We also compare these protocols in terms of communication and computation complexity. Table 1 summarises the results.

Properties. The protocols in [12,13] require clients to interact with each other at setup. In [12] clients need to generate jointly the key of the pseudorandom permutation used to encode the datasets, while in [13] they need to jointly compute some parameters that are used in the encryption of their datasets. In contrast to

Table 1. Comparison of different delegated PSI protocols. Set cardinality and intersection cardinality are denoted by d and k respectively.

Property	O-PSI	[12]	[13]	[14]	[15]	[16]
Non-interactive setup	✓	✗	✗	✓	✓	✓
Hiding the intersection size from the server	✓	✓	✓	✗	✓	✗
Many set intersections without re-preparation	✓	✗	✗	✗	✗	✗
Multiple clients	✓	✓	✓	✓	✗	✓
Computation integrity verification	✗	✓	✗	✗	✗	✓
Communication complexity	$O(d)$	$O(d)$	$O(d^2)$	$O(d)$	$O(d^2)$	$O(k)$
Computation complexity	$O(d)$	$O(d)$	$O(d^2)$	$O(d^2)$	$O(d^2)$	$O(d)$

these protocols, in [14–16] and O-PSI the clients can independently prepare and outsource their private datasets. This is desirable in a cloud computing context as organizations and individuals can take advantage of the storage capabilities of the cloud and outsource their data at different points in time and without prior consideration of who is going to use them.

In a delegated PSI protocol, privacy should be maintained and the server should not learn anything about the intersection during the computation, including its cardinality. This is the case for the size-hiding variation of [12], protocols in [13,15], and O-PSI. However, as discussed in section 2 this is not the case for [14,16].

More interestingly, O-PSI is the only protocol in which clients can reuse their outsourced datasets on the server in multiple delegated PSI computations without the need to prepare their datasets for each computation, and computing PSI on the outsourced dataset multiple times does not reveal any information to the server. This is an important advantage in scenarios where outsourced datasets are expected to be used a lot of times, as it significantly reduces the overall communication and storage cost for the clients. This is not the case for any of the other protocols, because the clients either do not outsource their datasets, or need to re-encode them locally for each operation in order to prevent the server from inferring information about the intersection over time.

As we showed in section 6.2, O-PSI can be easily extended to support multiple clients. This is also the case for [12–14,16]. However, this is not possible for [15], as this requires an additional logical operation that is not supported by the homomorphic encryption scheme used.

O-PSI has been designed for the semi-honest security model and as a result does not consider the case where the server maliciously deviates from the protocol and computes the wrong result. This is a reasonable assumption in a cloud computing context where cloud providers are keen to preserve their reputation and this assumption is widely considered in the literature [13–15,23,24]. However [16] allows the client to verify the correctness of the results, while as we have seen in section 2, [12] can detect server misbehavior at an additional cost.

In conclusion, in contrast to other protocols, O-PSI has a unique combination of properties that make it particularly appealing for a cloud computing setting.

Communication Complexity. The communication complexity of O-PSI for the client who receives the result, client B, is $O(d)$, where d is the dataset size. This is because, client B sends to client A the $n = 2d + 1$ encrypted random values $E_{pk_B}(r_i^{(B)})$ for $0 \leq i \leq n - 1$ (see step 3a). The communication complexity for client A, who authorizes the operation on its dataset, is $O(d)$, as for each of the n values it receives from client B it sends to the server $E_{pk_B}(r_i^{(B)} \cdot (r_i^{(A)})^{-1})$ (see step 3b). The communication complexity for the server is $O(d)$, as it sends to client B the result vector **t** of size n (see step 3d). Thus, the overall communication complexity of our protocol is $3n$ which is linear, $O(d)$, to the dataset size.

In [13] for each set intersection, the client engages in a two-round protocol, one round to upload its elements in the form of RSA ciphertexts to the server with $O(d)$ communication complexity, and another to interactively compute private set intersection with the server with $O(d^2)$ communication complexity. For the protocol in [15], the communication complexity is also quadratic $O(sd^2)$, where s is the number of hash functions used for the bloom filter, and the messages contain BGN encryption ciphertexts. On the other hand, the protocols in [12,14] have $O(d)$ communication complexity with messages containing symmetric key encryption ciphertexts, while the protocol in [16] has $O(k)$ complexity, where k is the intersection size.

In conclusion, similar to the most efficient protocols, O-PSI has linear communication complexity, however at an increased message size, which results from the additional dataset outsourcing properties and privacy guarantees that it provides.

Computation Complexity. We evaluate the computational cost of O-PSI by counting the number of exponentiation operations, as their cost dominates that of other operations. More specifically, client B performs n exponentiations to encrypt the random values in step 3.a, and needs another n exponentiations to decrypt the polynomial sent by the server in step 3.e. So, in total it carries out $2n$ exponentiations. Client A performs n exponentiations to enable the set intersection in step 3.b, while the server carries out n exponentiations to encrypt client B's dataset and n exponentiations to transform client A's dataset in step 3.d, a total of $2n$ exponentiations. It is interesting to note that using the point-value representation increases the overall storage costs at the server. However, the modest increase in storage brings a significant decrease in the computational costs, from $O(d^2)$ (when using encrypted coefficients such as in [6]) to $O(d)$. In total O-PSI involves $5n$ exponentiations. Hence, its computation complexity is linear to the size of the dataset, $O(d)$.

The semi-honest variant of the protocol in [12] also has linear complexity $O(d)$, as the client computing the result and the server invoke the pseudorandom permutation (PRP) d times, while the other client invokes the PRP, $2d$ times. On the other hand, the computational overhead in [13] is quadratic $O(d^2)$, as it involves a joint PSI protocol (plus public key encryption of the dataset elements). The protocol in [15] also has quadratic complexity, as it involves $O(d^2)$ BGN public key encryption operations. In [14] the client performs $O(d)$ modular additions, while the server carries out $O(d^2)$ operations to compare the expanded sets of the users. Finally, the protocol in [16] is based on bilinear maps and requires $6d$ pairings at the server side and $2k$ exponentiations at the client side, resulting in $O(d)$ and $O(k)$ computation complexity at the server and client side respectively.

In conclusion, similar to the most efficient protocols, due to the use of polynomials in point-value form, O-PSI incurs only linear computational costs. However, the additional properties it provides come at the cost of more costly exponentiation operations.

8   Conclusions and Future Work

In this paper we have presented O-PSI, a protocol that allows clients to outsource their private datasets and delegate PSI computation to a server. A key building block of O-PSI is a novel representation of sets as polynomials in point-value form. The protocol allows clients to independently prepare and outsource their private datasets, while allowing, with the clients' permission, the server to compute multiple set intersections without revealing any information about the result or the sets, and no need for re-preparation of the sets. O-PSI has been shown to be secure in the semi-honest model, and has linear communication and computation complexity, with respect to the size of the datasets. O-PSI can be easily extended to support multiple clients and dataset integrity verification. As a result, O-PSI is a scalable protocol particularly suited for cloud computing environments. In the future, we plan to investigate how O-PSI can be extended to support additional set operations like set union or subset. We also plan to explore how clients can update their sets without the need to fully re-encode them, and verify the integrity of any computation.

Acknowledgments. We would like to thank the anonymous reviewers. Aydin Abadi is supported by a EPSRC Doctoral Training Grant studentship.

References

1. Fiore, D., Gennaro, R., Pastro, V.: Efficiently verifiable computation on encrypted data. In: 21st ACM Conference on Computer and Communications Security, Scottsdale, AZ, USA, pp. 844–855 (2014)
2. Backes, M., Fiore, D., Reischuk, R.M.: Verifiable delegation of computation on outsourced data. In: 20th ACM Conference on Computer and Communications Security, Berlin, Germany, pp. 863–874 (2013)
3. Agrawal, R., Srikant, R.: Privacy-preserving data mining. ACM Sigmod. Record **29**(2), 439–450 (2000)
4. Cristofaro, E.D., Tsudik, G.: Practical private set intersection protocols with linear complexity. In: 14th International Conference on Financial Cryptography and Data Security, pp. 143–159 (2010)
5. Freedman, M.J., Nissim, K., Pinkas, B.: Efficient Private Matching and Set Intersection. In: Cachin, C., Camenisch, J.L. (eds.) EUROCRYPT 2004. LNCS, vol. 3027, pp. 1–19. Springer, Heidelberg (2004)

6. Kissner, L., Song, D.: Privacy-Preserving Set Operations. In: Shoup, V. (ed.) CRYPTO 2005. LNCS, vol. 3621, pp. 241–257. Springer, Heidelberg (2005)
7. De Cristofaro, E., Kim, J., Tsudik, G.: Linear-Complexity Private Set Intersection Protocols Secure in Malicious Model. In: Abe, M. (ed.) ASIACRYPT 2010. LNCS, vol. 6477, pp. 213–231. Springer, Heidelberg (2010)
8. Dong, C., Chen, L., Wen, Z.: When private set intersection meets big data: an efficient and scalable protocol. In: 20th ACM Conference on Computer and Communications Security, pp. 789–800 (2013)
9. Pinkas, B., Schneider, T., Zohner, M.: Faster private set intersection based on OT extension. In: 23rd USENIX Security Symposium, San Diego, CA, USA, USENIX (2014)
10. Papamanthou, C., Tamassia, R., Triandopoulos, N.: Optimal Verification of Operations on Dynamic Sets. In: Rogaway, P. (ed.) CRYPTO 2011. LNCS, vol. 6841, pp. 91–110. Springer, Heidelberg (2011)
11. Canetti, R., Paneth, O., Papadopoulos, D., Triandopoulos, N.: Verifiable set operations over outsourced databases. In: 17th IACR International Conference on Theory and Practice of Public-Key Cryptography, pp. 113–130 (2014)
12. Kamara, S., Mohassel, P., Raykova, M., Sadeghian, S.: Scaling Private Set Intersection to Billion-Element Sets. In: Christin, N., Safavi-Naini, R. (eds.) FC 2014. LNCS, vol. 8437, pp. 193–213. Springer, Heidelberg (2014)
13. Kerschbaum, F.: Collusion-resistant outsourcing of private set intersection. In: 27th ACM Symposium on Applied Computing, Riva, Trento, Italy, pp. 1451–1456 (2012)
14. Liu, F., Ng, W.K., Zhang, W., Giang, D.H., Han, S.: Encrypted set intersection protocol for outsourced datasets. In: IEEE International Conference on Cloud Engineering, IC2E 2014, pp. 135–140. IEEE Computer Society, Washington, DC (2014)
15. Kerschbaum, F.: Outsourced private set intersection using homomorphic encryption. In: 7th ACM Symposium on Information, Compuer and Communications Security, ASIACCS 2012, Seoul, Korea, May 2–4, pp. 85–86 2012 (2012)
16. Zheng, Q., Xu, S.: Verifiable delegated set intersection operations on outsourced encrypted data. IACR Cryptology ePrint Archive, 178 (2014)
17. Goldreich, O.: The Foundations of Cryptography, vol. 2. Basic Applications. Cambridge University Press (2004)
18. Stefanov, E., Shi, E.: Multi-cloud oblivious storage. In: 20th ACM Conference on Computer and Communications Security, Berlin, Germany, pp. 247–258 (2013)
19. Raykova, M., Vo, B., Bellovin, S.M., Malkin, T.: Secure anonymous database search. In: First ACM Cloud Computing Security Workshop, Chicago, IL, USA, pp. 115–126 (2009)
20. Paillier, P.: Public-Key Cryptosystems Based on Composite Degree Residuosity Classes. In: Stern, J. (ed.) EUROCRYPT 1999. LNCS, vol. 1592, p. 223. Springer, Heidelberg (1999)
21. Aho, A.V., Hopcroft, J.E.: The Design and Analysis of Computer Algorithms, 1st edn. Addison-Wesley Longman Publishing Co., Inc., Boston (1974)
22. Ateniese, G., Burns, R.C., Curtmola, R., Herring, J., Kissner, L., Peterson, Z.N.J., Song, D.X.: Provable data possession at untrusted stores. In: 14th ACM Conference on Computer and Communications Security, pp. 598–609 (2007)
23. Wang, C., Ren, K., Wang, J.: Secure and practical outsourcing of linear programming in cloud computing. In: 30th IEEE International Conference on Computer Communications, Shanghai, China, pp. 820–828 (2011)
24. Hahn, F., Kerschbaum, F.: Searchable encryption with secure and efficient updates. In: 21st ACM Conference on Computer and Communications Security, Scottsdale, AZ, USA, pp. 310–320 (2014)

Flexible and Robust Privacy-Preserving Implicit Authentication

Josep Domingo-Ferrer[1]([✉]), Qianhong Wu[2], and Alberto Blanco-Justicia[1]

[1] Department of Computer Engineering and Mathematics,
UNESCO Chair in Data Privacy, Universitat Rovira i Virgili,
Av. Països Catalans 26, E-43007 Tarragona, Catalonia, Spain
{josep.domingo,alberto.blanco}@urv.cat
[2] School of Electronics and Information Engineering, Beihang University,
XueYuan Road No. 37, Beijing, Haidian District, China
qianhong.wu@buaa.edu.cn

Abstract. Implicit authentication consists of a server authenticating a user based on the user's usage profile, instead of/in addition to relying on something the user explicitly knows (passwords, private keys, etc.). While implicit authentication makes identity theft by third parties more difficult, it requires the server to learn and store the user's usage profile. Recently, the first privacy-preserving implicit authentication system was presented, in which the server does not learn the user's profile. It uses an *ad hoc* two-party computation protocol to compare the user's fresh sampled features against an encrypted stored user's profile. The protocol requires storing the usage profile and comparing against it using two different cryptosystems, one of them order-preserving; furthermore, features must be numerical. We present here a simpler protocol based on set intersection that has the advantages of: i) requiring only one cryptosystem; ii) not leaking the relative order of fresh feature samples; iii) being able to deal with any type of features (numerical or non-numerical).

Keywords: Privacy-preserving implicit authentication · Privacy-preserving set intersection · Implicit authentication · Active authentication · Transparent authentication · Risk mitigation · Data brokers

1 Introduction

The recent report [10] by the U.S. Federal Trade Commission calls for transparency and accountability of data brokers. On the one hand, the report describes the pervasive data collection carried out by data brokers as clearly privacy-invasive. On the other hand, it presents risk mitigation services offered by data brokers as the good side of data collection, to the extent that such services protect consumers against identity theft. Indeed, storing information on how a consumer usually interacts with a service (time of the day, usual places, usual sequence of keystrokes, etc.) allows using this information to *implicitly authenticate* a user: implicit authentication [12] (a.k.a. transparent authentication [5] or active

© IFIP International Federation for Information Processing 2015
H. Federrath and D. Gollmann (Eds.): SEC 2015, IFIP AICT 455, pp. 18–34, 2015.
DOI: 10.1007/978-3-319-18467-8_2

authentication [1]) is the process of comparing the user's current usage profile with the stored profile. If both profiles disagree, maybe someone is impersonating the user, *e.g.* after some identity theft (password theft, etc.).

The above risk mitigation argument is part a long-standing simplistic tendency in digital services (and elsewhere) to justify privacy invasion in the name of legitimate interests, as if the latter were incompatible with privacy (another old example is intellectual property protection, which was portrayed as being incompatible with the anonymity of digital content consumers until anonymous fingerprinting was proposed [8,14,16]). In fact, implicit authentication turns out to be a weak excuse to justify the storage and/or access by servers to the usage profiles of users. In [17] it was shown how to make implicit authentication compatible with the privacy of users. The idea is that the server only needs an *encrypted* version of the user's usage profile.

1.1 Contribution and Plan of this Paper

The protocol in [17] needs the server to store the users' accumulated usage profiles encrypted under *two* different cryptosystems, one that is homomorphic and one that is order-preserving. We present here a protocol for privacy-preserving implicit authentication based on set intersection, which has the advantage that the server only needs to store the users' accumulated usage profiles encrypted under *one* (homomorphic) cryptosystem. This allows saving storage at the carrier and also computation during the protocol. Also, unlike [17], our protocol does not leak the relative order of fresh feature samples collected by the user's device for comparison with the encrypted profile. Finally, our protocol can deal with any type of features (numerical or non-numerical), while the protocol [17] is restricted to numerical features.

The rest of this paper is organized as follows. Section 2 gives background on implicit authentication and on the privacy-preserving implicit authentication protocol of [17]. Section 3 discusses how to compute the dissimilarity between two sets depending on the type of their elements. Section 4 presents a robust privacy-preserving set intersection protocol that can effectively be used for implicit authentication. The privacy, security and complexity of the new protocol are analyzed in Section 5. Experimental results are reported in Section 6. Finally, conclusions and future research directions are summarized in Section 7. Appendix A gives background on privacy-preserving set intersection, Appendix B recalls the Paillier cryptosystem and Appendix C justifies the correctness of the least obvious steps of our protocol.

2 Background

We first specify the usual setting of implicit authentication and we then move to privacy-preserving implicit authentication.

2.1 Implicit Authentication

The usual scenario of implicit authentication is one in which the user carries a mobile networked device (called just user's device in what follows) such as a cell phone, tablet, notebook, etc. The user wishes to authenticate to a server in order to use some application. The user may (or not) use a primary password authentication mechanism. To strengthen such a primary authentication or even to replace it, the user resorts to *implicit authentication* [12]. In this type of authentication, the history of a user's actions on the user's device is used to construct a profile for the user that consists of a set of features. In [12] empirical evidence was given that the features collected from the user's device history are effective to distinguish users and therefore can be used to implicitly authenticate them (instead or in addition to explicit authentication based on the user's providing a password).

The types of features collected on the user's actions fall into three categories: (i) device data, like GPS location data, WiFi/Bluetooth connections and other sensor data; (ii) carrier data, such as information on cell towers seen by the device, or Internet access points; and (iii) cloud data, such as calendar entries. It is not safe to store the accumulated profile of the user in the user's device, because an intruder might compromise the device and alter the stored profile in order to impersonate the legitimate user. Hence, for security, the profile must be stored by some external entity. However, the user's profile includes potentially sensitive information and storing it outside the user's device violates privacy.

Implicit authentication systems try to mitigate the above privacy problem by using a third party, the *carrier* (i.e. the network service provider) to store the user's profiles. Thus, the typical architecture consists of the user's device, the carrier and the application servers. The latter want to authenticate the user and they collaborate with the carrier and the user's device to do so. The user's device engages in a secure two-party computation protocol with the carrier in order to compare the fresh usage features collected by the user's device with the user's profile stored at the carrier. The computation yields a score that is compared (by the carrier or by the application server) against a threshold, in order to decide whether the user is accepted or rejected. In any case, the application server trusts the score computed by the carrier.

2.2 Privacy-Preserving Implicit Authentication

In the privacy-preserving implicit authentication system proposed in [17], the user's device encrypts the user's usage profile at set-up time, and forwards it to the carrier, who stores it for later comparison. There is no security problem because during normal operation the user's device does not store the user's profile (it just collects the fresh usage features). There is no privacy problem either, because the carrier does not see the user's profile in the clear.

The core of proposal [17] is the algorithm for computing the dissimilarity score between two inputs: the fresh sample provided by the user's device and the profile stored at the carrier. All the computation takes place at the carrier and both inputs are encrypted: indeed, the carrier stores the encrypted profile and the user's device sends the *encrypted* fresh sample to the carrier. Note that the keys to both encryptions are only known to the user's device (it is the device who encrypted everything).

The carrier computes a dissimilarity score at the feature level, while provably guaranteeing that: i) no information about the profile stored at the carrier is revealed to the device other than the average absolute deviation of the stored feature values; ii) no information about the fresh feature value provided by the device is revealed to the carrier other than how it is ordered with respect to the stored profile feature values.

The score computation protocol in [17] uses two different encryption schemes: a homomorphic encryption scheme HE (for example, Paillier's [15]) and an order-preserving symmetric encryption scheme $OPSE$ (for example, [4]). For each feature in the accumulated user's profile, two encrypted versions are created, one under HE and the other under $OPSE$. Similarly, for each feature in the fresh sample it collects, the user's device computes two encrypted versions, under HE and $OPSE$, respectively, and sends them to the carrier. The following process is repeated for each feature:

1. Using the HE ciphertexts the carrier performs some computations (additions and scalar multiplications) relating the encrypted fresh sampled feature value and the set of encrypted feature values in the stored encrypted user's profile.
2. The output of the previous computations is returned to the user's device, which decrypts it, re-encrypts it under $OPSE$ and returns the re-encrypted value to the carrier.
3. Using the order-preserving properties, the carrier can finally compute a dissimilarity score evaluating how different is the fresh sampled feature from those stored in the encrypted user's profile. This score can be roughly described as the number of feature values in the stored encrypted profile that are less dissimilar from the median of the stored values than the fresh sampled value.

The authors of [17] point out that, in case of a malicious user's device (*e.g.* as a result of it being compromised), one cannot trust the device to provide the correct HE-encrypted version of the fresh sampled feature. Nor can it be assumed that the device returns correct $OPSE$-encryptions in Step 2 above. In [17], a variant of the privacy-preserving implicit authentication protocol is presented in which the device proves the correctness of HE-encrypted fresh sampled features and does not need to provide $OPSE$-encrypted values. This version is secure against malicious devices, but its complexity is substantially higher.

Other shortcomings of [17]:

– It is restricted to numerical features, due to the kind of computations that need to be performed on them. However, among the example features listed in Section 2.1, there are some features that are not numerical, like the list of cell towers or Internet access points seen by the user's device.

– It discloses the following information to the user's device: i) how the fresh sample is ordered with respect to the stored profile feature values; ii) the average absolute deviation of the stored feature values.

We present a privacy-preserving implicit authentication protocol based on set intersection that deals with the above shortcomings.

3   Dissimilarity Between Sets Depending on the Data Type

Based on [2], we recall here how the dissimilarity between two data sets X and Y can be evaluated using set intersection. If we let X be the user's profile and Y be the fresh sample collected by the user's device, our privacy-preserving implicit authentication setting presents the additional complication (not present in [2]) that X is only available in encrypted form (the carrier stores only the encrypted user's profile). Anyway, we describe here the case of two plaintext sets X and Y and we will deal with encrypted sets in the following sections.

3.1   Case A: Independent Nominal Feature Values

Assume X and Y consist of qualitative values, which are independent and binary, that is, the relationship between two values is equality or nothing. Take as an example the names of the network or phone providers seen by the user's device, the operating system run by the device and/or the programs installed in the device. In this case, the dissimilarity between X and Y can be evaluated as the multiplicative inverse of the size of the intersection of X and Y, that is $1/|X \cap Y|$, when the intersection is not empty. If it is empty, we say that the dissimilarity is ∞.

Clearly, the more the coincidences between X and Y, the more similar is the profile stored at the carrier to the fresh sample collected by the device.

3.2   Case B: Correlated Categorical Feature Values

As in the previous case, we assume the feature values are expressed as qualitative features. However, these may not be independent. For example, if the feature values are the IDs of cell towers or Internet access points seen by the device, nearby cell towers/access points are more similar to each other than distant cell towers/access points.

In this case, the dissimilarity between X and Y cannot be computed as the size of their intersection.

Assume we have an integer correlation function $l : E \times E \mapsto \mathbb{Z}_+$ that measures the similarity between the values in the sets of features held by the device and the carrier, where E is the domain where the sets of features of both players take values. For nominal features, semantic similarity measures can be used for this purpose [18]; for numerical features that take values over bounded and discrete domains, standard arithmetic functions can be used. Assume further that both the device and the carrier know this function s from the very beginning.

Here the dissimilarity between the set X and the set Y can be computed as

$$1/(\sum_{x \in X} \sum_{y \in Y} l(x, y))$$

when the denominator is nonzero. If it is zero, we say that the distance is ∞.

3.3   Case C: Numerical Feature Values

In this case, we want to compute the dissimilarity between two sets of numerical values based on set intersection. Numerical features in implicit authentication may include GPS location data, other sensor data, etc. Assume $U = \{u_1, \cdots, u_t\}$ and $V = \{v_1, \cdots, v_t\}$. A way to measure the dissimilarity between X and Y is to compute $\sum_{i=1}^{t} |u_i - v_i|$.

4   Robust Privacy-Preserving Set Intersection for Implicit Authentication

It will be shown further below that computing dissimilarities in the above three cases A, B and C can be reduced to computing the cardinality of set intersections. Furthermore, this can be done without the carrier revealing X and without the user's device revealing Y, as required in the implicit authentication setting. The idea is that, if the dissimilarity stays below a certain threshold, the user is authenticated; otherwise, authentication is refused.

In Appendix A, we give some background on privacy-preserving set intersection protocols in the literature. Unfortunately, all of them assume an honest-but-curious situation, but we need a privacy-preserving set intersection protocol that works even if the adversary is a malicious one: notice that the user's device may be corrupted, that is, in control of some adversary. Hence we proceed to specifying a set intersection protocol that remains robust in the malicious scenario and we apply it to achieving privacy-preserving implicit authentication in Case A. We then extend it to Cases B and C. We make use of Paillier's cryptosystem [15], which is recalled in Appendix B.

4.1   Implicit Authentication in Case A

Set-up. Let the plaintext user's profile be $(a_1, \cdots, a_s)$. In this phase, the user's device transfers the encrypted user's profile to the carrier. To do so, the user's device does:

1. Generate the Paillier cryptosystem with public key $pk = (n, g)$ and secret key sk.
2. Compute the polynomial $p(x) = \prod_{i=1}^{s}(x - a_i) = p_0 + p_1 x + p_2 x^2 + \cdots + p_s x^s$.
3. Compute $Enc(p_0), \cdots Enc(p_s)$ where $Enc(p_i) = g^{p_i} r_i^n \mod n^2$.

4. Randomly choose $R' \in Z_{n^2}$. Find $r'_0, \cdots, r'_s \in Z_{n^2}$ such that

$$R' = r'_0 \cdot r'^{a_j}_1 \cdot r'^{a_j^2}_2 \cdots r'^{a_j^s}_s \quad \bmod n^2, \quad j = 1, \cdots, s \qquad (1)$$

Note that the system (1) has a trivial solution $r'_0 = R'$ and $r'_1 = \cdots = r'_s = 1$, but, since it is underdetermined ($s+1$ unknowns and s equations), it has many non-trivial solutions too (see correctness analysis in Appendix C).

5. Compute $R_i = r'_i / r_i \bmod n^2$. Randomly choose integer $d \in Z_n$. Send

$$pk, Enc(p_0), \cdots Enc(p_s); R_0{}^d, \cdots, R_s{}^d \quad \bmod n^2$$

to the carrier. Locally delete all data computed during the set-up protocol, but keep (d, R') secretly.

Implicit Authentication Protocol. As discussed in Section 3.1, in case of independent nominal feature values (Case A), dissimilarity is computed as $1/|X \cap Y|$. Hence, to perform implicit authentication the carrier just needs to compute the cardinality of the intersection between the fresh sample collected by the user's device and the user's profile stored at the carrier. *The challenge is that the carrier only holds the encrypted user's profile and the user's device does no longer hold the plaintext user's profile either in plaintext or ciphertext.*

Let $Y = \{b_1, \cdots, b_t\} \subseteq E$ be the fresh sample collected by the user's device. Then the device and the carrier engage in the following protocol:

Step 1 The carrier randomly chooses θ, and sends pk, $Enc(p_0)^\theta, \cdots Enc(p_s)^\theta$; $R_0{}^d, \cdots, R_s{}^d$ to the user's device.

Step 2 The user's device picks a random integer $r(j) \in Z_{n^2}$ for every $1 \leq j \leq t$. The device computes for $1 \leq j \leq t$

$$Enc(r(j) \cdot d \cdot \theta \cdot p(b_j)) = Enc(p(b_j))^{d \cdot \theta \cdot r(j)}$$

$$= (Enc(p_0) \cdots Enc(p_s)^{b_j^s})^{d \cdot \theta \cdot r(j)}$$

$$= g^{r(j) \cdot d \cdot \theta p(b_j)} \gamma_j^{n \cdot d \cdot \theta} \quad \bmod n^2$$

where $\gamma_j = (r_0 \cdot r_1{}^{b_j} \cdot r_2{}^{b_j^2} \cdots r_s{}^{b_j^s})^{r(j)} \bmod n^2$. The user's device then computes $\Upsilon_j = (R_0 \cdot R_1{}^{b_j} \cdot R_2{}^{b_j^2} \cdots R_s{}^{b_j^s})^{dr(j)} \bmod n^2$. For all j, the device randomly orders and sends

$$\{(Enc(r(j) \cdot d \cdot \theta \cdot p(b_j)), \Upsilon_j, R'^{r(j)d})\} \qquad (2)$$

to the carrier.

Step 3 For $1 \leq j \leq t$, the carrier does:
- Compute $Enc(r(j) \cdot d \cdot \theta \cdot p(b_j)) \cdot \Upsilon_j^{n\theta}$;
- From Expression (1), if $b_j = a_i$ for some $i \in \{1, \cdots, s\}$, then $p(b_j) = 0$ and hence $Enc(r(j)d \cdot \theta \cdot p(b_j)) \cdot \Upsilon_j^{n\theta} = R'^{r(j)dn\theta}$; note that the carrier can recognize $R'^{r(j)dn\theta}$ by raising $R'^{r(j)d}$ received in Expression (2) to $n\theta$. Otherwise (if $b_j \neq a_i$ for all $i \in \{1, \cdots, s\}$) $Enc(r(j) \cdot d \cdot \theta \cdot p(b_j))$ looks random. See correctness analysis in Appendix C.

If both parties are honest, then the carrier learns $|X \cap Y|$ but obtains no information about the elements in X or Y.

4.2 Implicit Authentication in Case B

Here, the carrier inputs X and the user's device inputs Y, two sets of features, and they want to know how close X and Y are without revealing their own set. In the protocol below, only the carrier learns how close X and Y are.

We assume that the domain of X and Y is the same, and we call it E. The closeness or similarity between elements is computed by means of a function s. In particular, we consider functions $l : E \times E \to \mathbb{Z}_+$. Observe that Case A is a particular instance of this Case B in which $l(x,x) = 1$ and $l(x,y) = 0$ for $x \neq y$.

Let Y be the input of the user's device. For every $z \in E$, the device computes $\ell_z = \sum_{y \in Y} l(z,y)$. Observe that ℓ_z measures the overall similarity of z and Y. Let $Y' = \{z \in E : \ell_z > 0\}$. It is common to consider functions satisfying $l(z,z) > 0$ for every $z \in E$, and so in general $Y \subseteq Y'$.

An implicit authentication protocol for such a computation can be obtained from the protocol in Case A (Section 4.1), by replacing Steps 2 and 3 there with the following ones:

Step 2' For every $z \in Y'$, the user's device picks ℓ_z random integers $r(1), \cdots, r(\ell_z) \in \mathbb{Z}_{n^2}$ and for $1 \leq j \leq \ell_z$ does

– Compute

$$
\begin{aligned}
Enc(r(j) \cdot d \cdot \theta \cdot p(z)) &= Enc(p(z))^{d \cdot \theta \cdot r(j)} \\
&= (Enc(p_0) \cdots Enc(p_s)^{z^s})^{d \cdot \theta \cdot r(j)} \\
&= g^{r(j) \cdot d \cdot \theta p(z)} \gamma_j^{n \cdot d \cdot \theta} \quad \bmod n^2
\end{aligned}
$$

where $\gamma_j = (r_0 \cdot r_1^{z} \cdot r_2^{z^2} \cdots r_s^{z^s})^{r(j)} \bmod n^2$.

– Compute $\Upsilon_j = (R_0 \cdot R_1^{z} \cdot R_2^{z^2} \cdots R_s^{z^s})^{dr(j)} \bmod n^2$.

– Let $E_j = \{(Enc(r(j) \cdot d \cdot \theta \cdot p(z)), \Upsilon_j, R'^{r(j)d})\}$.

Finally, the user's device randomly re-orders the sequence of all computed E_j for all $z \in Y'$ (a total of $\sum_{z \in Y'} \ell_z$ elements) and sends the randomly re-ordered sequence of E_j's to the carrier.

Step 3' For every received E_j, the carrier does

– Compute $Enc(r(j)d\theta \cdot p(z)) \cdot \Upsilon_j^{n\theta}$;

– From Expression (1), if $z \in X$, then $p(z) = 0$ and hence $Enc(r(j)d \cdot \theta \cdot p(z)) \cdot \Upsilon_j^{n\theta} = R'^{r(j)dn\theta}$ (see correctness analysis in Appendix C); otherwise (if $z \notin X$) $Enc(r(j)d\theta \cdot p(z))$ looks random.

Hence, at the end of the protocol, the total number of E_j which yield $R'^{r(j)dn\theta}$ is

$$
\sum_{x \in X} \ell_x = \sum_{x \in X} \sum_{y \in Y} l(x,y),
$$

that is, the sum of similarities between the elements of X and Y. This clearly measures how similar X and Y are. At the end of the protocol, the carrier knows $|Y'|$ and the device knows $|X|$. Besides that, neither the carrier nor the device can gain any additional knowledge on the elements of each other's set of preferences.

4.3   Implicit Authentication in Case C

Let the plaintext user's profile be a set U of t numerical features, which we denote by $U = \{u_1, \cdots, u_t\}$. The device's fresh sample corresponding to those features is $V = \{v_1, \cdots, v_t\}$. The carrier wants to learn how close X and Y are, that is, $\sum_{i=1}^{t} |u_i - v_i|$.

Define $X = \{(i,j) : u_i > 0 \text{ and } 1 \leq j \leq u_i\}$ and $Y = \{(i,j) : v_i > 0 \text{ and } 1 \leq j \leq v_i\}$. Now, take the set-up protocol defined in Section 4.1 for Case A and run it by using X as plaintext user profile. Then take the implicit authentication protocol for Case A and run it by using Y as the fresh sample input by the device. In this way, the carrier can compute $|X \cap Y|$. Observe that

$$|X \cap Y| = |\{(i,j) : u_i, v_i > 0 \text{ and } 1 \leq j \leq \min\{u_i, v_i\}\}| = \sum_{1 \leq i \leq t} \min\{u_i, v_i\}.$$

In the set-up protocol for Case A, the carrier learns $|X|$ and during the implicit authentication protocol for Case A, the carrier learns $|Y|$. Hence, the carrier can compute

$$|X| + |Y| - 2|X \cap Y| = \sum_{i=1}^{t} (\max\{u_i, v_i\} + \min\{u_i, v_i\}) - 2 \sum_{i=1}^{t} \min\{u_i, v_i\}$$

$$= \sum_{i=1}^{t} (\max\{u_i, v_i\} - \min\{u_i, v_i\}) = \sum_{i=1}^{t} |u_i - v_i|.$$

5   Privacy, Security and Complexity

Unless otherwise stated, the assessment in this section will focus on the protocols of Case A (Section 4.1), the protocols of Cases B and C being extensions of Case A.

5.1   Privacy and Security

We define privacy in the following two senses:

- After the set-up is concluded, the user's device does not keep any information about the user's profile sent to the carrier. Hence, compromise of the user's device does not result in compromise of the user's profile.
- The carrier learns nothing about the plaintext user's profile, except its size. This allows the user to preserve the privacy of her profile towards the carrier.

Lemma 1. *After set-up, the user's device does not keep any information on the user's profile sent to the carrier.*

Proof. The user's device only keeps (d, R') at the end of the set-up protocol. Both d and R' are random and hence unrelated to the user's profile.   □.

Lemma 2. *The carrier or any eavesdropper learn nothing about the plaintext user's profile, except its size.*

Proof. After set-up, the carrier receives $pk, Enc(p_0), \cdots Enc(p_s); R_0{}^d, \cdots, R_s{}^d$ mod n^2. Since d is random and unknown to the carrier, $R_0{}^d, \cdots, R_s{}^d$ mod n^2 look random to the carrier and will give him no more information about the plaintext user's profile than the Paillier ciphertexts $Enc(p_0), \cdots Enc(p_s)$. That is, the carrier learns nothing about the user's plaintext profile $X = \{a_1, \cdots, a_s\}$ except its size s. The same holds true for an eavesdropper listening to the communication between the user's device and the carrier during set-up.

At Step 2 of implicit authentication, the carrier only gets the fresh sample Y encrypted under Paillier and randomly re-ordered. Hence, the carrier learns no information on Y, except its size t. At Step 3, the carrier learns $|X \cap Y|$, but not knowing Y, the size $|X \cap Y|$ of the intersection leaks to him no information on X. $\qquad\square$

If we define security of implicit authentication as the inability of a dishonest user's device to disrupt the authentication outcome, we can state the following result.

Lemma 3. *A dishonest user's device has no better strategy to alter the outcome of implicit authentication than trying to randomly guess the user's profile.*

Proof. At the end of the set-up protocol, the (still uncompromised) user's keeps no information about the user's profile (Lemma 1). Hence, if the user's device is later compromised and/or behaves dishonestly, it still has no clue on the real user's profile against which its fresh sample is going to be authenticated. Hence, either the user's device provides an honest fresh sample and implicit authentication will be correctly performed, or the user's device provides a random fresh sample with the hope that it matches the user's profile. $\qquad\square$

5.2   Complexity

Case A. During the set-up protocol, the user's device needs to compute:

- $s + 1$ Paillier encryptions for the polynomial coefficients;
- values $r'_0, \cdots, r'_s$; as explained in Appendix C, this can be done by randomly choosing r'_0, then solving an $s \times s$ generalized Vandermonde system (doable in $O(s^2)$ time using [7]) and finally computing s modular powers to find the $r'_1, \cdots, r'_s$;
- $s + 1$ modular powers (raising the R_i values to d).

During the implicit authentication protocol, the user's device needs to compute (Step 2):

- t Paillier encryptions;
- ts modular powers (to compute the Υ_j values);
- t modular powers (to raise R' to $r(j)d$).

Also during the implicit authentication protocol, the carrier needs to compute:

- At Step 1, $s + 1$ modular powers (to raise the encrypted polynomial coefficients to θ);
- At Step 3, t Paillier encryptions;
- At Step 3, t modular powers (to raise the Υ_j values to $n\theta$).

Case B. The set-up protocol does not change w.r.t. Case A. In the implicit authentication protocol, the highest complexity occurs when $Y' = E$ and the similarity function l always takes the maximum value in its range, say L. In this case,

$$\sum_{z \in Y'} \ell_z = \sum_{z \in Y'} \sum_{y \in Y} l(z, y) = |E|sL.$$

Hence, in the *worst case* the user's device needs to compute (Step 2'):

- $|E|sL$ Paillier encryptions;
- $|E|sL$ modular powers (to compute the Υ_j values);
- $|E|sL$ modular powers (to raise R' to $r(j)d$).

Also during the implicit authentication protocol, the carrier needs to compute:

- At Step 1, $s + 1$ modular powers (to raise the encrypted polynomial coefficients to θ);
- At Step 3', $|E|sL$ Paillier encryptions;
- At Step 3', $|E|sL$ modular powers (to raise the Υ_j values to $n\theta$).

Note that the above complexity can be reduced by reducing the range of the similarity function $l(\cdot, \cdot)$.

Case C. Case C is analogous to Case A but the sets X and Y whose intersection is computed no longer have s and t elements, respectively. According to Section 4.3, the maximum value for $|X|$ occurs when all u_i take the maximum value of their range, say, M, in which case X contains tM pairs (i, j). By a similar argument, Y also contains at most tM pairs.

Hence, the *worst-case* complexity for Case C is obtained by performing the corresponding changes in the assessment of Case A. Specifically, during the set-up protocol, the user's device needs to compute:

- $tM + 1$ Paillier encryptions for the polynomial coefficients;
- Solve a Vandermonde system $tM \times tM$ (doable in $O((tM)^2)$ time) and then compute tM modular powers to find the r_i' values;
- Compute $tM + 1$ modular powers (raising the R_i values to d).

During the implicit authentication protocol, the user's device needs to compute (Step 2):

- tM Paillier encryptions;
- $t^2 M^2$ modular powers (to compute the Υ_j values);
- tM modular powers (to raise R' to $r(j)d$).

Also during the implicit authentication protocol, the carrier needs to compute:

- At Step 1, $tM + 1$ modular powers (to raise the encrypted polynomial coefficients to θ);
- At Step 3, tM Paillier encryptions;
- At Step 3, tM modular powers (to raise the Υ_j values to $n\theta$).

Note that the above complexities can be reduced by reducing the range of the numerical values in sets U and V.

6 Experimental Results

As stated in the previous section, the complexity of our implicit authentication protocol ultimately depends on the sizes of the input sets. In Case A, the sizes of the sets are directly given by the user inputs; in Case B, these sizes are the product of the size of the input sets times the range of the similarity function ℓ; and in Case C, the sizes are given by the size of the original sets times the range of their values. We ran an experiment to test the execution times of our protocol, based on Case A, to which the other two cases can be reduced.

The experiment was implemented in Sage-6.4.1 and run on a Debian7.7 machine with a 64-bit architecture, an Intel i7 processor and 8GB of physical memory. We instantiated a Paillier cryptosystem with a 1024-bit long n, and the features of preference sets were taken from the integers in the range $[1 \dots 2^{128}]$. The input sets ranged from size 1 to 50, and we took feature sets of the same size to execute the set-up and the authentication protocols.

Step 4 of the set-up protocol (Section 4.1), in which a system of equations is solved for r_i' for $1 \leq i \leq s$, is the most expensive part of the set-up protocol. As a worst-case setting, we used straightforward Gaussian elimination which takes time $O(s^3)$, although, as mentioned above, specific methods like [7] exist for generalized Vandermonde matrices that can run in $O(s^2)$ (such specific methods could be leveraged in case of smartphones with low computational power). On the other hand, Step 2 of the authentication protocol (Section 4.1), computed by the user's device, is easily parallelizable for each feature in the sample set. Since parallelization can be exploited by most of the current smartphones in the market, we also exploited it in our experiment. The results are shown in Table 1 (times are in seconds).

Note that the set-up protocol is run only once (actually, maybe once in a while), so it is not time-critical. However, the authentication protocol is to be run at every authentication attempt by the user. For example, if a user implicitly authenticates herself using the pattern of her 20 most visited websites, authentication with our proposal would take 3.37 seconds, which is perfectly acceptable in practice.

Table 1. Execution times (in seconds) for different input set sizes

	1	5	10	15	20	25	30	35	40	45	50
Set-up	0.89	0.79	1.1	1.83	4.67	11.45	24.65	47.6	84.99	144.81	228.6
Authentication	0.08	0.47	1.05	2.0	3.37	5.4	8.27	12.13	17.3	23.39	31.2

7   Conclusions and Future Research

To the best of our knowledge, we have presented the second privacy-preserving implicit authentication system in the literature (the first one was [17]). The advantages of our proposal with respect to [17] are:

- The carrier only needs to store the user's profile encrypted under *one* cryptosystem, namely Paillier's.
- Dishonest behavior or compromise at the user's device after the initial set-up stage neither compromises the privacy of the user's profile nor affects the security of authentication.
- Our proposal is not restricted to numerical features, but can deal also with all sorts of categorical features.
- In case of numerical or categorical ordinal features, our proposal does not disclose how the fresh sample is ordered with respect to the feature values in the stored user's profile.

For binary or independent nominal features, the complexity of our proposal is quite low (quadratic in the number of values in the user's profile). For correlated categorical feature values, the complexity is higher, but it can be reduced by decreasing the range of the similarity function used. Finally, in the case of numerical values, the complexity is also higher than in the binary/independent nominal case, but it can be reduced by decreasing the range of the numerical feature values.

Future research will include devising ways to further decrease the computational complexity in all cases.

Acknowledgments. The following funding sources are gratefully acknowledged: Government of Catalonia (ICREA Acadèmia Prize to the first author and grant 2014 SGR 537), Spanish Government (project TIN2011-27076-C03-01 "CO-PRIVACY"), European Commission (projects FP7 "DwB", FP7 "Inter-Trust" and H2020 "CLARUS"), Templeton World Charity Foundation (grant TWCF0095/AB60 "CO-UTILITY"), Google (Faculty Research Award to the first author) and Government of China (Natural Science Foundation of China under projects 61370190 and 61173154). The first author is with the UNESCO Chair in Data Privacy. The views in this paper are the authors' own and do not necessarily reflect the views of UNESCO, the Templeton World Charity Foundation or Google.

A   Background on Privacy-Preserving Set Intersection

Secure multiparty computation (MPC) allows a set of parties to compute functions of their inputs in a secure way without requiring a trusted third party.

During the execution of the protocol, the parties do not learn anything about each other's input except what is implied by the output itself. There are two main adversarial models: honest-but-curious adversaries and malicious adversaries. In the former model, the parties follow the protocol instructions but they try to obtain information about the inputs of other parties from the messages they receive. In the latter model, the adversary may deviate from the protocol in an arbitrary way.

We will restrict here to a two-party setting in which the input of each party is a set, and the desired output is the cardinality of the intersection of both sets. The intersection of two sets can be obtained by using generic constructions based on Yao's garbled circuit [20]. This technique allows computing any arithmetic function, but for most of the functions it is inefficient. Many of the recent works on two-party computation are focused on improving the efficiency of these protocols for particular families of functions.

Freedman, Nissim, and Pinkas [9] presented a more efficient method to compute the set intersection, a *private matching scheme*, that is secure in the honest-but-curious model. A private matching scheme is a protocol between a client C and a server S in which C's input is a set X of size i_C, S's input is a set Y of size i_S, and at the end of the protocol C learns $X \cap Y$. The scheme uses polynomial-based techniques and homomorphic encryption schemes. Several variations of the private matching scheme were also presented in [9]: an extension to the malicious adversary model, an extension of the multi-party case, and schemes to compute the cardinality of the set intersection and other functions. Constructing efficient schemes for set operations is an important topic in MPC and has been studied in many other contributions. Several works such as [3,6,11,13,19] present new protocols to compute the set intersection cardinality.

B   Paillier's Cryptosystem

In this cryptosystem, the public key consists of an integer n (product of two RSA primes), and an integer g of order n modulo n^2, for example, $g = 1 + n$. The secret key is $\phi(n)$, where $\phi(\cdot)$ is Euler's totient function.

Encryption of a plaintext integer m, with $m < n$ involves selecting a random integer $r < n$ and computing the ciphertext c as

$$c = Enc(m) = g^m \cdot r^n \bmod n^2 = (1 + mn)r^n \bmod n^2.$$

Decryption consists of first computing $c_1 = c^{\phi(n)} \bmod n^2 = 1 + m\phi(n)n \bmod n^2$ and then $m = (c_1 - 1)\phi(n)^{-1} \bmod n^2$.

The homomorphic properties of Paillier's cryptosystem are as follows:

- *Homomorphic addition of plaintexts.* The product of two ciphertexts decrypts as the sum of their corresponding plaintexts:

$$D(E(m_1, r_1) \cdot E(m_2, r_2) \bmod n^2) = m_1 + m_2 \bmod n.$$

Also, the product of a ciphertext times g raised to a plaintext decrypts as the sum of the corresponding plaintexts:

$$D(E(m_1, r_1) \cdot g^{m_2} \bmod n^2) = m_1 + m_2 \bmod n.$$

- *Homomorphic multiplication of plaintexts.* An encrypted plaintext raised to the power of another plaintext will decrypt to the product of the two plaintexts:

$$D(E(m_1, r_1)^{m_2} \bmod n^2) = D(E(m_1, r_1)^{m_2} \bmod n^2) = m_1 m_2 \bmod n.$$

More generally, given a constant k, $D(E(m_1, r_1)^k \bmod n^2) = k m_1 \bmod n$.

C   Correctness

In general, the correctness of our protocol follows from direct algebraic verification using the properties of Paillier's cryptosystem. We go next through the least obvious steps.

C.1   Set-up Protocol

In the set-up protocol, $r'_0, \cdots, r'_s$ are found as a solution of the following system

$$\begin{bmatrix} R' \\ \vdots \\ R' \end{bmatrix} = \begin{bmatrix} r'_0 \cdot r'^{a_1}_1 \cdot r'^{a^2_1}_2 \cdots r'^{a^s_1}_s & \bmod n^2 \\ \vdots \\ r'_0 \cdot r'^{a_s}_1 ? \cdot r'^{a^2_s}_2 \cdots r'^{a^s_s}_s & \bmod n^2 \end{bmatrix}.$$

The above system has $s + 1$ unknowns and s equations. Therefore it has one degree of freedom. To avoid the trivial solution $r'_0 = R'$ and $r'_1 = \cdots = r'_s = 1$, we choose a random r'_0. Then we divide the system by r'_0 and we take logarithms to get

$$\begin{bmatrix} \log(R'/r'_0) \\ \log(R'/r'_0) \\ \vdots \\ \log(R'/r'_0) \end{bmatrix} \bmod n = \begin{bmatrix} a_1 & a^2_1 & \cdots & a^s_1 \\ \vdots & \vdots & \vdots \\ a_s & a^2_s & \cdots & a^s_s \end{bmatrix} \cdot \begin{bmatrix} \log r'_1 \\ \log r'_2 \\ \vdots \\ \log r'_s \end{bmatrix} \bmod n.$$

The matrix on the right-hand side of the above system is an $s \times s$ generalized Vandermonde matrix (not quite a Vandermonde matrix). Hence, using the techniques in [7] it can be solved in $O(s^2)$ time for $\log r'_1, \cdots, \log r'_s$. Then s powers modulo n^2 need to be computed to turn $\log r'_i$ into r'_i for $i = 0, \cdots, s$.

C.2   Implicit Authentication Protocol

We specify in more detail the following derivation in Step 2 of the implicit authentication protocol of Section 4.1:

$$Enc(r(j) \cdot d \cdot \theta \cdot p(b_j)) = Enc(p(b_j))^{d \cdot \theta \cdot r(j)} \mod n^2$$

$$= (Enc(p_0) \cdots Enc(p_s)^{b_j^s})^{d \cdot \theta \cdot r(j)} \mod n^2$$

$$= (g^{p_0} r_0^n \cdots (g^{p_s} r_s^n)^{b_j^s})^{d \cdot \theta \cdot r(j)} \mod n^2$$

$$= (g^{p(b_j)})^{d \cdot \theta \cdot r(j)} (r_0 \cdot r_1^{b_j} \cdots r_s^{b_j^s})^{r(j) \cdot n \cdot d \cdot \theta} \mod n^2$$

$$= g^{r(j) \cdot d \cdot \theta p(b_j)} \gamma_j^{n \cdot d \cdot \theta} \mod n^2.$$

Regarding Step 3 of the implicit authentication protocol, we detail the case $b_j = a_i$ for some $i \in \{1, \cdots, s\}$. In this case, $p(b_j) = 0$ and hence

$$Enc(r(j)d\theta \cdot p(b_j)) \cdot \Upsilon_j^{n\theta} \mod n^2 = Enc(0)^{r(j)d\theta} \cdot \Upsilon_j^{n\theta} \mod n^2$$

$$= (r_0 \cdot r_1^{b_j} \cdots r_s^{b_j^s})^{nr(j)d\theta} \cdot \Upsilon_j^{n\theta} \mod n^2$$

$$= (r_0 \cdot r_1^{b_j} \cdots r_s^{b_j^s})^{nr(j)d\theta} \cdot (R_0 \cdot R_1^{b_j} \cdots R_s^{b_j^s})^{dr(j)n\theta} \mod n^2$$

$$= (r'_0 \cdot r'_1^{a_i} \cdots r'_s^{a_i^s})^{r(j)dn\theta} \mod n^2 = R'^{r(j)dn\theta} \mod n^2. \tag{3}$$

If in Step 3, if we have $b_j \neq a_i$ for all $i \in \{1, \cdots, s\}$, then Derivation (3) does not hold and a random number is obtained instead. On the one side, the powers of g does not disappear from $Enc(r(j)d\theta \cdot p(b_j))$. On the other side, the exponents $b_j, \cdots, b_j^s$ cannot be changed by $a_i, \cdots, a_i^s$ as done in the last step of Derivation (3). Hence, a random number different from $R'^{r(j)dn\theta}$ is obtained.

References

1. Aksari, Y.: Active authentication by mouse movements. In: 24th Intl. Symposium on Computer and Information Sciences, ISCIS 2009, pp. 571–574. IEEE (2009)
2. Blanco, A., Domingo-Ferrer, J., Farràs, O., Sánchez, D.: Distance Computation between Two Private Preference Functions. In: Cuppens-Boulahia, N., Cuppens, F., Jajodia, S., Abou El Kalam, A., Sans, T. (eds.) SEC 2014. IFIP AICT, vol. 428, pp. 460–470. Springer, Heidelberg (2014)
3. Blanton, M., Aguiar, E.: Private and oblivious set and multiset operations. In: ASIACCS 2012, pp. 40–41. Springer (2012)
4. Boldyreva, A., Chenette, N., Lee, Y., O'Neill, A.: Order-Preserving Symmetric Encryption. In: Joux, A. (ed.) EUROCRYPT 2009. LNCS, vol. 5479, pp. 224–241. Springer, Heidelberg (2009)
5. Clarke, N., Karatzouni, S., Furnell, S.: Flexible and Transparent User Authentication for Mobile Devices. In: Gritzalis, D., Lopez, J. (eds.) SEC 2009. IFIP AICT, vol. 297, pp. 1–12. Springer, Heidelberg (2009)
6. De Cristofaro, E., Gasti, P., Tsudik, G.: Fast and Private Computation of Cardinality of Set Intersection and Union. In: Pieprzyk, J., Sadeghi, A.-R., Manulis, M. (eds.) CANS 2012. LNCS, vol. 7712, pp. 218–231. Springer, Heidelberg (2012)
7. Demmel, J., Koev, P.: The accurate and efficient solution of a totally positive generalized Vandermonde linear system. SIAM Journal on Matrix Analysis and Applications **27**(1), 142–152 (2005)
8. Domingo-Ferrer, J.: Anonymous fingerprinting of electronic information with automatic identification of redistributors. Electronics Letters **34**(13), 1303–1304 (1998)

9. Freedman, M.J., Nissim, K., Pinkas, B.: Efficient Private Matching and Set Intersection. In: Cachin, C., Camenisch, J.L. (eds.) EUROCRYPT 2004. LNCS, vol. 3027, pp. 1–19. Springer, Heidelberg (2004)
10. Federal Trade Commission, Data Brokers: A Call for Transparency and Accountability (May 2014)
11. Hohenberger, S., Weis, S.A.: Honest-Verifier Private Disjointness Testing Without Random Oracles. In: Danezis, G., Golle, P. (eds.) PET 2006. LNCS, vol. 4258, pp. 277–294. Springer, Heidelberg (2006)
12. Jakobsson, M., Shi, E., Golle, P., Chow, R.: Implicit authentication for mobile devices. In: Proc. of the 4th USENIX Conf. on Hot Topics in Security (2009)
13. Kissner, L., Song, D.: Privacy-Preserving Set Operations. In: Shoup, V. (ed.) CRYPTO 2005. LNCS, vol. 3621, pp. 241–257. Springer, Heidelberg (2005)
14. Megías, D., Domingo-Ferrer, J.: Privacy-aware peer-to-peer content distribution using automatically recombined fingerprints. Multimedia Systems $20(2)$, 105–125 (2014)
15. Paillier, P.: Public-Key Cryptosystems Based on Composite Degree Residuosity Classes. In: Stern, J. (ed.) EUROCRYPT 1999. LNCS, vol. 1592, pp. 223–238. Springer, Heidelberg (1999)
16. Pfitzmann, B., Waidner, M.: Anonymous Fingerprinting. In: Fumy, W. (ed.) EUROCRYPT 1997. LNCS, vol. 1233, pp. 88–102. Springer, Heidelberg (1997)
17. Safa, N.A., Safavi-Naini, R., Shahandashti, S.F.: Privacy-Preserving Implicit Authentication. In: Cuppens-Boulahia, N., Cuppens, F., Jajodia, S., Abou El Kalam, A., Sans, T. (eds.) SEC 2014. IFIP AICT, vol. 428, pp. 471–484. Springer, Heidelberg (2014)
18. Sánchez, D., Batet, M., Isern, D., Valls, A.: Ontology-based semantic similarity: A new feature-based approach. Expert Systems with Applications $39(9)$, 7718–7728 (2012)
19. Vaidya, J., Clifton, C.: Secure set intersection cardinality with application to association rule mining. Journal of Computer Security $13(4)$, 593–622 (2005)
20. Yao, A.C.-C.: How to generate and exchange secrets. FOCS $\mathbf{1986}$, 162–167 (1986)

Towards Relations Between the Hitting-Set Attack and the Statistical Disclosure Attack

Dang Vinh Pham$^{(\boxtimes)}$ and Dogan Kesdogan

University of Regensburg, Regensburg, Germany
{vinh.pham,dogan.kesdogan}@ur.de

Abstract. The Minimal-Hitting-Set attack (HS-attack) is a well-known, provably optimal exact attack against the anonymity provided by Chaumian Mixes (Threshold-Mixes). This attack allows an attacker to identify the fixed set of communication partners of a given user by observing all messages sent and received by a Chaum Mix. In contrast to this, the Statistical Disclosure attack (SDA) provides a guess of that user's contacts, based on statistical analyses of the observed message exchanges.

We contribute the first closed formula that shows the influence of traffic distributions on the least number of observations of the Mix to complete the HS-attack. This measures when the Mix fails to hide a user's partners, such that the user cannot plausibly deny the identified contacts. It reveals that the HS-attack requires asymptotically less observations to identify a user's partners than the SDA, which guesses them with a given bias. This number of observations is $O(\frac{1}{p})$ for the HS-attack and $O(\frac{1}{p^2})$ for the SDA, where p the probability that the attacked user contacts his least frequent partner.

1 Introduction

Anonymity in communication networks is an essential part of privacy. According to the definition of Pfitzmann et al. [24]: *"Anonymity is the state of being not identifiable within a set of subjects, the anonymity set"*. Anonymity systems commonly seek to establish anonymity sets. The most influential work in this area is the Chaumian Mix (also known as Threshold-Mix) [7] that forms the basis of many popular services offering anonymity in open and shared networks [29], e.g. the Internet. A Threshold-Mix collects in every *round* a batch of b encrypted messages from distinct senders, who all contribute the same number of messages[1] of identical size. It changes the appearance and time characteristics of the messages in the output batch to provide unlinkability between its input and output messages. Therefore, the senders and recipients that use the Mix in a round form the sender- and recipient-anonymity set in that round.

This work investigates the fundamental limit of anonymity provided by the anonymity sets established by the Threshold-Mix with respect to a *global passive*

---

[1] Otherwise, it would be trivial to identify a pair of sender and a recipient by the number of their exchanged messages in a round.

© IFIP International Federation for Information Processing 2015
H. Federrath and D. Gollmann (Eds.): SEC 2015, IFIP AICT 455, pp. 35–50, 2015.
DOI: 10.1007/978-3-319-18467-8_3

attacker[2]. Analogous to the fundamental work of Shannon's unicity distance [30], we focus on determining the number of observations of Mix rounds required to disclose a profile of an arbitrary user (say Alice) and thus to break the anonymity system. We consider the case that Alice's profile determines a static set of friends that are repeatedly contacted by Alice. It is motivated by the observation that human relationships tend to be persistent and by the fact that anonymity should also be provided in this case.

The immanent information leaked by the Mix to a global passive attacker is the observed set of senders and recipients using the Mix in a round. Traffic analysis attacks can learn Alice's profile by accumulating this information, although the Mix provides unlinkability between the input and output messages in a single round. We distinguish between two categories: *combinatorial* attacks [2,4,16,17,26,27] and *statistical* attacks [8–11,20,22,23,31]. Combinatorial attacks are basically concerned with the disclosure of exact information about Alice's profile that is consistent to the observations of the anonymity system. In contrast to that, statistical attacks are concerned with classifying whether a recipient is likely Alice's friend, or not. Their main advantage is the computational efficiency. However, combinatorial attacks (e.g., the HS-attack) can also be computational efficient [27] for non-trivial cases. The classification of recipients by statistical attacks can lead to a profile that deviates from Alice's profile, e.g., due to false-positive errors, which classify recipients as friends that are not Alice's friends, or due to omitting friends.

We consider in this work the *Minimal-Hitting-Set* attack (HS-attack) [17,27], a combinatorial attack that provably requires the least number of rounds to uniquely identify Alice's set of friends [16]. Therefore it determines the fundamental limit of anonymity provided by the Threshold-Mix. This number of rounds is dependent on the traffic distribution of the users and on the parameters of the anonymity system. We contribute a closed formula that estimates the mean of this number with respect to arbitrary distributions of Alice's communication and the parameters of the Threshold-Mix. This complements past works that could only model uniform traffic distributions [16,18,26], which are less realistic. Therefore, we are to the best of our knowledge the first to provide such an analytical estimate. Our estimate proves that the number of rounds to uniquely identify Alice's set of friends by the HS-attack is $O(\frac{1}{p})$, while it is $O(\frac{1}{p^2})$ to classify all friends with some error rate by the SDA. The probability $0 < p < 1$ denotes the least probability in the distribution of Alice's traffic to her friends.

Although this work mainly addresses the anonymity of the Threshold-Mix, it might be generalisable to analyse the anonymity of other Mix variants like the *Pool-Mix* [29] that models Mixmaster. There are initial works towards this direction [25, Chap.5.2] that extends the HS-attack for the Pool-Mix and identifies some conditions for the disclosure of Alice's set of friends in that Mix.

Our analyses refer to high-latency Mix systems, as they seek to protect against global passive attackers. In contrast to these, low-latency systems like

---

[2] This attacker can observe any link in the network and can thus observe the anonymity sets.

Tor [13] and JAP [3,19] (as applied in practice) do not try to withstand a global attacker in their design.

1.1   Related Works

Our work is concerned with *passive traffic analysis* attacks [29]. These rely solely on external traffic observations of an anonymity system.

The idea of combinatorial traffic analyses was first discussed by Raymond [29] who also sketched the "intersection attack". Later two implementations of combinatorial approaches have been suggested in parallel, the *Intersection attack* [4] and the *Disclosure attack* [2]. The first approach identifies the recipient of a targeted sender for the case that this sender repeatedly contacts a recipient from a singleton [4]. In contrast to this, the Disclosure attack uncovers an arbitrary large set of repeated contacts of the targeted sender, which is thus more general than the Intersection attack. These were followed by the HS-attack [17], that unambiguously identifies a user's communication partner set with a provably minimal number of observations [16].[3] The limitation to all these attacks are that they require the solution of an NP-complete problem [14] to succeed, placing a high computational burden on the attacker. However, the most recent HS-attack that uses the ExactHS algorithm [27,28] achieves a mean polynomial computational complexity for many non-trivial Mix configurations as proved in [27]. Due to the optimal nature of the HS-attacks, the observations required to conduct them provide a measurement for the anonymity provided by Mix system. Estimates of this number were suggested in [16,18,21,26] for a simple model of uniformly distributed communication traffic.

Statistical attacks identify users through statistical patterns in traffic data. These attacks, introduced by the *Statistical disclosure* attack (SDA) [8–11,20], and subsequently improved by the *Perfect-matching disclosure attack* (PMDA) [31] and the *Bayesian-interference* [12], achieve significant increases in computational efficiency by relaxing the requirement for absolute correctness and allowing misclassification or omission of actors. The *Least square approach*[23] attempts to analytically analyse the deviation between a user's profile and the classification provided by it for the Threshold-Mix. Provided the same Threshold-Mix model as in SDA [8] (that is often used in combinatorial analyses, as well as in this work in Section 2) this approach is identical to the SDA. A succeeding extension [22] of this approach considers analogous analyses for the Pool-Mix model.

1.2   Structure

We introduce a simple model for the Threshold-Mix and the attacker, as well as the scheme of the HS-attack in Section 2. Section 3 estimates the mean least number of rounds to uniquely identify Alice's set of friends by a closed formula, based on this model. It compares this estimate with the number of rounds

---

[3] The intersection attack is identical to the special case of the HS-attack, where a targeted sender has exactly one recipient.

required by the SDA mathematically which shows that the SDA requires asymptotically more observations. Our analyses are confirmed and illustrated by simulations and mathematical evaluations in Section 4. Section 5 finally concludes the work and suggests future works. The proofs of all claims are provided in Appendixes A.

2   Mix and Attacker Model

We consider the Mix system as a black box that outputs information that is visible to the attacker (i.e. the sender-anonymity sets and recipient sets), as illustrated in Fig. 1. It represents a generalised and simplified model of practical real-world Threshold-Mixes.

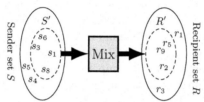

Fig. 1. Mix model

The Mix is abstractly described as follow:

- A communication system consists of a set of senders, S, a set of all recipients, R, and a Mix node as shown in Fig. 1. S and R represent all users with the ability to send or receive messages in the system[4]. If a sender $s \in S$ communicates with a recipient $r \in R$, then we say that r *is a recipient of s*.
- In each communication round, a subset $S' \subseteq S$ of all senders each send precisely one message to their recipients. Let $R' \subseteq R$ be the set of intended recipients.
- We call S' the *sender-anonymity set*, which is the set of all senders that may have sent a given message in a round. The *recipient set R'* is the set of all recipients that have received a message in a round.
- We label the size of the sender-anonymity set, $|S'|$, as b which is also called the *batch size*.
- The size of the *recipient set*, $|R'|$, is less than or equal to b, as each sender sends exactly one message per round, but several senders may communicate with the same recipient. The size of the set of all recipients is $|R| = u$.

2.1   Attacker Model

We consider a *global passive* attacker that observes the traffic on all links between the user and the Mix in the network. Therefore, he can observe all sending and

---

[4] This definition allows for cases of $S \neq R$, as well as $S = R$, i.e. the sender and recipient set might be distinct or identical.

receiving events in the Mix system, so that the pairs of sender anonymity set and recipient set (S', R') of every round is known to the attacker.

The goal of the attacker is to compute, from a set of traffic observations, all possible sets of friends of a target sender *Alice* $\in S$. These possibilities form *hypotheses* for the true set of Alice's set of friends, $_A\mathcal{H}$, which is assumed to be a fixed set of size $m = |_A\mathcal{H}|$. We call a recipient $r \in {}_A\mathcal{H}$ a *friend*; a recipient that does not communicate with Alice, $r \in R \setminus {}_A\mathcal{H}$, is called a *non-friend* and r is simply called a *recipient* if no distinction is required. To clarify that a variable $r \in R$ refers to a friend, it is also denoted by a, whereas it is denoted by n, if it refers to a non-friend.

The attacker focuses on revealing Alice's set of friends by observing only those pairs (S', R'), where Alice participates as a sender. Under this condition we refer to the corresponding recipient set R' as an *observation*, $\mathcal{O}$. The set of all observations collected during t communication rounds is referred to as the *observation set* $\mathcal{OS} = \{\mathcal{O}_1, \ldots, \mathcal{O}_t\}$.

2.2 Hitting-Set Attack

Alice's possible set of friends can be specified by computing all hitting-sets of size m with respect to the observation set $\mathcal{OS}$ collected by the attacker. A *hitting-set* is a set that intersects with all observations[5] in $\mathcal{OS}$. A hitting-set is a *minimal-hitting-set* if no proper subset of it is a hitting-set. We call a hitting-set $\mathcal{H}$ a *unique minimum-hitting-set*[6], if all hitting-sets $\mathcal{H}' \neq \mathcal{H}$ in $\mathcal{OS}$ fulfil the condition $|\mathcal{H}| < |\mathcal{H}'|$.

By collecting sufficiently many observations, until $\mathcal{OS}$ contains a unique minimum-hitting-set, the attacker can unambiguously identify Alice's set of friends $_A\mathcal{H}$. The intuition behind this attack is that at least one of Alice's friends in $_A\mathcal{H}$ appears in each observation (due to the definition of observations), while this does not hold for any set $\mathcal{H} \not\supseteq {}_A\mathcal{H}$. Therefore, if there are sufficiently many observations, then $_A\mathcal{H}$ becomes a unique minimum-hitting-set. This attack is known as the *Minimal-Hitting-Set attack* (HS-attack)[17]. We refer in the remaining paper to its most recent version that uses the ExactHS algorithm to compute the minimal-hitting-sets [27]. The HS-attack repeats aggregating new observations and computing all minimal-hitting-sets of a given size m' in the aggregated observation set $\mathcal{OS}$. It is successively applied for $m' = 1, \ldots, m$. If m' underestimates m, then there will be no hitting-set of size m' after a sufficient number of observation. This can be detected by the HS-attack to consider a larger value of m' in the HS-attack, until $m' = m$ and $_A\mathcal{H}$ becomes a unique minimum-hitting-set. As proved in [16], the HS-attack requires the least number of observations to uniquely identify Alice's set of friends with respect to the Threshold-Mix.

---

[5] Due to the definition of observations, $_A\mathcal{H} \cap \mathcal{O} \neq \emptyset$ for all $\mathcal{O} \in \mathcal{OS}$, therefore $_A\mathcal{H}$ is a hitting-set in $\mathcal{OS}$.

[6] Every unique minimum-hitting-set is a minimal-hitting-set, but not reversely.

Attack Scheme. In our Mix and attacker model, the effort of identifying Alice's set of friends is dependent on the *Mix parameters* (u, b, m) and the distribution of the *cover traffic* and of *Alice's traffic*. The cover traffic is induced by the communication of senders other than Alice to the recipients in the observations. We use the term *Mix configuration* to refer to a combination of Mix parameters and these traffic distributions. The basic scheme underlying the analysis of the HS-attack is illustrated in Fig. 2.

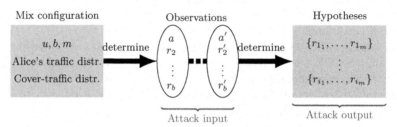

Fig. 2. Analysis scheme: Variables a, r represent arbitrary friend $a \in {}_A\mathcal{H}$ and recipient $r \in R$

Alice's traffic distribution is modelled by the probability mass function $P_A(a)$ for $a \in {}_A\mathcal{H}$, where $\sum_{a \in {}_A\mathcal{H}} P_A(a) = 1$. The cover traffic distribution is indirectly modelled by the probability function $P_N(r)$, which is the probability that any $b - 1$ senders (other than Alice) of a batch contact the recipient $r \in R$ in an observation.

3   Mean Number of Observations for Unique Identification

It was proved in [16] that the $2\times$-exclusivity of Alice's set of friends is a necessary condition for the unique identification of Alice's set of friends. The number of observations aggregated by the attacker, until the $2\times$-exclusivity condition is fulfilled provides a close estimate of the least number of observations to uniquely identify Alice's set of friends, as evaluated in [16].

We contribute a closed formula that estimates the expected least number of observations to fulfil $k\times$-exclusivity, which is for the general case of $k \in \mathbb{N}$. As defined in [16], a friend $a \in {}_A\mathcal{H}$ is *exclusive*, if there is an observation $\mathcal{O}$ that contains only a as an Alice's friend. This means $\mathcal{O} \cap {}_A\mathcal{H} = \{a\}$ and we call $\mathcal{O}$ the *observations that contains a exclusively*. A friend $a \in {}_A\mathcal{H}$ is $k\times$*-exclusive*, if it appears at least k times exclusively in observations, or at least one time alone in an observation (i.e. there is an observation $\mathcal{O}' = \{a\}$). The $k\times$*-exclusivity* is fulfilled, if all Alice's friends are $k\times$-exclusive.

3.1 Mean Number of Observations for $k\times$-Exclusivity

We estimate the mean of the least number of observations $E(T_{k\times e})$ for $k\times$-exclusivity by decomposing this mean in two sub means and estimating those sub means. These are the estimates of the following means[7]:

- The mean least number of observations $E(T_{k\times})$, until Alice contacts all her friends at least k times. This is regardless whether the observations are exclusive, or not.
- The maximum of the mean least number of times $E(T_{e,a})$ Alice has to contact a given friend $a \in {}_A\mathcal{H}$, until it is exclusive, with respect to all Alice's friends $a \in {}_A\mathcal{H}$. For each given friend $a' \in {}_A\mathcal{H}$, this mean only accounts those observations, where Alice contacts a', and the maximum of that mean is $\max_{a' \in {}_A\mathcal{H}} E(T_{e,a'})$.

The variables $T_{k\times e}$, $T_{k\times}$ and $T_{e,a}$ are random variables for: the least number of observations to fulfil $k\times$-exclusivity, the least number of observations until Alice contacts all friends at least k times and the least number of times Alice has to contact a friend a, until it is exclusive. We define $E(T_e) = \max_{a' \in {}_A\mathcal{H}} E(T_{e,a'})$ and set for $a = \operatorname{argmax}_{a' \in {}_A\mathcal{H}} E(T_{e,a'})$, the equality $T_e = T_{e,a}$.

Note that the value of $T_{k\times}$ is dependent on Alice's traffic to her friends, but is independent of the traffic of other senders. In contrast to that, the value of $T_{e,a}$ depends on whether any sender other than Alice contacts any friend in ${}_A\mathcal{H} \setminus \{a\}$ in observations where Alice contacts a. This is dependent on the cover-traffic, but is independent of Alice's traffic. Therefore, $T_{k\times}$ and T_e are statistically independent.

Claim 1. *Let $E(T_{e,a})$ be the mean least number of times Alice has to contact a friend $a \in {}_A\mathcal{H}$, [8]until a is exclusive and $E(T_e) = \max_{a \in {}_A\mathcal{H}} E(T_{e,a})$. Let $E(T_{k\times})$ be the mean least number of observations until Alice contacts all her friends at least k times[9], for $k \in \mathbb{N}$. The mean least number of observations until all Alice's friends are $k\times$-exclusive is estimated by:*

$$E(T_{k\times e}) \leq E(T_{k\times})E(T_e)$$

$$\approx \left(\frac{1}{p}(\ln m + \gamma) + (k-1)\frac{1}{p}\ln\ln m\right)\left(\frac{u-(m-1)}{u}\right)^{1-b}, \quad (1)$$

where $p = \min_{a \in {}_A\mathcal{H}} P_A(a)$ and $\gamma \approx 0,57721$ is the Euler-Mascheroni constant.

We conclude by (1) that the $2\times$-exclusivity of all Alice's friends requires on average $\left(\frac{1}{p}(\ln m + \gamma) + \frac{1}{p}\ln\ln m\right)\left(\frac{u-(m-1)}{u}\right)^{1-b}$ observations. The proof of this claim can be found in Appendix A.

---

[7] The composition of theses estimates in Claim 1 provide an estimate of $E(T_{k\times e})$.

[8] This only refers to observations, in that Alice contacts a, that is $\mathcal{OS}_A[a]$.

[9] This is regardless whether the observations are exclusive, or not.

3.2   Relation to Statistical Disclosure Attack

While the HS-attack aims at exact identification of friends; statistical attacks, as introduced by the SDA, cf. [9], aim at correct classification of friends with some probabilities. Although these two approaches are orthogonal, we can now analytically compare the number of observations required by these attacks by (1).

The SDA [9] considers the classification of each friend as a signal to noise problem. It virtually interprets Alice's traffic volume to a friend $a \in {}_A\mathcal{H}$ as a signal and the cumulative traffic volume of other senders to any recipient $r \in R$ as a noise. Let t be the number of observations and p be the probability that Alice contacts a in an observation, then the mean signal to a is pt with the variance $p(1-p)t$. To simplify the maths it is assumed that every non Alice sender contacts a recipient uniformly distributed, so that $\frac{1}{u}$ is the probability that r is contacted by a single non Alice sender. As there are $b-1$ non Alice senders in a batch, the mean noise to a recipient r after t observations is $P_N(r) = \frac{1}{u}(b-1)t$, with the variance $\frac{1}{u}(1 - \frac{1}{u})(b-1)t$.

The SDA classifies a friend a better than a random guess, if the mean signal to a is higher than the sum of the standard deviation of the signal and of the noise to a [9]. This is a necessary condition to distinguish the signal from the noise to the same recipient. The least number of observations, such that this condition is fulfilled with a probability determined by a confidence parameter l is, cf. [9],

$$\frac{1}{p^2}l^2\left[\sqrt{\frac{u-1}{u^2}(b-1)} + \sqrt{\frac{u-1}{u^2}(b-1) + p^2(\frac{1}{p}-1)}\right]^2 . \tag{2}$$

Setting $l = 2$, $l = 3$ in (2) leads to a classification with a true-positive rate of 95%, respectively 99%. Let us set $p = \min_{a \in {}_A\mathcal{H}} P_A(a)$, as the recipient which is least frequently contacted by Alice dominates the number of observations to classify all friends. In the case that Alice's traffic is uniformly distributed, $p = \frac{1}{m}$ as assumed in [9].

We can now compare (2) with (1) (for $k = 2$) with respect to the probability p by fixing all other parameters u, b, m, l; they are identical in both equations. This reveals that the SDA requires $O(\frac{1}{p^2})$ observations to classify all Alice's friends while the HS-attack only requires $O(\frac{1}{p})$ observations to uniquely identify all Alice's friends. This relation between the HS-attack and the SDA is visualised for some examples in Section 4.

4   Evaluation

This section illustrates the closeness of the estimate of the least number of observations to identify Alice's friends and compares this with the number of observations required by the SDA.

The first task applies the 2×-exclusivity evaluation an the HS-attack on simulated random observations of a Threshold-Mix. These empirically measure the least number of observations for the 2×-exclusivity and the identification of all friends. We use them to illustrate the closeness of the corresponding mathematical estimate by (1).

The second task compares the estimated mean number of observations required by the HS-attack and the SDA for some Mix configurations considered in the simulations. This illustrates that SDA requires asymptotically more observations than the HS-attack.

The traffic distributions that we use to model Alice's traffic and the cover traffic in all simulative and mathematical evaluations are described next.

- Alice contacts in each observation a friend that is randomly drawn from a $Zipf(m, \alpha)$ distribution of $_A\mathcal{H}$. The probability that she contacts her i-th most frequent contact is $P_A(a_i) = P_z^{m,\alpha}(i) = \frac{i^{-\alpha}}{\sum_{l=1}^{m} l^{-\alpha}}$, where $P_z^{m,\alpha}(i)$ is the probability mass function of the $Zipf(m, \alpha)$ distribution. Note that $_A\mathcal{H}$ is uniformly distributed if $\alpha = 0$.
- The remaining $b-1$ recipients of the cover traffic in an observation are drawn uniformly from the set of $|R| = u$ possible recipients. This means that for all $r \in R$, the probability that any of the $b-1$ senders other than Alice contacts r in an observation is $P_N = 1 - (\frac{u-1}{u})^{b-1}$.

Alice's traffic is modelled by a Zipf distribution, as it is known to closely model e-mail and internet traffic [1,6,15]. An example of this distribution is illustrated in Fig. 3 for distinct values of α, provide that Alice has $m = 23$ friends. The cover-traffic is for simplicity modelled by a uniform distribution that represents a bound of the real distribution. Note that an observation contains the recipients of senders who randomly communicate in

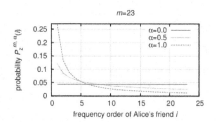

Fig. 3. $Zipf(m, \alpha)$ distribution of Alice's friends, for $m = 23$

the same round as Alice and is therefore a random variable. The distribution of this random variable and thus the number of observations to identify Alice's friends is dependent on the overall distribution of the cover-traffic and of Alice's traffic, regardless of differences in the communication distribution of the individual senders of the cover-traffic. Therefore we assume that all non-Alice senders behave the same to simplify the maths and the simulation.

The HS-attack is *successful* (or *succeeds*) if it uniquely identifies Alice's set of friends $_A\mathcal{H}$. For a given Mix configuration, the simulation generates new random observations until the HS-attack is successful and we call this an *experiment*. The average number of observations required by an attack is therefore the mean of the number of observations of all successful attacks (i.e. of all experiments with the same Mix configuration). Note that the results of these experiments, i.e., the number of observations to succeed the HS-attacks, are identically distributed independent random variables with unknown positive mean μ and standard deviation σ. By the law of large numbers, the empirical mean of the experiments' results approaches μ, while its standard deviation approaches 0, for large number of experiments[10]. To ensure that our results are statistically significant, experiments with the same Mix configuration are repeated until 95% of the results fall within an interval of 5% around the empirically observed mean. Every experiment is repeated at least 300 times and no experiment is dropped. We observed that most of our experiments require no more than 300 repeats to fulfil the statistical significance condition and therefore chose this number as a lower threshold. It is necessary to force a sufficiently large least number of repetitions to avoid cases like, e.g., after running two experiments, both results are within 5% around the empirical mean, which would be too few to represent a reliable measure.

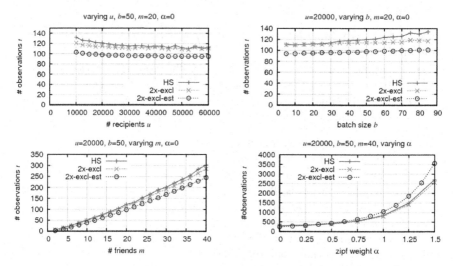

Fig. 4. Mean number of observations: to succeed HS-attack (HS) and to fulfil 2×-exclusivity (2x-excl) versus estimated mean for 2×-exclusivity (2x-excl-est)

Number of Observations Required by HS-attack. Fig. 4 visualises the empirical mean number of observations to succeed the HS-attack, labelled (HS) and to fulfil 2×-exclusivity labelled (2x-excl), obtained from simulations. These are compared with the estimate (1) of the mean of the least number of observations for 2×-exclusivity, labelled (2x-excl-est), which is: $E(T_{2\times e}) \approx \frac{1}{p}((\ln m + \gamma) + \ln\ln m)\left(1 - \frac{(m-1)}{u}\right)^{1-b}$. Since Alice's traffic is Zipf(m, α) distributed, we get $p = \min_{a \in {}_A \mathcal{H}} P_A(a) = P_z^{m,\alpha}(m)$.

The plots provide these comparisons for distinct Mix configurations that are modelled by the parameters u, b, m, α. The y-axis always shows the mean number of observations, while the x-axis vary one of the parameters u, b, m, α. We can observe that the estimate (1) provides reasonable approximations, even for the cases that Alice's traffic is non-uniformly distributed (i.e. $\alpha > 0$). According

---

[10] This law applies regardless of the magnitude of the variation of the results of single experiments.

to $[1,6,15]$, the value of $\alpha \approx 1$ typically models a user's Zipf(m, α) distributed traffic in the Internet. Due to a lack of experiences with running high-latency anonymity systems in a large user base, we have no authentic empirical values for the parameters u, b. Therefore, we choose parameter ranges that would be reasonable for JAP. JAP was designed to be close to the Chaum Mix, so that it contains batch mixing capabilities [19]. However, collecting messages for a batch increases the latency that is yet not accepted by many JAP users [19], so that this function is disabled in favour of low-latency. Therefore we refer to JAP as a low-latency system. The total number of users that repeatedly use the Dresden-Dresden JAP cascade is about 50000 [19] in 2009, therefore we consider u in the range up to 60000. In every minute, the cascade relays on average 17000 HTTP messages [19], which are 283 messages per second. JAP allows users to send multiple parallel messages, so that the number of messages per second would be lower, if every user is only allowed to send one message in a Mix round to prevent linking a communication by packet counting, as in the Chaum Mix [7]. Simulating batch sizes of up to 85 thus appears to be of reasonable order.

Number of Observations Required by HS-Attack vs. SDA. We illustrate that the SDA requires a number of observations that is by the factor of $O(\frac{1}{p})$ higher than those required by the HS-attack, where p is the least probability in the distribution of Alice's friends.

Table 1. Estimated number of required observations: HS-attack (2x-excl-est) versus SDA with 95% true-positive classification (SDA$_{95\%}$)

$u = 400$, $b = 10$, $m = 23$, varying α

α	p	2x-excl-est	SDA$_{95\%}$
0.0	0.0435	186	343
0.5	0.0253	319	840
1.0	0.0116	693	3282
1.5	0.0041	1960	23036

$p = \min_{a \in {}_A\mathcal{H}} P_A(a) = P_z^{23,\alpha}(23)$
in Zipf($23, \alpha$) distribution

$u = 20000$, $b = 50$, $m = 40$, varying α

α	p	2x-excl-est	SDA$_{95\%}$
0.0	0.0250	245	291
0.5	0.0140	437	637
1.0	0.0058	1047	2301
1.5	0.0017	3564	17586

$p = \min_{a \in {}_A\mathcal{H}} P_A(a) = P_z^{40,\alpha}(40)$
in Zipf($40, \alpha$) distribution

Table 1 provides evaluations for the Mix parameters ($u = 400, b = 10, m = 23$), respectively ($u = 20000, b = 50, m = 40$) and Zipf($m, \alpha$) distributed Alice's traffic. The cover-traffic is uniformly distributed. The tables list the estimated number of observations to succeed HS-attack based on (1) labelled by (2x-excl-est) and to classify Alice's friends with a true-positive rate of 95% by the SDA based on (2) (for $l = 2$) labelled by (SDA$_{95\%}$). We observe that the number of observations required by the SDA increasingly exceeds that required by the HS-attack for increasing value of α, as p decreases with increasing α.

Note that (2) solely considers the true-positive rate of the SDA; the classification of a given friend as a friend with a certain rate (e.g. 95% in Table 1). However, the false-positive rate can be larger. When SDA terminates, there is thus some number of non-friends that are classified as friends, whereas there is a unique identification of Alice's set of friends, when HS-attack terminates.

5   Conclusion

Anonymous communication systems seek to embed senders and recipients in anonymity sets to hide their communication relations. We measure in this work the anonymity provided by the anonymity sets constructed by the Threshold-Mix to analyse its limit of achievable protection. This limit is determined by the least number of observations of the Mix rounds, until Alice's set of friends can be exactly identified, so that the protection provided by the Mix is repealed. Alice's set of friends can be exactly identified with the least number of observations by the HS-attack [16].

We contribute by (1) (for $k = 2$) the first closed formula that estimates the mean least number of observations to uniquely identify Alice's set of friends for arbitrary distribution of her traffic. It reveals that this number is $O(\frac{1}{p})$, whereas the SDA requires $O(\frac{1}{p^2})$ observations to classify Alice's friends with some error. The variable $p = \min_{a \in {}_A\mathcal{H}} P_A(a)$ denotes the least probability in the distribution of Alice's communication to her friends [11]. This implies that the difference between these two number of observations is for more realistic (non-uniform) distribution of Alice's friends notably higher than for the uniform distribution considered in past mathematical analyses [8,16]. Section 4 experimentally confirms this difference for some zipf distributed communication of Alice which is known to model real e-mail traffic distribution [1,6,15]. Alice's set of friends can thus be exactly identified with a number of observations that is asymptotically less than required by the inexact SDA. This exact identification can be even computational feasible for non-trivial cases by using the HS-attack [27].

Our analysis shows that the mean least number of observations for the exact identification is lowest, if Alice's friends are uniformly distributed. Past works [16,18,21,26,27] that measure the anonymity of the threshold Mix by the time of exact identification assume for simplicity that uniform distribution. Therefore, we can now confirm that those works address a lower bound of the anonymity of Alice's set of friends.

This work explores the least number of rounds of the Threshold-Mix, such that the attacker's uncertainty about Alice's set of friends becomes 0, as a measure of anonymity. Future works might generalise this approach to quantify the attacker's uncertainty about the possible Alice's set of friends with respect to the number of observed rounds of some Mix. This would enable a more fine granular anonymity measure beyond the time of exact anonymity disclosure (i.e., 0 uncertainty), so that we can also analyse the anonymity provided by other Mix variants like the Pool-Mixe. Pool-Mixes [29] operate like the Threshold-Mix, but they can delay the relay of a random selection of messages in the Mix, as implemented in Mixmaster. Therefore, an attacker might observe a recipient set that misses the user that Alice contacts in the observed round. Such observations induce additional uncertainty about the possible Alice's set of friends in the

---

[11] If Alice's friends are uniformly distributed, then $p = P_A(a) = \frac{1}{m}$ for all $a \in {}_A\mathcal{H}$, otherwise $p < \frac{1}{m}$.

generalised anonymity quantification approach so that the attacker's uncertainty might remain above 0.

A   Proof of Claim

Proof (Claim 1). Let us consider the mean number of observations, such that all Alice's friends are observed at least k times exclusively, for the case that the cover-traffic is uniformly distributed. This uniform cover-traffic implies $E(T_{e,a_i})=E(T_{e,a_j}) = E(T_e)$ for all $a_i, a_j \in {}_A\mathcal{H}$. Since the random variables $T_{k\times}$ and T_e are statistically independent, the mean number of observations until every friend is observed at least k times exclusively, equals in this case: $E(T_{k\times})E(T_e)$.

Due to the definition of $k\times$-exclusivity, observing every Alice's friend at least k times exclusively implies $k\times$-exclusivity. Therefore, we deduce the following:

$$E(T_{k\times e}) \leq E(T_{k\times})E(T_e) \ . \tag{3}$$

We now estimate $E(T_{k\times e})$ and $E(T_e)$, for arbitrary distribution of Alice's traffic and cover-traffic.

$E(T_e)$: Assume that every recipient $r \in R$, $|R| = u$ is contacted uniformly distributed by any $(b-1)$ non-Alice senders in every observation, then the probability that r is contacted by any non-Alice sender is $P_N(r) = P_N = 1 - (\frac{u-1}{u})^{b-1}$. Given Alice contacts $a_j \in {}_A\mathcal{H}$ and the remaining $(b-1)$ non-Alice senders do not, then a_j is exclusive. That probability is $P_e(a_j) = (\frac{u-(m-1)}{u})^{b-1}$. The random variable T_{e,a_j} is geometrically distributed with mean:

$$E(T_{e,a_j}) = \frac{1}{P_e(a_j)} = (\frac{u-(m-1)}{u})^{1-b} \ , \text{ for } j = 1,\ldots,m \ . \tag{4}$$

Therefore $E(T_e) = E(T_{e,a_j})$ for all $a_j \in {}_A\mathcal{H}$, in the case of uniform cover-traffic distribution. This $E(T_e)$ serves as an upper bound for $E(T'_{e,a_j})$ of all cases, where $r' \in R'$ is non-uniformly contacted with $P'_N(r')$ and $\max_{r' \in {}_A\mathcal{H}} \{P'_N(r')\} \leq P_N$, for any recipient sets $R' \supset {}_A\mathcal{H}$.

$E(k\times)$: Let Alice contacts a friend $a \in {}_A\mathcal{H}$ (arbitrarily distributed) according to the probability mass function $P_A(a)$, where $\sum_{a \in {}_A\mathcal{H}} P_A(a) = 1$. Determining the mean number of observations $E(T_{k\times})$, until Alice contacts all her friends at least k times is equivalent to the *general coupon collector problem* (CCP) [5]. In that problem, there is a source of infinitely many coupons of the m types represented in ${}_A\mathcal{H}$, where $P_A(a)$ is the probability of drawing a coupon of type a from the source. The general CCP is to determine the mean least number of coupon collections $E(T_{k\times})$ to obtain all m coupon types. The following equality was proved for large value of m (i.e. $m \to \infty$) in [5]:

$$E(T_{k\times}) = \frac{m}{\delta}(\ln \kappa m + \gamma) + (k-1)\frac{m}{\delta}(\ln \ln \kappa m + \ln \frac{1}{\delta}) + o(1) \ .$$

The variables in this equation have the following meaning in our context:

- $m = |_A\mathcal{H}|$ is the number of coupon types, where w.l.o.g. $_A\mathcal{H} = \{1, \ldots, m\}$.
- $\delta = \min_{x \in (0,1]} f(x) \leq 1$, where $P_A(a) = \int_{(a-1)/m}^{a/m} f(x)dx$ and $\int_0^1 f(x)dx = 1$. δ is the continuous counterpart of the discrete probability $\min_{a \in _A\mathcal{H}} P_A(a)$. We therefore set $f(x) = mP_A(\lceil xm \rceil)$. Therefore $\delta = m(\min_{a \in _A\mathcal{H}} P_A(a))$.
- $\kappa = \gamma_1 \frac{\delta^{k-1}}{(k-1)!} \leq 1$, where $0 < \gamma_1 \leq 1$ is the size of the interval, where $f(x) = \delta$.
- $o(1)$ is a negligible value.

Let $p = \min_{a \in _A\mathcal{H}} P_A(a)$, then $\delta = mp$. We simplify and approximate the above equation by:

$$E(T_{k\times}) = \frac{1}{p}(\ln \frac{\gamma_1}{(k-1)!}m + \gamma) + (k-1)\frac{1}{p}\ln\ln \kappa m + o(1)$$

$$\approx \frac{1}{p}(\ln m + \gamma) + (k-1)\frac{1}{p}\ln\ln m \ . \tag{5}$$

The last estimate result from approximating $\frac{\gamma_1}{(k-1)!}$ and κ by its upper bound 1.

Applying the estimates (4) and (5) to inequality (3) result in (1) and completes the proof. □

References

1. Adamic, L.A., Huberman, B.A.: Zipf's Law and the Internet. Glottometrics **3**, 143–150 (2002)
2. Agrawal, D., Kesdogan, D., Penz, S.: Probabilistic treatment of MIXes to hamper traffic analysis. In: IEEE Symposium on Security and Privacy 0, p. 16 (2003)
3. Berthold, O., Federrath, H., Köpsell, S.: Web MIXes: a system for anonymous and unobservable internet access. In: Federrath, H. (ed.) Designing Privacy Enhancing Technologies. LNCS, vol. 2009, pp. 115–129. Springer, Heidelberg (2001)
4. Berthold, O., Langos, H.: Dummy traffic against long term intersection attacks. In: Dingledine, R., Syverson, P.F. (eds.) PET 2002. LNCS, vol. 2482, pp. 110–128. Springer, Heidelberg (2003)
5. Brayton, R.K.: On the Asymptotic Behavior of the Number of Trials Necessary to Complete a Set with Random Selection. Journal of Mathematical Analysis and Applications **7**(1), 31–61 (1963)
6. Breslau, L., Cao, P., Fan, L., Phillips, G., Shenker, S.: Web caching and Zipf-like distributions: evidence and implications. In: Proceedings of Eighteenth Annual Joint Conference of the IEEE Computer and Communications Societies, INFO-COM 1999, vol. 1, pp. 126–134. IEEE (1999)
7. Chaum, D.L.: Untraceable Electronic Mail, Return Addresses, and Digital Pseudonyms. Communications of the ACM **24**(2), 84–88 (1981)
8. Danezis, G.: Statistical disclosure attacks: traffic confirmation in open environments. In: Proceedings of Security and Privacy in the Age of Uncertainty, pp. 421–426 (2003)

9. Danezis, G.: Better Anonymous Communications. Ph.D. thesis, University of Cambridge (2004)
10. Danezis, G., Diaz, C., Troncoso, C.: Two-sided statistical disclosure attack. In: Borisov, N., Golle, P. (eds.) PET 2007. LNCS, vol. 4776, pp. 30–44. Springer, Heidelberg (2007)
11. Danezis, G., Serjantov, A.: Statistical disclosure or intersection attacks on anonymity systems. In: Fridrich, J. (ed.) IH 2004. LNCS, vol. 3200, pp. 293–308. Springer, Heidelberg (2004)
12. Danezis, G., Troncoso, C.: Vida: how to use Bayesian inference to de-anonymize persistent communications. In: Goldberg, I., Atallah, M.J. (eds.) PETS 2009. LNCS, vol. 5672, pp. 56–72. Springer, Heidelberg (2009)
13. Dingledine, R., Mathewson, N., Syverson, P.: Tor: the second-generation onion router. In: Proceedings of the 13th USENIX Security Symposium, pp. 303–320. USENIX (2004)
14. Garey, M.R., Johnson, D.S.: Computers and Intractability: A Guide to the Theory of NP-Completeness. Freeman (1990)
15. Glassman, S.: A Caching Relay for the World Wide Web. Computer Networks and ISDN Systems **27**(2), 165–173 (1994)
16. Kesdogan, D., Agrawal, D., Pham, V., Rauterbach, D.: Fundamental limits on the anonymity provided by the mix technique. In: Proceedings of the 2006 IEEE Symposium on Security and Privacy, pp. 86–99. IEEE (2006)
17. Kesdogan, D., Pimenidis, L.: The hitting set attack on anonymity protocols. In: Fridrich, J. (ed.) IH 2004. LNCS, vol. 3200, pp. 326–339. Springer, Heidelberg (2004)
18. Kesdogan, D., Pimenidis, L.: The lower bound of attacks on anonymity systems - a unicity distance approach. In: Quality of Protection, Advances in Information Security, vol. 23, pp. 145–158. Springer (2006)
19. Köpsell, S.: Entwicklung und Betrieb eines Anonymisierungsdienstes für das WWW. Ph.D. thesis, Technische Universität Dresden (2010) (in German)
20. Mathewson, N., Dingledine, R.: Practical traffic analysis: extending and resisting statistical disclosure. In: Martin, D., Serjantov, A. (eds.) PET 2004. LNCS, vol. 3424, pp. 17–34. Springer, Heidelberg (2005)
21. O'Connor, L.: Entropy Bounds for Traffic Confirmation. Cryptology ePrint Archive, Report 2008/365, August 2008. http://eprint.iacr.org/2008/
22. Perez-Gonzalez, F., Troncoso, C., Oya, S.: A Least Squares Approach to the Static Traffic Analysis of High-Latency Anonymous Communication Systems. IEEE Transactions on Information Forensics and Security **9**(9), 1341–1355 (2014)
23. Pérez-González, F., Troncoso, C.: Understanding statistical disclosure: a least squares approach. In: Fischer-Hübner, S., Wright, M. (eds.) PETS 2012. LNCS, vol. 7384, pp. 38–57. Springer, Heidelberg (2012)
24. Pfitzmann, A., Hansen, M.: Anonymity, Unobservability, Pseudonymity, and Identity Management - A Proposal for Terminology, August 2010 (version v0.34)
25. Pham, D.V.: Towards Practical and Fundamental Limits of Anonymity Protection. Ph.D. thesis, University of Regensburg (2013)
26. Pham, D.V., Kesdogan, D.: A combinatorial approach for an anonymity metric. In: Boyd, C., González Nieto, J. (eds.) ACISP 2009. LNCS, vol. 5594, pp. 26–43. Springer, Heidelberg (2009)
27. Pham, D.V., Wright, J., Kesdogan, D.: A practical complexity-theoretic analysis of mix systems. In: Atluri, V., Diaz, C. (eds.) ESORICS 2011. LNCS, vol. 6879, pp. 508–527. Springer, Heidelberg (2011)

28. Pham, V.: Analysis of the anonymity set of chaumian mixes. In: 13th Nordic Workshop on Secure IT-Systems (2008)
29. Raymond, J.-F.: Traffic analysis: protocols, attacks, design issues, and open problems. In: Federrath, H. (ed.) Designing Privacy Enhancing Technologies. LNCS, vol. 2009, pp. 10–29. Springer, Heidelberg (2001)
30. Shannon, C.: Communication Theory of Secrecy Systems. Bell System Technical Journal **28**, 656–715 (1949)
31. Troncoso, C., Gierlichs, B., Preneel, B., Verbauwhede, I.: Perfect matching disclosure attacks. In: Borisov, N., Goldberg, I. (eds.) PETS 2008. LNCS, vol. 5134, pp. 2–23. Springer, Heidelberg (2008)

POSN: A Personal Online Social Network

Esra Erdin[1], Eric Klukovich[1], Gurhan Gunduz[2],
and Mehmet Hadi Gunes[1](✉)

[1] University of Nevada, Reno, USA
mgunes@unr.edu
[2] Pamukkale University, Denizli, Turkey

Abstract. A growing concern for end users of Online Social Networks (OSNs) is the privacy and control of user data due to the client-server architecture of the current ecosystems. In this paper, we introduce a privacy preserving decentralized OSN platform, which mimics real life social interactions. In particular, we decentralize the OSN platform and give direct control of the information to the user. The distributed platform removes central authorities from the OSN and users share their content only with intended peers through mobile devices. This decentralized system ensures that interaction happens between friends and third parties cannot access the user content or relationships. To be able to efficiently share objects and provide timely access in the POSN platform, we take advantage of free storage clouds to distribute encrypted user content. The combination of phone-to-phone applications with cloud infrastructure would address the availability limitation of peer-to-peer systems, while enjoying the benefits of peer-to-peer systems, such as no central authority and scalability.

Keywords: Decentralize · Phone-to-phone · Privacy · Social networks

1 Introduction

Online social interactions are an integral part of our daily activity. As indicated in Milgram's experiment, we live in a small-world [10,21]. Connecting this small-world in the digital world has been a challenge and has been addressed in various ways. OSNs enable frequent social interaction and expansion of knowledge or gossip. The emergence of OSNs sparked a major reform in information spread and how users interact with each other. From data to search to social interactions, users around the world are now more deeply connected to the Internet as user-generated content undergoes perpetual growth and expansion.

The client-server architecture of the current OSN ecosystems have raised privacy concerns. In general, users have to trust corporations (and governments) with their personal data when using OSNs. OSNs collect considerable amount of personal information about their clients and provide new services based on collected or derived information. For instance, a provider can filter advertisements based on user profile or user's circle (i.e., friends). Additionally, OSNs have predictive

© IFIP International Federation for Information Processing 2015
H. Federrath and D. Gollmann (Eds.): SEC 2015, IFIP AICT 455, pp. 51–66, 2015.
DOI: 10.1007/978-3-319-18467-8_4

capabilities about the users as they continuously gather user data. Researchers have tried to address privacy concerns by user-based key management [6,12,14, 34], peer-to-peer architectures [8,9,11,13,25,27,32,36], or decentralized platforms [1,3,20,30,31,33,35,38]. In general, peer-to-peer OSN architectures suffer from inefficiency due to high churn rate of users. Even though some of the proposed decentralized platforms utilize cloud resources, they rely on compute clouds which are typically fee-based and could analyze user data.

In a decentralized architecture, efficient sharing and timely access of objects play a vital role [22]. In two-way friendship OSNs, users typically access a small number of objects among vast number of posts, with many users accessing only recently posted objects. Additionally, updates by a user must be available to his/her friends in a timely manner regardless of whether the posting user has become offline. To address these challenges, we take advantage of *free storage clouds* to distribute *encrypted user content*. Even though there are OSNs that utilize cloud, they either use it as an execution platform with plaintext or as a backup store to central servers. To best of our knowledge, this is the first study to promote a decentralized OSN relying on mobile devices and storage clouds with no central server. While peer-to-peer systems require a peer to be online for data exchange, we utilize cloud to greatly enhance data availability. The free cloud storage services allows POSN to function through user clients such as smart phone or tablet apps with no infrastructure of its own. Moreover, smart phones and tablets have considerable computing capabilities that is utilized to provide direct interaction between users.

In this paper, to address privacy concerns, we introduce a Privacy Preserving Decentralized Online Social Network (POSN) which mimics real life social interactions. Figure 1 presents sample snapshots of Android app in development. The main contribution

Fig. 1. Snapshots of the POSN prototype

of this paper is *the combination of phone-to-phone applications with cloud infrastructure* to address the main limitation of peer-to-peer systems, i.e., *availability*, due to high churn rate while enjoying the benefits of peer-to-peer systems, i.e., *no central authority and scalability*. This approach can be expanded to provide other forms of social communications where data privacy is a concern.

2   Cloud as Storage

In proposed POSN, each user's data is kept in a separate location and the owner is in charge of granting access to his or her friends. The cloud can provide this storage resource free of charge. Users upload encrypted data to their cloud and fetch data from the cloud's of their friends (see Section 5). Cloud providers could only observe encrypted data and share this encrypted data with users that have access to it as shown in Figure 2.

In order to find online friends, we need to check their cloud location file where their IP address and Port number is stored. In order to access posted content of a friend, a user should download the content i.e. the wall post file. In general, walls containing posts will be automatically downloaded but the mul-timedia content and comments will

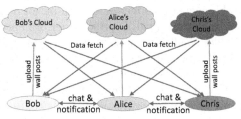

Fig. 2. Personal Online Social Network

be downloaded only when a user views it. Even though downloading a file is straightforward, checking hundreds of user's files across different clouds is not efficient. Knowing if your friends have a new content will speed up the process. Online friends can speed up the process as they can share their knowledge about common friends (see Section 8).

In order to see whether clouds can provide communication efficiency of OSNs, we compared the file upload/download timing of popular OSNs (i.e., Facebook and Google+) with popular clouds (i.e., Dropbox, Google Drive, Sky Drive, Mediafire, Copy Cloud). Figure 3 presents the average upload and download timing of 10 measurements using an Android tablet over WiFi at our campus. In these experiments to reduce bias due to background processes and radio status, we closed all unnecessary services, performed a small file transfer to ensure radio is on, and kept the measurement process in the foreground. As Facebook resizes and compresses pictures, we were not able to download a picture of about 1MB even though larger pictures were uploaded. Hence, 1MB and larger files are videos doubling in size whereas below 1MB are pictures resized by Facebook. We obtained comparable performances in our experiments at 10 different WiFi locations throughout the city as well (results not shown due to space limits).

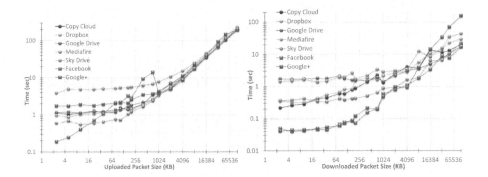

Fig. 3. Upload and Download times (log scale)

When uploading a photo, Facebook becomes progressively worse for pictures (likely due to re-rendering) but is comparable to the rest for videos. Google+ seems worse than all but one cloud provider. Our in depth analysis revealed that the Google+ API streams the videos, therefore the total download time is considerably increased. Overall, upload performances are similar as videos of 1MB and larger are uploaded. Download performance of OSNs are also better than clouds for files smaller than 1MB but are comparable for larger sizes. Even though this might impact interactive communications such as chat, performance difference of 1 sec or less would not be considerable for humans to affect adaptation of POSN. These experiments shows there is no significant performance difference when uploading/downloading a file to/from an OSN or a cloud provider.

Additionally, we performed measurements with 7 mobile phones over 3G in the Reno/SFO area. Figure 4 presents the ratio of Dropbox over Facebook performance for transfer of the same file by the phone around the same time. As each volunteer did not complete the same number of experiments, we present each point separately. Note that points above 1 indicate OSN is faster than cloud. Overall, we observe the OSN can be up to 10x faster or the cloud can be up to 9x faster, while in most cases OSN is faster. We believe such considerable performance variation in data transfers is due to the 3G traffic rate instability.

3   Friendship Establishment

Establishing friendship between interested people in a decentralized system is a challenge. Hence, in POSN, we need to rely on other mechanisms in establishing friendship and ensuring identities. POSN platform relies on users' existing contacts, i.e., phone numbers and email addresses, in order to establish friendship and ensure identities. POSN platform can exchange emails or SMS messages between users to establish certificates/tokens that will

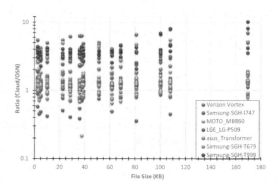

Fig. 4. 3G Performance Comparison (log scale)

inform the cloud location and public keys of friends as in Figure 5. As the temporal identities need to be unique, POSN generates identities based on hash of email addresses or phone numbers.

When a person wants to establish friendship with a contact, s/he sends a URI containing her/his identity, public key, and profile location. The receiving person may then respond with her/his information if s/he wants to establish a link. Note that, both messages should be exchanged via e-mail or SMS so that real identities are ensured. This approach is also in line with our focus on personalized OSN as the links in our network should correspond to real life friendships between users.

Note that, a malicious email provider might tamper with message and this is a research challenge we will focus on. To address this issue, public key certificates can be obtained or secure e-mails can be sent with PGP to assure validity of public keys against potential man-in-the-middle attackers. Distributed key agreement protocols can also be utilized to verify public keys among friends [5, 28, 29].

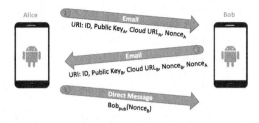

Fig. 5. Friendship establishment

4   Data Dissemination

POSN utilizes cloud storage system where users upload their content to a cloud and obtain wall posts of friends from their clouds. Even though one might think the overhead would be prohibitive (e.g., Facebook has 1.2 billion users), each user needs to manage content of their friends. On average, a Facebook user has 130 friends (while the number is 214 in the United States) [18] who are typically clustered into 12 groups [37]. We keep users in groups similar to most OSNs and have a wall post file for each group in addition to individual wall file. When the user makes a post it is appended to the appropriate group.

To better understand how data is being generated in OSNs, we monitored the activities of 16 Facebook users and their circles (i.e., posts shared by their friends) for 15 days with explicit permission from the users. On average; for analyzed users, number of friends is 220 (146 of whom used a smart device) who are divided into 9 groups. Similarly, per day, average number of text posts in the user's circle is 53, links is 37, pictures is 51, videos is 7, and chat messages is 85. The monitored users themselves uploaded just a total of 25 pictures and 2 videos in total over the same period.

Figure 6 shows how multimedia (i.e., pictures and videos) posts are generated by circles of each user. We observe majority of photos are less than 100KB while

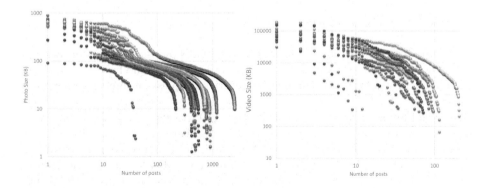

Fig. 6. Multimedia posting pattern of the circles of users (log-scale)

none is greater than 1MB. Likewise, majority of videos are less than 10MB but exceptionally there are videos larger than 100MB.

As multimedia can be very large, the multimedia should be distributed through the cloud where the user lets online friends know that there is a new post with a direct link to download data from the cloud. Otherwise, the user would send multiple copies of the file (i.e., as many as the number of online friends). Figure 7 shows the sender bandwidth overhead for a user if s/he was to post her/his

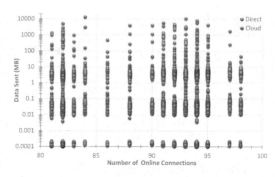

Fig. 7. Sender overhead for multimedia (log-scale)

friend's posts. It indicates that user overhead considerably increases if the user directly sends multimedia files to online friends. For sending average file of 93KB to 90 online friends, the user would need to send over 8MB data. Hence, rather than sending multiple copies of the file, the poster notifies online friends about the post that has been uploaded to the cloud.

Moreover, Figure 8 shows the frequency of non-multimedia posts (e.g., wall update, link, like, and comment) for the circle of a user. In the figure, points show the average number of posts when x number of friends were online and the line is the moving average. On average, during a session, a user posts 66 non-multimedia content while there are on average 81 online friends. Even though, cloud is utilized for efficient distribution of content, non-multimedia posts can directly be delivered to online friends.

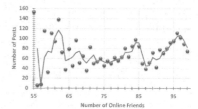

Fig. 8. Non-multimedia posts in a user's circle (log-scale)

5   Privacy Protection

In order to provide security and privacy in the POSN platform, data is encrypted before uploading into the cloud. Every user in the POSN would have a public key. This public key is exchanged at the time of friendship establishment and shared through the cloud. However, this would be very inefficient as a separate wall post would be made for each friend. Instead, POSN keeps a wall for each group as most users forms clusters of friends [17,24]. Therefore, each group needs a symmetric key for the group wall, and these keys need to be exchanged securely. In order to handle the access to the wall post that belongs to a specific group, the poster embeds a symmetric key into the file as shown in Figure 9. Using this mechanism, POSN ensures security without adding considerable overhead

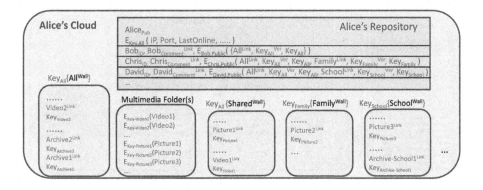

Fig. 9. Key Hierarchy to Protect User Content

to the system since the symmetric keys do not need to be exchanged but rather recovered through public keys. Furthermore, as multimedia files might be posted to different groups, we encrypt multimedia files with individual symmetric keys, which are shared in the wall post for the group.

Each user's repository provides group keys encrypted with each user's public key along with the comment file for that user (see Section 6 for commenting). In Figure 9, Bob just has access to the "All" group while Chris has access to "All" and "Family" groups. As the symmetric keys for groups can be updated, the Key^{ver} indicates the version number of the keys. Note that, each user has a different repository file and hence can not see other's by default.

In order to assess encryption overhead, we analyzed performance overhead of encryption (using standard Android AES library) using an Android tablet over WiFi at our campus. Figure 10 presents performance ratio of Dropbox over Facebook where blue points indicate transfer without encryption and red points indicate transfer with encryption for average of 10 measurements. Overall, we observe that encryption increases the ratio on

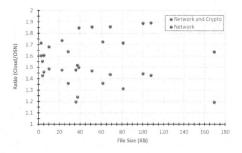

Fig. 10. Cryptography overhead

an average from 1.40 to 1.71, an average of 22% increase in time with encryption. This results are encouraging as the extra encryption is not adding significant delay overhead.

6   Commenting

Commenting is one of the important feature of OSNs since people typically care about their friends opinion and it should be incorporated into the framework. However, majority of the peer-to-peer and decentralized OSN platforms ignore

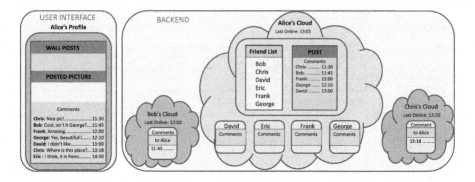

Fig. 11. Comment propagation

this feature as it is very challenging to provide in a decentralized structure (see Section 10). In POSN, each user posts her/his items into the cloud. In order for friends to post a comment, they should be granted with write permission to the wall. This might introduce security problems since friends might intentionally or accidentally mess up a shared file.

One way of incorporating commenting in this framework would be opening a file with a shared write permission for each friend (such as David, Eric, Frank, and George in Figure 11). If a friend wants to make a comment about a specific post, then this comment can be posted into a file that belongs to that specific friend. Associating the comments with the posts can be done by using the previously assigned IDs of wall posts. The next challenge is how to spread this comment to friends viewing the original post. So far, we assumed wall post file will be used to exchange data. Now, we would need to look into as many as the number of friends' files to see if they have a comment about posts. The owner can aggregate all the comments under friend's comment files to be included under the original post file and remove them from individual comment files. Unfortunately, this process can be accomplished only if the owner is online.

Moreover, users have different cloud providers and might not have an account with the poster's cloud (such as Bob and Chris in Figure 11). Such users will have comment files for their friends's post in their own cloud. To handle these distributed commenting files, the original poster needs to have a file that holds the friend's information where a link to each friends commenting location is provided (such as *Friend List* in Figure 11). In this case Alice will not be able to erase Bob's comment after populating it to her wall.

The last issue with the commenting is the efficiency. Gathering comments from each friends' cloud will introduce considerable overhead to the system. To minimize this overhead, we implement caching schemes as described in Section 8. When making a comment to a post, the user sends this comment to all (common) online friends who can further propagate to other common friends.

7 Search Optimization

Another feature of OSNs that is challenging in distributed platforms is the search for objects. In POSN, the cloud is used only for storage purposes and friends' encrypted content is scattered across several locations. In order to search for content of friends, the wall files from all friends should be downloaded to a client to be searched through. Such a scheme is very inefficient since the number of content belonging to a user's circle can be very high. In order to overcome this problem in POSN, an index structure is implemented as described in Figure 12. Whenever a post is made, its keywords or tags are inserted into the index file by the content creator and uploaded to the cloud along with the post.

Considering there are several groups for a user, one index file will not be enough to handle different groups. Because an owner might post a multimedia content to a specific group, inserting its tag information into a common index will hint other users of its existence. Hence, POSN keeps a different index file for each group encrypted with the symmetric key of the group that it belongs to as shown in Figure 9.

Since an index file is needed by all of our friends, it needs to be disseminated to them. If a user wants

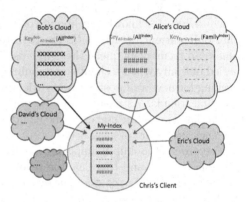

Fig. 12. Multi-level Indexing for Searching

to search for a multimedia content, s/he needs to download the index files of each friend. These index files are then searched for the desired content, which is not very efficient either. To improve search efficiency, POSN will preemptively process the index files of all friends and create a new index structure on the client whenever the user is online.

8 Data Distribution Optimization

The lack of a central server results in accessing several locations to gather the posts from friends. In the worst case, the user has to check all of friends' cloud locations, which may introduce significant overhead. In POSN framework clients establish direct connection with online friends' clients. When online, clients can exchange information about common friends that are not necessarily online. The number of connections that a client needs to aggregate the information from can

Fig. 13. Friends inter-connections

considerably be reduced as friends typically form clusters (i.e., communities). Figure 13 presents the network between 635 friends of a monitored user where they form several clusters among themselves. Online friends can exchange information about common friends' latest posts. As a result, the number of connections that a client needs to aggregate the information from will decrease.

In POSN, when a client (such as client **A** in Figure 14) becomes online, it will look for friends' cloud to see if they have a new post and learn their communication address (i.e., IP address and port number) if they are online. If the friend (such as client **D**) is online then the client can establish direct connection and ask the friend about common friends (clients **C**, **E**, **F**, and **G** in the example). The online friend then provides its knowledge about common friends. Once other online friends (such as **C**) are reported then the newcomer can recursively query these friends. This operation is

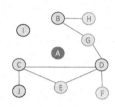

Fig. 14. Phone-to-Phone exchange

carried out only when a client comes online. Thereafter, rather than periodically checking for new wall posts at every friend's cloud, post notifications are pushed to online friends. As users might become online simultaneously, they need to first update the online status in the cloud and then look up for friends to assure that they are aware of each other.

The order of lookup is important as finding online friends early on has considerable benefits and there can be several approaches. The first one is to rank friends by the *number of common friends*. The second method is to rank friends by their expected *online duration*. In order to implement these approaches, a user needs to keep and share the relevant information. The success rate of these methods is a research issue that we will try to optimize in our system.

In Figure 15, we compare four methods namely, ideal, most online duration, most common friends, and random for our measured data. In the figure, the x-axis indicates the percentage of online friends when a user becomes online and the y-axis indicates percentage of connections that could

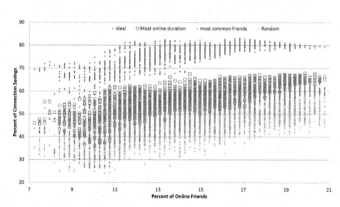

Fig. 15. Help from online friends

be eliminated. One issue is to determine when to take a snapshot of online activity. To mimic real user activity, we assumed the user came online one minute before one of her/his friends actually became online. Hence, we obtain a much larger number of data points than an individuals online pattern. The marks indicate one instance in our measurements for the user whose circle is shown in Figure 13. On average, 14.6% of friends were online while ideally one could save 76.5% of connections on average. Heuristics to first lookup at friends that are most online saves 57.9% of connections while prioritizing most common friends saves 53.2% of connections on average. Even, random ordering saves 45.7% of connections on average. Our evaluations with the user with 435 friends yield very close results (difference of less than 1% in each average).

Figure 16 presents the amount of multimedia data a user would need to download when s/he became online based on the measurement of user in Figure 13. Similar to Figure 15, we assume the friends' online pattern as the user's online duration. As the time between logins increase, the amount of data the user might download from her/his friends increases. In extreme cases, we observe there is about 1GB of data when the user has not logged in for about a day and friends have posted large

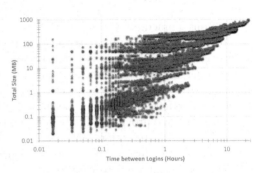

Fig. 16. Multimedia data to download when a user becomes online (log-scale in both axis)

videos. Hence, rather than auto-downloading all multimedia content, POSN would parse most recent posts and wait for the user to fetch subsequent content as s/he is scrolling through the posts (especially for large videos).

9 Discussion

9.1 Social Challenges

Friendships might not last forever or the level of friendship might change, as a result the content that friends exchange will change. The POSN framework should reflect changes in the friendship status. To reduce the level of information exchange with a friend, the group or groups that friend belongs to could be changed. As we might not want the person to be aware of unfriending, we move all other friends to new group(s) with new key(s). Hence, the unfriended person would think that there are no new posts even if they analyzed the raw data.

Another challenge in real life is *stalking*. In order to stalk someone in our system, s/he has to know the victim in real life and be a friend in the POSN platform. If the stalker is a friend of victims friend, s/he can only see the comments of the victim. There is no way that the stalker can see the shared content of the victim through POSN if they are not friends.

To allow third party application support without harming user privacy, each user can keep an App File for each authorized application in their cloud. This App file is encrypted with a key as any other group wall. Applications will write the relevant data into the files without revealing it to the app developer. Moreover, friends who want to partner in specific app can exchange their App file location and keys so that they can collaborate/compete. Online applications can also exchange information over the socket connection that is created by the online clients.

9.2 Security Challenges

Stolen devices pose a security risk. The owner of the stolen device should send notifications immediately. This notification could be send either by email or SMS or through some automated mechanisms to minimize the damage. Once a notification is received every key that is paired with that user would be renewed. On the other side, the mechanism should be carefully deployed so that this is not employed for denial of service attacks. Hence, we will investigate a solution that provides immediate notification mechanism while it can not be used for DoS.

Finally, a cloud provider might track who is accessing individual files and gain knowledge about interactions of a user [15,23]. Note that, to download content, a friend just uses direct link to the file without logging into the cloud. Also, online users do not need to connect to the cloud to exchange non-multimedia content. To prevent even IP based analysis by cloud provider, the user might utilize multiple clouds for different groups s/he is managing. Moreover, friends can utilize proxies and anonymizer technologies in her/his communications with the cloud [16,19]. Likewise, a user's online friends (who are not necessarily friend with the person whose encrypted data is downloaded) can be utilized in accessing clouds so that the cloud is not certain of who is accessing the content.

10 Related Work

We have analyzed some of the decentralized OSNs that we could identify, and found several decentralized OSNs currently in use: Diaspora [3], Friendica [1], and RetroShare [2]. Diaspora has tens of thousands of active users. Diaspora is a set of pods (currently about 130 are publicly available) that decentralize the system and is accessible through browsers. Even though an individual can deploy their private pod, the main issue with Diaspora is that each pod is a central server of many users. Similarly, Friendica builds a social web platform using set of decentralized servers. RetroShare is a peer-to-peer PC application that provides decentralized OSN support.

Additionally, there are several decentralized OSNs proposed in academia, but none of them seems to be actively used. Cachet [27], PeerSon [8], Safebook [9], and LifeSocial [13] build a peer-to-peer (p2p) system where peers are not necessarily trusted. Polaris [36], My3 [25] and Vegas [11] build a p2p network among friends to replicate data. Confidant [20], Tent [4], and Vis-a-Vis [31] build a distributed platform by building a protocol among servers that process user data. Persona [6] proposes to use attribute based encryption to store user data in untrusted storage servers with web based OSN platform. PrPl [30] allows a user to use personal or 3rd party server to store their encrypted content.

Finally, there are privacy preserving social networks that are not traditional OSNs. Pythia attempts to present a privacy aware p2p network for social search [26]. Gossple is an anonymous social network that helps users build new relationships with others based on mutual interests [7]. Priv.io [38] builds a decentralized web based platform to securely share data. Contrail is a communication platform that provides content filtering in decentralized social networks [33]. NOYB [14] and Lockr [34] can be integrated into current social networks in order to guarantee the users privacy in OSNs.

Friendship Establishment: The decentralized networks that provide security as a feature tend to be more careful with revealing the very existence of certain users, thus finding friends becomes a challenge. Others are more cavalier with this information so making more friends is easier. There is a tradeoff of how privacy protecting the system is and how difficult it is for users to find and add their friends. As Diaspora and Friendica has member directories, friends can can easily be found. In Cachet, LifeSocial, and Vis-a-Vis users can locate friends through a DHT. PeerSon, Persona, Polaris, RetroShare, and Vegas exchange certificate files to establish friendship. In proposed POSN, we rely on existing identities, i.e., email addresses, to exchange credentials and establish friendship.

Data Storage: In a decentralized OSN, the data is, by definition, not stored in a single location. Some applications store the data in a distributed manner as a security precaution, some do it in order to promote inter-connectivity between users, and others do it for a combination of reasons. Diaspora and Friendica store data in a set of servers, which can be private. P2p systems store encrypted data amongst all peers (i.e., Cachet, LifeSocial, and PeerSon) or only in trusted peers (i.e., My3, Safebook, and Vegas). Confidant, Tent, and Vis-a-Vis decentralize the data among the users selected servers (potentially cloud providers), but the servers actually process the user data. Persona stores data in servers but only stores encrypted data. Some store data only in the user's PC (i.e., RetroShare) or smart phone (i.e., Polaris). In the proposed POSN, we build a p2p platform between mobile devices and utilize the cloud for encrypted data storage.

Support for Content Search: Among analyzed systems only Confidant, Diaspora, and Friendica users can search for content in their own server (or other servers in case of Diaspora), and Vegas users can perform controlled friend flooding to search for content. Different from p2p platforms that typically do not allow search function, POSN provides search of encrypted content by preemptively building search indexes.

Support for Commenting: Among analyzed systems only Confidant, Diaspora, and Friendica allow comments to posts as content is stored on a set of servers. Different from p2p platforms that do not allow commenting function, POSN provides commenting by propagating comments through the system.

11   Conclusions

OSNs have gained a great importance in our daily life. People prefer to communicate and interact with their friends through OSNs. In this paper, we propose a privacy preserving decentralized OSN so that users have direct control of their information. POSN can be easily deployed by installing an application and using a free-of-charge cloud storage provider. The POSN platform focuses on the community of individuals and tries to optimize the system through encrypted cloud storage. The combination of phone-to-phone applications with cloud infrastructure addresses the main limitation of peer-to-peer systems, i.e., availability, while enjoying the benefits of peer-to-peer systems, i.e., no central authority and scalability. POSN ensures that interactions happen between friends and third parties cannot access the user content or relationships.

Acknowledgments. We would like to thank James Bridegum for initial App development and Davut Ucar for collecting public WiFi measurements.

This material is based upon work supported by the National Science Foundation under grant number EPS- IIA-1301726.

References

1. Friendica: The internet is our social network. http://friendica.com
2. Retroshare: secure communications with friends. http://retroshare.sourceforge.net
3. Diaspora: community-run, distributed social-network. https://joindiaspora.com
4. Tent: All your data in one place. https://tent.io
5. Ateniese, G., Steiner, M., Tsudik, G.: New multiparty authentication services and key agreement protocols. IEEE Journal on Selected Areas in Communications **18**(4), 628–639 (2000)
6. Baden, R., Bender, A., Spring, N., Bhattacharjee, B., Starin, D.: Persona: an online social network with user-defined privacy. In: ACM SIGCOMM 2009
7. Bertier, M., Frey, D., Guerraoui, R., Kermarrec, A.-M., Leroy, V.: The gossple anonymous social network. In: Gupta, I., Mascolo, C. (eds.) Middleware 2010. LNCS, vol. 6452, pp. 191–211. Springer, Heidelberg (2010)
8. Buchegger, S., Schiöberg, D., Vu, L.-H., Datta, A.: Peerson: P2p social networking: early experiences and insights. In: SNS 2009 (2009)
9. Cutillo, L., Molva, R., Strufe, T.: Safebook: feasibility of transitive cooperation for privacy on a decentralized social network. In: WOWMOM 2009 (2009)
10. Dodds, P.S., Muhamad, R., Watts, D.J.: An experimental study of search in global social networks. Science (2003)
11. Durr, M., Maier, M., Dorfmeister, F.: Vegas - a secure and privacy-preserving peer-to-peer online social network. In: SocialCom/PASSAT (2012)
12. Feldman, A.J., Blankstein, A., Freedman, M.J., Felten, E.W.: Social networking with frientegrity: privacy and integrity with an untrusted provider. In: USENIX Security 2012
13. Graffi, K., Gross, C., Mukherjee, P., Kovacevic, A., Steinmetz, R.: Lifesocial.kom: a p2p-based platform for secure online social networks. In: P2P 2010

14. Guha, S., Tang, K., Francis, P.: Noyb: privacy in online social networks. In: WOSN 2008
15. Gunes, M.H., Evrenosoglu, C.: Blind processing: securing data against system administrators. In: IEEE/IFIP NOMS 2010
16. Karaoglu, H.T., Akgun, M.B., Gunes, M.H., Yuksel, M.: Multi path considerations for anonymized routing: challenges and opportunities. In: IFIP NTMS 2012
17. Kardes, H., Sevincer, A., Gunes, M.H., Yuksel, M.: Six degrees of separation among US researchers. In: IEEE/ACM ASONAM 2012
18. Kirschner, P.A., Karpinski, A.C.: Facebook and academic performance. Computers in Human Behavior (2010)
19. Li, B., Erdin, E., Gunes, M.H., Bebis, G., Shipley, T.: An Overview of Anonymity Technology Usage. Computer Communications **36**(12), 1269–1283 (2013)
20. Liu, D., Shakimov, A., Cáceres, R., Varshavsky, A., Cox, L.P.: Confidant: protecting osn data without locking it up. In: Kon, F., Kermarrec, A.-M. (eds.) Middleware 2011. LNCS, vol. 7049, pp. 61–80. Springer, Heidelberg (2011)
21. Milgram, S.: The small world problem. Psychology Today (1967)
22. Narayanan, H.A.J., Gunes, M.H.: Ensuring access control in cloud provisioned healthcare systems. In: IEEE CCNC 2011
23. Naruchitparames, J., Gunes, M.H.: Enhancing data privacy and integrity in the cloud. In: HPCS 2011
24. Naruchitparames, J., Gunes, M.H., Louis, S.J.: Friend recommendations in social networks using genetic algorithms and network topology. In: IEEE CEC 2011
25. Narendula, R., Papaioannou, T., Aberer, K.: My3: a highly-available p2p-based online social network. In: Peer-to-Peer Computing (2011)
26. Nilizadeh, S., Alam, N., Husted, N., Kapadia, A.: Pythia: a privacy aware, peer-to-peer network for social search. In: WPES 2011
27. Nilizadeh, S., Jahid, S., Mittal, P., Borisov, N., Kapadia, A.: Cachet: a decentralized architecture for privacy preserving social networking with caching. In: CoNEXT 2012
28. Perrig, A.: Efficient collaborative key management protocols for secure autonomous group communication. In: CrypTEC 1999
29. Rafaeli, S., Hutchison, D.: A survey of key management for secure group communication. ACM Comput. Surv. **35**(3), 309–329 (2003)
30. Seong, S.-W., Seo, J., Nasielski, M., Sengupta, D., Hangal, S., Keat, S., Chu, T.R., Dodson, B., Lam, M.S.: Prpl: a decentralized social networking infrastructure. In: MCS 2010
31. Shakimov, A., Lim, H., Caceres, R., Cox, L., Li, K., Liu, D., Varshavsky, A.: Vis-a-vis: privacy-preserving online social networking via virtual individual servers. In: COMSNETS 2011
32. Sharma, R., Datta, A.: Supernova: super-peers based architecture for decentralized online social networks. In: COMSNETS 2012
33. Stuedi, P., Mohomed, I., Balakrishnan, M., Mao, Z.M., Ramasubramanian, V., Terry, D., Wobber, T.: Contrail: enabling decentralized social networks on smart-phones. In: Kon, F., Kermarrec, A.-M. (eds.) Middleware 2011. LNCS, vol. 7049, pp. 41–60. Springer, Heidelberg (2011)
34. Tootoonchian, A., Saroiu, S., Ganjali, Y., Wolman, A.: Lockr: better privacy for social networks. In: CoNEXT 2009

35. Yeung, C.-M.A., Liccardi, I., Lu, K., Seneviratne, O., Berners-lee, T.: Decentralization: the future of online social networking. In: W3C Workshop on the Future of Social Networking Position Papers (2009)
36. Wilson, C., Steinbauer, T., Wang, G., Sala, A., Zheng, H., Zhao, B.Y.: Privacy, availability and economics in the polaris mobile social network. In: HotMobile 2011
37. Wilson, R.E., Gosling, S.D., Graham, L.T.: A review of Facebook research in the social sciences. Perspectives on Psychological Science, May 2012
38. Zhang, L., Mislove, A.: Building confederated web-based services with priv.io. In: COSN 2013

Strategic Noninterference

Wojciech Jamroga[1] and Masoud Tabatabaei[2]([✉])

[1] Institute of Computer Science, Polish Academy of Sciences, Warsaw, Poland
w.jamroga@ipipan.waw.pl
[2] Interdisciplinary Centre for Security and Trust, University of Luxembourg,
Walferdange, Luxembourg
masoud.tabatabaei@uni.lu

Abstract. Noninterference is a property that captures confidentiality of actions executed by a given process. However, the property is hard to guarantee in realistic scenarios. We show that the security of a system can be seen as an interplay between functionality requirements and the strategies adopted by users, and based on it we propose a weaker notion of noninterference which we call *strategic noninterference*. We also give a characterization of strategic noninterference through unwinding relations for specific subclasses of goals and for the simplified setting where a strategy is given as a parameter.

1 Introduction

The term *noninterference* was first introduced in the seminal work by Goguen and Meseguer [4] as a formalisation of information flow security. The concept can be informally described as follows: one group of users, using a certain set of actions, is noninterfereing with another group of users if what the first group does has no effect on what the second group of users can see. The idea is to prevent any information about the behaviour of the first group (which we call High players) to flow to the second group (which we call Low players). From its appearance in [4], noninterference has been vastly used to define confidentiality properties in programs and concurrent processes.

As much as the notion is appealing in theory, several challenges make it less useful in practice. Noninterference is a very restrictive concept, and implementing a practical system that satisfies it entirely is hard or even impossible. It becomes even harder when integrating an already implemented infrastructure with an information flow policy defined on top of it (cf. [28]). Last but not least, in many applications, downward flow of information is either permitted or is inevitable in some possible runs of the system. In this paper, we propose to restrict the property of noninterference to only a subset of possible behaviors of the system. The proposal follows an observation that, in most systems, not all possible behaviors actually happen. If the High players pursue a particular goal, they may do so by executing a *strategy*. Then, only those runs of the system can occur, which are consistent with the strategy. But in that case it should suffice to preserve confidentiality only in the runs that can happen when the strategy

© IFIP International Federation for Information Processing 2015
H. Federrath and D. Gollmann (Eds.): SEC 2015, IFIP AICT 455, pp. 67–81, 2015.
DOI: 10.1007/978-3-319-18467-8_5

is executed. In other words, High do not need to worry about the leakage of information that their own strategy prevents.

Examples of strategies include institutional policies in organizations, implementation guidelines for programs etc. The following scenario shows how one may ensure noninterference in an intrinsically insecure system, by committing to a strategy which both satisfies a desired goal and prevents information flow.

Example 1 (Motivating example). A health care data center is responsible for gathering medical data from the hospitals in the area and storing them in the servers of the center. The center also provides limited internet access for public users who can run allowed queries on the database. The querying interface is accessible all of the time. Moreover, the data center runs an updating procedure whenever new data is available at one of the hospitals. In order to ensure integrity of answers, the querying interface returns "out of service" while the update is running. Unfortunately, it has turned out that a user may be able to relate the time of update (= the time of observing the "out of service" message) to the hospital from which the data comes, and then by checking the results of queries before and after the update, gain unauthorized information about the hospital.

The data center provides multiple functionalities (storing, updating, and providing access to the data). Moreover, requirements on the functionalities can be specified differently. Our main observation is that, depending on the actual functionality requirement, there might a strategy that fulfils the requirement *and* satisfies a given security property (in our case, noninterference). Consider, for instance, the following requirement: *"the system should be updated as soon as new data is available, and the querying interface should be running all day"*. It is easy to see that, for this functionality requirement, the system is bound to be vulnerable. More formally, there is no strategy that satisfies the requirement and at the same time guarantees noninterference. However, if the functionality requirement is changed to a weaker one: *"the system should be updated at most 24 hours after new data is available, and the querying interface should be running at least 22 hours a day"*, then there exist a strategy for the data center which both satisfies the requirement and prevents the unwanted information flow. The strategy can be to close the interface for one hour every day, and to postpone the updates to the nearest closing time of the interface.   □

The main idea behind this paper can be summarized as follows. For sophisticated systems, different security strategies are available that constrain the behavior of the system. Such a strategy can consist in fixing some parameters of the software (e.g., the schedule of automated updates, time windows for entering new data, etc.) as well as imposing constraints on the behavior of human components (e.g., who is allowed to enter new data). We propose that security of the system can be seen as an interplay between the goal of the system, phrased in terms of a functionality requirement, and the security strategy being used.

We begin by recalling the standard notion of noninterference and formally defining agents' strategic behavior (Section 2). Then, we propose our new concept of strategic noninterference in Section 3, and present its theoretical characterization for certain types of objectives in Section 4.

Related Work. Since the introduction of noninterference in [4], several variations have been suggested for the concept, such as *nondeducibility* [22], *noninference* [12], and *restrictiveness* [10]. Although noninterference was originally introduced for systems modeled as finite state machines, it was later redefined, generalized, and extended in the framework of process algebras [1,14–16,18]. Noninterference and its variants have been studied from different perspectives. Some works dealt with composability of noninterference [10,20,27]. Another group of papers studied the properties of intransitive noninterference [2,3,15,25]. Probabilistic noninterference and quantitative noninterference have been investigated, e.g., in [6,9,11,13,21,26]. Out of all the works, only [18] comes closer to our proposal, as the authors suggest that, for systems that do not satisfy noninterference in general, the property can be possibly restored for a suitably constrained version of the system. However, the behavioral constraint has to be given explicitly, and it can be of a completely abstract nature. In particular, it does not have to specify an executable strategy for any participants. Moreover, the functionality-related side (i.e., goals) is not treated explicitly in [18].

When reasoning about information leakage, it is important to distinguish between two methodological views on confidentiality. According to the first view, the Low users may attempt to read directly or deduce indirectly information that they are not authorized to obtain, and they are trying to do this on their own. The second view assumes possible cooperating agents among the High players, for example malicious spy processes, that help the Low players to get the unauthorized information. This is usually done through *covert channels* [8,26]. In our approach we assume that either the High players are not malicious, or the commitment mechanism is powerful enough so that even malicious players follow the selected strategy. We should also mention that our proposal is inherently different from so called *nondeducibility on strategies* [26]. While in [26] strategies are considered as a means to transfer information from the High player to the Low player, in our approach it is used by the High player to prevent the leakage of information.

2 Preliminaries: Noninterference and Strategies

2.1 Standard Concept of Noninterference

We first recall the standard notion of noninterference by Goguen and Meseguer [4]. The system is modeled by a multi-agent asynchronous transition network $M = \langle St, s_0, \mathfrak{U}, \mathfrak{A}, do, Obs, obs \rangle$ where: St is the set of *states*, s_0 is the initial state, $\mathfrak{U}$ is the set of *agents* (or *users*), $\mathfrak{A}$ is the set of *actions*, $do : St \times \mathfrak{U} \times \mathfrak{A} \rightarrow St$ is the transition function that specifies the (deterministic) outcome $do(s,u,a)$ of action a if it is executed by user u in state s; Obs is the set of possible *observations* (or *outputs*); $obs : St \times \mathfrak{U} \rightarrow Obs$ is the observation function. We will sometimes write $[s]_u$ instead of $obs(s,u)$. Also, we will call a pair *(user, action)* a *personalized action*. We construct the multi-step transition function $exec : St \times (\mathfrak{U} \times \mathfrak{A})^* \rightarrow St$ so that, for a finite string $\alpha \in (\mathfrak{U} \times \mathfrak{A})^*$ of personalized actions, $exec(\alpha)$ denotes the state resulting from execution of α from s_0 on.

If $U \subseteq \mathfrak{U}$, $A \subseteq \mathfrak{A}$, and $\alpha \in (\mathfrak{U} \times \mathfrak{A})^*$, then by $Purge_U(\alpha)$ we mean the subsequence of α obtained by eliminating all the pairs (u, a) with $u \in U$. Also, $Purge_{U,A}(\alpha)$ denotes the subsequence of α obtained by eliminating all the pairs (u, a) with $u \in U$ and $a \in A$.

Definition 1 (Noninterference [4]). *Given a transition network M and sets of agents H and L, we say that H is non-interfering with L iff for all $\alpha \in (\mathfrak{U} \times \mathfrak{A})^*$ and all $u_l \in L$ we have $[exec(\alpha)]_{u_l} = [exec(Purge_H(\alpha))]_{u_l}$. We denote the property by $NI_M(H, L)$. Throughout the paper, we assume that H, L are disjoint.*

In other words, for every sequence of actions α_H that H can execute, there is no "response" sequence from L which, interleaved with α_H, might reveal that H have done anything. Assuming that H need to hide only occurrences of some "sensitive" actions $A \subseteq \mathfrak{A}$, the concept of noninterference is refined as follows.

Definition 2 (Noninterference on sensitive actions [4]). *Given a transition network M, sets of agents H, L, and a set of actions $A \subseteq \mathfrak{A}$, we say that H is non-interfering with L on A iff for all $\alpha \in (\mathfrak{U} \times \mathfrak{A})^*$ and all $u_l \in L$ we have $[exec(\alpha)]_{u_l} = [exec(Purge_{H,A}(\alpha))]_{u_l}$. We denote the property by $NI_M(H, L, A)$.*

It is easy to see that $NI_M(H, L)$ iff $NI_M(H, L, \mathfrak{A})$.

2.2 Strategies and Their Outcomes

Strategy is a game-theoretic concept which captures behavioral policies that an agent can consciously follow in order to realize some objective. We assume that each subset of agents $U \subseteq \mathfrak{U}$ is assigned a set of available coalitional strategies Σ_U. The most important feature of a strategy is that *it constrains the possible behaviors of the system*. We represent it formally by the *outcome function* out_M as follows. First, let T' be a U-*trimming* of tree T iff T' is a subtree of T starting from the same root and obtained by removing an arbitrary subset of transitions labeled by actions of agents from U. Moreover, let $T(M)$ be the *tree unfolding* of M. Then, for every $\sigma_U \in \Sigma_U$, its outcome $out_M(\sigma_U)$ is a U-trimming of $T(M)$.

Let h be a node in tree T corresponding to a particular finite history of interaction. We denote the sequence of personalized actions leading to h by $act^*(h)$. Furthermore, $act^*(T) = \{act^*(h) \mid h \in nodes(T)\}$ is the set of finite sequences of personalized actions that can occur in T.

Observation 1. *In a transition network M, if $u \in \mathfrak{U}$, $\sigma_H \in \Sigma_H$, and $u \notin H$ then for all $\alpha \in act^*(out_M(\sigma_H))$ and $a \in \mathfrak{A}$ we have that $\alpha.(u, a) \in act^*(out_M(\sigma_H))$, where $\alpha.(u, a)$ denotes concatenation of α and (u, a). This is because M is asynchronous and in each state any agents may get its action executed before the others. On the other hand, σ_H only restricts the behaviour of agents in H. Therefore any outgoing transition from a node in $T(M)$ by an agent outside H must remain in the trimmed tree given by $out_M(\sigma_H)$.*

How do strategies and their outcomes look in concrete scenarios? We mention here one natural type of strategies. *Positional strategies* represent conditional plans where the decision is solely based on what the agents see in the current state of the system. Formally, for $u \in \mathfrak{U}$, the set of individual positional strategies of u is $\Sigma_u^{\mathfrak{Pos}} = \{\sigma_u : St \to \mathcal{P}(\mathfrak{A}) \mid [q]_u = [q']_u \Rightarrow \sigma_u(q) = \sigma_u(q')\}$, where $\mathcal{P}(X)$ denotes the powerset of X. Notice the "uniformity" constraint which enforces that the agent must specify the same action(s) in states with the same observations. Now, coalitional positional strategies for group of agents $U \subseteq \mathfrak{U}$ are simply tuples of individual strategies, i.e., $\Sigma_U^{\mathfrak{Pos}} = \times_{u \in U}(\Sigma_u^{\mathfrak{Pos}})$. The outcome of $\sigma_U \in \Sigma_U^{\mathfrak{Pos}}$ in model M is the tree obtained from $T(M)$ by removing all the branches that begin from a node containing state q with a personalized action $(u, a) \in U \times \mathfrak{A}$ such that $a \notin \sigma_U(q)$. We will assume positional strategies throughout the paper to make our presentation more accessible.

3   Strategic Noninterference

Our main idea can be summarized as follows. If the High agents H are going to behave in a certain way, they do not need to worry about information leakage in *all* executions of the system but only in those executions that can actually happen. In particular, if H execute strategy σ_H then they should not care about the traces that are outside the outcome traces of σ_H. Moreover, the agents can actually choose σ_H in such a way that they avoid leaks. This leads to the following attempt at refining noninterference for agents who play strategically.

Definition 3 (Strategic Noninterference, first attempt). *Given a transition network M, a set of High agents H with coalitional strategies Σ_H, a set of Low agents L, and a set of "sensitive" actions A, we say that H is strategically non-interfering with L on A iff there exists a strategy $\sigma_H \in \Sigma_H$ such that for all $\alpha \in act^*(out_M(\sigma_H))$ and all $u_l \in L$ we have $[exec(\alpha)]_{u_l} = [exec(Purge_{H,A}(\alpha))]_{u_l}$.*

Unfortunately, the above definition is not very practical. True, in many cases the High agents could avoid leakage of information – for instance, by refraining from doing anything but the most conservative actions. In that case, however, they would never obtain what they want. Thus, we need to take into account the *goals* of H in the definition of noninterference.

3.1   Goal-Driven Strategic Noninterference

Let $traces(M)$ be the set of finite or infinite sequences of states that can be obtained by subsequent transitions in M. Moreover, $paths(M)$ will denote the set of maximal traces, i.e., those sequences that are either infinite or end in a state with no outgoing transitions. Additionally, we will use $paths_M(\sigma)$ as a shorthand for $paths(out_M(\sigma))$.

Definition 4 (Goal). *A goal in M is any $\Gamma \subseteq traces(M)$. Note that traces $(M) = traces(T(M))$, so a goal can be also seen as a subset of traces in the tree unfolding of M.*

A goal is a property that some agents may attempt to enforce by selecting their behavior accordingly. Note that, in the models of Goguen and Meseguer, strategies of any group except for the grand coalition $\mathfrak{U}$ yield only infinite paths. We will typically assume goals to be sets of paths definable in Linear Temporal Logic [19]. Most common examples of such goals are safety and reachability goals. For example, a goal of user u_1 can be that message m is, at some future moment, communicated to user u_2. Or, the users u_1 and u_2 may have a joint goal of keeping the communication channel c operative all the time. The former is an example of a *reachability goal*, the latter a *safety goal.*

Definition 5 (Safety and reachability goals). *Formally, given a set of safe states $\mathbb{S} \subseteq St$, the safety goal $\Gamma_{\mathbb{S}}$ is defined as $\Gamma_{\mathbb{S}} = \{\lambda \in paths(M) \mid \forall i.\lambda[i] \in \mathbb{S}\}$. Moreover, given a set of target states $\mathbb{T} \subseteq St$, the reachability goal $\Gamma_{\mathbb{T}}$ can be defined as $\Gamma_{\mathbb{T}} = \{\lambda \in paths(M) \mid \exists i.\lambda[i] \in \mathbb{T}\}$.*

We can now propose a weaker concept of noninterference, parameterized with the goal that the High agents pursue.

Definition 6 (Strategic Noninterference). *Given a transition network M, a set of High agents H with goal Γ_H and coalitional strategies Σ_H, a set of Low agents L, and a set of "sensitive" actions A, we say that H is strategically non-interfering with L on actions A for goal Γ_H iff there exists a strategy $\sigma_H \in \Sigma_H$ such that: (i) $paths_M(\sigma_H) \subseteq \Gamma_H$, and (ii) for every $\alpha \in act^*(out_M(\sigma_H))$ and $u_l \in L$ we have $[exec(\alpha)]_{u_l} = [exec(Purge_{H,A}(\alpha))]_{u_l}$.*
We will denote the property by $SNI_M(H, L, A, \Gamma_H)$.

Example 2 (Strategic noninterference). Consider the model in Figure 1 for the health care scenario from Example 1. There are two agents H and L, and the initial state is s_0. The possible observations for agent H are *updated* and *outdated*, showing if the data center is up-to-date or not. The possible observations for agent L are *on* and *off*, showing if L sees the working interface or the "out of service" message. The available actions are: *newData* used by H to signal that new data is available from a hospital, *startUpdate* used by H to start the updating process, *endUpdate* used by H to finish the process, *openInt* and *closeInt* used by H to open and close the interface, and *query* used by L to run a query.

Let $A = \{newData, startUpdate, endUpdate\}$. Clearly, it is not the case that H noninterferes with L on A, because $Purge_{H,A}(\langle(H, newData), (H, start Update)\rangle) = \langle\rangle$, but $[s_2]_L \neq [s_0]_L$. However, if the goal Γ_H is defined as the system being updated after any opening of the interface, then player H can obtain Γ_H by avoiding action *startUpdate* in state s_1 and avoiding *openInt* in s_4. For this strategy, H's behavior is noninterfering with L on A.   □

Note that the variant of strategic noninterference from Definition 3 is captured by $SNI_M(H, L, A, traces(M))$. Moreover, the following is straightforward:

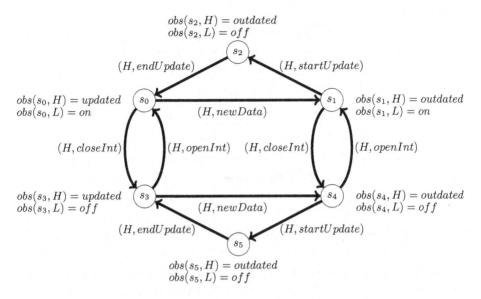

Fig. 1. Transition network for the healthcare example. Reflexive arrows for transitions that do not change the state of the system are omitted from the picture.

Proposition 1. $SNI_M(H, L, A, \Gamma_H)$ *if and only if there exists* $\sigma_H \in \Sigma_H$ *such that* $paths_M(\sigma_H) \subseteq \Gamma_H$ *and* $NI_{out_M(\sigma_H)}(H, L, A)$.

3.2   Private vs. Public Strategies

According to Definition 6, L can only use what they observe to determine if H have done a sensitive move. We implicitly assume that L do not know the strategy being executed by H; in this sense, the strategy of H is private. Another possibility is to assume that L are aware of the strategy of H. Then, L can detect in two ways that an action of H has occurred: (i) by getting to an observation that could not be obtained with no interleaved action from H, or (ii) by passing through a state where H's strategy forces H to execute something.

It is often appropriate to assume that H's strategy is known to the adversaries. This can be adopted as a worst case assumption, e.g., when a long-term pattern of H's behavior is used by L to predict their future strategy. A similar situation arises when H's goals and/or incentives are easy to guess. It is also known that announcing a strategy publicly and committing to it can sometimes increase security, especially in case of a government agency (cf. e.g. [7,23]).

Definition 7 (Strategic Noninterference in Public Strategies). *Given a transition network* M, *a set of High agents* H *with goal* Γ_H *and coalitional strategies* Σ_H, *a set of Low agents* L, *and a set of "sensitive" actions* $A \subseteq \mathfrak{A}$, *we say that* H *is strategically non-interfering with* L *on* A *for goal* Γ_H *in public strategies iff there exists a strategy* $\sigma_H \in \Sigma_H$ *such that: (i)* $paths_M(\sigma_H) \subseteq \Gamma_H$,

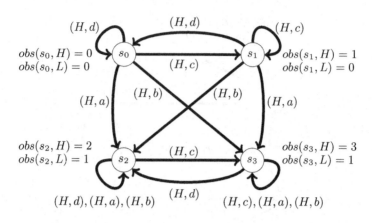

Fig. 2. Noninterference in public and private strategies

and *(ii) for every $\alpha \in act^*(out_M(\sigma_H))$ and $u_l \in L$ we have that $[exec(\alpha)]_{u_l} = [exec(Purge_{H,A}(\alpha))]_{u_l}$ and $Purge_{H,A}(\alpha) \in act^*(out_M(\sigma_H))$.*
We will denote the property by $SNI\text{-}Pub_M(H, L, A, \Gamma_H)$.

Example 3 (Public vs. private strategies). Consider the transition system in Figure 2, with two agents H and L and the initial state s_0. The set of possible actions is $\mathfrak{A} = \{a, b, c, d\}$ and the set of sensitive actions is $A = \{c, d\}$. The observations for both agents are shown in the picture. Let goal Γ_H be that whenever system goes to s_3, it must have been at some previous point in s_2. Agent H can obtain this goal by using strategy σ_1 of avoiding action b in s_0 and avoiding action a in s_1. Moreover, when using σ_1, H noninterferes with L on A in private strategies but not in public strategies. To see why, note that if $\alpha = \langle (H, c)(H, b) \rangle$ then $\alpha \in act^*(out(\sigma_1))$ but $Purge_{H,A}(\alpha) = \langle (H, b) \rangle$ is not in $act^*(out(\sigma_1))$. Therefore, although H can obtain Γ_H by using strategy σ_1 while preserving noninterference, the security can be only achieved if L does not know the strategy of H.   □

Strategic noninterference is a weaker notion than ordinary noninterference. Out of the two notions of SNI, noninterference in public strategies is stronger.

Proposition 2. $NI_M(H, L, A) \Rightarrow SNI\text{-}Pub_M(H, L, A, \Gamma_H) \Rightarrow SNI(H, L, A, \Gamma_H)$. *The converse implications do not universally hold.*

Proof. The implications are straightforward from the definitions. Non-validity of the converse implications follows from Examples 2 and 3.

Models of Goguen and Meseguer allow only to represent systems that are fully asynchronous and where all actions are available to each user at each state. As it turns out, revealing H's strategy makes a difference only when H have both sensitive and insensitive actions. Thus, if H are to conceal all their actions then it actually doesn't matter whether their strategy is publicly known. Before showing this formally, we make the following observation.

Observation 2.   *In the tree given by* $out_M(\sigma_H)$, *sequences of actions are prefix-closed. In other words, for every sequence* α, *we have* $\alpha.(u, a) \in act^*(out_M(\sigma_H)) \Rightarrow \alpha \in act^*(out_M(\sigma_H))$.

Proposition 3. $SNI_M(H, L, \mathfrak{A}, \Gamma_H)$ *iff* $SNI\text{-}Pub_M(H, L, \mathfrak{A}, \Gamma_H)$.

Proof. By Proposition 2 we have that $SNI\text{-}Pub_M(H, L, A, \Gamma_H)$ implies SNI_M (H, L, A, Γ_H). For the other direction it suffices to show that if $SNI_M(H, L, \mathfrak{A}, \Gamma_H)$ then for every $\alpha \in act^*(out_M(\sigma_H))$ and $\sigma_H \in \Sigma_H$ it holds that $Purge_{H,\mathfrak{A}}(\alpha) \in act^*(out_M(\sigma_H))$. We prove this by induction on the size of α.

Induction base: if $\alpha = \langle\rangle$, then $Purge_{H,A}(\alpha) = \langle\rangle$ and also $\langle\rangle \in act^*(out_M(\sigma_H))$, therefore $Purge_{H,A}(\alpha) \in act^*(out_M(\sigma_H))$.

Induction step: We want to show that if

(I) $\alpha \in act^*(out_M(\sigma_H)) \Rightarrow Purge_{H,A}(\alpha) \in act^*(out_M(\sigma_H))$

then for all $u \in \mathfrak{U}$ and $a \in \mathfrak{A}$:

(II) $(\alpha.(u, a)) \in act^*(out_M(\sigma_H)) \Rightarrow Purge_{H,A}(\alpha.(u, a)) \in act^*(out_M(\sigma_H))$

We prove it as follows. If (I) then either $\alpha \notin act^*(out_M(\sigma_H))$, in which case by Observation 2 we have $\alpha.(u, a) \notin act^*(out_M(\sigma_H))$ and therefore (II) is true; or $Purge_{H,A}(\alpha) \in act^*(out_M(\sigma_H))$, in which case we have two possibilities: (a) If $u \in H$ then $Purge_{H,A}(\alpha.(u, a)) = Purge_{H,A}(\alpha)$. We assumed that $Purge_{H,A} \in act^*(out_M(\sigma_H))$ so $Purge_{H,A}(\alpha.(u, a)) \in act^*(out_M(\sigma_H))$ and hence (II) is true. (b) If $u \notin H$ then $Purge_{H,A}(\alpha.(u, a)) = Purge_{H,A}(\alpha).(u, a)$. This together with Observation 1, $u \notin H$ and $Purge_{H,A}(\alpha) \in act^*(out_M(\sigma_H))$ implies that $Purge_{H,A}(\alpha.(u, a)) \in act^*(out_M(\sigma_H))$, therefore (II) is true.

4   Formal Characterization of Strategic Noninterference

Noninterference is typically characterized through so called unwinding relations [5,17,24]. Intuitively, an unwinding relation connects states that are indistinguishable to the Low agents, in the sense that Low have no "diagnostic procedure" that would distinguish one from the other. Thus, if High proceed from one such state to another, no information leaks to the adversaries. Unwinding relations are important because they characterize noninterference in purely structural terms, similar to well-known bisimulation relations. Moreover, existence of an unwinding relation is usually easier to verify than proving noninterference directly.

4.1   Unwinding Relations for Standard Noninterference

We first recall the unwinding characterization of the original noninterference .

Definition 8 (Unwinding for Noninterference [5, 17]). $\sim_{NI_L} \subseteq St \times St$ *is an* unwinding relation *iff it is an equivalence relation satisfying the conditions of* output consistency (OC), step consistency (SC), *and* local respect (LR). *That is, for all states* $s, t \in St$:

(OC) *If* $s \sim_{NI_L} t$ *then* $[s]_L = [t]_L$;
(SC) *If* $s \sim_{NI_L} t$, $u \in L$, *and* $a \in \mathfrak{A}$ *then* $do(s, u, a) \sim_{NI_L} do(t, u, a)$;
(LR) *If* $u \in H$ *and* $a \in \mathfrak{A}$ *then* $s \sim_{NI_L} do(s, u, a)$.

Proposition 4 ([5,17]). $NI_M(H, L)$ *iff there exist an unwinding relation* $\sim_{NI_L}$ *on the states of* M *that satisfies (OC), (SC) and (LR).*

4.2   Unwinding for Strategic Noninterference

In this part, we try to characterize strategic noninterference in a similar way. That is, we look for unwinding relations corresponding to strategies that obtain a given goal and at the same time prevent information leakage. There are two possible perspectives to this. First, we can look for unwinding relations whose existence corresponds to *existence* of a suitable strategy. Secondly, we may look for unwindings whose existence guarantees strategic noninterference *for a given strategy*. We focus on the former here; the latter will be studied in Section 4.3. We begin with the following negative result.

Proposition 5. *There is no succinct characterization of strategic noninterference with respect to goals definable in Linear Time Logic.*

Proof. Suppose, to the contrary, that there exists a deterministic[1] condition Φ which: (i) is of polynomial size with respect to the size of the model and the length of the goal formula, and (ii) guarantees that $SNI_M(H, L, \mathfrak{A}, \Gamma)$ iff there is an unwinding relation satisfying Φ for $M, H, L, \mathfrak{A}, \Gamma$. Note that the model checking problem for Linear Time Logic can be embedded in checking strategic noninterference by assuming that $H = \emptyset$ and that L have the same observation in every state. Then, $SNI_M(H, L, \mathfrak{A}, \Gamma)$ iff Γ is satisfied on every possible path in M. But this, together with our assumption, would give us a nondeterministic polynomial-time procedure for model checking Linear Time Logic, which is impossible since the problem is **PSPACE**-complete [19]. □

It is clear from the proof that the impossibility stems from the hardness of finding a strategy that obtains a given goal, and not necessarily from the noninterference part. We will now show that strategic noninterference can indeed be succinctly characterized for a specific class of goals, namely safety goals.

Definition 9 (Unwinding Relation for Safety Goal). *Let* M, H, L *be as usual, and* $\Gamma_{\mathbb{S}}$ *be a safety goal with safe states* $\mathbb{S} \subseteq St$. *Moreover, let* $reach(U) = \{s \mid \exists \alpha \in (U, \mathfrak{A})^* , \ s = exec(\alpha)\}$ *denote the set of reachable states for agents* U. *We say that* $\sim_{\Gamma_{\mathbb{S}}} \subseteq St \times St$ *is an unwinding relation for* $\Gamma_{\mathbb{S}}$ *iff* $\sim_{\Gamma_{\mathbb{S}}}$ *satisfies the following properties:*

---

[1] By "deterministic", we essentially mean "quantifier-free". Note that quantification over elements of the model (e.g., states, agents, and actions) is not a problem, since it can always be unfolded to a quantifier-free form by explicitly enumerating all the possible values. Such an unfolding incurs only polynomial increase of the size of Φ.

(OC$_\mathbb{S}$) For all $s, t \in reach(L)$, if $s \sim_{\Gamma_\mathbb{S}} t$ then $[s]_L = [t]_L$;

(SC$_\mathbb{S}$) For all $s, t \in reach(L)$, $u \in L$, and $a \in \mathfrak{A}$, if $s \sim_{\Gamma_\mathbb{S}} t$ then $do(s, u, a) \sim_{\Gamma_\mathbb{S}}$ $do(t, u, a)$.

Proposition 6. $SNI(H, L, \mathfrak{A}, \Gamma_\mathbb{S})$ iff $reach(\mathfrak{U} \setminus H) \subseteq \mathbb{S}$ and there exists an unwinding relation $\sim_{\Gamma_\mathbb{S}}$ for the safety goal $\Gamma_\mathbb{S}$.

Proof. "$\Leftarrow$" Suppose that $reach(\mathfrak{U} \setminus H) \subseteq \mathbb{S}$ and there exists an unwinding relation $\sim_{\Gamma_\mathbb{S}}$. We show that there exists a strategy σ_H for agents H such that (i) $path_M(\sigma_H) \subseteq \Gamma_\mathbb{S}$, and (ii) for every $\alpha \in act^*(out_M(\sigma_H))$ and $u_l \in L$ we have $[exec(\alpha)]_{u_l} = [exec(Purge_{H,\mathfrak{A}}(\alpha))]_{u_l}$. We choose σ_H to be a positional strategy defined as $\sigma_H(s) = \emptyset$ for all $s \in St$.

i) By the definition of σ_H, we know that $act^*(out_M(\sigma_H)) \subseteq (\mathfrak{U} \setminus H, \mathfrak{A})^*$. This together with $reach(\mathfrak{U} \setminus H) \subseteq \mathbb{S}$ and the definition of safety goal, implies that $path_M(\sigma_H) \subseteq \Gamma_\mathbb{S}$.

ii) For every $\alpha \in act^*(out_M(\sigma_H))$ and $u_l \in L$, we have $\alpha \in (\mathfrak{U} \setminus H, \mathfrak{A})^*$ by (i), and hence $Purge_{H,\mathfrak{A}}(\alpha) = \alpha$. Therefore $[exec(Purge_{H,\mathfrak{A}}(\alpha)]_{u_l} = [exec(\alpha)]_{u_l}$.

By i) and ii) we have that $SNI(H, L, \mathfrak{A}, \Gamma_\mathbb{S})$ holds.

"$\Rightarrow$" Suppose that $SNI(H, L, \mathfrak{A}, \Gamma_\mathbb{S})$, and σ_H is a strategy that satisfies the conditions of strategic noninterference. We show that there exists an unwinding relation $\sim_{\Gamma_\mathbb{S}}$ for the safety goal $\Gamma_\mathbb{S}$. Let $\sim_{\Gamma_\mathbb{S}}$ be the relation such that $s \sim_{\Gamma_\mathbb{S}} t$ if $s, t \in nodes(out_M(\sigma_H))$ and for all $\alpha \in (L, \mathfrak{A})^*$ and $u_l \in L$, $[exec(s, \alpha)]_{u_l} = [exec(t, \alpha)]_{u_l}$. We show that $\sim_{\Gamma_\mathbb{S}}$ is an unwinding relation for the safety goal $\Gamma_\mathbb{S}$.

i) If $\alpha \in (\mathfrak{U} \setminus H, \mathfrak{A})^*$ then by Observation 1 we have that $\alpha \in act^*(out_M(\sigma_H))$, and therefore $exec(\alpha) \in \mathbb{S}$ (by strategic noninterference). So $reach(\mathfrak{U} \setminus H) \subseteq \mathbb{S}$.

ii) If we take $\alpha = \langle \rangle$, then by definition of $\sim_{\Gamma_\mathbb{S}}$ we have that for all $u_l \in L$ and all $s, t \in reach(L)$, $[exec(s, \alpha)]_{u_l} = [exec(t, \alpha)]_{u_l}$. So $[exec(s, \langle \rangle)]_{u_l} = [exec(t, \langle \rangle)]_{u_l}$, or $[s]_{u_l} = [t]_{u_l}$ which proves that $\sim_{\Gamma_\mathbb{S}}$ satisfies (OC$_\mathbb{S}$).

iii) Lastly, we need to prove that $\sim_{\Gamma_\mathbb{S}}$ satisfies (SC$_\mathbb{S}$). Suppose there exists $s, t \in reach(L)$, $u \in L$ and $a \in \mathfrak{A}$ such that $s \sim_{\Gamma_\mathbb{S}} t$ and $do(s, u, a) \not\sim_{\Gamma_\mathbb{S}} do(t, u, a)$. Then there exists $\alpha \in (L, \mathfrak{A})^*$ such that $[exec(do(s, u, a), \alpha)]_{u_l} \neq [exec(do(t, u, a), \alpha)]_{u_l}$ for some $u_l \in L$. It implies that $[exec(s, ((u, a).\alpha))]_{u_l} \neq [exec(t, ((u, a).\alpha))]_{u_l}$, which contradicts $s \sim_{\Gamma_\mathbb{S}} t$. Therefore $\sim_{\Gamma_\mathbb{S}}$ satisfies (SC$_\mathbb{S}$).

It would be interesting to characterize strategic noninterference for other subclasses of goals in a similar way. We are currently working on a characterization result for reachability goals. Goals that can be achieved by fixpoint computation of strategies are another promising class that we leave for future work.

4.3   Strategy-Specific Unwinding Relations

We now turn to characterizing strategic noninterference when a strategy is given as a parameter of the problem. Let σ_H be a strategy for H in M. We define the maximum coverage of σ_H in state s as $maxcover(\sigma_H, s) = \{a \in \mathfrak{A} \mid \exists \alpha \in act^*(out_M(\sigma_H)), u_h \in H, \text{such that } exec(\alpha) = s \text{ and } \alpha.(u_h, a) \in act^*(out_M(\sigma_H))\}$.

Definition 10 (Strategy-Specific Unwinding Relation). *Let M, H, L be as usual, Γ be a goal, and σ_H a strategy for H. We call $\sim_{\sigma_H} \subseteq St \times St$ a strategy-specific unwinding relation for σ_H iff it satisfies the following properties:*

(OC$_\sigma$) *For all $s, t \in nodes(out_M(\sigma_H))$ and $u \in L$, if $s \sim_{\sigma_H} t$ then $[s]_u = [t]_u$;*

(SC$_\sigma$) *For all $s, t \in nodes(out_M(\sigma_H))$, $u \in L$, and $a \in \mathfrak{A}$, if $s \sim_{\sigma_H} t$ then $do(s, u, a) \sim_{\sigma_H} do(t, u, a)$;*

(LR$_\sigma$) *For all $s \in nodes(out_M(\sigma_H))$, $u \in H$, and $a \in maxcover(\sigma_H, s)$, we have that $s \sim_{\sigma_H} do(s, u, a)$.*

Proposition 7. *Let M, H, L, Γ be as before, and σ_H be a positional strategy for H that obtains Γ (formally: $paths_M(\sigma_H) \subseteq \Gamma_H$). If there exists a strategy-specific unwinding relation for σ_H then M satisfies strategic noninterference with respect to σ_H (formally: for every $\alpha \in act^*(out_M(\sigma_H))$ and $u_l \in L$ we have that $[exec(\alpha)]_{u_l} = [exec(Purge_{H,A}(\alpha))]_{u_l}$).*

Proof. By (OC$_\sigma$) it is enough to show that for all $\alpha \in act^*(out_M(\sigma_H))$, $exec(\alpha) \sim_{\sigma_H} exec(Purge_{H,\mathfrak{A}}(\alpha))$. We prove this by induction on the size of α.

Induction base: For $\alpha = \langle \rangle$, we have $\langle \rangle \in act^*(out_M(\sigma_H))$ and $Purge_{H,\mathfrak{A}}(\langle \rangle) = \langle \rangle$. Therefore $exec(\langle \rangle) \sim_{\sigma_H} exec(Purge_{H,\mathfrak{A}}(\langle \rangle))$, because $\sim_{\sigma_H}$ is reflexive.

Induction step: Suppose that for some $\alpha \in act^*(out_M(\sigma_H))$, $exec(\alpha) \sim_{\sigma_H} exec(Purge_{H,\mathfrak{A}}(\alpha))$. We show that for any (u, a) such that $u \in L$ and $a \in \mathfrak{A}$, either $exec(\alpha.(u, a)) \sim_{\sigma_H} exec(Purge_{H,\mathfrak{A}}(\alpha.(u, a))$, or $\alpha.(u, a) \notin act^*(out_M(\sigma_H))$. We consider three cases:

(i) If $u \in H$ and $a \notin \sigma_H(exec(\alpha))$, then $\alpha.(u, a) \notin act^*(out_M(\sigma_H))$.

(ii) If $u \in H$ and $a \in \sigma_H(exec(\alpha))$, then $Purge_{H,\mathfrak{A}}(\alpha.(u, a)) = Purge_{H,\mathfrak{A}}(\alpha)$. By (LR$_\sigma$) we have that $exec(\alpha) \sim_{\sigma_H} exec(\alpha.(u, a))$. This together with induction step assumption and transitivity of $\sim_{\sigma_H}$ implies that $exec(Purge_{H,\mathfrak{A}}(\alpha)) \sim_{\sigma_H} exec(\alpha.(u, a))$. By substituting $Purge_{H,\mathfrak{A}}(\alpha)$ with $Purge_{H,\mathfrak{A}}(\alpha.(u, a))$ we have $exec(\alpha.(u, a)) \sim_{\sigma_H} exec(Purge_{H,\mathfrak{A}}(\alpha.(u, a)))$.

(iii) If $u \in L$ then $exec(Purge_{H,\mathfrak{A}}(\alpha.(u, a))) = do(exec(Purge_{H,\mathfrak{A}}(\alpha)), u, a)$. This, together with the induction step assumption and (SC$_\sigma$), implies that $do(exec(\alpha)), u, a) \sim_{\sigma_H} do(exec(Purge_{H,\mathfrak{A}}(\alpha)), u, a)$. Therefore $exec(\alpha.(u, a)) \sim_{\sigma_H} exec(Purge_{H,\mathfrak{A}}(\alpha.(u, a)))$.

Proposition 8. *Let $M, H, L, \Gamma, \sigma_H$ be as in Proposition 7. If M satisfies strategic noninterference with respect to σ_H then there exists a strategy-specific unwinding relation for σ_H.*

Proof. Let $\sim_{\sigma_H}$ be the relation such that $s \sim_{\sigma_H} t$ if $s, t \in nodes(out_M(\sigma_H))$ and for all $\alpha \in (L, \mathfrak{A})^*$ and $u_l \in L$, $[exec(s, \alpha)]_{u_l} = [exec(t, \alpha)]_{u_l}$. We show that $\sim_{\sigma_H}$ has the conditions of strategy-specific unwinding relation for strategy σ_H.

(i) Proving (OC$_\sigma$) for $\sim_{\sigma_H}$ is analogous to the proof of part $\Rightarrow$.(ii) in Proposition 6.

(ii) Proving (SC$_\sigma$) for $\sim_{\sigma_H}$ is analogous to the proof of part $\Rightarrow$.(iii) in Proposition 6.

(iii) Suppose that $s \in nodes(out_M(\sigma_H))$, $a \in maxcover(\sigma_H, s)$, $\alpha \in (L, \mathfrak{A})^*$, $u_l \in L$ and $u_h \in H$. Then there exist $\lambda \in act^*(out_M(\sigma_H))$ such that $exec(\lambda) = s$. By strategic noninterference property, $[exec(\lambda.\alpha)]_{u_l} = [exec(Purge_{H,\mathfrak{A}}(\lambda.\alpha)]_{u_l}$ and $[exec(\lambda.(u_h, a).\alpha)]_{u_l} = [exec(Purge_{H,\mathfrak{A}}(\lambda.(u_h, a).\alpha))]_{u_l}$. We also know that $Purge_{H,\mathfrak{A}}(\lambda.(u_h, a).\alpha) = Purge_{H,\mathfrak{A}}(\lambda.\alpha)$. Using these equalities we have that $[exec(\lambda.\alpha)]_{u_l} = [exec(\lambda.(u_h, a).\alpha)]_{u_l}$, i.e $[exec(s, \alpha)]_{u_l} = [exec(do(s, u_h, a), \alpha)]_{u_h}$, therefore $s \sim_{\sigma_H} do(s, u_h, a)$ (by the definition of $\sim_{\sigma_H}$) and so (LR_{σ_H}) holds.

5   Conclusions

In this paper, we propose how to relax the classical requirement of noninterference by taking into account a strategy that the High players may follow in order to achieve their goals. The idea is especially important for analysis and design of confidentiality in realistic systems where full noninterference and nondeducibility can seldom be guaranteed. Moreover, strategic noninterference in a system can be obtained not only by strengthening security measures, but also by "fine-tuning" functionality requirements: even if it does not hold for the current goals, there may exist weaker yet still acceptable goals that allow for confidentiality-preserving behavior. Thus, the new concept helps to realize which objectives can be achieved while avoiding information leakage.

In terms of technical results, we study characterization of strategic noninterference through unwinding relations. On one hand, we prove that a general characterization result is impossible for arbitrary goals. On the other hand, we present some characterizations for specific subclasses of goals and for the simplified setting where a strategy is given as a parameter. The proofs are constructive and can be used to obtain practical algorithms that check for strategic noninterference. We also show that, in the classical models of Goguen and Meseguer, knowing the strategy of High usually does not increase the ability of Low to break noninterference. The models used in this paper are deterministic asynchronous transition networks of the original definition of noninterference [4]. We plan to extend our study to richer models in future work. In particular, the generalized form of non-interference by Ryan and Schneider [18] seems very promising for a formulation of strategic noninterference in process-algebraic models.

It is worth mentioning that, in a realistic system, the usefulness of strategic noninterference relies heavily on the ability of High to select specific behaviors. In a system where High has no such ability, the notions of noninterference and strategic noninterference coincide.

Acknowledgments. Wojciech Jamroga acknowledges the support of National Research Fund (FNR) Luxembourg under project GALOT (INTER/DFG/12/06), as well as the support of the 7th Framework Programme of the European Union under the Marie Curie IEF project ReVINK (PIEF-GA-2012-626398). Masoud Tabatabaei also acknowledges the support of the National Research Fund Luxembourg under project GAIVS (AFR Code:5884506).

References

1. Allen, P.G.: A comparison of non-interference and non-deducibility using CSP. In: Proceedings of CSFW, pp. 43–54 (1991)
2. Backes, M., Pfitzmann, B.: Intransitive non-interference for cryptographic purposes. In: Proceedings of S&P, pp. 140–152. IEEE (2003)
3. Engelhardt, K., van der Meyden, R., Zhang, C.: Intransitive noninterference in nondeterministic systems. In: Proceedings of CCS, pp. 869–880 (2012)
4. Goguen, J.A., Meseguer, J.: Security policies and security models. In: Proceedings of S&P, pp. 11–20. IEEE Computer Society (1982)
5. Goguen, J.A., Meseguer, J.: Unwinding and inference control. In: IEEE Symposium on Security and Privacy, pp. 75–75. IEEE Computer Society (1984)
6. Gray III, J.W.: Probabilistic interference. In: Proceedings of S&P, pages 170–179. IEEE (1990)
7. Korzhyk, D., Yin, Z., Kiekintveld, C., Conitzer, V., Tambe, M.: Stackelberg vs. Nash in security games: An extended investigation of interchangeability, equivalence, and uniqueness. Journal of Artif. Intell. Research **41**, 297–327 (2011)
8. Lampson, B.W.: A note on the confinement problem. Communications of the ACM **16**(10), 613–615 (1973)
9. Li, P., Zdancewic, S.: Downgrading policies and relaxed noninterference. In: ACM SIGPLAN Notices, vol. 40, pp. 158–170. ACM (2005)
10. McCullough, D.: Noninterference and the composability of security properties. In: Proceedings of S&P, pp. 177–186. IEEE (1988)
11. McIver, A., Morgan, C.: A probabilistic approach to information hiding. Programming Methodology, pp. 441–460 (2003)
12. O'Halloran, C.: A calculus of information flow. In: Proceedings of ESORICS, pp. 147–159 (1990)
13. Di Pierro, A., Hankin, C., Wiklicky, H.: Approximate non-interference. Journal of Computer Security **12**(1), 37–81 (2004)
14. Roscoe, A.W.: CSP and determinism in security modelling. In: Proceedings of S&P, pp. 114–127. IEEE (1995)
15. Roscoe, A.W., Goldsmith, M.H.: What is intransitive noninterference? In: Proceedings of CSF, pp. 228–228. IEEE (1999)
16. Roscoe, A.W., Woodcock, J.C.P., Wulf, L.: Non-interference through determinism. In: Proceedings of ESORICS, pp. 31–53. Springer (1994)
17. Rushby, J.: Noninterference, transitivity, and channel-control security policies. SRI International, Computer Science Laboratory (1992)
18. Ryan, P.Y.A., Schneider, S.A.: Process algebra and non-interference. Journal of Computer Security **9**(1), 75–103 (2001)
19. Schnoebelen, Ph.: The complexity of temporal model checking. In: Advances in Modal Logics, Proceedings of AiML 2002. World Scientific (2003)
20. Seehusen, F., Stølen, K.: Information flow security, abstraction and composition. IET Information Security **3**(1), 9–33 (2009)
21. Smith, G.: On the foundations of quantitative information flow. In: de Alfaro, L. (ed.) FOSSACS 2009. LNCS, vol. 5504, pp. 288–302. Springer, Heidelberg (2009)
22. Sutherland, D.: A model of information. In: Proc. 9th National Computer Security Conference, pp. 175–183 (1986)
23. Tabatabaei, M., Jamroga, W., Ryan, P.Y.: Preventing coercion in e-voting: be open and commit. In: Proceedings of the 1st Workshop on Hot issues in Security Principles and Trust (HotSpot) (2013)

24. van der Meyden, R., Zhang, C.: A comparison of semantic models for noninterference. Theoretical Computer Science **411**(47), 4123–4147 (2010)
25. van der Meyden, R.: What, Indeed, Is Intransitive Noninterference? In: Biskup, J., López, J. (eds.) ESORICS 2007. LNCS, vol. 4734, pp. 235–250. Springer, Heidelberg (2007)
26. Wittbold, J.T., Johnson, D.M.: Information flow in nondeterministic systems. In: IEEE Symposium on Security and Privacy, pp. 144–144 (1990)
27. Zakinthinos, A., Lee, E.S.: The composability of non-interference. Journal of Computer Security **3**(4), 269–281 (1995)
28. Zdancewic, S.: Challenges for information-flow security. In: Proceedings of the 1st International Workshop on the Programming Language Interference and Dependence (PLID04) (2004)

Verifying Observational Determinism

Jaber Karimpour, Ayaz Isazadeh, and Ali A. Noroozi$^{(\boxtimes)}$

Computer Science, University of Tabriz, Tabriz, Iran
{karimpour,isazadeh,noroozi}@tabrizu.ac.ir

Abstract. This paper proposes an approach to verify information flow security of concurrent programs. It discusses a hyperproperty called observational determinism which aims to ensure secure information flow in concurrent programs, and proves how this hyperproperty can be verified by stutter equivalence checking. More precisely, it defines observational determinism in terms of stutter equivalence of all traces having the same low initial value and shows how stutter trace equivalence can be verified by computing a divergence stutter bisimulation quotient. The approach is illustrated by verifying a small example.

Keywords: Secure information flow · Observational determinism · Verification · Bisimulation

1 Introduction

To perform an effective security analysis of a given program, program model, *security policy* and attacker (observer) model should be defined precisely [1]. In secure information flow analysis, the program model can be represented as a state machine, which produces a set of executions and is considered public knowledge. In this model, program variables are classified into different security levels. A nave classification is to label some variables as L, meaning low security, public information; and other variables as H, meaning high security, private information. The goal of a security policy is to prevent information in H from flowing to L and being leaked [2], [3]. Other classifications of program variables are possible via a lattice of security levels [4]. In this case, the security policy should ensure that information flows only upwards in the lattice.

The security policy is a property that needs to be satisfied by the program model. The attacker is assumed to be able to observe program executions. *Confidentiality policies* are of major concern in security policies. These policies are connected to the ability of an attacker to distinguish two program executions that differ only in their confidential inputs. Noninterference is a confidentiality policy that stipulates an observer able to see only low security data (low observer) learns nothing about high security inputs by watching low security outputs [5]. *Observational determinism* is another confidentiality policy which is a generalized notion of noninterference for concurrent programs. Inspired by earlier work by McLean [6] and Roscoe [7], Zdancevic and Myers [5] proposed observational determinism which requires the program to produce indistinguishable traces to

© IFIP International Federation for Information Processing 2015
H. Federrath and D. Gollmann (Eds.): SEC 2015, IFIP AICT 455, pp. 82–93, 2015.
DOI: 10.1007/978-3-319-18467-8_6

avoid information leaks. Thus, a program satisfying this condition appears deterministic to a low observer who is able to observe low variables and unable to distinguish states which differ only in high variables. As stated by Huisman et al. [8] *"concurrent programs are often used in a context where intermediate states can be observed."* That's why Zdancevic and Myers require determinism on all the states of a trace, instead of final states. Observational determinism is a widely accepted security property for concurrent programs. Observational deterministic programs are immune to *refinement attacks* [5], because observational determinism is preserved under refinement [9].

This paper concentrates on the problem of verifying observational determinism for concurrent programs. We define observational determinism in terms of stutter equivalence on all low variables. Our contributions include (1) a theorem showing that verifying secure information flow can be reduced to equivalence checking in the quotient system and (2) a sound model checking approach for verifying secure information flow in concurrent programs. In fact, our approach is the first that uses quotient space to reduce the state space and check for secure information flow simultaneously. We illustrate the progress made by the verification of a small example program. It is expected that these contributions constitute a significant step towards more widely applicable secure information flow analysis.

The remainder of the paper is organized as follows. In section 2, preliminaries are explained. In section 3, observational determinism is formally defined and section 4 discusses how to verify it. In section 5, some related work is discussed. Finally, Section 6 concludes, and discusses future work.

2   Preliminaries

In this section, at first we introduce the program model considered throughout the paper. Then, some preliminary concepts about bisimulation are discussed. Most of these preliminaries are taken from [10].

Definition 1 (Kripke structure). A *Kripke structure* KS is a tuple $(S, \rightarrow, I, AP, La)$ where S is a set of states, $\rightarrow \subseteq S \times S$ is a transition relation, $I \subseteq S$ is a set of initial states, AP is the set of atomic propositions, and $La : S \rightarrow 2^{AP}$ is a labeling function. Here, atomic propositions are possible values of the low variables. KS is called *finite* if S and AP are finite. The set of successors of a state s is defined as $Post(s) = \{s' \in S | s \rightarrow s'\}$. A state s is called *terminal* if $Post(s) = \varnothing$. For a Kripke structure modelling a sequential program, terminal states represent the termination of the program.

Definition 2 (Execution or Path). A finite *path fragment* $\hat{\pi}$ of KS is a finite state sequence $s_0 s_1 \ldots s_n$ such that $s_i \in Post(s_{i-1})$ for all $0 < i \leq n$. An *infinite path fragment* π is an infinite state sequence $s_0 s_1 s_2 \ldots$ such that $s_i \in Post(s_{i-1})$ for all $0 < i$. A *maximal* path fragment is either a finite path fragment that ends in a terminal state, or an infinite path fragment. A path fragment is called *initial* if it starts in an initial state, i.e., if $s_0 \in I$. A *path* of KS is an initial, maximal path fragment. $Paths(s)$ denotes the set of paths starting in s. All paths of a Kripke structure with no terminal state are infinite.

Definition 3 (Trace). The *trace* of a path $\pi = s_0 s_1 \ldots$ is defined as $T = trace(\pi) = La(s_0) La(s_1) \ldots$. Thus, the trace of a path is the sequence of sets of atomic propositions that are valid in the states of the path. $T[0]$ extracts the first atomic proposition of the trace, i.e., $T[0] = La(s_0)$. Let $Traces(s)$ denote the set of traces of s, and $Traces(KS)$ the set of traces of the initial states of KS: $Traces(s) = trace(Paths(s))$ and $Traces(KS) = \cup_{s \in I} Traces(s)$.

Definition 4 (Combination of Kripke structures $KS_1 \oplus KS_2$). For $KS_i = (S_i, \rightarrow_i, I_i, AP, La_i)$, $i = 1, 2$: $KS_1 \oplus KS_2 = (S_1 \uplus S_2, \rightarrow_1 \cup \rightarrow_2, I_1 \cup I_2, AP, La)$ where $\uplus$ stands for disjoint union and $La(s) = La_i(s)$ if $s \in S_i$.

Definition 5 (Stutter equivalence). Traces T_1 and T_2 over 2^{AP} are *stutter equivalent*, denoted $T_1 \triangleq T_2$, if they are both of the form $A_0^+ A_1^+ A_2^+ \ldots$ for $A_0, A_1, A_2, \cdots \subseteq AP$ where A_i^+ is the *Kleene plus* operation on A_i and is defined as $A_i^+ = \{x_1 x_2 \ldots x_k | k > 0$ and each $x_i = A_i\}$. Kripke structures KS_i over AP, $i = 1, 2$, are *stutter trace equivalent*, denoted $KS_1 \triangleq KS_2$, if $KS_1 \trianglelefteq KS_2$ and $KS_2 \trianglelefteq KS_1$, where $\trianglelefteq$ is defined by:

$$KS_1 \trianglelefteq KS_2 \text{ iff } \forall T_1 \in Traces(KS_1)(\exists T_2 \in Traces(KS_2). \ T_1 \triangleq T_2)$$

Definition 6 (Stutter bisimulation). A *stutter bisimulation* for KS is a binary relation R on S such that for all $(s_1, s_2) \in R$, the following three conditions hold: (1) $La(s_1) = La(s_2)$. (2) If $s_1' \in Post(s_1)$ with $(s_1', s_2) \notin R$, then there exists a finite path fragment $s_2 u_1 \ldots u_n s_2'$ with $0 \le n$ and $(s_1, u_i) \in R$, $i = 1, \ldots, n$ and $(s_1', s_2') \in R$. (3) If $s_2' \in Post(s_2)$ with $(s_1, s_2') \notin R$, then there exists a finite path fragment $s_1 v_1 \ldots v_n s_1'$ with $0 \le n$ and $(v_i, s_2) \in R$, $i = 1, \ldots, n$ and $(s_1', s_2') \in R$.

Definition 7 (Divergence stutter bisimulation). Let R be an equivalence relation on S. A state $s \in S$ is R-*divergent* if there exists an infinite path fragment $\pi = s s_1 s_2 \cdots \in Paths(s)$ such that $(s, s_j) \in R$ for all $0 < j$. Stated in words, a state s is R-divergent if there is an infinite path starting in s that only visits states in $[s]_R$. $[s]_R$ is the equivalence class of s under the equivalence relation R. R is *divergence-sensitive* if for any $(s_1, s_2) \in R$: if s_1 is R-divergent, then s_2 is R-divergent. States s_1, s_2 are *divergent stutter bisimilar*, denoted $s_1 \approx^{div} s_2$, if there exists a divergence sensitive stutter bisimulation R such that $(s_1, s_2) \in R$.

Definition 8 (Divergent stutter bisimilar paths). For infinite path fragments $\pi_i = s_{0,i} s_{1,i} s_{2,i} \cdots$, $i = 1, 2$ in KS, π_1 is *divergent stutter bisimilar* to π_2, denoted $\pi_1 \approx^{div} \pi_2$ if and only if there exists an infinite sequence of indices $0 = j_0 < j_1 < j_2 < \ldots$ and $0 = k_0 < k_1 < k_2 < \ldots$ with:

$$s_{j,1} \approx^{div} s_{k,2} \text{ for all } j_{r-1} \le j < j_r \text{ and } k_{r-1} \le k < k_r \text{ with } r = 1, 2, \ldots$$

The following lemma follows directly from the definition of $\approx^{div}$ on paths and $\triangleq$ on paths.

Lemma 1. *For all infinite paths π_1 and π_2, we have $\pi_1 \approx^{div} \pi_2$ implies $\pi_1 \triangleq \pi_2$.*

Lemma 2. *Divergent stutter bisimilar states have divergent stutter bisimilar paths:*

$$s_1 \approx^{div} s_2 \ \text{implies} \ \forall \pi_1 \in Paths(s_1) \ (\exists \pi_2 \in Paths(s_2). \ \pi_1 \approx^{div} \pi_2)$$

Proof: see [10], page 549.

Definition 9 (Divergence stutter bisimulation quotient $KS/ \approx^{div}$). The *quotient* of a Kripke structure KS is defined by $KS/ \approx^{div} = (S/ \approx^{div}, \rightarrow'$, $I', AP, La')$, where $S/ \approx^{div} = \{[s]_{\approx^{div}} | s \in S\}$, $La'([s]_{\approx^{div}}) = La(s)$, and $\rightarrow'$ is defined by

$$\frac{s \rightarrow s' \ \wedge \ s \not\approx^{div} s'}{[s]_{\approx^{div}} \rightarrow' [s']_{\approx^{div}}} \quad \text{and} \quad \frac{s \ is \ \approx^{div} -divergent}{[s]_{\approx^{div}} \rightarrow' [s]_{\approx^{div}}}$$

Theorem 1. *For any Kripke structure KS, we have $KS \approx^{div} KS/ \approx^{div}$.*

Proof: Follows from the fact that $R = \{(s, [s]_{\approx^{div}}) | s \in S\}$ is a divergence stutter bisimulation for $(KS, KS/ \approx^{div})$. ∎

3   Observational Determinism

A concurrent program is secure if it appears deterministic to a low observer and produces indistinguishable executions. Zdancevic and Myers [5] call this observational determinism and define it as:

$$\forall \ T, T' \in Traces(P). \ T[0] =_L T'[0] \Longrightarrow T \approx_L T'$$

where KS is a model of the program (e.g., a Kripke structure, modelling the program executions). Indistinguishability to a low observer is expressed as state equivalence relation $=_L$ and trace equivalence relation $\approx_L$. Zdancevic and Myers define trace equivalence as prefix and stutter equivalence of the sequence of states in each trace. However, Huisman et al. [8] argue that allowing prefixing causes information flows. That's why they propose stutter equivalence instead of prefix and stutter equivalence. For example, consider the following program:

```
l:=0;  while(h>0)  then  {l++}                        (P1)
```

where h is a high variable and l is a low veriable. The set of traces of this program is $\{< 0 >, < 0, 1 >, < 0, 1, 2 >, \dots\}$. These traces are prefix and stutter equivalent, hence considered secure by the definition of Zdancevic and Myers; But, the attacker can easily get the value of h by observing the traces. Huisman et al. [8] require stutter equivalence of traces of each low variable, but as Terauchi [11] shows, this kind of definition is not as restrictive as possible and accepts leaky programs. Thus, Terauchi requires prefix stutter equivalence of all traces w.r.t. all low variables.

Consequently, we define observational determinism in terms of stutter equivalence on all low variables:

$$\forall\, T, T' \in Traces(P). \;\; T[0] =_L T'[0] \Longrightarrow T \triangleq_L T'$$

where $\triangleq_L$ is stutter trace equivalence. For example, consider the following insecure program that can reveal the value of h:

```
l₁:=0; l₂:=0;
l₁:=1 || if(l₁=1) then l₂:=h                               (P2)
```

where $\|$ is the parallel operator. If the right program is executed first, the corresponding trace of low variables would be: $< (0,0), (0,0), (1,0) >$. Each ordered pair (l_1, l_2) shows the values of low variables in each state of the program. If the left program is executed first, the following traces are produced: $< (0,0), (1,0), (1,h) >$. As you can see, these traces are not stutter equivalent, so the program is insecure. As another example, consider the following secure program:

```
l₁:=0; l₂:=0;
l₁:=2 || if(l₁=1) then l₂:=h                               (P3)
```

If the right program is executed first, the corresponding trace would be: $< (0,0), (0,0), (2,0) >$, but if the left program is executed first, the following trace is produced: $< (0,0), (2,0), (2,0) >$. These two traces are stutter equivalent, hence the program is secure. Thus, this paper defines trace indistinguishability in observational determinism as stutter equivalence.

4   Verification of Observational Determinism

Let us assume $KS = (S, \rightarrow, I, AP, La)$ is a Kripke structure that models the behavior of the concurrent execution of the processes (or threads) of a concurrent program. AP is the set of the values of low variables and the function La labels each state with these values. It is assumed that the state space of KS is finite. If KS has a terminal state s_n, we include a transition $s_n \rightarrow s_n$, i.e., a self-loop, ensuring that the Kripke structure has no terminal state. Therefore, all traces of KS are infinite.

The main steps of the verification algorithm are outlined in Algorithm 1. The input of this algorithm is a finite Kripke structure KS modeling the program, and the output is yes or no. The first step is to partition the set I of initial states into sets of low equivalent initial states called initial state clusters $ISC_1, \ldots, ISC_m$, and define $ISC = \{ISC_1, \ldots, ISC_m\}$. The second step is to extract an arbitrary trace T_i from KS for each initial state cluster and build a Kripke structure KST_i from the path in KS corresponding to trace T_i. As the next step, we combine Kripke structures KST_i $(i = 1, \ldots, |ISC|)$, forming a single Kripke structure $KST = (S_{KST}, \rightarrow_{KST}, I_{KST}, AP_{KST}, La_{KST})$, where $KST = KST_1 \oplus KST_2 \oplus \ldots KST_{|ISC|}$. The following theorem reduces the problem of verifying observational determinism to checking divergence stutter bisimulation of KS and KST.

---

input : finite Kripke structure KS modeling the program
output: *yes* if the program satisfies observational determinism;
        Otherwise, *no*

1 Partition the set I of initial states into initial state clusters;
2 Take an arbitrary trace T_i of KS for each initial state cluster;
3 Construct Kripke structure KST_i from the path in KS corresponding to trace T_i;
4 Construct Kripke structure $KST = KST_1 \oplus KST_2 \cdots \oplus KST_{|ISC|}$;
5 Compute divergence stutter bisimulation quotient of $KS \oplus KST$;
6 **for** *each initial state cluster ISC_i* **do**
7   **for** *each pair of initial states s_0 and s_0' in ISC_i* **do**
8   **if** $[s_0]_{\approx_{KS \oplus KST}^{div}} \neq [s_0']_{\approx_{KS \oplus KST}^{div}}$ **then**
9   **return** *no*;
10   **else**
11   **end**
12   **for** *an arbitrary state s_0 in ISC_i and its correspondent initial state st_0 in KST* **do**
13   **if** $[s_0]_{\approx_{KS \oplus KST}^{div}} \neq [st_0]_{\approx_{KS \oplus KST}^{div}}$ **then**
14   **return** *no*;
15   **else**
16   **end**
17 **end**
18 **return** *yes*;

Algorithm 1. Verification of observational determinism

Theorem 2. *The problem of the verification of observational determinism is reduced to the following problem:*

$$\forall C \in (S \uplus S_{KST}) / \approx_{KS \oplus KST}^{div}, \ \forall s_0, s_0' \in ISC_i, \ 1 \leq i \leq |ISC|.$$
$$s_0 \in C \Leftrightarrow s_0' \in C \quad \text{and} \quad ISC_i \cap C \neq \phi \Leftrightarrow I_{KST} \cap C \neq \phi$$

where $\uplus$ stands for disjoint union and $(S \uplus S_{KST}) / \approx_{KS \oplus KST}^{div}$ denotes the quotient space with respect to $\approx_{KS \oplus KST}^{div}$, i.e., the set of all divergence stutter bisimulation equivalence classes in $S \uplus S_{KST}$.

Proof: To prove that KS is observational deterministic, one should prove that for every initial state of KS, all traces starting in that state are stutter equivalent. Thus, for all traces starting from an initial state s_0 of KS, there should be a stutter equivalent trace of KST starting from an initial state st_0 of KST. By Lemma 1, stutter equivalence of traces reduces to divergence stutter bisimulation. From Lemma 2, it follows that each initial state of KS should be divergent stutter bisimilar to an initial state in KST, and vice versa. Thus, KS and KST should be divergent stutter bisimilar. Then, $KS \approx^{div} KST$ if and only if

$$\forall C \in (S \uplus S_{KST})/ \approx^{div}_{KS \oplus KST} . \quad I \cap C \neq \phi \Longleftrightarrow I_{KST} \cap C \neq \phi$$

where $(S \uplus S_{KST})/ \approx^{div}_{KS \oplus KST}$ denotes the quotient space with respect to $\approx^{div}_{KS \oplus KST}$. Considering that some initial states may be low equivalent and consequently they form initial state clusters, it is sufficient to take an arbitrary trace for only each initial state cluster. Of course, all states of an initial state cluster should have stutter equivalent traces and thus should be divergent stutter bisimilar. As a result, KS is observational deterministic if and only if

$$\forall C \in (S \uplus S_{KST})/ \approx^{div}_{KS \oplus KST}, \; \forall s_0, s_0' \in ISC_i, \; 1 \leq i \leq |ISC|.$$
$$s_0 \in C \Leftrightarrow s_0' \in C \quad \text{and} \quad ISC_i \cap C \neq \phi \Leftrightarrow I_{KST} \cap C \neq \phi \qquad \blacksquare$$

The input finite Kripke structure KS has no terminal states. Hence, all traces are infinite and form a cycle in KS. To take an arbitrary trace from KS, we can use *cycle detection* algorithms of graphs. In order to detect cycle, a modified depth first search called *colored DFS* may be used. In colored DFS, all states are initially marked white. When a state is encountered, it is marked grey, and when its successors are completely visited, it is marked black. If a grey state is ever encountered, then there is a cycle and sequence of states pushed in the stack of the DFS so far forms a path.

It remains to explain how to compute divergence stutter bisimulation quotient of $KS \oplus KST$. The algorithm to compute the quotient relies on a partition refinement technique, where the finite state space $S \uplus S_{KST}$ is partitioned in blocks. Starting from a straightforward initial partition, where all states with the same label (low variable values) form a partition, the algorithm successively refines these partitions until a stable partition is reached. A partition is stable if it only contains divergent stutter bisimilar states and no refinement is possible on it. Further details can be found, e.g. in [12], [10].

Complexity. The time complexity of finding an arbitrary trace is $O(M)$, where M denotes the number of transitions of KS. Thus, the time complexity of constructing KST is $O(|I|.M)$. The quotient space of $KS \oplus KST$ under $\approx^{div}$ can be computed in time $O((|S| + M) + |S|.(|AP| + M))$ under the assumption that $M = |S|$ [10]. Thus, the costs of verifying observational determinism for concurrent programs are dominated by the costs of computing the quotient space under $\approx^{div}$, which is polynomial-time.

Using the quotient space to verify observational determinism has two advantages: (1) Instead of analyzing the concrete model of the program, a minimized abstract model is analyzed. Provided the quotiening preserves stutter equivalence, the analysis of the minimized model suffices to decide the satisfaction of observational determinism in the program. (2) The proposed approach can easily be adapted to verify programs with infinitely many states, as there are efficient algorithms for computing the quotient space of infinite state programs [13].

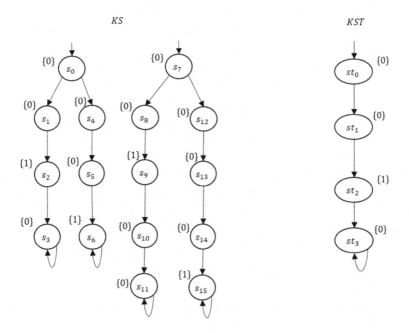

Fig. 1. The Kripke structure KS of P5 and the Kripke structure KST of an arbitrary trace of KS

Example. Consider the following program from [14]:

```
l:=0;
if(h) then {l:=0; l:=1} || l:=0
else {l:=0; l:=1} || {l:=0; l:=0}          (P4)
```

where h is a boolean and high variable and l is a low variable. The Kripke structure KS of the program P4 and the Kripke structure KST of an arbitrary trace of KS are shown in Figure 1. The equivalence classes of $KS \oplus KST$ under $\approx^{div}$ are $[s_0]_{div} = \{s_0, s_7\}$, $[s_1]_{div} = \{s_1, s_8, st_0, st_1\}$, $[s_2]_{div} = \{s_2, s_9, st_2\}$, $[s_3]_{div} = \{s_3, s_{10}, s_{11}, st_3\}$, $[s_4]_{div} = \{s_4, s_5, s_{12}, s_{13}, s_{14}\}$ and $[s_6]_{div} = \{s_6, s_{15}\}$. Therefore, the divergence stutter bisimulation quotient of it is computed as depicted in Figure 2. Since the initial state s_0 of KS and the initial state st_0 of KST are not in the same equivalence class, the program is labelled as insecure.

5   Related Work

Zdancevic and Myers [5] define observational determinism in terms of prefix and stutter equivalence each low variable. Huisman et al. [8] show that allowing pre-fixing permits some leaks, so they define observational determinism in terms of stutter equivalence on each low variable. Terauchi [11] shows that independent consideration of low variables is not correct and information flows may occur.

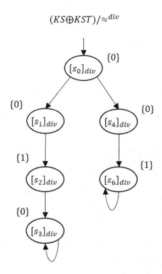

Fig. 2. The divergence stutter bisimulation quotient of $KS \oplus KST$ for P5

Hence, he proposes prefix and stutter equivalence on all low variables. Huisman and Blondeel [15] define observational determinism in terms of stutter equivalence on all low variables. Ngo et al. [16] defines observational determinism with two conditions: condition 1 requires stutter equivalence on each low variable and condition 2 requires stutter equivalence on all low variables. Ngo et al. argue that a concurrent program satisfying both of these conditions is secure.

A common approach to verify information flow properties is the use of type systems. A type system is a collection of type inference rules for assigning types to variables of a programming language and making judgments about programs [17]. With a type system developed for secure information flow, a program can be type checked for secure-flow violations [18]. But type systems are not extensible, as for each variation of confidentiality policy and programming language to be verified, a new type system should be redefined and proven sound. For more details about disadvantages of type systems, see [19].

Accordingly, logic-based verification and model checking has been advocated. But as security policies are not trace properties [6], [21], standard logic-based verification and model checking methods can't be utilized and need to be modified. Trace properties, e.g. safety or liveness properties [10], are properties of individual traces; But most of security policies, such as secure information flow, are properties of sets of traces, called hyperproperties [21]. For instance, observational determinism is a hyperproperty because a trace is allowed if it is indistinguishable from all other traces having the same low vales. Various attempts for logical specification of information flow properties has been made. One promising one is self-composition which composes a program with a copy of it, with all variables renamed. Then, the problem of verifying secure information flow is reduced to a trace property for the composed program. Huisman and Blondeel [15] use this idea to model check observational determinism for multi-threaded programs. They specify observational determinism in μ-calculus. A disadvantage with these kinds of methods that exploit logical verification and self-composition is the common problem of state space explosion [22], [23].

The concept of stutter equivalence in the definition of observational determinism brings weak bisimulation to mind. Ngo et al. [16] use bisimulation to verify observational determinism in multi-threaded programs. They make a copy of the program for each initial state of the program and check bisimilarity of each pair of the programs after removing stutter steps and determinizing them. But the cost of determinizing a program is exponential in the size of the program. This method suffers from state space explosion problem too, as it makes a copy of the program for each initial state of it.

Another line of research for verifying hyperproperties is to extend temporal logics and introduce new logics to specify these properties. Many attempts have been made, including HyperLTL, HyperCTL* [9], HyperCTL [24], SecLTL [25], etc. Clarkson et al. [9] specify observational determinism and many other security properties in HyperLTL and provide model checking techniques for verifying HyperLTL and HyperCTL*. Finkbeiner et al. [24] introduce HyperCTL, which extends CTL* with path variables. They reduce the model checking problem for HyperCTL to the satisfiability problem for QPTL to obtain a model checking algorithm for HyperCTL. Dimitrova et al. [25] add a new modal operator, the hide operator, to LTL and name the resulting logic SecLTL. They propose an automata-theoretic technique for model checking SecLTL.

A similar research to our work is Mantel's unwinding possibilistic security properties [26]. In this work, he proposes a modular framework in which most security properties can be composed from a set of basic security predicates (BSPs); he also presents unwinding conditions for most BSPs. These unwinding conditions can be seen as simulation relations on system states. Intuitively, unwinding conditions require that each high transition is simulated in such a way that a low observer cannot infer whether such high transition has been performed or not. Thus the low observation of the process is not influenced in any way by its high behavior. In 2011, D'Souza et al. [27] propose an automata-theoretic technique for model checking Mantel's BSPs. The proposed model checking approach is based on deciding set inclusion on regular languages.

6   Conclusion

This paper discusses a bisimulation-based approach for model checking observational determinism in concurrent programs. Concretely, we extract some trace(s) of the program and check stutter trace equivalence between the trace(s) and the program. This is done by computing a bisimulation quotient. The time complexity of the verification is polynomial. The advantage of our proposed approach is that the analysis is done on a minimized abstract model of the program. Hence, the state explosion problem may be avoided. Another advantage is that the approach can be easily adapted for infinite state programs.

As future work, we plan to implement the proposed approach. We will also study whether bisimulation-based modular minimization algorithms are appropriate for verifying observational determinism. We also aim to modify our algorithm and use compositional verification techniques to benefit from modular structure of the concurrent program.

References

1. Balliu, M.: Logics for information flow security: from specification to verification (2014)
2. Smith, G.: Principles of secure information flow analysis. In: Malware Detection, pp. 291–307. Springer, US (2007)
3. Sabelfeld, A., Myers, A.C.: Language-based information-flow security. IEEE Journal on Selected Areas in Communications **21**(1), 5–19 (2003)
4. Denning, D.: A lattice model of secure information flow. Communications of the ACM **19**(5), 236–243 (1976)
5. Zdancewic, S., Myers, A.C.: Observational determinism for concurrent program security. In: Computer Security Foundations Workshop, Proceedings. 16th IEEE (2003)
6. McLean, J.: Proving noninterference and functional correctness using traces. Journal of Computer security **1**(1), 37–57 (1992)
7. Roscoe, A.W.: CSP and determinism in security modelling. In: IEEE Symposium on Security and Privacy, Proceedings (1995)
8. Huisman, M., Worah, P., Sunesen, K.: A temporal logic characterisation of observational determinism. In: Computer Security Foundations Workshop, 19th IEEE (2006)
9. Clarkson, M.R., Finkbeiner, B., Koleini, M., Micinski, K.K., Rabe, M.N., Sánchez, C.: Temporal logics for hyperproperties. In: Abadi, M., Kremer, S. (eds.) POST 2014 (ETAPS 2014). LNCS, vol. 8414, pp. 265–284. Springer, Heidelberg (2014)
10. Baier, C., Katoen, J.P.: Principles of model checking, vol. 26202649. MIT press, Cambridge (2008)
11. Terauchi, T.: A type System for observational determinism. In: Computer Security Foundations, pp. 287–300 (2008)
12. Groote, J.F., Vaandrager, F.: An Efficient Algorithm for Branching Bisimulation and Stuttering Equivalence. Springer, Berlin Heidelberg (1990)
13. Chutinan, A., Krogh, B.H.: Verification of infinite-state dynamic systems using approximate quotient transition systems. IEEE Transactions on Automatic Control **46**(9), 1401–1410 (2001)
14. Ngo, T.M.: Qualitative and quantitative information flow analysis for multi-thread programs. University of Twente (2014)
15. Huisman, M., Blondeel, H.-C.: Model-checking secure information flow for multi-threaded programs. In: Mödersheim, S., Palamidessi, C. (eds.) TOSCA 2011. LNCS, vol. 6993, pp. 148–165. Springer, Heidelberg (2012)
16. Ngo, T.M., Stoelinga, M., Huisman, M.: Effective verification of confidentiality for multi-threaded programs. Journal of Computer Security **22**(2), 269–300 (2014)
17. Volpano, D., Irvine, C., Smith, G.: A sound type system for secure flow analysis. Journal of computer security **4**(2), 167–187 (1996)

18. Smith, G., Volpano, D.: Secure information flow in a multi-threaded imperative language. In: Proceedings of the 25th ACM SIGPLAN-SIGACT symposium on Principles of programming languages, pp. 355–364. ACM (1998)
19. Barthe, G., D'argenio, P.R., Rezk, T.: Secure information flow by self-composition. Mathematical Structures in Computer Science **21**(06), 1207–1252 (2011)
20. McLean, J.: A general theory of composition for trace sets closed under selective interleaving functions. In: IEEE Computer Society Symposium on Research in Security and Privacy, Proceedings, pp. 79–93 (1994)
21. Clarkson, M.R., Schneider, F.B.: Hyperproperties. Journal of Computer Security **18**(6), 1157–1210 (2010)
22. Clarke, E.M.: The Birth of Model Checking. In: Grumberg, O., Veith, H. (eds.) 25 Years of Model Checking. LNCS, vol. 5000, pp. 1–26. Springer, Heidelberg (2008)
23. Emerson, E.A.: The beginning of model checking: a personal perspective. In: Grumberg, O., Veith, H. (eds.) 25 Years of Model Checking. LNCS, vol. 5000, pp. 27–45. Springer, Heidelberg (2008)
24. Finkbeiner, B., Rabe, M.N., Snchez, C.: A temporal logic for hyperproperties. In: arXiv preprint arXiv:1306.6657 (2013)
25. Dimitrova, R., Finkbeiner, B., Kovcs, M., Rabe, M.N., Seidl, H.: Model checking information flow in reactive systems. In: Verification, Model Checking, and Abstract Interpretation, pp. 169–185. Springer, Berlin Heidelberg (2012)
26. Mantel, H.: Unwinding possibilistic security properties. In: Computer Security-ESORICS 2000, pp. 238–254. Springer, Berlin Heidelberg (2000)
27. D'Souza, D., Holla, R., Raghavendra, K.R., Sprick, B.: Model-checking trace-based information flow properties. Journal of Computer Security **19**(1), 101–138 (2011)

Web Security

Cache Timing Attacks Revisited: Efficient and Repeatable Browser History, OS and Network Sniffing

Chetan Bansal[1(✉)], Sören Preibusch[2], and Natasa Milic-Frayling[2]

[1] Microsoft Research, Bangalore, India
chetanb@microsoft.com
[2] Microsoft Research, Cambridge, UK

Abstract. Cache Timing Attacks (CTAs) have been shown to leak Web browsing history. Until recently, they were deemed a limited threat to individuals' privacy because of their narrow attack surface and vectors, and a lack of robustness and efficiency. Our attack implementation exploits the Web Worker APIs to parallelise cache probing (300 requests/second) and applies time-outs on cache requests to prevent cache pollution. We demonstrate robust cache attacks at the browser, operating system and Web proxy level. Private browsing sessions, HTTPS and corporate intranets are vulnerable. Through case studies of (1) anti-phishing protection in online banking, (2) Web search using the address bar in browsers, (3) publishing of personal images in social media, and (4) use of desktop search, we show that CTAs can seriously compromise privacy and security of individuals and organisations. Options for protection from CTAs are limited. The lack of effective defence, and the ability to mount attacks without cooperation of other websites, makes the improved CTAs serious contenders for cyber-espionage and a broad consumer and corporate surveillance.

Keywords: Privacy · Cache timing attacks · Cyber-security · Cyber-espionage · Browser history sniffing

1   Introduction

Web caching is a common performance enhancing mechanism. It improves Web browsing speed, for the convenience of the consumer, and reduces the network traffic, thus decreasing the cost for the provider and the user. Caching is not limited to the Web browser but also used by the operating system and network proxies to improve the user experience (Fig. 1). This convenience comes at the cost of decreased user privacy since caches store persistent information that can be interrogated by attacker websites.

Since the early Internet days, browsers have adopted the *same-origin principle* to limit the interaction between websites from different domains and to have cookies and JavaScript's from different sites coexist without interfering [1]. However, this principle is not applied to the entire persistent browser state.

© IFIP International Federation for Information Processing 2015
H. Federrath and D. Gollmann (Eds.): SEC 2015, IFIP AICT 455, pp. 97–111, 2015.
DOI: 10.1007/978-3-319-18467-8_7

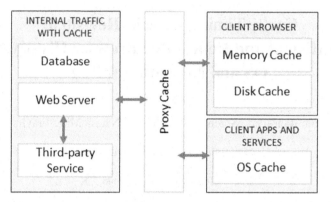

Fig. 1. Interaction among different caching facilities with the user PC and Web network

The ability for one site to learn about visits of individuals to other sites has fuelled a lucrative Internet economy around advertising services and user tracking across websites [2]. Despite the privacy risks, only rudimentary technical support and policy-based protection have been offered to users to control their exposure. At the same time, browsing history is considered personal information [3], and consumers dislike advertisers using their browsing history even when they are assured to remain anonymous [4].

While cookie-based user tracking is gaining attention of the general public and policy makers, privacy violations due to cache timing attacks (CTAs) are still an obscure matter. Whereas history sniffing through 'coloured hyperlinks' has been fixed by browser manufacturers, CTAs are harder to detect and difficult to prevent [5] [6]. Instead of placing new objects into the cache, CTAs probe the cache for the existence of specific items and make inferences about user activities that leave traces in the cache (e.g., visits to websites). More precisely, the attackers time the browser's response to an item request to determine whether the item was cached (fast response) or fetched from the website (slow response). In the former case, they can conclude that the user has visited the Web resource in the recent past.

Since CTAs require active probing for specific items and careful measurement of the time responses, they have been considered limited in the damage they can cause and the scale they can achieve. A limiting factor in CTAs is the need to lure the victim to the attacker's Web page that hosts the JavaScript for carrying out the attack. Furthermore, a simplistic probing of the cache only allows one-time inquiry since checking for the presence of an item requires reading the corresponding file which is then added to the cache. This side effect contaminates (or 'pollutes') the cache and precludes iterative probing. We revisit the implementation of CTAs and investigate the scope of their effectiveness in the contemporary ecosystem.

New Web paradigms (e.g., HTML5 and AJAX) enable rich, interactive end-user applications. Modern browsers expose comprehensive APIs and position the browser as an 'operating system' that hosts third-party applications (e.g., Chrome OS). At the same time, the scope of Web activities has expanded considerably to include high-stakes activities such as banking, e-commerce, and e-governance that are attractive targets for attacks. Also, in online social media activities, personal information flows in abundance.

In this paper we demonstrate how CTAs can be implemented to overcome the discussed limitations. We use two specific techniques: (a) time-outs on cache requests and (b) multi-threaded cache probing using Web Worker APIs, to create repeatable and efficient CTAs, making them a serious contender for cyber-espionage and for individual and enterprise-level surveillance by any third party. As a consequence, CTAs become a serious privacy threat both to individuals and enterprises.

Our research makes the following contributions: (1) *extended the scope* of CTAs by including practical attacks on operating systems, browser components, banking and social websites, as well as first real-world, practical attacks on proxy caches that open door for enterprise level tracking and surveillance and (2) improved *efficiency* and *repeatability* of CTAs by eliminating cache 'contamination' during cache probing.

We begin by situating our work within CTA research and follow with the technical description of our approach. We present four case studies that demonstrate the improvements in CTAs. We then discuss remedies to reduce the damage of CTAs before concluding with the summary of our contributions and an outlook on future work.

2   Related Work

2.1   Browsing History Extraction

The ability of a website to probe whether a hyperlink is displayed as a visited link, through a CSS a:visited rule, was at the heart of the first sniffing attacks on browser history [7]. Fortunately, the vulnerability due to the leak of the visited link colour has now been fixed by all major browser manufacturers, defending from attacks based upon it.

Timing attacks have been well-known for over a decade but remained limited to browser caches and were not considered in detail to achieve robustness and scale. Image-loading times in a browser are a cache-based side channel that can leak information about browsing history. The initial discussion dates back to 2000 by Felten et al. [5] who introduced web timing attacks and showed how they can be used to compromise users' browsing histories. They also discussed timing attacks on DNS and proxy caches.

Considering further the cache timing for DNS and browser, Jackson et al. [6] refined the same-origin policy to also cover the browser cache. They implemented their proposal as a Firefox extension, but the impact on the overall ecosystem remained small. The add-on gained no traction amongst users and browser vendors did not adopt the design [8]. We discuss mitigations in more detail in Section 5.

2.2   Cache Timing for Inference of Private Information and Identity

More recently, targeted timing attacks have been shown to leak very specific information about the users. Jia et al. demonstrated leakage of users' geo-location through CTAs [9]. According to them, 62% of the Alexa top 100 websites enable attackers to infer users' geo-location based on cached resources. For instance, websites like Google or Craigslist are personalised by user location (e.g., country or city specific domains and URLs or location-sensitive images). However, due to the lack of empirical studies, user damages from the described leakage of country or city information are unclear. It seems that, unless geo-location attack is combined with other non-trivial attacks, it can only be exploited for targeted phishing attacks. The robustness and accuracy of the attack are questionable, as is the effectiveness with a cache lookup frequency of 5 to 10 URLs per second. In our work, we consider these limitations, as well as the repeatability of the attacks.

Cache timing techniques also misuse the browser cache as a persistent data store, similar to cookies, and thus support identity attacks. Cache cookies can be created by interpreting each cache hit or miss as a single bit [5]. In this manner, a series of URLs can be used to persist several bits of information such as session ids or even unique tracking ids, despite the users' efforts to suppress cookies in their browsers. In the absence of access control for the browser cache, cache fingerprints can be read or written across origins akin to third-party cookies.

3   Attack Principles and Improvements

3.1   Attack Mechanics

Attack Principle. Although the same-origin policy [1] restricts cross-origin access to security critical APIs, such as DOM, Cookies, Local Storage, XMLHttpRequest, it allows for shared caches and cross-origin embedding of resources—a fundamental principle of hypermedia. For instance, if the domain A.com embeds a resource A.com/file.ext then the resource is cached by the browser on page load. Subsequently, any other origin can load A.com/file.ext and measure the loading time to infer whether the resource already existed in the cache or not. This can be further used to imply that the targeted user requested A.com/file.ext earlier.

Delivery of the Attacks. CTAs can be executed without help from the legitimate site and by any Web-savvy user who is able to implement (or copy) a cache probing Java-Script. Delivery of a malicious JavaScript is not difficult to achieve due to the many ways to distribute URLs, including emails and social media. Advertisements and social networks are the most common channels to distribute JavaScript based malware [10] [11]. Cache probing JavaScripts can be embedded in advertising banners, or delivered through the attacker page by ensuring that it ranks high in search results.

Unlike other JavaScript attacks, like CSR, XSS, etc., timing attacks are based on a polling mechanism. The malicious script has to make a request for each URL and time the response to make an inference. The larger the number of URLs, the longer the script has to run. Thus, cache probing requires a very speed-efficient attack. Otherwise, the victim needs to be exposed to the attack for a prohibitively long time. Finally, previous attacks were limited in their scope; they could only be executed once due to cache contamination with requested URLs.

Attack deployment. Our CTA implementation does not require any custom hardware or software. We have tested the attacks on common browsers, OS, services and real world proxies and banking websites. Our exact setup was a Windows 8.1 PC, on the corporate network of the authors. Attacks are done using JavaScript which can be hosted on any website. The minimum browser requirements for the Web Worker API are Internet Explorer 10, Chrome 4 and Firefox 3.5. Some attacks, like the one described in Section 4.4, require the attacker to host a website within the intranet.

```javascript
function isRequestCached(URI, callback) {
  var timeStamp, timedOut = false;
  var xhr = new XMLHttpRequest();
  xhr.open('GET', URI, true);
  xhr.onreadystatechange = function() {
    setTimeout(function() { callback(!timedOut); }, 2);
  };
  xhr.timeout = 5; // milliseconds
  xhr.ontimeout = function() { timedOut = true; }

  timeStamp = getTimeStamp();
  xhr.send(null);
}
```

Listing 1: JavaScript function snippet for timing queries

3.2   Improved CTAs

Overall Performance. In order to make the timing attacks scalable and avoid cache contamination, we use Web Workers and timeouts on probing requests. Previously, cache contamination was avoided through the same-origin policy and iframes [12]. However, that approach requires DOM access which creates a considerable overhead and leads to poor performance. Furthermore, the DOM is not available to Web Workers due to concurrency issues. As seen in Fig. 2, our parallel implementation of cache attacks is 15 times more efficient than the best-performing approach so far: it takes 0.5 seconds to complete 150 requests, compared to 7.4 sec for the same 150 requests using the CoreDump algorithm [12]. It is also more resilient to cache contamination.

Web Workers. Prior to HTML5, JavaScript did not have any notion of multi-threading. All the scripts on a given web page executed in a single thread. Asynchronous timers using setTimeout and setInterval functions were used to simulate multi-threading. With the introduction of Web Workers, concurrent background tasks can be spawned as OS-level threads. The worker thread can perform tasks without interfering with the user interface. The feature is supported by all major desktop and mobile browsers. Our experimental setup included successful tests with Internet Explorer, Firefox, Chrome, and Opera.

Time-out. We use high resolution timeouts for the XMLHttpRequests to avoid cache contamination during attacks. Listing 1 shows a code snippet where we use very small

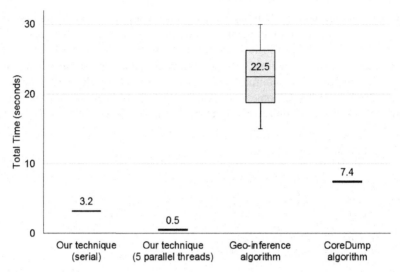

Fig. 2. Total time in seconds to complete 150 requests. Benchmark of our cache probing technique (single-threaded or multi-threaded) against the existing geo-inference algorithm [9] and the CoreDump algorithm [12]. Smaller numbers are better.

timeout values (5ms) to terminate the request before it is completed. This makes sure that the cache does not include the requested URLs due to probing.

The timeout value depends on the type of cache we probe (e.g., a browser or a proxy cache). We extensively tested the timeout technique using Chrome and Opera; similar can be done for other browsers. For attacking the browser cache, the timeout value of 5ms was sufficient while for proxies it was 15ms. The values vary based on the client configuration, bandwidth and network latency. The attacker can pre-compute these values for a specific victim by running benchmarks. We apply a simple method; for browser and proxy caches we make 5 requests, each for cached and un-cached resources, and calculate the mean and max timeout values.

Extended Attack Surfaces. First, we consider scenarios beyond the browsing history attacks and show that sensitive resources like security images, commonly used on banking website, and XML/JSON based API calls can be targeted to leak user's private information. Second, we exploit Web caches that are not limited to browsers but included in the operating system and network proxies.

4   Case Studies

In this section we demonstrate how CTAs render existing anti-phishing defences useless (Section 4.1) and how they can be used to revive and improve previous user de-anonymisation attacks (Section 4.2). We also present two novel case studies of CTAs applied to monitoring Web search and OS file-system queries (Sections 4.3 and 4.4).

4.1   Online Banking Security Images

Site-to-user is an anti-phishing product by RSA Security based on the challenge-response model. The product is used by major financial institutions like Virgin Money, HDFC Bank Ltd., and many others. Through Site-to-user a legitimate website can authenticate itself to the user and prove that it is not a phishing site. When a user creates her account, she is asked to choose an image and a text phrase as part of the Site-to-user protection. Now, whenever the user visits the website to log-in, the same Site-to-user image and text are displayed after she enters her customer id and before she enters her password. Thus, the user can verify that the site is legitimate.

The Site-to-user protection is not completely secure. It is vulnerable to man-in-the-middle attacks [13] where a malicious phishing website first asks the user to enter the customer id. Subsequently, serving as a proxy, the attacker makes a request to the real banking website to fetch the image and display it back to the user. Albeit simple to implement, this attack is also easy to detect in real-time because of multiple requests from different clients for the same customer id, in a very short time span.

We describe a new attack against Site-to-user that is difficult to detect by the banking service and equally difficult to prevent. In this instance a phishing site recovers the image directly from the user through a CTA. We confirmed the attack against a real banking website (Fig. 3).

Attack Implementation. Since the Site-to-user images are accessible to any individual at the time of subscribing to the service, the attacker has an opportunity to acquire the entire collection of images used by the service. This one-off effort in preparing the resources enables phishing attack across a broad population of customers. Figure 3 illustrates the time (in milliseconds) to get a response from the cache of the selected 283 Site-to-user images.

Responses by Manufacturer. RSA Security acknowledged the vulnerability in both the on-premise and hosted versions of RSA Adaptive Authentication. They fixed the vulnerability by setting no-cache headers for the hosted deployment and they also communicated the mitigation to their on-premise customers.

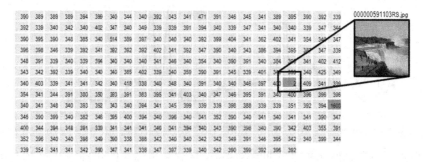

Fig. 3. Request response times in milliseconds for 283 Site-to-user images, colour-coded by magnitude. Green and framed, the correctly identified, cached image (2ms). Red, an outlier that does not impact the success of the attack (1600ms).

4.2   User Identification in Social Networks

Social Networking Sites (SNS) like Facebook, Twitter or LinkedIn are among the most popular destinations on the Web [14]. Facebook has more than 800 million daily active users [15]. SNS store and expose more current and historical personal information about their users and their relations than any other public websites. Personal data on SNS is not limited to personal information, like demographics (age, name, sex, etc.) and profile pictures, but often includes real-time location and status of off-line/online friends [16].

Social networking services used in the workplace include data about the organisation, internal team documents, and internal communication. They may also include more personal matter, such as job applications and inquiries of the team members. Linking and exposing such information could be incriminatory. Consequently, security and privacy attacks on these sites could have detrimental effects for their users.

Past SNS attacks involved methods for browser history sniffing based on CSS visited link vulnerability [7], aiming to de-anonymise a person within a set of known users. While the CSS vulnerability has been fixed, alternative attacks resorted to the analysis of the Transport Layer Security (TLS) traffic. Because TLS does not hide the length of the response, user identification can be done based on the pre-computed size of the users' profile images [17].

Attack Scenario. Methods for de-anonymising users can be applied to track audiences beyond SNS. For example, a marketing campaign team posts a link to the new promotion on the corporate Facebook page and wants to know who among the company's followers have clicked on the link. Such data is normally concealed from the company by the SNS platform due to privacy reasons. Similarly, in the case of a professional network like LinkedIn, clicks on job adverts could be traced and linked back to employees' profiles. The attack can also be used to circumvent privacy-enhancing techniques built into SNS, such as anonymous groups.

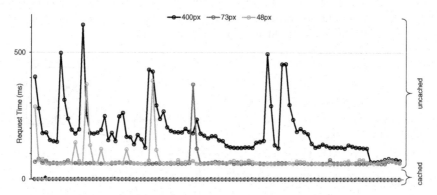

Fig. 4. Request response times in milliseconds for the same Twitter profile picture in the three standard sizes (100 repetitions). For un-cached media, response times vary but are always above response times for cached media, which are all consistently negligible.

Attack Implementation. Our attack enables any malicious website to de-anonymise an SNS user by checking if she is within a pre-defined set of users. It exploits the mapping between SNS users and their unique, self-uploaded profile images, a defining feature of SNS [16]. Uploaded pictures are assigned public, stable and unique URLs, cacheable by browsers for long durations. The user's cache is probed for all the images to determine which might be the user's. Figure 4 demonstrates the ability of our attack to consistently measure the difference in response times for cached versus un-cached Twitter profile pictures.

Our attack is easier to execute than previously described de-anonymisation attacks. As noted, history sniffing through differential colouring of visited links has long been fixed and is no longer possible. Furthermore, in contrast to the traffic analysis, our adversary only needs to set up a third-party website; there is no need for network eavesdropping. This increases the effectiveness of the attack because SNS members can be geographically distributed, i.e., not confined to a single physical network.

Mitigation. SNS like Twitter have two options to prevent the attack: first, by making profile pictures un-cacheable; second, by making URLs of profile pictures dependent on the requesting users, so that attackers cannot compile a set of probing URLs.

4.3   Monitoring Search Queries in Real-time

The CTA scenarios covered in the existing literature are limited to targeting image objects. As we noted in Section 3, images are not the only cacheable content type. Other types include XML, JSON, CSV, and HTML. XML and JSON objects are particularly interesting because they typically carry users' personal data in the requested URLs, for example, user identifiers and search keywords.

We demonstrate the threat of XML/JSON caching by constructing attacks that target information entered by the user into the address bar of a Web browser. The implications are serious because the address bars of modern browsers allow users to type in search queries and have them processed directly by a default search engine. Thus, such queries are exposed to malicious websites which can scan the browser cache. As per our tests, these attacks work on most of the commonly used browsers (Internet Explorer, Firefox, and Chrome) and across multiple search providers such as Bing, Yahoo!, Google, and Wikipedia; Ask and AOL do not show the same vulnerability.

Attack Scenario. In many instances, browsers are configured to provide real-time suggestions to the users as they type in their queries or Web addresses. Continuous AJAX calls are made to the search provider during this user interaction. For instance, a call made by Chrome to Yahoo! (non-essential parameters omitted):

http://ff.search.yahoo.com/gossip?output=fxjson&command=userquery.

where "userquery" refers to the query typed by the user in the Omnibox. Calls made to Google, Bing and other search engines look similar. The following sequence of AJAX calls are made when the user types in "sec15":

/gossip?output=fxjson&command=s
/gossip?output=fxjson&command=se

$$/gossip?output=fxjson\&command=sec$$
$$/gossip?output=fxjson\&command=sec1$$
$$/gossip?output=fxjson\&command=sec15.$$

The search engine responds to each call with a JSON or XML object that is placed in the browser cache. Because this cache is shared with Web domains, a malicious website can use CTAs to extract the queries using the techniques described in Section 3. Our attack is stronger than the packet size based attacks by Chen et al. [18] in two ways: (1) their adversary model is a network eavesdropper [18], while ours is simply a third party website; (2) their attack is based on the packet sizes of responses [18], while ours is based on cache timing and enables the attacker to leak information at any later time as well. Listing 1 shows our script to carry out the probing.

Mitigation. Ideally, the cache for the address bar, search box and all other browser components should be isolated. Furthermore, one could append a user specific nonce to the requests (Section 5).

Responses by Manufacturers. After our report, Bing enabled no-caching headers, effectively preventing CTAs on searches entered into the Browser address bar.

Fig. 5. Windows search provide auto-suggest across PC settings, local and cloud documents, the Web and Windows Store

4.4   Windows Operating System Caches

Windows 8.1 comes with an integrated search feature based on Bing SmartSearch. Search results are fetched from the local computer and from the Internet, as seen in Fig. 5. To provide auto-suggest, all keystrokes are forwarded to a Web service: https://www.windowssearch.com/suggestions?q=whateveryoutype that returns a cacheable XML response ("Cache-Control: private" response header). The search requests are cached by the INET cache built into Windows. This cache is shared between Internet Explorer, Windows components and even applications such as the Outlook mail client. Hence, SmartSearch and query completion work as side channels which can potentially leak data.

Attack Implementation. Any intranet hosted web page opened in Internet Explorer can probe the cache. The intranet requirement stems from the security model of the Internet Explorer (IE) whereby Web content is classified into five security zones, each with a separate cache. However, from our observations, the auto-suggest feature is powered by requests made to Bing by the IE process running in the local intranet zone. The attacker has to be associated with an intranet site rather than the local network; that is lowering the hurdle.

Impact. The attack is critical because any attacker that can publish in the intranet zone can sniff users' activities in the OS from within the browser. Brute force and dictionary techniques can recover users' searches which might contain software names (e.g., unreleased codenames, confidential intellectual property), personal files or Web searches. The requirement for the attacker to publish a website within an intranet is a hurdle but much lower than for traffic analysis-attacks that require access to the local network.

Mitigation. The cache for each OS component should be isolated, from any Internet or intranet Web pages.

Response by Manufacturer. After our report, Bing enabled no-caching headers, effectively preventing CTAs on searches entered into the Windows SmartSearch.

5   Potential Defences and Their Limits

Despite the previous research in this area, browser vendors have not yet taken actions to mitigate against CTAs. With deeper integration of Web services, it is critical that Web caches are carefully designed, by considering the timing side channel. Furthermore, with significant performance improvements of browsers in recent years [19], timing attacks have become more precise. Finally, as described in Section 3, multi-threading in JavaScript makes highly scalable brute force CTAs efficient. Thus, it is necessary to re-evaluate previously proposed mitigations and implement additional ones to address these issues.

5.1   Failed Mitigations

Felten et al. [5] proposed various hypothetical solutions such as disabling caches and JavaScript, and altering hit or miss timings. Unfortunately, disabling JavaScript will break most of the modern websites and disabling caching will lead to significant performance degradation for the Internet. Furthermore, altering hit or miss timings is not possible without affecting user experience and slowing Web applications. Solutions in the form of "domain tagging" [5], i.e., tagging each request with the domain that is making a request, could help with stopping attackers but poses a problem when resources need to be shared across multiple domains. That is the case for content delivery networks (CDNs), in use at over 55% of the top Alexa 1000 websites [20]. The same applies to the "domain tagging" method by Jackson et al. [6].

5.2   HTTPS and Private Browsing Don't help

HTTPS responses that are cached in the browser or by the OS are as vulnerable as HTTP responses. Caching is controlled only through the headers; thus, there is no differentiation between HTTPS and HTTP requests [21, 22]. *Private browsing* is a feature of modern browsers designed to sandbox a session. Data (history, cookies, local storage) pertaining to the private session are discarded when the session is closed. This may seem like a reasonable mitigation; however, the cache is shared between all websites, tabs, and the search-box/address bar opened within the private session. A malicious website can still leak data from any website accessed within the private session. Furthermore, it can still sniff data from the proxy cache.

5.3   Our Proposed Mitigations

We have demonstrated how various Web caches can be exploited to leak data using CTAs. Any counter-measure which impacts performance or requires Web scale changes cannot be expected to be implemented. Furthermore, there is no single mitigation that can fix all the attacks we have described.

Cache Segmentation: Browser and OS. As discussed in Section 4.4, browser and OS components currently leak information because they share the cache with Web pages. Unlike proxy caches, even HTTPS requests are stored in browser caches, making this more critical. Segmentation is an easy yet effective fix. Each component, plugin or extension should have a separate cache so that there is no side channel leak to a malicious Web page or a malicious component.

Proxy Cache. To prevent CTAs on Web proxies, appropriate no-cache headers should be set on all responses with any private data (e.g., API calls, image requests, etc.). The "Cache-control: private" header can be set to prevent any public proxy caching.

Browser Cache. Because of the current design of the browser cache, this is the hardest case of CTAs to fix. To begin with, we recommend that none of the security critical resources (such as Site-to-user images) are cached at all. Website developers should disable caching by setting the appropriate no-cache headers. Eliminating caching altogether is simply not practical; the Web architecture relies on caches.

Issues with the "domain tagging" method can be resolved by using the recently introduced Web standard for "resource timing" API [23]. By default, the cache is shared among all origins. However, for privacy sensitive resources, a list of origins can be provided in the response. These are allowed to load a resource from the cache without having requested it earlier. However, this requires changes in the standards, browsers and also Web servers.

A more pragmatic approach is to append a user or session specific nonce ('number used once') to all URLs with privacy-sensitive data. The CTAs attacker would then need to know or guess the URL in order to probe for it. This mediation does not require Web-scale changes and can be implemented with a minimal effort by developers. Most of the requests by Google and YouTube, for instance, append a nonce.

Probing Detection and Prevention. As an alternative defence, JavaScript engines could be augmented to detect and then prevent cache probing, thereby blocking the attack vector. Detection could be through the source code [24], or through behavioural analyses. Such mitigation adopts the route of antivirus software: instead of fixing the vulnerability we hinder its exploitation. Despite its near-term effectiveness, this approach incurs long-term costs and may result in an arms' race between attackers and their targets.

6   Discussion and Concluding Remarks

6.1   Cyber-Espionage of Corporate Intranets

We have demonstrated how an attacker can de-identify users even on professional social networks (Section 4.2), monitor Web search queries in real-time (Section 4.3), and trace files that users are searching for on their desktop PCs (Section 4.4). An attacker can combine these mechanisms to harvest data from corporate intranets as well. For the exploitation of OS search, the attacker has to be on the intranet (e.g., a rogue employee), but for the rest, any Internet website can deploy the attack.

The caches built into Web proxies (Fig. 1) expand the CTA surface. All major commercial proxy server software have a built-in cache to enable faster loading of frequently accessed resources across users behind the proxy. They are susceptible to the same side channel attack as the browser cache. However, such CTAs are more critical since a malicious Web page can sniff traffic from closed intranets such as hospitals and educational institutions and corporate networks. In some cases, users may not be aware that they share a proxy with others, or cannot change the proxy settings. That particularly applies to the mobile Internet. In our experiments we were able to use a malicious web page to sniff users' queries and traffic from a corporate network.

Taken together, cache attacks at the browser, operating system, and proxy level open door to targeted cyber-espionage. Confidential information can be sniffed from a corporate network. Gathered information can also be used to mount a credible social engineering attack in a second step, for instance, in combination with targeted individuals, identified over Facebook (Section 4.2).

6.2   Policy Recommendations and Managerial Implications

Finding the balance between surveillance and national security is an essential challenge for each society that recognises its citizens' preference for privacy and self-determination. Availability of ad-hoc surveillance "of anyone by anyone", within and outside the workspace, can be easily monetised by a service and, without proper intervention, can become a common practice and an economically viable enterprise. Once such practices take root, they are hard to weed out, as was the case with super cookies [25]. Thus, one would need to act swiftly to prevent the emergence of services that allow attack at scale.

At the corporate level, CIOs and system administrators need to be vigilant in guarding corporate information that can be revealed through employees' activities. This needs to go hand-in-hand with the policy recommendations and work with standardisation bodies to consider adaptations of the cache design.

7   Summary and Future Work

In this paper, we broadened the scope of cache timing attacks by demonstrating CTAs against banking sites, social networks, browser components, and operating systems. Our case studies show that cache timing attacks are applicable to much more critical scenarios than those previously considered. Our technique leverages fine-grained timeouts and HTML5 Web Workers to make the attacks more efficient, without contaminating the cache while probing. The robustness, effectiveness, and the non-cooperative nature of the attack increase the risk to undetectable, widespread attacks as part of the cyber espionage, ad-hoc surveillance of individuals and groups, un-consented identification and de-anonymisation. We discussed potential countermeasures and identified practical mitigations for each scenario that can be easily incorporated in the application design without requiring Web-scale changes.

Our future research will involve empirical studies of attack scenarios to evaluate both the applicability and the effectiveness of the CTAs. We plan a large-scale survey of cache implementations in operating systems across platforms (desktop, mobile, embedded), Web browsers and Web and desktop applications (e.g., mail, document authoring). Our work on systems security will be complemented by a user study to gauge reactions to the unexpected privacy invasions. We foresee outreach efforts to raise awareness amongst consumers and IT professionals.

Acknowledgements. The authors would like to thank Pushkar Chitnis, B. Ashok, Cedric Fournet, Sriram Rajamani and the reviewers for their helpful comments leading to significant improvements to this paper. We would also like to acknowledge the Microsoft and RSA Security teams for prompt and constructive discussions about our attacks.

References

1. Mozilla Developer Network and individual contributors, Same-origin policy (2014). https://developer.mozilla.org/en-US/docs/Web/Security/Same-origin_policy
2. Gomer, R., Rodrigues, E.M., Milic-Frayling, N., Schraefel, M.: Network analysis of third party tracking: User exposure to tracking cookies through search. In: IEEE/WIC/ACM Int. J. Conf. on Web Intelligence and Intelligent Agent Tech. (2013)
3. Carrascal, J.P., Riederer, C., Erramilli, V., Cherubini, M., de Oliveira, R.: Your browsing behavior for a big mac: economics of personal information online. In: Proceedings of the 22nd International Conference on World Wide Web (WWW 2013) (2013)
4. TRUSTe, Behavioral Targeting: Not that Bad? TRUSTe Survey Shows Decline in Concern for Behavioral Targeting, March 4, 2009. http://www.truste.com/about-TRUSTe/press-room/news_truste_behavioral_targeting_survey
5. Felten, E.W., Schneider, M.A.: Timing attacks on web privacy. In: Proceedings of the 7th ACM Conference on Computer and Communications Security (2000)

6. Jackson, C., Bortz, A., Boneh, D., Mitchell, J.C.: Protecting browser state from web privacy attacks. In: Proc. of the 15th Int. Conf. on World Wide Web (WWW) (2006)
7. Wondracek, G., Holz, T., Kirda, E., Kruegel, C.: A Practical attack to de-anonymize social network users. In: IEEE Symposium on Security and Privacy (SP) (2010)
8. Jackson, C.: SafeCache: Add-ons for Firefox (2006). https://addons.mozilla.org/en-US/firefox/addon/safecache/
9. Jia, Y., Dongy, X., Liang, Z., Saxena, P.: I Know Where You've Been: Geo-Inference Attacks via the Browser Cache. IEEE Internet Computing (2014) (forthcoming)
10. Yan, G., Chen, G., Eidenbenz, S., Li, N.: Malware propagation in online social networks: nature, dynamics, and defense implications. In: Proceedings of the 6th ACM Symposium on Information, Computer and Communications Security (ASIACCS) (2011)
11. Provos, N., McNamee, D., Mavrommatis, P., Wang, K., Modadugu, N: The ghost in the browser: analysis of web-based malware. In: First Workshop on Hot Topics in Understanding Botnets (HotBots) (2007)
12. Zalewski, M.: Chrome & Opera PoC: rapid history extraction through non-destructive cache timing, December 2011. http://lcamtuf.coredump.cx/cachetime/chrome.html
13. Youll, J.: Fraud vulnerabilities in sitekey security at Bank of America (2006). www.cr-labs.com/publications/SiteKey-20060718.pdf
14. Alexa Internet, Inc., Top Sites in United States (2014). http://www.alexa.com/topsites/countries/US
15. Facebook, Company Info | Facebook Newsroom (2014). https://newsroom.fb.com/company-info/
16. Bonneau, J., Preibusch, S.: The privacy jungle: on the market for data protection in social networks. In: Eighth Workshop on the Economics of Information Security (WEIS 2009) (2009)
17. Pironti, A., Strub, P.-Y., Bhargavan, K.: Identifying Website Users by TLS Traffic Analysis: New Attacks and Effective Countermeasures. INRIA (2012)
18. Chen, S., Wang, R., Wang, X., Zhang, K.: Side-Channel Leaks in Web Applications: A Reality Today, a Challenge Tomorrow. In: IEEE Symposium on Security and Privacy (SP 2010) (2010)
19. The BIG browser benchmark (January 2013 edition). http://www.zdnet.com/the-big-browser-benchmark-january-2013-edition-7000009776/
20. Datanyze.com, CDN market share in the Alexa top 1K (2014). http://www.datanyze.com/market-share/cdn/?selection=3
21. MSDN, HTTPS Caching and Internet Explorer - IEInternals (2010). http://blogs.msdn.com/b/ieinternals/archive/2010/04/21/internet-explorer-may-bypass-cache-for-cross-domain-https-content.aspx
22. MozillaZine Knowledge base, Browser.cache.disk cache ssl (2014). http://kb.mozillazine.org/Browser.cache.disk_cache_ssl
23. W3C, Resource Timing (2014). http://www.w3.org/TR/resource-timing
24. Acar, G., Juarez, M., Nikiforakis, N., Diaz, C., Gürses, S., Piessens, F., Preneel, B.: FPDetective: dusting the web for fingerprinters. In: ACM SIGSAC Conference on Computer and Communications Security (CCS) (2013)
25. Holter, M.: KISSmetrics Settles ETags Tracking Class Action Lawsuit. Top Class Actions LLC, October 22, 2012. http://topclassactions.com/lawsuit-settlements/lawsuit-news/2731-kissmetrics-settles-etags-tracking-class-action-lawsuit/

Enforcing Usage Constraints on Credentials for Web Applications

Jinwei Hu$^{(\boxtimes)}$, Heiko Mantel, and Sebastian Ruhleder

Department of Computer Science, TU Darmstadt, Darmstadt, Germany
{hu,mantel}@mais.informatik.tu-darmstadt.de
sebastian.ruhleder@googlemail.com

Abstract. For using credential-based access control effectively, recent work identified the need to enforce usage constraints also on credentials. The enforcement of such constraints has not yet been investigated for web applications, although it is relevant when credential-based access control is employed in a web application. This article proposes an approach suitable for enforcing usage constraints on credentials in web applications. More concretely, we present a novel algorithm and an implementation of this algorithm that construct constraint-compliant proofs for credential-based access control policies. We proved that our solution is correct and showed that it is also efficient through extensive experiments.

1 Introduction

Many web applications control access to their resources using policies that state which attributes a client must have in order to obtain access. For example, an online svn system in a university might allow a client to view a directory if some employee of the university owns the directory and if the employee nominates the client as a collaborator. One promising approach to enforce a policy like this is credential-based access control (CBAC) [1].

In CBAC, credentials are used to encode attributes of clients. The representation of credentials may vary, but usually digitally-signed certificates are used as representation. Which credentials a client must provide in order to obtain a particular access is specified by an access control policy. Hence, before granting access, an enforcement mechanism needs to check that the provided credentials legitimate the desired access. This last step is known as proof construction.

Recent work on CBAC identified a need to also restrict the usage of credentials [2,3], in particular, if CBAC is employed in open systems. In an open, distributed system, a credential might be issued with a particular purpose, but it is hardly possible for a credential issuer to exclude the possibility that the credential might be exploitable in other, unintended ways. The danger is that a credential is used in the construction of proofs that result in authorizations unforeseen by the issuer. Usage constraints on credentials enable credential issuers to better control the use of their credentials. They allow issuers to encode the purpose of a credential, thus, reducing the threat of misuse.

© IFIP International Federation for Information Processing 2015
H. Federrath and D. Gollmann (Eds.): SEC 2015, IFIP AICT 455, pp. 112–125, 2015.
DOI: 10.1007/978-3-319-18467-8_8

Usage constraints on credentials are obviously relevant for web applications that employ CBAC. However, the enforcement of usage constraints on credentials has not been investigated in this domain yet. Moreover, solutions in other domains cannot be transferred to web applications in a straightforward manner, as web applications pose new challenges to enforcing usage constraints on credentials. For instance, if a web application needs to respond to requests with low latencies, even under high workloads, then a web application developer is likely reluctant to adopt a usage constraint for credentials that causes substantial overhead. This is the challenge that we address in this article.

We present a novel algorithm for constructing proofs (1) that soundly certify compliance with a given CBAC policy and (2) that respect all usage constraints of credentials used during proof construction. Moreover, our algorithm is complete in the sense that it is able to generate all proofs that comply with (1) and (2). The feature of generating all constraint-compliant proofs is driven by the need to strategically manage credential disclosure to, for example, minimize the number or sensitivity of credentials sent to an application [4,5]. With all proofs at hand, one could choose a proof that meets a strategy.

In the implementation of our solution, we followed the idea of proof-carrying authorization to web applications [6]. More concretely, we implemented a browser extension for deploying our proof-construction algorithm. A client adds this extension for requesting resources at a web application. A web application simply checks the validity of a proof received from a client which uses the browser extension. In this way, the application only needs to incorporate a proof-checking functionality.

To sum up, our main technical contribution is a novel algorithm for constructing constraint-compliant proofs. We proved the correctness of our algorithm and demonstrated its effectiveness and efficiency in experiments.

The rest of the article is organized as follows. We present preliminaries and our problem statement in Section 2. In Section 3, we present our algorithm, including the algorithm description and the correctness theorem. We describe our implementation in Section 4, followed by the performance evaluation of our algorithm in Section 5. Finally, we discuss related work and conclude in Section 6.

2   Preliminaries and Problem Statement

Credential-based access control. We use the policy language RT_0 [7], a role-based trust management language, to express credentials. RT_0 has four types of credentials:

- *Simple membership* $A.R \leftarrow D$: principal D is assigned to role $A.R$.
- *Simple containment* $A.R \leftarrow B.R_1$: principals assigned to role $B.R_1$ are also assigned to role $A.R$.
- *Linking containment* $A.R \leftarrow A.R_1.R_2$: principals assigned to role $B.R_2$ with B being assigned to role $A.R_1$ are also assigned to role $A.R$.

$$\frac{A.R \leftarrow D}{D \text{ in } A.R} \, sm \qquad \frac{D \text{ in } B.R_1 \quad A.R \leftarrow B.R_1}{D \text{ in } A.R} \, sc$$

$$\frac{B \text{ in } A.R_1 \quad D \text{ in } B.R_2 \quad A.R \leftarrow A.R_1.R_2}{D \text{ in } A.R} \, lc$$

$$\frac{D \text{ in } B_1.R_1 \quad \cdots \quad D \text{ in } B_k.R_k \quad A.R \leftarrow B_1.R_1 \cap \ldots \cap B_k.R_k}{D \text{ in } A.R} \, ic$$

Fig. 1. The inference rules for RT_0 credentials

– *Intersection containment $A.R \leftarrow B_1.R_1 \cap \ldots \cap B_n.R_n$*: a principal is assigned to role $A.R$ if the principal is also assigned to all the roles $B_1.R_1$, ..., and $B_n.R_n$.

The semantics of RT_0 credentials is formalized by the inference rules in Figure 1, where D **in** $A.R$ denotes the principal D's membership of role $A.R$. For a credential of the form $X \leftarrow Y$, we say X is the head and Y is the body of the credential. Readers are referred to [7] for more details of RT_0.

In RT_0, roles are used to model particular accesses to particular resources. For example, one could introduce a role $Univ.network$, where $Univ$ is a principal and $network$ is a role name, to model access to networks of $Univ$. In turn, to access a particular resource one needs to have a membership in the role to which this resource corresponds.

Role memberships are granted based on credentials. For example, the credential $Univ.network \leftarrow Alice$ grants the membership in $Univ.network$ to $Alice$. For another example, the credentials in the following set jointly grant to Alice the membership in the role $Univ.network$. In both cases, one actually derives a proof of the membership using the provided credentials.

$$Univ.network \leftarrow Univ.guest \qquad Univ.guest \leftarrow Univ.Prof.collaborator$$
$$Univ.Prof \leftarrow Bob \qquad Bob.collaborator \leftarrow Alice$$

Definition 1 (Proofs). *Given a principal p, a role r, and a set CS of credentials, we say a tuple $(p, r, c, \emptyset)$ is a base proof of p **in** r based on CS if c is a simple membership credential $r \leftarrow p$. We say (p, r, c, s) is a proof of p **in** r based on CS if either it is a base proof or s is a set of proofs based on CS, called sub-proofs, such that for any $(p_i, r_i, c_i, s_i) \in s$, (1) there exists $c \in CS$ such that*

$$\frac{p_1 \text{ in } r_1 \quad \ldots \quad p_k \text{ in } r_k \quad c}{p \text{ in } r} \, l$$

for some $l \in \{sm, sc, lc, ic\}$ and (2) (p_i, r_i, c_i, s_i) is also a proof based on CS.

A proof (p, r, c, s) shows the membership of p in r. Thus, upon seeing the proof, a system deploying credential-based access control allows the access of p to the resource represented by r. We say a proof (p, r, c, s) *uses* a credential if it is c or it is used by the sub-proofs in s.

Usage Constraints on Credentials. As discussed in [2,3], credential issuers are in need of specifying constraints on how their credentials are used, in addition to the language support (e.g., RT). Typical example constraints include delegation depth and final-usage constraints. Following [3], we define a constraint as a deterministic finite automaton (DFA) $(Q, \Sigma, \delta, q_0, F)$, where Q is a finite set of states, Σ is a finite set of input symbols, $\delta \colon Q \times \Sigma \mapsto Q$ is a transition function, $q_0 \in Q$ is an initial state, and $F \subseteq Q$ is a set of final states. The input set Σ of a constraint shall be instantiated with the set of roles in the set CS of credentials when constructing proofs based on CS.

To define the semantics of constraints, we let $words(P)$ be *words* of a proof $P = (p, r, c, s)$ such that $words(P) = \{r\}$ if $s = \emptyset$ and, otherwise, $words(P) = \{r; w \in \Sigma^* \mid \exists P' \in s : w \in words(P')\}$. A proof (p, r, c, s) based on CS *satisfies* a constraint if all words of the proof are accepted by the constraint. Informally, a constraint restricts which roles may appear in a proof and where they may appear in the proof.

For example, suppose that $Univ$ wants to prevent its credential $c1 = Univ.network \leftarrow Univ.guest$ from being used for proving memberships in role $Univ.internal$, regardless of whichever credentials have been issued or may be issued later. This is a final usage constraint on $c1$; $Univ$ could specify the DFA in Figure 2 as a constraint and attach the constraint to $c1$. This constraint excludes any proof of the form $(p, Univ.internal, c, s)$. Receiving words of such a proof, the automaton transits from state q_0 to q_1 with the input $Univ.internal$; if $s \neq \emptyset$, the automaton stays at state q_1 with

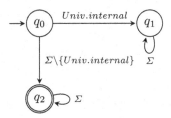

Fig. 2. An example constraint

input r_i for any sub-proofs $(p_i, r_i, c_i, s_i) \in s$. Hence, the automaton could not reach a final state, which means that the proof does not satisfy the constraint. On the other hand, for a proof of the form (p, r, c, s) where $r \neq Univ.internal$, its words are accepted by the automaton and thus the proof satisfies the constraint.

In principle, each credential may come along with a constraint specifying its usage. We say a proof is *constraint-compliant* if it satisfies all constraints that are attached to the credentials used in the proof.

Definition 2 (Problem statement). *Given a set CS of credentials, a principal p, and a role r, the problem is to find all constraint-compliant proofs of p in r based on CS.*

SAGE-PROVE(*credentials*, r, p)

 let *nodes* = CREATE-NODES(*credentials*) and *cons* = ∅
 return CONSTRUCT-PROOFS(r, p, *nodes*, (), *cons*)

CONSTRUCT-PROOFS(r, p, *nodes*, *rolepath*, *cons*)

```
1   r′ = EXTEND-ROLE-PATH(rolepath, r)
2   for every constraint con ∈ cons
3          if con cannot reach a final state after the input r′
4                 return ∅
5   if nodes contains no node for r
6          return ∅
7   let node = node for r and proofs = ∅
8   for each {c, p′} ∈ node.members with p′ == p
9          let proofs = proofs ∪ NEW-PROOF(r, p, c, ∅)
10  for each credential c ∈ node.credentials
11         let sets = ∅ and cons′ = cons ∪ {c's constraint}
12         if c is a simple containment credential
13                let sets = HANDLE-SC(c, p, nodes, r′, cons′)
14         elseif c is an intersection containment credential
15                let sets = HANDLE-IC(c, p, nodes, r′, cons′)
16         elseif c is a linking containment credential
17                let sets = HANDLE-LC(c, p, nodes, r′, cons′)
18         for each set of subproofs s ∈ sets
19                let proofs = proofs ∪ NEW-PROOF(r, p, c, s)
20  return FILTER-VALID-PROOFS(proofs)
```

Fig. 3. The Sage algorithm for constructing constraint-compliant proofs

3   Algorithm

This section presents our algorithm Sage that solves the problem in Definition 2. We first describe the algorithm and then discuss its correctness.

Overview. The Sage algorithm, as shown in Figure 3, is essentially a depth-first search algorithm. It makes use of a dependency between c and s in a proof $P = (p, r, c, s)$: The inference rule used to conclude the role membership p **in** r must take the credential c and all sub-proofs $s_i \in s$ as its premise; further, the rule must match one of the four inference rules sm, sc, ic, and lc. Consequently, the type of the credential c directly determines what proofs must be present in s for this to be possible. The Sage algorithm utilizes this dependency between c and s to construct proofs recursively: When a role membership p **in** r shall be proven, (1) select all credentials with r as the head; (2) for every such credential, (2i) identify the role memberships that must be proven in order to satisfy the premise of an appropriate inference rule, and (2ii) then call the Sage algorithm again with the same principal for every identified role membership. If all necessary role memberships can be proven, construct (and later return) a proof with the recursively constructed proofs and the associated, previously selected credential.

Main Procedure. The entry point of Sage is the SAGE-PROVE function: It takes a set of credentials, a role, and a principal as input and returns a set of proofs showing the membership of the principal in the role. Sage consists mainly of two parts: initialization and proof construction.

Initialization. Sage first converts the credentials into nodes. Sage uses *nodes*, each of which is a container for credentials with the same head role. Sage stores every credential $c \in CS$ in exactly one node, i.e. the node associated to its head role. The use of nodes provides a simplified way to access different credentials in the set CS. Sage initializes the constraints as an empty set, as no credential has been used for proofs yet.

Proof Construction. Sage calls the CONSTRUCT-PROOFS function to compute the set of proofs. Function CONSTRUCT-PROOFS consists of three stages: pre-processing (Lines 1 - 7), sub-proof construction (Lines 8 - 19), and post-processing (Line 20). The pre-processing stage checks whether any proofs may be constructed; the sub-proof construction stage proceeds to construct sub-proofs with different types of credentials. The post-processing stage checks additional constraints that proofs should comply with.

Pre-processing. Line 1 extends the role path with the provided role r. Given a proof (p, r, c, s), a *role path* is a sequence of roles, starting with r and being followed by a role path of a proof in s. Note that a proof may have multiple role paths. This extended role path serves as a trace at which point the algorithm is in relation to the overall structure of the constructed proofs. In lines 2 - 4, this extended role path is used to check whether all constraints in the set *constraints* can still reach a final state from it. If not, any further proofs do not comply with at least one of the constraints. Line 5 checks whether there is any credential available to construct further proofs. If so, the associated node is then assigned to the variable *node* and the set *proofs* is initialized as an empty set. The set *proofs* serves as a container for proofs.

Sub-proof Construction. Lines 8 - 19 construct sub-proofs for each type of credentials. First, lines 8 - 9 traverse all simple member credentials of *node* and add to the set *proofs* a proof for each credential $r \leftarrow p$. Lines 10 - 19 traverse the set of credentials of *node* to construct proofs for the three remaining types of credentials (simple, intersection, or linking containment). Depending on the type of credentials, a helper function is invoked (lines 12 - 17). Each function returns a collection of sets of sub-proofs that can be used to construct proofs in combination with c. Note that the helper functions also call CONSTRUCT-PROOFS for proof construction. Please see Appendix A for the helper functions. Line 19 combines the returned sets of sub-proofs with credential c to a proof of p's membership in r.

Post-processing. Line 20 (FILTER-VALID-PROOFS) filters proofs that satisfy all remaining constraints. Recall that the filtering at lines 2 - 4 checks constraints of a selected credential; this check does not concern constraints introduced posterior to the selected credential. FILTER-VALID-PROOFS checks those latter constraints. In combination, these two checks ensure that Sage returns only constraint-compliant proofs.

Algorithm Correctness. Given a set of credentials CS, a principal p, and a role r, we let *Proofs*(C, r, p) be the set of constraint-compliant proofs of p in r. That is, *Proofs*(C, r, p) contains all the proofs that show the membership of p in r, according to the semantics of RT_0 and constraints. Let SAGE-PROVE(C, r, p) be the set of proofs returned by the algorithm in Figure 3.

Theorem 1. *Given a set of credentials CS, a principal p, and a role r,*

$$\text{SAGE-PROVE}(C, r, p) = Proofs(C, r, p).$$

Proof sketch: We prove two lemmas:

1. SAGE-PROVE$(C, r, p) \subseteq$ *Proofs*(C, r, p) (i.e., any proof returned by the algorithm is constraint-compliant), and
2. SAGE-PROVE$(C, r, p) \supseteq$ *Proofs*(C, r, p) (i.e., any constraint-compliant proof will be generated by the algorithm).

We first map a proof (p, r, c, s) to a tree where the root is the proof itself and its children are the sub-proofs in the set s. The height of a proof is then defined as the height of this tree. We then prove the two lemmas by induction on the height. The full proof of the theorem is available on the authors' website.

4   Implementation

To implement the proposed approach for web applications, we first adapt the communication process between a client and a web application. As shown in Figure 4, the communication takes four steps: (1) The client sends a request for a resource to the application. (2) Upon receiving a request, the application returns a policy for the client to prove. (3) The client constructs a proof of the policy and sends the proof and the credentials together to the application. (4) The application sends the response to the client. If the proof is checked constraint-compliant, the resource is sent to the client; otherwise not.

Among the four steps, step (2) employs the Sage algorithm proposed in Section 3. We implement the algorithm in a browser extension. As such, users at the client need not interact with CBAC when requesting resources. At the web application side, we implement a reference monitor which checks the proof and returns the check results to the application.

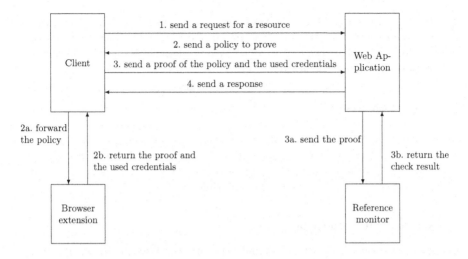

Fig. 4. The proposed architecture of CBAC in web applications

4.1 Browser Extension

We developed a Chrome[1] extension. This extension intercepts policies from web applications at step (2) in Figure 4. With the policy, the extension then invokes a library *Sage.js*, which is a JavaScript implementation of Sage. Obtaining the proofs, the extension selects one proof and re-sends the request to the web application. Note that we leave the investigation of proof selection as future work.

Alternatively, one may write client-side scripts to construct proofs. This will remove the need of a browser extension. However, based on our experiences, a browser extension could use more computational resources and thus lead to better performance. Hence, we chose the extension over client-side scripts.

4.2 Reference Monitor

We chose to implement a reference monitor for Ruby on Rails[2] (or Rails in short) applications. This choice is motivated by the use of model-view-controller pattern of Rails applications. In such a pattern, the notion of resources are directly linked to that of models; each resource is associated with a model. This logical connection between resources and models provides an entry point for incorporating a reference monitor. Also, at the code level, the separation of the view of resources from the model enables us to introduce custom methods to intercept resource requests.

Function-wise, our reference monitor maintains a relation between resources and policies that should be proved in order to access the respective resources.

---

[1] https://www.google.com/chrome/browser/
[2] http://rubyonrails.org/

The monitor also enforces the policies by checking proofs of the policies provided by each requester. To make the monitor effective, we modify Rails controllers which handle authorization logics. We implemented a reference monitor for BrowserCMS[3] as a case study.

5 Experiments

We evaluated the performance of our Javascript implementation of the algorithm Sage with synthetic credentials. The experimental results demonstrate the efficiency of Sage. We first describe a generator we used to synthesize credentials for experiments. Then, we present the experimental results.

5.1 Credential Generator

In order to generate credentials, we make use of a template of credentials available for proving p **in** r for randomly chosen principal p and role r. In a template, leaf nodes are labeled "sm", indicating simple membership credentials shall be generated, and non-leaf nodes are labeled "sc", "ic", or "lc", indicating the other three types of credentials shall be generated, respectively. A template with a root node rn means that a proof (p, r, c, s) can be obtained where c is a type rn credential and rn has a child node ch corresponding to a sub-proof (p', r', c', s') in s such that c' is a type ch credential. Then random, concrete credentials are generated whenever a node is reached when traversing a template. In addition, we also generate some "noisy" credentials which are useless for proving p **in** r.

The generator takes as input four parameters: (1) a tree template, (2) the height of a tree, (3) variant: the number of credentials that shall be created for each type of credentials at each node of the template, and (4) the number of noisy credentials. The generator outputs, in addition to credentials, the following parameters: the size of a generated credential set (i.e., the number of credentials in the set) and the number of credentials of each type in a credential set.

5.2 Experimental Credential Sets

We generated credentials by letting, all uniformly, the template be one of templates in Figure 6, height range from 1 to 5, the number of variant be 1 or 2, and the number of noisy credentials range from 0 to 20. We obtained 945 generated credential sets in total and used them as input to Sage. Note that the templates cover example policies like "Co-workers can see all photos and music" in the case studies of [8].

Figure 7 shows the distribution of the size of the generated credential sets, when the size is smaller than 200. The most of the generated credentials sets have a size smaller than 80. On the other hand, for the ranges between 80 and 180, each range contains 2-10 credentials sets. Also, there are 147 generated credential sets whose size is larger than 200.

---

[3] http://www.browsercms.org/

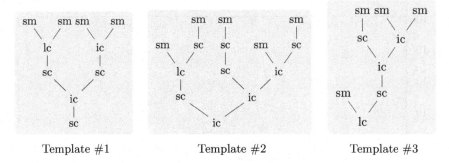

Template #1   Template #2   Template #3

Fig. 6. Templates that were used to generate credentials

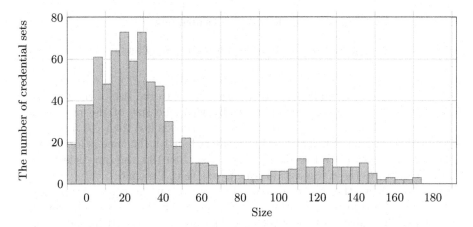

Fig. 7. The size distribution of the generated credential sets of size smaller than 200

5.3 Experimental Results

For each of the 945 generated credential sets, we invoked Sage, which is implemented as a JavaScript library, to compute all constraint-compliant proofs of p in r, where p and r were chosen when generating the credential set. For each credential set, we attached usage constraints to 30% of the credentials in the set: half are delegation depth constraints and the other half are final-usage constraints. The experiments were performed on a machine with 8 GB 1600 MHz DDR3 memory and Intel Core i5-3570 3.4 GHz RAM.

Figure 8 shows the time Sage took to return proof sets for each generated credential set. When the size of the credential sets is smaller than 100, the time is less than 1 ms, with four exceptions. When the size is smaller than 200, the time is always less than 10 ms. And when the size is smaller than 1000, the time is always less than 100 ms. In all cases, the time is less than 1 second. The computation time grows exponentially with the size of the credential sets. However, assuming the size of credential sets used in practice is smaller than 1000, the overhead, being less than 100 ms, is moderate.

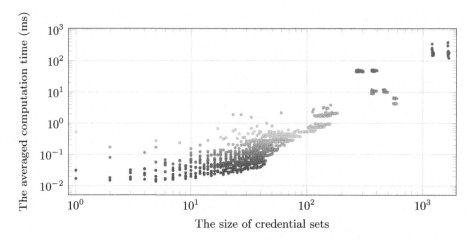

Fig. 8. The time Sage took to return proof sets

Figure 9 depicts the time Sage took with respect to the size of the returned proof sets. The time increases exponentially with the size of the proof sets. However, when the size is smaller than 1000, the time is less than 100 ms, which we think is moderate. When the size is smaller than 10, the time is less than 1 ms except for two cases. When the size is smaller than 100, the time is less than 10 ms. In all cases, the computation time is less than 1 second.

Figure 10 shows the impact of noisy credentials on the computation time. In the figure, the computation time is the average of the time needed for the generated credential sets of the same size. The ratio of noisy credentials in the generated credential sets ranges from 0% to 50%. When the ratio is greater than 10%, the computation time is less than 100 ms. In all cases of the ratios, the time increases along with the growth of the size of the credential sets. Comparing the ratios, however, it appears that the higher the ratio is, the less computation time Sage took on average; the reason for this remains unclear to us.

6   Related Work and Conclusion

Seamons et al. [9] define two variants of the compliance checking problem: type-1 and type-2. The type-1 problem is to determine whether a policy is entailed by a set of credentials. The type-2 problem is to find a proof of a policy together with the used credentials in the proof. Lee and Winslett [4] propose a type-3 compliance checking problem – find all minimal proofs of a policy for a given set of credentials. While an algorithm for the type-2 problem shall be more efficient than an algorithm for the type-3 problem, the latter enables to apply strategies to proof and credential disclosure. This is also the main reason why we address a variant of the type-3 problem.

This variant of the type-3 problem is different in that we construct all constraint-compliant proofs of a policy. With respect to usage constraints on

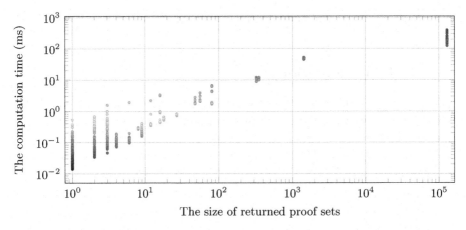

Fig. 9. The time Sage took when the size of returned proof sets varies

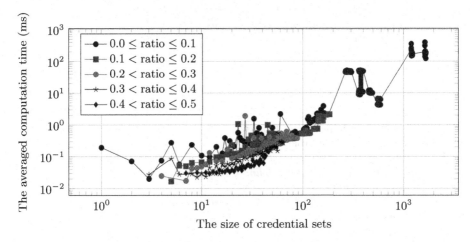

Fig. 10. The averaged computation time with different ratios of noisy credentials

credentials, this work shares the same problem with [3]. While Hu et al. propose a solution by encoding credentials in answer set programming, we develop a novel algorithm and implement it for web applications. Unlike [4] and [3], this work did not consider searching only *minimal* proofs of a policy. Concerning usage constraints on credentials, Bauer et al. [2] propose an approach for proof-carrying authorization. It is not clear how to generate all constraint-compliant proofs with their approach. Approaches to CBAC for web applications include, for example, [1,6]. However, neither of them addresses enforcing usage constraints on credentials.

We have presented a new algorithm for constructing constraint-compliant policy proofs. We have proved the correctness of the algorithm and shown its efficiency by experiments. The algorithm is implemented as a JavaScript library, used in a browser extension, and integrated for an example Ruby on Rails application.

A The Helper Functions

This appendix lists the helper functions that are called by the Sage algorithm in Figure 3. More details of the algorihtm can be found on authors' website.

HANDLE-SC($c, p, nodes, rolepath, cons$)
1 **return** CONSTRUCT-PROOFS(BODY(c), $p, nodes, rolepath, cons$)

HANDLE-IC($c, p, nodes, rolepath, cons$)
1 $sets = \emptyset$
2 $ip = \emptyset$
3 **for** each role $r_i \in$ BODY(c)
4      $ip = ip \cup$ CONSTRUCT-PROOFS($r_i, p, nodes, rolepath, cons$)
5 let $a_1, \ldots, a_n$ denote all sets in ip, with $a_i = a_j \Leftrightarrow i = j$
6 **for** each combination $e = \{e_1, \ldots, e_n\}$ with $e_i \in a_i$
7      $sets = sets \cup e$
8 **return** $sets$

HANDLE-LC($c, p, nodes, rolepath, cons$)
1   $sets = \emptyset$
2   $defining\text{-}role = $ defining role of BODY(c)
3   $linked\text{-}role\text{-}term = $ linked role of BODY(c)
4   **for** each principal p who defines a role r with the role term $linked\text{-}role\text{-}term$
5       $dp = $ CONSTRUCT-PROOFS($defining\text{-}role, p, nodes, (), \emptyset$)
6   **if** dp is not empty
7           $lp = $ CONSTRUCT-PROOFS($r, p, nodes, rolepath, cons$)
8   **for** each $e \in dp \times lp$
9               $sets = sets \cup e$
10 **return** $sets$

If the input credential c is a simple containment credential, HANDLE-SC is called. It simply calls CONSTRUCT-PROOFS with a new role parameter: the roles in the body of c. Every such proof is then later used in CONSTRUCT-PROOFS in combination with c to add proofs to the set *proofs*.

If c is an intersection containment credential, HANDLE-IC is called. In lines 3 - 4, for every role in the intersection of the body of c proofs are created by evaluating CONSTRUCT-PROOFS and then assigned to the variable ip. Finally, in lines 5 - 7, the Cartesian product of all proofs in ip is calculated. Note that the Cartesian product is used to model that an intersection containment credential allows a principal to obtain the head role if the principal is assigned to all roles in the body.

If c is a linking containment credential, HANDLE-LC is called. First, in line 4, all principals who define a role using the linked role term are traversed. For each such principal, CONSTRUCT-PROOFS is called in line 5 to calculate proofs showing the principal is assigned to the defining role of c, which are assigned to the variable dp. If there exist proofs of this form, i.e., if dp is non-empty, CONSTRUCT-PROOFS is called again for the actual principal and the linked role, and the result is assigned to the variable lp. Then, in line 8, the Cartesian product of dp and lp is calculated and later returned.

Acknowledgments. This work was supported by CASED (www.cased.de).

References

1. Vimercati, S.D.C.D., Foresti, S., Jajodia, S., Paraboschi, S., Psaila, G., Samarati, P.: Integrating trust management and access control in data-intensive web applications. ACM Trans. Web **6**(2), 6:1–6:43 (2012)
2. Bauer, L., Jia, L., Sharma, D.: Constraining credential usage in logic-based access control. In: CSF pp. 154–168 (2010)
3. Hu, Jinwei, Khan, Khaled M., Bai, Yun, Zhang, Yan: Compliance checking for usage-constrained credentials in trust negotiation systems. In: Gollmann, Dieter, Freiling, Felix C. (eds.) ISC 2012. LNCS, vol. 7483, pp. 290–305. Springer, Heidelberg (2012)
4. Lee, A.J., Winslett, M.: Towards an efficient and language-agnostic compliance checker for trust negotiation systems. In: Proceedings of the 2008 ACM Symposium on Information, Computer and Communications Security, ASIACCS 2008. pp. 228–239 (2008)
5. Oster, Zachary J., Santhanam, Ganesh Ram, Basu, Samik, Honavar, Vasant: Model checking of qualitative sensitivity preferences to minimize credential disclosure. In: Păsăreanu, Corina S., Salaün, Gwen (eds.) FACS 2012. LNCS, vol. 7684, pp. 205–223. Springer, Heidelberg (2013)
6. Bauer, L.: Access Control for the Web via Proof-carrying Authorization. Ph.D thesis, Princeton University (2003)
7. Li, N., Winsborough, W.H., Mitchell, J.C.: Distributed credential chain discovery in trust management. Journal of Computer Security **11**(1), 35–86 (2003)
8. Mazurek, M.L., Liang, Y., Melicher, W., Sleeper, M., Bauer, L., Ganger, G.R., Gupta, N., Reiter, M.K.: Toward strong, usable access control for shared distributed data. In: Proceedings of the 12th USENIX Conference on File and Storage Technologies (2014)
9. Seamons, K.E., Winslett, M., Yu, T., Smith, B., Child, E., Jacobson, J., Mills, H., Yu, L.: Requirements for policy languages for trust negotiation. In: 3rd International Workshop on Policies for Distributed Systems and Networks (POLICY 2002) pp. 68–79 (2002)

A Survey of Alerting Websites: Risks and Solutions

Amrit Kumar$^{(\boxtimes)}$ and Cédric Lauradoux

INRIA, Grenoble, France
{amrit.kumar,cedric.lauradoux}@inria.fr

Abstract. In the recent years an incredible amount of data has been leaked from major websites such as ADOBE, SNAPCHAT and LINKEDIN. There are hundreds of millions of usernames, email addresses, passwords, telephone numbers and credit card details in the wild. The aftermath of these breaches is the rise of *alerting websites* such as http:// haveibeenpwned.com, which let users verify if their accounts have been compromised. Unfortunately, these seemingly innocuous websites can be easily turned into phishing tools. In this work, we provide a comprehensive study of the most popular ones. Our study exposes the associated privacy risks and evaluates existing solutions towards designing *privacy-friendly alerting websites*. In particular, we study three solutions: private set intersection, private set intersection cardinality and private information retrieval adapted to membership testing. Finally, we investigate the practicality of these solutions with respect to real world database leakages.

Keywords: Data leakages · Phishing · Private set intersection · Private information retrieval · Bloom filter

1 Introduction

In the recent years, we have witnessed an increasing number of data leaks from major Internet sites including ADOBE, SNAPCHAT, LINKEDIN, eBAY, APPLE and YAHOO ! (see bit.ly/19xscQO for more instances). While in most of the cases passwords' files have been targeted; database of identifiers, phone numbers and credit card details have also been successfully exfiltrated and published. These leakages dealt a substantial blow to the trust of people in computer security.

The aftermath of these leakages has led to three pivotal developments. First, the bad security policies of major websites have been exposed, and better policies have been proposed to survive leakages (see [27], [20], [18]). In [27], Parno et al. design an architecture to prevent database leakage. At CCS 2013, Kontaxis et al. propose SAuth [20], an authentication scheme which can survive password leakage. At the same conference, Juels and Rivest present the Honeywords [18] to detect if a passwords' file has been compromised.

Second, security community has obtained datasets to study the password habits of users. In [7], Das et al. consider several leaked databases to analyze

© IFIP International Federation for Information Processing 2015
H. Federrath and D. Gollmann (Eds.): SEC 2015, IFIP AICT 455, pp. 126–141, 2015.
DOI: 10.1007/978-3-319-18467-8_9

password reuse. De Carnavalet et al. [8] use these datasets to test the effectiveness of password meters.

Third, a new kind of websites has appeared: *alerting website*. Users can check through these sites whether their accounts have been compromised or not. In order to check whether a user is a victim of data leakage, alerting websites ask for an identifying data such as username or email address and sometimes even password. These websites are maintained by security experts such as haveibeenpwned.com by Troy Hunt, security companies e.g., LASTPASS, and even government institutions like the German Federal Office for Information Security (BSI): sicherheitstest.bsi.de.

On one hand, these websites are very useful in alerting users, while on the other hand, they are real *"booby traps"*. The problem is the following: when a user submits a username or an email address or a password, the site searches whether it exists or not in the leaked database. If it exists, the user is warned and the website has accomplished its purpose. However, if it is not present in the database, the site owner learns for free a username/email address/password.

Most of these sites advert to the users that they do not indulge in phishing activities but this is the only guarantee available to the user. **The goal of alerting websites is to reduce the effect of data leakage but not amplify it!** Considering the risks of using alerting websites, we naturally raise the following question: How to design alerting websites which cannot be turned into a phishing trap? The user must have a guarantee that it is not possible for the database owner to collect his information during a search query.

With the increasing frequency of data leakages, these websites are fast becoming a *sine qua non* for the victims of data leakages. Consequently, an analysis of these websites and their service is necessary. Our work presents a comprehensive study of alerting websites from two angles: the associated privacy risks and possible solutions to improve the service.

Contribution. The contribution of the paper is threefold:

1. We examine 17 popular alerting websites (Section 2) and analyze their working mechanism, and their approach to deal with privacy. Our findings reveal that several of these websites have huge phishing potential and hence users should be careful while visiting any of these websites.
2. We evaluate existing solutions for designing *privacy-friendly alerting websites*. Two different scenarios have been considered depending on whether or not the database is public. In case of private database (Section 4), *private set intersection protocol* and its variant *private set intersection cardinality protocol* yield an immediate solution. The scenario of public database (Section 5) requires us to adapt *private information retrieval protocol* for membership testing. This is achieved by combining it with *Bloom filters* (Section 5.1). These protocols subsumed under the name of *Private Membership Query* protocols ensure user's privacy in the *honest-but-curious* model.
3. Finally, we experimentally analyze the merits of these solutions with respect to real world data leakages (Section 6).

2   Alerting Websites: Risks

Users can be alerted on the fact that their account or personal information has been leaked. We discuss the characteristics of these websites which evidently offer opportunities for sophisticated phishing attacks.

Websites alerting users about their account or data leakage can be divided into three types according to their sources of information. In the sequel, we categorically discuss our findings.

SINGLE-SOURCE (S). Some websites are associated with a single data leakage. This is the case for adobe.cynic.al, bit.ly/1by3hd9, lucb1e.com/credgrep and adobe.breach.il.ly. These websites are related to the ADOBE data leakage of 153 million accounts which occurred in October 2013. The last three websites were successfully tested on 22/12/2014 but cannot be accessed anymore. Other websites for instance snapcheck.org,[1] findmysnap.com, and lookup.gibsonsec.org are similarly associated with the SNAPCHAT leakage (4.6 million usernames, phone numbers and city exposed in January 2014).

AGGREGATOR (A). We observe that 5 of these websites search through several databases to inform users if their data has been exposed. For instance, shouldichangemypassword.com (bit.ly/1aJubEh for short) allegates to use 3346 leaked databases while only 194 are officially known. The remaining four are maintained by private companies: lastpass.com, bit.ly/1fj0SqV, bit.ly/1aJubEh and dazzlepod.com/disclosure. The last remaining site haveibeenpwned.com is designed and maintained by security expert Troy Hunt.

HARVESTER (H). Three sites claim to have created their own databases from harvested data. Two of these are maintained by famous security companies hacknotifier.com and pwnedlist.com/query. The last site is maintained by the German Federal Office for Information Security (BSI).

The rue89.nouvelobs.com site is slightly different from the others. In September 2014, this French news website bought on the Darknet 20 million French email addresses for 0.0419 bitcoins (see article bit.ly/1lKAxsB). The article offers the opportunity to check if the reader's addresses are included in the leak.

We have reviewed 17 alerting sites and our findings are summarized in Table 1. To measure if a user can trust the service offered by these sites, we have considered four criteria:

- The usage of a secure connection through HTTPS.
- The existence or not of a security/privacy statement.
- The fact that the site responds or not with an answer.
- A technical description of all the operations performed on the data.

From Table 1, we observe that ten of these sites do not use HTTPS which means that the traffic towards them can be easily eavesdropped. Single-source

---

[1] The database cannot be accessed anymore (10/12/2014).

Table 1. Analysis of 17 alerting websites (* result as on 22/12/2014).

Websites	Type	Database(s)	https	Statement	Answer	Descrip.
rue89.nouvelobs.com	S	Unknown	✗	✓	✓	✗
adobe.cynic.al	S		✗	✗	✓	✓
bit.ly/1by3hd9[*]	S	ADOBE	✓	✓	✓	✗
lucb1e.com/credgrep[*]	S		✗	✗	✗	✗
adobe.breach.il.ly[*]	S		✗	✗	✗	✗
snapcheck.org	S		✗	✗	✓	✗
findmysnap.com	S	SNAPCHAT	✗	✗	✓	✗
lookup.gibsonsec.org	S		✗	✗	✓	✗
didigetgawkered.com	S	GAWKER	✗	✗	✗	✗
lastpass.com	A	6	✓	✓	✓	✗
haveibeenpwned.com	A	9	✓	✓	✓	✓
bit.ly/1fj0SqV	A	12	✓	✗	✗	✗
dazzlepod.com/disclosure	A	28	✗	✓	✓	✗
bit.ly/1aJubEh	A	3346/194	✓	✗	✓	✗
hacknotifier.com	H	Unknown	✗	✓	✓	✗
pwnedlist.com/query	H	Unknown	✓	✗/✓	✓	✓
sicherheitstest.bsi.de	H	Botnets	✓	✓	✓	✗

alerting sites are the least trustworthy of all because most of them do not have a privacy statement. The website bit.ly/1by3hd9 is a notable exception. Aggregator sites in general perform better. Most of them use HTTPS and have a statement concerning privacy or phishing. The website haveibeenpwned.com even has a description of how it works.

The harvesters are more controversial: hacknotifier.com claims that *"we use a 256-bit secured and encrypted SSL connection"*, but does not use HTTPS or any encryption.[2] The website pwnedlist.com/query claims that *"this is not a phishing site"*, but they also state (pwnedlist.com/faq) that *"Over the past years we've built an advanced data harvesting infrastructure that crawls the web 24/7 and gathers any potentially sensitive data ..."*.

Four sites do not give any answer: either they are not working anymore (like lucb1e.com/credgrep) or they are real phishing traps.

Almost all the sites receive account information in clear. However, there are two notable exceptions lastpass.com and dazzlepod.com/disclosure. The former uses cryptographic hash functions and truncation to obfuscate the query and seems to be the most transparent and trustworthy of all. Table 2 presents a summary of our observations on lastpass.com. The latter source, dazzlepod.com/disclosure only recommends to truncate the email address. With pwnedlist.com/query, it is also possible to submit the SHA-512 digest of the email address instead of the address itself.

Cryptographic hash functions, e.g. MD5, SHA-1 or SHA-3 are however not enough to ensure the privacy of passwords, identifiers or email addresses: these

---

[2] Actually, subscribing for the hacknotifier.com watchdog is also not secure.

Table 2. Detailed analysis of lastpass.com.

Victim	Query	Policy	Privacy method
Adobe	Email	non-storage	None
LinkedIn	password	non-storage and non-logging	SHA-1
Snapchat	user name	non-storage and non-logging	SHA-1
Apple	UDID		Truncation
Last.fm	password	non-storage and non-logging	MD5
eHarmony	password	non-storage and non-logging	MD5

data do not have full entropy. Email addresses were recovered from Gravatar digests [2] as well as passwords (see [25] for instance). Apple's **U**nique **D**evice **ID**s *aka* UDIDs are no exceptions. They are computed by applying SHA-1 on a serial number, IMEI or ECID, the MAC address of WiFi and the MAC address of Bluetooth. The values used to produce a UDID can be guessed and LastPass asks only for the first 5 characters of UDID. It reduces the amount of information submitted to the site but the user is not warned if he provides more than 5 characters.

As a general conclusion, the measures taken by these websites are clearly not adequate to ensure the privacy of users' queries. In the remainder of the paper, we evaluate how existing cryptographic and privacy preserving primitives can solve the problems associated to alerting websites. These privacy-friendly solutions should guarantee that the websites cannot harvest any new data from a user's query.

3   Privacy-Friendly Solutions: Private vs. Public Database

As previously discussed, the existing alerting websites in general do not respect the privacy of a user and entail huge phishing potential. The need of the hour is to design *privacy-friendly alerting websites*. These websites would rely on what we refer as *Private Membership Query* protocols – allowing a user to privately test for membership in a given set/database. Such a protocol would guarantee that no new data can be harvested from a user's query.

To this end, two different privacy objectives can be defined depending on the privacy policy of the database owner. One that we henceforth refer as *Private Membership Query to Public Database*, and the other as *Private Membership Query to Private Database*. This classification arises due to the fact that most of these leaked databases are available on the Internet (as hackers have acquired the database dump) and hence can be considered as public in nature. However, even though they are public in terms of availability, an ethical hacker might want to ensure that the leaked information is not used for malicious purposes and hence the database cannot be accessed in a public manner to consult private information corresponding to other users. Rendering the database private could also be of interest for government agencies such as BSI sicherheitstest.bsi.de.

We highlight that a private membership query protocol provides a direct solution to the problem of designing privacy-friendly alerting websites. A user wishing to know whether his data has been leaked would be required to invoke the private membership protocol with the database owner and learns whether he is a victim of the breach. Thanks to the user's privacy provided by the protocol, no new data can then be harvested by the website. Consequently, in the rest of this work, we concentrate on evaluating solutions for private membership query problem. In the sequel, we formalize the privacy policies and examine viable solutions in the two database scenarios.

4   Solutions for Private Databases

The scenario of private membership query to private database involves a private database $\mathcal{DB}$ and a user $\mathcal{U}$. The database $\mathcal{DB} = \{y_1, \ldots, y_n\}$, where $y_i \in \{0,1\}^\ell$ consists of n bit-strings each of length ℓ. User $\mathcal{U}$ owns an arbitrary string $y \in \{0,1\}^\ell$. Private membership query to $\mathcal{DB}$ consists in knowing whether or not user's data y is present in the database while keeping y private to the user and $\mathcal{DB}$ private to the database.

Adversary model: The client and the database-owner are supposed to be *honest-but-curious* i.e. each follows the protocol but tries to learn information on the data held by the other player.

The above problem is very closely related to the problem of *Private Set Intersection*, hence we examine its applicability to designing privacy-friendly alerting websites.

Private Set Intersection (PSI). PSI protocol introduced by Freedman et al. [13] considers the problem of computing the intersection of private datasets of two parties. The scenario consists of two sets $\mathcal{U} = \{u_1, \ldots, u_m\}$, where $u_i \in \{0,1\}^\ell$ and $\mathcal{DB} = \{v_1, \ldots, v_n\}$, where $v_i \in \{0,1\}^\ell$ held by a user and the database-owner respectively. The goal of the user is to privately retrieve the set $\mathcal{U} \cap \mathcal{DB}$. The privacy requirement of the scheme consists in keeping $\mathcal{U}$ and $\mathcal{DB}$ private to their respective owner. Clearly, the private membership query to private database problem reduces to PSI for $m = 1$.

There is an abounding literature on novel and computationally efficient PSI protocols. The most efficient protocols are the ones by De Cristofaro et al. [10], Huang et al. [17] and Dong et al. [12]. The general conclusion being that for security of 80 bits, protocol by De Cristofaro et al. performs better than the one by Huang et al., while for higher security level, the latter protocol supersedes the former. The most efficient of all is the protocol by Dong et al. as it primarily uses symmetric key operations. We however note that the communication and the computational complexity of these protocols is linear in the size of the sets.

Private Set Intersection Cardinality (PSI-CA). PSI-CA is a variant of PSI where the goal of the client is to privately retrieve the cardinality of the intersection rather than the contents. While generic PSI protocols immediately provide a solution to PSI-CA, they however yield too much information. While several PSI-CA protocols have been proposed [13], [19], [16], [29], we concentrate on PSI-CA protocol of De Cristofaro et al. [9], as it is the most efficient of all. We also note that PSI-CA clearly provides a solution to the membership problem: if the size of the intersection is 0, then the user data is not present in the database.

5   Solutions for Public Databases

This scenario is modeled using a public database $\mathcal{DB}$ and a user $\mathcal{U}$. The database as in the previous scenario is $\mathcal{DB} = \{y_1, \ldots, y_n\}$, where $y_i \in \{0,1\}^\ell$. User $\mathcal{U}$ owns an arbitrary string $y \in \{0,1\}^\ell$ not necessarily in $\mathcal{DB}$. Private membership query consists in knowing whether or not user's data y is present in the database while keeping y private to the user.

The difference to the previous problem (Section 4) is that the database in this context is public. This leads to a trivial solution ensuring absolute privacy consisting in sending the database to the user, who using the available resources performs a search on the database. With huge databases of order GB, the trivial solution is not the most desirable one for low memory devices. In this scenario, a user would wish to securely outsource the search to the database-owner. In the following we present tools which provide a solution in the public database case.

5.1   Tools

In the first place we present a protocol called *Private Information Retrieval* [6], which is the closest to our needs. In the sequel we present Bloom filter and finally show that combining these tools allows us to obtain a protocol for private membership query to public database.

Private Information Retrieval (PIR). PIR first introduced in the seminal work by Chor et al. [6] is a mechanism allowing a user to query a public database while keeping his intentions private. In the classical setting of PIR [6], a user wants to retrieve the bit at index $1 \leq j \leq n$ in a database $\mathcal{DB} = \{y_1, \ldots, y_n\}$, where $y_i \in \{0,1\}$, but does not want the database to learn j.

Adversary model: The database owner is supposed to be honest-but-curious.

Since the work by Chor et al., several variants of PIR have been studied which include Private Block Retrieval (PBR) scheme – where the goal is to retrieve a block instead of a bit and **PrivatE Retrieval by KeYwords** (PERKY) [5] – where the user only holds a keyword kw instead of an index j. While PIR may either be built on single or replicated database copies, most of the latter works only consider the more realistic single database scenario. These works improve on the communication complexity [3,4], [14], [21,22]. The current best bound of $\mathcal{O}(\log^2 n)$ is independently achieved in [22], [14]. In this work, we only consider single database protocols. The principle reason being that in our context a user interacts with only one website.

Bloom Filter. Bloom filter [1] is a space and time efficient probabilistic data structure that provides an algorithmic solution to the *set membership query problem,* which consists in determining whether an item belongs to a predefined set.

Classical Bloom filter as presented in [1] essentially consists of k independent hash functions $\{h_1, \ldots, h_k\}$, where $\{h_i : \{0,1\}^* \to [0, m-1]\}_k$ and a bit vector $z = (z_0, \ldots, z_{m-1})$ of size m initialized to 0. Each hash function uniformly returns an index in the vector z. The filter z is incrementally built by inserting items of a predefined set S. Each item $x \in S$ is inserted into a Bloom filter by first feeding it to the hash functions to retrieve k indices of z. Finally, insertion of x in the filter is achieved by setting the bits of z at these positions to 1.

In order to query if an item $y \in \{0,1\}^*$ belongs to S, we check if y has been inserted into the Bloom filter z. Achieving this requires y to be processed (as in insertion) by the same hash functions to obtain k indexes of the filter. If any of the bits at these indexes is 0, the item is not in the filter, otherwise the item is present (with a small *false positive probability*).

The space and time efficiency of Bloom filter comes at the cost of false positives. If $|S| = n$, i.e., n items are to be inserted into the filter and the space available to store the filter is m bits, then the optimal number of hash functions to use and the ensuing optimal false positive probability f satisfy:

$$k = \frac{m}{n} \ln 2 \quad \text{and} \quad \ln f = -\frac{m}{n} (\ln 2)^2. \tag{1}$$

Membership Query to Bloom Filter: 2-party setting. Let us assume that *Alice* wants to check if her value y is included in the Bloom filter z held by *Bob*. The easiest way to do so consists for Alice to send y to Bob. Bob queries the filter on input y. He then sends 0 or 1 to Alice as the query output. If the canal between Alice and Bob has limited capacity, another strategy is possible and is described in Fig. 1.

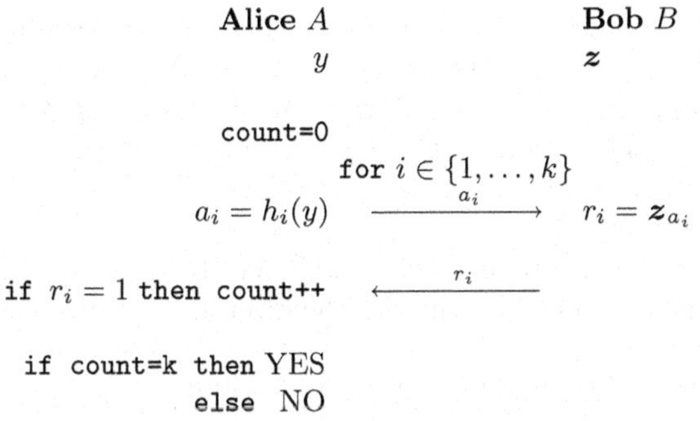

$$
\begin{array}{lll}
\text{Alice } A & & \text{Bob } B \\
\quad y & & \quad z \\
\\
\text{count=0} & & \\
& \text{for } i \in \{1, \ldots, k\} & \\
a_i = h_i(y) & \xrightarrow{\quad a_i \quad} & r_i = z_{a_i} \\
\\
\text{if } r_i = 1 \text{ then count++} & \xleftarrow{\quad r_i \quad} & \\
\\
\text{if count=k then YES} & & \\
\quad \text{else NO} & &
\end{array}
$$

Fig. 1. Verification on a constraint channel.

Alice cannot send y due to some channel constraints but she can send $a_i = h_i(y)$, for $1 \le i \le k$. We suppose that Alice and Bob first agree on the hash functions to be used. Then Alice sends a_i to Bob. In reply, Bob returns the bit at index a_i of z to her. If she only receives 1, y is included in z (with a small false positive probability f) otherwise it is not.

Remark 1. A possible private membership query protocol in the case of private database can be built by combining PSI/PSI-CA and Bloom filter. The idea would be to build a Bloom filter corresponding to the database entries and generate the set $\mathcal{DB} = \text{supp}(z)$, where $\text{supp}(z)$ represents the set of non-zero coordinate indices of z. The client on the other hand generates $\mathcal{U} = \{h_1(y), \ldots, h_k(y)\}$ for a data y. Finally, the client and the database owner invoke a PSI/PSI-CA protocol to retrieve the intersection set/cardinality of the intersection respectively. However, this solution is less efficient than a PSI/PSI-CA protocol on the initial database itself. The reason being the fact that, with optimal parameters the expected size of $\text{supp}(z) = m/2 = 2.88kn$ (see [24] for details) . Hence, the number of entries of the database in PSI/PSI-CA when used with Bloom filter is greater than the one of the original database.

We note that despite the similarity of the two problems: PIR and private membership to public database, PIR stand-alone does not provide a solution to our problem. Nevertheless, we show that when combined with a Bloom filter, PIR behaves as a private membership query protocol. Details are given in the following section.

5.2   Membership Query Using PIR

To start with, we note that classical PIR *per se* cannot be applied to our context since the user holding a data (email address, password, etc.) present in a database does not know its physical address in the database. Furthermore, PIR does not support non-membership queries as the database is constructed in a predefined manner and has only finite entries, while the set of all possible queries is infinite. PERKY resolves the problem of physical address as it only needs kw, and not the index. However, stand-alone it still suffers from the non-membership issue for the same reason as that in case of PIR.

Despite these issues, we can still design a private membership query protocol using PIR as a subroutine and by changing the database representation to Bloom filters which support non-membership queries as well. The idea then is to invoke PIR on each query to the filter.

The protocol explained below requires that the database owner builds a bloom filter z using the entries and a user queries the filter and not the database.

- Database owner builds the Bloom filter z using k hash functions $\{h_1, \ldots, h_k\}$.
- User for a data y generates $\{h_1(y), \ldots, h_k(y)\}$.
- For each $1 \leq i \leq k$, the user invokes a single-server PIR on index $h_i(y)$ and retrieves $z_{h_i(y)}$.
- If $z_{h_i(y)} = 0$ for any i, then y is not in the database, else if all the returned bits are 1, then the data is present (with a false positive probability f).

The only difference with the classical use of Bloom filter (Fig. 1) in the protocol is that the bit is retrieved using PIR.

Remark 2. As in the case of PIR, the database owner in our scenario is honest-but-curious. This attack model for instance does not allow the database owner to return a wrong bit to the user. Under this adversary model, the above protocol modification is private (i.e., keeps user's data private), if the underlying PIR scheme is private. PIR hides any single query of the user from the database owner. Therefore, any k different queries of the user are also hidden by PIR.

5.3   Extension with PBR Protocol

The adapted protocol in its current form requires a bit retrieval PIR scheme. Nevertheless, it can be easily modified to work even with a block retrieval *aka* PBR protocol. The essential advantage of using a PBR protocol instead of a classical PIR protocol would be to increase the throughput i.e. decrease the number of bits communicated to retrieve 1 bit of information. In fact, the most efficient PIR schemes [14], [22] are block retrieval schemes. The modification required to incorporate PBR would consist in using a *Garbled Bloom filter* (see [12]) instead of a Bloom filter. We briefly explain below the garbled Bloom filter construction, and later we present the modification required.

Garbled Bloom Filter.   At a high level Garbled Bloom Filter $(k, m, \mathcal{H}_k, \lambda)$ GBF [12] is essentially the same as a Bloom filter. The parameter k denotes the number of hash functions used, while $\mathcal{H}_k$ is a family of k independent hash functions as in a Bloom filter. The size of the filter is denoted by m, and λ is the size of the items to be included in the filter. The difference with respect to a Bloom filter is that at each index in GBF, a bit string of length λ is stored instead of just storing the bit 1. In order to include an item $y \in \{0, 1\}^\lambda$, one randomly generates k shares $\{r_1^y, \ldots, r_k^y\}$, where $r_i^y \in \{0, 1\}^\lambda$ such that $y = \oplus_i r_i^y$. As in a Bloom filter, one then generates the k indices $i_1^y, \ldots, i_k^y$ by computing the hashes as $i_j^y = h_j(y)$ and truncating them by taking modulo m. Finally, at index i_j^y of the filter, the bit string r_j^y is stored. Collisions on two values y and y' for a certain hash function h_j are handled by choosing the same r_j for both the values.

To check if a given item is in GBF, one computes the truncated hashes and retrieves the shares stored at these indices in GBF. If the XOR of these shares is the same as the given item, then the item is in the filter, or else not. More details on the probability of collisions and the probability of false positives can be found in [12].

Private Membership Query using PBR.   This protocol essentially follows the same principle as the one which combines PIR and a Bloom filter. The database owner now builds a GBF $(k, m, \mathcal{H}_k, \lambda)$ using the entries and a user queries the GBF instead of the database. Again k PBR invocations are required to retrieve the k random shares. This adapted protocol is private if the underlying PBR scheme is private, i.e., does not reveal the user's queries.

Remark 3. At this juncture, we have two solutions for private membership query to public database: 1) k invocations of single server PIR/PBR to Bloom filter/GBF, 2) Send the complete filter for a local query. On one hand, any PIR based solution only provides computational privacy, has a communication cost, the best being $\mathcal{O}(\log^2 m)$ and involves cryptographic computations and hence entails a significant time complexity. While on the other hand sending the filter ensures absolute privacy, but has a larger communication complexity m bits (still much better than the trivial PIR i.e., sending the initial database) but has a very low time complexity (has to invoke the protocol in Fig. 1 locally). Since the size of the database gets drastically reduced with Bloom filter, this solution provides a competitive alternative to trivial PIR even for low memory devices.

6   Practicality of the Solutions

We reiterate that a private membership query protocol provides an immediate solution for designing privacy-friendly alerting websites. For the sake of practicality, any realistic privacy-friendly alerting websites should provide response to a user's query in real time. It is hence highly important to evaluate the practicality of the underlying protocol.

We first discuss the practicality of the solutions based on PIR/PBR and Bloom filter in case of public database and in the sequel we discuss the practicality of PSI/PSI-CA protocol in case of private database.

Since Bloom filter is highly efficient in space and time, the practicality of PIR/PBR based protocol depends on the practicality of the underlying PIR/PBR scheme. Hence we first discuss its practicality as perceived in the literature and later by experimentally evaluating PIR/PBR protocols.

For experimental evaluation, the tests were performed on a 64-bit processor desktop computer powered by an Intel Xeon E5410 3520M processor at 2.33 GHz with 6 MB cache, 8 GB RAM and running 3.2.0-58-generic-pae Linux. We have used GCC 4.6.3 with -O3 optimization flag.

6.1   Applicability of PIR

Sion and Carbunar [28] evaluate the performance of single database PIR scheme. The authors show that the deployment of non-trivial single server PIR protocols on real hardware of the recent past would have been orders of magnitude less time-efficient than trivially transferring the entire database. The study primarily considers the computational PIR protocol of [21]. The authors argue that a PIR is practical if and only if per-bit server side complexity is faster than a bit transfer. With a normal desktop machine, trivial transfer (at 10MBps) of the database is 35 times faster than PIR. This ultimately restricts the use of PIR protocols for low bandwidths (tens of KBps).

Olumofin and Goldberg [26] refute the general interpretation [28] that no PIR scheme can be more efficient that the trivial one. Authors evaluate two multi-server information-theoretic PIR schemes by Chor et al. [6] and by Gold-berg [15] as well as a single-server lattice-based scheme by Aguilar-Melchor and Gaborit [23]. The later scheme is found to be an order of magnitude more efficient over the trivial scheme for situations that are most representative of today's average consumer Internet bandwidth. Specifically, for a database of size 16 GB, the trivial scheme outperforms the lattice based scheme only at speeds above 100 Mbps.

6.2   Experimental Analysis

We have implemented two PIR/PBR protocols: 1) Cachin et al. [3], which is the most efficient (in terms of communication) bit retrieval scheme 2) Aguilar-Melchor and Gaborit [23] (implemented in parig-gp[3]) which is the most computationally efficient PBR protocol. We have also implemented RSA-OPRF PSI protocol of De Cristofaro et al. [10] and PSI-CA protocol of De Cristofaro et al. [9]. The existing implementation[4] of protocol by Dong et al. [12] seems not to execute correctly. Even after correcting the initial compilation errors, the code seems not to be executing the protocol till the end. We hence do not consider it for our evaluation.

Table 3. Results for the leaked databases using SHA-1. Databases contain single data for a user, for instance Snapchat contains only username and ignores other auxiliary leaked information.

Database	Size	n	$-\log_2 f$	m (MB)	Build time (mins)	Compress. ratio
SNAPCHAT	49 MB	4609621	128	102	6	0.48
			64	52	2	0.94
			32	26	1	1.88
LINKEDIN	259 MB	6458019	128	142	10	1.82
			64	72	3	3.60
			32	36	1.5	7.19
ADOBE	3.3 GB	153004872	128	412	198	8.20
			64	206	72	16.4
			32	102	30	33.13

Public Database. The cost of using PIR-based schemes reduces to the cost of building the filter combined with the cost of k PIR invocations on the filter. We present the time required to build a Bloom filter for the leaked databases corresponding to SNAPCHAT, LINKEDIN and ADOBE in Table 3. The filter is constructed using SHA-1 which generates 20 bytes' digest.

From Table 3, we can observe that the filter size grows slowly and that the computational time of the filter is reasonable. Initially, all the computations are performed in a sequential manner. We have then distributed the computation

---

[3]   pari.math.u-bordeaux.fr/
[4]   Available at bit.ly/1k75nu6

on 4 computers (with similar characteristics). Parallelizing the creation of the Bloom filter is straightforward and we nearly achieved a 4× speedup (50 mins). With a few computers, it is possible to reduce the computational time for creating the filter to a desired threshold. We further note that building a Bloom filter involves only a one-time cost.

Despite the space and time efficiency of Bloom filter, the huge cost of PIR invocation (using the existing primitives) makes such protocols impractical. The protocol [3] takes over 6 hours in case of Snapchat database for one invocation. If the probability of false positive is 2^{-32} i.e. $k \approx 32$, the estimated time for 32 PIR invocations is over 32×6 hours i.e. over 8 days. The PBR protocol [23], takes around 2 hours for 1 PBR invocation on Snapchat garbled Bloom filter. The security level considered here is of 100 bits. However, considering the household network bandwidth of 10 Mbps, the time to download the filter would take 20 seconds. The time efficiency of the trivial PIR with Bloom filter seems unmatchable.

Private Database. Table 4 presents results obtained for the PSI protocol by De Cristofaro et al. [10] for 80 bits of security.

Table 4. Cost for PSI protocol [10] with 80 bits of security using SHA-1

Database	Cost (mins)
SNAPCHAT	48
LINKEDIN	68
ADOBE	1600

Table 5. Cost for PSI-CA protocol [9] with 80 bits of security using SHA-1

Database	Cost (mins)
SNAPCHAT	9
LINKEDIN	12
ADOBE	301

As the user's set has only one data, his computational cost is negligible. To be precise, a user's computational cost consists in computing a signature and n comparisons. The authors in [11] claim that the result of the server's computation over its own set can be re-used in multiple instances. Hence, the server's cost can be seen as a one-time cost, which further makes it highly practical.

Table 5 presents results obtained using PSI-CA protocol by De Cristofaro et al. [9]. Recommended parameters of $|p| = 1024$ and $|q| = 160$ bits have been chosen.

Clearly, PSI-CA outperforms PSI by a factor of 5. The reason behind this performance leap is that the exponents in modular exponentiations are only 160 bits long in PSI-CA as opposed to 1024 bits in PSI.

Table 6 summarizes the results obtained on Snapchat database for $f = 2^{-32}$. Clearly, in the public database case, sending the Bloom filter is the most computationally efficient solution. While, in the private database scenario, PSI-CA provides a promising solution. Comparing the two cases, we observe that the private database slows down the query time by a factor of 9.

Table 6. Summary of the results on Snapchat with $f = 2^{-32}$

		Cost	
Protocol	Type	Commun.	Comput.
Trivial PIR with Bloom filter	PIR	26 MB	1 min
Cachin et al. [3]	PIR	7.8 KB	> 8 days
Melchor et al. [23]	PBR	12.6 TB	> 2.5 days
De Cristofaro et al. [10]	PSI	562 MB	48 mins
De Cristofaro et al. [9]	PSI-CA	87.92 MB	9 mins

We highlight that PSI/PSI-CA protocols perform much better than PIR/PBR protocols. This is counter-intuitive, as in case of PIR the database is public while in PSI the database is private. A protocol on private data should cost more than the one on public data. With a theoretical stand-point, there are two reasons why private set intersection protocols perform better than PIR protocols: 1) the computational cost in PSI/PSI-CA protocols is reduced at the cost of communication overhead, 2) the size of the security parameter is independent of the size of the database. More precisely, the communication cost of the most efficient PSI/PSI-CA protocols [9,10], [17], [12] is linear while the goal of PIR protocols is to achieve sub-linear or poly-logarithmic complexity. This indeed comes at a cost, for instance the size of RSA modulus in PSI [10] for 80 bits of security is 1024 bits and hence independent of the size of the sets involved. While in case of PIR [3], the size of the modulus used is $\log^{3-o(1)}(n)$ bits. Hence for a million bit database, the modulus to be considered is of around 8000 bits, which leads to a very high computational cost.

7   Conclusion

In this work, we examined websites alerting users about data leakage. With the current rate of leakage, these websites will be needed for a while. Unfortunately, it is currently difficult to determine whether or not these websites are phishing sites since they do not provide any privacy guarantee to users. Our work exposes the privacy risks associated to the most popular alerting websites. We further evaluate how state-of-the-art cryptographic primitives can be applied to make private query to an alerting site possible. Two different scenarios have been considered depending on whether the database is public. While PSI/PSI-CA protocols provide a straightforward solution in the private database scenario, a tweak using Bloom filter transforms PIR/PBR into private membership protocols for public database.

Our experimental evaluation shows that PSI/PSI-CA protocols perform much better than PIR/PBR based protocol. This is an encouraging result for the ethical hacking community or security companies. Yet the cost incurred by these ad hoc solutions is considerable and hence there remains the open problem of designing dedicated and more efficient solutions.

Acknowledgements. This research was conducted with the partial support of the Labex PERSYVAL-LAB(ANR-11-LABX-0025) and the project-team SCCyPhy.

References

1. Bloom, B.H.: Space/time trade-offs in hash coding with allowable errors. Communications of the ACM **13**, July 1970
2. Bongard, D.: De-anonymizing users of french political forums. In: Passwords 2013 (2013)
3. Cachin, C., Micali, S., Stadler, M.A.: Computationally private information retrieval with polylogarithmic communication. In: Stern, J. (ed.) EUROCRYPT 1999. LNCS, vol. 1592, pp. 402–414. Springer, Heidelberg (1999)
4. Chang, Y.-C.: Single database private information retrieval with logarithmic communication. In: Wang, H., Pieprzyk, J., Varadharajan, V. (eds.) ACISP 2004. LNCS, vol. 3108, pp. 50–61. Springer, Heidelberg (2004)
5. Chor, B., Gilboa, N., Naor, M.: Private information retrieval by keywords (1998)
6. Chor, B., Goldreich, O., Kushilevitz, E., Sudan, M.: Private information retrieval. In: Annual Symposium on Foundations of Computer Science, FOCS 1995 (1995)
7. Das, A., Bonneau, J., Caesar, M., Borisov, N., Wang, X.: The tangled web of password reuse. In: Network and Distributed System Security Symposium, NDSS 2014 (2014)
8. de Carné de Carnavalet, X., Mannan, M.: From very weak to very strong: analyzing password-strength meters. In: Network and Distributed System Security Symposium, NDSS 2014 (2014)
9. De Cristofaro, E., Gasti, P., Tsudik, G.: Fast and private computation of cardinality of set intersection and union. In: Pieprzyk, J., Sadeghi, A.-R., Manulis, M. (eds.) CANS 2012. LNCS, vol. 7712, pp. 218–231. Springer, Heidelberg (2012)
10. De Cristofaro, E., Tsudik, G.: Practical private set intersection protocols with linear complexity. In: Proceedings of the 14th International Conference on Financial Cryptography and Data Security (2010)
11. De Cristofaro, E., Tsudik, G.: Experimenting with fast private set intersection. In: Katzenbeisser, S., Weippl, E., Camp, L.J., Volkamer, M., Reiter, M., Zhang, X. (eds.) Trust 2012. LNCS, vol. 7344, pp. 55–73. Springer, Heidelberg (2012)
12. Dong, C., Chen, L., Wen, Z.: When private set intersection meets big data: an efficient and scalable protocol. In: ACM Conference on Computer and Communications Security (2013)
13. Freedman, M.J., Nissim, K., Pinkas, B.: Efficient private matching and set intersection. In: Cachin, C., Camenisch, J.L. (eds.) EUROCRYPT 2004. LNCS, vol. 3027, pp. 1–19. Springer, Heidelberg (2004)
14. Gentry, C., Ramzan, Z.: Single-database private information retrieval with constant communication rate. In: Caires, L., Italiano, G.F., Monteiro, L., Palamidessi, C., Yung, M. (eds.) ICALP 2005. LNCS, vol. 3580, pp. 803–815. Springer, Heidelberg (2005)
15. Goldberg, I.: Improving the robustness of private information retrieval. In: IEEE Symposium on Security and Privacy, 2007. S&P 2007 (2007)
16. Hohenberger, S., Weis, S.A.: Honest-verifier private disjointness testing without random oracles. In: Danezis, G., Golle, P. (eds.) PET 2006. LNCS, vol. 4258, pp. 277–294. Springer, Heidelberg (2006)
17. Huang, Y., Evans, D., Katz, J.: Private set intersection: are garbled circuits better than custom protocols? In: NDSS (2012)

18. Juels, A., Rivest, R.L.: Honeywords: making password-cracking detectable. In: ACM SIGSAC Conference on Computer and Communications Security, CCS 201313 (2013)
19. Kissner, L., Song, D.: Privacy-preserving set operations. In: Shoup, V. (ed.) CRYPTO 2005. LNCS, vol. 3621, pp. 241–257. Springer, Heidelberg (2005)
20. Kontaxis, G., Athanasopoulos, E., Portokalidis, G., Keromytis, A.D.: SAuth: protecting user accounts from password database leaks. In: ACM SIGSAC Conference on Computer and Communications Security, CCS 2013 (2013)
21. Kushilevitz, E., Ostrovsky, R.: Replication is not needed: single database, computationally-private information retrieval. In: Proceedings of the 38th Annual Symposium on Foundations of Computer Science (1997)
22. Lipmaa, H.: An oblivious transfer protocol with log-squared communication. In: Zhou, J., López, J., Deng, R.H., Bao, F. (eds.) ISC 2005. LNCS, vol. 3650, pp. 314–328. Springer, Heidelberg (2005)
23. Melchor, C.A., Gaborit, P.: A fast private information retrieval protocol. In: IEEE International Symposium on Information Theory, 2008. ISIT 2008 (2008)
24. Mitzenmacher, M.: Compressed bloom filters. In: ACM Symposium on Principles of Distributed Computing - PODC 2001 (2001)
25. Narayanan, A., Shmatikov, V.: Fast dictionary attacks on passwords using time-space tradeoff. In: ACM Conference on Computer and Communications Security, CCS 2005 (2005)
26. Olumofin, F., Goldberg, I.: Revisiting the computational practicality of private information retrieval. In: Danezis, G. (ed.) FC 2011. LNCS, vol. 7035, pp. 158–172. Springer, Heidelberg (2012)
27. Parno, B., McCune, J.M., Wendlandt, D., Andersen, D.G., Perrig, A.: CLAMP: Practical prevention of large-scale data leaks. In: IEEE Symposium on Security and Privacy - S&P 2009 (2009)
28. Sion, R., Carbunar, B.: On the Practicality of Private Information Retrieval. In: NDSS (2007)
29. Vaidya, J., Clifton, C.: Secure set intersection cardinality with application to association rule mining. J. Comput. Secur. **13**(4), 593–622 (2005)

Access Control, Trust and Identity Management

A Generalization of ISO/IEC 24761 to Enhance Remote Authentication with Trusted Product at Claimant

Asahiko Yamada[⊠]

National Institute of Advanced Industrial Science and Technology,
1-1-1 Umezono, Tsukuba, Ibaraki 305-8568, Japan
yamada.asahiko@aist.go.jp

Abstract. In this paper, a data structure to enhance remote authentication is proposed generalizing the concept of ISO/IEC 24761. Current technologies do not provide sufficient information on products which are used in the authentication process at the Claimant to the Verifier. As a result, the Verifier cannot sufficiently distinguish the authentication result executed with a trusted product from that without a trusted product. The difference is made clear if an evidence data of the execution of authentication process at the Claimant is generated by the trusted product and used for verification by the Verifier. Data structure for such a data is proposed in this paper as client Authentication Context (cAC) instance. Relation to other works and extension of the proposal are also described for further improvement of remote authentication. For this proposal to realize, standardization activities are to be taken as the next steps.

Keywords: Biometric authentication · Cryptographic Message Syntax (CMS) · Digital signature · IC card · Initial authentication · Public Key Infrastructure (PKI) · Remote authentication · Tamper-resistant device · Trusted device

1 Introduction

In networked IT environments, remote authentication is essential. Remote authentication is one of the most important elements of the security of innumerous applications of governmental, commercial, academic systems and so forth and it is applied to them. Although policy-based authorization makes the Relying Party (RP) possible to change the service level reflecting the level of assurance of the identity, the level of trust of the environment of the Claimant where the authentication protocol is executed is not taken into account appropriately and sufficiently. This paper proposes a mechanism with which the Verifier can know the level of trust in the authentication process executed at the Claimant of remote authentication under the condition that a trusted product with the digital signature generation function such as a tamper-resistant IC card is used for authentication at the Claimant. There are two cases for the activation of the private key, with passphrase or biometrics. Both cases are discussed in this paper, extending the former to the latter.

© IFIP International Federation for Information Processing 2015
H. Federrath and D. Gollmann (Eds.): SEC 2015, IFIP AICT 455, pp. 145–158, 2015.
DOI: 10.1007/978-3-319-18467-8_10

2   Current Technologies

Progresses in authentication technologies have been significant in the last decade. Single Sign-On (SSO) technologies such as Security Assertion Markup Language (SAML) and OpenID have made general service providers free from authentication itself and only consume the assertion generated by the Verifier, which is called Identity Provider (IdP) in SAML and OpenID Provider (OP) in OpendID. While the technologies in subsequent authentication between the Verifier and the RP, the consumer of the assertion, have been progressed, the technologies in initial authentication between the Claimant and the Verifier have been stable. In Web systems, Transport Layer Security (TLS) protocol including its predecessor Secure Sockets Layer (SSL) has been dominant for about twenty years and is still the most major and standard technology. The variation of tokens has not changed, something you know, something you have, and something you are.

In SAML [1], authentication context is optionally used in assertions to give additional information for the RP in determining the authenticity and confidence of assertions. Authentication context contains information how the user is authenticated at the Claimant. Although the IdP generates an authentication context at the initial authentication, the IdP does not always have sufficiently trustable information about the authentication process at the Claimant in order to generate an authentication context, considering that the execution environment of the Claimant is not always so sufficiently trustable to the IdP as that of the IdP to the RP. For example, the IdP does not have sufficient information to judge whether a tamper-resistant IC card with digital signature function is used at the Claimant or not. It is true that a private key stored in a tamper-resistant IC card can be distinguished with the qualified certificate specified in RFC 3739[16] with the qualified certificate statement 5.2.4 in ETSI TS 101 862 [3] which is for secure signature-creation devices with the conditions in Annex III of Directive 1999/93/EC of the European Parliament and of the Council of 13 December 1999 on a Community framework for electronic signatures [4]. But the purpose of X.509 certificate itself is to describe the attributes of the user and his/her public key. So the use of the extension of X.509 certificate in such ways does not match its original purpose.

Guidelines and requirements on authentication have been also studied well. One of the most important results in this area is NIST SP 800-63-2 Electronic Authentication Guideline [13]. It assigns requirements on tokens, token and credential management, authentication process, and assertions to each Level of Assurance (LoA) from Level 1 to Level 4 each of which was introduced in OMB M-04-04 [14]. Although SP 800-63-2 requires Level 4 to use Multi-Factor (MF) hardware cryptographic token such as tamper-resistant cryptographic IC card, any of the current authentication protocols does not show sufficient evidence that such a token is used at the Claimant. At Level 4, such a protocol may be unnecessary because only in-person registration is allowed at Level 4 and it can be assured that such a token is issued and used in authentication process at the Claimant. But in Level 2 and Level 3 to which remote registration is allowed, it is not evident for the Registration Authority (RA) or the Credential Service Provider (CSP) whether a public key pair is generated and stored in a tamper-resistant IC card in registration process or not, and it is not evident either to the Verifier whether such a product is used in authentication process or not, for example. In Level

2 and Level 3, it would be desirable for the RP to know more information about the trust level of the authentication process executed at the Claimant. Then the RP can provide its services according to the level of trust.

In the area of biometric authentication, a similar motivation and the solution can be found in ISO/IEC 24761 Authentication Context for Biometrics (ACBio) [10]. The work in this paper is a generalization of the idea in ISO/IEC 24761.

In the following, terms and definitions in SP 800-63-2 are basically applied unless otherwise specified.

3   ISO/IEC 24761, A Related Work in Biometric Authentication

ISO/IEC 24761 referred as ACBio is an enhancement using evidence data generated by execution environment for biometric authentication while this proposal is that for PKI based authentication.

ACBio is a solution to the technological issues of biometric authentication used in the Internet environment. The issues are listed in the threat analysis done in [15] and they are categorized into three. The first is that subprocesses may be replaced with malware. Here a subprocesses is an execution component in biometric authentication, namely data capture to sense human body to output raw biometric sample, intermediate signal processing to process raw biometric sample to intermediate processed biometric sample, final signal processing to process intermediate biometric sample to processed biometric sample, storage to store and retrieve enroled biometric reference template , biometric comparison to compare and calculate the score of similarity of processed biometric sample to biometric reference template, or decision to decide match or non-match from the score. The second is that the enroled biometric reference template may be replaced with that of another person such as an attacker. The last is that the data transmitted between subprocesses may be replaced with another data.

ACBio has solved these issues by generation and verification of evidence data of the executed biometric processing under the assumption that trusted biometric products are used. Authentication using the specification of ACBio is called ACBio authentication. A trusted biometric product is called a Biometric Processing Unit (BPU) in ACBio.

In production process, the BPU manufacturer has to generate the BPU report to BPU product in ACBio authentication. In the BPU report which is a data of type `SignedData` digitally signed by the BPU manufacture, information about the BPU such as the modality which the BPU processes, the subprocesses implemented and the data flow in the BPU are contained. In ACBio authentication, a key pair for the BPU is generated and the X.509 certificate for the public key of the BPU is issued. The data generated at production process are all stored in the BPU.

At registration process, Biometric Reference Template (BRT) certificate is issued to BRT by BRT certificate authority in ACBio authentication. The BRT certificate is a digitally signed data by a BRT certificate authority and links a BRT to a user. For privacy reasons, the BRT certificate does not contain the BRT itself but contains the hash value of the BRT. There is an evidence data named ACBio instance for enrolment, which is digitally signed with the private key of the BPU, to show the generation and storage of the BRT is securely done in the BPU. In ACBio authentication, each BPU used in the enrolment generates its ACBio instance for enrolment. The ACBio instances for enrolment show the BPUs used in the enrolment and the integrity of the data transmitted between the BPUs if the enrolment is done with multiple BPUs. The ACBio instances for enrolment are optionally set in the BRT certificate. From the ACBio instances for enrolment, the BPU where the BRT is stored is also identified. ACBio instances for enrolment may be used to check whether the enrolment satisfies the security requirement or not by the BRT certificate authority to issue the BRT certificate, and also by the Verifier later in authentication process, depending on the security policies of the BRT certificate authority and the Verifier respectively.

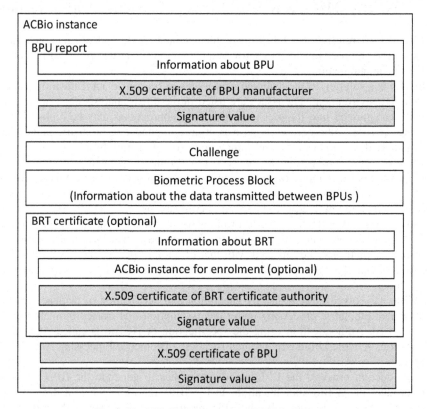

Fig. 1. Simplified data structure of ACBio instance

At authentication process, ACBio authentication assumes challenge response mechanism. An ACBio instance is generated in each BPU which takes part in biometric authentication process. Fig. 1 overviews the data structure of ACBio instance.

An ACBio instance contains the BPU report. This gives information to the Verifier about the product which executes authentication protocol at the Claimant.

The triple of the challenge which is called Control Value in ACBio, the Biometric Process Block, and the BRT certificate, which is contained only if the BPU stores the BRT, is contained in an ACBio instance. This shows that the authentication process at the Claimant is successfully executed.

The ACBio instance contains all the data mentioned above and the digital signature of those with the private key of the BPU. This gives the evidence of the successful execution of the authentication protocol done at the Claimant.

Toshiba Solutions Corporation in Japan has already implemented ACBio authentication into a product. Using this product, its customer company has built an in-house system.

The idea of ACBio enhances biometric authentication used in the Internet but the name ACBio (Authentication Context for Biometrics) is inappropriate. As written in 2, authentication context in SAML is information in assertions, i.e., information sent from the Verifier to the RP while ACBio instance is not but is sent form the Claimant to the Verifier. In this context, the name cAC (client Authentication Context) is used in this paper.

4   Problem Definition

In an environment where a trusted product is not used at the Claimant for PKI based authentication protocol, there may be possibilities that the private key is compromised, i.e., an attacker may get and misuse it for spoofing. When a trusted product is used, it will be assured that the private key is not stolen under certain conditions, as assumptions listed in 5. There should be an authentication protocol for the Verifier to distinguish the above two cases.

5   Assumptions

In this paper, suppose that the trusted products considered have the following assumptions.

(A)   The trusted product has digital signing function.

(B)   The trusted product has generation function of public key pairs.

(C)   The private key embedded in production process or generated in the trusted product cannot be exported.

(D)   The trusted product has a function to manage the triples of private key, public key, and X.509 certificate of the public key.

(E)   The trusted product can digitally sign only with a private key embedded in production process or one generated in the trusted product.

(F)   The trusted product has functions proposed in this paper for authentication process.

In addition to the above assumption to the trusted products, assume that the whole production process of trusted products is trusted. Therefore the private key embedded to the trusted product is never leaked in the production process.

The assumptions (A) and (D) are necessary to generate data such as SignedData in a product. If a trusted product can digitally sign with an imported private key, then the private key may have been already compromised before it is imported. Therefore the assumption (E) is necessary to assure that the digital signature is generated by the trusted product. To assume (E), the private key has to be generated in production process or it has to be generated in the trusted product after production process. Therefore the assumption (B) is necessary. Without (C) the private key may be misused.

These assumptions are appropriate since tamper-resistant PKI cards conformant to ISO/IEC 7816-4 [5] and 8 [6] satisfy (A) to (E). The implementation of (F) is not difficult as is to be seen later.

In the following, the detailed communication protocol including negotiation is not discussed.

6   Proposal

In this paper, a data structure named client Authentication Context (cAC) is proposed to enhance the PKI based authentication protocol under the condition that a trusted product with assumptions from (A) to (F) is used at the Claimant. Hereafter a trusted product with the assumptions is called a cAC product and authentication using cAC is called cAC authentication. The cAC authentication enables the Verifier to judge whether a cAC product is used for the authentication process or not. In short, this is done with a combination of product authentication and user authentication techniques, PKI based user authentication assured by PKI based product authentication. Authentication protocol for cAC authentication is also discussed. The problem cannot be solved only with the authentication protocol but with a series of processes beginning from the production process as in ACBio. This proposal tries to give a solution to the problem as universal as possible.

6.1   Production Process

In the production process of cAC products, the cAC product manufacturer needs several procedures for cAC authentication afterwards.

The cAC product manufacturer has to generate its public key pair and have the X.509 certificate issued in advance. The private key is used to digitally sign cAC product report which gives information about the cAC product. Digitally signed by the cAC product manufacturer, cAC product report becomes a trusted data if there is an assumption that the Verifier trusts the cAC product manufacturer. Hereafter certificateMnf denotes the X.509 certificate of the cAC product manufacturer.

In the following, type means ASN.1 type.

For generation of cAC product report, a type SignedData, specified in RFC 3852 [17] /RFC 5911 [18] Cryptographic Message Syntax (CMS), is applied. In SignedData, the signed object is the field encapContentInfo of type EncapsulatedContentInfo which consists of two fields. The first is a field to indicate the data type of the data which is DER encoded in the second field. To indicate the data type, OBJECT IDENTIFIER type is used. The second is the content itself carried as an octet string whose data type is identified with the first field.

There are some categories of cAC products. For example, in a category, a cAC products activates the private key with a passphrase, in another it may activate the private key with biometric authentication. Here only the former category is discussed. The latter will be discussed later.

There is another categorization of products into a category of software and one of hardware.

The type identifier for the content of cAC product report is defined as id-content-cPR-passphrase of type OBJECT IDENTIFIER. The corresponding content type ContentCPRPassphrase identified by id-content-cPR-passphrase, is define to have four fields. The first field productType gives information that the product is a software or hardware product. The second field levelCMVP is to show the level of Cryptographic Module Validation Program specified in FIPS 140-2 [12] and ISO/IEC 19790 [9] if the cryptographic module in the cAC product is certified. The third reqLengthPassPhrase and fourth minLength are a field to show whether there is a requirement for the length of passphrase, and a field for the required minimal length of passphrase if there is. With the above information, the Verifier knows the extent to which it can trust the cAC product. In ASN.1 notation, ContentCPRPassphrase is specified as follows:

```
ContentCPRPassphrase :: = SEQUENCE {
     productType           ProductType,
     levelCMVP             LevelCMVP,
     reqLengthPassPhrase BOOLEAN,
     minLength             INTEGER OPTIONAL}
ProductType ::= ENUMERATED {
     software   (0),
     hardware   (1) }
LevelCMVP ::= ENUMERATED {
     none       (0),
     level1     (1),
     level2     (2),
     level3     (3),
     level4     (4) }
```

Let SIGNEDDATA(eCTypeID, ContentType) denote a type which is derived from SignedData where the fields eContentType in encapContentInfo is specified to take eCTypeID and eContent in encapContentInfo is OCTET STRING of the DER encoding of a data of type ContentType.

Then a type CACProductReport for cAC product report is defined as SIGENDDATA(id-content-cPR-passphrase, ContentCPRPassphrase). A data of this type shall be digitally signed with the private key of a cAC product manufacturer. Therefore certificateMnf is set in one of certificates in the cAC product report.

At the last of production process of cAC product, a public key pair shall be generated and the X.509 certificate for the public key, which is denoted by certificatePrd hereafter, shall be issued. In the X.509 certificate, the field subject of type Name in the field tbsCertificate of type TBSCertificate shall contain the name of the cAC product and that of the cAC product manufacturer. The name of the cAC product manufacturer in the field subject shall be the same as that in the field subject in the X.509 certificate of the cAC product manufacturer in the cAC product report. The public key pair and the X.509 certificate shall be stored in the cAC product together with the already generated cAC product report.

6.2   Registration Process

To become a Claimant in PKI based authentication process, a user has to generate the public key pair and get the X.509 certificate. It is also the same in cAC authentication, but the Claimant has to generate the key pair in the cAC product. Otherwise, if the public key pair is generated outside the cAC product, the imported key pair cannot generate digital signature because of assumption (E).

There is no corresponding data in cAC authentication to the ACBio instance for enrolment. There seems to have to be "key generating context" in cAC authentication. But it is redundant because the private key used in authentication process is assured to have been generated in the same cAC product in registration process by assumptions (B) and (E). Furthermore it is assured that the digital signature is generated in the cAC product by assumption (C) and (E).

6.3   Authentication Process

In the cAC product, the pair of the private key and X.509 certificate for the cAC product, the pair of the private key and X.509 certificate for the user, and the cAC product report are stored before the authentication process starts. With these data, a cAC instance, an evidence data of the cAC authentication process at the Claimant, is defined. In this paper, challenge response mechanism is assumed to be applied in the authentication protocol in order to prevent replay attacks. This assumption is appropriate since most of the protocols used in remote authentication apply challenge response mechanism. But before defining the authentication protocol, the data structure is defined.

A type `ChallengeSignedByUser` is defined as `SIGNEDDATA(id-data, OCTET STRING)`. When the Claimant receives a challenge from the Verifier, a data of type `ChallengeSignedByUser` is generated at the Claimant setting the challenge of type `OCTET STRING` into `eContent` and digitally signing with the user's private key which is activated with a passphrase input by the user. Hereafter a data of type `ChallengeSignedByUser` is called a CSBU. A type `ContentClientAC` identified by the type identifier `id-contentClientAC` is defined as:

```
ContentClientAC :: = SEQUENCE {
    cACProductReport        CACProductReport,
    challengeSignedByUser ChallengeSignedByUser }
```

Then a type `ClientACInstance` is defined as:
`SIGNEDDATA(id-contentClientAC, ContentClientAC)`. To generate a cAC instance of type `ClientACInstance`, the cAC product report and the data of `ChallengeSignedByUser` generated as in the above are used. For digital signing, the private key of the cAC product is used. Therefore the X.509 certificate set in certificates in the cAC instance is `certificatePrd`. Fig. 2 shows a simplified data structure of cAC instance where shaded boxes indicate data specified in RFC 3852.

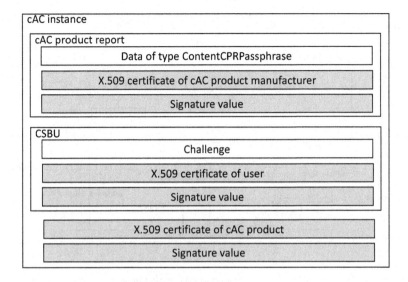

Fig. 2. Simplified data structure of cAC instance

At the Verifier, a cAC instance is verified as follows:

(1)   The Verifier checks the cAC product report. This consists of signature verification, checking of the product type, the level of cryptographic function, and the passphrase policy implemented on the cAC product. By checking the cAC product report, the Verifier can know if the cAC product satisfies the authentication policy of the RP for example, and that the cAC product is manufactured by the cAC product manufacturer with the X.509 certificate in the cAC product report.

(2)   The Verifier checks the CSBU. The Verifier can know whether there was a replay attack or not by checking the challenge in the CSBU, and whether the Claimant generated the digital signature or not. The digital signature of the challenge is verified with the public key in the X.509 certificate in the CSBU.

(3)   The Verifier verifies the digital signature of the cAC instance. With this verification, the Verifier can conclude that the Claimant has done the authentication process in the cAC product because the digital signature has been calculated with the private key of the cAC product which has been stored in the cAC product since key generation because of assumptions from (A) to (E). This solves the problem stated in 4.

Fig. 3 summarizes all the operations in all the processes that are proposed in this paper. In the region of processing in cAC product in Fig.3, surrounded by the dotted line, the relations of "contained" and "digitally sign" are assured by the assumption from (A) to (F). These make the evidence of the execution of authentication process in cAC product trusted.

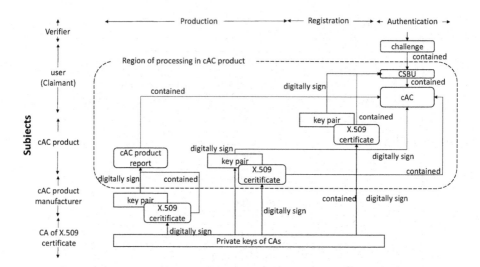

Fig. 3. Trust relation in cAC authentication

7   Considerations

7.1   Comparison with the Qualified Certificate Model

The qualified certificate can be used to show that the private key paired to the public key to which the certificate is issued is stored and used in a trusted product. If a vulnerability of the trusted product concerning the storage of the private key is found, then all the qualified certificates to the users who use the trusted product to digitally sign with have to be revoked while only one cAC product report of the trusted product has to be invalidated in the proposed model. There is a big difference in efficiency of the validation process at the Verifier. For the CA to revoke the qualified certificates, the information about the trusted product has to be stored to each of the qualified certificates issued.

The qualified certificate does not show which trusted product the private key is stored and used in. As a result, the Verifier can know nothing about the trusted product used in the authentication process and can give less information about the authentication process to the RP than in the proposed model. This information to the RP is important for policy-based authorization. Therefore the proposed model is more appropriate for the policy-based authorization than the qualified certificate model.

7.2   Application of the Proposal to ITU-T X.1085 | ISO/IEC 17922 BHSM

In ITU-T SG 17 and ISO/IEC JTC 1/SC 27, a project to make a common text on Biometric Hardware Security Module (BHSM) is going on. It is at Committee Draft stage in SC 27 at the time of writing this paper. A typical example of BHSM is a PKI card in which the private key is activated by biometric authentication. To show that a BHSM is used in the authentication process, cAC can be applied with modification where the modification depends on the security policy on authentication. If only the modality used has to be known by the Verifier, then replacement of `ContentCPRPassphrase` in `CACProductReport` with `ContentCPRBiometicsSimple`, which is defined as follows, suffices to apply cAC to BHSM:

```
ContentCPRBiometicsSimple ::= SEQUENCE {
    productType         ProductType,
    levelCMVP           LevelCMVP,
    biometricType       BiometricType,
    biometricSubype     BiometricSubtype OPTIONAL }
```

Here `BiometricType` and `BiometricSubtype` are types for modalities defined in ISO/IEC 19785-3 [8]. This is the simplest case of the application of cAC to BHSM.

If the Verifier needs to validate the biometric authentication executed in the BHSM through the authentication protocol, the combination of cAC and ACBio will be required. This is the most complex case of the application of cAC to BHSM. To deal with this issue, `ContentCPRBiometicsFull` shall be defined as follows to replace `ContentCPRBiometicsSimple`:

```
ContentCPRBiometicsFull ::= SEQUENCE {
    productType         ProductType,
    levelCMVP           LevelCMVP,
    bpuFunctionReport   BPUFunctionReport,
    bpuSecurityReport   BPUSecurityReport}
```

Here `BPUFunctionReport` and `BPUSecurityReport` are types defined in ACBio to show the specification of function and security of BPU. In this case, a BHSM is also considered as a BPU from the view point of ACBio. A cAC product report with `ContentCPRBiometicsFull` is regarded as an extension of BPU report with two fields, `productType` and `levelCMVP`, added to the data structure of `BPUReportContentInformation` in a BPU report.

In registration process, X.509 certificate and BRT certificate shall be issued. The issuance of these two types of certificate will be done at different TTPs. In ACBio, harmonization with PKI authentication has been considered. When both PKI and biometrics are used, the X.509 certificate shall be issued before the BRT certificate is issued. From a BRT certificate, the corresponding X.509 can be referenced with the field `pkiCertificateInformation` of type `PKICertificateInformation` in the BRT certificate. This correlates PKI authentication and biometric authentication.

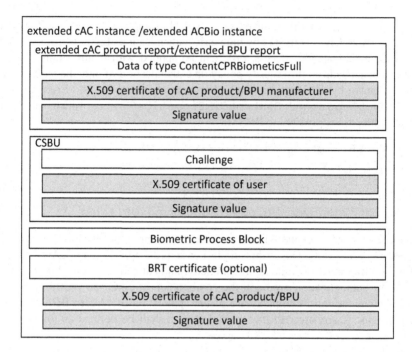

Fig. 4. Simplified data structure of extended cAC instance

In authentication process, extended cAC instance whose data structure is depicted in Fig.4 shall be used. The extended cAC instance can be also regarded as extended ACBio instance. If it is regarded as extended ACBio instance, the BPU report and the control value shall be replaced with the above defined cAC product report and CSBU respectively. With this extended cAC instance (or extended ACBio instance), cAC authentication and ACBio authentication are unified.

7.3   Future Works

In this paper, there is an assumption that the Verifier trusts the cAC product manufacturer. This is a strong assumption because it is difficult for the Verifier to know all the cAC product manufacturers that are trusted beforehand. It is desirable to weaken this assumption.

For security evaluation and certification of products, there is a scheme Common Criteria (CC) [2] which is also internationally standardized as ISO/IEC 15408 [7]. In the CC world, there is a movement to specify collaborative Protection Profile (cPP) to share security requirements for certain categories of security related products. At the time of writing this paper, Full Disk Encryption cPPs are posted for comments. For informing security features of a CC certified product, it is appropriate to show the cPPs which the product conforms to because cPPs are security requirements.

Let `CPPsConformantTo` be a type defined as follows:

```
CPPsConformantTo ::= SEQUENCE OF IdentifierCPP
IdentifierCPP ::= OBJECT IDENTIFIER
```

Here `IdentifierCPP` is used to assign an object identifier to a cPP. Then the type `CPPsConformantTo` can mean a set of cPPs which a CC certified product conforms to. Let `ContentCCCertificate` be a type defined as follows:

```
ContentCCCertificate::= SEQUENCE {
    nameProduct        Name,
    cPPsConformantTo CPPsConformantTo }
```

and let `id-content-CCCertificate` be the object identifier for the type `ContentCCCertificate`. Then the type `CCCertificate` defined as `SIGNEDDATA(id-cPPs-ConformantTo,CPPsConformantTo)` is used to express a CC certificate of a product if the private key of a CC certificate authority is used to digitally sign in generating a data of this type. The operation of the verification of this digital CC certificate will be easy to deal with for the Verifier since it needs to prepare only seventeen X.509 certificates in advance as there are only seventeen CC certification authorities worldwide (See http://www.commoncriteriaportal. org/ccra/members/). If signed CC certificate is standardized, the Verifier only needs to trust seventeen CC certification authorities. This will weaken the assumption stated at the beginning of this subsection. When `CCCertificate` becomes commonly used, the redefinition of type `ContentCPRPassphrase` adding a new field of type `CCCertificate` will make the cAC product report a more trustable data to the Verifier.

As is written at the end of 5, the communication protocol including negotiation is not discussed and to be specified in the next step. Adding new authentication contexts corresponding to cAC authentications to the OASIS standard related to authentication context is also necessary.

8   Conclusion

A new data cAC instance is proposed to improve the authentication process between the Claimant and the Verifier in remote authentication by giving the evidence data of execution of authentication process at the Claimant. To realize this proposal, standardization activities on the specification of cAC instance, the authentication protocol applying cAC authentication are necessary as the next steps.

Acknowledgement. The author appreciates Mr. Tatsuro Ikeda of Toshiba Solutions Corporation for a lot of discussions related to this work. Without these discussions, the author could not have reached the basic concept of this proposal.

References

1. Advancing open standards for the information society (OASIS). Authentication Context for the OASIS Security Assertion Markup Language (SAML) V2.0, OASIS Standard (2005)
2. Common Criteria Recognition Arrangement. Common Criteria for Information Technology Security Evaluation, Part 1: Introduction and general model, September 2012, Version 3.1 Revision 4, CCMB-2012-09-001 (2012)
3. Directive 1999/93/EC of the European Parliament and of the Council of 13 December 1999 on a Community framework for electronic signatures (2000)
4. European Telecommunications Standards Institute (ETSI). ETSI TS 101 862 V1.3.1 Qualified Certificate profile (2004)
5. International Organization for Standardization (ISO), International Electrotechnical Committee (IEC). ISO/IEC 7816-4:2013, Identification cards – Integrated circuit cards — Part 4: Organization, security and commands for interchange (2013)
6. International Organization for Standardization (ISO), International Electrotechnical Committee (IEC). ISO/IEC 7816-8:2004, Identification cards – Integrated circuit card — Part 8: Commands for security operations (2004)
7. International Organization for Standardization (ISO), International Electrotechnical Committee (IEC). ISO/IEC 15408-1:2009, Information technology — Security techniques — Evaluation criteria for IT security — Part 1: Introduction and general model (2009)
8. International Organization for Standardization (ISO), International Electrotechnical Committee (IEC). ISO/IEC 19785-3:2007, Information technology — Common Biometric Exchange Formats Framework — Part 3: Patron format specifications (2007)
9. International Organization for Standardization (ISO), International Electrotechnical Committee (IEC).ISO/IEC 19790:2012, Information technology — Security techniques — Security requirements for cryptographic modules (2012)
10. International Organization for Standardization (ISO), International Electrotechnical Committee (IEC). ISO/IEC 24761:2009, Information technology — Security techniques — Authentication context for biometrics (2009)
11. International Organization for Standardization (ISO), International Electrotechnical Committee (IEC). ISO/IEC 24761:2009/Cor 1:2013 (2013)
12. National Institute of Standards and Technology (NIST). Federal Information Processing Standardization (FIPS) 140-2 (2001)
13. National Institute of Standards and Technology (NIST). NIST Special Publication (SP) 800-63-2 Electronic Authentication Guideline (2013)
14. Office of Management and Budget (OMB). E-Authentication Guidance for Federal Agencies, M-04-04 (2003)
15. Ratha, N.K., Connell, J.H., Bolle, R.M.: A biometrics-based secure authentication system, Proc. of IEEE Workshop on Automatic Identification Advanced Technologies (AutoId 99), Summit, NJ, pp. 70-73 (1999)
16. Santesson, S., Nystrom, M., Polk, T.: Requests for Comments (RFC) 3739, Internet X.509 Public Key Infrastructure: Qualified Certificates Profile, The Internet Engineering Task Force (IETF) (2004)
17. Housley, R.: Requests for Comments (RFC) 3852, Cryptographic Message Syntax (CMS), The Internet Engineering Task Force (IETF) (2004)
18. Hoffman, P., Schaad, J.: Requests for Comments (RFC) 5911, New ASN.1 Modules for Cryptographic Message Syntax (CMS) and S/MIME, The Internet Engineering Task Force (IETF) (2010)

Enhancing Passwords Security Using Deceptive Covert Communication

Mohammed H. Almeshekah[(✉)], Mikhail J. Atallah,
and Eugene H. Spafford

Computer Science Department and CERIAS, Purdue University,
305, N. University St., West Lafayette, IN 47907, USA
{malmeshe,spaf,matallah}@purdue.edu
https://www.cs.purdue.edu/

Abstract. The use of deception to enhance security has shown promising results as a defensive technique. In this paper we present an authentication scheme that better protects users' passwords than in currently deployed password-based schemes, without taxing the users' memory or damaging the user-friendliness of the login process. Our scheme maintains comparability with traditional password-based authentication, without any additional storage requirements, giving service providers the ability to selectively enroll users and fall-back to traditional methods if needed. The scheme utilizes the ubiquity of smartphones; however, unlike previous proposals it does not require registration or connectivity of the phones used. In addition, no long-term secrets are stored in any user's phone, mitigating the consequences of losing it. Our design significantly increases the difficulty of launching a phishing attack by automating the decisions of whether a website should be trusted and introducing additional risk at the adversary side of being detected and deceived. In addition, the scheme is resilient against Man-in-the-Browser (MitB) attacks and compromised client machines. We also introduce a covert communication mechanism between the user's client and the service provider. This can be used to covertly and securely communicate the user's context that comes with the use of this mechanism. The scheme also incorporates the use of deception that makes it possible to dismantle a large-scale attack infrastructure before it succeeds. As an added feature, the scheme gives service providers the ability to have full-transaction authentication.

With the use of our scheme, passwords are no longer communicated in plaintext format to the server, adding another layer of protection when secure channels of communication are compromised. Moreover, it gives service providers the ability to deploy risk-based authentication. It introduces the ability to make dynamic multi-level access decisions requiring extra authentication steps when needed. Finally, the scheme's covert channel mechanisms give servers the ability to utilize a user's context information — detecting the use of untrusted networks or whether the login was based on a solicitation email.

Keywords: Authentication · Smartphone · Deception · Covert channel

© IFIP International Federation for Information Processing 2015
H. Federrath and D. Gollmann (Eds.): SEC 2015, IFIP AICT 455, pp. 159–173, 2015.
DOI: 10.1007/978-3-319-18467-8_11

1   Introduction

A recent American Banking Association (ABA) report identified internet banking as the preferred method for customer banking [4]: 62% of customers named online banking as their preferred banking method, a substantial rise from 36% in 2010. At the same time, phishing has been an increasing threat — rising at an alarming rate despite all the security mechanisms banks have in place. Criminals have been stealing money by means of exploiting the ubiquity of online banking. It is estimated that the Zeus trojan alone resulted in $70 million dollars stolen from bank accounts [22]. Many of the currently deployed two factor authentication schemes by banks remain vulnerable to a number of attacks [17]. Zeus managed to bypass two factor authentication schemes employed by banks [22]. Adham et al. presented a prototype of a browser add-ons that, even with two factor authentication, can successfully manipulate banking transactions on-the-fly [1]. There is clearly a need to improve the currently deployed schemes and address their shortcomings.

Deployed schemes need to tackle the issues of stolen credentials and phishing, and to mitigate man-in-middle (MitM) and man-in-the-browser (MitB) attacks – we discuss these two attacks in the next section. In this paper we present a mechanism that address these challenges. The scheme has the following desirable characteristics:

1. It automates the decision whether a website should be trusted before the user submits her password. This enhances the ability to detect, and further deceive, an adversary launching a phishing attack by increasing the risk of conducting such attacks.
2. Resilience against the common case of using an untrusted computer and/or network for a login session (e.g., at a hotel lobby or using a guest-account when visiting another organization).
3. A hidden/covert channel facility to convey information to the server about the current authentication context. This can be utilized by the user herself and/or her client – without user involvement. Users can convey their status or doubts they harbor about the trustworthiness of the computer or network they are using for the login session. Users often know that an activity is hazardous yet engage in it nevertheless because of perceived necessity (they need to check their account balance, even in unsafe circumstances). The bank can use this user-conveyed information to grant limited access (e.g., reading account balances and paying utility bills but not carrying out transfers to other bank accounts).
4. Unlike previous schemes, our use of smartphones does not necessitate storing any permanent information on the phone, does not require the phone to have network connectivity or ability to communicate with the computer, and does not require the phone to be registered. It merely uses the smartphone's computing capability.
5. The user-friendly covert channel facility facilitates the use of honeyaccounts through which service providers can learn about the attackers, their methods of operation, which other banks and laundering accounts they use, etc.

Throughout the paper we are using the notion of a bank generically, for two reasons. First, banking is one of the prominent use-cases necessitating the use of secure authentication. Second, banks are quickly becoming the target of choice for malfeasance by evildoers. The scheme we propose is, of course, more generally applicable.

2 Background

2.1 Authentication Schemes

We are concerned with two general classifications of attacks against client-server communication: man-in-the-middle (MitM) and man-in-the-browser (MitB) as shown in figure 1. In the former case, the adversary places herself in the communication channel between the user's computer and the server. End-to-end encryption schemes, such as SSL/TLS and IPSec, are intended to address this so that the adversary cannot observe or alter the data in the communication channel. Attackers overcome this protection by forcing the user to have an end-to-end encrypted channel with them instead of the real server, which is the case in phishing attacks. In the latter case, MitB, the attacker places herself between the user and his computer by altering the interface (browser) and manipulates the information displayed to the user in real-time. In this case even if the user employs an end-to-end encryption scheme, such as SSL/TLS, the attacker accesses the information when it is decrypted and can actively modify it before it is shown to the user.

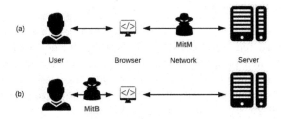

Fig. 1. Man-in-the-Middle (MitM) vs. Man-in-the-Browser (MitB)

Adham et al. identified three main authentication schemes built on the traditional username and password in the area of online banking [1]. These schemes are one-time password (OTP), partial transaction authentication, and full transaction authentication. They have shown that OTP schemes such as HMAC-Based One-time Password (HOTP) [18] or Time-based One-time Password (TOTP) [19] are not secure against active man-in-the-middle attacks (MitM) or man-in-the-browser (MitB) attacks [1]. The former can be orchestrated using an active phishing attack, in which the adversary immediately uses the stolen credentials to impersonate the user to the bank, while the latter can be seen, as an example, in the Zeus trojan.

To address the problem of active MitB attacks, banks started to use transaction authentication [1,7]. The Chip Authentication Program (CAP) introduced by many banks requires a piece of dedicated hardware, and its protocol has a number of vulnerabilities [7]. A number of these hardware devices degrade the full transaction authentication to authenticate only part of the transaction, as a consequence of usability challenges [1]. CrontoSign [8] is a smartphone-based full-transaction authentication that uses the smartphone to verify the information. The scheme requires a new phone registration process that stores information on the phone, which makes the user vulnerable if her phone is compromised or stolen. In addition, it ties the user to a specific phone, hindering the usability of the scheme if the user does not have this particular phone at transaction time. Moreover, this scheme only deals with transaction authentication, and does not focus on providing enhanced user authentication.

Full transaction authentication gives a bank the ability to ask the user to confirm her banking transaction to detect if MitB attacks are taking place and modifying the transaction *on-the-fly*. It is an essential step to enhance the security of online banking, as pointed out by Adham et al. [1]. The scheme we present in this paper achieves such goals without the need for additional hardware, as in CAP [7] or hPIN/hTAN [15], or for a long term secret stored in the user's smartphone. It also has the other features mentioned earlier, of covertly conveying information to the bank and supporting deceiving the adversary (honeyaccounts).

2.2   Use of Smartphones

Clarke et al. were the first to suggest the use of a camera-based device when connecting from untrusted computers [6]. While they did not explicitly discuss the use of QR codes, their paper is considered seminal in this approach of enhancing authentication. A number of follow-on proposals presented other camera-based schemes, using smartphones and other devices to improve authentication (see, e.g., [11,13,14,16,20,23], to mention a few).

Each one of these schemes suffers from one or more of the following shortcomings; (i) requiring an extra piece of hardware; (ii) storage of long-term secret on the smartphone; (iii) requiring a new registration process for associating the user's bank account with a particular smartphone; (iv) requiring the smartphone to have (network or cellular) connectivity to carry out the authentication process. The scheme we present in this paper does not suffer from any of these shortcomings.

2.3   Use of Deception and Covert Messages

The use of deception has shown a number of promising results in aiding computer defenses. Almeshekah et al. discussed the advantages of incorporating deception into computer security defenses [3]. We incorporate deceptive elements in our scheme in two ways: (i) active MitM will be deceived such that he is forwarding the covert messages back-and-forth that sends an alarm to the service provider, (ii) we introduce honeyaccounts in our scheme to dismantle an attack before it takes place, and to gather information about the attacker's goals, objectives, and resources.

The *covert channel* term was introduced by Lampson in 1973 and defined as *"channels not intended for information transfer at all"* [12]. Such a channel has been extensively studied as a security vulnerability that undermines the security of a system and leaks out private information. The covert channel we are introducing in this scheme is observed to "not carry information" by the adversary and is created by design to *enhance* the overall security of the system. In this work we are overloading the term, although we see the functionality as similar.

Our method introduces the use of covert deceptive messages between the user and/or her client and the service provider. One of the choices of covert message is that the user is logging in as a response to an email; we discuss how this can be achieved in the next section. If the bank has no record of a recent communication, that response may trigger an enhanced defense, such as enabling read-only access. This would directly address many forms of phishing. Other messages can be automatically embedded by the user's client, such as the use of a public network.

Honeyaccounts are fake bank accounts that banks can use to lure attackers and deceive them into believing that they have successfully broken into the user's account at the bank. They provide an effective mechanism to monitor attackers' activities – to learn who is targeting a certain bank, and learn the other accounts being used to launder users' stolen funds. This information is usually gathered by banks during the forensic investigations following a money-theft episode (when it is too late to follow the money trail leading overseas). A user who covertly conveys to the bank her belief in the present transaction offers some hope of dismantling the financial infrastructure of a large-scale phishing campaign before it does real damage. We all experience situations where we *know* that an email is a phishing attempt, yet many of us limit our reaction to not falling prey to it — it would be nice to have an easy-to-use mechanism for conveying our belief and thereby triggering the deception mechanisms of the bank. The covert communication we propose can achieve this.

3   Technical Specification

This section discusses the technical specifications of our scheme. We show how to perform the initial setup at the server and seamlessly enroll users. We also discuss how the covert channel can be deployed within the authentication scheme. At the end of this section, we discuss some the potential enhancements that our scheme brings which can be incorporated in future work.

3.1   Attack Scenarios

There are many attacks against password-based authentication systems including the following common attacks.

- **Stolen Passwords.** The security of password-based authentication systems fundamentally relies on the fact that each user's password is only known to the user alone. When an adversary obtains the user's password he has the ability to *continuously* impersonate the user to the server, without any of the two parties noticing. Many attacks, such as phishing, keylogging, and shoulder-surfing are centered on the goal of obtaining users' passwords to gain unbounded access to their accounts.
- **Stolen Password Hashes File.** An adversary who obtains the passwords hashes file of many users can apply an offline cracking process (such as dictionary attacks) to retrieve the users' passwords from their hashes.
- **Poor/Easily Guessable Passwords.** When the user chooses an easily guessable password, an adversary can easily guess it and impersonate the user to the server.
- **Repeated Password Use.** A person may use the same passwords across multiple systems where a compromise against one system undermines the security of all other systems.

The focus of our design is primarily to address the first attack scenario. In addition, it provides a minor improvement to address the problem of cracking passwords.

3.2   Scheme – Setup

As depicted in figure 2, there is no new registration required for bank customers, and the bank can roll out the deployment of the scheme either all at once, or progressively by selecting a specific subset of their customers (in which case a user who prefers the old system can easily be accommodated). In addition to a cryptographic one-way hash function H and a cryptographic message authentication code such as HMAC, we use a one-way accumulator function A whose output is to have the same number of bits as H (so that the format of the bank server's password file does not need to be modified – only the nature of the bits stored changes).

As discussed by Fazio and Nicolosi, an accumulator function can be constructed such that it behaves as a one-way function [10]. In addition to the usual one-way property required of cryptographic hashes, a one-way accumulation of n items has the properties that (i) the order of the accumulation does not matter (i.e., any two permutations of the same n items give rise to the same result) [i.e. $A(x_1, x_2) = A(x_2, x_1)$]; and (ii) given a new item/s and the accumulation of a previous item $A(x_1)$, a new accumulation that includes the new item/s (as well as the old one) can be efficiently obtained without needing to know the previous item (x_1) which equals $A(x_1, new\_items)$. To illustrate the second property using an example, if we have the modular exponentiation of x_1 (g^{x_1}) and we want to compute the new accumulation including a new item x_2, we compute this as $g^{x_1^{x_2}} = g^{x_1 * x_2}$. A real world realization of such a function can be done by using a modular exponentiation where the accumulation of x_1 can be implemented as $A(x_1) = g^{x_1}$.

As the most common ways of implementing such an accumulator A function involve modular exponentiation, it is typically the case that $A(x, y) = A(x * y)$ (where arithmetic is modular). In that case the security of A hinges on the Computational Diffie-Hellman assumption: That given $A(x_1)$ and $A(x_2)$ it is computationally intractable to compute $A(x_1, x_2)$ without knowing either x_1 or x_2. We give our presentation assuming the existence of such an A, without going into any details of how it is actually implemented (our scheme depends only on A's one-way property, its above-mentioned order-independence, and its above-mentioned incremental accumulation).

Recall that a user's entry in a traditional password file contains $h = H(passwd \parallel salt)$ and $salt$, where the purpose of the salt bits is to make a wholesale dictionary attack against all users harder (but it does not make it harder to attack an individual user, because the salt is in-the-clear). To switch to the new system, the bank simply replaces h with $A(h)$. This can handle users who select to remain in the traditional username/password authentication (in the obvious way). But replacing h by $A(h)$ is essential for users who select to switch to our proposed smartphone-based scheme, which we describe next.

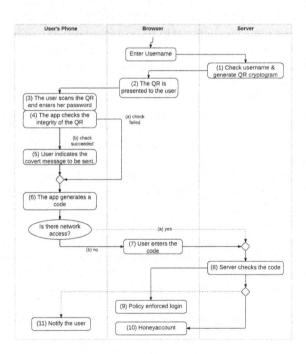

Fig. 2. Protocol Run

3.3   Scheme – Login

As usual, the login starts with the user entering her username on the computer. We assume that the smartphone has the needed app (which knows nothing about the user or the bank).

- The bank verifies that the username exists and, if so, generates a nonce R. Then it computes and sends the following information to the user's browser, encoded in a QR-code (recall that a QR code is an optically machine-readable two-dimensional barcode).
    - $A(R)$.
    - $\mathrm{HMAC}_{key}(A(R))$ where $key = A(A(h), R) = A(h, R)$.
    - The user's salt.
- The user scans the QR code using the smartphone app and inputs his password to the smartphone. The app computes $h' = H(password \parallel salt)$ and then generates the HMAC key by computing $A(A(R), h') = A(R, h')$ — the user's phone does not need a copy of R to make this computation. The HMAC is recomputed locally and then the app verifies that the received HMAC matches the HMAC it just computed. If the check succeeds (meaning the user entered the correct password and $h == h'$) the user moves into the next step of the protocol – phase 5. If the check fails there are two scenarios for what comes next: A *safe case* (branch a), and a *decoy case* (branch b). With the *safe case* the scheme continues to phase 5; in the *decoy case* the scheme jumps to phase 6 to send the MitM/MitB to a honeyaccount. In the latter case, the app can simply skip the covert messaging part if it detects a MitM/MitB impersonating the bank, and either terminate or continue with a honeyaccount. In this case, the failure of the HMAC verification can be treated as a special kind of covert message.
- In phase (5), the user is provided with the optional facility to covertly signal a simple message to the server. This covert messaging mechanism enables different behaviors from the current practice of "all-or-nothing" authentication and access. We give users the ability to choose from a fixed set of possible messages they could convey to the server. Giving users the ability to convey their level of trust in the computing or network facilities being used, e.g., using a public or a friend's computer, wireless network at an airport, etc. Later in this section, we show how these messages can be easily embedded in the code generated, in phase (6) of the scheme. Users can use this same facility to covertly request a limited-access login (e.g., read-only), in cases where they are following an email-solicited invitation to login to view an "important message." This covert message can alternatively be realized by other means than the above, such as those proposed by Almeshekah et al. [2].
- In phase (6), a one-time code is generated by the smartphone by computing the following accumulation:

$$y = A(A(R), h, msg_1, .., msg_i) = A(R, h, msg_1, .., msg_i)$$

The covert messages are conveyed by setting up the bit of any *covert message* (of the i possible messages) to one.

- In phase (7), the user types the generated code into the computer (copied from the smartphone screen). To make the code readable we can use base64 encoding and selecting the first n characters (the size of n is discussed later). Branch (a) of the previous phase, i.e. the existence of networking facility in the phone, will be discussed shortly.
- When the bank receives the code, in phase (8), it will check the validity of the code and whether a covert message has been signaled or not. It first accumulates into $A(h)$ the item R, if it matches the y sent by the user sent then the login succeeds (and the user did not convey a message), if it does not match y then the bank further accumulates (in turn) every possible covert message until the result matches y (or, if none matches, the login fails). In the *safe case*, if the bank receives a valid code with no message, phase (9) of the protocol is reached. However, if a message is sent, there are two possible options depending on the message:

  1. Take policy-specified action as per to the message conveyed before reaching phase (9). This can incorporate a variety of policies including the requirement of carrying out additional authentication measures or offer limited access. This gives service providers the ability to implement risk-based authentication and access control, and enforce a rich set of policies.
  2. Redirect the authentication session to a honeyaccount and, optionally, notifying the user of this access decision.

Length of code (y). As we will discuss below, the accumulator function is a one-way function and its output can be viewed as a random sequence of bits. As a result, the adversary succeeds if he can guess all the characters in this code. If we have 64 possible characters (including alphanumeric characters and symbols), the probability of guessing a single character is 2^{-6}. If we set the length of y to 5, the probability of guessing the code y is roughly equal to 2^{-30}.

In addition, as presented above, the calculation of y includes a random number R. As a result, the adversary gains no advantage by learning any previous runs of the protocol and the value of y as it is a one-way function of a number of variables including a random variable.

3.4 Incorporating Deception and Covert Communication

The introduction of covert channels in our scheme gives the user and app the ability to convey a number of pre-determined messages without the knowledge of any party positioning itself at any place in the communication channels. This can be done by appending a number of bits to the input of the accumulation function in step (6). To give an example, assume the protocol is designed to signal two different messages to the server; (i) msg_1 the user is accessing from a new wireless network, (ii) msg_2 the user selected read only access. When the app computes y in step (6) it can append two bits to the hash output as the following;

$y = A(A(R), h(passwd\|salt)\|msg_1\|msg_2)$ where msg_1 and msg_2 are single bits that are set to 1 if the user want to signal this message and 0 if the message is not being signaled.

The multitude of applications that can utilize such a mechanism is large and it incorporates status communication as part of the authentication protocol. For example, the bank can take extra precautions if the user is authenticating from a new networking environment. Another example, is the user can signal duress if he has been threatened and forced to transfer money to other accounts. Duress can be signaled covertly, for example, by measuring rapid changes in the phone's built-in accelerometer where the user can subtly shake his phone during login. Another example to signal duress is when the user presses the physical volume buttons during the authentication process.

3.5   Security Analysis

Within our scheme when the bank sends $A(R)$, the only party that can successfully respond with y is one who knows the password and gets the smartphone to compute $h = H(password\|salt)$ and thus the code y that is conveyed back to the server. This is true because an adversary who gets $A(h)$ and $A(R)$ is unable to compute $y = A(h, R)$ without knowing either R or h, neither of which is available to the attacker. Also note that, if the credentials database at the bank is leaked, no one can impersonate the user without cracking the passwords, as in traditional password schemes. One minor advantage this scheme provides is that cracking is slower for the adversary because of the introduction of the accumulation function A – it is significantly slower to accumulate every password in the cracking dictionary than to simply hash it.

Central to the security of our scheme is the fact that the only information of use to an adversary (the password) is entered on the cell phone and not on the client computer being used to remotely access the bank. The cell phone has no permanent record of any sensitive information. In addition, the bank's server never contains (even ephemerally) the user's password in the clear, providing a measure of defense against a snooping insider at the bank.

Finally, we point out that there are a number of additional security advantages of entering the user's password in a smartphone application instead of the browser:

- **The use of Software Guards.** Traditional password based-schemes ask the user to enter her password in the browser running on the client operating system. Current browsers are not self-protected, as identified in [5], and they are a complex piece of software that is exposed to many vulnerabilities. For that, our scheme uses a specific phone application that can have an intrinsic software protection against tampering as illustrated in [5,9].
- **Automated Trust Decision.** Adversaries using social-engineering attacks to lure users to give up their credentials, such as in the case of phishing, exploit the users' decision-making process by presenting them with legitimate-looking web pages. Our scheme aids users in making trust decision

about the authenticity of a web page mandating that the website provides a cryptographic proof of their knowledge of a shared secret; namely the password. This process is done in total transparency to the user and the user is only asked to capture the picture of a QR code.

This cryptographic proof can be computed by the web server without the need of explicitly storing the password value and, more importantly, without storing any information on the user's phone. This significantly increases the difficulty of social engineering attacks, such as phishing, as it reverses the game – demanding that the web site provides proof of authenticity before the user logs in.

– **Smaller Chance for Shoulder-Surfing.** Traditionally, users enter their passwords using a large keyboard where shoulder surfing is an easy task for adversaries. Asking the user to input their password on their phone increases the difficulty of such activity.

It worth noting that if the user logs-in to the service provider using a phone browser, our scheme cannot be directly used to scan the QR code as we discussed above. However, the basic protocol and feature can still be applicable with only a change in how the QR is input. This can be achieved by developing a browser extension that can automatically detect a QR code in the webpage and button on the corner of such codes to be clicked by users to launch the authentication app where the QR is automatically read. Nevertheless, the advantages of separating the service login, previously done on the computer, and the authentication process on the phone are slightly degraded. If the phone browser is infected with a MitB trojan, it would be easier to circumvent the security on the scheme as it can communicate directly with the authentication app. However, we note that most security sensitive transactions on a phone are done using dedicated apps that are hardened for a specific application. In addition, the underlying principle of using a covert channel presented in this paper can be incorporated in these dedicated apps.

3.6   Scheme – Enhancements

Full-Transaction Authentication – After the user logs in, the same steps can be repeated for every sensitive transaction with two main differences: (i) instead of sending the username, it is the transaction information that is sent, so that the QR code will contain additional information about the transaction details along with the HMAC and the user can verify those details on the app itself and make sure it is what they really want; and (ii) the covert message part can be eliminated, only keeping the part related to the failure of MAC checks. This part can be used, as we discussed before, to lure attackers who are launching MitB attacks manipulating transactions "on-the-fly."

Phone Connectivity – If the smartphone happens to have (optional) network connectivity (step (a) in figure 2), it can spare the user the trouble of manually entering the code displayed on its screen, and send it itself to the bank's server (user sessions can be uniquely identified by the server using the nonce R).

Storage of Insensitive Information – The security of our scheme does not require the long term storage of any information in the phone itself. Nevertheless, we can benefit from storing information that can increase the utility of the covert communication. As an example, the app can store the name(s) of user's home network(s) and automatically send a covert message when the user is using a non-trusted network to login. Such knowledge gives service providers the ability to deploy a risk-based authentication. For example, when the user is using an untrusted network to login, a limited control can be provided and extra level of authentication can be enforced when powerful transactions are required.

4   Comparison with Other Schemes

In table 1 we evaluate the different schemes using the following criteria.

Requirement of phone enrollment — schemes such as CrontoSign and QRP [21] require the user to register her phone with the bank, i.e. phone enrollment. Such schemes store phone information, such as IMEI number, and use it as part of their protocol to achieve assurances about the user's identity. One of the major issue of tying the user's identity to his phone is that the user may lose his phone, forget it or run out of battery. In these circumstances, the user wants to be able to use an alternative phone to login to his account. If the user loses his phone he is vulnerable to the threat of impersonation until he reports the incident to every bank he banks with. In the case where he does not have his phone the usability of such a scheme becomes an issue as the user cannot login to his account anymore. This could result in lost business if the user moves to other banks that are using more usable schemes.

Our approach addresses these concerns in two ways. First, we allow users to use many phones without degrading the security of the scheme or asking the user to register all his phones. Second, we challenge the all-or-nothing assumption allowing users to fall back to other authentication mechanisms dynamically, possibly setting the privileges to only allow non-sensitive transactions.

Requirement of long-term secrets — many of the previously proposed schemes require the storage of long-term secret(s) either on the users' phones or on another piece of specialized hardware [15, 21, 23]. To the best of our knowledge, our scheme is the first scheme that provides full transaction authentication and user authentication that resist MitB without the need to store long-term secrets or require additional hardware.

Resisting MitB — a recent paradigm in banking Trojans is to bypass two factor authentication by launching MitB attacks that change transaction information on-the-fly. We compare the schemes in table 1 based on their resistance to MitB. When our scheme is used to authenticate transactions, as discussed in section 3.6, a MitB attack can be defeated. This is because the MitB needs to send the modified transaction information to the bank, where an HMAC is created. However, when the user verifies this information on his phone after scanning the QR-code he can see that the transaction details have been changed. He can click on a button to say that the details have been changed and a *deceptive* code can be generated. The MitB attacker would end up in phase (10) where they will be deceived.

Table 1. Schemes Comparison

	no phone enroll-ment	no long-term secret	resists MitB	no special hard-ware	no phone connec-tivity	compatible with exist-ing
Our Scheme	✓	✓	✓	✓	✓	✓
CrontoSign [8]	–	–	✓	✓	✓	–
QR-Tan [23]	–	–	✓	✓	✓	–
hPin/hTan [15]	N/A	–	✓	–	N/A	–
QRP [21]	–	–	✓	✓	✓	–

Use of special Hardware — many proposals introduce a new piece of hardware to the authentication scheme to achieve a higher level of assurance and to verify banking transactions, such as the CAP scheme [7]. There are two major disadvantages with those approaches: cost and usability. As an illustrative example, Barclay's bank in the UK equipped users with special full-transaction authentication hardware, but ended up having to reduce the functionality to only partial transaction authentication because of many customer complaints. This degradation led to a number of security vulnerabilities [1].

Requiring phone connectivity — a number schemes are intended to maximize their usability by making the smartphone or the special hardware act on the users' behalf. In all the mechanisms we examined this comes with the cost of either requiring the phone to have network connectivity, which is not always possible, or requiring a direct communication between the users' computers and their smartphones, which hinders usability. In our proposal we share the same goals and enhance the usability of our scheme by giving users the ability to login even though they do not have any connectivity in their phone and without having to connect their phones to their computers.

Compatible with existing infrastructure — banks perceive security as an economic and risk reduction activity. Protocols that require radical changes to current infrastructure usually do not get adopted because of the associated high cost. In addition, the ability to dynamically fall back to traditional authentication methods is a preferred property giving banks the ability to dynamically deploy their new scheme and progressively enroll their users. This is why we use this as a comparison factor with other schemes.

5   Conclusion

We propose an authentication mechanism that has many attractive features, including compatibility with deployed authentication infrastructure; flexible use of smartphones without requiring phone registration or storage of permanent information in the phone; without any requirement of phone connectivity (i.e., using the phone as a computational device rather than as a storage or communication device); resistance to many common forms of attack; and a facility for user-friendly (pull-down menu on the cell phone app) covert communication from the user to the bank. The covert communication in turn makes possible different levels of access (instead of the traditional all-or-nothing), and the use of deception (honeyaccounts) that makes it possible to dismantle a large-scale attack infrastructure before it succeeds (rather than after the painful and slow forensics that follow a successful phishing attack).

References

1. Adham, M., Azodi, A., Desmedt, Y., Karaolis, I.: How to attack two-factor authentication internet banking. In: Financial Cryptography (2013)
2. Almeshekah, M.H., Atallah, M.J., Spafford, E.H.: Back channels can be useful! – layering authentication channels to provide covert communication. In: Christianson, B., Malcolm, J., Stajano, F., Anderson, J., Bonneau, J. (eds.) Security Protocols 2013. LNCS, vol. 8263, pp. 189–195. Springer, Heidelberg (2013)
3. Almeshekah, M.H., Spafford, E.H.: Planning and integrating deception into computer security defenses. In: New Security Paradigms Workshop (NSPW 2014), Victoria, BC, Canada (2014)
4. American Banking Association (ABA). Popularity of Online Banking Explodes, September 2011
5. Chang, H., Atallah, M.J.: Protecting software code by guards. In: Sander, T. (ed.) DRM 2001. LNCS, vol. 2320, p. 160. Springer, Heidelberg (2002)
6. Clarke, D., Gassend, B., Kotwal, T., Burnside, M., van Dijk, M., Devadas, S., Rivest, R.L.: The untrusted computer problem and camera-based authentication. In: Mattern, F., Naghshineh, M. (eds.) PERVASIVE 2002. LNCS, vol. 2414, pp. 114–124. Springer, Heidelberg (2002)
7. Drimer, S., Murdoch, S.J., Anderson, R.: Optimised to fail: card readers for online banking. In: Dingledine, R., Golle, P. (eds.) FC 2009. LNCS, vol. 5628, pp. 184–200. Springer, Heidelberg (2009)
8. Drokov, I., Punskaya, E., Tahar, E.: System and Method For Dynamic Multifactor Authentication (2006)
9. Falcarin, P., Collberg, C., Atallah, M., Jakubowski, M.: Software Protection. IEEE Software **28**(2), 24–27 (2011)
10. Fazio, N., Nicolosi, A.: Cryptographic accumulators: Definitions, constructions and applications
11. Harini, N., Padmanabhan, T.R.: 2CAuth: A New Two Factor Authentication Scheme Using QR-Code. International Journal of Engineering and Technology (2013)
12. Lampson, B.W.: A note on the confinement problem. Communications of the ACM **16**(10), 613–615 (1973)

13. Lee, Y., Kim, J., Jeon, W., Won, D.: Design of a simple user authentication scheme using QR-code for mobile device. In: Park, J.H.J., Kim, J., Zou, D., Lee, Y.S. (eds.) Information Technology Convergence, Secure and Trust Computing, and Data Management. LNCS, vol. 180, pp. 241–247. Springer, Dordrecht (2012)
14. Lee, Y.S., Kim, N.H., Lim, H., Jo, H., Lee, H.J.: Online banking authentication system using mobile-OTP with QR-code. In: 2010 5th International Conference on Computer Sciences and Convergence Information Technology (ICCIT), pp. 644–648. IEEE (2010)
15. Li, S., Sadeghi, A.-R., Heisrath, S., Schmitz, R., Ahmad, J.J.: hPIN/hTAN: a lightweight and low-cost e-banking solution against untrusted computers. In: Danezis, G. (ed.) FC 2011. LNCS, vol. 7035, pp. 235–249. Springer, Heidelberg (2012)
16. Liao, K.-C., Lee, W.-H.: A novel user authentication scheme based on QR-code. Journal of Networks 5(8), 937–941 (2010)
17. Mimoso, M.: Two-Factor Authentication No Cure-All for Twitter Security Woes
18. M'Raihi, D., Bellare, M., Hoornaert, F., Naccache, D., Ranen, O.: RFC 4226 - HOTP: An HMAC-Based One-Time Password Algorithm. Technical report, IETF (2005)
19. M'Raihi, D., Machani, S., Pei, M., Rydell, J.: RFC 6238 - TOTP: Time-Based One-Time Password Algorithm. Technical report, IETF (2011)
20. Mukhopadhyay, S., Argles, D.: An Anti-Phishing mechanism for single sign-on based on QR-code. In: 2011 International Conference on Information Society (i-Society), pp. 505–508. IEEE (2011)
21. Pintor Maestre, D.: QRP: An improved secure authentication method using QR codes (2012)
22. Risk Analytics. $70 Million Stolen From U.S. Banks With Zeus Trojan
23. Starnberger, G., Froihofer, L., Goeschka, K.M.: QR-TAN: Secure mobile transaction authentication. In: International Conference on Availability, Reliability and Security, 2009. ARES 2009, pp. 578–583. IEEE (2009)

Information Sharing and User Privacy in the Third-Party Identity Management Landscape

Anna Vapen[1]([⊠]), Niklas Carlsson[1], Anirban Mahanti[2],
and Nahid Shahmehri[1]

[1] Linköping University, Linköping, Sweden
{anna.vapen,niklas.carlsson,nahid.shahmehri}@liu.se
[2] NICTA, Sydney, Australia
anirban.mahanti@nicta.com.au

Abstract. The cross-site information sharing and authorized actions of third-party identity management can have significant privacy implications for the users. In this paper, we use a combination of manual analysis of identified third-party identity management relationships and targeted case studies to (i) capture how the protocol usage and third-party selection is changing, (ii) profile what information is requested to be shared (and actions to be performed) between websites, and (iii) identify privacy issues and practical problems that occur when using multiple accounts (associated with these services). By characterizing and quantifying the third-party relationships based on their cross-site information sharing, the study highlights differences in the privacy leakage risks associated with different classes of websites, and provides concrete evidence for how the privacy risks are increasing. For example, many news and file/video-sharing sites ask users to authorize the site to post information to the third-party website. We also observe a general increase in the breadth of information that is shared across websites, and find that due to usage of multiple third-party websites, in many cases, the user can lose (at least) partial control over which identities they can merge/relate and the information that is shared/posted on their behalf.

1 Introduction

Many popular web services, such as Facebook, Twitter, and Google, rely heavily on their large number of active users and the rich data and personal information these users create or provide. In addition to monetizing the high service usage and personal information, the rich user data can also be used to provide personalized and customized user experiences that add value to their services.

With this in mind, it is perhaps not surprising that many websites are using third-party single sign-on (SSO) [5,14] services provided by popular websites. With SSO, a website such as Soundcloud will partner with one or more other third-party websites (e.g., Facebook and Google), which will be responsible for user authentication on behalf of Soundcloud. As illustrated in Figure 1(a), a user

H. Federrath and D. Gollmann (Eds.): SEC 2015, IFIP AICT 455, pp. 174–188, 2015.
DOI: 10.1007/978-3-319-18467-8_12

(a) IDP selection   (b) Authentication   (c) App rights

Fig. 1. Soundcloud example illustrating the login process when using IDPs, as well as the app rights requested by Soundcloud when using Google as IDP

is given the option of using Facebook and Google for authentication. Assuming that the user selects Google, the user is redirected to Google for authentication (Figure 1(b)). We refer to Soundcloud as a relying party (RP) and Facebook/Google as a third-party identity provider (IDP).

In addition to providing an authentication service, at the time of account creation or first login, the user is typically asked to approve an app-rights agreement (e.g., Figure 1(c)) between the user and the RP, which (i) gives permission to the RP to download agreed-upon information from the user's IDP account, and (ii) authorizes the RP to perform certain actions on the IDP, such as posting information. Such permissions place great responsibility on the RPs, and can raise significant privacy concerns for users.

Privacy concerns related to the rich information shared across websites will likely increase as more sophisticated statistical methods are used to reveal private information using only public data [3,10,18]. For example, public Twitter feeds can be used to determine political views and ethnicity [10], users can be identified across websites even when they lie about their identity [18], and even relatively innocent information such as the music that people listen to can reveal personal information many users want to keep private [3]. Despite many interesting case studies of how this information can be misused, and our previous basic characterization of the geographic and service-based biases in how RPs select their IDPs [15], we are not aware of any study that characterizes the cross-site information sharing and RP authorization in this third-party landscape. Such a study is important to assess the current privacy risks.

This paper provides the first broad empirical analysis of the cross-site information sharing, app-rights agreements, and account management complexities in the current third-party identity management landscape. We place particular attention on the personal information shared and accessed between different sites, and discuss potential privacy implications for end users. Motivated by a high skew in website popularities [7], our analysis primarily focuses on the cross-site information sharing associated with the 200 most popular websites.[1]

---

[1] Alexa (official website), www.alexa.com.

Focusing on these sites allows us to manually identify and analyze the information sharing, account creation process, and website interactions as observed by the user.

1.1   Contributions and Roadmap

A high-level summary of the results were reported in a short (3-page) poster paper [16]. Here, we first briefly present a high-level characterization of the protocol and IDP usage observed in the wild (Section 2). Our results confirm that the use of authorization protocols such as OAuth is significantly more common than the use of pure authentication protocols such as OpenID and that OAuth is becoming increasingly dominant. Since OAuth allows richer cross-site information sharing and can authorize RPs to perform actions on the IDPs, on behalf of the user, these results reaffirm the importance of characterizing today's app-rights agreement usage and their privacy risks. We find that many RPs likely select IDPs on other criteria than protocol compatibility. We also find that some IDPs are much more frequently used in combination than on their own, and that there is a high concentration in IDP usage. This can be a potential privacy and security concern in itself, as the user credentials for the most popular IDPs become more valuable to an impersonator, for each RP that adds that IDP.

Thereafter, we characterize the cross-site information sharing and authorized app rights associated with the most popular IDPs (Section 3), responsible for the majority of RP-IDP relationships. We categorize app-rights agreements based on the type of information and actions granted to the RPs (Section 3.1) and identify the most commonly observed privacy risk categories (Section 3.2). We find significant differences in the information leakage risks associated with different RP classes (Section 3.3) and IDPs (Section 3.4).

Finally, we use targeted login and account creation tests to analyze the information sharing in scenarios in which the users have accounts with multiple IDPs (Section 4). Among other things, we find that there often is significant overlap in the information that an RP may request from different IDPs (Section 4.1), that there are significant differences in how well RPs combine the information from multiple IDPs (Section 4.2), and that some IDPs (e.g., Facebook) are much more likely to implicitly enable information leakage between IDP accounts through the RP than others (Section 4.3). In many cases, we have also found that the results depend on the order IDPs are added and that users often lose control of what is shown in their public profile with the RP. We even found several cases in which account merging is not possible or additional IDPs cannot be added/used.

The significant differences observed from case to case also illustrate that there is no common API, and that RPs typically pick IDPs based on IDP popularity and the information sharing and actions they enable, rather than protocol compatibility. With each RP implementing its own solution, the user must trust the RP and its implementation. Both OpenID and OAuth have many security issues [1,5], even when used alone, especially if implemented incorrectly [12,17]. Many privacy issues discussed here will therefore likely take time to address.

2   Protocol and IDP Selection

Today's RP-IDP relationships are typically implemented using OpenID or OAuth. While OpenID was designed purely for authentication and OAuth primarily is an authorization protocol, both protocols provide an SSO service that allows the user to access the RP by authenticating with the IDP without needing local RP credentials. With OAuth, a local RP account is always linked with the users IDP account, allowing information sharing between the RP and IDP. Local RP accounts are optional with OpenID.

We primarily focus on all RP-IDP relationships that we have manually identified on the 200 most popular websites on the Web (as observed in Apr. 2012, Feb. 2014, and Sept 2014), but will also leverage the 3,203 unique RP-IDP relationships (3,329 before removing false positives) identified using our custom designed Selenium-based crawling tool [15].

OAuth is the dominant protocol as observed in both manual and crawled datasets. For example, in Apr. 2012, 121 of 180 (67%) relationships in the manual dataset and 2,543 of 3,203 (79%) relationships in the crawled dataset are directly classified as OAuth, compared to only 20 (11%) and 180 (6%) as OpenID relationships in the two datasets. Of the remaining relationships, 39 and 441 used an IDP that supports both OpenID and OAuth. Since then, as measured in Sept. 2014, we have seen a further increase of OAuth usage (+24%) and drop in OpenID usage (-10%) among the top-200 websites.

We have found that IDP selection differs significantly depending on how many IDPs an RP selects, and some IDPs are more likely to be selected together with others. In total the top-5 ranked IDPs are responsible for 92% (33 of 36) and 90% (1,111 of 1,233) of the relationships of RPs selecting one single IDP. For RPs with 2-3 IDPs, 83% and 75% of the relationships are to the top-5, but for RPs with 4 or more IDPs only 38% and 55% are to the top-5 IDPs. Facebook+Twitter is the most popular pairing with 37% (125 of 335) of all IDP pairs, Chinese QQ+Sina place second (19%), and Facebook+Google third (12%).

3   App Rights and Information Flows

This section considers the information sharing and actions that RPs are permitted. Although it is impossible to know exactly *how* each RP uses the information they obtain from the IDPs (e.g., if they use data mining to present targeted ads, provide better services, or if they simply store the information for potential future use), the app-rights agreements between RPs and users reveal (i) the information that the RP *will obtain* from the IDP, and (ii) the actions the RP *will be allowed* to perform on behalf of the user.

For this study, we have carefully recorded the app-rights agreements for the RP-IDP relationships identified in the manual top-200 dataset. We created fake accounts on the IDPs, initiated the account creation process for each identified RP-IDP relationship involving this IDP, and recorded the app-rights agreements that our fake users were requested to agree to. For the tests in this section, we interrupt the login process after recording the app rights. Due to limited translation support, we only recorded statistics that provided app-rights agreements in English. The use of fake identities helps remove potential biases in the app-rights agreements presented to the users.

A few IDPs required the use of phone numbers in the registration process. Although these phone numbers or advanced data mining techniques [18] can be used to link the fake profiles with real identities, we have not observed anything that would suggest that these phone numbers have impacted our results.

For this analysis we focus on the RP-IDP relationships in the top-200 dataset from Feb. 2014. However, as Facebook has significantly changed their API since then, from version 1.0 (Apr. 2010) to 2.0 (Apr. 2014), and again to 2.1 (Aug. 2014), we analyze recorded app rights from both Feb. 2014 and Sept. 2014.

3.1 Classification of Information

When analyzing app-rights restrictions as described in the APIs of the three major IDPs (Facebook, Twitter and Google) as well as the actual app-rights usage across the top-200 websites in our datasets, we have identified five different classes of app rights, each with their own privacy implications. The first four classes (B, P, C, and F) capture information (or content) transferred from the IDP to the RP. The last class (A) has to do with actions being performed by the RP, on the IDP, on behalf of the user.

- **Basic information (B):** Relatively non-private information that the user is often asked to provide websites, including identifiers (e.g., email address) to identify existing accounts, age range, language, and public information.
- **Personal information (P):** This class includes personal information, common in many basic "bundles" (e.g., gender, country, time zone, and friend list), but also more sensitive information such as political views, religion, and sexual orientation.[2]
- **Created content (C):** This class contains content directly or indirectly created by the user, and includes images, likes, and check-in history. The sensitivity of the data varies. For example, in some cases the user may want to share images and video across sites, while in other cases this content may be considered private. Also the sensitivity of "logged" content (e.g., likes, watched video clips, location history) varies significantly on the situation.
- **Friends' data (F):** This class consists of data of other users (e.g., friends of the user). Even when of a non-sensitive nature, this data is privacy critical since it belongs to another, potentially non-consenting, user.
- **Actions taken on behalf of the user (A):** This final class includes the right to actively export data from the RP to the IDP and the right to perform *actions* on behalf of the user. This may include posting information on a

---

[2] One current Facebook bundle and two Google bundles named "Basic information" and similar (from which the RP selects which bundle to use in the app-rights agreement presented to the user) include both class B and P information.

user's IDP timeline or feed. The transferred data may include content the user creates at the RP (e.g., images), or information about the user's actions on the RP (e.g., sharing read articles, or music the user has listened to).

While the current example considers a scenario with a single RP-IDP pair, Section 4 briefly considers the multi-IDP case, in which information may be shared/leaked across multiple sites. Here, the action (A) class is particularly interesting when used in combination with friends' data (F). In this case, the RP may enable the actions by one user at one IDP to be leaked (through the RP) to other users at another IDP.

It is perhaps for this reason that Facebook, in their recent (Sept. 2014) multi-step app-rights agreements, does not share friend (F) data, and first request that the user approve data sharing permissions (B, P, and C), before the RP can ask the user to agree to optional action (A) permissions of different types. Regardless how these action permissions were classified in Feb. 2014, in the Feb. 2014 dataset, we include the most recent optional Facebook action (A) permissions from Sept. 2014. For the other big IDPs there have been no major changes in their APIs since Feb. 2014.

3.2   Risk Types

Today, many IDPs bundle the information requested into larger "bundles", and RPs must select which bundle to present to the users.[3] This simplifies the agreements, but reduces the granularity of control over information sharing, often resulting in the user being asked to grant permissions to share more information than the RP requires to perform the desired service.

Figure 2 summarizes all the observed app-rights agreements in our Feb. 2014 dataset. We use a Venn diagram to show all relationships involving actions in the left square and all others in the right square. Any relationship that is not in any of the three classes P, C, and F is in class B.

Only a handful of cases (4) limit themselves to only the basic (B) information (without actions (A)), and most RPs are requesting significantly more personal information from their users. These observations suggest that there is an expectation of trust in the RPs, beyond what the user would share publically. Generally, RPs that are performing actions (A) on behalf of their users are more likely to request access to content (C) from the IDP. In total, 40 of the 87 classified relationships include actions (A). Of these, 14 RPs also request access to content (C). Of the 47 app-rights agreements that does not request actions to be performed, only 12 (9+3) also request access to content (C).

Another important observation is that within each of the two boxes there is a clear ordering in risk types observed, suggesting that there is a natural ordering of the risk types observed in practice. In particular, class F is only used in

---

[3] For Twitter, the RP selected bundles (either "read", "read + write", or "read + write + direct messages") are translated into an explicit list of app rights presented to the users.

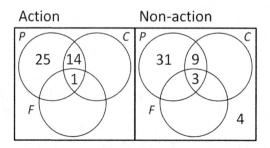

Fig. 2. RP-IDP relationships of different app-rights classes in the top-200 dataset

Table 1. Risk types identified in dataset

Risk type	Class combination	Risk type	Class combination
$\mathcal{R}_A^-$	$A \cap B$	$\mathcal{R}^-$	$\neg A \cap B$
$\mathcal{R}_A$	$A \cap P$	$\mathcal{R}$	$\neg A \cap P$
$\mathcal{R}_A^+$	$A \cap P \cap C$	$\mathcal{R}^+$	$\neg A \cap P \cap C$
$\mathcal{R}_A^{++}$	$A \cap P \cap C \cap F$	$\mathcal{R}^{++}$	$\neg A \cap P \cap C \cap F$

combination with both C and P. This combination clearly has the highest privacy risks associated with it. Similarly, class C is only used in combination with P, clearly distinguishing its risks with those of sites that only request personal (P) or basic (B) information.

Motivated by these observations, we identify eight semi-ordered risk types (strict ordering within columns). Table 1 summarizes the observed risk types. We note that there is a strict privacy ordering in each column (from (-) to (++)), and with regards to each row (as allowing actions implies some risk), but that further ordering is not possible without making assumptions.

3.3   RP-Based Analysis

Using the above RP-IDP relationship type classification, we next compare the app rights for different classes of RPs. In particular, we compare the app rights of RPs with different (i) primary web services, or (ii) number of IDPs.

Table 2 shows the number of relationships of each type, for websites that provides different web services. Here, we use a basic service categorization inspired by categories defined by Gill et al. [7]. With this categorization, each of the top-200 websites was manually classified as one of nine classes.

Among the classes with at least 10 RPs, News sites and File sharing sites are the most frequent users of actions (risk types $\mathcal{R}_A$ and $\mathcal{R}_A^+$), with 55% and 50% of their relationships including actions, respectively. Also Video sharing (67%) and Tech (63%) sites have a large fraction of relationships that include action (A) permissions. The high action (A) permission usage is likely an effect of these sites often wanting to promote articles, files, or videos to friends of the user. While we express privacy concerns regarding $\mathcal{R}_A^+$ relationships, these sites

Table 2. Breakdown of risk types of the RP-IDP relationships for RPs belonging to different websites categories, as classified based on their primary service

	Sites		Relationship type						
Categ.	RPs/Tot	Tested/Tot	$\mathcal{R}^-$	$\mathcal{R}$	$\mathcal{R}^+$	$\mathcal{R}^{++}$	$\mathcal{R}_A$	$\mathcal{R}_A^+$	$\mathcal{R}_A^{++}$
Ads/CDN	0/9	-/-	-	-	-	-	-	-	-
Commerce	8/26	7/16	0	5	0	0	2	0	0
File sharing	6/10	12/17	2	3	1	0	3	3	0
Info	9/14	10/16	0	5	0	1	4	0	0
News	12/20	22/40	0	4	6	0	7	5	0
Social/portal	26/81	22/65	1	10	2	2	3	4	0
Tech	7/23	8/21	1	2	0	0	2	2	1
Video	9/17	6/21	0	2	0	0	4	0	0
Total	77/200	87/196	4	31	9	3	25	14	1

Table 3. Breakdown of risk types of the RP-IDP relationships for RPs with different numbers of IDPs

			Relationship type						
IDPs	RPs	Tested/Tot	$\mathcal{R}^-$	$\mathcal{R}$	$\mathcal{R}^+$	$\mathcal{R}^{++}$	$\mathcal{R}_A$	$\mathcal{R}_A^+$	$\mathcal{R}_A^{++}$
1	36	24/36	0	11	3	2	7	1	0
2	15	19/30	1	7	0	1	7	2	1
3	11	21/33	1	6	3	0	6	5	0
4+	15	23/97	2	7	3	0	5	6	0
Total	77	87/196	4	31	9	3	25	14	1

would in fact desire that the information that their articles/content are being read to propagate across many sites. This is also reflected in the relatively large number of IDPs per RP for these four website categories (3.3, 2.83, 2.33, and 3.0, respectively, compared to an overall average of 2.5).

We next compare RPs with different numbers of IDPs (Table 3). Interestingly, relationships including actions ($\mathcal{R}_A$ and $\mathcal{R}_A^+$) are primarily associated with RPs that have many IDPs. For example, while RPs with a single IDP use actions in 33% (8 of 24) of their relationships (all using Facebook), RPs with multiple IDPs (2, 3, or 4+) use actions in 48-53% of their relationships. As with our discussion about News sites and File sharing sites, the many IDPs of these RPs increases the risk for cross-site information leakage.

The most restrictive type ($\mathcal{R}^-$) includes only OpenID relations. For content sharing without actions ($\mathcal{R}^+$), OAuth is the primary protocol, even if it is possible to transfer personal data and (links to) content over OpenID. Naturally, all relationships including actions use (and must use) OAuth.

3.4   Head-to-Head IDP Comparison

We have found that the top-three English speaking IDPs (Facebook, Twitter, and Google) are used differently by their RPs and that the usage is relatively independent of which other IDPs the RPs are using.

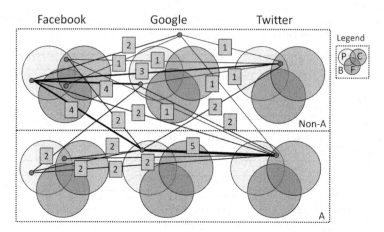

Fig. 3. Dependencies between app rights for the top-three English speaking IDPs. Here, the top-right legend shows the labeling of RP-IDP relationship types for each IDP, and link weights specify the number of RPs with such a relationship pair.

Table 4. Breakdown of risk types of the RP-IDP relationships associated with the top-three English speaking IDPs

IDP	Relationship type								
	Tot	$\mathcal{R}^-$	$\mathcal{R}$	$\mathcal{R}^+$	$\mathcal{R}^{++}$	$\mathcal{R}_A$	$\mathcal{R}_A^+$	$\mathcal{R}_A^{++}$	**Unk**
Facebook	55	0	24	5	3	13	3	1	6
Twitter	15	0	0	4	0	0	11	0	0
Google	29	4	7	0	0	12	0	0	6

Table 4 breaks down the app rights for RPs using each of these three IDPs. Google is the only IDP with type $\mathcal{R}^-$ relationships. Most of these relationships are due to use of Google's OpenID-based API, which in comparison to Google's OAuth API typically share less information and does not allow actions.

Overall, Google's mix of OpenID-based and OAuth-based relationships share less information (large fraction of $\mathcal{R}^-$, $\mathcal{R}$, and $\mathcal{R}_A$) than Twitter and Facebook (who also have many $\mathcal{R}^+$, $\mathcal{R}^{++}$, and $\mathcal{R}_A^+$ relationships). Furthermore, compared to Twitter and Facebook, Google allows more fine-grained personalization of app-rights agreements. The user is sometimes able to select which contacts (if any) to share information with (e.g., using Google's concept of "circles"). The most privacy preserving choice is, however, typically not selected by default.

Facebook is dominated by $\mathcal{R}$ and $\mathcal{R}_A$ relationships, and typically allows rich datasets to be imported to the RP. For Twitter, public messages and contacts are normally the only shared data (counted as content (C)); however, it should be noted that there are Twitter relations in which even private messages are shared with the RP. Twitter has the largest fraction of relationships with actions ($\mathcal{R}_A$ and $\mathcal{R}_A^+$). Twitter is particularly attractive for RPs wanting to perform actions on behalf of their users, as it provides an API that allows a wide of range of such actions to be performed and has a relatively active user population.

While we have not found any major statistical biases when comparing the fraction of relationship types observed when two IDPs (an IDP pairing) are used by the same RP vs. when they do not appear in such a pairing, we have found that there are some relatively common combinations. Figure 3 shows appropriate rights selections for IDP pairs consisting of Facebook/Google (19 pairs), Facebook/Twitter (11 pairs), and Google/Twitter (12 pairs). For example, we note that RPs importing personal data (P) from Facebook, often do the same with Google (with or without actions). We also observe several cases where Google and Twitter are used together and both IDPs use actions (A) and importing personal (P) data (being classified as $\mathcal{R}_A$). In general, there is a bias for selecting to use actions (A) with one IDP, given that actions are used with the other IDP. For example, in 24 of 40 cases (60%) in which an RP-IDP relationship of a pairing uses action (A) the other relationship uses actions (A) too. In contrast, only in 16 of 44 cases (37%) in which the first RP-IDP relationship does not use actions (A), the other does. Using one-sided binomial hypothesis testing, these differences are significant with 98% confidence ($p = 0.015, z = 2.167$).

4   Multi-account Information

It is becoming increasingly common that users have accounts with multiple of the RP's IDPs. For example, in our original Soundcloud example (Figure 1), a user may have accounts with both Google and Facebook. In addition, a local RP account may be created either before connecting the account to one of the IDPs, or when first creating the account using one of the IDPs. The use of all these accounts and their relative dependencies can complicate the situation for the end user, potentially increasing privacy risks.

In this section we present the highlights from a set of targeted scenario-driven case studies that we have performed to analyze the interaction between the different accounts, as observed in the wild. (Due to space limitations detailed results and tables are omitted.) For this analysis, we performed tests for each pairing of the three most popular English-speaking IDPs: Facebook, Twitter, and Google. For each possible IDP pairing, we allowed both IDPs in the pair to be used first in a sequence of tests. The tests were also performed both with and without first creating local accounts at the RPs. For each test sequence, we recorded all information $I_{u(\alpha \to \gamma)}$ (of class B, P, C or F) that a user u agrees that the RP γ can import from IDP α, all information $I_{u(\gamma \to \alpha)}$ that user u agrees that the RP can post on the IDP (through actions (A)), all information $I_{u(u \to \gamma)}$ that the user manually inserts into its local profile, and the information $I_{u(p)}$ which ends up in the user profile.

4.1   Information Collision

When looking closer at the overlap between the information shared by the IDPs (i.e., $I_{u(\alpha \to \gamma)}$ and $I_{u(\beta \to \gamma)}$) with the RP, we observe that contact lists (26 of 42) are the most common overlap. As Twitter does not explicitly list email address, profiles picture, and names in their agreements or bundles, the overlaps for these categories are limited to Facebook+Google scenarios: 14 out of 42 cases for email addresses, 10 of 42 for profile pictures, and 10 of 42 for names. Having said this, we did observe cases where the profile picture and name were imported from Twitter without asking (or being listed in the app-rights agreement), suggesting that these numbers only provide a lower bound of the potential information collisions.

As the shared information can be both conflicting and complementary, significant identity management complications can arise because of overlapping information. Yet, we have found little to suggest that the RPs provide users with identity/information management for these instances. In fact, even among the typically very small subset of information transferred to the user profile (Section 4.3) there often is an overlap. For example, regardless if there exists an initial local account or not, in 9 of 42 cases, at least some potentially conflicting information is imported to the user's RP profile from both IDPs.

4.2 Account Merging and Collisions

We next evaluate how well the RPs allow multiple accounts to be associated with a single user, and if the RPs allow multiple accounts to be merged. For merging to take place, the RP must allow the user to connect an IDP to an existing local account, or to connect a second IDP to an account that already have an IDP associated to it, such that both IDPs can be used to login to the RP.

Interestingly, we have found that both account merging and the information transferred between accounts often are highly dependent on the order in which accounts are added. Furthermore, in many cases the user is not able to merge accounts, or control if merging should take place. For example, out of the 42 (6x7) first-login cases when using a local account, only 10 cases resulted in optional merging and 11 in automatic merging. In 6 of the remaining cases, temporary accounts were created that did not have full functionality, in 7 cases the login failed altogether (typically due to collisions of email accounts between the original local account and that used at the IDP), and in the remaining cases a new account is created.

Similarly, out of the 2x42 (2x6x7) second-login cases with a second IDP, starting both with and without a local account, we observe few merging opportunities: 9 optional cases and 2 automatic cases, when there is no local account (12 and 10 cases when there is a local account). In total, a second IDP can be added (and merged) in 33 (11+22) of 84 cases.

Our results suggest that many RPs are not designing for multi-IDP scenarios, but that Facebook is doing the best job allowing for such relationships. The lack of multi-IDP support can have serious negative consequences as many of these IDPs are popular services with many users; increasing the chance that users have accounts with multiple IDPs. In the following, we take a closer look at information flow in the cases when two IDPs could be added.

4.3   Cross-IDP Information Leakage

Not only can information $I_{u(\alpha \rightarrow \gamma)}$ be shared from an IDP α to an RP γ, but in some cases the app-rights agreements with another IDP β may (intentionally or unintentionally) allow information to be moved from one IDP to another IDP (through the RP). This occurs when this agreement allows the RP γ to post some subset of this information to IDP β. Looking at the overlap $I_{u(\alpha \rightarrow \gamma)} \cap I_{u(\gamma \rightarrow \beta)}$ we observed multiple cases where such cross-IDP sharing is possible. For example, six RPs allow personal (P) and/or content (C) from Facebook to be posted on Twitter, and five RPs allow basic (B) information from Facebook or Google to be transferred. We have also observed two RPs that have general posting rights on Facebook that allow transfer from Google, and two RPs that allow Facebook to transfer data from Twitter (although in this case Twitter would only transfer profile picture and name to the RPs). While these results show that all IDPs can be potential information sources and publishers of leaked information, in general, we see that Facebook allows the richest cross-IDP leakage and Twitter is the most likely publisher of cross-IDP leaked information.

5   Related Work

The third-party authentication landscape has gone from a situation with many OpenID enabled accounts but very few RPs supporting login with an IDP [13] to a landscape dominated by OAuth and Web 2.0 services that share data between sites. Limited work has been done on characterizing this emerging landscape.

In this paper, we leverage our RP-IDP relationship identifications and manual collection methodology [15], previously used to characterize and compare the relative biases (geographic and service-based) that RPs have in their IDP selection relative to the biases in the third-party content delivery landscape. In contrast, this paper looks closer at the information sharing and privacy risks associated with the observed RP-IDP relationships.

Sun et al. [14] have shown that there are misconceptions about how SSO works and the information transfers using OAuth, which leads to many users avoiding SSO. However, it can perhaps be argued that the users' fear is partially justified, as it has been shown that users become increasingly susceptible to phishing attacks as they get used to being redirected between sites and providing their credentials [5].

Others have proposed recommendation systems to help users make informed choices about what data to allow on different IDPs [11] and frameworks that provide users added control over how third-party applications (TPAs) can access data from an online social network (OSN) [4,6]. Many of the insights in these works are directly applicable to ours, as TPAs play a similar role as our RPs and the OSN acts as IDP. Extending these frameworks to the general RP-IDP landscape, characterized here, provides interesting future work.

Many researchers have used the data available on the popular IDPs, sometimes generated with the help of RPs, to illustrate how data mining and other statistical methods can be used to determine potentially private information from public data (such as likes, twitter feeds, etc.) [3,10,18], or correlating user data from several websites to identify a user based on behavior [8]. This type of cross correlations is, of course, even easier if RPs and IDPs are linked. We see these examples as motivation for looking more closely into the increased cross-site sharing and potential information leakage associated with the RP-IDP relationships. Cross-site leakage and the associated privacy risks have also been studied in the context of ad services and trackers [9].

Birrell and Schneider [2] present a privacy-driven taxonomy of the design choices in the third-party identity management landscape. Protocol related security problems that enable identity theft and blackmailing [17], and economic factors [5] have also been discussed in the literature.

6 Discussion and Conclusions

This paper characterizes the cross-site information sharing and privacy risks in the third-party identity management landscape. We show that OAuth is the dominant protocol, and OpenID is decreasing in usage. Not only is OAuth used by the most popular IDPs (e.g., Facebook, QQ, and Twitter) but it also enables sharing of much richer information with RPs.

We also observe high concentration in usage of a few popular IDPs, and that some IDPs are more frequently used in combination with others. The skew towards a few popular IDPs, which often allow RPs to act on behalf of the users, has privacy implications for the end users, regardless of whether the users choose to create an account with the RP or not. For example, a user with a compromised IDP account could easily be impersonated across all the RPs using a particular IDP, even if the user did not originally have an account with these RPs.

We then carefully classify and analyze the app-rights agreements of the most popular websites. Our classification of RP-IDP relationships is based on both the information that the RPs are allowed to import (e.g., basic, personal, generated content, or friend data) from the IDP, and if the RP is allowed to perform actions (e.g., create, update, or delete information) on behalf of the user on the IDP. Although we observe significant differences in the information leakage risks seen both across classes of RPs and across popular IDPs, we find multiple high-risk sites (e.g., RPs that both import private information and that are authorized to perform actions) among the top-200 websites for all website classes except Ads/CDN services. Such sites can easily become a source of information leakage.

Our multi-account case studies show that users are often asked to allow the RP to import more information from the IDP than is needed for the local user profile, and to enter redundant information. Furthermore, we find significant incompatibilities and inconsistencies in scenarios involving multiple IDPs. Often it is not possible to merge accounts with different IDPs, and the user can be stuck with a wide range of undesirable account situations. Clearly, many RPs are not designed to simply and securely use multiple IDPs.

We believe that more focus must be placed on multi-IDP scenarios when defining future policies for OpenID Connect (based on OAuth2), for example.

Ideally, the user should remain in control of exactly what is being shared between the involved parties, and which information should be used and shared with each IDP. Similar to how Google+ (and to some extent Facebook) allows users to define circles, we believe that carefully designed protocols with added user control can be defined in this context. Already today, these IDPs allow some degree of personalization in their RP-IDP permission agreements, so generalizing this concept to the context of multiple IDPs could be one possible approach. Future work will include the definition and evaluation of such policies.

References

1. Armando, A., Carbone, R., Compagna, L., Cuellar, J., Pellegrino, G., Sorniotti, A.: From multiple credentials to browser-based single sign-on: are we more secure? In: Camenisch, J., Fischer-Hübner, S., Murayama, Y., Portmann, A., Rieder, C. (eds.) SEC 2011. IFIP AICT, vol. 354, pp. 68–79. Springer, Heidelberg (2011)
2. Birrell, E., Schneider, F.B.: Federated identity management systems: A privacy-based characterization. IEEE Security & Privacy 11(5), 36–48 (2013)
3. Chaabane, A., Acs, G., Kaafar, M.A.: You are what you like! information leakage through users' interests. In: Proc. NDSS (2012)
4. Cheng, Y., Park, J., Sandhu, R.: Preserving user privacy from third-party applications in online social networks. In: Proc. WWW, May 2013
5. Dhamija, R., Dusseault, L.: The seven flaws of identity management: Usability and security challenges. IEEE Security & Privacy 6(2), 24–29 (2008)
6. Felt, A., Evans, D.: Privacy protection for social networking APIs. In: Proc. W2SP, May 2008
7. Gill, P., Arlitt, M., Carlsson, N., Mahanti, A., Williamson, C.: Characterizing organizational use of web-based services: Methodology, challenges, observations, and insights. ACM Trans. on the Web 5(4), 19:1–19:23 (2011)
8. Goga, O., Lei, H., Parthasarathi, S.H.K., Friedland, G., Sommer, R., Teixeira, R.: Exploiting innocuous activity for correlating users across sites. In: Proc. WWW, May 2013
9. Malandrino, D., Petta, A., Scarano, V., Serra, L., Spinelli, R., Krishnamurthy, B.: Privacy awareness about information leakage: Who knows what about me? In: Proc. ACM WPES (2013)
10. Pennacchiotti, M., Popescu, A.-M.: Democrats, republicans and starbucks afficionados: user classification in twitter. In: Proc. ACM SIGKDD (2011)
11. Shehab, M., Marouf, S., Hudel, C.: Roauth: recommendation based open authorization. In: Proc. SOUPS, July 2011
12. Sun, S.-T., Beznosov, K.: The devil is in the (implementation) details: an empirical analysis of oauth sso systems. In: Proc. ACM CCS (2012)
13. Sun, S.-T., Boshmaf, Y., Hawkey, K., Beznosov, K.: A billion keys, but few locks: the crisis of web single sign-on. In: Proc. NSPW (2010)
14. Sun, S.T., Pospisil, E., Muslukhov, I., Dindar, N., Hawkey, K., Beznosov, K.: Investigating user's perspective of web single sign-on: Conceptual gaps, alternative design and acceptance model. ACM Trans. on Internet Technology 13(1), 2:1–2:35 (2013)

15. Vapen, A., Carlsson, N., Mahanti, A., Shahmehri, N.: Third-party identity management usage on the Web. In: Faloutsos, M., Kuzmanovic, A. (eds.) PAM 2014. LNCS, vol. 8362, pp. 151–162. Springer, Heidelberg (2014)
16. Vapen, A., Carlsson, N., Mahanti, A., Shahmehri, N.: Information sharing and user privacy in the third-party identity management landscape. In: Proc. ACM CODASPY (2015)
17. Wang, R., Chen, S., Wang, X.: Signing me onto your accounts through facebook and google: a traffic-guided security study of commercially deployed single-sign-on web services. In: Proc. IEEE Symposium on S&P, May 2012
18. Zafarani, R., Liu, H.: Connecting users across social media sites: A behavioral-modeling approach. In: Proc. ACM SIGKDD (2013)

An Iterative Algorithm for Reputation Aggregation in Multi-dimensional and Multinomial Rating Systems

Mohsen Rezvani[1]($\boxtimes$), Mohammad Allahbakhsh[2], Lorenzo Vigentini[1], Aleksandar Ignjatovic[1], and Sanjay Jha[1]

[1] University of New South Wales, Sydney, Australia
{mrezvani,ignjat,sanjay}@cse.unsw.edu.au, l.vigentini@unsw.edu.au
[2] University of Zabol, Zabol, Iran
allahbakhsh@uoz.ac.ir

Abstract. Online rating systems are widely accepted as a means for quality assessment on the web, and users increasingly rely on these systems when deciding to purchase an item online. This fact motivates people to manipulate rating systems by posting unfair rating scores for fame or profit. Therefore, both providing useful realistic rating scores as well as detecting unfair behaviours are of very high importance. Existing solutions are mostly majority based, also employing temporal analysis and clustering techniques. However, they are still vulnerable to unfair ratings. They also ignore distance between options, provenance of information and different dimensions of cast rating scores while computing aggregate rating scores and trustworthiness of raters. In this paper, we propose a robust iterative algorithm which leverages the information in the profile of raters, provenance of information and a prorating function for the distance between options to build more robust and informative rating scores for items as well as trustworthiness of raters. We have implemented and tested our rating method using both simulated data as well as three real world datasets. Our tests demonstrate that our model calculates realistic rating scores even in the presence of massive unfair ratings and outperforms well-known ranking algorithms.

Keywords: Online rating · Voting · Trust · Provenance · Multi-dimensional

1 Introduction

Nowadays, millions of people generate content or advertise products online. It is very unlikely for a customer to have a personal experience with a product or to know how trustworthiness a seller might be. One of the widely used methods to overcome this problem is to rely on the feedback received from the other users who have had a direct experience with a product or have already bought it. *Online rating systems* collect feedback from users of an online community and,

© IFIP International Federation for Information Processing 2015
H. Federrath and D. Gollmann (Eds.): SEC 2015, IFIP AICT 455, pp. 189–203, 2015.
DOI: 10.1007/978-3-319-18467-8_13

based on the feedback, assign a quality score to every product or trustworthiness of a user in the community. The Amazon[1] online market and the eBay[2] are some of the well-known outlets which incorporate an online rating systems.

One of the big issues with the online rating systems is the credibility of the quality ranks that they produce. For various reasons, users might have interest to post unfair feedback, either individually or as an organised, colluding group. If such unfair feedback is taken into account when ranks are computed, the resulting quality ranks are no longer reliable. Many pieces of evidence show that the online rating systems are widely subject to such unfair ratings [10,16]. Some studies propose methods for dealing with this problem which rely on clustering techniques to analyze the behaviour of raters and find the abnormal ones [8,11]. The main problem with such solutions is that the clustering techniques are generally based on solutions to NP-Hard graph problems; thus their performance is severely degraded when the size of an online systems is too large. The other type of solutions to such problems is based on iterative filtering (IF) techniques [4,6,20]. These techniques, while performing better than the simple aggregation techniques, are still vulnerable to sophisticated collusion attacks [13].

We have recently proposed an algorithm [1], *Rating Through Voting (RTV)*, which outperforms the previous IF algorithms in terms of detection and mitigation of unfair behaviour. Although RTV shows a promising robustness against unfair ratings, it still has limitations that require more investigations.

The first limitation is that in RTV the order of the choices is not important and the distance between the choices is not defined. For example, when a rater chooses the Nominee$_1$ as the most popular candidate and another rater selects the Nominee$_2$, it does not make sense to talk about the distance between these two options. However, in a movie rating system, if one of the raters chooses 4 star rating of a movie and another chooses a 3 star rating then a distance between there ratings is well defined and might be important for rating methods. The distance between choices is not taken into account in the RTV algorithm.

Moreover, in a rating system, raters may assess quality of a product, a service or a person from different aspects. For instance, in eBay's detailed seller rating system, buyers express their opinion on the quality of a transaction form four different aspects[3]. For a reputation to be more credible, it is necessary that the reputation system aggregates the scores received for all different aspects to build the final reputation score. This is another limitation of the RTV algorithms.

Finally, the provenance of a rating score is another piece of information that is ignored in the RTV algorithm. The contextual information around a cast rating score can give the system useful hints to adjust its weight. The profile of the rater, the time a feedback has been cast, etc., are examples of contextual meta data that can be taken into account in the computation of the ranks.

---

[1] http://www.amazon.com/

[2] http://www.ebay.com/

[3] http://www.ebay.com/gds/

In this paper we propose a novel reputation system which is based on the RTV algorithm[4]. The proposed method takes into account the distance between options to fairly propagate credibility among options. We also, consider the different dimensions of the cast rating scores and utilize them in order to build more realistic and credible reputation aggregation. Finally, our proposed method takes advantage from the provenance of the cast feedback when calculating reputation and rating scores and consequently computes more informative and reliable scores. We have assessed the effectiveness of our approach using both synthetic and three real-world datasets. The evaluation results show superiority of our method over three well-known algorithms in the area, including RTV.

The rest of this paper is organized as follows. Section 2 formulates the problem and specifies the assumptions. Section 3 presents our novel reputation system. Section 4 describes our experimental results. Section 5 presents the related work. Finally, the paper is concluded in Section 6.

2 Preliminaries

2.1 Basic Concepts and Notation

Assume that in an online rating system a set of n users cast ratings for m items. Each user rates several items (but not necessarily all) and each item might be rated from K different perspectives. We represent the set of ratings by a three dimensional array $A_{n \times m \times K}$ in which $A_{i,j,k}$ ($1 \le i \le n, 1 \le j \le m, 1 \le k \le K$) is the rating cast by user i on the item j from the kth perspective. We suppose that rating scores are selected from a discrete set of numbers each of which represent a quality level, for example 1-star to 5-stars.

2.2 Rating Through Voting

The RTV algorithm [1] reduces the problem of rating to a voting task. In the algorithm, when a rater chooses a quality level, say 4-stars, to represent quality of a product, one can say that the rater believes that 4-stars represents the quality of the product better than the other options; thus, in a sense, he has voted for it out of the list of 1-star to 5-stars options.

RTV assigns a credibility degree to each quality level in order to show how credible this quality level is for representing the real quality of the item. Thereafter, it aggregates the credibility of all quality levels a users has voted for to build the users' trustworthiness. Assume that for each item l, there is a list of options $\Lambda_l = \{I_1^l, \ldots, I_{n_l}^l\}$ and each user can choose maximum one option for each item. We define the credibility degree of a quality level I_i on list Λ_l, denoted by ρ_{li} as follow:

$$\rho_{li} = \frac{\sum_{r:r \to li} (T_r)^{\alpha}}{\sqrt{\sum_{1 \le j \le n_l} \left(\sum_{r:r \to lj} (T_r)^{\alpha} \right)^2}} \tag{1}$$

---

[4] An extended version of this paper has been published as a technical report in [12].

where $r \to li$ denotes that user r has chosen option I_i^l from list Λ_l. $\alpha \geq 1$ is a parameter which can be used to tune the algorithm for a particular task. T_r is the trustworthiness of user r which is obtained as:

$$T_r = \sum_{l,i\,:\,r \to li} \rho_{li} \tag{2}$$

Equations (1) and (2) show that there is an interdependency between the credibility and trustworthiness. RTV leverages such interdependency through an iterative procedure. Given the credibility degrees obtained by such iterative algorithm, the aggregate rating score of item l, denoted as $R(\pi_l)$, is obtained as:

$$R(\pi_l) = \sum_{1 \leq i \leq n_l} \frac{i \times \rho_{li}^p}{\sum_{1 \leq j \leq n_l} \rho_{lj}^p} \tag{3}$$

where $p \geq 1$ is a parameter for controlling the averaging affect.

3   Reputation Aggregation System

In this section, we extend RTV by taking into account the rating provenance as well as credibility propagation in a multi-dimensional rating system.

3.1   Distance Between Nominal Values

In most of social rating systems, such as eBay 5-star feedback system, there is a numerical distance between the existing options. In order to take into account such distance in our reputation propagation method, we formulate the distance using a decaying function.

One can use any decreasing function, symmetric around the origin, i.e., such that $d(x) = d(-x)$. Here we define the distance of two options i and j as $d(i,j) = q^{|i-j|}$, where q is the *base distance*, $0 < q < 1$ and is defined as the distance value between two consecutive options. We assume that there is a limited range for the ratings in the rating system. The main condition is that the sum of all distances must be equal to a constant value, we call it *propagation parameter* and is denoted as b. The propagation parameter is a positive value which controls the proportion of credibility propagation among options. By taking into account this condition, we have

$$q + q^2 + \cdots + q^{n_l-j} + q + q^2 + \cdots + q^{j-1} = b \iff$$

$$q \left(\frac{1 - q^{n_l-j}}{1 - q} \right) + q \left(\frac{1 - q^{j-1}}{1 - q} \right) = b \iff$$

$$2 - q^{j-1} - q^{n_l-j} = b \frac{1 - q}{q} \tag{4}$$

Note that since $0 < q < 1$, Eq. (4) has only one real solution for each positive value of b.

3.2   Provenance-Aware Credibility Propagation

Given the distance function $d(i,j)$ for computing the numerical distance between options i and j, we update our computation equations for the credibility degree as well as users' trustworthiness. Firstly, we define β_{li} as the non-normalized credibility degree of quality level li. Considering the idea of credibility propagation among the options, the credibility degree of a quality level is obtained not only from the raters who have chosen such particular level, but also from all raters who rated such item with proportion to the distance of their choices from such level. In other words, we define the credibility degree for a quality level in an item as amount of credibility which such level can obtain from all raters who rated such an item. Therefore, we reformulate the Eq. (1) for computing the non-normalized credibility degree of quality level li as follows:

$$\beta_{li} = \sum_{j,r\,:\,r \to lj} (T_r)^{\alpha} d(i,j) \tag{5}$$

As we mentioned some rating systems provide contextual information about the ratings, we call it *rating provenance*. It contains attributes such as watching duration in a movie ratings system and educational level of raters in a student feedback system, which provides more information about either the raters or the environment of ratings. Since the rating provenance provides informative data about the quality of ratings, a reputation system needs to take into account these data in the its computations. In this paper, we propose a provenance model based on the attributes provided by a student feedback system which includes two contextual attributes: staff/non-staff and watching behaviour of students. We note that the approach can be easily adapted for other contextual attributes. This provenance model is based on the approach from [17], originally proposed in the context of participatory sensing.

The main idea of our provenance model is to define a weight function for considering the contextual attributes provided by the rating system. To this end, we define a weight function for each attribute and then we aggregate all the weights from these functions using the simple product of the weights to obtain the provenance weight. Such provenance weight is used to assess the credibility level as well as users' trustworthiness.

In the student feedback system, users are asked to rate the movies in an online course. In this system, each user has an status which indicates whether such user is staff or non-staff. Moreover, the system provides for each rating the time spent for watching the movie. We utilize both the staff status and watching duration as two contextual attributes to model the rating provenance. To this end, we consider a somewhat higher credibility for the staff raters. Thus, we define the *staff weight*, denoted as w_s, which is set $w_s = 0.98$ for staff raters and $w_s = 0.95$ for non-staff raters. Moreover, we take into account the watching time due to the fact that a student who spends enough time to watch a movie can provide higher quality ratings. We denote the watching time provided for each rating and the original duration of its corresponding movie as T_r and T_v, respectively. Thus, we compute the gap between them by $|\min\{T_r, T_v\} - T_v|$. Now, we define the *watching time weight*, denoted as w_t:

$$w_t = e^{-|\min\{T_r, T_v\} - T_v| \times \beta} \tag{6}$$

where $0 \leq \beta \leq 1$ is the *duration sensitivity* parameter which controls the watching time weight. Note that Eq. (6) makes w_t equal to 1 when the time gap between the watching and duration is 0 and w_t approaches 0 when such gap is large. Given both staff and watching time weights, we define *provenance weight*, denoted as w_p through aggregating these two weights as:

$$w_p = w_s \times w_t \tag{7}$$

Note that in general the provenance weight can be define as the product of the weight values for all contextual attributes, where such weights are in the range of [0,1]. Given the provenance weight, we re-write Eq. (5) as follows:

$$\beta_{li} = \sum_{j,r \, : \, r \rightarrow lj} (T_r)^\alpha \times d(i,j) \times w_p \tag{8}$$

For normalizing the credibility degree, we use the same method used in our previous approach which is:

$$\rho_{li} = \frac{\beta_{li}}{\sqrt{\sum_{1 \leq j \leq n_l} (\beta_{lj})^2}} \tag{9}$$

The trustworthiness of a user is the weighted sum of all credibility degrees from all quality levels of items which has been rated by such user. The weight here is the distance between the chosen level by such user and the credible level. Thus, we have

$$T_r = \sum_{l,i \, : \, r \rightarrow li} \sum_{1 \leq j \leq n_l} \rho_{li} \times d(i,j) \times w_p \tag{10}$$

Note that we formulated the uncertainty in rating systems through both credibility propagation among options and rating provenance. Thus, we considered them in computing both credibility degrees and users' trustworthiness.

3.3 Iterative Vote Aggregation

Given equations (8), (9) and (10), we have interdependent definitions for credibility degree and trustworthiness. Clearly, the credibility degree of a quality level in for item depends on the trustworthiness of users who rated such item. on the other hand, the trustworthiness of a user depends on the credibility of the quality levels of the items which have been rated by such user. Thus, we propose an iterative algorithm to compute both the credibility degrees and trust scores simultaneously in a single recursive procedure. We denote the non-normalized credibility, normalized credibility and trustworthiness at iteration l as $\beta_{li}^{(l)}$, $\rho_{li}^{(l)}$

and $T_r^{(l)}$, respectively which are computed from the values obtained in the previous iteration of the algorithm.

Algorithm 1 shows our iterative process for computing the credibility and trustworthiness values. One can see that the algorithm starts with identical trust scores for all users, $T_r^{(0)} = 1$. In each iteration, it first compute the non-normalized credibility degree β_{li}. After obtaining the normalized credibility degree ρ_{li} for all options, the trustworthiness for all users are updated. The iteration will stop when there is no considerable changes for the credibility degrees.

Algorithm 1. Iterative algorithm to compute the credibility and trustworthiness.

1: **procedure** CREDTRUSTCOMPUTATION(A, b, α, n_l)
2:     Compute q using (4)
3:     $d(i, j) \leftarrow q^{|i-j|}$ for each $1 \leq i, j \leq n_l$
4:     $T_r^{(0)} \leftarrow 1$
5:     $l \leftarrow 0$
6:     **repeat**
7:         Compute β_{li} using (5) for each level i and item l
8:         Compute ρ_{li} using (9) for each level i and item l
9:         Compute T_r using (10) for each each use r
10:         $l \leftarrow l + 1$
11:     **until** credibilities have converged
12:     **Return** ρ and T
13: **end procedure**

3.4   Multi-dimensional Reputation

As we discussed, a reputation system needs to consider the correlation among raters' perceptions among multiple categories. The eBay's feedback system and student course evaluation in educational systems are two examples of rating systems with multiple categories. A traditional approach is to apply the computations over the ratings of each category, separately. However, the correlation among ratings in various categories can help a reputation system to accurately assess the quality of ratings [15].

In Eq. (3) we proposed a aggregation method for single category rating system. In this method, the final reputation of an item is obtained from an aggregate of the credibility values of different options for such item. In order to extend this method to multi-dimensional rating systems, we first perform Algorithm 1 over each category to obtain K weights for each user (Note that we have K dimensions in the ratings). Then, we aggregate the weights using simple averaging to obtain the final users' trustworthiness. Thereafter, we employ a weighted averaging method to compute the final reputation of item l in category k, as follows

$$R(\pi_{lk}) = \frac{\sum_{i,r\,:\,r\to lik} i \times (\hat{T}_r)^p}{\sum_{i,r\,:\,r\to lik} (\hat{T}_r)^p} \qquad (11)$$

where $r \rightarrow lik$ denotes that user r chose option I_i^l from list Λ_l for category k. $\hat{T}_r$ is the average of weights of user r obtained by applying Algorithm 1 over the ratings of different categories. Moreover, constant $p \geq 1$ is a parameter for controlling the averaging affect.

4 Experiments

In this section, we detail the steps taken to evaluate the robustness and effectiveness of our approach in the presence of faults and unfair rating attacks.

4.1 Experimental Environment

Although there are a number of real world datasets for evaluating reputation systems such as MovieLens[5] and HetRec 2011[6], none of them provides a clear ground truth. Thus, we conduct our experiments by both real-world datasets and generating synthetic datasets.

We generate the synthetic datasets by using statistical parameters of the MovieLens 100k dataset, as shown in Table 1. The quality of each movie has been uniformly randomly selected from the range [1,5]. In addition, we consider a zero mean Gaussian noise for ratings of each user with different variance values for the users. All ratings are also rounded to be discrete values in the range of [1,5]. We conducted parameter analysis experiments to find the values of parameters α, p and b. The results of these experiments are reported in [12] and consequently we choose $\alpha = 2$, $p = 2$ and $b = 0.5$ for our subsequent experiments.

Table 1. MovieLens 100k dataset statistics

Parameter	MovieLens 100k
Ratings	100,000
Users	943
Movies	1682
# of votes per user	Beta($\alpha = 1.32, \beta = 19.50$)

In all experiments, we compare our approach against three other IF techniques proposed for reputation systems. Table 2 shows a summary of discriminant functions for these IF methods. We also call our new method *PrRTV* and the previous one *BasicRTV*, briefly presented in Section 2.2.

4.2 Robustness Against False Ratings

In order to evaluate robustness of our algorithm against false ratings, we conduct experiments based on two types of malicious behaviour proposed in [4] over

---

[5] http://grouplens.org/datasets/movielens/
[6] http://grouplens.org/datasets/hetrec-2011/

Table 2. Summary of different IF algorithms

Name	Discriminant Function
dKVD-Affine [4]	$w_i^{l+1} = 1 - k\frac{1}{T} \left\| \mathbf{x}_i - \mathbf{r}^{l+1} \right\|_2^2$
Zhou [20]	$w_i^{l+1} = \frac{1}{T} \sum_{i=1}^{T} \left(\frac{x_i^t - \bar{\mathbf{x}}^t}{\sigma_{x_i}} \right) \left(\frac{r^t - \bar{\mathbf{r}}}{\sigma_r} \right)$
Laureti [6]	$w_i^{l+1} = \left(\frac{1}{T} \left\| \mathbf{x}_i - \mathbf{r}^{l+1} \right\|_2^2 \right)^{-\frac{1}{2}}$

the MovieLens dataset: *Random Ratings*, and a *Promoting Attack*. For random ratings, we modify the rates of 20% of the users within the original MovieLens dataset by injecting uniformly random rates in the range of [1,5] for those users.

In slandering and promoting attacks, one or more users falsely produce negative and positive ratings, respectively, about one or more items [2]. The attacks can be conducted by either an individual or a coalition of attackers. We evaluate our approach against a promotion attack by considering 20% of the users as the malicious users involved in the attack. In this attack, malicious users always rate 1 except for their preferred movie, which they rate 5.

Let r and $\tilde{r}$ be the reputation vectors before and after injecting false ratings in each scenario (random ratings and promoting attack), respectively. In the proposed reputation system, the vectors are the results of Eq. (11). Table 3 reports the 1-norm difference between these two vectors, $\|r - \tilde{r}\|_1 = \sum_{j=1}^{m} |r_j - \tilde{r}_j|$ for our algorithm along with other IF algorithms. Clearly, all of the IF algorithms are more robust than *Average*. In addition, the *PrRTV* algorithm provides higher accuracy than other methods for both false rating scenarios. The results can be explained by the fact that the proposed algorithm effectively filters out the contribution of the malicious users.

Table 3. 1-norm absolute error between reputations by injecting false ratings

	$\|r - \tilde{r}\|_1$				
	Average	dKVD-Affine	Laureti	BasicRTV	PrRTV
Random Ratings	205.32	152.40	171.55	152.75	151.54
Promoting Attack	579.65	378.29	377.72	894.25	368.81

4.3 Rating Resolutions and Users Variances

In this section, we investigate the accuracy of *PrRTV* over the low resolution ratings and different variance scales using synthetic datasets. The ratings scale is in the range of $[1, R]$, where R is an integer number and $R \geq 2$. Also, the standard deviation σ_i for user i is randomly selected by a uniform distribution $U[0; \sigma_{max}]$, where σ_{max} is a real value in the range of $[0, R-1]$. We also evaluate a normalized RMS error, $RMSE/(R-1)$ (see [12] for RMS Error) for each experiment. In this section, we investigate the accuracy of our reputation system against various values for both rating resolution R and variance scale σ_{max}.

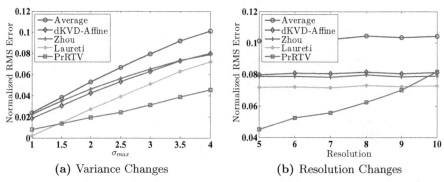

(a) Variance Changes   (b) Resolution Changes

Fig. 1. Accuracy with different variances and resolutions

For the first experiment, we set $R = 5$ and vary the value of σ_{max} in the range of $[1, 4]$. By choosing such a range at the worst case, a highest noisy user with $\sigma_i = \sigma_{max} = 4$ could potentially report a very low reputation for an item with a real reputation of 5, and vice versa. Fig. 1a shows the accuracy of the *PrRTV* algorithm along with the accuracy of the other IF algorithms for this experiment. We observe that *PrRTV* is the least sensitive to the increasing error level, maintaining the lowest normalized RMS error.

In order to investigate the effect of changing the ratings' resolution, we set $\sigma_{max} = R - 1$ and vary the value of R in the range of $[5, 10]$, so that the maximum possible users' errors cover the ratings' scale. Fig. 1b shows the accuracy of the algorithms for this experiment. As we can see, although the accuracy of the *PrRTV* algorithm is higher than the accuracy of other IF algorithms, the algorithm provides more sensitivity for the high resolution values. In other words, the accuracy of our reputation system significantly drops as the ratings resolution increases. The reason of this behaviour is that Eq. (11) for computing the final rating scores gives more credibility to the options with higher numerical values, particularly when there is a large distance between lowest and highest options in the ratings scales. We plan to extend our reputation aggregation method to provide more robustness for high resolution rating systems.

4.4   Accuracy Over HetRec 2011 MovieLens Dataset

In this section, we evaluate the performance of our reputation system based on the accuracy of the ranked movies in the HetRec 2011 MovieLens dataset. This dataset links the movies in the MovieLens dataset with their corresponding web pages at Internet Movie Database (IMDb)[7] and Rotten Tomatoes movie critics systems[8]. Thus, we use the top critics ratings from Rotten Tomatoes as the domain experts for evaluating the accuracy of our approach.

There are 10,109 movies in the HetRec 2011 MovieLens dataset rated by users. The dataset also includes the average ratings of the top and all critics of

---

[7] http://www.imdb.com/

[8] http://www.rottentomatoes.com/critics/

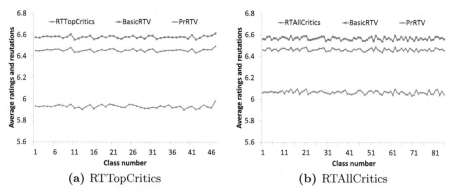

(a) RTTopCritics   **(b)** RTAllCritics

Fig. 2. Average reputations obtained by our algorithms and RTCritics

Rotten Tomatoes for 4645 and 8404 movies, respectively. We consider such average ratings as two ground truth to evaluate the accuracy of our approach and we call them *RTTopCritics* and *RTAllCritics*, respectively. In order to clearly compare the results of our reputation system with those provided by RTTopCritics and RTAllCritics, we first classify the movies by randomly assigning every 100 movies in a class. We then compute two average values for each class: the average of reputation values given by our algorithm and the average of rating given by RTTopCritics and RTAllCritics. Now, we use such average values to compare the reputations given by our algorithm with the ratings of RTTopCritics and RTAllCritics. Note that this method is employed only for clarifying this comparison over such large number of movies.

Fig. 2a and 2b illustrate the comparison between the results of our algorithm with the ratings provided by RTTopCritics and RTAllCritics, respectively. The results confirm that the reputation values given by our algorithm is very close to the experts opinions given by RTCritics. Moreover, comparing the results of *PrRTV* with *BasicRTV* shows that the *PrRTV* algorithm provide a better accuracy than the *BasicRTV* algorithm as its aggregate ratings are more closer to the ratings provided by Rotten Tomatoes critics. As one can see, our algorithm ranks the movies slightly higher than RTCritics ratings for all classes. This can be explained by the fact that the ratings of our algorithm are based on the scores provided by public users through the MovieLens web site. However, both RTTopCritics and RTAllCritics ratings provided by Rotten Tomatoes critics who tend to rank the movies more critically.

4.5   Accuracy Over Student Feedback Dataset

In this section, we evaluate the effectiveness of our reputation system using a privately accessed student feedback dataset provided by the Learning and Teaching Unit at UNSW, called *CATEI*. The dataset consists of 17,854 ratings provided by 3,910 students (221 staffs and 3,690 non-staffs) for 20 movies in an online course presented in UNSW. In the CATEI dataset, students were asked to

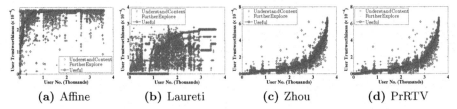

(a) Affine   (b) Laureti   (c) Zhou   (d) PrRTV

Fig. 3. Users' weights obtained by the IF algorithms over three categories

Table 4. Correlation among users' weights over three categories

	dKVD-Affine	Laureti	Zhou	PrRTV
U and UC	0.52	0.42	0.58	0.96
U and FE	0.61	0.40	0.61	0.97
UC and FE	0.45	0.50	0.63	0.97

rate the movies in the range of [1-5] and for three different categories: *Useful* (U), *UnderstandContent* (UC), *FurtherExplore* (FE). Moreover, the dataset includes the starting and ending times of the watching of the movie for each rating which allow us to compute the watching duration for each rating. We also set the duration sensitivity, $\beta = 0.2$ for computing the watching time weight of each rating. As we mentioned in Section 3.2, the rating provenance is obtained as the product of staff weight and watching weigh for each rating.

In the first part of the experiments over the CATEI dataset, we apply the IF algorithms over each rating category separately and then investigate the correlation between the obtained users' weights. We expected to observe high correlation among the weights on different categories. We first obtained all the users' weights, then sorted them in an increasing order based on the *Useful* category. Fig. 3 compares the users' weights among three categories obtained by each IF algorithm. Moreover, Table 4 reports the Pearson correlation coefficient among such weight values. One can see in the results that our reputation system provides the highest correlation among the weights for various categories. This can validate the effectiveness of our approach over the CATEI dataset.

In Section 3.4, we proposed the idea of aggregation of users' weights obtained for each category to obtain the final reputation values over multi-dimensional rating datasets. A traditional approach is to separately apply the reputation system over each dimension. In order to investigate the effectiveness of the proposed approach, we evaluate the correlation among the reputation values for various categories over the CATEI dataset for these two methods. To this end, we first perform the IF algorithms over each category and compute the correlation among the obtained reputation vectors for each category. After that, we perform the proposed method in Section 3.4, and compute the correlation among the new reputation vectors. Table 5 reports the percentage of increasing such correlation among categories by performing our multi-dimensional reputation method. One can see that our approach improved the average correlation value for all four algorithms. The results also show a significant improvement in the *Zhou* algorithm. This can be explained by some negative correlations obtained by the algorithm using the traditional reputation computation method.

Table 5. Percentage of increasing correlation among reputations by aggregating the weights obtained through each category

	dKVD-Affine	Laureti	Zhou	PrRTV
U and UC	0.70	2.79	2.80	13.90
U and FE	0.03	8.54	72.12	-0.65
UC and FE	-0.26	0.12	0.09	-0.73
Average	**0.16**	**3.81**	**25.00**	**4.17**

5   Related Work

According to several research evidences, as the reliance of the users of online stores on the rating systems to decide on purchasing a product constantly increases, more efforts are put in building up fake rating or reputation scores in order to gain more unfair income [16]. To solve this problem, Mukherjee et al., [11] proposed a model for spotting fake review groups in online rating systems. The model analyzes feedbacks cast on products in Amazon online market to find collusion groups. In a more general setup, detection of unfair ratings has been studied in P2P and reputation management systems; good surveys can be found in [14]. EigenTrust [3] is a well known algorithm as a robust trust computation system. However, Lian et al. [7] demonstrate that it is not robust against collusion. Another series of works [9,18,19] use a set of signals and alarms to point to a suspicious behavior. The most famous ranking algorithm of all, the PageRank algorithm [5] was also devised to prevent collusive groups from obtaining undeserved ranks for webpages.

Several papers have proposed IF algorithms for reputation systems [4,6,20]. While such IF algorithms provide promising performance for filtering faults and simple cheating attacks, we recently showed that they are vulnerable against sophisticated attacks [13]. In this paper, we compared the robustness of our approach with some of the existing IF methods.

The method we propose in this paper is different from the existing related work, mainly from its ancestor RTV, from three various aspects. First, the distance between the options is taken into account in this work. Second, reputation scores are in fact multi dimensional. Finally, the provenance of rating scores are considered while giving credit and weight to them. To the best of our knowledge, no existing work considers all of these issues in reputation systems.

6 Conclusions

In this paper, we proposed a novel reputation system which leverages the distance between the quality levels, provenance of cast rating scores and multidimensional reputation scores to address the problem of robust reputation aggregation. The experiments conducted on both synthetic and real-world data show the superiority of our model over three well-known iterative filtering algorithms. Since the proposed framework has shown a promising behaviour, we plan to extend the algorithm to propose a distributed reputation system.

References

1. Allahbakhsh, M., Ignjatovic, A.: An iterative method for calculating robust rating scores. IEEE Transactions on Parallel and Distributed Systems **26**(2), 340–350 (2015)
2. Hoffman, K., Zage, D., Nita-Rotaru, C.: A survey of attack and defense techniques for reputation systems. ACM Comput. Surv. **42**(1), 1:1–1:31 (2009)
3. Kamvar, S.D., Schlosser, M.T., Garcia-Molina, H.: The eigentrust algorithm for reputation management in P2P networks. In: Proceedings of the 12th International Conference on World Wide Web, pp. 640–651 (2003)
4. de Kerchove, C., Van Dooren, P.: Iterative filtering in reputation systems. SIAM J. Matrix Anal. Appl. **31**(4), 1812–1834 (2010)
5. Langville, A.N., Meyer, C.D.: Google's PageRank and Beyond: The Science of Search Engine Rankings. Princeton University Press, February 2012
6. Laureti, P., Moret, L., Zhang, Y.C., Yu, Y.K.: Information filtering via Iterative Refinement. EPL (Europhysics Letters) **75**, 1006–1012 (2006)
7. Lian, Q., Zhang, Z., Yang, M., Zhao, B.Y., Dai, Y., Li, X.: An empirical study of collusion behavior in the maze P2P file-sharing system. In: Proceedings of the 27th IEEE International Conference on Distributed Computing Systems. ICDCS 2007, pp. 56–56 (2007)
8. Lim, E.P., Nguyen, V.A., Jindal, N., Liu, B., Lauw, H.W.: Detecting product review spammers using rating behaviors. In: Proceedings of the 19th ACM International Conference on Information and Knowledge Management, pp. 939–948. ACM (2010)
9. Liu, Y., Yang, Y., Sun, Y.: Detection of collusion behaviors in online reputation systems. In: 2008 42nd Asilomar Conference on Signals, Systems and Computers, pp. 1368–1372. IEEE (2008)
10. Morgan, J., Brown, J.: Reputation in online auctions: The market for trust. California Management Review **49**(1), 61–81 (2006)
11. Mukherjee, A., Liu, B., Glance, N.: Spotting fake reviewer groups in consumer reviews. In: Proceedings of the 21st International Conference on World Wide Web. WWW 2012, pp. 191–200 (2012)
12. Rezvani, M., Allahbakhsh, M., Ignjatovic, A., Jha, S.: An iterative algorithm for reputation aggregation in multi-dimensional and multinomial rating systems. Tech. Rep. UNSW-CSE-TR-201502, January 2015
13. Rezvani, M., Ignjatovic, A., Bertino, E., Jha, S.: Secure data aggregation technique for wireless sensor networks in the presence of collusion attacks. IEEE Transactions on Dependable and Secure Computing **12**(1), 98–110 (2015)
14. Sun, Y.L., Liu, Y.: Security of online reputation systems: The evolution of attacks and defenses. IEEE Signal Process. Mag. **29**(2), 87–97 (2012)

15. Tang, J., Gao, H., Liu, H.: mTrust: Discerning multi-faceted trust in a connected world. In: Proceedings of the Fifth ACM International Conference on Web Search and Data Mining. WSDM 2012, pp. 93–102 (2012)
16. Wang, G., Wilson, C., Zhao, X., Zhu, Y., Mohanlal, M., Zheng, H., Zhao, B.Y.: Serf and turf: crowdturfing for fun and profit. In: Proceedings of the 21st International Conference on World Wide Web. WWW 2012, pp. 679–688 (2012)
17. Wang, X.O., Cheng, W., Mohapatra, P., Abdelzaher, T.F.: ARTSense: anonymous reputation and trust in participatory sensing. In: INFOCOM, pp. 2517–2525. IEEE (2013)
18. Yang, Y.F., Feng, Q.Y., Sun, Y., Dai, Y.F.: Dishonest behaviors in online rating systems: cyber competition, attack models, and attack generator. J. Comput. Sci. Technol. 24(5), 855–867 (2009)
19. Yang, Y., Feng, Q., Sun, Y.L., Dai, Y.: RepTrap: a novel attack on feedback-based reputation systems. In: Proceedings of the 4th International Conference on Security and Privacy in Communication Netowrks. SecureComm 2008, pp. 8:1–8:11 (2008)
20. Zhou, Y.B., Lei, T., Zhou, T.: A robust ranking algorithm to spamming. EPL (Europhysics Letters) 94(4), 48002–48007 (2011)

A Comparison of PHY-Based Fingerprinting Methods Used to Enhance Network Access Control

Timothy J. Carbino$^{(\boxtimes)}$, Michael A. Temple, and Juan Lopez Jr.

Air Force Institute of Technology, Electrical and Computer Engineering,
WPAFB, Ohio 45433, USA
{timothy.carbino,michael.temple,juan.lopez.ctr}@afit.edu

Abstract. Network complexity continues to evolve and more robust measures are required to ensure network integrity and mitigate unauthorized access. A physical-layer (PHY) augmentation to Medium Access Control (MAC) authentication is considered using PHY-based Distinct Native Attribute (DNA) features to form device fingerprints. Specifically, a comparison of waveform-based Radio Frequency DNA (RF-DNA) and Constellation-Based DNA (CB-DNA) fingerprinting methods is provided using unintentional Ethernet cable emissions for 10BASE-T signaling. For the first time a direct comparison is achievable between the two methods given the evaluation uses the same experimentally collected emissions to generate RF-DNA and CB-DNA fingerprints. RF-DNA fingerprinting exploits device dependent features derived from instantaneous preamble responses within communication bursts. For these same bursts, the CB-DNA approach uses device dependent features derived from mapped symbol clusters within an adapted two-dimensional (2D) binary constellation. The evaluation uses 16 wired Ethernet devices from 4 different manufacturers and both Cross-Model (manufacturer) Discrimination (CMD) and Like-Model (serial number) Discrimination (LMD) is addressed. Discrimination is assessed using a Multiple Discriminant Analysis, Maximum Likelihood (MDA/ML) classifier. Results show that both RF-DNA and CB-DNA approaches perform well for CMD with average correct classification of %C=90% achieved at Signal-to-Noise Ratios of $SNR \geq$ 12.0 dB. Consistent with prior related work, LMD discrimination is more challenging with CB-DNA achieving %C=90.0% at SNR=22.0 dB and significantly outperforming RF-DNA which only achieved %C=56.0% at this same SNR.

Keywords: Network Access Control · Physical-layer distinct native attribute · RF-DNA · CB-DNA · Device fingerprinting · MDA/ML

1 Introduction

Network Access Control (NAC) solutions implement strategies which allow devices and/or users access to a given network. There are many NAC solutions that

© IFIP International Federation for Information Processing 2015
H. Federrath and D. Gollmann (Eds.): SEC 2015, IFIP AICT 455, pp. 204–217, 2015.
DOI: 10.1007/978-3-319-18467-8_14

can be employed by a network administrator to include mapping Medium Access Control (MAC) addresses to specific ports, device credentials, and querying the hardware and software of a device. Each of these potential solutions suffer from weakness to include an attackers ability to spoof specific device information or steal device credentials. As each year passes technical capability expands and more devices are able to connect to a network. This expansion creates unique security challenges and increases the potential for unauthorized access. Physical-layer (PHY) augmentation of MAC based authentication processes provides one means to improve security and network authentication reliability. The envisioned PHY-augmented authentication process utilizes a device's digital ID (e.g., MAC address) and PHY features extracted from the device's communication signal. Ideally, the device's fingerprint consists of unique PHY features that enable reliable discrimination. The final authentication decision, to allow or deny network access, is based on 1) presentation of an authorized MAC address and 2) a statistical match between the current Distinct Native Attribute (DNA) features of the device presenting the MAC address and the stored DNA for the actual device assigned the MAC address.

The majority of PHY-based fingerprinting methods are based on features generated from transient, invariant or entire burst responses as discussed in the review presented in [1]. It is concluded in [1] that many of the PHY fingerprinting techniques discussed lack proper performance evaluation. It is the goal of this work to conduct performance evaluation between the two most prevalent approaches in [1]. The contributions of the research presented in this paper includes: 1) a direct comparison of performance in waveform-based Radio Frequency DNA (RF-DNA) and Constellation-Based DNA (CB-DNA) approaches by, 2) utilizing for the first time the same collected emissions for both approaches, 3) the CB-DNA approach is expanded for the first time to include *conditional* constellation point sub-clusters, and 4) expand CB-DNA classification to include Like-Model Discrimination (LMD).

The paper is organized as follows. Section 2 provides background information and related work on some of the most recent works in device fingerprinting. Section 3 discusses the experimental setup and outlines the PHY-based RF-DNA and CB-DNA device fingerprinting approaches. This is followed by device discrimination results in Sect. 4 and a summary and conclusions in Sect. 5.

2 Background

Device hardware fingerprinting is possible due to variations in manufacturing processes and device components. These variations inherently induce PHY feature differences that vary across devices [2]. Amplifiers, capacitors, inductors and oscillators also possess slight imperfections that influence device fingerprints [2–5]. The resultant variation can cause deviation in communication symbol rate, center frequency, and induce AM/FM/PM conversion [2]. Thus, it is possible to exploit device imperfections even when the intrinsic components used are supposedly identical [1,6].

As noted previously, the review in [1] focused primarily on PHY based finger-printing techniques, with non-PHY based approaches prior to 2009 only briefly addressed. Non-PHY based fingerprinting techniques as in [7–12] are relevant and can be used to fingerprint devices by actively probing or passively monitoring network packet traffic. Fingerprinting is accomplished by exploiting clock-skew via round trip time and inter-arrival time estimation in the collected network traces. These non-PHY based approaches are noted here for completeness and a comparison of PHY based and non-PHY based approaches is the subject of subsequent research.

PHY based device fingerprinting works in [6, 15–19, 21] generally rely on invariant *non-data modulated* Region of Interest (ROI) within the burst (turn-on transient, preamble, midamble, etc.) to extract fingerprint features. Additional works [1–5], utilize the *data modulated* burst response regions to extract their fingerprint features from device dependent modulation errors. Transient-based approaches are generally avoided given 1) the limited duration of the transient response, and 2) the transient response being influenced by environmental conditions that affect the communication channel and limit its usefulness [4]. As noted in Sect. 3.2, the CB approaches require a signal constellation for calculating error statistics and thus are only applicable for CB communication applications. This is not a constraint of the RF-DNA approach presented in Sect. 3.1 which has been successfully used for both communication applications [15, 16, 18, 19, 21], and non-communication applications such as discriminating between device components and operational states [6, 17, 22, 23].

A new approach to CB-DNA was first introduced in [20] which included development of a 2D binary signal constellation for unintentional wired Ethernet emissions using features from two binary *composite* constellation point clusters. Nearest Neighbor (NN) and Multiple Discriminant Analysis, Maximum Likelihood (MDA/ML) classifiers were used to assess device discrimination for Cross-Model (manufacturer) Discrimination (CMD) with the MDA/ML classifier out performing NN. Results here extend this earlier work by 1) exploiting discriminating feature information in multiple *conditional* constellation point sub-clusters that form the binary composite clusters, and 2) assessing Like-Model (serial number) Discrimination (LMD) capability as required for the envisioned network device ID authentication process.

3   Experimental Methodology

This work varies from traditional PHY fingerprinting approaches in that it is fingerprinting wired network devices via the unintentional RF emissions given off by the Ethernet cable. The experimental methodology here was adopted from [24] and is summarized briefly for completeness. The emission collection setup included interconnecting two computers using 10BASE-T Ethernet signaling over a category 6 Ethernet cable. A LeCroy WavePro 760Zi-A oscilloscope operating at a sample frequency is f_s=250M Samples/Sec (MSPS) and a high sensitivity Riscure 205HS near-field RF probe were used to collect the unintentional RF emissions. An in-line baseband filter with bandwidth of W_{BB}=32Mhz

was used to limit the collection bandwidth. The Ethernet cable and RF probe were placed in a test fixture to maintain relative cable-to-probe orientation while the Ethernet cards were swapped in and out for collection.

As shown in Table 1 [20], a total of 16 network cards were tested, with four cards each from D-Link (DL), Intel (IN), StarTech (ST), and TRENDnET (TN). The last four MAC address digits show that some devices vary only by a single digit and are likely from same production run. Four unique LAN transformer markings are provided and used to analyze results. The LAN transformer is the last part that the signal goes through prior to reaching the RJ45 output jack [20].

Table 1. Ethernet Cards Used for Emission Collection [20]

Manufacturer	Reference	MAC Address Last Four	LAN Transformer Markings		
D-Link	DL1	D966	Bi-Tek	IM-1178LLF	1247I
	DL2	DA06	Bi-Tek	IM-1178LLF	1247I
	DL3	DA07	Bi-Tek	IM-1178LLF	1247I
	DL4	60E0	Bi-Tek	IM-1178LLF	1247I
TRENDnET	TN1	9B55	Bi-Tek	IM-1178LLF	1247I
	TN2	9334	Bi-Tek	IM-1178LLF	1247I
	TN3	9B54	Bi-Tek	IM-1178LLF	1247I
	TN4	9B56	Bi-Tek	IM-1178LLF	1247I
Intel	IN1	1586	BI	HS00-06037LF	1247
	IN2	1A93	BI	HS00-06037LF	1247
	IN3	1A59	BI	HS00-06037LF	1247
	IN4	1A9E	BI	HS00-06037LF	1247
Star Tech	ST1	32CB	FPE	G24102MK	1250a1
	ST2	32B4	FPE	G24102MK	1250a1
	ST3	96F4	FPE	G24102MK	1320G1
	ST4	3048	FPE	G24102MK	1250a1

3.1 RF-DNA Fingerprinting

The RF-DNA fingerprinting approach has been most widely used for *intentional* signal responses of wireless devices [15,16,18,19]. For this work, the RF-DNA approach adopts the technique introduced in [24] for collecting *unintentional* RF emissions from Ethernet cables and producing RF-DNA fingerprints on a burst-by-burst basis. Useful RF-DNA has been historically extracted from invariant signal amble regions [6,15,16] and thus the 10BASE-T preamble response was targeted here for initial assessment. RF-DNA features can be extracted from various ROI responses, a few of which include Time Domain (TD) [16], Spectral Domain (SD) [18], Fourier Transform (FT) [18], and Gabor Transform (GT) [15].

Instantaneous amplitude $\{a(k)\}$, phase $\{\phi(k)\}$, and frequency $\{f(k)\}$ are TD sequences used for RF-DNA fingerprint generation using the preamble as the ROI; k denotes discrete time samples. Composite RF-DNA fingerprints are generated by 1) centering (mean removal) and normalizing $\{a(k)\}$, $\{\phi(k)\}$, and

$\{f(k)\}$, 2) dividing each TD sequence into N_R equal length subregions as illustrated in Fig. 1, 3) calculating three statistical features of variance (σ^2), skewness (γ), and kurtosis (κ) for *each* TD sequence to form *Regional Fingerprint* $F_{R_i}^{a,\phi,f}$ as in (1) for $i=1, 2, \ldots, N_R$, and 4) concatenating $F_{R_i}^{a,\phi,f}$ to form the final $1 \times (3 \times N_R)$ *Composite RF-DNA Fingerprint* F_C^{RF} as in (2) [17]. Statistical features across entire ROI response are commonly included as well, hence the regional indexing in (2) to N_R+1 total elements.

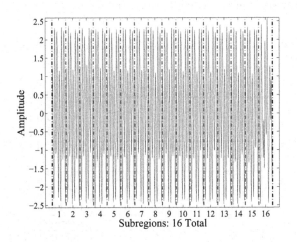

Fig. 1. Representative 10BASE-T Preamble Time Domain Amplitude Response Used for Fingerprint Generation. The 6.4 μs Preamble is Divided into $N_R=16$ Subregions.

The total number of RF-DNA features in (2) is a function of N_R, TD responses, and statistics. Varying N_R provides a means to investigate performance for various feature vector sizes. Fingerprints were generated over the preamble ROI using three TD responses ($\{a(k)\}$, $\{\phi(k)\}$, $\{f(k)\}$), three statistics (σ^2, γ, κ) per response, for $N_R=16, 31, 80$ with (2) and produced RF-DNA fingerprints having $N_{Feat}=144, 279$, and 720 total features, respectively.

$$F_{R_i}^{a,\phi,f} = [\sigma_{R_i}^2, \gamma_{R_i}, \kappa_{R_i}]_{1 \times 3} \tag{1}$$

$$F_C^{RF} = [F_{R_1}^{RF} : F_{R_2}^{RF} : F_{R_3}^{RF} : \cdots : F_{R_{N_R+1}}^{RF}]_{1 \times (3 \times N_R)} \tag{2}$$

3.2   CB-DNA Fingerprinting

As with RF-DNA fingerprinting approach, the majority of CB fingerprinting works utilize intentional RF emissions from wireless devices with unique features derived from modulation errors in the constellation space, i.e., differences (error) between received projected symbol points and ideal transmitted constellation points [1–3,5]. The CB-DNA approach adopted here differs from previous approaches by utilizing statistical features from *unconditional* and *conditional* projected symbol clusters (not modulation errors) in a 2D constellation space.

The CB-DNA fingerprinting process used here was adopted from [20] and is summarized here for completeness. CB-DNA fingerprints were generated from a single burst with example constellations being illustrated in Fig. 2 for the four card manufacturers with blue circles and black squares clusters representing Binary 0 and Binary 1, respectively. This research expands on [20] by utilizing for the first time *conditional* subclusters illustrated in Fig. 3 for card manufacturer StarTech. The *conditional* subclusters are based not only on the current demodulated bit but the proceeding and succeeding bit as well. The eight distinct *conditional* sub-clusters correspond to the eight possible bit combinations that can precede and succeed the bit being estimated i.e., bit combinations of [0 **X** 0], [0 **X** 1], [1 **X** 0], and [1 **X** 1], where **X** denotes the bit being estimated.

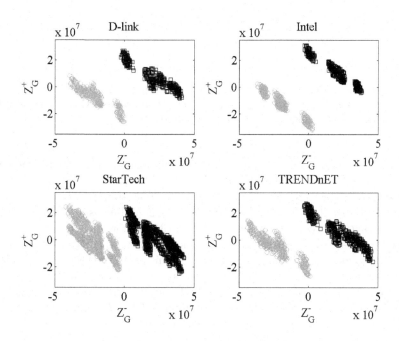

Fig. 2. Device Constellations Consisting of Approximately 1,400 Symbols (1 Burst) for Each of the Four Card Manufacturers. Each *Composite Cluster* Represents a Binary 0 (Blue Circle) or Binary 1 (Black Square).

CB-DNA fingerprint generation begins by dividing constellation points into their respective *unconditional* and *conditional* cluster regions for a total of $N_{CR}=2+8=10$. Statistical CB-DNA features are then calculated for each cluster region using the mean (μ), variance (σ^2), skewness (γ), and kurtosis (κ) along the Z_G^- and Z_G^+ dimensions shown in Fig. 3. Joint statistics in both the Z_G^- and Z_G^+ direction are also considered and include covariance (cov), coskewness ($\beta_{1\times2}$),

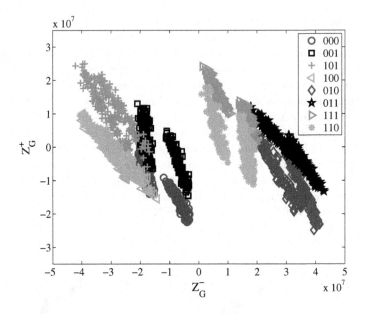

Fig. 3. 2D Binary Constellation for ST1 showing each *Composite Cluster* Comprised of Four Distinct *Sub-Clusters* Corresponding to the Four Possible Combinations of Bits Preceding and Succeeding the Bit Being Estimated

and cokurtosis ($\delta_{1\times3}$) which provide an extra six features per region. The resultant statistics form a *Regional Cluster Fingerprint* $F_{R_i}^{CB}$ given by (3), where the superscripted $-/+$ sign denotes constellation dimension and $i = 1, 2, \ldots, N_{CR}$. The final *Composite CB-DNA Fingerprint* F_C^{CB} is of dimension $1 \times (14 \times N_{CR})$ and constructed by concatenating $F_{R_i}^{CB}$ from (3) as shown in (4) [20]. The total number of CB-DNA features in (4) is a function of N_{CR}, statistics, and dimensions i.e., Z_G^- and Z_G^+. Varying N_{CR} provides a means to investigate performance for various feature vector sizes. Fingerprints were generated using $N_{CR}=2, 8$, and 10 (μ, σ^2, γ, κ, cov, $\beta_{1\times2}$, $\delta_{1\times3}$) with 4 statistics from each of the Z_G^- and Z_G^+ dimensions and 6 joint statistics producing CB-DNA fingerprints having $N_{Feat}=28, 112$, and 140 total features, respectively.

$$F_{R_i}^{CB} = \left[\mu_{R_i}^-, \mu_{R_i}^+, \sigma_{R_i}^{2-}, \sigma_{R_i}^{2+}, \gamma_{R_i}^-, \gamma_{R_i}^+, \kappa_{R_i}^-, \kappa_{R_i}^+, cov, \beta_{1\times2}, \delta_{1\times3}, \right]_{1\times14} \quad (3)$$

$$F_C^{CB} = \left[F_{R_1}^{CB} : F_{R_2}^{CB} : F_{R_3}^{CB} : \cdots : F_{R_{N_{CR}}}^{CB} \right]_{1\times(14\times N_{CR})} \quad (4)$$

3.3 Device Discrimination

The effect of varying SNR on discrimination performance was assessed to characterize the effect of varying channel conditions. This was done by adding independent like-filtered Additive White Gaussian Noise (AWGN) N_{Nz} realizations to each experimentally collected emission to achieve the desired SNR for Monte

Carlo simulation. Given an average collected SNR=30.0 dB, device discriminability was assessed for simulated $SNR \in [12\ 32]$ dB in 2 dB steps. For Monte Carlo simulation results in Sect. 4, a total of N_{Nz}=6 independent AWGN realizations were generated, filtered, power-scaled and added to the collected signal responses to generated signals at the desired SNR. Given N_{Nz} =6 AWGN realizations and N_S=1000 collected signal responses per card, a total of N_F=$N_S \times N_{Nz}$=6000 independent fingerprints per card were available for discrimination assessment.

Consistent with prior related work [6,15,16], device discriminability was assessed using a MDA/ML classification process. MDA/ML processing was implemented for N_C=4 and 16 classes using an identical number of *Training* (N_{Tng}) and *Testing* (N_{Tst}) fingerprints for each class. A total of N_F=24,000 (CMD) and N_F=6,000 (LMD) fingerprints were generated for each N_C per Sect. 3.1 and Sect. 3.2 for RF-DNA and CB-DNA methods, respectively. MDA/ML *training* was completed for each N_C using N_{Tng}=$N_F/2$ fingerprints and K-fold cross-validation with K=5 to improve MDA/ML reliability. This involves: 1) dividing the training fingerprints into K equal size disjoint blocks of $N_{Tng}/5$ fingerprints, 2) holding out one block and training on K-1 blocks to produce projection matrix $\mathbf{W}$, and 3) using the holdout block and $\mathbf{W}$ for validation [25]. The $\mathbf{W}$ from the best training iteration is output and used for subsequent MDA/ML *testing* assessment. The process is repeated to generate an SNR-dependent $\mathbf{W}(SNR)$ for each analysis SNR.

4   Discrimination Results

The MDA/ML classification results are presented for CMD (manufacturer) and LMD (serial number) performance using the 16 devices in Table 1. Device fingerprint generation occurs using identical burst-by-burst emissions per methods in Sect. 3.1 and Sect. 3.2, with RF-DNA using only the burst preamble and CB-DNA using the entire burst to include preamble. A total of 1000 bursts are processed from each device with three AWGN realizations added to each burst to create 3000 fingerprints per device for classification. Discrimination results are based on two classification models created per Sect. 3.3. The CMD results are based on N_{Tst}=12,000 testing fingerprints and LMD results are based on N_{Tst}=3,000 fingerprints. An arbitrary performance benchmark of %C=90% correct classification is used for comparative assessment with summary analysis based on CI=95% binomial confidence intervals. Given the large number of independent trials for all results in Sect. 4, the resultant CI=95% confidence intervals are less than the vertical extent of data markers in Fig. 4 through Fig. 6 and therefore omitted for visual clarity.

Fig. 4 shows average RF-DNA results for CMD and LMD. The %C=90% benchmark is achieved for CMD with all three N_R values at $SNR \geq 21$ dB, with N_R=80 performance starting out with %C=92% at SNR=12 dB and the other N_R=16 and N_R=31 cases requiring an additional 6.0 dB and 10.0 dB gain in SNR, respectively, to achieve %C=92%. At $SNR \approx 26$ dB the markers

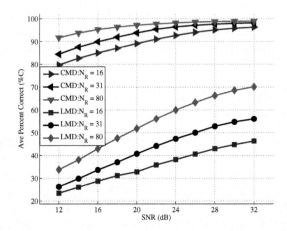

Fig. 4. RF-DNA Fingerprinting Averages for *Cross-Model Discrimination* (CMD) Using N_C=4 Classes and *Like-Model Discrimination* (LMD) Using N_C=16 Classes with N_R=16, 31 and 80 Sub-Regions

for N_R=80 and N_R=31 begin to overlap suggesting those two MDA/ML models yield statistically equivalent performance at SNR=26.0 dB and higher with N_R=16 %C being slightly lower. The LMD results for RF-DNA in Fig. 4 never reach the %C=90% benchmark. However, the N_R=80 case outperforms the others by approximately 15% and 20% at SNR=30 dB. Thus, the RF-DNA model for N_R=80 was chosen for comparison with the CB-DNA model.

Fig. 5 shows CMD and LMD results for CB-DNA fingerprinting while varying the use of composite clusters and sub-clusters. The CMD and LMD results using N_{CR}=2 are about 5% and 25% respectively worse in correct classification with respect to the N_{CR}=10 cases. For CMD the N_{CR}=10 model achieves 96% correct classification on average at 12 dB where the N_{CR}=2 model peaks out at 94% at 32 db, which shows that the N_{CR}=10 model is superior. The results for CMD with N_{CR}=8 are similar to N_{CR}=10. LMD results for N_{CR}=8 are constantly a few percentage points lower than N_{CR}=10 and requires an additional 4 dB gain to achieve %C=90 over N_{CR}=10 at 22 dB. LMD increases the complexity of the classification and reaches an average of %C=90% across all 16 device for N_{CR}=10 with average collected SNR=22.0 dB.

%C classification results for RF-DNA and CB-DNA Fingerprinting are provided in Fig. 6 for CMD and LMD. The CMD comparison shows that CB-DNA reaches %C=96% at SNR=12 dB while RF-DNA reaches %C=96% at $SNR \approx 18$ dB (approximately 6.0 dB higher). The LMD comparison shows that CB-DNA consistently out performs RF-DNA by at least 24% at all SNR levels.

The results in Fig. 6 enable direct comparison of RF-DNA and CB-DNA Fingerprinting however, average %C performance hides individual class interactions. Thus, MDA/ML confusion matrix results for SNR=24.0 dB are introduced to highlight cross-class misclassification for CMD (Table 2) and LMD (Table 3);

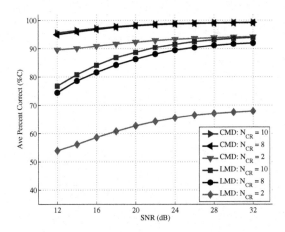

Fig. 5. CB-DNA Fingerprinting Averages for *Cross Model Discrimination* (CMD with N_C=4) and *Like Model Discrimination* (LMD with N_C=16) Using Composite (N_{CR}=2), Sub-Cluster (N_{CR}=8), and Combined (N_{CR}=10) Constellation Statistics

matrix rows represent *input class* and matrix columns represent *called class*. The table entries are presented as %C CB-DNA / %C RF-DNA with bold entries denoting best or equivalent performance.

The CMD confusion matrix in Table 2 is nearly symmetric with *all* misclassification occurring between DL and TN devices. This is attributable to DL and TN devices using identical LAN transformers as indicated in Table 1. The diagonal entries show that CMD performance, for CB-DNA is better than or equivalent to RF-DNA. The resultant CMD averages for CB-DNA (%C=98.9%) and RF-DNA (%C=98.21%) are pursuant with Fig. 6.

Table 2. CMD confusion matrix for CB-DNA and RF-DNA Fingerprinting at SNR=24 dB and 12,000 trials per class. Entries presented as % CB-DNA / % RF-DNA with bold entries denoting best or equivalent performance.

	DL	IN	ST	TN
DL	**98.10** / 96.05	0.0 / 0.0	0.0 / 0.0	1.90 / 3.95
IN	0.0 / 0.0	**100.00** / **100.00**	0.0 / 0.0	0.0 / 0.0
ST	0.0 / 0.0	0.0 / 0.0	**100.00** / **100.00**	0.0 / 0.0
TN	2.49 / 3.20	0.0 / 0.0	0.0 / 0.0	**97.51** / 96.80

The LMD confusion matrix results in Table 3 summarize misclassification of the complete 16-by-16 confusion matrix. Results are presented as individual manufacturer confusion matrices with "Other" entries representing all misclassifications outside the manufacturing group. The results here are consistent with prior CMD results in Table 2, with 1) the IN and ST devices are never misclassified as another manufacturer, and 2) nearly 100% of the DL "Other" misclassifications

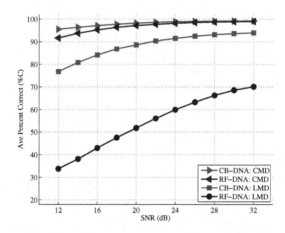

Fig. 6. RF-DNA vs. CB-DNA Fingerprinting Averages for *CMD* (Manufacturer Discrimination) Using $N_C=4$ Classes with ($N_R=16$) Sub-Regions and *LMD* (Serial Number Discrimination) Using $N_C=16$ Classes with ($N_{CR}=10$) Cluster Regions

Table 3. LMD confusion matrix for CB-DNA and RF-DNA Fingerprinting at $SNR=24.0$ dB and 3,000 trials per class, highlighting errors within manufacturing groups. The "Other" column represents all other manufacturers. Entries presented as % CB-DNA / % RF-DNA with bold entries denoting best or equivalent performance.

	DL1	DL2	DL3	DL4	Other
DL1	**86.27** / 43.10	0.0 / 9.43	13.73 / 20.47	0.0 / 25.77	0.0 / 1.23
DL2	0.03 / 10.83	**97.57** / 72.80	0.80 / 6.50	0.63 / 3.50	0.97 / 6.37
DL3	15.77 / 22.47	0.03 /5.40	**83.93** / 57.77	0.27 / 12.40	0.0 / 1.96
DL4	0.0 / 29.30	0.37 / 7.13	0.10 / 17.07	**97.20** / 45.67	2.33 / 0.83

	TN1	TN2	TN3	TN4	Other
TN1	**97.90** / 43.37	1.10 / 16.44	0.03 / 8.13	0.67 / 30.13	0.30 / 1.93
TN2	1.36 / 23.90	**89.57** / 43.60	1.77 / 6.80	3.07 / 19.13	4.23 / 6.57
TN3	0.0 / 4.43	2.83 / 4.60	**84.87** / 85.07	11.90 / 5.50	0.40 / 0.40
TN4	1.60 / 32.60	5.20 / 16.60	6.76 / 8.13	**84.27** / 39.84	2.17 / 2.83

	IN1	IN2	IN3	IN4	Other
IN1	**91.67** / 78.43	5.63 / 9.00	2.40 / 11.40	0.30 / 1.17	0.0 / 0.0
IN2	4.50 / 9.73	**94.30** / 60.67	1.20 / 14.60	0.00 / 15.00	0.0 / 0.0
IN3	1.46 / 11.00	0.67 / 17.10	**97.67** / 61.77	0.20 / 10.13	0.0 / 0.0
IN4	0.0 / 4.07	0.0 / 19.13	0.0 / 12.07	**100.00** / 64.73	0.0 / 0.0

	ST1	ST2	ST3	ST4	Other
ST1	**90.53** / 67.63	0.70 / 1.20	4.40 / 13.27	4.37 / 17.90	0.0 / 0.0
ST2	0.43 / 0.83	**97.47** / 77.80	0.77 / 13.40	1.33 / 7.97	0.0 / 0.0
ST3	4.46 / 10.93	1.07 / 14.30	**83.57** / 60.60	10.90 / 14.17	0.0 / 0.0
ST4	3.63 / 19.33	1.30 / 6.93	7.50 / 17.50	**87.57** / 56.24	0.0 / 0.0

being TN devices, and vice versa–this confusion is again attributed to DL and TN devices using identical LAN transformers as indicated in Table 1. Most notably in Table 3 are bold diagonal entries showing that CB-DNA outperformed RF-DNA performance for *all* devices.

5   Summary and Conclusions

A PHY augmentation to MAC-based authentication is addressed using PHY-based Distinct Native Attribute (DNA) features to form device fingerprints. Specifically, a previous Radio Frequency (RF-DNA) fingerprinting approach and new Constellation Based (CB-DNA) fingerprinting approach that exploits 2D constellation statistics are considered. The two methods are compared using fingerprints generated from the same set of unintentional 10BASE-T Ethernet cable emissions. Prior to this preliminary investigation it was hypothesized that CB-DNA would outperform RF-DNA. Considerable differences in the amount of burst information being exploited was the basis for this conjecture, i.e., RF-DNA fingerprinting only exploits a fraction of the Ethernet burst (64 preamble symbols) while CB-DNA exploits the entire Ethernets burst (average of 1,400 symbols here).

When comparing RF-DNA results here to previous related work [15–17], it is noted that Cross-Model Discrimination (CMD) results are consistent but Like-Model Discrimination (LMD) results are poorer. One reason for this is more stringent signaling characteristics of the Ethernet standards as well as the devices here sharing similar LAN transformer markings.

As measured by average percentage of correct classification (%C), the final RF-DNA vs. CB-DNA outcome shows that CB-DNA outperforms RF-DNA for the 16 devices considered. For CMD there was only a marginal difference at SNR=24 dB with CB-DNA at %C=98.9% and RF-DNA at %C=98.21%. Of particular note for CMD is that 100% of the misclassification error occurred between DL and TN devices which use the same LAN transformer. For LMD there was considerable improvement at SNR=24 dB, with CB-DNA at %C=91.5% and RF-DNA at %C=59.9%. LMD is generally more challenging than CMD and results show that both approaches suffer when classifying LMD. However, CB-DNA performance remained above the 90% threshold and only suffered a 6.2% degradation in %C while RF-DNA dropped by more than 30%.

From a device authentication and network security perspective, LMD performance is most important. Results here show that CB-DNA outperformed RF-DNA by a considerable margin. LMD results at the collected SNR=30.0 dB include like model %C=94% for CB-DNA and only %C=69% for RF-DNA.

These CB-DNA results are encouraging and work continues to improve performance. This includes investigating alternatives such as the Generalized Relevance Learning Vector Quantized-Improved (GRLVQI) classifier which provides a direct indication of feature relevance on classifier decision [21,26]. Feature relevance enables dimensional reduction analysis, which in-turn reduces processing complexity and enhances real-world applicability. Furthermore, the use of CB-DNA for device verification and rogue detection and rejection remains under investigation as well.

References

1. Danev, B., Zanetti, D., Capkun, S.: On Physical-Layer Identification of Wireless Devices. ACM Computing Surveys (CSUR) **45**(1), 6 (2012)
2. Huang, Y., Zheng, H.: Radio frequency fingerprinting based on the constellation errors. In: 2012 18th Asia-Pacific Conf. on Communications (APCC), pp. 900–905. IEEE (2012)
3. Brik, V., Banerjee, S., Gruteser, M., Oh, S.: Wireless device identification with radiometric signatures. In: Proc. of the 14th ACM Intl. Conf. on Mobile computing and Networking, pp. 116–127. ACM (2008)
4. Danev, B., Luecken, H., Capkun, S., El Defrawy, K.: Attacks on physical-layer identification. In: Proc. of the Third ACM Conf. on Wireless Network Security, pp. 89–98. ACM (2010)
5. Edman, M., Yener, B.: Active Attacks Against Modulation-Based Radiometric Identification. Technical report 0902, Rensselaer Institute of Technology (2009)
6. Cobb, W.E., Laspe, E.D., Baldwin, R.O., Temple, M.A., Kim, Y.C.: Intrinsic Physical-Layer Authentication of Integrated Circuits. IEEE Trans on Information Forensics and Security **7**(1), 14–24 (2012)
7. Desmond, L.C.C., Cho, C.Y., Tan, C.P., Lee, R.S.: Identifying unique devices through wireless fingerprinting. In: Proceedings of the first ACM Conference on Wireless Network Security. ACM (2008)
8. Kohno, T., Broido, A., Claffy, K.C.: Remote physical device fingerprinting. IEEE Transactions on Dependable and Secure Computing **2**(2), 93–108 (2005)
9. Franklin, J., McCoy, D., Tabriz, P., Neagoe, V., Randwyk, J.V., Sicker, D.: Passive data link layer 802.11 wireless device driver fingerprinting. In: Usenix Security, vol. 6 (2006)
10. Gao, K., Corbett, C., Beyah, R.A.: A passive approach to wireless device fingerprinting. In: Proc. of IEEE/IFIP DSN, pp. 383–392 (2010)
11. Uluagac, A., Radhakrishnan, S., Corbett, C., Baca, A., Beyah, R.: A passive technique for fingerprinting wireless devices with wired-side observations. In: Proceedings of the IEEE Conference on Communications and Network Security (CNS), pp. 305–313 (2013)
12. Francois, J., Abdelnurt, H., State, R., Festort, O.: Ptf: passive temporal fingerprinting. In: Proc. of IFIP/IEEE International Symposium on Integrated Network Management, pp. 289–296 (2011)
13. Gubbi, J., Buyya, R., Marusic, S., Palaniswami, M.: Internet of Things (IoT): A Vision, Architectural Elements, and Future Directions. Future Generation Computer Systems **29**(7), 1645–1660 (2013)
14. Zhou, L., Chao, H.C.: Multimedia Traffic Security Architecture for the Internet of Things. IEEE Network **25**(3), 35–40 (2011)
15. Reising, D.R., Temple, M.A., Oxley, M.E.: Gabor-based RF-DNA fingerprinting for classifying 802.16e WiMAX mobile subscribers. In: 2012 Intl. Conf. on Computing, Networking and Communications (ICNC), pp. 7–13. IEEE (2012)
16. Ramsey, B.W., Temple, M. A., Mullins, B. E.: PHY foundation for multi-factor ZigBee node authentication. In: Global Communications Conf. (GLOBECOM), 2012, pp. 795–800. IEEE (2012)

17. Cobb, W.E., Garcia, E.W., Temple, M.A., Baldwin, R.O., Kim, Y.C.: Physical Layer Identification of Embedded Devices using RFDNA Fingerprinting. MILITARY COMMUNICATIONS Conf., MILCOM **2010**, 2168–2173 (2010)
18. Williams, M.D., Munns, S., Temple, M.A., Mendenhall, M.J.: RF-DNA fingerprinting for airport WiMax communications security. In: 2010 4th Intl. Conf. on Network and System Security (NSS), pp. 32–39 (2010)
19. Williams, M.D., Temple, M.A., Reising, D.R.: Augmenting bit- level network security using physical layer RF-DNA fingerprinting. In: Global Telecommunications Conf. (GLOBECOM 2010), pp. 1–6. IEEE (2010)
20. Carbino, T.J., Temple, M.A., Bihl, T.: Ethernet card discrimination using unintentional cable emissions and constellation-based Fingerprints. In: 2015 Intl. Workshop on Computing, Networking and Communications (IWCNC) (to appear, February 2015) (Accepted)
21. Reising, D.R.: Exploitation of RF-DNA for Device Classification and Verification Using GRLVQI Processing. Technical report DTIC Doc (2012)
22. Stone, S.J., Temple, M.A., Baldwin, R.O.: RF-based PLC IC design verification. In: 2012 DMSMS and Stand Conf. (DMSMS12) (2012)
23. Wright, B.C.: PLC Hardware Discrimination using RF-DNA Fingerprinting. Technical Report DTIC Document (2014)
24. Carbino, T.J., Baldwin, R.O.: Side channel analysis of ethernet network cable emissions. In: 9th Intl. Conf. on Cyber Warfare and Security, ICCWS (2014)
25. Duda, R.O., Hart, P.E., Stork, D.G.: Pattern Classification. John Wiley and Sons (2012)
26. Mendenhall, M.J., Merényi, E.: Relevance-Based Feature Extraction for Hyperspectral Images. IEEE Trans on Neural Networks **19**(4), 658–672 (2008)

Model-Driven Integration and Analysis of Access-control Policies in Multi-layer Information Systems

Salvador Martínez[1](✉), Joaquin Garcia-Alfaro[2], Frédéric Cuppens[3],
Nora Cuppens-Boulahia[3], and Jordi Cabot[4]

[1] AtlanMod Team (Inria, Mines Nantes, LINA), Nantes, France
salvador.martinez_perez@inria.fr
[2] RST Department, Télécom SudParis, CNRS Samovar UMR 5157, Evry, France
joaquin.garcia_alfaro@telecom-sudparis.eu
[3] Télécom Bretagne, LUSSI Department,
Université Européenne de Bretagne, Rennes, France
nora.cuppens-boulahia@telecom-bretagne.eu
[4] ICREA - UOC, Barcelona, Spain
jcabot@uoc.edu

Abstract. Security is a critical concern for any information system. Security properties such as confidentiality, integrity and availability need to be enforced in order to make systems safe. In complex environments, where information systems are composed of a number of heterogeneous subsystems, each must participate in their achievement. Therefore, security integration mechanisms are needed in order to 1) achieve the global security goal and 2) facilitate the analysis of the security status of the whole system. For the specific case of access-control, access-control policies may be found in several components (databases, networks and applications) all, supposedly, working together in order to meet the high level security property. In this work we propose an integration mechanism for access-control policies to enable the analysis of the system security. We rely on model-driven technologies and the XACML standard to achieve this goal.

1 Introduction

Nowadays systems are often composed of a number of interacting heterogeneous subsystems. Access-control is pervasive with respect to this architecture, so that we can find access-control enforcement in different components placed in different architectural levels, often following different AC models. However, these policies are not independent and relations exist between them, as relations exist between components situated in different architecture layers. Concretely, dependency relations exist between access-control policies, so that the decision established by rules in a policy will depend on the decisions established in another policy.

© IFIP International Federation for Information Processing 2015
H. Federrath and D. Gollmann (Eds.): SEC 2015, IFIP AICT 455, pp. 218–233, 2015.
DOI: 10.1007/978-3-319-18467-8_15

Thus, ideally, a global policy representing the access-control of the whole system should be available, as analysing a policy in isolation does not provide enough information. However, normally, this global policy only exist in an implicit and not always consistent manner. Consequently, integration mechanisms are needed in order to 1) facilitate the analysis of the security status of the whole system and 2) achieve the global security goal of the security property.

In order to tackle the aforementioned problems, we propose here a model-driven solution to integrate policies from different concrete components collaborating in an information system in a single model representation. Two requirements need to be met for achieving this goal: The use of a common access-control policy model for representing the policies of each component and the recovery/representation of the implicit dependency relations between them.

Translating all the recovered access-control policies to the same policy language, thus, representing them in a uniform way, eases the manipulation and reusability of analysis operations. In our approach, the component policies will be translated to the XACML[9] policy language while domain-specific information is added/kept by the use of profiles. Then, we complete the integration framework with a semi-automatic process for detecting the policy dependencies and to organize the policies within a single XACML model. This enables us to see the policies in our information systems as a whole. Finally, we provide a set of OCL[16] operations making use this global model and an approach to detect inter-component anomalies.

Our framework relies on the existence of high-level model representations of the policies implemented by concrete systems and on the use of model-driven tools and techniques. Consequently, as a previous step, our solution requires to perform policy recovery tasks. Concrete components often implement access-control policies by using diverse, low-level mechanisms (low level languages, database tables) to represent the rules, adding complexity to the analysis and manipulation tasks. Conversely, recovering these implemented policies and representing them in form of higher-level, more abstract models reduces the complexity and enables the reusability of a plethora of proved model-driven tools and techniques. We rely on state of the art recovery approaches [11–13] for this task.

The rest of the paper is organized as follows. In Section 2 we present a running example and motivation. Section 3 is devoted to the presentation of the proposed approach while in Sections 4, 5 and 6 we describe each of its steps. In Section 7 we provide details about the implementation. Finally, Section 8 discusses related work and Section 9 presents conclusions and future work.

2   Motivation

In order to motivate our approach, we present here an information system (IS) example that will be used through the rest of the paper.

In Figure 1, a simple, yet very common IS is depicted. This IS is composed of several components working in different architecture layers, namely, a network layer, providing networking services and enforcing access control through

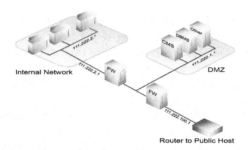

Fig. 1. Information System Architecture

the firewalls (using Rule-based lists implementing Non-discretionary AC), a database layer, providing storage services and implementing role-based access-control (RBAC)[18] through its built-in permissions schema and an application level, where a Content Management System (CMS) provides publication services. This CMS also enforces RBAC by using a built-in permission schema.

As we can see, three different systems enforce access-control. These systems are not isolated but collaborate to build up the functionality of a global system that encompasses them. Concretely, and in the case of subsystems located in different architecture layers, the collaboration relation is a dependency relation where systems in higher layers depend on services provided by lower layers. Access-control reproduces this behaviour. Consider access-control rules as functions where a decision is taken w.r.t. to a subject accessing a resource to perform a given action under certain conditions and having the following form:
$R(Subject, Resource, Action, Condition) \rightarrow Decision$

Let us take a look to the following examples:

Example 1:

$R_{DB}(RoleX, TableX, Write, 8{:}00 - 16{:}00) \rightarrow accept$
$R_{FW}(Local, DBServer, Send/receive, 8{:}00 - 14{:}00) \rightarrow accept$

In this example, a given role is granted permission to access a table for modification between 8:00 and 16:00. However, the access to the database server in constrained by a firewall rule, that only allows local access to the server between 8:00 and 14:00. As the database policy depends on the firewall policy, when the latter is more restrictive, it prevails. When asking if the role can access the table under which conditions, both policies need to be taken into account in order to provide a complete answer.

Example 2:

$R_{CMS}(BlacklistedIPs, Admin, Access) \rightarrow deny$
$R_{DB}(CMSRole, CMSSchema, Write) \rightarrow accept$
$R_{FW}(0.0.0.0, DBServer, Send/receive,) \rightarrow accept$

This example concerns the three subsystems in our IS. A rule in the CMS forbids the access to the admin pages to users located in blacklisted countries as identified by its IP address. However, the user the CMS uses to connect to the database has access for modification to the CMS database backend as stated by

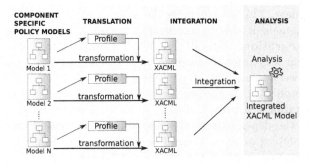

Fig. 2. Policy Integration Approach

the second rule. Moreover, the third rule, that belongs to the firewall systems, allows to connect to the database to users in any location. Combining these three rules, a user located in a blacklisted area may be able to access the admin information on the CMS through the database backend.

From the examples, we can conclude that Access-control policies can not be regarded as isolated when they belong to systems situated in different architecture layers. Analysing the AC rules of a component for the absence of anomalies requires information from the AC policies of other components it depends on. However, this comprehensive analysis is hampered by two factors: 1) dependencies between component's policies are not explicit 2) the AC information may be represented following a different AC model and stored in different technical spaces requiring domain experts for its analysis.

3 Approach

In order to tackle the problems we have shown in Section 2, we propose a model-driven approach that integrates all the policies collaborating in the enforcement of access-control in a single model. Our approach requires a previous step, namely the extraction of abstract models from concrete components, and then is structured in three steps (see Figure 2):

0. **Policy recovery.** AC policies are implemented in concrete systems using a diverse set of mechanisms, often low level and proprietary, like ad-hoc rule languages, specific database dictionaries, etc. As a preliminary step for our approach we require the policies of each component to be represented in the form of abstract models, from where the complexity arising from the specificities of a given vendor or implementation technology is eliminated and only the AC information is present. This requirement is met by several previous work that investigate the recovery of access-control policies from diverse components [11–13]. The outputs of those works are to be the inputs of our approach.

1. **Policy Translation.** Taking as input the models described in the preliminary step, our approach proposes to translate all the policies to the same

policy language. This step includes the description of extensions of the target language to make it able to represent component-specific information.
2. **Policy Integration.** With all the models translated to the same language, the next step is to integrate them all in a single model, along with the dependencies between them. This step requires the discovery of such dependencies, normally implicit.
3. **Policy Analysis Support.** Having all the policies represented in the same model and the dependencies between them made explicit enables the definition of complex analysis tasks. Prior to that, the definition of a number of operations taking advantage of the model organization is required to ease the building of those analysis tasks. The third step is meant to provide that set of operations.

The following sections are devoted to a detailed description of each of the steps.

4   Policy Translation

All the policies in the IS, potentially conforming to different access-control models and containing domain specific information need to be translated into the same language as a previous step for the integration in a single policy. In order to do so, first, we need to chose a policy language able to represent policies following different policy models and to represent multiple policies in the same resource.

4.1   XACML Policy Language

XACML[9] is an access control policy language and framework fulfilling these requirements. It follows the Attribute-based access-control model (ABAC)[7] what, along with its extensibility, provides to the language enough flexibility to represent policies following different access-control models. Other approaches [15, 19] describe languages and tools able to produce flexible access-control models. However, several reason inclined us to choose XACML. First of all, thanks to its ABAC philosophy, XACML is able to represent a wider range of security policies (see [7] for the capabilities of ABAC to cover other AC models), while other extensible languages like SecureUML[10] will impose the use of RBAC. Secondly, being an standard language, we expect a wider adoption and a more consistent maintenance and evolution of the language.

XACML policies are composed of three main elements *PolicySet*, *Policy* and *Rule*. A *PolicySet* can contain other *PolicySets* or a single *Policy* that is a container of *Rules* (Policy and PolicySet also specify a rule-combining algorithm, in order to solve conflicts between their contained elements). These three elements can specify a *Target* that establishes its applicability, i.e., to which combination of *Subject*, *Resource* and *Action* the *PolicySet*, *Policy* and *Rule* applies. *Subject*, *Resource* and *Action* identifies subjects accessing given resources to perform actions. These elements can hold *Attribute* elements, that represent additional characteristics (e.g., the role of the subject). Optionally, a *Rule* element can hold a *Condition* that represents a boolean condition over a subject resource or action. Upon an access request, these elements are used to get an answer of the type: permit, deny or not applicable.

4.2 Translation to XACML and Profiles

Our goal is to translate all the existing policies of the system in hand to XACML policies. However, the component-specific models will typically represent the access-control information in a component-specific way, i.e., they will include concepts of the domain for easing the comprehension and elaboration of policies by domain experts. Those concepts should be preserved in order to keep the expressivity of the policy. For that purpose, XACML profiles need to be defined. These profiles will basically specialize the core concepts of the XACML policy language. In general, a profile will contribute new attributes specializing the concepts of Subject, Resource and Action although specializing other concepts may be necessary mostly when the profile needs to reflects some special feature of the original policy model (take as an example the XACML RBAC Profile[1], where the concepts of PolicySet and Policy are extended as well as describing how to arrange these elements in a specific way to achieve the desired goal).

In order to demonstrate the process of defining a XACML profile, in the following, we describe the development of a XACML profile for the domain of relational database management systems (RDBMSs). The concepts of the domain are extracted from a security database metamodel described in [11].

First of all, note that the domain of relational databases usually relies on a RBAC model, what should be represented in the profile. There exists already a XACML profile for RBAC. Therefore, our profile will complement the use of this profile by contributing domain specific attributes for Subject, Resource and Action.

We start by defining the profile identifier that shall be used when an identifier in the form of a URI is required:

```
urn:oasis:names:tc:xacml:3.0:rdbms
```

Regarding the Resources, we will describe the following attributes.

```
urn:oasis:names:tc:xacml:3.0:rdbms:resource:database
urn:oasis:names:tc:xacml:3.0:rdbms:resource:schema
urn:oasis:names:tc:xacml:3.0:rdbms:resource:table
urn:oasis:names:tc:xacml:3.0:rdbms:resource:column
urn:oasis:names:tc:xacml:3.0:rdbms:resource:view
urn:oasis:names:tc:xacml:3.0:rdbms:resource:procedure
urn:oasis:names:tc:xacml:3.0:rdbms:resource:trigger
```

As for the actions, we will describe the following attributes, being all of type string.

```
urn:oasis:names:tc:xacml:3.0:rdbms:action:tableOpt:insert
urn:oasis:names:tc:xacml:3.0:rdbms:action:tableOpt:delete
urn:oasis:names:tc:xacml:3.0:rdbms:action:tableOpt:select
```

---

[1] http://docs.oasis-open.org/xacml/cd-xacml-rbac-profile-01.pdf

```
urn:oasis:names:tc:xacml:3.0:rdbms:action:tableOpt:update
urn:oasis:names:tc:xacml:3.0:rdbms:action:dbOpt:alter
urn:oasis:names:tc:xacml:3.0:rdbms:action:dbOpt:drop
urn:oasis:names:tc:xacml:3.0:rdbms:action:dbOpt:create
urn:oasis:names:tc:xacml:3.0:rdbms:action:permissionOpt:grant
urn:oasis:names:tc:xacml:3.0:rdbms:action:permissionOpt:revoke
urn:oasis:names:tc:xacml:3.0:rdbms:action:sessionOpt:set
urn:oasis:names:tc:xacml:3.0:rdbms:action:sessionOpt:connect
urn:oasis:names:tc:xacml:3.0:rdbms:action:codeOpt:execute
```

Finally, and regarding the subjects, the concept of role is already included in the RBAC profile. We will only add an attribute to identify the database elements owned by a subject, as this attribute influences the permissions (commonly, in RDBMS, the owner of a resource has all the permissions and moreover, is allowed to delegate those permissions to others).

```
urn:oasis:names:tc:xacml:3.0:rdbms:subject:owner
```

Once the profile is available, a transformation between the metamodel of the model recovered from the subsystem and the XACML (plus profiles) metamodel is defined, providing as an output XACML instance models. Note that to reflect the access-control model used in the RDBMS, we have to explicitly create a rule that in RDBMS is implicit, i.e., the owner has all the rights on the owned element.

The definition of any other profile will follow a similar process. Concretely, for the CMS we will define attributes extending the core concepts of XACML following the types defined in [13] and then combining its use with the use of the RBAC profile. As for the firewalls, several mappings to use as a basis for the profile exists, including the use of roles [4] or not [12]. We decide to extend the latter to include domain concepts (as host, zone, protocol, etc), discarding the discovery/creation of implicit roles.

5   Integration

Once we have all the policies represented within the same policy language, the next step is to organize the policies in a single global model. A key issue in this step is to unveil the implicit dependencies between policies situated at different architecture levels to make them explicitly appear in the model.

First of all, we need to decide the structure we will follow to represent the policies and their dependencies in a single XACML resource. The policy of each component will be stored in single XACML PolicySet, so that we can use the PolicySetIdRef to link it (without inheritance semantics) to other policies in the system. Note that some scenarios will require the policy of the component to be split in several PolicySet and Policy elements as is the case when using the RBAC profile. For simplicity, in the rest of the paper we will consider the policy of a component as the element containing its rules, disregarding how they are internally organized using XACML structural elements. Note also that the proposed structure is only intended to enable analysis capabilities and not to mimic a structure suitable, for instance, for code-generation and system deployment.

Starting from the individual policies, we need a process to discover the dependencies between them, so that the references can be properly set. We propose here

Algorithm 1

```
1:  P←All Policies
2:  for each P_i ∈ P do
3:      Dependency[P_i]← ∅
4:      Candidates[P_i]←P\{P_i}
5:  end for
6:  for each P_i ∈ P do
7:      C← All Context Attributes in P_i
8:      for each C_i ∈ C do
9:          for each P_j ∈ Candidates[P_i] do
10:             A← All Rule Attributes in P_j
11:             if C_i in A then
12:                 Dependency[P_i]←Dependency[P_i]∪{P_j}
13:                 Candidates[P_j]←Candidates[P_j]\{P_i}
14:             end if
15:         end for
16:     end for
17: end for
```

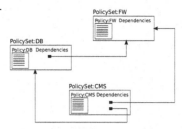

Fig. 3. Policy Organization

a process based on exploiting context information (e.g., IP address or database-backend user for a CMS) that suggests relationships between subsystem. Note that we do not deal here with the possible heterogeneity of the properties storing the context information (different names or types) by considering that the matching of such heterogeneities may be performed, if needed, as a previous step. This context information is relevant not only to unveil the dependencies but also for the analysis of the system, thus, it needs to be stored along with the policy representation. As XACML does not provide a specific place to store this kind of information and to minimize the language extension it may require, we add this information in the description field of the PolicySet element. In this field we store a string representing a key and value map with the corresponding environment values for the Policy or PolicySet:

$$Context\{dbUserName : anonyme; IpAddress : 192.000.111.0\}$$

With the context information available, the process to find the dependencies between policies is described in Algorithm 1. Basically, for each context parameter in a given policy it searches if there is any rule using that attribute value in any of the other policies. If this is the case, a dependency exists between both policies and as such it is registered. Note that the algorithm has been optimized by considering that no circular dependencies exist. The set of candidate policies for a Policy Pj (i.e., policies it may depend on), initialized to all the other policies in line 3, is modified in line 13 to remove Policies Pi that already depend on it. This assumption stems from the nature of multi-layer ISs where upper components depend only on components in lower layers. This optimization can be dropped for other scenarios if needed.

Figure 3 shows the result of applying our approach to the IS example in Section 2. A *policySet* element has been created for each of the system components: firewall, database and CMS. These *policySets* contain the translated to XACML access-control *policy* of each component along with references to its dependencies as calculated by algorithm 1.

Table 1. OCL Operations

Operation	Description
getDependents(p:Policy) : Sequence{Policy}	Given a policy P, returns the sequence of policies having this policy as dependency.
getDependencies(p:Policy): Sequence{Dependency}	Given a policy P, returns the sequence of direct dependencies.
getAllDependencies(p:Policy): Sequence{Dependency}	Given a policy P, returns the sequence of ALL the dependencies, direct and indirect.
resolveDependency(d:Dependency) : Policy	Given a dependency D, returns its target Policy P.
getDependencySource(d:Dependency): Policy	Given a dependency D, returns its source Policy P.
getContextAttributes(p:Policy) : Sequence{Tuple{key:String,val:String}}	Given a Policy P, returns a sequence of tuples{key:String,Value:String}, representing the context attributes
getRelevantRules(p:Policy,p2:Policy) : Sequence{Rule}	Given two policies, Pi and Pj, with Pi dependent on Pj, returns the rules in Pj related to the context attributes of Pi, i.e., the set of rules of Pj Pi depends on

Considering the following set of context attributes for each component: *IpAddress : 111.222.1.10* for the database; *dbUserName:anonyme* and *IpAddress: 111.222.1.12* for the CMS; the empty set for the firewall, the results is that the database *policySet* holds a dependency on the firewall *policySet* (due to the IP address context attribute) while the CMS *policySet* holds dependencies to the firewall and the database *policySets* (due to the database user and IP address context attributes).

6   Global Analysis of Inter-Component Anomalies

We are now able to perform all kinds of security analysis and manipulation tasks unavailable when focusing only on individual policies. The implementation of such tasks will benefit from the use of a common XACML representation which abstracts from irrelevant technical details and facilitates their reusability regardless the specific components those policies come from.

In this paper we focus on one of such analysis tasks that we believe is specially critical: the detection of inter-component anomalies. As a preparation, we will first present a number of basic operations introduced with the purpose of easing the manipulation of our integrated model (for this and other possible analysis).

6.1   Basic Operations

Our model can be easily queried to extract useful information by using the OCL [16] standard query language. However, there is a set of operations that will be commonly used and as such, we consider worth it to define them as a reusable library. In that sense, we present here a list of useful model manipulation operations implemented with OCL.

Table 1 presents a description of this set of basic operations. Basically, we present operations to work with the dependencies, *getDependents*, *getDependencies*, *getAllDependencies resolveDependency* and *getDependencySource*; operations to obtain the context attributes of a policy, *getContextAttributes*; and operations to obtain the rules related with context attributes in a dependency relation, *getRelevantRules*.

6.2 Detection of Rule Anomalies

One important analysis task is the detection of anomalies that appear when several policies work together, as shown in the examples in Section 2. The problems these anomalies cause vary from simply increasing the complexity of policies to the introduction of unexpected behaviour of a component w.r.t. its defined policy.

Focusing on the undesired effects these anomalies may produce and considering rule r_i depending on r_j (as indicated by the policy dependency structure presented in 5), we identify the following risks (defining risk as a threat caused by an anomaly that may lead to loses in terms of money and/or reputation):

- **Security Risk**: The combination of r_i and r_j may cause a security hole. This happens when r_j allows requests for values r_i does not allow. We consider the risk partial when r_j only allows some of the r_i denied values. Example 2 in Section 2 belongs to this category, as the network layer, combined with the database layer, allows request the CMS does not.
- **Service Risk**: The combination of r_i and r_j may cause the component to which r_i provides access-control not to be able to provide the expected service. This happens when r_j denies requests for values r_i allows. We consider the risk partial when r_j only denies some of the r_i allowed values. Example 1 in Section 2 shows a partial service risk.
- **Redundancy**: r_i or r_j may be eliminated without impact to the behaviour in the system. This may happen when both rules deny requests for the same values. Policies containing those rules may be refactored to reduce complexity.
- **No Risk**: The combination of r_i and r_j does not generate any risk.

As we have seen, these anomalies depend on the relations that hold between the set of request matched by a pair of rules. For determining that relation we need to compare security rules. This comparison is done for the purpose of checking if 1) Conditions in different rules hold for the same set of values 2) The rule effect when the conditions hold are conflicting. This process, which we call rule similarity evaluation following the terminology in [14], can be performed following different approaches. Here, due to the relative simplicity of the syntactical analysis they propose, we adapt the approach proposed in [14] to the case of policies in different architectural layers. Other approaches could however be also adapted to our specific case.

Rule Similarity. For risk analysis purposes, the similarity of rules can be classified in five values { *Converges, Diverges, Restricts, Extends, Shuffles* } with the following definition (see the second column in Table2 for a graphical representation):

Table 2. Policy rule similarity type instantiated

Rule similarity type	Matched requests	$R_i^{Accept},$ R_j^{Accept}	R_i^{Deny}, R_j^{Deny}	$R_i^{Deny},$ R_j^{Accept}	$R_i^{Accept},$ R_j^{Deny}
$Ri\,Converges\,Rj$	$\left(R_i = R_j\right)$	No Risk	Redundancy	Security Risk	Service Risk
$Ri\,Diverges\,Rj$	R_i $\quad$ R_j	Service Risk	No Risk	No Risk	No Risk
$Ri\,Restricts\,Rj$	$R_j\,(R_i)$	No Risk	No Risk	Security Risk	Service Risk
$Ri\,Extends\,Rj$	$R_i\,(R_j)$	Service Risk*	No Risk	Security Risk*	Service Risk*
$Ri\,Shuffles\,Rj$	$R_i\!\!\times\!\!R_j$	Service Risk*	No Risk	Security Risk*	Service Risk*

* partial risk

Converge: Two rules 'converge' if the sets of values are equal with respect to which their conditions hold.

Diverge: Two rules 'diverge' if the sets of values do not intersect with respect to which of their conditions hold.

Restrict and extend: A rule 'restricts' (or 'extends') another rule if the sets of values with respect to which its conditions hold contain (or is contained in) the set of values computed for the other rule.

Shuffle: Two rules 'shuffle' if the sets of values for which their conditions hold intersect, but no one is contained in the other.

These values are calculated by a similarity calculation algorithm presented in [14]. We instantiate the Rule similarity types for the case of rules situated in different architectural layers by assigning them the previously defined risk types.

Risk calculation. The assignment of risk types to rule similarity types depends on their effect (deny, accept) and matched request sets. Table 2 shows the assignment for all the possible combinations. Notice that the actual presence of anomalies between two rules depends on the nature of the involved systems and how they interact.

Algorithm 2 describes the process of instantiating the risks of rules over our infrastructure given a rule and an attribute to check. Basically, the algorithm iterates over the policies the policy containing the rule depends on, retrieving relevant rules (lines 9 and 13) and retrieving the similarity value (line 18) to produce an anomaly report (line 19). It is important to note that when the dependency is indirect, i.e., the dependency relationship is established through another policy, we need to get the relevant rules w.r.t. this latter policy having the direct dependency (line 11 to 15). This is specially important because a given policy may have both, a direct and an indirect dependency with another policy, each one yielding a different set of relevant rules. As this information is relevant

---

Algorithm 2. Risk evaluation

```
 1: r← Initialrule, a← Initialattribute
 2: P← P/r ∈ P, D← getAllDependencies(P), S← getDependencies(P)
 3: for each Dᵢ ∈ D do
 4:     Pᵢ ← resolveDependency(Dᵢ)
 5:     if Dᵢ in S then
 6:         R← getRelevantRules(P, Pᵢ)
 7:         tagRules(R, P)
 8:     else
 9:         Pⱼ ← getDependencySource(Dᵢ)
10:         R← getRelevantRules(Pⱼ, Pᵢ)
11:         tagRules(R, Pⱼ)
12:     end if
13:     for each rᵢ ∈ R do
14:         if a ∈ rᵢ then
15:             sim← calculateSimilarity(rᵢ, r, a)
16:             reportAnomalyCheck(sim, rᵢ, r, )
17:         end if
18:     end for
19: end for
```

---

for performing further analysis, each rule is tagged with its dependent policy (lines 10 and 14).

Let us take a look of how the risk types instantiation is calculated for the examples presented in Section 2. Regarding the first example, we want to know if given the database rule R_{DB} and its time attribute there exists an anomaly:

$$R_{DB}(RoleX, TableX, Write, 8{:}00 - 16{:}00) \rightarrow accept$$

Following the proposed algorithm, the policy dependencies are retrieved, that in this case consists only in a dependency towards the firewall policy. Using the context attributes, the rules in the firewall policy related to the database are retrieved. Finally, from this set of rules, the ones containing the time attribute are checked for similarity with the database rule and tagged in consequence. We can then show only those having a similarity implying an anomaly. In that subset we will have the second rule in the example, R_{FW}, as it uses a context attribute, the time attribute, and the calculated similarity has the value of extend, which may cause an anomaly of partial service risk, as shown in the Table 2.

$$R_{FW}(Local, DBServer, Send/receive, 8{:}00 - 14{:}00) \rightarrow accept$$

As for the second example, the process starts in a similar way, by retrieving the dependencies of the CMS policy containing the rule R_{CMS} and the attribute to be checked, in this case, the source IP address.

$$R_{CMS}(BlacklistedIPs, Admin, Access) \rightarrow deny$$

However, now we will have two kinds of dependencies. The CMS policy depends directly on the database and firewall policies, but it also holds an indirect dependency to the firewall policy through the database one. Thus, three sets of rules are retrieved, those of the firewall and database policies related to the CMS context attributes (IP address and database user) and those of the firewall related with the context attributes of the database (IP address of the server).

The risk type instantiation calculated on the set of retrieved rules will exhibit not only the possible anomalies the policy of the CMS has with respect to the database and the firewall directly, but also those anomalies arising from the combination of the effects of rules in the database and firewall together. Thus, among other possible anomalies present in the firewall or database configuration we will retrieve the one associated with the following rule:

$$R_{FW}(0.0.0.0, DBServer, Send/receive,) \rightarrow accept$$

It gives access to the database server (back-end of the CMS) to users in a location forbidden by the CMS policy. This rule retrieved from the database dependency and tagged that way, informs us about an anomaly (shadowing) between the CMS and the firewall involving the database system. The security expert will only need to retrieve the database relevant rules w.r.t. the CMS policy to have a complete picture of the problem.

$$R_{CMS}(BlacklistedIPs, Admin, Access) \rightarrow deny$$
$$R_{DB}(CMSRole, CMSSchema, Write) \rightarrow accept$$
$$R_{FW}(0.0.0.0, DBServer, Send/receive,) \rightarrow accept$$

Obtaining this information would not have been possible without the integration of the policies and the discovery of their dependencies.

7   Implementation

In order to validate the feasibility of our approach, a proof-of-concept prototype implementation has been developed under the Eclipse environment[2] by using Model-driven tools and techniques. Concretely, our implementation is based on two features:

Model Representation. Our approach takes as input domain-specific access-control models extracted from different components in order to translate them to XACML models. To be able to do that, a XACML policy metamodel (models conform to metamodels, which define the main concepts and relationships of the domain) is required, so that models conforming to it can be created. We have used, EMF, the de-facto modeling framework for that purpose.

Providing the XACML XSD schema[3] as an input to EMF, the framework allowed us to generate the XACML policy metamodel, and in turn, to generate Java code plugins for the manipulation of model instances, including a tree-based editor. Note that these models instances can be, in turn, serialized using a XML syntax. XACML identifiers, datatypes, etc, are integrated in a similar way i.e., by extracting a metamodel through EMF and linking it to the XACML metamodel.

Model Query and Transformations. Once the means to represent XACML models are available, we can perform the transformations from the domain models and the operations and algorithms described in Sections 5 and 6. We have

---

[2] https://www.eclipse.org/
[3] http://docs.oasis-open.org/xacml/3.0/XSD/cs-xacml-schema-policy-01.xsd

used the ATL[8] model-to-model transformation language for that purpose. ATL is a hybrid (declarative with imperative facilities) language and framework that provides the means to easily specify the way to produce target models from source models. The following model-to-model transformation have been created:

1) A model transformation for each component model to a XACML model.

2) A library of helpers, an ATL mechanism to factorize OCL operations, representing the basic operations in section 6

3) A model transformation for the integration algorithm in 1.

4) A model query for the detection of anomalies, following the algorithm 2.

8   Related Work

The integration of security policies is a research problem that has attired the attention of the security research community in the recent years. Consequently, different approaches to tackle the problem have been proposed.

From a formal perspective, in [3] the authors provide the foundations of a formal framework to represent policies in different architectural layers. Similarly, in [2] the authors analyze different combination operations for AC policies. Among them, the combination of heterogeneous policies and the integration of hierarchical policies through refinement. [1] provides a logical framework to encode multiple authorization policies into a proof-carrying authorization formalism. In [17] Method-B is used to formalize the deployment of AC policies on systems composed of several (network) components. Finally, by using model-driven techniques, in [5] the authors formalize the policy continuum model, that represent policies at different inter-related abstraction layers although it does not tackle the problem of inter-related architectural layers.

The aforementioned works are valuable contributions that could be eventually used to enforce a forward engineering process to generate correct policies. However, none of these formalization works provide the bridges necessary to fill the gap between real deployed policies and the proposed formalisms as they mostly aim at providing a formal framework to deploy/analyse/manipulate synthetic policies. Conversely, our approach works the other way round by proposing a more pragmatic approach, aimed at providing a solution for the integration of real, already deployed policies.

More similar to us and working on XACML policies, in [6] the authors describe an approach to detect anomalies while in [14] integration analysis for policies belonging to different authorization entities is proposed. None of them deals with dependencies between policies as we do here for the case of multi-layer architectures. Finally, we have adapted the similarity process proposed in [14] to compare rules and policies to the case of inter-dependent access control policies.

9   Conclusions and Future Work

We have presented an approach to integrate the Access-control policies collaborating in an Information System. It translates all the policies to the XACML policy language and organizes them in an unique model by unveiling the implicit dependencies between them. Finally, we have presented useful operations taking advantage of the proposed infrastructure that lead to detect possible anomalies between the policies.

As a future work, we plan to extend our approach to include other sources of information. Concretely, we would like to integrate in our approach the information provided by the audit and logging systems of IS components. So far, we can point the security experts to possible anomalies. By analysing the audits together with them, we believe we can determine whether the anomaly is taking place/being exploited or not. Finally, we also intend to extend our approach to integrate different kinds of policies. Privacy, Integrity and Secrecy policies may collaborate between them and thus, we believe they may benefit of an integration approach as the one we have presented here.

References

1. Bauer, L., Appel, A.W.: Access Control for the Web via Proof-Carrying Authorization. PhD thesis, Princeton University (2003)
2. Bonatti, P., De Capitani di Vimercati, S., Samarati, P.: An Algebra for Composing Access Control Policies. TISSEC **5**(1), 1–35 (2002)
3. Casalino, M.M., Thion, R.: Refactoring multi-layered access control policies through (de)composition. In: CNSM, pp. 243–250 (2013)
4. Cuppens, F., Cuppens-Boulahia, N., Sans, T., Miège, A.: A formal approach to specify and deploy a network security policy. In: FAST 2004, pp. 203–218 (2004)
5. Davy, S., Jennings, B., Strassner, J.: The Policy Continuum-Policy Authoring and Conflict Analysis. Computer Communications **31**(13), 2981–2995 (2008)
6. Hu, H., Ahn, G.-J., Kulkarni, K.: Anomaly discovery and resolution in web access control policies. In: SACMAT 2011, pp. 165–174. ACM (2011)
7. Jin, X., Krishnan, R., Sandhu, R.: A unified attribute-based access control model covering DAC, MAC and RBAC. In: Cuppens-Boulahia, N., Cuppens, F., Garcia-Alfaro, J. (eds.) DBSec 2012. LNCS, vol. 7371, pp. 41–55. Springer, Heidelberg (2012)
8. Jouault, F., Allilaire, F., Bézivin, J., Kurtev, I.: ATL: A Model Transformation Tool. Science of Computer Programming **72**(1), 31–39 (2008)
9. Lockhart, H., Parducci, B., Anderson, A.: OASIS XACML TC (2013)
10. Lodderstedt, T., Basin, D., Doser, J.: SecureUML: a UML-based modeling language for model-driven security. In: Jézéquel, J.-M., Hussmann, H., Cook, S. (eds.) UML 2002. LNCS, vol. 2460, pp. 426–441. Springer, Heidelberg (2002)
11. Martínez, S., Cosentino, V., Cabot, J., Cuppens, F.: Reverse engineering of database security policies. In: Decker, H., Lhotská, L., Link, S., Basl, J., Tjoa, A.M. (eds.) DEXA 2013, Part II. LNCS, vol. 8056, pp. 442–449. Springer, Heidelberg (2013)
12. Martínez, S., Garcia-Alfaro, J., Cuppens, F., Cuppens-Boulahia, N., Cabot, J.: Model-driven extraction and analysis of network security policies. In: Moreira, A., Schätz, B., Gray, J., Vallecillo, A., Clarke, P. (eds.) MODELS 2013. LNCS, vol. 8107, pp. 52–68. Springer, Heidelberg (2013)
13. Martínez, S., García-Alfaro, J., Cuppens, F., Cuppens-Boulahia, N., Cabot, J.: Towards an access-control metamodel for web content management systems. In: ICWE Workshops, pp. 148–155 (2013)

14. Mazzoleni, P., Crispo, B., Sivasubramanian, S., Bertino, E.: XACML Policy Integration Algorithms. TISSEC **11**(1), 4 (2008)
15. Mouelhi, T., Fleurey, F., Baudry, B., Le Traon, Y.: A model-based framework for security policy specification, deployment and testing. In: Czarnecki, K., Ober, I., Bruel, J.-M., Uhl, A., Völter, M. (eds.) MODELS 2008. LNCS, vol. 5301, pp. 537–552. Springer, Heidelberg (2008)
16. OMG. OCL, version 2.0. Object Management Group, June 2005
17. Preda, S., Cuppens-Boulahia, N., Cuppens, F., Garcia-Alfaro, J., Toutain, L.: Model-driven security policy deployment: property oriented approach. In: Massacci, F., Wallach, D., Zannone, N. (eds.) ESSoS 2010. LNCS, vol. 5965, pp. 123–139. Springer, Heidelberg (2010)
18. Sandhu, R., Ferraiolo, D., Kuhn, R.: The NIST Model for Role-Based Access Control: Towards A Unified Standard. RBAC 2000, pp. 47–63. ACM (2000)
19. Trninic, B., Sladic, G., Milosavljevic, G., Milosavljevic, B., Konjovic, Z.: PolicyDSL: towards generic access control management based on a policy metamodel. In: SoMeT, pp. 217–223 (2013)

Network Security

Authenticated File Broadcast Protocol

Simão Reis[1]([✉]), André Zúquete[2]([✉]), Carlos Faneca[1], and José Vieira[2]

[1] IEETA, University of Aveiro, Aveiro, Portugal
{simao.paulo,carlos.faneca}@ua.pt
[2] DETI/IEETA/IT, University of Aveiro, Aveiro, Portugal
{andre.zuquete,jnvieira}@ua.pt

Abstract. The File Broadcast Protocol (FBP) was developed as a part of the DETIboot system. DETIboot allows a host to broadcast an operating system image through an 802.11 wireless network to an arbitrary number of receivers. Receivers can load the image and immediately boot a Linux live session. The initial version of FBP had no security mechanisms. In this paper we present an authentication protocol developed for FBP that ensures a correct file distribution from the intended source to the receivers. The performance evaluations have shown that, with the best operational configuration tested, the file download time is increased by less than 5%.

1 Introduction

The DETIboot system is a solution that was designed and developed to quickly install a temporary, live Linux image in an arbitrarily large number of computers [1–3]. It uses a wireless 802.11 network (WiFi), operating in ad hoc mode, and broadcast communication to send the Linux image to nearby clients. These load the image and immediately boot a Linux live session, which can disappear without leaving a trace after a power down. This system has potential applications in both academic and enterprise environments. Currently we are working on a security ecosystem for DETIboot in order to allow its use in exams using students' personal laptops and an hardened Linux image.

The DETIboot system uses a broadcast file distribution protocol (FBP). The first version of FBP had no security mechanisms, which is not advised for ensuring a correct distribution of the intended Linux image among all receivers. In this paper we propose a broadcast authentication protocol for FBP, which enables FBP receivers to make a correct download from an intended FBP server.

Our authentication protocol kept the basic behaviour of FBP. The authentication is performed with extra messages (authenticators) interleaved at unpredictable places within the original FBP frame transmission flow. These authenticators enable a set of future frames to be authenticated by the receivers. The option for sending an authenticator before its target frames was taken for preventing receivers from accumulating frames that may never be authenticated.

Authenticators use well-known technology: SHA-1 frame digests, signed with an RSA private key. For the envisioned exploitation scenarios we use

© IFIP International Federation for Information Processing 2015
H. Federrath and D. Gollmann (Eds.): SEC 2015, IFIP AICT 455, pp. 237–251, 2015.
DOI: 10.1007/978-3-319-18467-8_16

high-performance RSA setups (1024 bit modulus, small public exponents) for increasing performance without compromising security. The setup of an FBP session is driven by parameters derived from the public key of the FBP server, which guaranties that receivers cannot be fooled by networks deployed by attackers.

For evaluating the performance of our proposal, we did measurements in multiple operational scenarios, considering different reception conditions, different timings for sending authenticators and the presence of an attacker. Without attacks, the overhead in the total download time for a more aggressive transmission of authenticators, the one with better results, was below 5%.

This paper is structured as follows. In Section 2 we present the FBP concepts that are fundamental to understand the options we took for adding authentication, as well as its security weaknesses. In Sections 3 and 4 we present our FBP authentication protocol and some implementation details. In Section 5 we present the performance evaluation of FBP with authentication. In Section 6 we present some related work in the area of broadcast authentication. Finally, in Section 7 we present our conclusions.

2   File Broadcast Protocol

In this section the File Broadcast Protocol (FBP) is described in order to clarify the scenario that needs to be protected.

FBP [1–3] uses Fountain Codes [4,5] to broadcast a file. Fountain Codes create a sequence of codewords that can be generated from a given set of source symbols such that those symbols can be recovered from any subset of the codewords of size equal to, or only slightly larger than, the number of source symbols.

FBP starts by slicing the file to be transmitted into a set of equally-sized segments (source symbols). Pseudo-random XOR combinations of those segments are then calculated, yielding Fountain Code codewords. FBP repetitively and indefinitely broadcast codewords from a server to multiple clients. The transmitter encodes file segments into codewords and the clients decode those codewords, obtaining the original file segments.

FBP clients may enter at any time in the broadcast session, they do not need to be present at the begging of the FBP transmission. Furthermore, they are tolerant to packet losses since, in theory, it does not matter the exact set of codewords one needs to receive (all codewords are equality good to get the original symbols). After a given threshold of received codeword it should be highly probably to complete the decoding and get all the original symbols.

FBP is a network protocol (layer 3 of the OSI model), identified through the Ethernet code 0x1986 in 802.11 frames. An 802.11 codeword frame conveys the codeword itself and the indexes of all symbols used to generate it. The indexes are not transmitted directly, they are derived by receivers from parameters included in the frame: total number of symbols (K), degree of the codeword (number of symbols used in its generation), and a random seed (cf. Figure 1). The degree and the seed, together with a universal pseudo-random generator, are used to generate the index set of the symbols contained in the codeword. A codeword frame also includes a codeword index (a sequence number) for performance evaluation purposes. We used it also for defining authentication windows.

2.1 Security Vulnerabilities/Attacker Model

FBP uses a wireless medium, through 802.11 ad-hoc networks, to broadcast codewords of a boot image from a source to many destination laptops. Thus, an attacker can try to impersonate a legitimate source in order to provide its own boot image. Alternatively, the attacker may provide only a few codewords that would act as a Trojan Horse, i.e., could change the final behavior of the boot image while keeping most of its functionality unchanged. This is not easy, but certainly not impossible.

Besides those attacks, where the attacker could attempt to control the downloaded boot image, an attacker can use Denial of Service (DoS) attacks. In this case, it can (i) repeat previously sent codewords or (ii) prevent legitimate codeword transmissions or receptions.

In the first case, which is a typical replay attack, it would increase the receivers' memory with useless codewords, but not ruin the codeword decoding process (repeated codewords can, in fact, happen). In any case, it is advised to discard repeated codewords if we are able to detect such situation.

In the second case, involving interference with a legitimate transmission and reception, there is no definitive solution, because jamming or abusive 802.11 medium occupancy is always possible. Nevertheless, we can make an attacker's task harder by forcing it to interfere continuously with the legitimate transmitter. In fact, since FBP codewords do not need to be strictly ordered and can be lost, as long as a receiver is able to get codewords, even at a lower rate, it will continuously evolve towards a complete codeword decoding. The only way to avoid this is by preventing receivers to get any codewords at all.

Another type of attack involves the name resolution used in ad hoc networks. These networks, formally referred as Independent Basic Service Sets (IBSS), can be identified by names, which are assigned to 48-bit values (BSS IDentifiers, BSSID). Usually, the binding between a network name and a BSSID is made by any node that attempts a network name resolution within the neighbors and gets no answer. Thus, it is perfectly possible to have a legitimate FBP transmitter and an attacker with the same network name bound to different BSSID values. In this case, FBP receivers should not resolve network names to BSSID values, because they may get the attacker's BSSID, thus entering its network thereafter. In such case, the attacker could impersonate the legitimate FBP transmitter, providing its own boot image, or remain silent, this way deploying a DoS black hole attack. Since the name resolution is a basic 802.11 feature, which cannot be changed or protected in any way, the obvious solution is to force the BSSID of FBP receivers to a value known to be in use by the legitimate FBP transmitter.

Finally, assuming that FBP needs some mechanism to enable receivers to check the validity of the codewords they receive, this mechanism should be designed in a way that does not allow an attacker to interfere with it with a minimum effort. Otherwise, it would be easy for an attacker to force receivers to discard all legitimate codewords. The autonomous authentication of each and every codeword could be a solution, but the overhead costs, both in terms of data transmission and CPU processing, could as well be excessive. On the other hand, the transmission of a few, critical authentication control frames, which could be used to authenticate many codewords, cannot be predictable (i.e., nobody should be able to guess their transmission slot). Otherwise, an attacker could simply jam those control frames to interfere with, an completely ruin, the entire codeword reception process.

2.2   Authentication Requirements and Alternatives

As referred in [6], the solutions to reliable, point-to-point packet communications do no scale well to broadcast environments. In point-to-point is usual that receivers request retransmission of the data in case of failure. FBP solves this issue for broadcast communication by using Fountain Codes, which do not require feedback. Furthermore, authentication in point-to-point communications can be achieved with a pure symmetrical solution, such as a Message Authentication Code (MAC). Both parties share a common secret key, and when a message with a correct MAC arrives the receiver is assured that the correct transmitter generated it. However, in a broadcast environment a MAC is not safe. Every party knows the MAC key, therefore anyone could impersonate the genuine source and assume the broadcast transmission. The obvious approach is the use of an asymmetric mechanism, such as a digital signature. These have the asymmetrical authentication property required by FBP: each source generates signatures with its private key and the receivers can verify the signatures with the public key of the intended source.

An FBP receiver needs to know something about a legitimate FBP transmitter to authenticate it, or the codewords it sends. However, an FBP receiver should process codewords immediately upon their reception, to maximize the decoding CPU cycles between the reception of consecutive frames. Consequently, it is advised to either (i) authenticate each codeword independently from the others or (ii) to transmit a multi-codeword authentication frame prior to a transmit the respective codewords.

The natural solution for the first option is to include in each codeword a signature, produced by the FBP transmitter and that could be verified by each an every receiver. However, ordinary signatures, such as the ones made with RSA, can take a relevant space in the codeword frame. For a typical codeword with nearly 1500 bytes, an RSA signature using a 1024-bit modulus would add 128 more bytes to a codeword. This means about 9% more data to transmit per codeword. Since to overall decoding time is a function of the time it takes to receive a minimum number of codewords, with this authentication strategy the overall decoding time would increase by no less than 9%. This is not dramatic, but we thought we could get a better solution, and we did.

The second option is to transmit authentication frames with authentication material for the frame itself and for checking a set of codewords following it. A simple strategy for implementing this authentication policy would be to include in a authentication frame a set of references and digests of future codewords, all signed by the FBP transmitter. With a 1500-byte frame and an 128-byte RSA signature we have room for about 60 20-byte SHA-1 digests. Without frame losses, this strategy has an overhead lower than 2% relatively to the data transmitted, because we only need to transmit an authenticator (and the correponding public key to validate it) before a batch of 60 codewords. However, with frame losses the overhead is higher, because upon the loss of an authenticator the receiver would have to discard all codewords until getting the next authenticator.

Regarding attacks, the second option is potentially weaker than the first against DoS attacks. In fact, if an attacker could predict the instant when authenticators are transmitted, then it could jam the network during such transmission and, with a minimum effort, could prevent the validation of all received codewords. However, this weakness can be mitigated by adding some randomness to the instants when authenticators are transmitted. For instance, the transmitter can insert a variable number of codewords between authenticators, ranging from 1 and up to the maximum of digests present in the previous authenticator. With this strategy, an attacker could never anticipate the transmission of an authenticator, therefore selective jamming would not be possible any more.

3 Authenticated File Broadcast Protocol

This section presents the authentication extension developed for the FBP protocol. In this extension we used the last solution presented in the previous section: special authentication packets, interleaved from time to time with codewords, which authenticate a fixed number of following codewords.

3.1 Design Assumptions and Options

Our authentication protocol was conceived for an operational environment where a new, fresh asymmetric key pair can be create and used in a time-limited file download session. For instance, it can be use to download a particular live Linux distribution in the beginning of a class, possibly taking no more then a few minutes. Or we can use a daily key pair for on-demand distribution of live Linux distributions for the computers of an organization (e.g. a demonstration distribution for all laptops being presented in shelfs of a computer store).

In both cases, we take the two following assumptions: (i) key pairs can be changed frequently, on a per-session basis, and do not need to stay stable for a long time; and (ii) the receivers can get, from a reliable source, some elements that allow them to verify if a public key is the correct one they should use. In this last case, we did not consider any automatic validation strategies, such as public key certificates or certification chains, but rather some human-driven mechanisms, such as the validation of the equality between digests.

Taking into consideration the first assumption, there is no need to use very long asymmetric keys; we chose 1024-bit RSA keys. Furthermore, we used the smallest Fermat prime (3), as the public exponent, which reduces to the minimum the computation overhead in the receivers without bringing known security vulnerabilities. We have chosen SHA-1 as the algorithm to compute the digest of each codeword. Currently it has no known vulnerabilities and the digests are not excessively long.

3.2   Key Distribution and Validation

Each authenticator carries the modulus of the public key of its generator, as well as a signature produced by the corresponding private key. When a receiver starts, it waits for an authenticator, checks its signature, presents a digest of the public key to the user and waits for an accept/reject decision. This decision must be taken upon checking, by some means, if the digest is the expected one. For instance, in a classroom, the teacher controlling the source machine can get the same digest and write it in the board.

For segregating communications involved in different FBP sessions, the overall key-related setup is slightly more complex:

1. The sender initiates the FBP server, this generates a fresh key pair for the transmission session. Then, it computes (and displays) a digest from its public modulus and uses part of that digest to compute (and display) the BSSID of its ad hoc network. This BSSID can or cannot be already in use, that is irrelevant for FBP.
2. The receiver initiates the FBP client with the BSSID being used by the intended server, in order to enter its ad hoc network.
3. The FBP client waits for an authenticator, which it will use to present the digest of its public modulus. If the user approves its value, the modulus is recorded for checking future authenticators.
4. The FBP client waits for a valid (properly authenticated) codeword for extracting the download operational parameters – number of symbols K and size of each symbol/codeword. Once having this, the decoding process can start (using this and the following valid codewords).

Ethernet packets have a payload of 1500 bytes. Subtracting the size of the public RSA modulus (128 bytes), the size of the corresponding signature (128 bytes), the remaining space can, at the maximum, accommodate 62 20-byte codeword digests. We decided to use only 60, leaving some space in the authenticator for some extra fields that could be necessary.

Each authenticator can authenticate 60 consecutive codewords. Considering that authenticators are equal in size to codewords (the difference is small), at least $\frac{1}{61}$ ($\sim$1.6%) of all transmitted bytes will be exclusively used for authentication. By increasing the transmission frequency of authenticators we increase accordingly such overhead. This can be a low price to pay when transmission losses increase, affecting the number of received authenticators. We will address this issue in Section 5.

codeword index	(4 bytes)
K	(4 bytes)
seed	(4 bytes)
degree	(4 bytes)
codeword	(1484 bytes)

last codeword index: $x + 59$	(4 bytes)
0	(4 bytes)
session identifier	(4 bytes)
SHA-1 digests: $d_x, d_{x+1}, \cdots, d_{x+59}$	(1200 bytes)
RSA signature & public key modulus	(256 bytes)

Fig. 1. FBP frame payloads for codewords (left) and authenticators for transmitting before codeword index x (right)

3.3 Authenticator Generation

Before sending a set of $1 \leq N \leq 60$ previously generated codewords, the FBP server creates an authenticator to protect the next $60 \geq N$ codewords $(C_x, \cdots, C_{x+59})$. For each codeword C_i, with $i \in [x, x + 59]$, a digest $d_i = h(C_i)$ is calculated and inserted into the authenticator. The authenticator also carries the index $x + 59$ of the codeword used to compute the last digest (d_{x+59}), an RSA signature of the transmitter over this index and all the digests and the signer public key modulus (see Figure 1).

Upon checking the validity of an authenticator, an FBP client saves all its digests to validate future codewords. For instance, if the last codeword index in the authenticator is 2000, only the 60 codewords with an index between 1941 and 2000 can be checked and possibly accepted by the client. If in the meanwhile another valid authenticator is received, this validation information is updated accordingly for authenticating the following codewords.

Figure 1 shows the complete physical mapping of an authenticator's fields. The second field, corresponding in terms of location to a codeword's field K, is always 0. Since K is never 0 in codeword frames, this field can be used by clients to distinguish codewords from authenticators. The session identifier is used to efficiently discard authenticators belonging to a different download session (sharing, by a very unlikely coincidence, the same 802.11 channel and the same BSSID value). This identifier is randomly chosen by an FBP server and adopted by a receiver upon the acceptance of an authenticator that carries the public modulus that will be used to authenticate the traffic.

3.4 Replay Attacks Against Clients

To prevent replay attacks, authenticators with an outdated latest codeword index (lower than the one of the current authenticator being used) are discarded by clients without further validation.

The codewords' index is also checked to avoid replay attacks. The client saves the index of the last (valid) codeword and discards codewords with a previous or equal index without further validation. Note that we are working with a one-hop wireless network, where frames, in principle, do not get out of order.

4   Implementation Details

4.1   Key Generation and Distribution

The FBP server was modified to generate an RSA key pair with the public exponent 3. Besides including the modulus of this key in all authenticators, the server outputs for its administrator an SHA-1 digest of the modulus and a 48-bit BSSID extracted from part of such digest. These two values need to be conveyed, by the best suited means, to all the users running the FBP client and wishing to download a file from this server. The BSSID is used by the server to initiate the ad hoc network prior to start using it.

The FBP client was modified to accept a BSSID (formerly it was using a name-BSSID translation). Then it waits for an authenticator, displays the SHA-1 digest of its public key modulus, and prompts the user if that is the key to be used. The user has the options to (i) use it, (ii) do not use it once, (iii) do not use it forever, or (iv) input the SHA-1 digest or the desired modulus. Thus, flooding attacks exploring constant or always changing modulus on each authenticator can be overcome by either (i) choosing not to use a modulus forever or (ii) providing the digest of the correct modulus, respectively.

4.2   Production of Authenticators

The server was implemented as a pipeline of 3 tasks: (i) produce the codewords, (ii) build the authenticators and (iii) send both the codewords and the authenticators. Most laptops nowadays are multiprocessor so these tasks can be assigned to an equal number of threads (Producer, Signer and Sender), each on its own CPU, in order to maximize the CPU usage. These tasks manage two circular buffers that are used for queueing codewords and authenticators (see Figure 2).

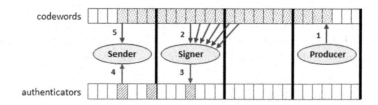

Fig. 2. Tasks, buffers and actions used to coordinate the production and transmission of codewords and authenticators

The Producer thread is the first to start. It produces as many codewords as possible (action 1 in Figure 2). As soon as there are enough codewords (at least 60) to fill an authenticator with their digests, the Signer thread starts. Upon having at least one authenticator, the Sender thread starts.

There are 4 synchronization points, implemented with semaphores: two between the Producer and the Signer; one between the Producer and the Sender and one between the Sender and the Producer. These are represented by the thick vertical lines in Figure 2. Preliminary tests indicated that synchronization points between any pair of buffer items would cause to much computational of overhead. So, these 4 synchronization points are done in blocks of 60 items. The Producer needs only one block; while inside it, it produces as many codewords as possible. The Signer needs two blocks, because each authenticator must always protect the next 60 codewords, and some may be in the next adjacent block. The Sender only needs one block. In total, 4 blocks of 60 items are needed.

As we can see in actions 2 and 3 in Figure 2, the Signer always saves the authenticator in the same index as the first codeword it authenticates. In actions 4 and 5 in Figure 2, the Sender at index i of a block b checks if in the authenticators' queue there is a authenticator for the same index. If there is, it sends it, and then it sends the codeword in the same position of the codewords' queue. Otherwise, it only sends the codeword in that position.

5   Performance Evaluation

The performance evaluation involved reaching two fundamental conclusions: (i) what is the overhead, under normal conditions (i.e., when not being attacked), of our FBP authentication and (ii) what is the preferable frequency for sending authenticators.

To reach these conclusions we have made a series of live measurements considering all possible scenarios combining the following parameters:

- A receiver near or far away from the transmitter. For the near case we experienced an average RSSI (Received Signal Strength Indicator) of -25 dBm, while for the far case we experienced an average RSSI of -75 dBm) (evaluated with Android mobile phones using the Wifi Analizer application).
- A variable number C of codewords between each authenticator, uniformly distributed in the intervals $[1, 30]$ and $[1, 60]$. The first interval leads to an higher frequency in the transmission of authenticators.
- The presence of another transmitter using the same wireless network (same 802.11 channel, same BSSID) and close to the receiver.

For transmissions without authentication we obtained the following indicators: (i) decoding elapsed time (**Time**); (ii) the number of codewords effectively used for reaching the complete file decoding (**Used**); (iii) the number of codewords received by the decoder but not effectively decoded (**Unused**); and (iv) the number of codewords lost in the transmission, due to physical transmission problems or overruns of reception buffers (**Lost**). This last value is computed from the indexes of the first and last codewords (F and L, respectively) received by the decoder and the total number of codewords received by the decoder (R):

$$\text{Lost} = L - F + 1 - R$$

Since $R = \text{Used} + \text{Unused}$, then

$$\text{Lost} = L - F + 1 - (\text{Used} + \text{Unused})$$

The (percentage of) codeword loss in the decoding process is given by

$$\text{Loss} = \frac{\text{Lost}}{R + \text{Lost}} = \frac{\text{Lost}}{\text{Used} + \text{Unused} + \text{Lost}}$$

For transmissions with authentication we obtained all the previous indicators plus the following: (i) the number of codewords from the correct source that failed authentication (**Invalid**); and (ii) the number of codewords from other sources that also failed authentication (**Other**). To distinguish codewords from the correct or incorrect source we used the K of each codeword and all codeword sources broadcast files with a different K. With authentication the calculation of Lost is different, being given by

$$\text{Lost} = L - F + 1 - (\text{Used} + \text{Unused} + \text{Invalid})$$

and the (percentage of) codeword loss in the decoding process is calculated as

$$\text{Loss} = \frac{\text{Invalid} + \text{Lost}}{\text{Used} + \text{Unused} + \text{Invalid} + \text{Lost}}$$

In the measurements we used the following systems and data:

Legitimate transmitter: Toshiba Portégé 830-10R, with an Intel Core i7-2620M at 2.7 GHz, 8 GiB of RAM, with an external (USB) Thomson TG123g WiFi interface (with the TxOP option [7] for fast transmission[1]), running a 64-bit Linux Lubuntu. It was used to transmitted a file with 104, 792, 660 bytes (~100 MiB, 70615 symbols, each with 1484 bytes).

Receiver: Asus K55VM-SX083V, with an Intel Core i5-3210M Dual Core at 2.5 GHz, 8 GiB of RAM, Atheros AR9485 WiFi interface, running a 64-bit Linux Lubuntu at runlevel 1 (single user administration mode).

Attacker: Asus F3SC-AP260C, with an Intel Core 2 Duo T5450 at 1.67 GHz, 1 GiB of RAM, running a 32-bit Linux Lubuntu.

Note that the attacker can be as powerful as intended, as it can be deployed with different machines. In our case, the attacker was made intensionally less powerful than the correct FBP source.

In all transmissions we used 802.11g broadcast at the maximum speed allowed by interface drivers. For the legitimate transmitter we could set that speed to 54 Mbit/s, the 802.11g maximum. When combined with the TxOP, the non-authenticated FBP can achieve a download performance of about 40 Mbit/s. Without such option, the maximum performance drops to about 25 Mbit/s.

Tables 1, 2 and 3 present the average and standard deviation values observed for the elements previously referred in the several scenarios considered. All values were computed after 10 experiments in the same exact circumstances.

---

[1] TxOP allows a transmitter to send batches of frames separated by the minimum possible time, a SIFS (Short Interframe Space).

Table 1. Results at the end of the file decoding without authentication

	Time (s)		Used		Unused		Loss (%)	
Distance	Avg	σ	Avg	σ	Avg	σ	Avg	σ
Near	20.8	0.9	72102.0	171.3	913.6	540.2	0.09	0.09
Far	70.6	6.4	72238.4	137.3	151.3	111.6	3.72	0.12

Table 2. Results at the end of the file decoding with authentication and no attackers

		Time (s)		Used		Unused		Invalid		Lost		Loss (%)	
Distance	C	Avg	σ	Avg	σ	Avg	σ	Avg	σ	Avg	σ	Avg	σ
Near	[1, 30]	21.5	0.1	72141.1	212.5	493.6	328.9	25.6	5.4	42.6	28.2	0.09	0.04
	[1, 60]	21.0	0.1	72212.7	236.4	591.3	343.0	161.2	53.5	437.7	87.4	0.82	0.12
Far	[1, 30]	74.0	14.5	71989.3	132.0	228.0	310.6	8107.3	2069.3	168894.7	46626.2	69.95	6.27
	[1, 60]	121.5	40.3	71943.1	156.3	147.2	270.7	30170.0	6624.8	314448.3	132831.6	81.34	4.94

Table 3. Results at the end of the file decoding with authentication and an attacker

		Time (s)		Used		Unused		Invalid		Lost		Loss (%)		Other	
Dist.	C	Avg	σ	Avg	σ	Avg	σ	Avg	σ	Avg	σ	Avg	σ	Avg	σ
Near	[1, 30]	35.5	0.4	71949.3	145.4	616.8	262.8	820.2	101.5	23006.3	681.2	24.7	0.6	20436.3	23.9
	[1, 60]	36.0	2.1	72155.2	409.9	548.2	281.4	7144.1	1329.5	20811.5	4384.4	27.6	4.0	20917.0	20.5
Far	[1, 30]	87.8	32.7	72061.8	363.9	238.3	330.3	9925.3	3728.8	209600.6	105077.0	72.3	9.3	2610.0	68.9
	[1, 60]	135.8	37.2	72033.8	174.8	38.8	68.2	35275.0	5758.2	358082.8	126205.5	83.7	4.1	3265.3	75.8

Table 4. Overheads in the decoding time and codeword losses due to authentication

Distance	C	Δ Time (%)	Δ Loss (%)
Near	1-30	3.5	0.5
	1-60	1.3	773.9
Far	1-30	4.8	1780.1
	1-60	72.2	2086.5

5.1   Analysis of Results

The results show a typical result of our coding policy: the number of codewords required for completing the file decoding is fairly stable in all cases. However, the time to get those codewords varies a lot depending on the scenario.

Regarding our first goal, compute the overhead introduced by the authentication in normal circumstances (when not being attacked), we see that the overhead is small. Table 4 shows the overheads due to the introduction of authentication. In terms of decoding time, the increment ranged from 3.5 to 4.8% when the frequency of authenticators is higher ($C \in [1, 30]$), and 1.3 to 72.2% when such frequency is lower ($C \in [1, 60]$). In terms of codeword losses, this value increased due to the discarding of invalid codewords. The increase was between 0.5 and 1780.1% when authenticators are more frequent, and between 773.9 and 2086.5% when authenticators are less frequent.

There is an apparently strange outcome, which is the fact that, despite a major increase of losses with authentication, the total decoding time does not increase on the same proportion. Notice, however, that if we have erasure rates (total losses) ϵ_n and ϵ_f for a nearby and far way transmissions, respectively, for reaching a threshold X of codewords in the decoder enabling it to complete the decoding we need to transmit N_n and N_f codewords, in each case, such that

$$X = N_n \times (1 - \epsilon_n)$$
$$X = N_f \times (1 - \epsilon_f)$$

which means that

$$N_f \times (1 - \epsilon_f) = N_n \times (1 - \epsilon_n) \Leftrightarrow \frac{N_f}{N_n} = \frac{1 - \epsilon_n}{1 - \epsilon_f}$$

Now, for $\epsilon_n = 0.0009$ and an $\epsilon_f = 0.6995$ (observed with high frequency authenticators, see Table 2), we get $\frac{N_f}{N_n} \approx 3.325$. Since there is some linear correlation between the decoding time T and the total number of transmitted codewords during the decoding (N), we can also anticipate that $\frac{T_f}{T_n}$ should yield a similar value, which it does: $\frac{74.0}{21.0} = 3.442$. This demonstration is also applicable to the results obtained for transmissions with less frequent authenticators.

Regarding our second goal, finding a preferable frequency for sending authenticators, the tests allow us to conclude that, except in one case, it is preferable to use a higher frequency ($C \in [1, 30]$) than a lower one ($C \in [1, 60]$). With an higher frequency the Time and Loss indicators, the ones that are relevant to evaluate the transmission efficiency, are usually lower than with a low frequency. The increase of Loss is partially due to the increase of the Invalid indicator, which grows when authenticators are transmitted less frequently.

The exception happens when the receiver is very close to the transmitter and there is not an attack. Besides being an hard-to-find scenario (not all receivers can be this close, specially when there are many or they are scattered along a classroom), the difference in the average decoding time is negligible ($\sim 2\%$) for deciding for a lower frequency.

When an attacker is present and competes for the transmission media, it will succeed in reducing the FBP performance. This is evident from the comparison of the results of Tables 2 and 3. However, such results show a curious behaviour: when the attacker and the victim are close to each other, an far away from the genuine source, the Other indicator drops when comparing with the scenario were all three hosts are near each other. This is probably due to transmission collisions between the genuine source and the attacker, which have difficulties in listening to each other traffic.

We have used SHA-1 both for computing the digests of codewords and the authenticators' signatures. Since SHA-1 is deprecated for digital signatures [8], we should probably use stronger digest functions, such as SHA256 or SHA512, for handling signatures. We did some experiments with SHA256 and the performance results were very similar to the ones observed with SHA-1, which means we can increase security without compromising performance.

6   Related Work

Regarding the authentication of Fountain Code transmissions, in [9] the authors developed a solution for authenticating Fountain Code codewords used in the distribution of a new image in multi-hop wireless sensor networks. Their solution is totally different from ours: they recode the original symbols to include digests of other symbols, forming an hash chain up to a new root symbol that needs to be transmitted authenticated and without Fountain Codes. The digests can only be recovered when original (recoded) symbols are recovered, and for building the complete digest tree one needs to recover (recoded) symbols with a particular order. In the mean time, recovered symbols that could not be verified are dropped. Although using Fountain Codes, there is an initial time for the transmission, when the root symbol is transmitted.

Regarding the authentication of other broadcast transmissions, there are numerous contributions using various strategies. We will not go through all individual contributions, but rather highlight those strategies with some references.

Signature amortization methods are similar to our approach: they compute a signature relatively to a set of frames to reduce the signature generation and verification overhead. This approach can be complex to implement if one could not verify a signature upon loosing a related frame (as in [10]) or if we could not verify a signature until receiving a set of frames (as in [11]). We solved these problems, as we tolerate codeword losses and we can immediately verify the validity of a codeword upon its reception at the decoder, with a false negative rate that is a function of the frequency of authenticators.

Symmetric key schemes were used in some secure broadcast approaches, such as TESLA [12], but TESLA requires a synchronized start by all receivers (which we do not) and frames cannot be immediately authenticated, only after receiving a few other frames (which we do not want and we do not need to).

In [13] the author developed a mechanism, called Rapid Authentication, that enables the use of precomputed data in the creation of RSA signatures. His goal was to accelerate the individual signature of Command & Control Messages for an efficient, real-time transmission. This is not a problem for us, since we do not need to sign each and every codeword, just authenticators, and this can be done in parallel with the production and transmission of codewords.

7   Conclusions

In this paper we have presented a solution for adding a lightweight source authentication to codewords transmitted by an FBP server. The goal was to prevent a nearby attacker to compromise codeword receptions by adding wrong codewords.

The solution we have presented uses well-known and widely accepted technologies (SHA-1 digests and RSA key pairs and signatures) to produce and check codeword authenticators. These are transmitted before the actual transmission of the codewords they authenticate, which enables receivers to validate codewords immediately upon their reception. Authenticators are transmitted at a variable and unpredictable pace, which prevents attackers to make surgical jamming strikes against them. Using a higher rate for sending authenticators we achieved very good performance result, with a maximum overhead of less then 5% in the total file decoding time. Note that this overhead already includes the public key distribution, which is performed by all authenticators.

The distribution of the public module of the RSA key pair used to authenticate an FBP session was adapted to the operational scenarios where FBP was designed to be used within DETIboot: for transmitting a file (usually a Linux live distribution image) to an arbitrarily large population of nearby receivers (e.g. in a classroom). Since these are sufficiently close to the transmission source to make eye contact, the critical information regarding the public key modulus (its digest) and the ad hoc network BSSID can be conveyed in a simple and straightforward way: by writing somewhere where it could be seen by all receivers (e.g. on the classroom board).

Acknowledgments. This research work was supported by the projects PTDC/EEI-TEL/3006/2012 (CodeStream) and PEst-OE/EEI/UI0127/2014, both from FCT (Foundation for Science and Technology).

References

1. Cardoso, J.: DETIboot: distribuição e arranque de sistemas Linux com redes WiFi. Master's thesis, University of Aveiro, Portugal (2013)
2. Faneca, C., Vieira, J., Zúquete, A.: Fast image file distribution with fountain codes via a Wi-Fi Ad-hoc network, using low power processors. In: 16th Int. Telecommunications Network Strategy and Planning Symposium (NETWORKS 2014), Funchal, Madeira, Portugal, September 2014
3. Faneca, C., Vieira, J., Zúquete, A., Cardoso, J.: DETIboot: A fast, wireless system to install operating systems on students laptops. In: 2nd Int. Conf. on Advances in Computing, Electronics and Communication (ACEC 2014), Zurich, Switzerland, October 2014
4. Byers, J., Luby, M., Mitzenmacher, M.: A digital fountain approach to asynchronous reliable multicast. IEEE Journal on Selected Areas in Communications **20**(8), 1528–1540 (2002)
5. MacKay, D.J.C.: Fountain codes. IEE Proceedings Communications **152**(6), 1062–1068 (2005)
6. Perrig, A., Tygar, J.D.: Secure Broadcast Communication: In Wired and Wireless Networks. Springer, New York (2003)
7. IEEE Std 802.11e: Wireless LAN Medium Access Control (MAC) and Physical Layer (PHY) Specifications, Amendment 8: Medium Access Control (MAC) Enhancements for Quality of Service (QoS) (2005)
8. Barker, E.B., Roginsky, A.L.: Transitions: Recommendation for Transitioning the Use of Cryptographic Algorithms and Key Lengths. NIST SP - 800–131A (2011)
9. Bohli, J.M., Hessler, A., Ugus, O., Westhoff, D.: Security enhanced multi-hop over the air reprogramming with fountain codes. In: IEEE 34th Conference on Local Computer Networks (LCN 2009), pp. 850–857, October 2009

10. Park, J.M., Chong, E.K.P., Siegel, H.J.: Efficient multicast packet authentication using signature amortization. In: Proc. of IEEE Symposium on Security and Privacy, Washington, DC, USA (2002)
11. Wong, C.K., Lam, S.S.: Digital Signatures for Flows and Multicasts. IEEE/ACM Transactions on Networking 7(4), 502–513 (1999)
12. Perrig, A., Canetti, R., Tygar, J., Song, D.: Efficient authentication and signing of multicast streams over lossy channels. In: Proc. of the IEEE Symposium on Security and Privacy, pp. 56–73 (2000)
13. Yavuz, A.: An Efficient Real-Time Broadcast Authentication Scheme for Command and Control Messages. IEEE Transactions on Information Forensics and Security 9(10), 1733–1742 (2014)

Automated Classification of C&C Connections Through Malware URL Clustering

Nizar Kheir[1]([✉]), Gregory Blanc[2], Hervé Debar[2], Joaquin Garcia-Alfaro[2], and Dingqi Yang[2]

[1] Orange Labs, 92794 Issy-Les-Moulineaux, France
nizar.kheir@orange.com
[2] Institut Mines-Telecom, Telecom SudParis,
CNRS Samovar UMR 5157, 91011 Evry, France

Abstract. We present WebVisor, an automated tool to derive patterns from malware Command and Control (C&C) server connections. From collective network communications stored on a large-scale malware dataset, WebVisor establishes the underlying patterns among samples of the same malware families (e.g., families in terms of development tools). WebVisor focuses on C&C channels based on the Hypertext Transfer Protocol (HTTP). First, it builds clusters based on the statistical features of the HTTP-based Uniform Resource Locators (URLs) stored in the malware dataset. Then, it conducts a fine-grained, noise-agnostic clustering process, based on the structure and semantic features of the URLs. We present experimental results using a software prototype of WebVisor and real-world malware datasets.

1 Introduction

Malware constitutes a serious threat to the Internet. Once it infects a terminal, malware may perform a variety of actions, such as taking over the system, connecting to Command and Control (C&C) servers, leaking information to a dropzone, and recruiting the terminal to a botnet involved in activities such as spam and denial of service. Efforts in the literature aim to handle malware both at the system and network level. While traditional host-based malware detection systems suffer from low detection coverage [19], network-based detection offers a complementary approach to detect malware through its network activity [6,7,10,12]. It usually adds network-level patterns, i.e., patterns referring to any network activity triggered by malware instances. For instance, they can leverage C&C activity, which is a key feature of malware operation. By comparing the network traffic of different malware samples, it is possible to identify similar patterns that can be further used for malware detection.

To keep pace with the large number of malware being collected daily, current solutions aim at automatically classifying malware and extracting appropriate detection signatures [11,20,24]. For example, the behavioral classification system in [20] correlates HTTP traffic from different malware samples and extracts network signatures for detection. It observes common HTTP artifacts in order

© IFIP International Federation for Information Processing 2015
H. Federrath and D. Gollmann (Eds.): SEC 2015, IFIP AICT 455, pp. 252–266, 2015.
DOI: 10.1007/978-3-319-18467-8_17

to find trends that are shared among a large set of malware samples, and that may characterize a given malware family. Another approach provided earlier by [14] also observes network traffic for a large set of malware samples and identifies pattern signatures for detection. However, malware avoids being correctly classified by these systems as it uses several network obfuscation mechanisms such as encrypting its C&C traffic, injecting noise, using Domain Generation Algorithms (DGA) [1], or embedding efficient failover strategies [17].

In this paper, we present WebVisor, an automated tool to classify malware instances based on the features of their web-based C&C applications. These are the set of web server applications that are installed by an attacker (i.e. botmaster) in order to establish C&C communications with the remote infected bots. WebVisor implements a behavioral-based approach that observes the network activity of malware when executed in a sandbox. It classifies malware into families and generates family detection signatures. WebVisor targets malware C&C communication channels supported by standard network protocols, such as the Hypertext Transfer Protocol (HTTP). HTTP-based malware belonging to the same botnet family connects to a shared infrastructure that involves the same set of web C&C applications. Such malware C&C applications are uniquely identified and accessed using Uniform Resource Locators (URLs). The classification process conducted by WebVisor assumes that malware belonging to the same family shares similar C&C connection patterns, including similar sets of C&C attributes, both in terms of parameter names, semantics, and values.

The benefits of WebVisor are threefold. First, it provides a behavioral approach that classifies malware into families based on features of their network traffic, with no need to analyze the system-level activity of malware on the infected terminals. Second, it provides a malware detection system that operates semantical enrichment and density-based clustering in order to automatically reduce the impact of noise and common obfuscation mechanisms used by malware up to a certain level. Third, it identifies URL features common to a given malware family. Such features are further used to detect and classify other malware instances. To verify our claims, we present an experimental validation of a first prototype against live Internet traffic collected from a large ISP provider.

This paper is organized as follows. Section 2 provides the background and components underlying WebVisor. Section 3 describes our experimental results. Section 4 surveys related work. Section 5 concludes the paper.

2   Background and System Overview

Network-based malware detection solutions can be classified into two main categories. First, solutions addressing network activities attributed to synchronized botnet operations (e.g. [6,15]). Second, solutions executing the malware and analyzing its associated traces, to learn new malware techniques (e.g. [7,11]). The first category works only when multiple infected terminals are using the same botnet architecture and are controlled by a single entity. Modern botnets avoid this type of detection through the hiding of their C&C activity by, e.g., using

fake connections and adding statistical inconsistencies in their network traffic
[21]. The second category assumes that malware belonging to the same family (e.g., in terms of development tools) shares similar behavioral patterns that
reflect its origin and purpose [24].

WebVisor belongs to the second category. It observes HTTP traffic triggered
by malware during dynamic analysis, and identifies URL patterns that are shared
among samples of the same family. Hereinafter, we interchangeably use the terms
C&C patterns and *URL patterns* to refer to specific character strings in the URLs
triggered by malware during its execution in a sandbox. When these patterns are
shared among multiple variants of the same family, they characterize specific
features of their C&C applications. In the end, the patterns are used to build
appropriate detection signatures. Remaining malware URL instances that do not
convey shared C&C activity, and so they do not characterize specific malware
families, are automatically discarded by WebVisor and they are no longer used
during detection. We detail next the main blocks underlying WebVisor.

Input Data – The malware C&C communication channels addressed by Web-
Visor are supported by standard network protocols, such as HTTP, which is the
most common type of malware communication on the Internet today [4]. Malware
using HTTP-based C&C channels may efficiently bypass firewall and proxy settings, by hiding the C&C exchanges within benign HTTP traffic. Furthermore,
HTTP-based malware may also evade detection by leveraging infected or legitimate websites, which makes the detection very challenging [9]. The input HTTP
data processed by WebVisor are the URL methods (e.g. Get, Post, Head), the
absolute paths, and the parameters of the URLs associated to the C&C communication channels. They are captured during the dynamic analysis of malware instances on a sandbox. Domain names from the stored URLs are ignored,
since they do not convey information about the structure and content of the
C&C applications. As opposed to domain names, URL paths provide the precise applications at the C&C server to handle malware requests. This highlights
common patterns that are likely to be shared among multiple variants of the
same malware family. In addition to paths, WebVisor also uses the URL parameters, leveraging attribute names, their semantics and values. The stored URLs
handled by WebVisor are grouped into an initial set of coarse-grained clusters,
using the statistical clustering process that we outline next.

Statistical URL Clustering – This process partitions the input data into
a collection of coarse-grained clusters based on common URL statistical features. URLs often include patterns (e.g., `/images/`, `/adi/`, `/generate_204/`)
and keywords (e.g., `.php`, `.exe`, `.gif`) that refer to the nature and type of
resources accessible on a remote server. WebVisor leverages the distribution of
characters within URLs in order to group together malware URLs that include
similar or redundant patterns. It builds a features vector that captures the
distribution of characters within the URL. Paths and parameters are handled
separately, since they hold different structural nature and semantics. In turn,
the parameters are separated into keys and values. For instance, the following
URL '`/doc/lat/widget?tp=2&nbr=1111&tag=11`', whose protocol identifier and

domain name are already removed, is split up into the path '/doc/lat/widget'; keys 'tp','nbr', and 'tag'; and values '2','1111', and '11'.

Since high-level features such as the URL length, the number of paths and number of attributes do not capture relevant pattern signatures, WebVisor leverages string based features that capture shared patterns among different URL instances. The frequency of occurrence of each single character in a given URL is computed. For example, assuming the following path '/doc/lat/widget', the occurrence frequency of character 'o' is 1, 't' is 2, '/' is 3, 'z' is 0, and so on. Following such a rationale, each URL is transformed into an m-ary vector that captures the distribution of characters within the URL. Given that the HTTP standard sets to 128 the number of acceptable ASCII codes for a character in a given URL; and given that paths, keys and values in each URL are treated separately, the value of m is settled to 384 (i.e., 3×128). Based on the m-ary vector associated to each URL, the initial set is partitioned into coarse-grained clusters. A vector quantization clustering method is used to drive the process. For instance, the process can be conducted using incremental k-means [22], as reported in Section 3. Finally, each coarse-grained cluster is further processed by a second clustering process, to build the eventual fine-grained clusters whose structure and semantic shall characterize common C&C applications. Density-based clustering drives this second process that we outline next.

Density-based URL Clustering – After the statistical coarse-grained process, a fine-grained density-based clustering is conducted within each of the statistical coarse-grained clusters. The process starts by an enrichment procedure that adds meta-data to characterize the type and semantics of each URL value field, based on the types listed in Table 1. The first column in table 1 introduces a shortlist of the attribute types used by WebVisor, column 2 illustrates some examples, and column 3 provides a brief description. Such meta-data is further used to build fine clusters where URLs are associated to semantically equivalent instances. This way, and instead of comparing values as strings via, e.g., string distance functions, the density-based clustering process considers that two values are similar when they share the same semantics (e.g., both are timestamps). The rationale behind this configuration is that botnets usually add encryption and use URL encodings to evade network detection signatures, since it alters the entropy of characters distribution in a URL. The proposed enrichment process aims to handle such evasion techniques and remove the encoded values when it compares two different URLs. Other non-encoded parameters in the URL, such as IP or MAC addresses, country code and timestamps, are also compared semantically. A 'No_Type' entry is introduced in order to handle unknown types.

After the semantic enrichment process, fine-grained clusters are built up using a density-based classifier. For instance, assuming a density-based classifier based on DBScan [5], WebVisor builds up a similarity matrix containing the distance between each couple of URLs. Inputs to the URL distance function include the URL method (e.g., Get, Post, Head), the URL path, and the URL parameters. The similarity between two URLs is computed by using the Jaro-Winkler distance [8] to compare URL paths as string chains, and by comparing

Table 1. Non-exhaustive list of types used during the semantic enrichment process

Type	Example	Description
URL redirection	http://example.com	Phishing attacks or obfuscation using URLs similar to legitimate websites
File path	C:\test.txt	File location on the victim terminal
SHA1	97d07314f735998585bb-8e2d6b5acb5ac7956690	Cryptographic hash function including 40 hexadecimal characters
Base64	dG90bw==	Encoding schemes that represent binary data using ASCII or UTF-8 formats
MD5	4f863423326e85d44aae-147d2d86e1c0	Cryptographic hash function consisting of 32 hexadecimal figures.
MAC address	0a:00:27:00:00:01	MAC address of the infected terminal
IP address	192.168.0.10	IP address of the infected terminal
Serial number	06AE-B34D	The volume serial number on the infected terminal
Timestamp	Mar 30 2014 00:30:08	The local time on the victim terminal
No_type	utv42	Any value not matching a previous type

the parameters and values semantically, i.e., two parameters in two different URLs are similar in case they have the same key and the same semantic type.

Generation of Signatures – Detection signatures are created by extracting the longest common substrings for all URLs in a given dense cluster, using the Generalized Suffix Trees algorithm [3]. It builds a token-subsequence starting with the longest token in the ordered list of longest common substrings. Selected tokens are further used as input to the Best Alignment Algorithm [18] in order to build a pattern-based signature that characterizes all URLs that belong to the same dense cluster.

WebVisor Prototype – A software prototype of WebVisor is available for testing purposes at http://j.mp/WVProto. It implements all the processes introduced in this section, i.e., statistical clustering, semantic enrichment, density-based clustering, and signature generation processes. The prototype has been used in order to process some real-world malware datasets that we describe in section 3, with the objective of generating detection signatures. The set of signatures has also been tested against live Internet traffic from a large ISP provider. Results and discussions about our findings are provided in the following section.

3   Experimental Results

Experiments were conducted using the WebVisor prototype, on an Intel 8-core 2.67Ghz server, with 16Gb RAM. The statistical URL clustering process was conducted using incremental k-means [22] and Euclidean distance to compare the feature vectors. The density-based URL clustering process was conducted using DBScan [5]. Finally, a python script is used to transform the fine-grained clusters into regular expressions as detection signatures.

The malware URL C&C communication dataset used to generate the detection signatures was collected from multiple public and private sources, including commercial feeds, public repositories (e.g., http://malware.lu/ and Malicia [16]), and HTTP traces triggered by malware from the Anubis database [2] (during their execution in a dynamic analysis environment). Almost a quarter million malware samples were considered, and more than two million HTTP traces were collected, from which duplicates and empty URLs were excluded. The MD5 hashes of malware binaries associated to each URL were also used to label our dataset. To ease the analysis, the dataset was divided into three separate categories, according to the year of collection of the URLs (24 months, from June 2011 until July 2013). Using WebVisor, we separately processed each category, and generated the corresponding family clusters and detection signatures.

Table 2. Dataset summary

Year	Samples	Families	URLs	Get	Post	Head	Coarse Clusters	Signatures	Process Time
2011	75,398	127	886,077	68%	20%	12%	27	120	1h15min
2012	87,648	129	592,104	65%	24%	11%	27	182	2h01min
2013	85,597	84	848,998	76%	17%	7%	29	315	2h50min

To properly validate the experiments, ground truth labels indicating malware families were generated. More than two-hundred distinct families, including each more than a dozen malware samples, were settled by using AntiVirus (AV) signatures from services such as VirusTotal (cf. http://virustotal.com/). Notice that AV editors usually assign conflicting signatures for the same malware sample. For example, the SpyEye malware has a *kaspersky* signature of Trojan-Spy.-Win32.SpyEyes and a *McAfee* signature of PWS-Zbot.gen.br. To avoid errors, the AV labels were associated to multiple keywords, and common prefixes such as W32, Mal and Trojan were discarded. Generic malware identifiers, such as Heur, Worm, Gen, and malware, were also discarded. The site http://spywareremove.com/ was used to group together all aliases of a given family. For example, the signatures win32.spammy by *kaspersky* and W32/Sality by *McAfee* were identified as aliases for the same sality malware, and considered as part of the Sality family. Multiple malware families may cover two or more years, including examples such as Zeus, ZeroAccess, and Sality. This overlap in families between years is explained by the fact that samples of the same malware family can be distributed through multiple infection campaigns.

Table 2 summarizes some of the above information, as well as the time required for WebVisor to generate the detection signatures. We provide in the following sections a more elaborated analysis of the experimental results, such as evaluation of the obtained clusters and signatures, and evaluation of the signatures against live Internet traffic.

3.1   Cluster Validation

The malware clustering problem is assumed to be a classification subproblem. We use two distinct quality metrics, precision and recall, to evaluate the quality of each individual behavioral cluster. A cluster family is defined as being the ground truth label associated with a maximal number of samples in a cluster. Note that malware belongs to a cluster when it has at least one URL that is classified by WebVisor into this same cluster. Moreover, malware may belong to multiple clusters in case it interacts with multiple C&C applications during analysis, and whose associated URLs are classified by our system into different clusters. The cluster precision captures the level of *mis-classifications* within the cluster, which is the rate of samples in the cluster that are not associated with the cluster family. Let η_c be the number of malware samples in cluster c, and $|Sig_c| \leq \eta_c$ the maximal number of samples in c that have the same ground truth label. Then, the precision index of c is computed as $\mathcal{P}_c = \frac{|Sig_c|}{\eta_c}$. The cluster recall captures the proportion of samples that should belong to a cluster, but misclassified into other clusters. Let $|\overline{Sig_c}|$ be the number of samples in the ground truth dataset that should be classified in c, but that were misplaced into other clusters. Then, the cluster recall index of c is computed as $\mathcal{R}_c = \frac{|\overline{Sig_c}|}{|Sig_c|+|\overline{Sig_c}|}$. Tables 3 and 4 contain the distributions of the cluster precision ($\mathcal{P}_c$) and recall ($\mathcal{R}_c$) coefficients for the 617 fine-grained clusters provided by WebVisor during our experiments (cf. Table 2, fine-grained clusters used to generate the detection signatures of the 2011, 2012, and 2013 subsets). Left columns provide the index ranges. Right columns provide the percentage of clusters having similar indexes. With regard to

Table 3. Cluster precision index results

Index Range	Percentage
$0.98 \leq \mathcal{P}_c < 1.0$	65%
$0.96 \leq \mathcal{P}_c < 0.98$	15%
$0.94 \leq \mathcal{P}_c < 0.96$	8%
$0.92 \leq \mathcal{P}_c < 0.94$	7%
$0.00 \leq \mathcal{P}_c < 0.92$	6%

Table 4. Cluster recall index results

Index Range	Percentage
$0.6 \leq \mathcal{R}_c < 1.0$	4%
$0.4 \leq \mathcal{R}_c < 0.6$	6%
$0.2 \leq \mathcal{R}_c < 0.4$	21%
$0.04 \leq \mathcal{R}_c < 0.2$	14%
$0.00 \leq \mathcal{R}_c < 0.04$	55%

the cluster precision metric, we can observe that almost 94% of the fine-grained clusters held more than a 92% precision index. In other words, 92% of malware in each fine-grained cluster is properly classified in the correct malware family. This validates the accuracy of the clustering process of WebVisor. Concerning the cluster recall metric, 67% of the fine-grained clusters hold a recall index lower than 10%. This means that only 10% of malware were misclassified by WebVisor into other clusters. Most of the remaining 33% of the fine-grained clusters held a recall index ranging between 20% and 40%. A manual analysis of these clusters revealed that certain clusters included different versions of the same malware family (e.g., different versions of the `conficker` malware family). Some other clusters were also associated with generic ground truth labels such as `Heur` and `Agent`. These anomalies rather depend on the quality of the ground truth labels. Therefore, they should not be considered a weakness of the system.

3.2 Evaluation of the Detection Signatures

To verify the quality of the detection signatures generated by WebVisor, we evaluate them in terms of false positives and false negatives. We recall that in density-based clustering, a cluster represents an area that has a relatively higher density in the dataset, whereas the noise concept is represented as isolated objects that belong to sparse areas in the same dataset. DBScan [5], used by WebVisor to conduct the fine-grained clustering process, is a density-based algorithm that implements the aforementioned concept. It takes as input the minimum number of objects in a cluster and the maximum neighborhood radius between two objects. Although these parameters affect the total number of clusters, the latter is a result of the clustering process and is not required as input of the process. DBScan creates multiple clusters. Each cluster represents a dense area in the initial dataset. URLs belonging to sparse areas are grouped into a single noise cluster which is further discarded by WebVisor. Each dense cluster includes similar URLs that are shared among multiple variants of a malware family, and that characterize a specific C&C application. Therefore, and since WebVisor automatically discards noise into separated clusters, we also evaluate the corresponding noise clusters.

The coverage of the signatures is evaluated by analyzing their ability to detect malware communication not included in the experimental dataset. We separately processed the malware samples at our disposal by the year of collection. We tested each set of signatures against the input dataset, and the datasets collected in the following years. Due to space limitations, we discuss only the evaluation in terms of the 2011 traffic collection. Similar results were obtained with the other collections. Table 5 illustrates the distribution of URLs across the

Table 5. Distribution of statistical clusters

URL Range	Percentage
0 to 2000	14%
2000 to 4000	37%
4000 to 8000	11%
more than 8000	38%

Table 6. Noise rate distribution

Noise Rate	Percentage
less than 0.02	33%
0.02 to 0.1	30%
0.1 to 0.2	22%
more than 0.2	15%

27 statistical clusters. The left column represents the number of distinct URLs in each statistical cluster. The right column represents the percentage of clusters having similar number of URLs. We recall that the 2011 dataset (cf. Table 2) contains 75, 398 distinct malware samples. According to the ground truth labels, these samples were classified into 127 distinct families. We use the incremental k-means algorithm for statistical clustering. It starts from one centroid and incrementally adds new centroids when the distance between a new entry and all

existing centroids exceeds an input threshold τ_h. Incremental k-means iterates over the input dataset until k - *which is the number of output clusters* - reaches its optimal value based on the value of τ_h.

The output of the statistical clustering, using an experimental threshold $\tau_h = 0.15$, includes 27 clusters. Almost 14% of clusters in table 5 contained less than two-thousand URLs, mostly including very short URLs such as '*/a/*', '*/2/*', and '*/?src=integer*'. These are irrelevant URLs that were later discarded as noise by the density-based clustering. In terms of outliers, 6 clusters were also discarded. These outliers contained more than twenty thousand URLs. Because of their small number, these clusters were manually analyzed. Almost all URLs in these clusters were associated with generic web operations, including URLs like '*/json?c=resolution*', and '*/addserver/www/...*'.

After the statistical clustering, URL enrichment and density-based clustering was applied to each statistical cluster. An overall number of 120 distinct fine-grained clusters (represented as detection signatures in Table 2) were generated. The processing of each statistical cluster during the density-based clustering led to a stable average of noise rate. We recall that noise here represents those URLs that were further classified during the density-based clustering, by DBScan, as noise clusters. Table 6 summarizes these results. The left column provides the rate of noise in each statistical cluster, and that were further discarded by Web-Visor. The right column provides the percentage of statistical clusters leading to similar noise rates. Few outlier clusters, mostly consisting of very small clusters or including a large number of URLs, contained noise rates exceeding 20%. The resulting 120 signatures were identified by WebVisor as being associated with URLs that carry true C&C activity. They only describe fine-grained clusters including URLs that have almost identical structure and semantics.

Detection Rate – We cross-validated the set of signatures against the initial malware dataset. A signature is considered to detect malware when it matches at least one URL during its dynamic analysis. Note that we would not expect 100% detection rate as WebVisor is grouping irrelevant URLs that belong to sparse areas in the dataset into noise clusters during the fine-grained clustering, and so it may mistakenly discard relevant C&C URLs during this process. Table 7 illustrates the detection rates that we obtained during the experiments. According to Table 2, the whole dataset was divided into three subsets (from year 2011 to 2013), according to the year at which malware samples were collected. A 10-fold experiment was applied, where a 10% of the samples from the initial dataset were repeatedly removed before building the detection signatures. Each set of signatures was matched against the samples collected during the corresponding year, as well as for the remainder years. The goal is to evaluate the ability of WebVisor for detecting malware that belongs to the families defined in the initial training dataset. The ability of the signatures to detect samples that were unknown at the time of generating such signatures was also evaluated. As a result, it was obtained that WebVisor achieves near 84% average detection rates when tested against the same year dataset. This means that the remaining 16% of undetected malware had their C&C activity mistakenly classified into

Table 7. Detection rates

Signa-	Malware Dataset		
tures	2011	2012	2013
2011	87%	64%	21%
2012	NA	86%	57%
2013	NA	NA	81%

Table 8. Samples signatures generated by WebVisor

Signature	Family
POST /includes/inc/helps/[.*].php	Zeus
GET /logos[.]*.gif?[0-0,a-z]6=[0-9]*	Sality
GET /streamrotator/thumbs/[a-z]2/[0-9]*.jpg	Srizbi
GET /generate/software/?[A-Z]3RND=[0-9]*	Zango

noise clusters (discarded by WebVisor). The detection rate drops to near 60% for malware collected in the next year following the signatures generation, and to almost 20% in the third year. The decrease in detection rates is explained by new emerging malware families that use new C&C applications. To overcome such weakness, WebVisor can be continuously fed with streams of new malware HTTP traffic. New malware families that appear in the wild would have their HTTP traffic processed by WebVisor to update its signatures database.

The experiment proves the ability of WebVisor to capture URL patterns that are shared among samples of the same malware family, and that characterize common features of their C&C applications. In fact, binary polymorphism modifies the malware signature but it does not affect the network behavior of malware, including the web toolkit that is shared among samples of the same family. While network obfuscation, including fake connections, attacks and connectivity checks, makes generic network signatures less efficient, WebVisor eliminates noise using density-based clustering. It discards noise into separate sparse clusters and builds detection signatures only for the main C&C connections which are shared among samples of the same malware family.

False Positives – To evaluate false positives, we collected one day of network activity, at March 2014, from a well protected corporate network. Terminals connected to this network are all equipped with updated antivirus software. Access to this network is possible only through firewall gateways and monitored using web proxies. Although we cannot rule out the possibility of few terminals being infected, these would be limited with respect to the large set of terminals being connected. Hence, we may still reasonably consider this traffic to include only benign web activity. We further developed a python script that extracts URLs and matches them against our signatures. We collected near 1.8 million distinct URLs, including both regular web activity and scheduled software updates, and that we tested against our entire set of 617 signatures. The collected dataset includes all distinct URLs that are triggered by up to 3,500 active network terminals. It includes URLs towards thousands of distinct remote domains. Almost 9% of URLs were dedicated to Google search queries, while remaining URLs included regular browsing activity such as webmails, advertising, media websites, social networks and content downloads. Although our malware dataset is relatively old compared to the benign traffic at our disposal, this does not affect our experimental setup as we are only considering false positives. We consider all matching signatures to be false positives. In the end, 72 alerts out of the initial 1.8 million URLs were matched with only 21 distinct signatures. Hence, WebVisor achieved 0.004% false positives, and we only identified 3.4% *weak* signatures (i.e., signatures that triggered false positives during evaluation). We recall that a main property of our system is that WebVisor does not need to implement a pruning step in order to eliminate rogue signatures. This is a tedious step as it would require a large set of benign traffic, as well as an automated process to generate valid ground truth from the collected benign traffic.

3.3   Evaluation Against Live Internet Traffic

We tested WebVisor against two days of real live Internet traffic from a large ISP network. More than 150 GB of anonymized traffic, collected during September 2013, and including the entire network communications for near ten thousand distinct IP addresses, was analyzed. We extracted URLs using the same Python scripts that we used for the previous experiment, and we tested against our entire set of 617 signatures. Our system triggered 173 alerts, associated with 19 distinct signatures that were matching with 93 distinct IP addresses. Since the traffic at our disposal was few months old, we checked the domain names reputation using the domain search functionality on services like virusTotal, and searched for evidence on the Internet about the matching URLs. Unfortunately we could not check the status on the infected terminals since all traffic at our disposal was anonymized, and the ISP did not offer to contact infected clients in order to validate our findings.

We could not verify 95 alerts that were triggered by 15 detection signatures, including 9 weak signatures that triggered false positives in our previous experiment. Domains contacted through these URLs seem to be benign domains. We could not find signs of infection on the remote websites. Possibly these websites have been used temporarily or as stepstones through web or system vulnerabilities. Since we could not validate the exactness of these alerts, we considered them as false positives. In addition, the 4 signatures in Table 8 triggered almost 78 alerts, associated with 11 IP addresses. The first signature was matching with 3 IP addresses. The detected URLs were all associated with the domain name *marytraders.in*, which is identified by Zeus Tracker (cf. https://zeustracker.abuse.ch/) as a C&C domain. The second signature was triggered by two IP addresses (and associated with the `Sality-A` label in the dataset). The corresponding domain included pornographic content and is associated with botnet activity according to Google safe browsing. We also detected six other IP addresses that matched with the two remaining signatures. They were confirmed malware infections, validating the reliability of WebVisor.

3.4   Resilience to Malware Evasion

To evaluate the resilience of our system against noise, we trained WebVisor using a dataset that we obtained by adding random benign URLs to the malware dataset. We used for this purpose the traffic that we collected from the corporate network. We computed the average cluster precision and recall indexes for different values of Signal to Noise Ratio (SNR). Our main assumption is that malware can use fake benign URLs in order to evade our detection system.

Therefore, we evaluate the ability of our system to discard fake URLs and keep only common C&C patterns as input to build detection signatures. As described in [21], malware may also trigger specific noise patterns in order to evade our system. However, there still need to be multiple samples of such malware in our dataset in order to interleave with our dense clusters. Although it is interesting to evaluate the resilience of our system against such specific evasion techniques, we focus in this paragraph only on random noise patterns. We plan in future work to conduct a deeper evaluation of WebVisor against targeted evasion techniques, taking into account the fact that malware herders may be aware of the process implemented by our system. The results of our experiments are illustrated with the ROC curve in Figure 1. WebVisor has an overall good resilience against noise. While its performance decreases at slow rate for decreasing values of SNR, WebVisor achieves almost 80% cluster precision for SNR values around 40%. Yet, we noticed a significant degradation of the quality of our malware families for noise rates exceeding 50%. The degradation of the precision index is mainly due to the threshold τ_h that we use for statistical clustering. Since we experimentally set the value of this threshold using our malware dataset, adding 50% benign URLs to this dataset alters its statistical consistency. WebVisor would thus classify URLs that are associated with similar C&C activities into different statistical clusters. While the degradation of malware clusters comes as a reasonable consequence to the increasing noise ratio, our system still achieves stable clustering results for up to 40% noise in our initial malware dataset. This is a main contribution of our system compared to other state of the art solutions where a pruning process is usually required in order to eliminate rogue signatures.

Another property of WebVisor is that it processes URL parameters using regular expressions that characterize all attributes shared between malware and its remote C&C applications. Although WebVisor captures specific obfuscation mechanisms such as encodings (e.g., base64) and hash functions (MD5 or SHA-1), it would be unable to correctly build expressions for URLs that have their entire set of parameters encrypted within a single chain of characters.

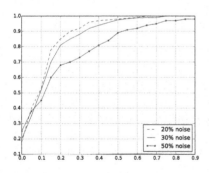

Fig. 1. ROC curve and SNR ratios

It associates these parameters with the 'No_type' label, and handles them as string values. Note that the density-based clustering process may still identify shared patterns in case they appear in all encrypted URLs for a given malware family, as previously shown in [14]. However, malware that fully encrypts its URLs, with no shared patterns between URLs of the same family, would be unlikely to be detected using our system, and so it is more likely to be dropped into noise clusters. This is a common limitation to all network-based malware detection systems, as long as they are unable to access the content of malware communications with its remote C&C applications.

4 Related Work

Multiple contributions in the literature propose the use of supervised machine processing to classify malware activities and build behavioral models for detection. Solutions in this category include tools such as Firma [23], PhishDef [13], and JackStraws [7]. As opposed to them, WebVisor uses an unsupervised clustering approach. It does not require an initial set of benign network traffic to train the classifier prior to generating detection signatures. This is an important issue, since obtaining valid ground truth labels for benign network activity is a tedious task that cannot be easily automated.

Similarly to WebVisor, Perdisci et al. propose in [20] the use of unsupervised clustering processing to analyze malware HTTP connections and build detection signatures. As opposed to our work, their approach classifies malware families using all kinds of HTTP requests triggered by malware executed in a sandbox. This includes not only C&C traffic, but also any other kinds of malware activity such as benign connectivity checks. Therefore, the approach is not robust against malware obfuscation, since it may reduce the accuracy of the resulting detection signatures. To handle the issue, i.e., to avoid a high rate of false positives, Perdisci et al.'s approach requires to carefully verify all those generated signatures against benign web activity. This is a tedious and error prone task. First, obtaining a large-scale representative ground truth dataset of benign network traffic to prune out unnecessary signatures is very challenging. Second, it makes infeasible to automatically build and deploy effective detection signatures. WebVisor offers an alternative approach to classify malware using only relevant C&C traffic. Although it is difficult to detect C&C connections during a single malware analysis, the C&C activity becomes more apparent when observing a larger set of malware. Furthermore, WebVisor automatically discards noise and identifies common C&C requests used by variants of the same malware family.

5 Conclusion

We have presented WebVisor, an automated tool for the generation of malware detection signatures. WebVisor targets HTTP malware belonging to the same family, e.g., malware that uses the same C&C applications and equivalent sets of URLs. We have outlined the main design properties underlying WebVisor and evaluated a software prototype against real-world malware datasets. Our experiments verify the capability of WebVisor at identifying the main and invariant features of malware C&C activity.

Acknowledgments. The authors thank A. Gupta, S. Martinez-Bea and A. Verez for all their work on the implementation of the WebVisor prototype.

References

1. Antonakakis, M., Perdisci, R., Nadji, Y., Vasiloglou, N., Abu-Nimeh, S., Lee, W., Dagon, D.: From throw-away traffic to bots: detecting the rise of dga-based malware. In: USENIX Security, pp. 24–40 (2012)
2. Bayer, U., Kruegel, C., Kirda, E.: TTAnalyze: a tool for analyzing malware. In: 15th EICAR Conference (2006)
3. Bieganski, P., Riedl, J., Cartis, J., Retzel, E.: Generalized suffix trees for biological sequence data: applications and implementation. In: Proc. of International Conference on System Sciences, vol. 5, pp. 35–44 (1994)
4. Bu, Z., Bueno, P., Kashyap, R., Wosotowsky, A.: The new era of botnets. White paper from McAfee (2010)
5. Ester, M., Kriegel, H.-P., Sander, J., Xu, X.: A density-based algorithm for discovering clusters in large spatial databases with noise. In: Proc. of KDD (1996)
6. Gu, G., Perdisci, R., Zhang, J., Lee, W.: Botminer: clustering analysis of network traffic for protocol and structure independent botnet detection. In: Proc. of IEEE SSP (2008)
7. Jacob, G., Hund, R., Kruegel, C., Holz, T.: JackStraws: picking command and control connections from bot traffic. In: USENIX Security (2011)
8. Jaro, M.A.: Advances in record-linkage methodology as applied to matching the 1985 census of tampa, florida. Journal of the American Statistical Association 4 (1989)
9. Kartaltepe, E.J., Morales, J.A., Xu, S., Sandhu, R.: Social network-based botnet command-and-control: emerging threats and countermeasures. In: Zhou, J., Yung, M. (eds.) ACNS 2010. LNCS, vol. 6123, pp. 511–528. Springer, Heidelberg (2010)
10. Kheir, N.: Behavioral classification and detection of malware through http user agent anomalies. Journal of Information Security and Applications (2013)
11. Kheir, N., Han, X.: PeerViewer: behavioral tracking and classification of P2P malware. In: Wang, G., Ray, I., Feng, D., Rajarajan, M. (eds.) CSS 2013. LNCS, vol. 8300, pp. 282–298. Springer, Heidelberg (2013)
12. Kheir, N., Wolley, C.: BotSuer: suing stealthy P2P bots in network traffic through netflow analysis. In: Abdalla, M., Nita-Rotaru, C., Dahab, R. (eds.) CANS 2013. LNCS, vol. 8257, pp. 162–178. Springer, Heidelberg (2013)
13. Le, A., Markopoulou, A., Faloutsos, M.: Phishdef: URL names say it all. In: IEEE INFOCOM (2011)
14. Li, Z., Sanghi, M., Chen, Y., Kao, M.-Y., Chavez, B.: Hamsa: fast signature generation for zero-day polymorphic worms with provable attack resilience. In: Proc. of IEEE SSP (2006)
15. Nagaraja, S., Mittal, P., Hong, C.-Y., Caesar, M., Borisov, N.: BotGrep: finding p2p bots with structured graph analysis. In: USENIX Security (2010)
16. Nappa, A., Rafique, M.Z., Caballero, J.: Driving in the cloud: an analysis of drive-by download operations and abuse reporting. In: Rieck, K., Stewin, P., Seifert, J.-P. (eds.) DIMVA 2013. LNCS, vol. 7967, pp. 1–20. Springer, Heidelberg (2013)
17. Neugschwandtner, M., Comparetti, P.M., Platzer, C.: Detecting malware's failover C&C strategies with squeeze. In: Proc. of ACSAC (2011)
18. Newsome, J., Karp, B., Song, D.: Polygraph: automatically generating signatures for polymorphic worms. In: Proc. of IEEE SSP, pp. 226–241. IEEE (2005)
19. Oberheide, J., Cooke, E., Jahanian, F.: CloudAV: N-version antivirus in the network cloud. In: USENIX Security (2008)

20. Perdisci, R., Ariu, D., Giacinto, G.: Scalable Fine-Grained Behavioral Clustering of HTTP-Based Malware. Special Issue on Botnet Activity: Analysis, Detection and Shutdown **57**, 487–500 (2013)
21. Perdisci, R., Dagon, D., Lee, W., Fogla, P., Sharif, M.: Misleading worm signature generators using deliberate noise injection. In: Proc. of IEEE SSP (2006)
22. Pham, D.T., Dimov, S.S., Nguyen, C.D.: An incremental K-means algorithm. Journal of Mechanical Engineering Science **218**, 783–795 (2004)
23. Rafique, M.Z., Caballero, J.: FIRMA: malware clustering and network signature generation with mixed network behaviors. In: Stolfo, S.J., Stavrou, A., Wright, C.V. (eds.) RAID 2013. LNCS, vol. 8145, pp. 144–163. Springer, Heidelberg (2013)
24. Rieck, K., Holz, T., Willems, C., Düssel, P., Laskov, P.: Learning and classification of malware behavior. In: Zamboni, D. (ed.) DIMVA 2008. LNCS, vol. 5137, pp. 108–125. Springer, Heidelberg (2008)

B.Hive: A Zero Configuration Forms Honeypot for Productive Web Applications

Christoph Pohl[1], Alf Zugenmaier[2], Michael Meier[3], and Hans-Joachim Hof[1(✉)]

[1] MuSe - Munich IT-Security Research Group,
Munich University of Applied Sciences, Munich, Germany
{christoph.pohl0,hof}@hm.edu
[2] Munich University of Applied Sciences, Munich, Germany
alf.zugenmaier@hm.edu
[3] Fraunhofer FKIE Cyber Defense, Bonn, Germany
michael.meier@fkie.fraunhofer.de

Abstract. Honeypots are used in IT Security to detect and gather information about ongoing intrusions by presenting an interactive system as attractive target to an attacker. They log all actions of an attacker for further analysis. The longer an attacker interacts with a honeypot, the more valuable information about the attack can be collected. Thus, it should be one of the main goals of a honeypot to stay unnoticed as long as possible. Also, a honeypot should appear to be a valuable target system to motivate attackers to attacks the honeypot. This paper presents a novel honeypot concept (B.Hive) that fulfills both requirements: it protects existing web application in productive use, hence offering an attractive attack target, and it uses a novel technique to conceal the honeypot components such that it is hard to detect the honeypot even by manual inspection. B.Hive does not need configuration or changes of existing web applications, it is web framework agnostic, and it only has a slight impact on the performance of the web application it protects. The evaluation shows that B.Hive can be used to protect the majority of the 10,000 most popular web sites (based on the Alexia Global Top 10,000 list), and that the honeypot cannot be identified by humans.

Keywords: Web application · Honeypot · Security · Web security · Network security

1 Introduction

Honeypots are well known and valuable components for the protection of networks. They can be used for attack detection or for research purposes. Usually, a honeypot is a *fake* system without any function that runs in parallel to other productive systems. Thus, all activities detected on the honeypot can be considered attacks (or unintended use). However, a honeypot can only monitor ongoing attacks if it succeeds in tricking attackers into attacking the honeypot at first. To do so, a honeypot must be known to an attacker and it should appear like a real

© IFIP International Federation for Information Processing 2015
H. Federrath and D. Gollmann (Eds.): SEC 2015, IFIP AICT 455, pp. 267–280, 2015.
DOI: 10.1007/978-3-319-18467-8_18

application or service. In order to maintain the attackers interest and to maximize the attackers interactions to gather as much information about the attack as possible, attackers should not be able to notice that the system they are attacking is a honeypot. The approach presented in this paper, B.Hive, blends into already existing and running web applications (further called target applications). As the honeypot components are completely invisible to benign users, any interaction with it is likely an attack. As an existing, productive web application is used, attacks on this system are likely.

The contribution of this paper is twofold: It presents a zero configuration Low Interaction Honeypot that can blend into any existing and running web application. Furthermore, it employs a technique that makes it substantially harder for an attacker to detect that honeypot components were integrated into a web application, even when manually inspected by humans. B.Hive does not need configuration for the integration, and the protected web application does not need to be changed. B.Hive is ideal to be integrated into active protection components like the web application firewall "All-Seeing Eye" [10].

The paper is structured as follows: The next Section 2 gives an overview on B.Hive. Related work is described in Section 3. Design and implementation is explained in Section 4. Section 5 validates the concept and shows that performance of the prototype implementation would allow augmentation of all but the busiest web applications. Section 6 summarizes the paper and gives an outlook on future work.

2   Overview

The Open Web Application Project (OWASP) maintains a list of the ten most prevalent attacks on web application in [7]. For four of these attacks, named A1 (Injection), A3 (Cross-Site Scripting (XSS)), A8 (Cross-Site Request Forgery (CSRF)), and A9 (Using Components with Known Vulnerabilities), an attacker usually inject malicious data into form fields of websites. As these attacks are very common, using form fields as a honeypot component allows a honeypot to detect many attackers and many different attacks. B.Hive transparently injects form fields into existing forms of the target application. To do so, B.Hive acts as a proxy between Internet and target web application. It intercepts web pages served by the target web application and modifies forms if present. Additional form fields are added to detected forms. Changes to these additional form fields are monitored to detect attackers inserting malicious data to test for common vulnerabilities (e.g. A1, A3, A8, A9, see above). As field manipulation is usually part of early phases of an attack (reconnaissance phase), detecting attacks at this point of time helps to monitor attacks. The fields injected by B.Hive can for example be hidden fields, or the fields are made invisible using CSS or JavaScript. In all cases, these fields are invisible to legitimate users of the web application. B.Hive also intercepts incoming HTTP requests to the target application and removes the injected fields again. Hence, B.Hive is invisible for the web application as well as legitimate users. There is no impact on the functionality of the web application.

The crucial point in injection fields into existing form field is to find suitable names and default values for the injected form fields. Most web applications use a consistent naming of form fields of a form, and the naming is consistent with the context of the web application. Hence, using random names as well as using the same name all the time is prohibitive. Involving web developers or administrators to define suitable field names for security components opposes the goal to build a zero configuration honeypot suitable for a large number of frameworks. It is the main contribution of this paper to propose a way to select suitable form field names and field parameters for the injected form fields. B.Hive selects suitable form fields and other parameters from a database of form fields harvested from a large number of existing applications. B.Hive detects the context of a form and selects a suitable field name and field parameters from this database.

3   Related Work

There are some approaches that use real applications to construct honeypots, for example [5]. However, the honeypot is directly integrated into the target application. Changing existing, already deployed applications is not desirable in a productive environment with already deployed applications. In contrast, B.Hive does not require changes of the target application. [3] describes an automated honeypot generation using search engines output. The resulting honeypot is a standalone non-productive web application. B.Hive in contrast protects an existing, productive web application.

Injection form fields in a form was already described in [9,12]. However, the developer has to implement these fields on his own in the target application or using jQuery. In both cases, the undetectability of the honeypot heavily depends on the developer to select suitable form field names and parameters. B.Hive does not need any configuration to adopt the look and feel from the original web application, hence relieves the developer from the burden of selecting suitable form field names and parameters. The approach in [6] also uses form fields as honeypot. In this case, form fields are duplicated and it is disguised, which is the form field to use. For a human, such a form is easy to spot. B.Hive in contrast puts special emphasize on staying undetected.

In comparison to related approaches, the presented zero configuration honeypot solution has the advantage that it integrates into the target application without the need of configuration. The integration is almost independent of target application technology, framework or system. The injected form fields adapt to the context of the web page in which they are injected to stay unnoticed even from manual inspection of the web page by a human attacker.

4   Design and Implementation

This Section describes the design of B.Hive with a special focus on the generation of suitable form fields for the forms to protect.

4.1 Generation of Plausible Fields

The goal of the form field generation is to generate a form field for injection that is plausible in the context of the form where it should be inserted. Plausible means that attackers as well as automated attack tools cannot distinguish inserted fields from original fields of the form. B.Hive tries to find plausible fields in a database of web forms harvested from the 10,000 most popular websites according to Alexa [1]. Important key figures of the Global Top 10,000 list of Alexa are described in Table 1.

Table 1. Initial database for Alexa Global Top 10,000

Websites	10,000
Extracted forms	15,255
Different field names	18,210
Average fields per form	3.8
Maximum fields per form	182
Minimum fields per form	0

For the purpose of optimized storage, the extracted form data gets preprocessed. In a first step, the attribute *name*, the field name (f), is extracted from every field. This attribute gets normalized as described in equation 1 where a character at index i in f is described as c_i. Ξ denotes a technical control character for further usage in B.Hive, Θ stands for an alphabet of lowercase letters, and Υ names an alphabet of uppercase letters. Allowed other characters are termed by ϑ. Let $u(x)$ be the function to bring an uppercase character to lowercase. The function $h(x)$ is used for preprocessing.

For $0 \leq i < length(f)$

$$h(c_i) = \begin{cases} c_i, & \text{if } c_i \in \Theta \vee c_i \in \vartheta \\ u(c_i), & \text{if } c_i \in \Upsilon \\ \Xi, & \text{if } (i - 1 \neq 0 \wedge c_{i-1} \neq \Xi \wedge c_{i-1} \neq \emptyset) \\ & \quad \vee (i - 1 = 0) \\ \emptyset, & \text{other} \end{cases} \tag{1}$$

Whenever $h(x) = \emptyset$, it will be ignored in further calculation. The result of this preprocessing gets stored in the new attribute f_{clean}.

The condition $b(x)$ to store f_{clean} in the B.Hive database is described in equation 2.

$$b(f_{clean}) = \begin{cases} true, & \text{if } length(f) > 0 \wedge f_{clean} \neq \{\Xi\} \\ false, & \text{other} \end{cases} \tag{2}$$

The final result f_{clean} is stored in a special Trie-structure (see [15] for details), optimized for calculation operations with the Levenshtein Distance [4]. The Levenshtein Distance is used in B.Hive as a metrics for similarity between field names. The Levenshtein Distance is defined as *"Minimum number of insertion, deletion and substitution edits required to change one word into another"* [4]. It is ideal to handle typical abbreviations used by web application developers, e.g. to compare field names like "passwd" and "password". Formally the Levenshtein Distance $lev(r, s)$ is defined in equation 3, using a search word s and a reference word r as input. The search word is compared to the reference word. The recursive function of $lev(r, s)$ is $k(|r|, |s|)$.

$$
\begin{aligned}
\omega_1(i,j) &= max(i,j) \\
\omega_2(i,j) &= min(k(i-1,j)+1, k(i,j-1)+1), \\
&\quad k(i-1,j-1)+0) \\
\omega_3(i,j) &= min(k(i-1,j)+1, k(i,j-1)+1, \\
&\quad k(i-1,j-1)+1) \\
k(i,j) &= \begin{cases} \omega_1(i,j) & \text{,if } min(i,j)=0 \\ \omega_2(i,j) & \text{,if } min(i,j) \neq 0 \wedge r[i]=s[j] \\ \omega_3(i,j) & \text{,other} \end{cases}
\end{aligned}
\tag{3}
$$

The Trie-structure holds the preprocessed field names extracted from the Alexa Global Top 10,000 list. At the end of a field name (the last node in a Trie-structure) a link to the original field(s) is stored. Other parameters like field default values, raw HTML code, forms, and pages are stored in a separate database.

During run-time, the honeypot generator needs to find plausible form field names for the form fields that should be injected into forms in the output of the target application. Plausible means that attackers as well as automated attack tools cannot distinguish inserted fields from original fields of the form. This is done by finding forms in the candidate pool, which have similar form field names to the original response. B.Hive includes a LR-Parser with a state machine to extract form field names from the response. This means the full HTML source gets parsed. While parsing, it recognizes each form and each field of a form with its attributes. These forms and their form fields will be further used as input for B.Hive.

To find similar forms, it is necessary to define the similarity of field names (see equation 4). A field name is described with f and the length of f with $l(f)$. Φ is the set of all field names. Let $\Phi = \{f_1, f_2, \ldots, f_n\}$. A form F is described as $F \subseteq \Phi$ and the set of forms is denoted by Γ where $\Gamma = \{F_1, F_2, \ldots, F_n\}$. λ is a system parameter for tuning performance and precision. It describes the maximum acceptable Levenshtein Distance. The other system parameter δ ensures that short field names (shorter than $\delta + \lambda$) get compared with a lower Levenshtein Distance than longer field names. The key variable for the upper bound of similarity (what is least similar) is denoted by μ.

$$\mu = \begin{cases} \lambda, & \text{if } min(l(f_1), l(f_2)) \geq \delta + \lambda \\ min(l(f_1), l(f_2)) - \lambda, & \text{if } \delta \leq min(l(f_1), l(f_2)) < \delta + \lambda \\ 0, & \text{other} \end{cases}$$

For the similarity between two fields f_1, f_2 let

$$f_1 \sim f_2 \Leftrightarrow lev(f_1, f_2) \leq \mu \tag{4}$$

The calculation for the best matching form is described in equation 5. Based on the similarity between field names, the definition of similarity between two Forms F_1 and F_2 is: $F_1 \sim F_2 \Leftrightarrow \{\exists f_1 \in F_1 \exists f_2 \in F_2 : f_1 \sim f_2\}$. The function $a(F_1, F_2)$ describes the number of similar fields in F_1, F_2 where: $a(F_1, F_2) = |\{f_1 \in F_1 | \exists f_2 \in F_2 : f_1 \sim f_2\}|$. Further, the number of similar forms with a field similar to f is defined as $s(f)$ where: $s(f) = \sum_{F \in \Gamma} a(\{f\}, F)$. The set of different forms is denoted by Ψ (in contrast to Γ that could include similar forms). Ψ is defined as: $\Psi := \{F_1 \in \Gamma | \exists f_1 \in F_1 \forall F_2 \in \Gamma \backslash F_1 : \forall f_2 \in F_2 : lev(f_1, f_2) > 0\}$. To identify the best matching form Ψ_{Best} for a reference form R (the form of the target application that should be protected) equation 5 is used.

$$\Psi_{Best} = \{F_1 \in \Psi | \forall F_2 \in \Psi : a(R, F_1) \geq a(R, F_2)\} \tag{5}$$

In the last step, possible plausible fields for injection are identified. First, possible candidate fields Ω for injection are collected where:

$\Omega = \{f \in \bigcup_{F \in \Psi_{Best}} F | \forall r \in R : lev(r, f) > 0\}$.

Let $L^{[1]}$ be the list of field names of Ω descendingly ordered by the number of appearances in similar forms: $L^{[1]} = \{f_1, f_2, \ldots, f_n\}$. Such that: $i < j \Rightarrow s(f_i) \geq s(f_j)$).

Let $L^{[2]}$ be the list of field names of Ω descendingly ordered by the minimum Levenshtein Distance to any of the fields of the form in that the plausible field should be inserted: $L^{[2]} = \{f_1, f_2, \ldots, f_n\}$. Such that: $i < j \Rightarrow lev_{min}(f_i, R) \geq lev_{min}(f_j, R)$ where $lev_{min}(f, R) = \min_{r \in R}(lev(f, r))$ The index of f in L^k is denoted by $index_k(f)$.

The result score $score(f)$ for a field f is defined by: $score(f) = (\alpha * index_1(f)) + (\beta * index_2(f))$ where α, β are factors to weight the ordering of $L^{[1]}$ and $L^{[2]}$. In this approach, let $\alpha = \beta = 1$ List $L^{[3]}$ is the list of the field names of Ω ascendingly sorted by the result score $score(f)$. $L^{[3]} = \{f_1, f_2, \ldots, f_n\}$. Such that: $i < j \Rightarrow score(f_1) \leq score(f_2)$.

The field with the lowest $score(f)$, respectively the first field in $L^{[3]}$, is selected by B.Hive as the most plausible field name.

4.2   Position of Form Fields

For the injected field to be unnoticed, it is necessary to find a plausible position of the injected form field in the form. B.Hive will inject the honeypot field at a position in the target form F than is similar to the position in the form H from that the honeypot field was harvested.

$L^{[H]}$ is a list of field names from form H ascendingly ordered by the index of the field names in H: $L^{[H]} = (h_1, h_2, \ldots, h_i)$. $L^{[F]}$ defines a similar list for the form F: $L^{[F]} = (f_1, f_2, \ldots, f_i)$. Let h_k be the honeypot field to inject into the target form F. Let l be the index, where $|l - k|$ is minimal and $\exists m : f_m \sim h_l$. The result form is defined in equation 6:

$$L^{[F']} = \begin{cases} (f_1, f_2, \ldots, f_{m-1}, h_k, f_m, \ldots, f_j) & \text{,if } l - k \geq 0 \\ (f_1, f_2, \ldots, f_m, h_k, f_{m+1}, \ldots, f_j) & \text{,if } l - k < 0 \end{cases} \tag{6}$$

4.3 Field Type and Default Value

In most of the cases from the Alexa Top 10,000 the type of a fields with the same name is the same. Hence, it is possible to let the injected field have the same type and default value as any one of the fields in the database. B.Hive injects the honeypot field using the same type and default value it had in the form from which it was originally harvested. The fields are hidden by hidden attribute. Whenever the field from the result form contains an id, the honeypot field will get this id too, except this id already occurs in the original page. The algorithm for the ordering of the attributes is naive but effective. B.Hive computes the most frequently used ordering from the original page. As ordering attributes, *name, value,id* and *style* is used. The injected form field gets constructed with this ordering.

5 Evaluation

This chapter provides the evaluation results of B.Hive. First, the choice of system parameters for the evaluation is presented. Subsection 5.2 evaluates the effectiveness of B.Hive. The following subsection evaluates the quality of the honeypot. The last subsection evaluates the performance of B.Hive.

Every analysis uses the full set of data without snipping outliers. For the sake of readability, histograms only show forms with less then 16 fields. Only 292 out of the 15,255 harvested forms have more than 15 fields.

5.1 Choice of System Parameters

The most relevant system parameter for the performance and the effectiveness of the honeypot is the maximum edit distance λ. When choosing λ there are two computing factors: Whenever the allowed Levenshtein Distance grows, the similarity check gets more accurate but the performance drops.

For the evaluation, one honeypot field for every Alexa Top 10,000 has been generated with different values for λ in the range $\{0, 1, \ldots, 5\}$. Table 2 shows

Table 2. Percentage of cases in which no plausible field could be found and run-time for different values of λ

λ	No result	$\varnothing$ run-time sec
0	9.34%	0.026
1	6.90%	0.079
2	5.20%	0.227
3	**3.78%**	**0.459**
4	2.64%	0.731
5	1.99%	1.027

the resulting run-time as well as the percentage of cases where no plausible field could be found for different values of λ. B.Hive has been started single threaded with a sequential calculation.

A value of $\lambda = 3$ was chosen for all other evaluations as it provides a balanced result for run-time and success rate. The system parameter δ was set to $\delta = 3$. Changing this parameter to a lower variable has no significant changes in the accuracy, but the subjective quality of honeypot fields drops in some cases. The subjective quality has been measured with a manual validation of the results.

5.2   Evaluation of Effectiveness

To prove that it is possible to generate honeypot fields for most existing web application, B.Hive was used to generate honeypot fields for each website of the Alexa Top 10,000 (list of most popular websites worldwide).

Table 3. Results of the Evaluation of Effectiveness of B.Hive when protecting each website of the Alexa Top 10,000 list

Number of forms	15,255
Trie-Nodes	140,298
Field names	18,210
Protectable forms	146,790 ~96.22%
$\varnothing$ similar fields	2.5
$\varnothing$ possible honeypot fields / form	1,023.4

Table 3 shows the results: A significant number of forms (96.22 % of all forms) can be protected by B.Hive. Successful protection of a form means in this context, that at least one plausible field was found for the form. B.Hive keeps a list of unprotectable forms. Whenever there is no plausible field for a form (3.78 % of all forms), B.Hive takes a random field from the list of unprotectable forms. In the following evaluation, this is not regarded as success.

The evaluation of the effectiveness shows, that in average there are 2.5 similar fields in the target form and the form from which a honeypot field is taken. In

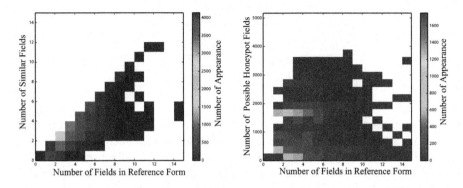

Fig. 1. Field similarity metric   **Fig. 2.** Possible honeypot fields/form

average, for each form there are 1023.4 possible honeypot fields. Figure 1 and Figure 2 describes these results in detail.

Figure 1 gives a more detailed view on the similarity of fields. This figure shows the similarity between the target form and the result form for each form in a site of the Alexa Top 10,000 list. This and all further histograms use less equal calculation. This means that the upper right corner of a bin represents the value. Figure 1 has the number of fields in the reference form (target form) on the x-axis. On the y-axis the number of fields in the similar form (the form from which the honeypot field was chosen by B.Hive) is given. The bins and their colors represent the number of occurrences of a combination.

Figure 2 shows the number of potential honeypot fields per target form for all forms of the Alexa Top 10,000 list. The x-axis describes the number of fields in the target form. The y-axis shows the number of potential honeypot fields for this form. The color denotes the number of occurrences of this combination. It could be seen that there is a significant number of potential honeypot fields for all but very small forms (forms with only one field).

In conclusion B.Hive is able to generate a proper protection for the vast majority of the most popular 10,000 web sites.

5.3   Evaluation of Honeypot Quality

It is one of the main goals of the work presented in this paper to keep an attacker unaware of the presence of the honeypot. Hence, it is very important, that humans (attackers) cannot identify the injected form fields when manually inspecting the HTML source code of a page. To evaluate, if attackers can identify injected form fields, an empirical study with 75 participants was executed. All participants are students in a computer science program (49 in a bachelor program, 26 in a master program). Participants of the study were presented the content of 50 different forms of the Alexa Top 10,000 list. With a probability of 0.5, a form field was injected by B.Hive, in the other cases the original form was presented. The students were told before that 50% of all forms include an injected

Table 4. Empirical study setting

Students	75
Evaluated number of forms	3,714
Forms without honeypot	1,798 (48.41%)
Forms with honeypot	1,916 (51.59%)

field. The students were asked to identify injected form fields or to state that there is no injected field in a form. The default answer for each form was *"I do not want to answer"* to make sure, that no "click-through" influences the results. Table 4 summarizes the setting. The students decided in 1,919 cases (51.67%) that a form includes an injected field. In 1,013 cases (52.79% or 27.28% of all choices) they were right and in 906 cases(47.21% or 24.39% of all choices) they were wrong. In 1,675 cases (45.1%) the students decided that no injected field was present. In 825 cases (49.25% or 22.21% of all choices) they were correct and in 850 cases (50.75% or 22.89% of all choices) they were wrong. In the remaining 120 cases (3.23% of all choices) the students did not want to answer.

In average, the students chose in 24.745 (out of 50) cases (49.49%) the correct answer (field injected or not). The standard deviation for a correct answer is 6.74 with a maximum of 35 correct answers and a minimum of 1 correct answer.

These results are significantly near random choices, hence showing that it is not possible for an attacker to identify the injected form fields when looking at the field names.

In 314 cases the injected field was detected. In average the students decided in 4.077 (out of 50) cases (8.154%) for the injected field and in median they decided in 3 cases for the injected field. The standard deviation is 2.818 with a maximum of 12 correct answers and a minimum of 0 correct answers for all student and 50 answers. With random choices the probability to detect the honeypot field is 10.748% (with 4.8 fields per form in average when a field was injected).

This result is also significantly near random choices.

There has been no significant difference between master and bachelor students.

In conclusion, the evaluation shows that B.Hive is able to hide itself in the vast majority of forms. Humans cannot successfully identify the injected form fields.

In order to show that B.Hive is useful for detecting automated attacks, and that attack tools do not avoid the fields injected by B.Hive, the breakable web application (BREW) [11] was augmented with B.Hive and then attacked using penetration testing tools Owasp Zed Attack Proxy Project (Owasp ZAP) [8] and Vega [13].

In average, each form of BREW has about 2.43 fields. In conclusion it is expected that a penetration testing tool will hit the honeypot field with about 40% of all requests. Table 5 concludes the result in one overview. In all cases B.Hive worked correct and the penetration testing tools identified all B.Hive fields as possible target. The row *touch quota* describes the expected calls to the

Table 5. Validation with penetration testing tools

	Owasp ZAP	Vega	$\sum$
Requests	783	2,097	2,880
Post Requests	524	814	1,338
Trapped Requests	206	342	548
Touch quota	99%	101%	100%

honeypot when the penetrations testing tool identify the honeypot as suitable target.

In conclusion, each penetration testing tool recognized the injected honeypot field as a possible target. Both tools showed the expected amount of attacks on the target. B.Hive was able to recognize and identify each attack.

5.4 Performance Evaluation

B.Hive works as a proxy for web applications, so all traffic to the target application passes B.Hive. Hence, it is important to evaluate if B.Hive is ready for productive usage.

Figure 3, 4 and 5 show the performance of B.Hive **without** caching and **without** the overhead of parsing.

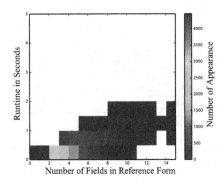 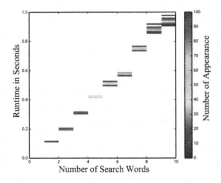

Fig. 3. Run-time of B.Hive without caching and without overhead of parsing

Fig. 4. Performance number of search words

In contrast, Figure 6 shows B.Hive under productive usage **with** enabled caching and **with** parsing.

Figure 3 shows the run-time for B.Hive for forms of the Alexa Top 10,000 list with a different number of fields in them. The x-axis shows the number of fields in the target form. The y-axis shows the run-time in seconds to find a similar field. The colored bins describes the number of appearance for this combination. It can be seen that B.Hive is able to protect a new website with a proper run-time. The vast majority of forms can be protected under 0.5 seconds. The average run-time for B.Hive is 0.46 seconds. However, for productive usage, it is highly recommended to use caching for optimized run-time.

Figure 4 shows the run-time for B.Hive with different number of form fields in the target form. The search words used are randomized strings with a length of ten characters. It is guaranteed that the field names of the target form have no similarity to any other word in the database. This avoids side effects during result set building. Every number of field names has been measured 100 times. The x-axis describes the number of reference words per evaluation. The y-axis shows the run-time of B.Hive. The color denotes the number of occurrences of this combination.

The evaluation shows that the run-time grows near linear with the number of form fields in the target form, hence protecting forms with a low number of fields is faster then protecting forms with a high number of field. Fortunately, the evaluation of the Alexa Top 10,000 showed, that the average number of fields per form is very low (average of 3.8).

Figure 5 shows the dependency between the run-time of B.Hive and the length of one field name. The x-axis shows the length a of field name. The y-axis

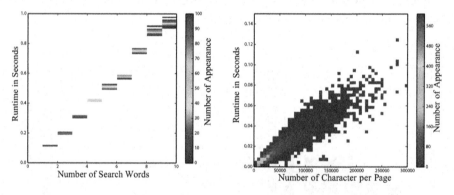

Fig. 5. Performance diff. word length   **Fig. 6.** Performance with caching and with parsing

shows the measured run-time. Each length between 1 − 50 has been measured for 100 times. The figure shows that the dependency is near linear. The falloff between a length of 1 and 6 shows the effect of the system parameter δ.

The B.Hive algorithm is designed with the possibility of multi-threading. Each form field name analysis is atomic, a number of form field names (forms with more fields) can be calculated in a parallel way. The result set assembling is designed that algorithm like map reduce [2] can be used.

In conclusion, the performance evaluation shows that without caching (or the protection of a new form, not known to the cache) B.Hive is able to protect a web application in productive usage.

Figure 6 shows B.Hive in a productive scenario: caching and parsing is enabled. Injected form fields get cached and further injections do not have to run the algorithm again but can look up a suitable field in the cache. The x-axis of the figure shows the number of characters for each page. The y-axis shows the measured run-time for each page. The colored bins shows the number of appearances of each combination. The figure shows the correlation between the number of characters in the raw HTML page and the runtime, which is near linear. In average, B.Hive needs 30.5258 milliseconds to protect one page, which is 15.072 times faster than without caching. The number of forms per page does not correlate with the runtime. The overhead to query the cache (measured without parsing) is insignificant with 0.000072 milliseconds in average.

The honeypot field generation for one page is done by a single process. A load balancing with more processes or different server can be done by starting more instances of B.Hive and a load balancer like nginx [14].

In conclusion, B.Hive is able to protect even large and busy web applications when using caching and parsing.

6 Conclusion and Outlook

This paper presents B.Hive, a honeypot that protects existing web applications in productive use by transparently adding form fields to forms with a special focus on the undetectability of the honeypot by human inspection. The evaluation of B.Hive shows that humans are not able to identify the injected form fields, hence an attacker cannot avoid the honeypot. This allows to gain valuable insights into attacks. The evaluation also showed, that B.Hive only adds a slight overhead to the total response time of a web application when using caching and parsing. It also shows that B.Hive can protect the vast majority of web applications.

Over the course of the next year we plan to deploy B.Hive on a public web server to gather data on how real attackers interact with it. This could also lead to classification of attack payloads. Future work includes a extension of B.Hive beyond form field injection.

References

1. Alexa Internet, I.: Alexa - The Web Information Company. http://www.alexa.com/ (last accessed March 13, 2014)
2. Dean, J., Ghemawat, S.: Mapreduce: simplified data processing on large clusters. Communications of the ACM **51**(1), 107–113 (2008)
3. John, J.P., Yu, F., Xie, Y., Krishnamurthy, A., Abadi, M.: Heat-seeking honeypots. In: The 20th International Conference, p. 207. ACM Press, New York (2011)
4. Levenshtein, V.I.: Binary Codes Capable of Correcting Deletions, Insertions and Reversals. Soviet Physics Doklady **10**, 707 (1966)
5. Mueter, M., Freiling, F., Holz, T., Matthews, J.: A generic toolkit for converting web applications into high-interaction honeypots. University of Mannheim (2008)

6. Nassar, N., Miller, G.: Method for two dimensional honeypot in a web application. In: 2012 8th International Conference on Collaborative Computing: Networking, Applications and Worksharing (CollaborateCom), pp. 681–686 (2012)

7. OWASP: Top 10 2013 - OWASP. https://www.owasp.org/index.php/Top_10_2013 (last accessed March 13, 2014)

8. Owasp: OWASP Zed Attack Proxy Project - OWASP (2014). https://www. owasp.org/index.php/OWASP_Zed_Attack_Proxy_Project (last accessed October 23, 2014)

9. Perry, K.: Honeypot Technique of Blocking Spam - Dex Media, May 2013. http:// www.dexmedia.com/blog/honeypot-technique/ (last accessed October 20, 2014)

10. Pohl, C., Hof, H.J.: The all-seeing eye: a massive multi-sensor zero-configuration intrusion detection system for web applications. In: SECURWARE 2013, The Seventh International Conference on Emerging Security Information, Systems and Technologies (2013)

11. Pohl, C., Schlierkamp, K., Hof, H.J.: BREW: a breakable web application. In: European Conference of Software Engineering Education, ECSEE 2014, November 2014

12. Squiid: Honeypot: Protecting web forms * Squiid, June 2011. http://squiid.tumblr. com/post/6176439747/honeypot-protecting-web-forms (last accessed October 20, 2014)

13. SubGraph: Vega Vulnerability Scanner (2014). https://subgraph.com/vega/ (last accessed October 23, 2014)

14. Sysoev, I.: nginx (2014). http://nginx.org/ (last accessed October 23, 2014)

15. Wang, Y., Peng, T., Zuo, W., Li, R.: Automatic filling forms of deep web entries based on ontology. In: Web Information Systems and Mining, pp. 376–380 (2009)

Security Management and Human
Aspects of Security

Investigation of Employee Security Behaviour: A Grounded Theory Approach

Lena Connolly[1(✉)], Michael Lang[1], and J.D. Tygar[2]

[1] Business Information Systems,
National University of Ireland Galway, Galway, Ireland
y.connolly1@nuigalway.ie
[2] Electrical Engineering and Computer Science,
University of California, Berkeley, Berkeley, USA

Abstract. At a time of rapid business globalisation, it is necessary to understand employee security behaviour within diverse cultural settings. While general deterrence theory has been extensively used in Behavioural Information Security research with the aim to explain the effect of deterrent factors on employees' security actions, these studies provide inconsistent and even contradictory findings. Therefore, a further examination of deterrent factors in the security context is required. The aim of this study is to contribute to the emerging field of Behavioural Information Security research by investigating how a combination of security countermeasures and cultural factors impact upon employee security behaviour in organisations. A particular focus of this project is to explore the effect of national culture and organisational culture on employee actions as regards information security. Preliminary findings suggest that organisational culture, national culture, and security countermeasures do have an impact upon employee security behaviour.

Keywords: Employee security behaviour · Security countermeasures · Organisational culture · National culture

1 Introduction

The majority of modern organisations are heavily relying on computerised information systems (IS). These systems store the sensitive data necessary to run businesses efficiently, including financial, customer, and product records. Therefore, managing risks associated with the loss of this vital information is essential. Threats can come from external as well as internal sources. External attacks are typically initiated by hackers who are seeking political or financial gain. The common way to prevent external attacks is an implementation of technical security controls, including firewalls, anti-malware software, and authentication controls. These measures are widely employed by organisations and are largely effective.

On the other hand, an insider threat refers to an intentional or unintentional misuse of an organisation's IS by employees that may negatively affect the confidentiality, integrity, or availability of that organisation's vital information. Maintaining employees' compliance with information security rules is a more problematic matter as

© IFIP International Federation for Information Processing 2015
H. Federrath and D. Gollmann (Eds.): SEC 2015, IFIP AICT 455, pp. 283–296, 2015.
DOI: 10.1007/978-3-319-18467-8_19

technical controls are unable to prevent all human blunders. For instance, employees tend to write passwords down, share them with colleagues or send confidential information in an unencrypted form. It is estimated that at least half of information security breaches are made by internal personnel [1]. Posey et al. [2] argue that deviant behaviour is best managed with a combination of technical and social measures.

Overcoming the issue of "human error" has received considerable attention in Behavioural Information Security (InfoSec) research. Various approaches designed to improve employee security behaviour have been suggested by IS scholars. These range from security awareness programmes [3] and security education and training [4] to approaches that take into account deterrent [5] as well as cognitive [6, 7] factors.

However, a comprehensive literature review conducted for this research revealed that a number of areas in Behavioural InfoSec research require further investigation. To begin with, while IS researchers demonstrate the influence of security countermeasures on employee security behaviour, the results of these studies are inconsistent and therefore require further clarification [8]. Several IS researchers suggested that the influence of deterrent factors may vary under the impact of other aspects [9]. A literature review conducted for this project revealed a limited amount of studies that investigate the influence of deterrent factors in combination with cultural aspects. Furthermore, cross-cultural studies are particularly rare in Behavioural InfoSec research, although prior research shows that national culture (NC) has an effect on organisational behaviour [10, 11]. Finally, Hu et al. [5] report that there is a general lack of studies that examine the effect of organisational culture (OC) on employee security behaviour and existing studies fail to illustrate strong theoretical foundations for linking OC and behaviour.

This research in progress addresses the aforementioned literature gaps and attempts to answer the following research questions:

1. How do organisational culture values affect employee security behaviour?
2. How does national culture affect employee security behaviour?
3. How do security countermeasures affect employee security behaviour?

This is a cross-cultural study conducted in the USA and Ireland. As is commonly the situation with comparative international studies, the initial choice of these two countries was more opportunistic than deliberate, arising as it did out of a research exchange programme which necessitated the lead author spending extended periods of time in both countries. Nevertheless, although the cultures of both Ireland and the USA are often referred in the extant literature as "Western", these two countries have similar as well as contrasting cultural characteristics [12] and therefore are worthy of comparison. Additionally, Ireland is an important commercial gateway between the USA and Europe, it being the location of the European headquarters of several American multinational corporations. Ireland is situated at the interface of two rather different perspectives on privacy and data protection (i.e. EU versus USA), which is a further reason why a cross-cultural study between Ireland and the USA is a useful undertaking.

2   Theoretical Context

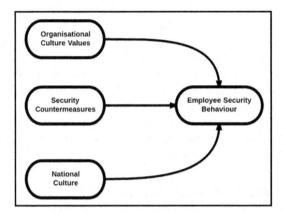

Fig. 1. Theoretical framework

2.1   Culture

The study of culture is rooted in sociology, social psychology, and anthropology [13]. Culture has been studied for over a hundred years in various disciplines. As a result, numerous definitions, conceptualisations, and dimensions of culture have been produced by researchers. For example, Kroeber and Kluckhohn [14] identify 164 definitions of culture. They range from simple to complex, incorporate and extend previous definitions, and even contradict prior definitions. Consequently, viewpoints on culture vary significantly. For example, some scholars perceive culture as a hidden or partly hidden force and therefore culture is problematic to assess as it is not directly observable [15]. In contrast, DeLong and Fahey [16] argue that culture embraces explicit and observable artifacts and therefore can be assessed.

The two most commonly used theoretical frameworks of culture are the socio-cultural system and the individual system [13]. Taking the socio-cultural perspective, Mead [17] defines culture as "shared patterns of behaviour". This definition implies that "culture is a group-level construct, situated between the personality of individuals and the human nature that is common to all of us" [13, p. 549]. Groups like societies, organisations and professions are considered to have their own cultures. Hence, studying culture entails more than observing and describing behaviour. On the other hand, the individual perspective treats culture as "an individual's characteristic way of perceiving the man-made part of one's environment" [18, p.3]. This definition assumes that culture can be assessed by analysing an individual's behaviour [13].

For the purpose of this research, culture is regarded as follows:

1. Culture is explicit and therefore can be observed.
2. Culture can be assessed by analysing an individual's behaviour.

2.2   Organisational Culture and Security Behaviour

Prior research shows that OC affects behaviour. For example, Kilmann [19] describes culture as a separate and hidden force that controls behaviours and attitudes in organisations. Furthermore, Philips [20] portrays culture as a set of tacit assumptions that guide acceptable perceptions, thoughts, feelings, and behaviour among members of the group. Finally, Baker [15] emphasises the importance of OC as a power that can lead a company to success or weaken its vitality because OC directly affects employee behaviour in an organisation. While the aforementioned studies show a link between OC and behaviour, this subject area has received very little attention in Behavioural InfoSec research. A literature review conducted for this study revealed a general lack of OC studies in the security context.

2.3   National Culture and Security Behaviour

Various academic works show that NC influences organisational behaviour. In particular, Hofstede [21] argues that organisations are bound by national cultures and underlines the cross-national differences in the functioning of organisations and people in them. He compares culture with an onion consisting of multiple layers, values being the inner layer of the onion, which are invisible until they become evident in behaviour. Ali and Brooks [13] define NC as a shared set of core values, norms and practices in a society that shapes individuals' behaviour within that society. However, cross-cultural research in Behavioural InfoSec is particularly scarce and urgent calls for more studies have been made [10]. For example, Dinev et al. [11] report differences in user behaviour toward protective information technologies in the USA and South Korea. Flores et al. [22] state that the effect of behavioural information security governance factors on the establishment of security knowledge sharing differs between Swedish and the USA organisations.

Cross-Cultural Dimensions. Hofstede's [12] original taxonomy describes culture in terms of four dimensions – *power distance, uncertainty avoidance, masculinity vs. femininity,* and *individualism vs. collectivism*. The score difference between the USA and Ireland's *individualism vs. collectivism* dimension is 21. Thus, it may be possible to explain the effect of NC on employee security behaviour from the perspective of the national trait of *individualism*. According to Hofstede [12], the United States has a highly individualistic culture, which affects relationships between individuals. For example, in the USA people typically take care of themselves and their immediate family. On the contrary, Irish people normally take into consideration group as well as individual interests. Propensity towards individualism or collectivism in a society can have an impact on organisational affairs. For example, Zhang et al.'s [23] study conducted in the United States and China, reveal that the level of *majority influence* (i.e. the attempt by the majority of group members to impose their common position on group dissenters during group decision making) on *group minorities* appears to be stronger in collectivist societies. Furthermore, Hofstede [12] points out that the level of individualism in society will affect the organisational members' reasons for complying with organisational rules and regulations. For example, in Ireland, *peer pressure* may have a stronger effect on employee security behaviour than in the USA.

Furthermore, Hofstede [12, p.217] claims that national characteristics have a strong affect on the "nature of relationships between a person and the organisation to which she or he belongs". Regardless of the nature of business, organisations in different countries vary in terms of organisational structures and processes [12]. Mintzberg [24] stresses that five distinct coordinating mechanisms explain the fundamental ways in which organisations manage their work, including *mutual adjustment, direct supervision, standardisation of work processes, standardisation of work outputs*, and *standardisation of worker skills*. These mechanisms form an organisational structure. Hofstede [12] argues that typically Irish organisations employ a *mutual adjustment* mechanism for coordinating activities and form a structure of *adhocracy*, in which the support staff is the key part. *Mutual adjustment* achieves the coordination of work by a simple process of informal communication and control of the work rests in the hands of the doers [24]. On the other hand, the structure of the United States organisations takes a *divisionalised form*, based on *standardisation of outputs*, in which the middle line is the key part. Typically, American firms standardise outputs by setting specific goals and results [12]. Prior studies show that employees tend to circumvent security rules when put under pressure to meet deadlines [25]. Therefore, factors that impel employees to break security rules may be different in the United States and Ireland due to different organisational structures.

2.4   Security Countermeasures and Security Behaviour

With the increasing occurrence of computer abuse by employees, organisations are searching for improved ways to deter it. According to the General Deterrence Theory (GDT), organisations can increase employee compliance with information security rules by implementing deterrence mechanisms, including *technical controls, information security policies*, and *security education, training and awareness programmes* [3, 4]. Deterrence theory is one of the most widely applied theories in IS security research [10]. Rooted in criminology [26], the classic deterrence theory posits that individuals weigh costs and benefits before committing a crime. If an individual believes that the risk of getting caught is high and that penalties will be applied if caught, then GDT states that the individual will not commit the crime.

D'Arcy et al. [3] present an extended deterrence theory model and report that security countermeasures such as *security policies, awareness programmes*, and *computer monitoring* influence perceived *severity of formal sanctions*, which leads to reduced intention to misuse IS, while *certainty of formal sanctions* does not have any effect on intention to misuse IS. Furthermore, Lee et al. [4] show that deterrence-based countermeasures, including *information security policy, security education and training awareness programmes*, and *security systems*, directly influence security behaviour in organisations. In contrast, Herath and Rao [27] report that *perceived severity of penalties* has significant but negative effect on *security policy compliance intention*. Additional studies inform that deterrence constructs do not have a significant influence on employee behaviour [28]. Overall, the extant literature provides inconsistent findings for deterrence theory in the information security context. Therefore, an additional examination of the influence of deterrence measures on actual behaviour is needed.

3   Research Methodology

The methodology adapted for this study draws on the *analytical grounded theory* (AGT) approach [29], employing the *constant comparative method* of Maykut and Morehouse [30]. This methodological framework draws on the work of Lincoln and Guba [31]. While none of the grounded theory principles were directly employed, nevertheless this project adapts a grounded theory approach insofar as the findings of this study are entirely rooted in the data. The AGT is the method of applying grounded theory analytical techniques (constant comparative method) to analyse data without a necessity to follow grounded theory principles. For example, a researcher may start with prior theory, then go on to collect empirical data, and analyse it using grounded theory coding techniques.

The *constant comparative method* is particularly appropriate for this research project because both OC and NC can be investigated within a single study. Due to similar characteristics, it may be hard to separate traits of OC and NC. For example, hierarchy in an organisation could be a result of a bureaucratic culture within the organisation [32] or the effect of a NC trait of high power distance [12]. A *constant comparative method* allows to overcome this challenge by first performing *in-case analysis* to analyse data within each country and then *cross-case analysis* to compare results between two research settings.

Data collection was carried out using semi-structured *in-person* interviews. Interviews are suitable to study behaviour [30] because interview participants are given an opportunity to describe their past experiences and incidents. Company selection for this project was partly opportunistic. Organisations from a diverse set of industries were selected. Using personal connections, seven companies were interviewed in the United States from September to November 2012, and eight companies in Ireland from June to August 2013. Details about US and Irish companies are given in Table 1 and Table 2.

Table 1. Facts about US companies

Name (aliases)	Industry type? When founded, size?	Number of people interviewed and their organisational roles
CloudSer	IT; 1998; large	One person – a software developer
RetCo	Finance; 1932; large	One person – a security executive
CivEngCo	Civil Engineering; 1945; SME	One person – a civil engineer
TechCorp	IT; 1968; large	Two security researchers
EducInst	Education; 1868; large	Two people – an administrator and a lecturer with substantial industry experience in the security field
FinCo	Finance; 1982; large	One person – a security consultant
PublCo	Publishing; 2005; SME	One person – a business owner

Table 2. Facts about Irish companies

Name (alias-es)	Industry type? When founded, size?	Number of people interviewed and their organisational roles
TechCorp	IT; 1968; large	Two people – a product manager and an IT executive
CharOrg	Charity; 1883; large	One person – a data protection officer
BevCorp	Food and Beverage Manufacturing; 1944; large	One person – an IT executive
PublOrg	Publishing; 2000; SME	One person – a chief editor
EducOrg	Education; 1845; large	Two people – an administrator and a lecturer with substantial experience in information security research
TelCommCorp	IT; 1984; large	One person – a software developer
ResReg	Energy Regulation; 1999; SME	One person – a policy analyst
BankOrg	Finance; 1982; large	One person – a security executive

The interview guide was constructed following a thorough analysis of the literature. The guide included questions about OC values and security countermeasures and their relationships with employee security behaviour. A list of the most prominent OC frameworks used in IS research was borrowed from Leidner and Kayworth's [33] work. Due to the evident similarity, these values were grouped into categories, including Solidarity, Sociability, People-Orientation, Task-Orientation, Rule-Orientation, and Hierarchy.

Table 3. Interview guide topics

Topics	Reference	Examples of questions
Organisational Culture		
Solidarity	Goffee and Jones [34]	Do you ever voluntary work overtime in order to complete some important task?
Sociability	Goffee and Jones [34]	Is it common to have non-work related chats with your colleagues during work hours?
People-orientation	Cooke and Lafferty [35]	How satisfying is the you are working for with respect to employee benefits?
Task-orientation	Cooke and Lafferty [35]	Do you think management expects you to put company goals before your personal goals?
Rule-orientation	Denison and Mishra [36]	Is it acceptable to break rules in your organisation?
Hierarchy	Ouchi [37]	Is it common in your organisation to disagree with your superior's opinion/decision?
Deterrent Security Countermeasures		
Technical Controls	D'Arcy et al. [3]	What information security rules and practices are utilised in your organisation?
Information Security Policy	D'Arcy et al. [3]	Is there an information security policy in your organisation?
Information Security Training	D'Arcy et al. [3]	Did you ever have to attend information security training?
Employee Awareness	D'Arcy et al. [3]	What information security values exist in your organisation?

With regards to security countermeasures, various classification have been offered by IS researchers on deterrent mechanisms. This research adapts D'Arcy et al.'s [3] taxonomy of security countermeasures, suggesting the following four topics for the interview guide – Employee Awareness, Information Security Policy, Information Security Training, and Technical Controls. Interview guide topics including corresponding references and questions are illustrated in Table 3.

4   Preliminary Findings

Data analysis is currently ongoing but a number of interesting preliminary results have emerged:

4.1   Organisational Culture Values and Security Behaviour

So far, preliminary results suggest that OC impacts upon employee security behaviour. CivEngCo is a bureaucratic organisation where rules and discipline prevail, and segregation between management and regular employees exists. Employees in this organisation generally comply with rules. A Civil Engineer, who is also an ambitious and creative individual, informs:

"…typically, employees conform with information security rules".

However, this is an organisation with established procedures and practices and normally higher management is reluctant to except new ideas and change traditional ways of conducting business. A motivated and striving employee would find it hard to survive in this type of environment. The same Civil Engineer shares her disappointment:

"I remember, one time I really wanted to change the design methodology…the manager of the project did not accept it but I had my supervisor backing me up… so we made a big meeting-fight…it was a very tough meeting…and finally I could convince them to change their approach… the type of practice they do is too old… and these old managers…it is so hard to change their minds…"

Furthermore, the same Civil Engineer adds that the fact that she cannot challenge management's decision discourages her and negatively affects every aspect of her job, including compliance with information security rules:

"…If I lose my motivation, it affects everything, in particular the quality of job that I do, such as how I archive things, how I back up things, how I care about everything, including organisation in general and security in particular. Of course, it affects everything".

EducOrg demonstrates similar traits of organisational culture, where ambitious employees are not encouraged to strive because promotions are scarce and some managers have a reputation of treating employees improperly. Since a promotion may entail a migration to a different department managed by an unfair manager, staff is reluctant to apply. Additionally, due to internal politics, promotions are not distributed justly. As a result, this atmosphere creates a lax attitude towards information security:

> "...For the last few years there have not been too many opportunities to be promoted...but if a promotion is coming up, I feel I don't stand a chance...I am happy in the place I am at the moment...if I go somewhere else, it might be like walking on a frying pan...Right now there is an opportunity for a promotion but I would not go there because a lot of managers in this department have a reputation of treating staff really, really, really badly. And this atmosphere creates a lax attitude towards sensitive information...the attitude is "it's not my job".

On the contrary, in CloudSer there is an environment where employees are welcome to express their opinions and contribute to various aspects of company's functioning. Employees are encouraged to provide feedback regarding information security rules and in some instances, they are trusted to make independent decisions as this organisation does not have rigid rules and procedures. A Software Developer reveals:

> "...a security team designs and implements an information security policy...however, there have been instances when software engineers did not agree with certain aspects of the policy...for example, two-factor authentication...but there is a communication channel...we talked it out and agreed that two-factor authentication is vital... but if I felt a requirement was too restrictive and I could not challenge it, I would really view my security policy differently...but the fact that I can challenge, changes my opinion...I feel I can contribute...I feel it is participative...I do not feel excluded..."

> "...in terms of security rules, nobody has tried to violate the rules...we have a fairly relaxed environment in terms of security rules...there is a lot of trust which is placed on the employees to make the right choices..."

RetCo is a financial organisation, where employees also are encouraged to provide feedback regarding security rules and changes have been made in the past based on this feedback. Staff are proud to work for this organisation. Subsequently, employees comply with organisational rules. A Security Executive Officer reports:

> "...I think in our organisation some of those unwritten assumptions would be that everybody matters in the organisation, so everybody has an opinion and equal voice...people are very proud to work here...and as a result, there is this assumption that everybody is going to conduct themselves in a manner that is appropriate for that value...they are happy to be there and working there..."

> "...I have not heard personally of any instance where somebody has broken a rule, a fixed rule..."

The above analysis leads us to conclude that OC affects employee security behaviour. A flat organisational structure and employees' involvement in a company's life have a positive effect on employee compliance with information security rules. However, employee-management segregation, poor management, and an unjust treatment of employees lead to disappointment and ultimately to a lax attitude towards information security.

4.2   National Culture and Security Behaviour

Although findings reveal that employees break rules in organisations in both countries, group non-compliance with rules in Ireland is more prevalent than in the United States. Besides, a larger amount of incidents was recorded in Irish organisations than in the United States. A Security Executive of an Irish financial institution shares the following:

> "...I would like to be a bit stricter on some of the rules. Sometimes, after implementing a certain security measure, someone in a managerial position may ask to have an access to something that is forbidden to access...the rules should be there for everybody...and they are not...once certain people ask, I have to circumvent the rule...the rule is broken then. At the moment, really senior people want to have access to Twitter...that will be another battle..."

An IT manager from BevCorp further confirms that rules get broken collectively in Ireland:

> "...I think breaking rules is kind of an Irish thing...'sure that rule does not apply to me because I have a good excuse or I can reason myself out of why I did not follow the rules'... I have definitely seen rules being broken...and the level of acceptance for that from peers...it is not like one person did it and everyone was shocked...they are not going to tell on somebody as well..."

Finally, a Software Developer at TelCommCorp verifies that Irish employees break rules as a group:

> "...One of my colleague's laptop was stolen from her work desk...I think there is a policy that if you leave your laptop at work, you are supposed to chain it to the desk...she did not anyway and I never do...I leave my laptop there every evening and I do not lock it...and a lot of people leave their laptops at work without locking them...the general attitude is: 'if it is robbed, it is not my problem...it is company's security is lacking' "

In the United States, however, employees seem to be breaking rules individually and collectively. A Civil Engineer from CivEngCo shares:

"...If I like the organisation, then I follow their security rules, of course. If I get disappointed with the organisation, then I don't care about anything, one of them would be security"

A Security Researcher from TechCorp adds:
"...My laptop is sitting on my desk upstairs and I am not supposed to leave it...so this is an example of a rule I have broken today...My laptop should be in a hibernated mode...I don't hibernate it, I usually just suspend it, so this is a violation of the policy"

Finally, a Professor from EducInst adds:
"...At EducInst we break rules all the time...When was the day I didn't break a rule?...Let me give you an example...a student needs a resource...there is a lot of rules about handling and allocating...I might just cut through them and make sure that a student gets the resource...and I am not interested about whether the right form is being filled out"

As can be seen from the above quotes, in Irish organisations breaking rules at a group level is more prevalent than in the United States.

4.3 Security Countermeasures and Security Behaviour

Results show that security countermeasure, including *security training*, *policies* and *awareness programmes*, inform employees about organisational security rules and encourage appropriate behaviour. A Software Developer from CloudSer shares:
"...educating employees to make the right choices is very important...employees should understand why they should not go to certain sites or why they should not do something within the corporate firewall..."

A Security Researcher from TechCorp reveals:
"Information security policy dictates things like what should I do with registered secret documents and I have to follow those rules... and this is one rule [related to secret documents] I would not want to break because if something happens, it is bad. Information security policy definitely affects what I do".

A Security Consultant from FinCo adds:
"...I think information security policy creates a framework that people shape their day-to-day work around".

Finally, Security Executive from RetCo further confirms:
"...training affects employees' behaviour...an alternative way to educate employees is to remind them of the safe security practices by

sending notifications and bulletins...I think this is another way employees interact with information security policy and it affects how they do their jobs..."

Generally, the above quotes suggest that procedural security countermeasures positively affect employee security behaviour in organisational settings.

5   Conclusion

Preliminary results indicate that security countermeasures, OC, and NC impact upon employee security behaviour in organisational settings. In terms of OC, in the organisations where employees are empowered to make changes and express their opinion, staff compliance with security rules is prevalent. However, in organisations where employees are discouraged to implement new ideas and employee-management segregation exists, security rules get broken. Wallach [32] labels culture based on power and control as bureaucratic. Organisations, where bureaucracy prevails, are resistant to implement changes. Therefore, a strong bureaucratic culture is unlikely to attract and retain creative and ambitious people [32]. On the contrary, in companies with supportive culture, employees are involved in organisation's matters and are given power to speak up. Supportive culture promotes employee autonomy, which leads to improved overall performance of an organisation [38]. Hence, if an organisation explicitly states that information security is its vital function, employees will be inclined to comply with rules.

Regarding NC, employee security behaviour in organisations in the United States and Ireland shows slightly different patterns. In particular, in the United States, employee security actions are driven by a combination of factors, including individual interests and group aspects. However, in Ireland, collective disobedience with security rules is more prevalent. The influence of peer pressure may be stronger in Ireland as opposed to the United States due to the difference in the score on *individualism*. Interestingly, Zhang et al.'s [23] work demonstrate that in collectivist China the pressure from group's *majority influence* on *minorities* is stronger than in the United States. Therefore, security practitioners may need to focus on *group participant-led security trainings* in collectivist countries as oppose to computerised security tests performed individually.

Security countermeasures, including *security policy*, *awareness programmes*, and *security training* encourage employee compliance with security rules. These deterrent countermeasures serve as important guidelines for employees to distinguish between appropriate and inappropriate actions. When employee are aware of company's security etiquette, they are less likely to engage in illicit behaviour, which is consistent with results reported by D'Arcy et al. [3]. Hence, companies are advised to have in place deterrent countermeasures. Overall, based on the aforementioned findings, this research in progress has a potential to make a valuable contribution to research and practice.

References

1. Spears, J.L., Barki, H.: User participation in information systems security risk management. MIS Quarterly **34**(3), 503–522 (2010)
2. Posey, C., Bennett, R., Roberts, T.L.: Understanding the mindset of the abusive insider: an examination of insiders' causal reasoning following internal security changes. Computers & Security **30**(6–7), 486–497 (2011)
3. D'Arcy, J., Hovav, A., Galletta, D.: User awareness of security countermeasures and its impact on information systems misuse: A deterrence approach. Information Systems Research **20**(1), 1–20 (2009)
4. Lee, S.M., Lee, S.G., Yoo, S.: An integrative model of computer abuse based on social control and general deterrence theories. Information & Management **41**(6), 707–718 (2004)
5. Hu, Q., Dinev, T., Hart, P., Cooke, D.: Managing employee compliance with information security policies: the role of top management and organizational culture. Decision Sciences **43**(4), 615–660 (2012)
6. Hu, Q., Xu, Z., Dinev, T., Ling, H.: Does deterrence work in reducing information security policy abuse by employees? Communications of the ACM **54**(6), 54–60 (2011)
7. Ifinedo, P.: Understanding information systems security policy compliance: An integration of the theory of planned behavior and the protection motivation theory. Computers & Security **31**, 83–95 (2012)
8. D'Arcy, J., Herath, T.: A review and analysis of deterrence theory in the IS security literature: Making sense of the disparate findings. European Journal of Information Systems **20**(6), 643–658 (2011)
9. Son, J.-Y.: Out of fear or desire? Toward a better understanding of employees' motivation to follow IS security policies. Information & Management **48**(7), 296–302 (2011)
10. Pavlou, P.A., Chai, L.: What drives electronic commerce across cultures? A cross-cultural empirical investigation of the theory of planned behavior. Journal of Electronic Commerce Research **3**(4), 240–253 (2002)
11. Dinev, T., Goo, J., Hu, Q., Nam, K.: User behaviour towards protective information technologies: the role of national culture differences. Information Systems Journal **19**(4), 391–412 (2009)
12. Hofstede, G.: Culture's Consequences: International Differences in Work-related Values. Sage Publications, Thousand Oaks (1980)
13. Ali, M., Brooks, L.: Culture and IS: National Cultural Dimensions within IS Discipline. In: Proceedings of the 13th Annual Conference of the UK Academy for Information Systems, pp. 1–14 (2009)
14. Kroeber, A.L., Kluckhohn, C.: Culture: A critical review of concepts and definitions. Peabody Museum, Cambridge (1952)
15. Baker, E.L.: Managing organizational culture. Management Review **69**, 8–13 (1980)
16. DeLong, D.W., Fahey, L.: Diagnosing cultural barriers to knowledge management. Academy of Management Executive. **14**(4), 113–127 (2000)
17. Mead, M.: National character. In: Tax, S. (eds.) Anthropology Today, pp. 396–421. University of Chicago Press, Chicago (1962)
18. Triandis, H.C.: The Analysis of Subjective Culture. Wiley, New York (1972)
19. Kilmann, R.H.: Managing your organization's culture. The Nonprofit World Report **3**(2), 12–15 (1985)
20. Phillips, M.E.: Industry mindsets: Exploring the cultures of two macro-organizational setting. Organization Science **5**(3), 363–383 (1994)

21. Hofstede, G.: Culture's Consequences. Comparing Values, Behaviors, Institutions, and Organizations Across Nations, 3rd edn. Sage Publications, Thousand Oaks (2001)
22. Flores, W.R., Antonsen, E., Edstedt, M.: Information security knowledge sharing in organizations: Investigating the effect of behavioral information security governance and national culture. Computers & Security 43, 90–110 (2014)
23. Zhang, D., Lowry, P.B., Zhou, L., Fu, X.: The Impact of Individualism-Collectivism, Social Presence, and Group Diversity on Group Decision Making under Majority Influence. Journal of Management Information Systems 23(4), 53–80 (2007)
24. Mintzberg, H.: Structure in fives: Designing effective organizations. Prentice-Hall Int., Englewood Cliffs (1983)
25. Besnard, D., Arief, B.: Computer security impaired by legitimate users. Computers & Security. 23(3), 253–264 (2004)
26. Beccaria, C.: On Crimes and Punishment. Macmillan, New York (1963)
27. Herath, T., Rao, H.: Encouraging information security behaviors in organizations: role of penalties, pressures and perceived effectiveness. Decision Support Systems 47(2), 154–165 (2009)
28. Siponen, M., Vance, A.: Neutralization: new insights into the problems of employee information systems security policy violations. MIS Quarterly 46(5), 487–502 (2010)
29. Matavire, R., Brown, I.: Profiling grounded theory approaches in information systems research. European Journal of Information Systems 22(1), 119–129 (2013)
30. Maykut, P., Morehouse, R.: Beginning Qualitative Research: A Philosophic and Practical Guide. The Falmer Press, London (1994)
31. Lincoln, Y., Guba, E.: Naturalistic Inquiry. Sage Publications, Beverly Hills (1985)
32. Wallach, E.J.: Individuals and organizations: The cultural match. Training and Development Journal 37(2), 28–36 (1983)
33. Leidner, D.E., Kayworth, T.: Review: A review of culture in information systems research: Toward a theory of information technology culture conflict. MIS Quarterly 30, 357–399 (2006)
34. Goffee, R., Jones, G.: What holds the modern company together? Harvard Business Review 74(6), 133–148 (1996)
35. Cooke, R.A., Lafferty, E.: Organizational Culture Inventory. Human Synergistics, Plymouth (1987)
36. Denison, D.R., Mishra, A.K.: Toward a theory of organizational culture and effectiveness. Organization Science 6(2), 204–223 (1995)
37. Ouchi, W., Theory, Z.: How American business can meet the Japanese challenge. Addison-Wesley Publishing Company, Reading (1981)
38. Shrednick, H.R., Stutt, R.J., Weiss, M.: Empowerment: key to is world-class quality. MIS Quarterly 16(4), 491–505 (1992)

Practice-Based Discourse Analysis of InfoSec Policies

Fredrik Karlsson[1(✉)], Göran Goldkuhl[2], and Karin Hedström[1]

[1] CERIS, Department of Informatics, Örebro University School of Business,
SE-701 82 Örebro, Sweden
{fredrik.karlsson,karin.hedstrom}@oru.se
[2] Department of Management and Engineering, Linköping University,
SE-581 83 Linköping, Sweden
goran.goldkuhl@liu.se

Abstract. Employees' poor compliance with information security policies is a perennial problem for many organizations. Existing research shows that about half of all breaches caused by insiders are accidental, which means that one can question the usefulness of information security policies. In order to support the formulation of practical, from the employees' perspective, information security policies, we propose eight tentative quality criteria. These criteria were developed using practice-based discourse analysis on three information security policy documents from a health care organisation.

Keywords: Information security policy · Discourse analysis · Communicative analysis · Quality criteria

1   Introduction

Information and information systems have become key assets in, for example, health care. Here is timely access to correct electronic medical records (EMR) essential in order to provide medical care of high quality. Consequently, the importance of information security increases; the confidentiality, availability and integrity of business information assets need to be kept at the level regulated by laws and public administration policies. It is argued that employees' poor compliance with information security policies is a perennial problem for many organizations [1, 2]. Having said that, existing research also shows that about half of all breaches caused by insiders are accidental [3], which means that one can question how useful today's information security policies are in guiding employees. Despite the importance of information security policies the design of such artefacts is an understudied area of information security research in general [4]. Gaskell [5], one of few who has studied the design process, has characterized the information security policy design process as ad-hoc. The main input that information security managers draw upon during such a design process is elicited information security requirements and international security standards [6]. Standards are general guidelines not addressing the specific context of an organisation [7], such as the specific needs of healthcare, making the elicited requirements an important complement.

© IFIP International Federation for Information Processing 2015
H. Federrath and D. Gollmann (Eds.): SEC 2015, IFIP AICT 455, pp. 297–310, 2015.
DOI: 10.1007/978-3-319-18467-8_20

If few studies focus information security policy design, even fewer studies have been carried out on information security policies as communicative objects and what constitutes a useful information security policy from a communicative point of view. Stahl et al. [8] is a notable exception, who based on a discourse analysis of information security policies provide six advices for the development of information security policies. Of course, this is a valuable contribution, but according to Baskerville's and Siponen's [4] taxonomy of information security policies, Stahl et al. [8] mainly focus on high-level policies. With this focus they seem to leave out the problematic aspect that employees often are exposed to several documents that together constitute the information security policy.

We therefore take an explicit starting point in a practice-based perspective. This means that a) we critically assess the role of the information security policy as a *practical tool* in the employee's every day work, including the use of both high-level *and* low-level policy documents, and b) we acknowledge the fact that there exist *multiple practices* in an organisation that *need to interact*. To this end we view information security policy documents as the results of the interaction (or lack thereof) between the information security practice and the health care practice. Information security policy documents are in this setting thus seen as communicative objectives.

The purpose of this paper is a) to illustrate the usefulness of practice-based discourse analysis for understanding information security policy design, and b) to provide a set of tentative quality criteria for information security policy design in health care from a practice-based perspective. For this purpose, we carried out a case study at a Swedish emergency hospital. We employed a *practice-based* discourse analysis on the hospital's information security policy. A practice-based discourse analysis means besides collecting and analysing information security policy texts, that we also have studied the mentioned practices through observations and interviewing. The latter is important in order to interpret the communicative limitations of the policy from the *employees'* perspective. Hence, this research responds to the call for more research on employees' behaviour with respect to information security policies within health care [9] and it focuses communicative aspects of the information security policy artefact, which is an even more understudied area. As far as we know there exist no quality criteria for information security policy design in health care anchored in a practice-based perspective.

2   Information Security Policy Theories

An information security policy is a general rule for directing acceptable behaviour of employees when using an organisation's information assets [10]; they provide information security management with a vehicle for establishing information security practices in organisations [11]. Given the strategic importance of information assets it is nowadays stressed that information security management should be integrated into corporate governance [12]. The executive management at the strategic level outlines a set of directives to indicate the importance of information assets, which are operationalized through the organisation's information security policy design. While information security governance research fail to offers detailed guidance on how to develop information security policies [e.g. 13], there exists practitioner-oriented literature that do [14, 15]. However, this literature focuses on design guidelines without reflecting on the end products' usefulness from an employee perspective. Scholarly studies about information security policy design exist as well. Gaskell [5] and Sibley [16] have described the information security policy formulation as an ad-hoc process, although, for example, Wood [17] has stressed the importance of a well thought out design process. It is common in information security literature to recommend that this process should be informed by information security standards [5, 18]. However, the use of information security standards has been criticised, since they do not take into account that organisations differ [4, 7], and Wood [17] argued that 'one must understand the special needs of an organization before one attempts to generate specific written management directives'. Knapp et al. [19] provided a more balanced view when proposing that both external and internal aspects of an organisation should influence information security policy work.

Research on techniques for eliciting local information security requirements [e.g. 20, 21] make a valuable contribution in such cases. Although there is a large body of research on information security policy, and much consensus can be found with regard to the importance of information security policies, less attention has been given to how to design the content of these policies. Wood [17] provided guidelines for the information security policy design process, arguing that different audiences often require tailored policies. Baskerville and Siponen [4] explored the design of information security policies, but their conclusions are limited to emerging organisations. Doherty et al. [22] stated that 'there are very few studies that explicitly address how the scope or content of information security policies support the employee in their daily work.' They concluded that there is a wide diversity of disparate policies in use and that they contain a low degree of detail. A somewhat broader take on how to design information security policy content also shows a debate about the ideal number of policies in an organisation and how they should be inter-related [e.g. 4, 23]. However, Lindup [24] has noted that in practice organisations often have one single information security policy.

In summary, existing research stresses the importance of congruent communication, and that information security policies should align both with business strategies and international standards. However, we found few empirical studies that address the communicative quality of information security policies. One exception is the study by Stahl et al. [8] who present six advices on how to design an information security policy, based on a critical discourse analysis of twenty-five information security policies.

3   Research Approach

3.1   The Study Object and Its Implication on Overall Research Strategy

The research approach taken in this study is discourse analysis [25]. Discourse in an open sense 'cover all forms of spoken interaction, formal and informal, and written texts of all kind' (ibid p 7). An inter-textual analysis is a natural element of discourse analysis. So is also an action perspective: 'Texts … do not just describe things; they *do* things.' (ibid p 6; emphasis in original). A discourse analysis of an information security policy will study how different text elements relate to each other; how well they congruently build up the whole text. The discourse analysis will also focus how the text is intended to influence the regulated practice and how it succeeds to comply with governing statements of higher order (standards and regulations). A discourse analysis of this kind is qualitative and interpretive with the purpose to reveal meanings of inter-textual and efficacious character. As a practice-based discourse analysis, we have besides collection and analysis of the information security policy texts also studied the mentioned practices through observations and interviewing.

3.2   Case Study and Data Collection

This study is as a case study [26], and the analysis is based on a reading of three documents that regulate the information security practice in one medium-size Swedish county council. The information security policy consists of one high-level policy document, and two low-level documents that more in detail describe information security instructions and rules. The findings in these documents were complemented with interviews with three high-level information security managers. The interviews gave us deeper knowledge about the county council's information security policies and how they were designed. In order get an understanding of the type of practice we studied, we selected one hospital within the county council for studies of information security policy compliance and translation in practice. We chose a hospital with about 750 employees, 142 places of treatment that serves around 90 000 citizens. Two clinics at the hospital were chosen as cases based on their different degrees of computerization of patient information: one clinic had manual handling of medical records; the other has used an EMR system for a number of years. This variety was important for providing us with rich data concerning information security in both light and heavy computerized settings, both of which are common in health care. We carried out twenty-four semi-structured interviews with health care staff (e.g., nurses, physicians, administrators) at the two clinics. The interviews lasted between one and two hours and concerned how information security were translated and carried out in practice, together with the reasons for the information security actions. The interviews were tape-recorded and transcribed. We complemented the interviews with 28 hours of observations of the information security practice. The observations were documented by note-taking and, when appropriate, by photographs (for example, how medical record were stored). The interviews and observations taken together gave us deeper knowledge about how information security was integrated in the health care practice. During observations we focused on the same categories as during the interviews, i.e., areas regulating the information security practice. This resulted in re-interviewing and further probing about the rationality for information security actions in practice.

3.3   A Conceptual Framework for Practice-Based Discourse Analysis

We characterize this type of discourse analysis as practice-based. A practice is considered to be 'embodied, materially mediated arrays of human activity centrally organized around shared practical understanding' [27, p 2]. This means that language and discourse is part of a practice. A practice consists of humans and their activities including material and semiotic elements. Thus, a study of documents (as e.g. information security policies) cannot be made without taking into account the practices where these documents are generated and used. Three important influences to be used in discourse analysis have been suggested: a semiotic understanding of different language functions; a speech act-based understanding of utterances; an ethnomethodological understanding of conversation. Consequently, they have stated these demands, but they have not synthesised and operationalised these theoretical orientations into a coherent approach for discourse analysis. Within information systems research there exists several studies that use different linguistic theories, but usually only one such theory at a time. Goldkuhl [28] has presented a socio-pragmatic communication framework adapted to studies in information systems. It is a synthesis of speech act theory [e.g. 29], ethnomethodological conversation analysis [30] and semiotics [e.g. 31]. Goldkuhl's [28] framework consists of nine communicative functions. It emphasises a multi-functional view of language and communication, i.e. we do several things at the same time while communicating. The nine functions are shown in Table 1 together with an explanation of each function, and the analytical questions we have used to assess each function.

Table 1. Goldkuhl's [28] framework of communicative functions

Communicative function	Explanation	Analytical question
Accountable	The message is comprehensible, i.e. include sufficient self-references and arguments to explain its role in the communication process.	What is meant?
Carried	The message is using the features of some medium.	How? By what means?
Constitutive	The message creates changes in social states between communicators and sometimes socially broader.	What is done?
Directed	The message is intended towards one or more addressees.	To whom?
Expressive	The message is an expression of the locutor's (the one who says the speech act) subjectivity (e.g. desires, emotions, values).	By whom?
Referential	The message is saying something about something in the world.	About what?
Pre-situationally compliant	The message is in accordance with general institutions and norms and specific pre-situational grounds.	Why? What reasons there?
Projected future actions	The message is an initiative for further actions.	For what?
Situationally responsive	The message is a response to prior messages and other situational features.	Why? What reasons there?

We have modified the terminology of two functions (carried, constitutive) in order to make them more intelligible. In our discourse analysis we have selected seven of these functions to use for our study of the information security policy. We have not used the functions of carried (since it is sufficient with a general characterization that policies are written documents), or situationally responsive (since the demand to write a policy has been excluded from our analysis).

3.4   Analytical Steps

A classical dilemma and choice in empirical social research is how to be open-minded vs. to be informed by previous theories in relation to the data material. In our study we used both strategies. We studied the text in an inductive and open-minded way, and then in the further analysis of the text we applied Goldkuhl's [28] framework in a theory-informed way. We have adopted an inquiry attitude [32], i.e. searched for and recorded what seems problematic in some way from a communicative point of view. In our case these principles meant the following. First, the information security policy has been read through and we have noticed all things that caught our attention as being communicatively problematic. We made an open coding of data through this reading [33], just stating what kind problems or other peculiarities we identified. This means that we have selected a set of policy declarations and made annotations to be used for further analysis.

Second we carried out the theory-informed discourse analysis using the results from the open coding as input. The theory-informed analysis in our case meant employing the analytical questions in Table 1. Furthermore, in order to carry out this step the interviews and observations were necessary background information. We used this information to interpret the policy declarations (when asking the analytical questions) from an employee's point of view, since a practice-based discourse analysis of an information security policy requires taking into account the practice where it is used. For example, we used this background understanding when interpreting what the confidentiality instructions meant for the medical secretaries when they are to fax patient information to another care provider. The information security policy stated that 'Patients should be confident that sensitive information does not reach unauthorized'. A second guideline was the following: 'Whatever form the information has, or the way in which it is transmitted or stored, it must always receive adequate protection.' When reading these statements we concluded that the instructions were directed (to whom?) towards the medical secretaries. However, the instructions were vague when it came to projected future actions (for what?).

Our interviews and observations revealed that the instructions were interpreted as follows by the staff: First, the medical secretary checked whether or not the care provider requesting the medical record had the patient's consent or not, either documented in the medical records or provided by the inquiring part. Second, the medical secretary removed the social security number from the physical medical record. This was done to anonymise the medical record when sending it via fax. Third, she/he added a temporary code, for example 2020. Finally, after faxing the medical secretary called her/his contact person at the requesting care provider in order to tell the temporary code. However, this set of actions was difficult to understand of from only reading the information security policy.

The third step was carried out to organise the analysed policy declarations into overall themes. These themes, which were inductively generated, are to be seen as broader problem areas based on the detailed analysis. We ended up with four themes of importance for design of practical communicative information security policies: external congruence, goal conflicts, internal congruence, and target group. These themes were used when constructing the tentative quality criteria, which are found in Section 4.2.

4   From Discourse Analysis to Tentative Quality Criteria

At the hospital the employees had to deal with three different information security policy documents that together constituted the information security policy. One document contained a high-level description of the information security regulations, while additional two documents contained low-level descriptions. The presentation below is structured according to the thematic analysis we carried out. The analysis was brought further through the formulation of eight tentative quality criteria (Section 4.2). Table 2 shows examples from our analysis. The table has three columns. The left-most column contains identifiers referring to the policy documents. Passages from the high-level document are referred to using 1.x, while the two low-level documents are referred to as 2.x and 3.x. The second column shows the policy declarations. Finally, the right-most column contains the analysis. Due to the limited space we only present the communicative functions that were considered problematic when analysing the policy declarations.

4.1   Thematic Analysis of Information Security Policy

Internal congruence is our first theme. This theme includes concerns about projected future actions that arise from incomplete explanations and definitions, inconsistent use of terminology, inconsistent communicative function, inconsistent description of the information security mechanisms in use, inconsistent description of the same rule and unclear references between the different information security policy documents. The incomplete explanations and definitions found in the three policy documents can be exemplified with passage 2.7 in Table 2. This quote refers to 'sensitive information' that must be removed from the hard drive before the computer is handed over to external service. However, none of the three investigated policy documents contains a definition of 'sensitive information'. In addition, the same document also includes the term 'business critical information' which is never defined and the differences between these categories are not accounted for. It results in a lack of guidance of the employees due to lack of definitions.

Passage 1.4 in Table 2 is to some extent related to the use of definitions, however it is an example of inconsistent use of terminology once it is introduced. This passage gives the impression that information security is achieved through 'information security policies, guidelines, and instructions', which means that technical measures are not necessary. However, it contradicts, for example, passage 2.6 and 2.11 that clearly contain references to technical security controls. It is also contradicts other references to the existence of technical security controls, such as password controls: 'Do not reveal your password to others, or lend out your authorization'. Consequently, the first and second policy documents give different impressions of what types of information security measures that are needed, and also how the most fundamental concept in the policy, information security, is defined.

Table 2. Practice-based discourse analysis of information security policy

No	Policy declaration	Analysis
1.2	'Information security must protect patients, employees and the public from harm caused by deficiencies in information management or disruption in information systems. The protection of human life, health and privacy are valued the most.'	*Pre-situational grounds:* Based on health law and security standards. *Accountable:* A goal conflict between health and privacy is built into this policy statement. *Projected future actions:* There is no guidance to users for choice between conflicting goals.
1.3	'Laws and regulations shall constitute the lowest level when specifying security measures and controls.'	*Pre-situational grounds:* Difficulties to know which laws and regulations one is to pay attention to. *Projected future actions:* Risk that laws and regulations are neglected.
1.4	'Information security is achieved by developing and complying with appropriate management tools such as information security policies, guidelines, and instructions.'	*Pre-situational grounds:* Lack of compliance with standards; neglect of technical, physical and informal security. *Accountable:* Contradictory to other statements including technical security. *Projected future actions:* Risk of neglecting measures (e.g. technical).
2.6	'If you leave your work place, you must lock the PC using the "Ctrl-Alt-Del" or log out, even if it is just for a short while.'	*Accountable:* Very clear and detailed instruction implies a shift in the text from abstract explanations to concrete and detailed measures. Hard to understand how and when this type of shift occurs. *Projected future actions:* Very clear measures specified.
2.7	'If your personal computer is handed over - for external services, you must ensure that any sensitive information is removed from the hard drive. It is the organisation's responsibility to ensure that the drives are cleaned before the computer goes to scrapping or another organisation.'	*Directed:* Ambiguous addressee (you vs. organisation). *Accountable:* Sensitive information is. *Constitutive:* Ambiguous responsibility is constituted. *Projected future actions:* Limited guidance for the users to take actions concerning file deletion when the PC is handed over to external parties.

Table 2. (*Countinued*)

2.10	'Information classification should be performed according to documented rules for classification of information.'	*Directed:* This instruction does not target regular users.
2.11	Examples of advice for management of information: • 'Information shall not be stored on the "own" local disc' • Backup should always be taken • Unauthorized access shall be prevented'	*Accountable:* Why are "examples" given; not a complete list? *Constitutive:* What is meant by "advice" in this regulative context? *Directed:* These "advices" are addressed not only to regular users. Unclear who the addressees are. *Projected future actions:* Difficult for users to understand the scope of the instructions.
2.17	The 'Information security policy'-document is referred to as the IT-policy.	*Referential:* the reference to the documents is incorrect. The naming of the document is inconsistent.
3.5	'Do not save patient information or other sensitive information on your local hard drive.'	*Accountable:* Unclear what 'other sensitive information' means. *Projected future actions:* Unclear what information can be saved locally
3.7	'Sensitive information may only in exceptional cases be saved on the local hard drive.'	*Accountable:* Unclear what 'sensitive information' means. In addition, earlier they have stated that you are not allowed to store sensitive information on your local hard drive. Cf. 3.5 *Projected future actions:* Unclear what actions are allowed or not.

The three documents have inconsistent communicative functions. Information security management switches from being regulative to in some parts being educational. As discussed in Section 2 the main purpose of a policy is limiting acceptable behaviour of employees, meaning that its primary communicative function is to be regulative. Of course, it is sometimes necessary to educate employees, but the two types of communicative functions are highly intertwined in the documents, without clear indication which communicative function that is in focus. For example, the detailed instructions on how to lock a workstation (Passage 2.6), is followed by an educational passage on why functionality to log the employees' activities is used: 'Logging of activities and transactions are carried out in order to continuously monitor the security of the IT systems. The purpose is to trace important events if disturbances occur in the systems. Tracing is also used to free the innocent, and discover threats to the information security.' Another educational passage in the document is a discussion on malware: 'code in the form of viruses, trojans, or worms could damage, distort or destroy information, or make sensitive information available to persons not allowed to see the information … Malware can be said to be software'.

In addition, Passage 2.6 is also an example of how the available information security mechanisms are described using an inconsistent level of abstraction. This specific passage is a very clear and detailed instruction compared to a passage similar to the following one, which is found sentences earlier: 'Remember that you are responsible for everything that is registered with your user identity.' Hence, from an employee's point it becomes difficult to understand the role of the document. Passages 3.5 and 3.7 are examples of inconsistent descriptions of the same rule. In this case it concerns if the employee are allowed to store sensitive information on 'the local hard drive'. In passage 3.5 the regular user is not allowed to store sensitive information on the computer. While, passage 3.7 states that such information should only 'in exceptional cases be saved on the local hard drive'. This is an inconsistent description, where the employees are left in the dark on how to act. Finally, as discussed earlier the investigated information security policy consists of three documents, and they contain references to each other. But the naming of the documents is not consistent (2.17), which means that it is difficult for the employees to find the right related document. For example, the 'Information security policy'-document is referred to as the IT-policy in the 'Security instructions for county council IT users'-document.

Target group is the second theme, which covers the problem of ambiguous addressees in three policy documents. Passage 2.7 in Table 2 shows one such case. As discussed above, the example concerns how to handle the computer when it is handed over to a third, external, part for service. However, the regulation is ambiguous. In the first part of the example, there is a focus on 'you' as the addressee: 'If your personal computer is handed over - for external services, you must ensure that any sensitive information is removed from the hard drive'. But in the next sentence it is at the same time the responsibility of the organisation, which means that it is not the employee's responsibility. Finally, the third sentence reads 'IT Support provides software for cleaning and can assist with clean-up', which yet again signals that it is the employee's responsibility. A second example of ambiguous addresses is passage 2.10: 'Information classification should be performed according to documented rules for classification of information.' Information classification is carried out in order to determine the right level of information security measure. It is normally an activity of information security management or general management. If employees would carry out this activity they might start neglecting existing information security measure based on their own classifications. Consequently, it is not evident who the information security management is actually regulating, which in the end means that an ambiguous responsibility is constituted.

External congruence is the third identified theme. In several occasions the three policy documents reference other documents such as laws, regulation, or standards. However, the congruence with these sources is not clear. Passage 1.4 claims, as discussed earlier, that information security is achieved through 'information security policies, guidelines, and instructions.' Hence it is a focus on administrative routines, neglecting technical, physical and informal information security. The same document refers to the ISO-standard 17799, which does not described information security as something to be addressed by administrative means only. Another problem with the information security policy documents is that information security management references laws and regulations in general, without specifying exactly which laws and regulations (Passage 1.3). Consequently, it is difficult for the employees to know exactly which laws and regulations they are to pay attention to.

Goal conflicts are the fourth and final theme we identified. The three investigated policy documents included a number of goal conflicts. Passage 1.2 concerns the tension between protection of human life and health on one hand, and protection of patient information, i.e. privacy, on the other. In the policy document it is stated that 'protection of human life, health and privacy are valued the most.' Another example of conflicting goals is the following which is found in passage 2.1: 'In addition to legal requirements, there are additional demands from organisations and the public, stating that information must be correct, it must be available and must be handled with respect to privacy or publicity.' In this case the tension is between privacy and publicity. A third example is passage 2.11 gives advises 'for management of information'. However, these advises are not directed towards employees only. From an employee's point of view it is contradictory that information should not be stored on the local disc, but at the same time backup should always be taken. In all these cases the information security management leaves the employees without any guidance on how to choose between the conflicting goals.

4.2   Towards Tentative Quality Criteria

The practice-based discourse analysis of this case material has revealed problems with the information security policy. The analysis has aimed for abstraction and four themes have been formulated. These abstracted themes (designating problematic areas in the information security policy) were used for articulating general expectations on policy features. The underlying assumption in our work is that an information security policy should be functional in regulating employees' actions with respect to information security. The policy documents must be comprehensive and useful in guiding employees' actions. The discourse analysis has been a generative basis for formulation of tentative quality criteria for information security policies in health care. The quality criteria express what is considered a good information security policy in health care, i.e. they express positive design values. We have formulated them as criteria that can be useful both in a design/formulation situation and in an evaluation situation. Our criteria cover both the whole information security policy (possibly consisting of different documents of both high-level and low-level character) and different parts of such policy documents.

Quality criteria:

1. *The information security policy shall not introduce goal conflicts.* We identified several goal conflicts (1.2, 2.1) that the employees were left to manage. The policy was ambiguous with regard to employee prioritization. Theme: goal conflicts.
2. *External policies shall be translated and transformed to the current work practice when such parts are included in the information security policy.* Our analysis (1.3) showed that parts of laws and international standards were included in the policy without paying attention to the local context, or that only vague references were provide to laws. Theme: external congruence.
3. *The information security policy (or explicit parts thereof) shall have clear and uniformed user groups.* The analysis (2.7) showed that it was unclear who were affected by the instructions. Theme: target group.

4.   *The information security policy shall contain congruent guidelines for actions that are well adapted to the current work practice.* The analysis (2.6, 3.5, 3.7) showed that instructions are provided at a general level, which left room for interpretation on how to implement the guidelines in the work practice. Theme: internal congruence.

5.   *The information security policy shall have a clear and congruent conceptual framework adapted to the current work practice.* The analysis (1.4, 2.6, 2.11) showed an ambiguous use of concepts, where several concepts were used for the same phenomenon. As a consequence, the policy was ambiguous when referring to phenomena in the work practice. Theme: internal congruence.

6.   *The information security policy (in whole and parts) shall have a clear structure.* Our analysis (2.7, 2.17) showed ambiguously structured documents where phenomena concerning the same target group were discussed at multiple places. Thus it was difficult for employees to know when they had assimilated all information concerning a specific phenomenon. Theme: internal congruence.

7.   *The information security policy (in whole and parts) shall have clear objectives; implying clear communicative functions of the document.* Our analysis (2.6) showed that the communicative functions of specific parts of the documents were unclear (regulative and educational sections are highly intertwined). Making it difficult to identify regulatory instructions. Theme: internal congruence.

8.   *The information security policy shall be constitutively clear; clarifying responsibilities and social commitments and expectations.* The analysis (2.10) showed that the responsibilities of the employees were unclear. Hence, it was difficult to achieve accountability. Theme: target group.

5   Conclusions

An information security policy of high communicative quality has the potential to be a practical and useful tool for information security management. The purpose of this paper was a) to illustrate the usefulness of practice-based discourse analysis for understanding information security policy design, and b) to provide a set of tentative quality criteria for information security policies in health care from a practice perspective. Based on a practice-base discourse analysis that includes high-level and low-level information security policy documents we suggest eight quality criteria for design of information security policies in health care. Our findings are based on one case study. We therefore see interesting venues for future research to further validate the criteria and make them more precise. Another research task is to investigate if any of these criteria are applicable in other business sectors, and if so to what extent. Our quality criteria have, to some extent, similarities with the criteria presented by Stahl et al. [8]. If we are to highlight one similarity, both studies stress the importance of using a clear and congruent conceptual framework adapted to the current work practice. Otherwise, the policies are not accessible to the employees. However, unlike Stahl et al. [8] our quality criteria also address the importance of the structure of policy documents. This difference is a result from Stahl et al.'s [8] choice to limit their study to high-level policies, whereas we studied both high-level *and* low-level policy documents and their relationships. The criteria presented are all derived from a practice-based perspective. It means that they emphasize information security policies as *useful tools for employees.* This perspective represents an alternative and a contrast to the management perspective. When designing information security policies both perspectives need to be acknowledged in order to create a balanced solution. Our list of quality criteria is one important component in the discussion to find such a balance.

References

1. Ernst & Young: Ernst & Young 2008 Global Information Security Survey. Ernst & Young (2008)
2. Ernst & Young: Borderless security - Ernst & Young's 2010 Global Information Security Survey. Ernst & Young (2010)
3. Vroom, C., von Solms, R.: Towards information security behavioural compliance. Computers and Security **23**, 191–198 (2004)
4. Baskerville, R., Siponen, M.: An information security meta-policy for emergent organizations. Logistics Information Management **15**, 337–346 (2002)
5. Gaskell, G.: Simplifying the onerous task of writing security policies. In: 1st Australian Information Security Management Workshop (2000)
6. ISO: ISO/IEC 27002:2005, Information Technology - Secuirty Techniques - Code of Practice for Information Management Systems - Requirements. International Organization for Standardization (ISO) (2005)
7. Baskerville, R.: Information systems security design methods: Implications for information systems development. ACM Computing Surveys 25 (1993)
8. Stahl, B.C., Doherty, N.F., Shaw, M.: Information security policies in the UK healthcare sector: a critical evaluation. Information Systems Journal **22**, 77–94 (2012)
9. De Lusignana, S., Chanb, T., Theadoma, A., Dhoula, N.: The roles of policy and professionalism in the protection of processed clinical data: A literature review. International Journal of Medical Informatics 76(4), 261–268 (2007)
10. Davis, G.B., Olson, M.H.: Management information systems: conceptual foundations, structure, and development. McGraw-Hill Inc., New York (1985)
11. von Solms, R., von Solms, B.: From policies to culture. Computers and Security **23**, 275–279 (2004)
12. von Solms, B.: Corporate Governance and Information Security. Computer & Security **20**, 215–218 (2001)
13. von Solms, R., von Solms, S.H.: Information Security Governance: A model based on the Direct-Control Cycle. Computer & Security **25**, 408–412 (2006)
14. Peltier, T.R.: Information security policies and procedures - a practitioner's reference. Auerbach Publications, Boca Raton (2004)
15. Wood, C.C.: Information security policies made easy. Information Shield, Huston (2001)
16. Sibley, E.H.: Experiments in organizational policy representation: resuls to date. In: Proceedings of the International Conference on Systems, Man and Cybernetics, vol. 1, 337–342 (1993)
17. Wood, C.C.: Writing InfoSec Policies. Computer & Security **14**, 667–674 (1995)
18. Janczewski, L.: Managing Security Functions Using Security Standards. In: Janczewski, L. (ed.) Internet and Intranet Security Management: Risks and Solutions, pp. 81–105. IGI Global, Hershey (2000)

19. Knapp, K.J., Morris Jr., R.F., Marshall, T.E., Byrd, T.A.: Information security policy: An organizational-level process model. Computer & Security **28**, 493–508 (2009)
20. Fabian, F., Gürses, S., Heisel, M., Santen, T., Schmidt, H.: A comparison of security requirements engineering methods. Requirements Engineering **15**, 7–40 (2010)
21. Mellado, D., Blanco, C., Sánchez, L.E., Fernaández-Medina, E.: A systematic review of security requirements engineering. Computer Standards and Interfaces **32**, 153–165 (2010)
22. Doherty, N., Anastasakis, L., Fulford, H.: The information security policy unpacked: A critical study of the content of university policies. International Journal of Information Management **29**, 449–457 (2009)
23. Siponen, M.: Policies for construction of information systems' security guidelines. In: The 15th International Information Security Conference (IFIP TC11/SEC2000), Beijing, China (2000)
24. Lindup, K.: The Role of Information Security in Corporate Governance. Computer & Security **15**, 477–485 (1996)
25. Potter, J., Wetherell, M.: Discourse and social psychology. Beyond attitudes and behaviour. Sage, London (1987)
26. Yin, R.K.: Case study research: design and methods. Sage, Thousand Oaks (1994)
27. Schatzki, T.R.: Introduction: Practice theory. In: Schatzki, T.R., Knorr Cetina, K., von Savigny, E. (eds.) The Practice Turn in Contemporary Theory. Routledge, London (2001)
28. Goldkuhl, G.: The many facets of communication – a socio-pragmatic conceptualisation for information systems studies. In: Proceedings of the Workshop on Communication and Coordination in Business Processes, Kiruna (2005)
29. Habermas, J.: The theory of communicative action1. Reason and the rationalization of society. Polity Press, Cambridge (1984)
30. Sacks, H.: Lectures on conversation. Blackwell, Oxford (1992)
31. Bühler, K.: Theory of language. John Benjamins Publishing, Amsterdam (2011)
32. Dewey, J.: Logic: The theory of inquiry. Henry Holt, New York (1938)
33. Corbin, J., Strauss, A.: Basics of qualitative research. Techniques and procedures for developing Grounded Theory. Sage, Thousand Oaks (2008)

Understanding Collaborative Challenges in IT Security Preparedness Exercises

Maria B. Line[1,2]([✉]) and Nils Brede Moe[2]

[1] Norwegian University of Science and Technology (NTNU),
Trondheim, Norway
maria.b.line@item.ntnu.no
[2] SINTEF, Trondheim, Norway
nils.b.moe@sintef.no

Abstract. IT security preparedness exercises allow for practical collaborative training, which in turn leads to improved response capabilities to information security incidents for an organization. However, such exercises are not commonly performed in the electric power industry. We have observed a tabletop exercise as performed by three organizations with the aim of understanding challenges of performing such exercises. We argue that challenges met during exercises could affect the response process during a real incident as well, and by improving the exercises the response capabilities would be strengthened accordingly. We found that the response team must be carefully selected to include the right competences and all parties that would be involved in a real incident response process, such as technical, managerial, and business responsible. Further, the main goal of the exercise needs to be well understood among the whole team and the facilitator needs to ensure a certain time pressure to increase the value of the exercise, and both the exercise and existing procedures need to be reviewed. Finally, there are many ways to conduct preparedness exercises. Therefore, organizations need to both optimize current exercise practices and experiment with new ones.

Keywords: Information security · Incident management · Preparedness exercises · Training · Decision-making · Self-managing teams

1 Introduction

Preparing for information security incident management requires training. Basic structures such as well documented procedures and clear definitions of roles and responsibilities need to be in place, but during an incident, there is no time to study documentation in order to figure out the most appropriate response strategies; involved personnel needs to be well trained and well experienced, and hence able to make the right decisions under pressure [1]. Wrong decisions may cause the incident to escalate and lead to severe consequences.

The electric power industry is currently implementing major technological changes in order to achieve smart grids. These changes concern new technologies, higher connectivity and more integration, which increase the attack surface

© IFIP International Federation for Information Processing 2015
H. Federrath and D. Gollmann (Eds.): SEC 2015, IFIP AICT 455, pp. 311–324, 2015.
DOI: 10.1007/978-3-319-18467-8_21

and the potential consequences of attacks [2]. At the same time, current threat reports show that targeted attacks are on the rise, and critical infrastructures are attractive targets [3]. However, recent studies of the electric power industry show that preparedness exercises for IT security incidents are not commonly performed [4,5] though guidelines exist for how to plan and perform such exercises [6,7]. Reasons for not performing such exercises seem to relate to their perception of the probability of being attacked and their understanding of potential threats and consequences, and that more pressing tasks receive higher priority. Still, personnel from both the IT staff and the industrial control staff express confidence in their organization's incident response capabilities.

Motivated by the importance of collaborative training for responding to information security incidents, and the evident problem of adopting such training, the following research question is defined for our study:

What are the challenges of performing tabletop exercises for IT security incidents?

We will discuss how these challenges might affect the incident management process during a real-life incident and provide recommendations for how to reduce these challenges in the setting of an exercise, as that should positively affect a real-life incident management process as well.

The paper is structured as follows. Related work on preparedness exercises are described in Section 2. The research method and our case context are presented in Section 3, while Section 4 sums up the observations made during the case study. Challenges are discussed in Section 5 along with recommendations for preparedness exercises, and Section 6 concludes the paper.

2   Background

The purpose of an emergency preparedness exercise is to strengthen the response capabilities of an organization by training personnel in responding to situations that deviate from normal operations. A certain baseline of written plans and procedures should be present. However, during an emergency there is a need for a more dynamic process that requires coordination and improvisation, and where exceptions and violations are managed, and experienced incident handlers are valued. Relying on predefined documentation is what Hale and Borys refer to as Model 1 in the use of safety rules and procedures [8], while allowing for rules to be emerged from practical experience is referred to as Model 2. Exercises are a way of developing Model 2. In the following we elaborate on tabletop exercises specifically, and coordination and improvisation in the incident response process.

2.1   Tabletop Exercises

Tabletop exercises prepare personnel for responding to an emergency situation. They allow for discussions of roles, responsibilities, procedures, coordination, and decision-making, and are a reasonably cost-efficient way of reviewing and learning documented plans and procedures for incident response. Tabletop exercises are usually performed in a classroom without the use of any specific equipment. A facilitator presents a scenario and initiates the discussion. According to the National Institute of Standards and Technology (NIST), a tabletop exercise should consist of the following four phases; Design the event by identifying objectives and participants, Develop the scenario and guides for the facilitator and the participants, Conduct the exercise, and Evaluate by debriefing and identifying lessons learned [6]. As a training method it suffers from the weakness that it does not provide practical demonstrations of the effects of an incident or the emergency management's true response capabilities [9].

In his study of preparedness exercises initiated by the Norwegian Water and Energy Directorate (NVE), Gåsland [10] found that there is a positive attitude for participating in exercises and an understanding that collaboration is important in problem-solving processes. He still found that exercises compete with daily tasks for prioritization, and he considered it to be an obstacle to learning if exercises are not used as a means of making improvements afterwards. Further, he emphasized the importance of making exercises as realistic as possible. However, creating realistic scenarios is challenging [11], and even though a scenario is successfully responded to in an exercise, it does not give any guarantees that a real emergency situation will be successfully responded to [12].

2.2   Coordination in Preparedness Exercises

Coordination of work and making collaborative decisions are important aspects of the incident response process and hence also of preparedness exercises. Responding to an IT security incident usually implies personnel from different parts of an organization collaborating on solving complex problems. "Coordination is management of interdependencies between activities" [13] and coordination mechanisms are the organizational arrangements, which allow individuals to realize a collective performance [14]. Interdependencies include sharing of resources, synchronization of activities, and prerequisite activities. Coordination challenges in incident response are functions of the complexity, such as processes and technology.

Further, responding to an IT security incident is creative work, as there might not be one correct solution and a number of both uncertainties and interdependencies need to be taken into account. In creative work progress towards completion can be difficult to estimate [15] because interdependencies between different pieces of work may be uncertain or challenging to identify. This makes it difficult to know who should be involved in the work, and whether there is a correct order in which parties should complete their own specialized work [14]. Further, in creative work it is essential to improve the knowledge transactions between team members. This is captured in a transactive memory system (TMS), a shared cognitive system for encoding, storing and retrieving knowledge between members of a group [16]. TMS can be understood as a shared understanding of who knows what and also on the degree to which individual knowledge sets are differentiated.

Coordination can be either predefined or situated [17]. Predefined coordination takes place prior to the situation being coordinated and can be understood as what Hale and Borys refer to as Model 1 [8] and an incident response scheme as described by ISO/IEC 27035 – *Information security incident management* [18]. It typically consists of establishing written or unwritten rules, routines, procedures, roles, and schedules. Situated coordination, on the other hand, occurs when a situation is unknown and/or unanticipated, such as when an IT security incident strikes, and can be understood as Model 2 [8]. Those involved in the situation do not know in advance how they should contribute. They lack knowledge of what to achieve, who does what, how the work can be divided, in what sequence sub-activities should be done, when to act, etc. Consequently, they have to improvise and coordinate their efforts ad hoc. In most collaborative efforts there is a mix of predefined and situated coordination. Involved actors may for instance already know the goal, but not who performs what, or they may know who does what but not when to do it. To compensate for lacking predefined knowledge of how the actual unfolding of activities in an exercise will be, the participants must update themselves on the status of the situation.

To handle a crisis, not only does the team need to coordinate their work; they also need to take decisions together and be responsible for managing and monitoring their own processes and executing tasks, i.e they need to be able to self-manage [19].

3   Method

Since the goal of this research was to explore and provide insight into challenges experienced during IT security preparedness exercises, it was important to study such exercises in practice. We designed a holistic multiple case study [20] of three IT security preparedness exercises in three different organizations. According to Yin, case studies are the preferred research strategy when a "question is being asked about a contemporary set of events over which the investigator has little or no control" [ibid p. 9]. In the following, we present the scenario used, the organizations studied, and how data collection and analysis were performed.

3.1   Scenario

One scenario recently recommended by the authorities[1] was used by all organizations in our study. This scenario describes an information security incident that escalates through five phases:

1. Abnormally large amounts of data is sent to external recipients.
2. Two weeks later, the SCADA supplier wants to install a patch. The contact is made in a different way than what is regulated in the service agreement.

---

[1] Norwegian Water Resources and Energy Directorate (NVE).

3. Three months after the first event, one area suffers from power outage. The monitoring systems do not display any alarms.
4. Customers start calling as more areas suffer from power outage. The monitoring systems do still not display any alarms.
5. Mobile communications and Internet connections are down.

The participants had 20 minutes to discuss each phase before they were given information about the next. For each phase the participants had to describe how they would interpret the events and which actions they would take.

3.2   Case Context

The three organizations in our study are Norwegian Distribution System Operators (DSOs) and they are among the ten largest DSOs in Norway. For organizations A and B, this was their first execution of such a collaborative exercise for IT security. Organization C had performed a similar exercise once before, and the Emergency Management Team performs preparedness exercises regularly for a variety of incident types. In the following, we present the organizations and how each of them set up their exercise, as well as all participants and their number of years of experience in the organization.

Organization A. Three groups of personnel were represented in this exercise: IT operations, industrial control systems, and network infrastructure. Nine participants were present, including the Preparedness Coordinator[2], a representative from external supplier of SCADA systems, and the facilitator, cf. Table 1.

Table 1. Participants in organization A

Role	Exp.
IT production manager	5
IT security coordinator	25
Fiber networks manager	>20
Senior engineer, fiber networks	5
Control systems manager	20
Special advisor, remote control units	>30
Service engineer, supplier of control systems	>30
Emergency preparedness coordinator	>30
IT security coordinator for control systems (facilitator)	28

Organization B. Fourteen participants represented three different areas of expertise: IT, control systems, and control room operations. They were divided into three groups for the exercise, and there was one observer in each group, cf. Table 2. "GO" indicates who was the group observer. The intention was to have all three areas of expertise represented in each group, but last minute changes due to sudden business-related events caused group 1 to not have anyone from control systems. The HSE/Quality/Preparedness Coordinator, who has more than 20 years of experience, visited all three groups and is therefore not listed in the table in one specific group.

---
[2] All DSOs are required to have this role assigned to someone.

Table 2. Participants in organization B

Group 1		Group 2		Group 3	
Role	Exp.	Role	Exp.	Role	Exp.
Control operations eng.	10	Control operations eng.	25	Control systems engineer	6
IT infrastructures engr.	9	Control operations eng.	>20	Control room manager	8
IT operations engineer	1	IT operations engineer	29	IT operations engineer	>15
IT manager	4	IT operations engineer	8	IT operations engineer	8
Control sys. manager (GO)	1	IT business sys. manager	>20	IT security manager (GO)	12
		IT consultant	1		
		Control ops. manager (GO)	>10		

Organization C. Twelve employees took part in the exercise, cf. Table 3. Five belonged to the Emergency Management Team and were called for when their presence was needed. One person facilitated the exercise in close collaboration with the IT security coordinator.

Table 3. Participants in organization C

Technical personnel		Emergency Management Team	
Role	Exp.	Role	Exp.
Manager, Control room DSO	5	Main corporation, IT manager	3
Deputy manager, Control room DSO	34	Power production, CEO	19
Manager, Control systems	36	DSO Technical manager	28
IT operation manager	4	Emergency preparedness coordinator	30
IT network security engineer	6	DSO Manager, emerg. prep. manager	5
Marketing, Broadband, Tech. manager	8		

3.3 Data Collection and Analysis

The first author contributed to the planning of all the tabletop exercises. Before the scenario was presented to the participants, they were asked about their expectations for the exercise. A retrospective was facilitated after the exercise, where all participants reflected upon what worked well and what could have been done differently. Their expectations from beforehand were discussed; whether they were fulfilled and why/why not.

For the analysis, we described the tabletop exercises and evaluations from each organization to achieve an understanding of what was going on during the exercises. Then we categorized interesting expressions and observations, before we compared findings between the organizations.

4   Results

The three organizations carried out the preparedness exercises according to generally recommended NIST practices. Plans and goals of the exercise were established in advance, and they all discussed the five phases of the scenario. While the three organizations used the same scenario and main agenda for the exercise, they all had diversity in goals and the number and types of participants. Our observations are hereby presented, as characterized by the following descriptions:

1. Knowledge exchange and process improvement (org. A)
2. Cross-functional self-managing groups (org. B)
3. Involvement of Emergency Management Team (org. C)

4.1 Knowledge Exchange and Process Improvement

In organization A the IT security coordinator for control systems planned and facilitated the exercise. He presented his goals for the exercise in the beginning: *knowledge exchange across organizational boundaries, obtaining a common understanding of what is technically possible in todays' systems, identifying technical and organizational improvements, and ideas for future exercises.* The participants were seated around one big table. The scenario was already known to two of the participants; the fiber networks manager and the emergency preparedness coordinator; as they had participated in this exact same exercise the week before in a different context. This was the only organization that included one participant from their supplier.

A few participants dominated throughout the whole discussion and nobody seemed to take charge of the group as a chair person responsible for involving all participants and achieving consensus in the group. For the first three phases the IT security coordinator and the fiber networks manager appeared to be quite sure of what would be the right choices of action. Still, they were open about lacking knowledge of systems outside their own domain and asked questions in order to get the whole picture. The facilitator later commented that he had expected these two participants to dominate because of their roles, competences, and personality. He added that in a real emergency situation, only four of the participants would be involved in the crisis management group: the two most dominant participants, the control systems manager, and himself.

The participants were satisfied with this exercise being performed, as they see this as an important scenario for preparedness exercises and as lacks were revealed that they need to work on to improve their own response capabilities. Furthermore, they approved of the initiative of making different parts of the organization meet for an IT security exercise. However, some participants felt that the discussion was a bit out of control, as they did not manage to keep the focus on solving the actual problems presented in the scenario. They missed a person facilitating the discussion. The facilitator, on the other hand, was satisfied with the discussion, as he saw it as valuable knowledge exchange, which was one of his main goals. At the same time, some participants would have liked to have more time for discussions. Furthermore, some perceived the last phase of the scenario to be unrealistic and unlikely.

One important insight obtained was that they would not be able to relate the event in the third phase to the two events that occurred three months earlier. Their main priority is usually to get the systems back to normal operations, while understanding *why* the incident occurred typically receives less focus, if any. A number of improvements were identified, regarding both technical and organizational aspects, in order to strengthen the response capabilities for information security incidents affecting complex IT and control systems.

4.2   Cross-Functional Self-Managing Groups

The exercise in organization B was prepared by a group of three managers: of IT security, control systems, and the control room. The former had participated in a similar exercise before. The goal of the exercise was to practice collaboration between the departments of industrial control and IT systems. The subgoals were to get to know persons, tasks, and responsibilities across the two involved departments and identify improvements to existing procedures for emergency preparedness and information security in general. The three managers acted as observers; one for each group of participants. They were responsible for presenting the scenario, making sure the group made decisions for each phase of the scenario, and assisting the group in keeping the discussion going if necessary. Each group was seated around one table in three different meeting rooms.

The group observers reported that in general, the group discussions were good and nobody seemed to dominate. In group 3 the control room manager took to some extent on the role as a chair person for the group; the group observer perceived this as natural based on his role in the organization. This group observer further stated that the participants appeared curious on each others' competences and responsibilities as they lacked this insight in order to get the big picture. The observer in group 1 would like to see more involvement from the management level in preparedness exercises.

Each group was intended to be self-managing, with as little intervention from the group observers as possible. Reflections from the group observers indicated that it was difficult to keep quiet, as they wanted to contribute. This was particularly challenging for the observer in group 1, as this group suffered from the lack of control systems personnel, and he was the only one with this competence. He still chose to remain fairly passive. All group observers reported that they did not need to intervene in order for the discussions to keep going. They did not need to push their groups into making decisions either, as the groups were focused on solving the problems as described in the scenario. While all groups made several decisions on what would be appropriate actions for each phase of the scenario, they did not present clear solutions to all sub-problems.

There was some criticism to the scenario description: "It is stated here that we reinstalled (...), but we would never have done that because (...)". Some pointed out that the scenario was not realistic because of how their systems are integrated, while others found the scenario to be quite realistic.

The evaluation showed that the participants were overall satisfied with the exercise. They appreciated the opportunity to meet and get to know colleagues from other parts of the organization and to get insight into their areas of responsibilities and knowledge. The participants would have liked to have more time than 20 minutes for discussions for some of the phases. Furthermore, they lacked the opportunity to hear how the other groups had solved the problems. A separate meeting for this was arranged a couple of weeks later. One participant suggested they use the existing preparedness plans and procedures actively during such an exercise. The group observers found the thorough evaluation process to be very valuable, and they saw it as an advantage that it was lead by an external (one researcher) as it made the participants put extra effort into contributing.

4.3   Involvement of Emergency Management Team

In organization C the exercise was planned by the IT security coordinator and a facilitator from the communications department. The goal of the exercise was awareness raising and practice in responding to IT security incidents that occur in the control systems. The participants were seated around one big table. Five representatives from the Emergency Management Team were present during the introduction. Three of them left the room when the scenario was presented, while two chose to stay as passive observers. The intention was that the complete Emergency Management Team should be called for at a later phase of the scenario, when the seriousness of the incident required them to be involved, in order to resemble a realistic situation. They were called for twice.

When the first phase of the scenario was presented, the IT operation manager quickly claimed ownership of the incident. He said that he would be the one to get the first alert, and that he would be the one to initiate analyses and reporting to other stakeholders in the organization. One issue that was thoroughly discussed, was the reporting from IT to the control room: when would that be done, if at all; is this relevant information for the control room staff; and is this reporting line documented. This was identified as a lack in the documented procedures when one participant checked these during the discussion. The group still knew who to contact. Another issue that received a lot of attention, was the question of shutting down the control systems. The IT operation manager would recommend this at the stage where the control room supplier calls and wants to install a security patch in the control systems (phase two), as he was worried about the malware infections spreading further into the systems. The control system manager on the other hand claimed that shutting down the control systems has extensive financial consequences for the operations, as manual operations are expensive. The Emergency Management Team decided to shut down the control systems in the fourth phase of the scenario.

During the evaluation it was agreed that such an incident would pose a great challenge for the organization. They still concluded that the situation was resolved satisfactorily in this exercise, and that they would be able to maintain power production and distribution by manually operating power stations. The facilitators felt that relevant assessments and decisions were made, and that the Emergency Management Team was involved at the right points in time. The Emergency Management Team contributed with thorough analyses and unambiguous decisions.

5   Discussion

We have described a tabletop exercise as performed in three organizations. While they all relied on the same scenario, they organized the exercise differently.

In the following we discuss the importance of preparedness exercises, along with our results in the light of our research question: *What are the challenges of performing tabletop exercises for IT security incidents?* Then we discuss how observed challenges could affect a real-life incident response process. Finally, we provide recommendations for how to succeed with preparedness exercises.

Our study confirmed the importance of conducting preparedness exercises. In organization A they realized that in a real situation they would most probably not be able to link the third phase to the first two, i. e. events that occur three months apart. By training they became aware that such links exist. Further, the participants in organization B were not sufficiently aware of each others' needs for information. They realized how the information flow could be improved. In two of the organizations in our study, A and B, the participants had different views on whether the scenario was realistic or not. This difference shows a need for developing a common perception of possible threats and potential consequences, which can be partly achieved by performing exercises.

A single best practice on organizing tabletop exercises does probably not exist. However, we found a number of challenges that need to be understood in order to succeed with such training.

Having One Goal Only. For a team to have good performance and to be able to effectively solve a complex problem, they need shared understanding of the team goals [21]. Having several goals for the exercise might lead to the individual members heading towards different goals. In organization A the team focused on solving the given problem while the facilitator was just as focused on knowledge sharing and fruitful discussions. As a consequence they had problems staying focused during the exercise. The main goal of an exercise should be to solve the problem, while additional goals may rather be aimed for during the evaluation afterwards, as was done in organization B.

Recommendation: Define only one main goal for the preparedness exercise.

Enabling Self-Management and Growing Team Knowledge. For a team to solve a crisis and make good decisions it needs to be able to self-manage. Members of self-managing teams share decision authority jointly, rather than having a centralized decision structure where one person makes all the decisions, or a decentralized decision structure where team members make independent decisions. Organization A had problems self-managing as two persons made most of the decisions. It was later concluded that only a few of the team members would participate in a real situation. The others should have been present as observers to distinguish between who are part of the team and who are not.

Enabling self-management further requires the group to have the necessary competence; otherwise the group will be training for solving the problem without having the necessary competence available. However, because handling incidents is creative work, it might be challenging to identify everyone that should be present in the training up front. One of the teams in organization B clearly suffered from the lack of competence, and both organizations B and C lacked personnel from their external suppliers. The training outcome would have been better with the right personnel present.

In addition to the right competence, a shared understanding of who knows what is needed to solve a crisis effectively [16]. We found that in most teams people did not have a good overview of what the others knew, however, the team members became more aware of each others' knowledge during the exercise.

Recommendation: Ensure the presence of all required competence in the team, including personnel from external suppliers. Make it explicit who are part of the team and who are observers. Include a facilitator to support the team in making joint decisions and conduct exercises frequently to develop a shared understanding of who knows what.

Availability of Personnel. Business runs continuously and might require sudden and unforeseen actions, which in turn might cause personnel to cancel their presence in the exercise. This will affect the group composition as happened in organization B, where last minute changes led to the lack of one type of competence in one of the groups. Further, members of management groups tend to have little time for exercises, but their presence is needed to have realism to the exercise. Limiting the time spent on exercises would most likely make it easier for key personnel to participate. All organizations experience turnover. Hence, sudden absence of critical competence might be experienced during a real-life incident as well.

Recommendation: Perform preparedness exercises frequently to make sure that all personnel receive training regularly. Limit the time spent on each exercise to make it easier for key personnel to participate.

Time Management. Having 20 minutes for discussing each phase was perceived as too short for some, while sufficient for others, depending on both the participants and the complexity of the given problems. Creating a time-pressure for making quick decisions was understood as making the exercise more realistic. Still, according to FEMA [9] it is wise to take the time to resolve problems. A facilitator needs to balance the amount of time spent on the different phases based on the progress and how well the team performs. Further, making time for thorough reflections after the exercise is important to improve the benefits of the exercise, as was also recommended by NIST [6]. Both organizations A and B spent 60-70 minutes on such reflections and stated that one large benefit was that of having an external facilitator for this, as the participants clearly put more effort into contributing than they would usually do during internal evaluations. A similar evaluation was planned for organization C, but they ran out of time and did not prioritize a thorough evaluation after the exercise. A short around-the-table discussion was performed.

Recommendation: Ensure time pressure by limiting the time for problem-solving in the exercise. Allow for thorough reflections in a plenary session right after the exercise is completed. If there is more than one group, add time for reflection within each group as well, before the plenary session.

Use of Existing Documentation. None of the teams actively consulted written plans and procedures during the exercise. Such plans were made available to the team in organization C only. Although documentation needs to be in place, situated coordination is more important because the scenarios in the exercise are unknown. An organization therefore needs to rely on the individuals and their knowledge when handling a crisis. In organization C, a lack in the reporting procedures was identified, but the participants still knew who to contact and when. It was stated that in an emergency situation there is no time for consulting documentation. Exercises contribute to develop practical knowledge and the knowledge of who knows what, which is essential to make good decisions when handling an incident. Still, documentation would be available during a real situation, therefore it should also be available during an exercise. One of the main goals with a tabletop exercise is to review plans and procedures [9], and this should be performed shortly after the exercise.

Recommendation: Make existing written documentation available during the preparedness exercise and review the documentation in retrospective if needed. If the available documentation is not consulted, discuss why.

Involvement of Business Management. It is essential to involve those with the authority to make decisions influencing business operations. IT security involves more than IT personnel, as an incident might have severe consequences for both the organization, its customers, and society at large. In an emergency situation the goal from a business perspective is usually to maintain normal operations as continuously as possible. However, there are different strategies that may be used for this: to resolve the incident with as little disturbances to the operations as possible, to understand why the incident occurred, or to make sure that the incident will not repeat itself. These different strategies require slightly different approaches and priorities, and it is therefore crucial that the incident responders have a common understanding of the overall preferred strategy.

Organization C seemed to succeed with their model where the team called for the Emergency Management Team when severity of the incident required them to. In organization C the IT personnel wanted to shut down the control systems quite early, due to their fear of malware infections; the control room manager wanted to wait, due to high costs of manual operations. These costs were compared to the consequences of an uncontrolled breakdown. We found that priorities among different parts of the organization vary, which supports the need for collaborative exercises and practicing joint decision-making, at the same time as different authority levels come into play.

Recommendation: Include all personnel that will play a role during a real-life incident, including both technical personnel and business representatives.

6   Concluding Remarks and Future Research

For industrial control organizations to withstand and/or successfully respond to attacks, personnel from different parts of the organization need to collaborate:

IT, control systems, control room, networks/infrastructure, and business representatives. These groups of personnel do not have a tradition for collaborating with each other, as industrial control systems used to be isolated from administrative IT systems. A holistic view of the incident response process is needed so that the whole organization is included in training, as it would be during a real emergency situation.

There are many ways to conduct preparedness exercises. Therefore organizations need to both optimize current exercise practices and experiment with new ones. Regardless of how the exercises are conducted, there are a number of challenges to be aware of, as identified in our study. Functional exercises should be performed as a supplement to tabletop exercises in order to improve the operational capabilities as well.

We studied organizations doing such exercises for the first time. There is therefore a need to study which challenges are met by organizations that are more mature when it comes to performing preparedness exercises for IT security incidents. Such a study should also investigate what good practices these organizations are performing in their exercises. Further, challenges met during real-life incident response processes should be investigated, in order to make preparedness exercises even more useful.

Acknowledgments. The authors would like to thank the three DSOs that participated in this study, and Senior Research Scientist Martin G. Jaatun, SINTEF, and Professor Poul E. Heegaard, NTNU, for providing valuable feedback. This work was funded by the Norwegian Research Council through the *DeVID* project, grant no 217528, and by the Norwegian University of Science and Technology through the project *Smart Grids as a Critical Infrastructure*.

References

1. Hollnagel, E.: The four cornerstones of resilience engineering. In: Nemeth, C.P., Hollnagel, E., Dekker, S. (eds.) Preparation and Restoration, Resilience Engineering Perspectives. Ashgate Studies in Resilience Engineering, vol. 2. Ashgate Publishing, Ltd. (2009)
2. Line, M.B.: Why securing smart grids is not just a straightforward consultancy exercise. Security and Communication Networks **7**(1), 160–174 (2013)
3. Batchelder, D., Blackbird, J., Felstead, D., Henry, P., Jones, J., Kulkarni, A.: Microsoft Security Intelligence Report. Microsoft (2014)
4. Line, M.B., Tøndel, I.A., Jaatun, M.G.: Information security incident management: planning for failure. In: 8th International Conference on IT Security Incident Management and IT Forensics (IMF), pp. 47–61 (May 2014)
5. Line, M.B., Zand, A., Stringhini, G., Kemmerer, R.A.: Targeted attacks against industrial control systems: is the power industry prepared? In: 21st ACM Conference on Computer and Communications Security and Co-located Workshops, pp. 13–22 (November 2014)
6. Grance, T., Nolan, T., Burke, K., Dudley, R., White, G., Good, T.: NIST SP 800–84: Guide to Test, Training and Exercise Programs for IT Plans and Capabilities. National Institute of Standards and Technology (2006)

7. NVE: Øvelser: En veiledning i planlegging og gjennomføring av øvelser i NVE (in Norwegian). Norwegian Water Resources and Energy Directorate (2013)
8. Hale, A., Borys, D.: Working to rule, or working safely? Part 1: A state of the art review. Safety Science (2012)
9. FEMA: IS 139 Exercise Design - Unit 5: The Tabletop Exercise. Federal Emergency Management Agency - Emergency Management Institute (FEMA)
10. Gåsland, S.: Gjør øvelse mester? Om læringsfaktorer i beredskapsøvelser initiert av NVE (in Norw.). Technical report, University of Oslo (2014)
11. Hove, C., Tårnes, M., Line, M.B., Bernsmed, K.: Information security incident management: identified practice in large organizations. In: 8th International Conference on IT Security Incident Management and IT Forensics (IMF), pp. 27–46 (May 2014)
12. Rykkja, L.H.: Kap. 8: Øvelser som kriseforebygging. In: Organisering, Samfunnssikkerhet Og Krisehåndtering (in Norw.), 2 edn. Universitetsforlaget (2014)
13. Malone, T.W., Crowston, K.: The Interdisciplinary Study of Coordination. ACM Computing Surveys 26(1), 87–119 (1994)
14. Okhuysen, G.A., Bechky, B.A.: Coordination in Organizations: An Integrative Perspective. The Academy of Management Annals 3(1), 463–502 (2009)
15. Kraut, R.E., Streeter, L.A.: Coordination in Software Development. Communications of the ACM 38(3), 69–81 (1995)
16. Lewis, K., Herndon, B.: Transactive Memory Systems: Current Issues and Future Research Directions. Organization Science 22(5), 1254–1265 (2011)
17. Lundberg, N., Tellioğlu, H.: Understanding Complex Coordination Processes in Health Care. Scandinavian Journal of Information Systems 11(2), 157–181 (1999)
18. ISO/IEC: ISO/IEC 27035:2011 Information technology - Security techniques - Information security incident management (2011)
19. Hackman, J.R.: In: The psychology of self-management in organizations. American Psychological Association, Washington, D.C. (1986)
20. Yin, R.K.: Case Study Research - Design and Methods, 4th edn. Applied Social Research Methods, vol. 5. SAGE Publications (2009)
21. Moe, N.B., Dingsøyr, T., Dybå, T.: A teamwork model for understanding an agile team: A case study of a scrum project. Information and Software Technology 52(5), 480–491 (2010)

Social Groupings and Information Security Obedience Within Organizations

Teodor Sommestad[⊠]

Swedish Defence Research Agency (FOI),
Olaus Magnus väg 42, Linköping, Sweden
Teodor.Sommestad@foi.se

Abstract. Individuals' compliance with information security policies is important for the overall security of organizations. It has been suggested that obedience cultures exist in organizations and that social processes and structures play a role for the compliance intentions and compliance behavior of individuals. This paper investigates if individuals' compliance intention is more homogenous within social groups in the workplace than they are within the workplace overall workplace and the effect these groups have are in line with the theory of planned behavior. The results show that a considerable portion of variance in information security policy compliance intentions is explained by the respondents' organizational department (15%), professional knowledge area (17%), and the same lunch room (18%). While sizeable and significant effects can be found on intentions the effects on attitudes, norm and perceived behavior control are less clear. The only statistically significant (p<0.05) effect is from department on attitudes and perceived norm, each with 6% explained variance. This suggests that the theory of planned behavior fails to account for factors tied to these types of social groups.

Keywords: Information security culture · Theory of planned behavior · Information security behavior · Compliance · Obedience

1   Introduction

Information security behavior is important for the overall security of organizations. It is also a lively research area and a considerable number of studies have been performed to identify factors that influence individuals' information security behavior. In a recently published review we identified 29 quantitative empirical studies published before March 2012 testing antecedents of security policy compliance attitudes, intentions and behavior [1]. Meanwhile, social aspects related to information security have gained increased attention in recent years, often discussed as information security culture. Theory suggests that if managers can predict or control the information security culture(s) of their organization they can manage the information security of their organization more efficiently [2]. For instance, [3] suggests that educational efforts should be adapted to cultural differences.

© IFIP International Federation for Information Processing 2015
H. Federrath and D. Gollmann (Eds.): SEC 2015, IFIP AICT 455, pp. 325–338, 2015.
DOI: 10.1007/978-3-319-18467-8_22

Information security culture is a concept that is used and interpreted in many different ways. However, there is a wide agreement that it is a group phenomenon where something is shared in the group and that social context and communication play a role. For instance, Hofstede [4] states that "cultures of work organizations are acquired through socialization at the work place." It follows that the frequency and the way people interact ought to determine the culture they share. However, as will be shown below, there is little known about how social processes form individuals' information security compliance.

In this paper the relationship between social groups' and individuals' views of information security policy compliance is investigated. A questionnaire-based survey within a governmental research institute in Sweden is used to assess individuals' views on information security policy compliance and the social groups they belong. Individuals' views are measured as prescribed by the theory of planned behavior [5]. This theory states that the effect of social factors (like culture) on intentions to perform a behavior is fully mediated by attitude, perceived norms and perceived behavior control associated with the behavior [5]. The effect of social group membership on information security culture is measured by comparing the responses in the organization as a whole to the responses within three types of groups within the organization namely groups based on: organizational department, professional knowledge area, and lunch room.

The outline of this paper is as follows. Section 2 describes the theoretical background and presents the hypotheses that are addressed. Section 3 details the method. In section 4 the results are presented and in section 5 implications are discussed. In section 6 conclusions are drawn.

2   Theory and Research Questions

This section will introduce some of the more central ideas needed to understand the present focus and scope of the present study. The theory of planned behavior (TPB) is described in section 2.1 and a broad description of information security culture is given in 2.2. The hypotheses derived from this are described in section 2.3.

2.1   The Theory of Planned Behavior

The TPB [6] and its predecessor, the theory of reasoned action [7], offer an established framework for predicting behavioral intentions and actual behavior. According to the theory, illustrated in Figure 1, behavior is influenced by people's intentions and actual behavior control, where actual behavior control moderates the effect of intentions. Most applications use perceived behavior control as a proxy because of the difficulties associated with measuring actual behavior control, as advocated by [6]. Additionally, the moderating role of perceived behavior control has been difficult to establish empirically, and many models include it side-by-side with intentions in a simpler additive linear model [5].

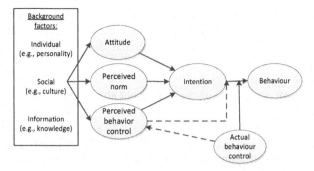

Fig. 1. The theory of planned behavior and culture, adapted from [5]

The TPB further states that intentions are influenced by attitude, perceived norms, and perceived behavior control. Their influences are assumed to be linear, i.e., the effects can be modeled using additive models. Although the theory claims that these three constructs are sufficient to explain the intentions concerning a behavior in question, there is no universal ordering of their importance. On the contrary, the relative importance of the constructs differs among populations and behaviors. For instance, for behaviors over which people feel they have almost full control, the variable perceived behavior control is of little value because it is equal for all respondents [6].

A recent meta-analysis of observational questionnaire based studies of information security policy compliance behavior found the following sample-weighted correlation coefficients between variables: attitude-intention 0.48, perceived norm-intention 0.52, perceived behavior control-intention 0.45, intention-behavior 0.83 and actual behavior control-behavior 0.35 [8]. Approximately 0.4 of the variance in security policy compliance intentions is explained by the variables in the theory, leaving approximately 0.6 of the variance in intentions to be explained by measurement error and missing variables.

As Figure 1 shows, the originators of the theory of planned behavior explicitly list culture as a primary antecedent to the constructs that the theory says influence behavior [5]. The study presented in this paper focuses on this link between culture and information security compliance. More precisely, this study aims to investigate if social groups at the work place influence the variables of the theory of planned behavior in this way.

2.2   Information Security Culture

Research on information security culture rests heavily on the more general concept of organizational culture and the theories developed related to culture in other fields. However, this is of little help when it comes to agreeing on a definition for the concept – already in 1998 a review found 54 different definitions of the concept of organizational culture in the literature [9].

Research on information security culture often focuses on policy compliance. For example, in [10] it is argued that information security obedience (i.e., compliance with policies) binds together information security, corporate governance and corporate culture and in [11] "culture" is described as the ideal state of "compliance. The most frequently cited their theoretical frameworks in r research on information security culture [12] are those of Edgar Schein and Geert Hofstede. Schein's framework is a three-tiered model that explains organizational culture on the levels of shared basic assumptions, espoused values and artifacts/behaviors [13]. Schein recently argued for a move away from discussions about abstract definitions and more concrete operationalizations instead, e.g., through measurement instruments [14]. Hofstede, known to have developed the first empirical model of dimensions of national cultures, provides a succinct definition of culture as "the collective programming of the mind that distinguishes the members of one group or category of people from another" [15].

In Hofstede's definition, and in Schein's model, culture can be tied to various groupings of humans, e.g., nations, cities, organizations, work groups, occupations, professions, and so on. Four levels of analysis for perception in organizational culture research are distinguished in [16]: 1) individuals, 2) workgroups or teams that interact on a face to face or virtual basis, 3) larger groups like whole organizations and 4) societies or countries. The current study is focused on level two and aims at examining the notion that social groupings in the workplace form individuals' information security policy compliance. There is little knowledge on the relative importance of different social groupings on this level, or what the relative importance depends on. Previous research on information security culture has primarily addressed the concept on an organizational level (e.g., [17] [2] [18]), surveyed how individuals perceive the culture (e.g., [19][20][21]) or group norms (e.g., [22]), and occasionally on a national level (e.g., [23]). Furthermore, there is also little known about the relative importance of different social groups for attitudes and values related to information security, such attitudes and values to safety. For example, no quantitative measurements on the relation between different groups and safety views can be found in the following reviews of safety climate and safety culture measurements [24][25][26].

To summarize, information security culture is (like culture in general) difficult to define and measure, it is relatively often coupled to policy compliance, and there is little research on information security culture between the levels of whole organizations and single individuals. The present study does not attempt to define the concept of culture, but use social groups within an organization as a proxy for the culture(s) individuals belong to and use these as proxies for the culture an individual belongs to. This paper follows the definition of Turner [27] and consider a social group to be two or more individuals who share a common social identification of themselves or two or more individuals who perceive themselves to be members of the same social category.

2.3   Hypotheses

Three main hypotheses together with nine sub-hypotheses are addressed in this study. These hypotheses concern how *organizational departments*, *professional knowledge areas*, and *lunch room* explain variation in constructs covered by the theory of planned behavior. They are discussed and presented below.

In most organizations, managers try to set goals, measure the achievement of goals and incentivize their staff through different types of social interactions (e.g., meetings, courses and documents). When it comes to information security, it can be expected that middle management plays the important role of implementing information systems strategies [28] and their behavior is believed to be vital to cultural change because of the feedback they give to employees [29]. In our study's organization, the management structure follows, as in many other organizations, the organizational structure and projects are heavily associated with this structure although they are not bound by it. Thus, the organizational department a person belongs to ought to shape its views on information security policies. The following hypotheses are therefore posed.

H1: Intentions to comply with information security policies are more homogenous within organizational department than within the organization as a whole.

H1.1: Attitudes to compliance with information security policies are more homogenous within organizational department than within the organization as a whole.

H1.2: Perceived norms with respect to compliance with information security policies are more homogenous within organizational department than within the organization as a whole.

H1.3: Perceived behavior control over compliance with information security policies is more homogenous within organizational department than within the organization as a whole.

In the studied organization eleven knowledge areas are defined by management. The knowledge area an individual is part of can also be expected to influence the culture an individual is a part of for several reasons. First, a professional knowledge area can be associated with certain codes of ethics, symbols, role models and professional goals. An example is the Hippocratic Oath sworn by those who practice medicine. Second, the professional knowledge area an individual works within often coincides with a particular type of schooling and knowledge. For instance, an individual who works with the secretive domain of electronic warfare can be expected to treat restrictions on electromagnetic leakage from information technology with more care than a person unaware of the risks associated with this. Third, it could be expected that individuals end up in social interactions with peers in the same knowledge area more often than they do with people from a randomly selected (other) knowledge area. In the studied organization most projects are within a particular knowledge area. Thus, the professional knowledge area ought to coincide with the workgroups and projects an individual belongs to. These factors lead to the following hypotheses.

H2: Intentions to comply with information security policies are more homogenous within professional knowledge areas than within the organization as a whole.

H2.1: Attitudes to compliance with information security policies is more homogenous within professional knowledge area than within the organization as a whole.

H2.2: Perceived norms with respect to compliance with information security policies are more homogenous within professional knowledge area than within the organization as a whole.

H2.3: Perceived behavior control over compliance with information security policies are more homogenous within professional knowledge area than within the organization as a whole.

Informal social interaction, like unstructured discussions and chattering, can be expected to play a role in the formation and conservation of information security culture. For instance, rumors, stories, gossip and opinions may be vetted during informal discussions and meetings might concern information security. To reliably group people according to how they socialize informally is of course difficult. However, in the present organization, located in Sweden, where "fika" (coffee breaks) is a social institution, and lunch rooms are places where informal meeting occur multiple times each day. Because of this, the lunch areas a person belong to captures much of an employee's informal social life and the following hypotheses are posed.

H3: Intentions to comply with information security policies are more homogenous within lunch areas than within the organization as a whole.

H3.1: Attitudes to compliance with information security policies are more homogenous within lunch areas than within the organization as a whole.

H3.2: Perceived norms with respect to compliance with information security policies are more homogenous within lunch areas than within the organization as a whole.

H3.3: Perceived behavior control over compliance with information security policies are more homogenous within lunch areas than within the organization as a whole.

None of the abovementioned hypotheses concerns actual behavior. The reason is not theoretical (culture is supposed to form behavior too); the reason is the costs and privacy issues associated with measuring actual policy compliance by monitoring employees behavior, especially without introducing observer bias.

3   Method and Materials

This section presents the measurement instrument used in this study (section 3.1), the data collection procedure (section 3.2) and assessment of instrument validity in (section 3.3).

3.1   Measurement Instrument

The questionnaire used contained an introductory section describing the purpose of the survey, a section explaining the question format, questions about the respondent's role and the social groups the respondent belonged to, questions operationalizing constructs in the theory of planned behavior, and other questions not directly related to the hypotheses addressed in this research.

Through a large number of applications, tests and reviews of the theory of planned behavior, a considerable amount of knowledge concerning how to best operationalize the theory in general has been accumulated. The parts of this measurement instrument associated with TPB was based on the example and template for direct scales given in [5] and followed the guidelines it provides. Thus, both instrumental (e.g., bad-good) and experiential (e.g., necessary-unnecessary) attitudes were measured; items of perceived norms measured both injunctive norms (i.e., what people that are important think) and descriptive norms (i.e., what people that are important do); perceived behavior control covered both autonomy (e.g., if it is under my control) and capability factors (e.g., if it is easy to do). Intentions were measured as outright intention predictions of future behavior. As recommended by [5] a questionnaire with open-ended questions was distributed in the target population to survey general beliefs related to the studied constructs before items were formulated. The answers were used as input in the formulation of the questionnaire items, e.g., to form bipolar scales for the attitude items. Three to four items were used for each TPB construct. Appendix contains a translation of the questions to English.

Questions regarding organizational department and knowledge area were formulated as multiple choice questions; lunch room was asked for in the form of a free text field with examples of the type of formulations to be used. All other questions in the questionnaire were associated with the behavior of complying with the information security policy and rules within the specific organization surveyed. These items were answered using a seven-point semantic differential scale. Their mean value is used to form the construct of interest, as proposed by [5].

The layout and understandability of the instrument was reviewed iteratively by six employees within the surveyed organization before a final version was established. In this review process it was also verified that respondents understood the questions related to organizational department, knowledge area and lunch area.

3.2   Data Collection Procedure

This study surveyed perceptions of individuals within the Swedish Defence Research Agency in Sweden (also the organization the author belongs to). This organization is distributed over four geographical sites and has approximately 1000 employees, with a median age of 45 years and a relatively even age distribution. Approximately 35 percent hold a PhD. Approximately 800 work as researchers and 200 as work as managers or with internal services (e.g., information systems or facilities).

The internal mail service distributed one printed copy of the survey to each employee during September 2013. A reminder was distributed electronically one week later. Surveys received within the first three months after the distribution were included in the analysis. A total of 311 questionnaires were returned within this time period. To ensure anonymity, respondents were encouraged to provide their department, knowledge area, and lunch area only if they wanted and felt comfortable doing so. Since many chose to only answer one or two of the three questions, a number of returned surveys could not be used for the test of research questions posed in this paper. In addition, it was deemed necessary to exclude respondents who belonged to groups of less than two persons to obtain a meaningful statistical measurement of the variance in the group. As a result of this filtering, only 176-178 questionnaires contained the responses necessary for the analysis of the 12 hypotheses.

Visual inspection of QQ-plots and histograms suggests that all constructs arc approximately normally distributed except attitude, which suffers from ceiling effects (with many respondents answering maximum). The results of tests with ANOVA (which is robust to deviations from the normality assumption (Schmider et al., 2010)) show that no mean differences of statistical significance (at the 5%-level) could be found between respondents returning the survey in different months for the four constructs. Nor was any statistical difference in mean values found between those who provided all the information that was required for the analysis and those that did not. Thus, the survey does not appear to suffer from problems due to non-response bias. Furthermore, the number of respondents from different departments, sites and roles match the overall distribution in the organization reasonably well, suggesting that the respondents are representative of the organization as a whole.

3.3   Instrument Validity

Only five respondents used the feedback section to report difficulties in answering the questions in the questionnaire. Three of these reports concerned difficulties in answering because of the abstraction level of overall policy compliance rather than specific behavior (e.g., practices related to passwords or USB sticks). Two complained about the language and understandability of the questions.

The constructs and relationships of the theory of planned behavior are well established and this survey does not posit new constructs and builds on previous work on how questions should be formulated. Therefore the construct validity of the present survey is to some extent already given. The reliability, i.e., accuracy, of psychological measurements can be measured using Cronbach's alpha [30]. The reliability of all constructs except perceived behavior control exceeded 0.70, a commonly used threshold [31]. The reliability values for perceived behavior control ($\alpha=0.69$) is on the border of acceptable, meaning that the answers to the three items used to measure these constructs are somewhat inconsistent. This might be because they are operationalized in two dimensions: perceived behavior control is supposed to capture both autonomy and capacity.

4   Results

The hypotheses stated in section 2.3 are evaluated by assessing if variance in peoples' views about information security policies is lower within groups than within the organization as a whole. In other words, it is expected that a part of the variance in respondents' responses is explained by the group they belong to.

Table 1. Variance explained by social groupings

		Attitude	Perceived Norm	Perceived behavior control	Intention
Departments (K=5, N=177)	Eta-squared	0.06	0.06	0.03	0.15
	P-value	0.01	0.00	0.09	0.00
Knowledge areas (K=11, 178)	Eta-squared	0.05	0.05	0.05	0.17
	P-value	0.17	0.16	0.20	0.00
Lunch areas (K=21, N=176)	Eta-squared	0.10	0.13	0.11	0.18
	P-value	0.69	0.36	0.57	0.04

K: The number of groups
N: The number of respondents

Table 1 describes the results of one-way ANOVA tests. The effect size Eta squared reflects the portion of variance explained by the social groups that respondents belong to, i.e., the quotient of sum of squares between groups and the sum of squares of the population as a whole. The p-value reflects the probability that the effect is due to chance.

As Table 1 shows, variance in all psychological constructs is lower within departments than within the organization as a whole. The effects are also statistically significant to the 0.05-level on all constructs except perceived behavior control. Thus, H1 and H1.1, and H1.2 are supported in this sample, but not H1.3.

The relationship to knowledge areas is not as straightforward. Considerable statistical significant reductions in variance are found for intention (H2), meaning that H2 is supported. However, a more modest measured and statistically insignificant effect is found for attitude, perceived norm, and perceived behavior control. Thus, H2.1, H2.2, and H2.3 are not supported.

As for knowledge areas, the effect measured by lunch areas is considerable and statistically significant for intentions to comply. However, even though the effect sizes are fairly large for attitude, perceived norm, and perceived behavior control, none of these effects are statistically significant. In other words, H3 can be accepted, but H3.1 H3.2, and H3.3 cannot be accepted.

Overall, the results confirm the hypotheses concerning an influence of social groups on intentions to comply with information security policies. Effects in terms of reduced variance (i.e., Eta-squared) on intentions are between 15 and 18 percent. These results suggest that social processes and structures play a large role in forming the information security obedience intentions. In other words, respondents' intentions to comply with the information security policy is to some extent explained by which department they work at, in which knowledge area they work, as well as who they drink coffee with and have their lunch with.

People within organizational departments are also more homogenous when it comes to attitudes and perceived norms. With a p-value of 0.09 the there is also a tendency that perceived behavior control is influenced by department. However, in contrast to what was predicted, professional knowledge areas and lunch rooms do not appear to explain variance in attitudes, perceived norms, and perceived behavior control. Thus, while people within the same professional knowledge areas and lunch room have homogenous intentions, there is no clear forming effect on attitudes, perceptions of norms and perceptions of how much control they have.

5   Discussion

The results of this study are far from clear-cut. To assist the reader in the interpretation of the results some of the major issues with the study are discussed below. Issues of dependence between the groups and confound variables are discussed in section 5.1, implications related to the theory of planned behavior in section 5.2, and measurement issues in section 5.3.

5.1   Dependence Between Social Groupings and Confounding Variables

There are apparent relationships between the three types of social groups in the studied organization. First, both knowledge areas and coffee rooms are, to some extent, determined by departments. Knowledge areas are highly concentrated to specific departments because of organizational reasons. In seven of the knowledge areas the respondents comes from only one or two departments; within each of the departments one to seven knowledge areas are represented. Because of a tendency to collocate departments geographically the lunch areas are more likely to be shared by two persons form the department than by two persons from different departments. Overall the respondents use 21 lunch rooms, but within departments between one and nine lunch rooms are used. In addition, 14 of the 21 lunch rooms are used by people from one department only. Second, people within the same knowledge area are often collocated because of the need to interact with each other, and therefore often share the same lunch room. Ten lunch rooms is used by one knowledge area only and most knowledge areas are keep within three lunch rooms.

Unfortunately, the sample size makes it difficult to control for these dependencies by further partitioning of the sample into sub groups (e.g., a particular knowledge area within a specific department). Readers are therefore cautioned to treat the effects as independent. It is likely that parts of the variance that one social grouping explains is also explained by the other social groupings.

Furthermore, the effects on the response variables may be due to confounding variables that have little to do with culture but are related to the social groupings. The explained variance may be due to more direct links to influential variables than the social interaction that follows from these three groupings. It is not necessarily because they share the same culture (e.g., underlying assumptions or values). For example, the effect of knowledge area on compliance intentions might simply be because information security requirements are trickier to live up to for some types employees than others (e.g., because of certain clients), because some researchers are better skilled in tasks required to be compliant (e.g., are schooled in information security) or because information security is a more important issue within some areas.

In addition, variables associated with the Swedish culture and with this particular organization's culture or policies may skew the results obtained. For instance, the managers in this organization may be unusually influential, particularly homogenous knowledge areas may not be present, and discussions during coffee breaks may be unusually relevant or irrelevant to information security.

5.2   Theory of Planned Behavior as a Mediator of Cultural Phenomena

The theory of planned behavior states that attitudes, perceived norm and perceived behavior control moderate the effect of culture on individuals' intentions. Based on this, one would expect that variables that predict behavioral intentions also predicts attitudes, perceived norm and perceived behavior control. For departments this is the case. Responses to all four variables within groups are more homogenous and the forming effect of these groups may be mediated as the theory of planned behavior claims. However, knowledge areas and lunch areas mean a significant reduction in variance in intentions to comply, but not attitudes, norms or perceived behavior control.

A direct effect on intentions, without mediation by attitude, perceived norm or perceived behavior control, suggests that something is missing in the theory of planned behavior which is common to members in the social groups. As noted above, this missing piece is not necessarily culture alone. It may be an effect of other factors already hypothesized as antecedents to the variables of the theory of planned behavior which are coupled to the social groups, like: knowledge, media exposure, interventions, age, gender, risk perception, moods or personality. Nevertheless, factors captured by knowledge areas and lunch areas seems to influence intentions without being mediated the way the theory of planned behavior say they should be. This warrants further investigations of the sufficiency of this theory with respect to social processes and structures.

5.3   Measurement Issues

The sample frame used to test the hypotheses addressed in research is well defined: a Swedish defense research organization with highly educated employees, a fairly even age distribution and approximately 1000 employees distributed over four geographical locations. This workplace definitely represents an organization in which information security is of relevance and security policies are important. However, it is only one organization, chosen because it was convenient. Clearly, to generalize from one single organization is risky. Furthermore, the response rate (as low as 18% for some tests) is problematic. Even though no clear signs of response bias can be observed there are problems associated with drawing general conclusions from these results. For example, seven managers in one organization can hardly be said to represent managers/departments in general. And group sizes as small as two or three persons pose another potential source of measurement error if the actual groups (e.g., using a lunch area) are substantially bigger.

The small sample also prohibits the use of more sophisticated statistical measures to address the hypotheses. A multilevel analysis was performed using LISREL to identify the effect of a second level on predictions of intention. This analysis suggests that around five percent of the variance in intentions is explained by the groups (department 8%; knowledge area 7%; lunch area 3%) when they are added to a model that already includes the other antecedents (attitude, perceived norm and perceived behavior control). However, with the sample size of this study the effects are insignificant and associated with considerable confidence intervals. With a larger sample, multi-level analysis could be used to better test if these types of social groups play a significant role in forming intentions without being mediated by attitude, perceived norms, and perceived behavior control. This would enable assessments of how much variance the social groupings add on top of the variables in the TPB.

6   Conclusion

In the studied organization, 15-18 percent of the variance in intentions to comply with information security policies can be explained by the department they belong to, knowledge area they work within and lunch room they use. The results are in line with the idea that group phenomena influence security behavior and those social processes and structures play a role for the information security obedience culture of organizations. In addition, the explanatory power of these social groupings based on professional knowledge areas and lunch rooms does not appear to be mediated by the constructs of the theory of planned behavior. This suggests that this theory misses important variables for explaining information security policy compliance.

Appendix: Questionnaire Items

Attitude

Adhering to the information security policy at [the organization] *is:*

(bad<->good)

(meaningless <->meaningful)

(unimportant<->important)

(unnecessary<->necessary)

Perceived norm

Most people who are important to me think I should adhere to the information security policy that exists at [the organization]. (false<->true)

Most people whose opinion I respect would tolerate that I adhere to the information security policy that exist at [the organization]. (improbable<->probable)

Most people I respect would adhere to the information security policy at [the organization] *if they were in my situation.* (unlikely<->likely)

Most people at [the organization] *who are like me follow our information security policy.* (false<->true)

Perceived behavior control

I am certain that I can adhere to the information security policy that exists at [the organization]. (false<->true)

If I really want to, I can adhere to the information security policy that exists at [the organization]. (disagree<->agree)

Whether I adhere to the information security policy that exists at [the organization] is entirely within my control. (false<->true)

Intention

My intention is to henceforth adhere to the information security policy that exists at [the organization]. (false<->true)

In the future, I will adhere to all of the information security policies that exist at [the organization]. (unlikely<->likely)

Regardless of what happens and which situations arise, I will adhere to the information security policy that exists at [the organization]. (unlikely<->likely)

I cannot imagine violating the information security policy that exists at [the organization] *even once in the future.* (false<->true)

References

1. Sommestad, T., Hallberg, J., Lundholm, K., Bengtsson, J.: Variables influencing information security policy compliance: a systematic review of quantitative studies. Inf. Manag. Comput. Secur. **22**, 42–75 (2014)
2. Da Veiga, A., Eloff, J.: A framework and assessment instrument for information security culture. Comput. Secur. **29**, 196–207 (2009)
3. Lacey, D.: Understanding and transforming organizational security culture. Inf. Manag. Comput. Secur. **18**, 4–13 (2010)
4. Hofstede, G.: National cultures, organizational cultures, and the role of management. In: González, F. (ed.) Values and Ethics for the 21st Century, pp. 385–403. BBVA, Madrid, Spain (2011)
5. Fishbein, M., Ajzen, I.: Predicting and Changing Behavior: The Reasoned Action Approach. Psychology Press, New York, NY, USA (2010)
6. Ajzen, I.: The theory of planned behavior. Organ. Behav. Hum. Decis. Process **50**, 179–211 (1991)
7. Fishbein, M.: A theory of reasoned action: Some applications and implications. Nebraska Symp. Motiv. **27**, 65–116 (1979)
8. Sommestad, T., Hallberg, J.: A review of the theory of planned behaviour in the context of information security policy compliance. In: Janczewski, E., Wolf, H., Shenoi, S. (eds.) International Information Security and Privacy Conference. Springer, Berlin / Heidelberg, Auckland (2013)
9. Verbeke, W., Volgering, M., Hessels, M.: Exploring the Conceptual Expansion within the Field of Organizational Behaviour: Organizational Climate and Organizational Culture. J. Manag. Stud. **35**, 303–329 (1998)
10. Thomson, K.-L., von Solms, R.: Information security obedience: a definition. Comput. Secur. **24**, 69–75 (2005)
11. Furnell, S., Thomson, K.-L.: From culture to disobedience: Recognising the varying user acceptance of IT security. Comput. Fraud Secur. **2009**, 5–10 (2009)
12. Karlsson, F., Åström, J., Karlsson, M.: Information security culture: State-of-the-art review between 2000 and 2013. Inf. Comput. Secur. (in press)
13. Schein, E.: Coming to a new awareness of organizational culture. Sloan Manage. Rev. **25** (1984)
14. Schein, E.: Preface. In: Ashkanasy, C., Wilderom, M.F. (eds.) Organizational Culture and Climate, pp. xi–xiii. Sage Publications, Inc, 2455 Teller Road, Thousand Oaks California 91320 United States (2012)
15. Hofstede, G.: Dimensionalizing cultures: The Hofstede model in context. Online readings Psychol. Cult. **2**, 1–26 (2011)
16. Yammarino, F.J., Dansereau, F.: Multilevel issues in organizational culture and climate research. In: Ashkanasy, N.M., Wilderom, C.P.M., Mark F. (eds.) The Handbook of Organizational Culture and Climate, pp. 50–76. SAGE Publications, Inc., 2455 Teller Road, Thousand Oaks California 91320 United States (2011)

17. Malcolmson, J.: What is security culture? Does it differ in content from general organisational culture? 43rd Annual 2009 International Carnahan Conference on Security Technology, pp. 361–366. IEEE (2009)
18. Schlienger, T., Teufel, S.: Information security culture-from analysis to change. IFIP TC11 International Conference on Information Security, Cairo, Egypt (2003)
19. Hu, Q., Dinev, T., Hart, P., Cooke, D.: Managing Employee Compliance with Information Security Policies: The Critical Role of Top Management and Organizational Culture*. Decis. Sci. **43**, 615–660 (2012)
20. Dugo, T.M.: The insider threat to organizational information security: a sturctural model and empirical test (2007). http://etd.auburn.edu/etd/handle/10415/1345
21. McCoy, B., Stephens, G., Stevens, K.: An Investigation of the Impact of Corporate Culture on Employee Information Systems Security Behaviour. In: Proceedings of ACIS 2009 (2009)
22. Herath, T., Rao, H.R.: Protection motivation and deterrence: A framework for security policy compliance in organisations. Eur. J. Inf. Syst. **18**, 106–125 (2009)
23. Furnell, S.: End-user security culture: A lesson that will never be learnt? Comput. Fraud Secur. **2008**, 6–9 (2008)
24. Guldenmund, F.W.: The use of questionnaires in safety culture research – an evaluation **45**, 723–743 (2007)
25. Flin, R.: Measuring safety culture in healthcare: A case for accurate diagnosis. Safety Science **45**, 653–667 (2007)
26. O'Connor, P., O'Dea, A., Kennedy, Q., Buttrey, S.E.: Measuring safety climate in aviation: A review and recommendations for the future. Saf. Sci. **49**, 128–138 (2011)
27. Turner, J.C.: Towards a cognitive redefinition of the social group. In: Tajfel, H. (ed.) Social Identity and Intergroup Relations, pp. 15–40. Cambridge University Press, Cambridge, Great britain (1982)
28. Leidner, D.E., Milovich, M.: Middle Management and Information Systems Strategy: The Role of Awareness and Involvement. 2014 47th Hawaii International Conference on System Sciences, pp. 4396–4405. IEEE (2014)
29. Niekerk, J. Van, Solms, R. Von: An holistic framework for the fostering of an information security sub-culture in organizations. Information Security South Africa (ISSA) (2005)
30. Cronbach, L.J., Shavelson, R.J.: My Current Thoughts on Coefficient Alpha and Successor Procedures. Educ. Psychol. Meas. **64**, 391–418 (2004)
31. Peterson, R.A.: Meta-analysis of Alpha Cronbach's Coefficient. J. Consum. Res. **21**, 381–391 (2014)

Attack Trees with Sequential Conjunction

Ravi Jhawar[1], Barbara Kordy[2]([✉]), Sjouke Mauw[1], Saša Radomirović[3],
and Rolando Trujillo-Rasua[1]

[1] CSC/SnT, University of Luxembourg, Luxembourg, Luxembourg
{ravi.jhawar,rolando.trujillo,sjouke.mauw}@uni.lu
[2] INSA Rennes, IRISA, Rennes, France
barbara.kordy@irisa.fr
[3] Institute of Information Security, Department of Computer Science, ETH Zürich,
Zürich, Switzerland
sasa.radomirovic@inf.ethz.ch

Abstract. We provide the first formal foundation of SAND attack trees which are a popular extension of the well-known attack trees. The SAND attack tree formalism increases the expressivity of attack trees by introducing the sequential conjunctive operator SAND. This operator enables the modeling of ordered events.

We give a semantics to SAND attack trees by interpreting them as sets of series-parallel graphs and propose a complete axiomatization of this semantics. We define normal forms for SAND attack trees and a term rewriting system which allows identification of semantically equivalent trees. Finally, we formalize how to quantitatively analyze SAND attack trees using attributes.

Keywords: Attack trees · Security modeling · Sequential operators · SAND

1 Introduction

Attack trees allow for an effective security analysis by systematically organizing the different ways in which a system can be attacked into a tree. The root node of an attack tree represents the *attacker's goal* and the children of a given node represent its refinement into *sub-goals*. A refinement is typically either disjunctive (denoted by OR) or conjunctive (denoted by AND). The leaves of an attack tree represent the attacker's actions and are called *basic actions*.

Since their inception by Schneier [19], attack trees have quickly become a popular modeling tool for security analysts. However, the limitations of this formalism, in particular with respect to expressing the order in which the various attack steps are executed, have been recognized by many authors (see e.g., [10]). In practice, modeling of security scenarios often requires constructs where conditions on the execution order of the attack components can be clearly specified. This is for instance the case when the time or (conditional) probability of an attack is considered, as in [2,21]. Consequently, several studies have extended attack trees informally with sequential conjunctive refinements. Such extensions

© IFIP International Federation for Information Processing 2015
H. Federrath and D. Gollmann (Eds.): SEC 2015, IFIP AICT 455, pp. 339–353, 2015.
DOI: 10.1007/978-3-319-18467-8_23

have resulted in improved modeling and analyses (e.g., [15,21,22]) and software tools, e.g., ATSyRA [16].

Even though the sequential conjunctive refinement, that we denote by SAND, is well understood at a conceptual level and even applied to real world scenarios [16], none of the existing solutions have provided a rigorous mathematical formalization of attack trees with SAND. Indeed, the extensions found in the literature are rather diverse in terms of application domain, interpretation, and formality. Thereby, it is infeasible to answer fundamental questions such as: What is the precise expressibility of SAND attack trees? When do two such trees represent the same security scenario? Or what type of attributes can be synthesized on SAND attack trees in the standard bottom-up way? These questions can only be precisely answered if SAND attack trees are provided with a formal, general, and explicit interpretation, i.e., if they are given a formal foundation.

Contributions: In this article we formalize the meaning of a SAND attack tree by defining its semantics. Our semantics is based on series-parallel (SP) graphs, which is a well-studied branch of graph theory. We provide a complete axiomatization for the SP semantics and show that the SP semantics for SAND attack trees are a conservative extension of the multiset semantics for standard attack trees [13] (i.e., our extension does not introduce unexpected equivalences w.r.t. the multiset semantics). To do so, we define a term rewriting system that is terminating and confluent and obtain normal forms for SAND attack trees. As a consequence, we achieve the rather surprising result that the domains of SAND attack trees and sets of SP graphs are isomorphic. We also extend the notion of attributes for SAND attack trees which enable the quantitative analysis of attack scenarios using the standard bottom-up evaluation algorithm.

Organization: Section 2 summarizes the related work and puts our work in context. Section 3 provides a formal definition of SAND attack trees and its semantics using series-parallel graphs. Section 4 defines a complete set of axioms for SAND attack trees and presents a term rewriting system which allows identification of semantically equivalent SAND attack trees. Section 5 outlines an approach to quantitatively analyze SAND attack trees using attributes. Finally, Section 6 concludes with an outlook on future work.

2   Related Work and Motivation

One of the goals of our work is to provide a level of abstraction that encompasses most of the existing approaches from literature. Several extensions of attack trees with temporal or causal dependencies between attack steps have been proposed. We observe that there are three different approaches to achieve this goal. The first approach is to use standard attack trees with the added assumption that the children of an AND node are sequentially ordered from left to right. The second approach is to introduce a mechanism for ordering events in an attack tree, for instance by adding a new type of edge to express causality or conditionality. In its most general case, any partial order on the events in an attack tree can be specified. The third approach consists of the introduction of a new type of node for sequencing. Most extensions fall in this category. This approach is used by authors who require their formalism to be backward compatible, or who need standard, as well as ordered conjunction. We discuss for each of these approaches the most relevant papers with respect to the present article.

Approaches with a sequential interpretation of AND. In their work on *Bayesian networks for security*, Qin and Lee define a transformation from attack trees to Bayesian networks [17]. They state that "there always exists an implicit dependent and sequential relationship between AND nodes in an attack tree." Most literature on attack trees seem to contradict this statement, implying that there is a need to explicitly identify such sequential relationships.

Jürgenson and Willemson developed an algorithm to calculate the *expected outcome* of an attack tree [22]. The goal of the algorithm is to determine a permutation of leaves for which the optimal expected outcome for an attacker can be achieved. In essence, their input is an attack tree where an AND node represents all possible sequences of its children. A peculiarity of their interpretation is that multiple occurrences of the same node are considered only once, implying that the execution of the same action twice cannot be expressed.

Approaches introducing a general order. Peine et al. introduce *security goal indicator trees* [14] in which nodes can be related by a notion of *conditional dependency* and Boolean connectors. The authors, however, do not formally specify the syntax and semantics of the model. A more general approach is proposed by Piètre-Cambacédès and Bouissou [15], who apply *Boolean logic driven Markov processes* to security modeling. Their formalism does not introduce new gates, but a (trigger-)relation on the nodes of the attack tree. Although triggers can express a more general sequential relation than the SAND operator, they lack the readability of standard attack tree operators.

Vulnerability cause graphs [1,3] combine properties of attack trees (AND and OR nodes) and attack graphs (edges express order rather than refinement). The interaction between the AND nodes and the order relation is defined through a graph transformation called *conversion of conjunctions*, which ignores the order between nodes. This discrepancy could be solved by considering distinct conjunctive and sequential conjunctive nodes, as we do in this paper.

Approaches introducing sequential AND. As noted by Arnold et al. [2], the analysis of time-dependent attacks requires attack trees to be extended with a sequential operator. This is accomplished by defining sequential nodes as conjunctive nodes with a notion of progress of time. The authors define a formal semantics for this extension based on cumulative distribution functions (CDFs), where a CDF denotes the probability that a successful attack occurs within time t. The main difference with our work is that their approach is based on an explicit notion of time, while we have a more abstract approach based on causality. In their semantics, the meaning of an extended attack tree is a CDF, in which the relation to the individual basic attacks is not explicit anymore. In contrast, in our semantics the individual basic attacks and their causal ordering remain visible. As such, our semantics can be considered more abstract, and indeed, we can formulate their semantics as an *attribute* in our approach.

Enhanced attack trees [4] (EATs) distinguish between OR, AND and OAND (Ordered AND). Similarly to the approach of Arnold et al. [2], ordered AND nodes are used to express temporal dependencies between attack components. The authors evaluate EATs by transforming them into tree automata. Intermediate states in the automaton support the task of reporting partial attacks. However, because every intermediate node of the tree corresponds to a state in the tree automaton, their approach does not scale well. This problem can be addressed by considering the normal form of attack trees, as proposed in this article.

Not every extension of attack trees with SAND refinements concerns time-dependent attack scenarios; some aim at supporting risk analyses with conditional probabilities. For that purpose, Wen-Ping and Wei-Min introduce *improved attack trees* [21]. The concepts, however, are described at an intuitive level only.

Unified parameterizable attack trees [20] unify different extensions of attack trees (structural, computational, and hybrid). The authors consider two types of ordered AND connectors: priority-based connectors and time-based connectors. The children of the former are ordered from highest to lowest priority, whereas the children of the latter are ordered temporally. Our formalism gives a single interpretation to the SAND operator, yet it can capture both connectors.

Khand [7] extends attack trees with a set of gates from dynamic fault tree modeling, which includes the priority AND gate. Khand assigns truth values to his attack trees by giving truth tables for all gates. When restricted to AND, OR, and priority AND, the truth tables constitute an attribute which is compatible (in the sense of [9]) with our SP semantics for SAND attack trees.

We observe that the extensions of attack trees with sequential conjunction are rather diverse in terms of application domain, interpretation, and formality. In order to give a clear and unambiguous interpretation of the SAND operator and capture different application domains, it is necessary to give a formal semantics as a translation to a well-understood domain. Note that, neither the multiset [13] nor the propositional semantics [11] can express ordering of attack components. Therefore, a richer semantical domain needs to be defined. The purpose of this article is to address this problem.

3   Attack Trees with Sequential Conjunction

We extend the attack tree formalism so that a refinement of a (sub-)goal of an attacker can be a sequential conjunct (denoted by SAND) in addition to disjuncts and conjuncts. We first give a definition of attack trees with the new sequential operator and then define series-parallel graphs on which the semantics for the new attack trees is based.

3.1   SAND Attack Trees

Let $\mathbb{B}$ denote the set of all possible basic actions of an attacker. We formalize standard attack trees introduced in [19] and call them simply *attack trees* in the

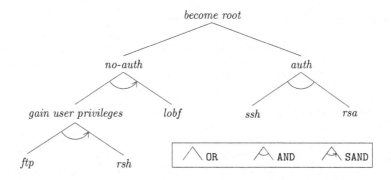

Fig. 1. An attack tree with sequential and parallel conjunctions

rest of this paper. Attack trees are closed terms over the signature $\mathbb{B} \cup \{\text{OR}, \text{AND}\}$, generated by the following grammar, where $b \in \mathbb{B}$ is a terminal symbol

$$t ::= \quad b \mid \text{OR}(t, \ldots, t) \mid \text{AND}(t, \ldots, t). \tag{1}$$

The universe of attack trees is denoted by $\mathbb{T}$. SAND *attack trees* are closed terms over the signature $\mathbb{B} \cup \{\text{OR}, \text{AND}, \text{SAND}\}$, where SAND is a non-commutative operator called *sequential conjunction*, and are generated by the grammar

$$t ::= \quad b \mid \text{OR}(t, \ldots, t) \mid \text{AND}(t, \ldots, t) \mid \text{SAND}(t, \ldots, t). \tag{2}$$

The universe of SAND attack trees is denoted by $\mathbb{T}_{\text{SAND}}$. The purpose of OR and AND refinements in SAND attack trees is the same as in attack trees. The sequential conjunctive refinement SAND allows us to model that a certain goal is reached if and only if all its subgoals are reached in a precise order.

The following attack scenario motivates the need for extending attack trees with sequential conjunctive refinement.

Example 1. Consider a file server S, offering ftp, ssh, and rsh services. The attack tree in Figure 1 shows how an attacker can gain root privileges on S (*become root*), in two ways: either without providing any user credentials (*no-auth*) or by breaching the authentication mechanism (*auth*). In the first case, the attacker must first gain user privileges on S (*gain user privileges*) and then perform a local buffer overflow attack (*lobf*). Since the attack steps must be executed in this particular order, the use of SAND refinement is substantial. To gain user privileges, the attacker must exploit an ftp vulnerability to anonymously upload a list of trusted hosts to S (*ftp*).[1] Finally, she can use the new trust condition to remotely execute shell commands on S (*rsh*). The second way is to abuse a buffer overflow in both the ssh daemon (*ssh*) and the RSAREF2 library (*rsa*) used for authentication. These attacks can be executed in any order, which is modeled with the standard AND refinement. Using the term notation introduced

---

[1] For readability, attack actions are named after the services that are exploited.

in this section, we can represent the SAND attack tree from Figure 1 as

$$t = \texttt{OR}\big(\texttt{SAND}(\texttt{SAND}(\textit{ftp}, \textit{rsh}), \textit{lobf}), \texttt{AND}(\textit{ssh}, \textit{rsa})\big),$$

where $\textit{ftp}, \textit{rsh}, \textit{lobf}, \textit{ssh}, \textit{rsa} \in \mathbb{B}$ are basic actions.

3.2 Series-Parallel Graphs

A *series-parallel graph* (SP graph) is an edge-labeled directed graph that has two unique, distinct vertices, called *source* and *sink*, and that can be constructed with the two operators for sequential and parallel composition of graphs that we formally define below. A source is a vertex which has no incoming edges and a sink is a vertex without outgoing edges.

Our formal definition of SP graphs is based on *multisets*, i.e., sets in which members are allowed to occur more than once. We use $\{\!|\cdot|\!\}$ to denote multisets and $\mathcal{P}(\cdot)$ to denote the powerset of a set or multiset. The *support* $M^\star$ of a multiset M is the set of distinct elements in M. For instance, the support of the multiset $M = \{\!|b_1, b_2, b_2|\!\}$ is $M^\star = \{b_1, b_2\}$. In order to define SP graphs, we first introduce the notion of source-sink graphs labeled by the elements of $\mathbb{B}$.

Definition 1. *A source-sink graph over $\mathbb{B}$ is a tuple $G = (V, E, s, z)$, where V is the set of vertices, E is a multiset of labeled edges with support $E^\star \subseteq V \times \mathbb{B} \times V$, $s \in V$ is the unique source, $z \in V$ is the unique sink, and $s \neq z$.*

The sequential composition of a source-sink graph $G = (V, E, s, z)$ with a source-sink graph $G' = (V', E', s', z')$, denoted by $G \cdot G'$, is the graph resulting from taking the disjoint union of G and G' and identifying the sink of G with the source of G'. More precisely, let $\dot{\cup}$ denote the disjoint union operator and $E^{[s'/z]}$ denote the multiset of edges in E, where all occurrences of vertex z are replaced by vertex s. Then we define

$$G \cdot G' = (V \setminus \{z\} \dot{\cup} V', E^{[s'/z]} \dot{\cup} E', s, z').$$

The parallel composition, denoted by $G \parallel G'$, is defined similarly, except that the two sources are identified and the two sinks are identified. Formally, we have

$$G \parallel G' = (V \setminus \{s, z\} \dot{\cup} V', E^{[s'/s, z'/z]} \dot{\cup} E', s', z').$$

It follows directly from the definitions that the sequential composition is associative and that the parallel composition is associative and commutative.

We write $\xrightarrow{b}$ for the graph with a single edge labeled with b and define SP graphs as follows.

Definition 2. *The set $\mathbb{G}_{SP}$ of series-parallel graphs (SP graphs) over $\mathbb{B}$ is defined inductively by the following two rules*

- *For $b \in \mathbb{B}$, $\xrightarrow{b}$ is an SP graph.*
- *If G and G' are SP graphs, then so are $G \cdot G'$ and $G \parallel G'$.*

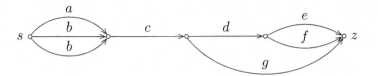

Fig. 2. A series-parallel graph

It follows directly from Definition 2 that SP graphs are connected and acyclic. Moreover, every vertex of an SP graph lies on a path from the source to the sink. We consider two SP graphs to be *equal* if there is a bijection between their sets of vertices that preserves the edges and edge labels.

Example 2. Figure 2 shows an example of an SP graph with the source s and the sink z. This graph corresponds to the construction

$$\left(\xrightarrow{a} \| \xrightarrow{b} \| \xrightarrow{b} \right) \cdot \xrightarrow{c} \cdot \left(\left(\xrightarrow{d} \cdot (\xrightarrow{e} \| \xrightarrow{f}) \right) \| \xrightarrow{g} \right).$$

3.3 SP Semantics for SAND Attack Trees

Numerous semantics have been proposed to interpret attack trees, including propositional logic [12], multisets [13], De Morgan lattices [11], tree automata [4], and Markov processes [2,15]. The choice of a semantics allows us to accurately represent the assumptions made in a security scenario, e.g., whether actions can be repeated or resources reused, and to decide which trees represent the same security scenario. The advantages of formalizing attack trees and the need for various semantics have been discussed in [9]. Since attack trees are AND/OR trees, the most natural interpretation is based on propositional logic. However, because the logical operators are idempotent, this interpretation assumes that the multiplicity of an action is irrelevant. As a consequence, the propositional semantics is not well suited to reason about scenarios with multiple occurrences of the same action. Due to this lack of expressivity a semantics was proposed [13] in which the multiplicity of actions is taken into account. This was achieved by interpreting an attack tree as a set of multisets that represent different ways of reaching the root goal. This multiset semantics is compatible with computations that depend on the number of occurrences of an action in the tree, such as the minimal time to carry out the attack represented by the root goal.

We now extend the multiset semantics to SAND attack trees. Since SP graphs naturally extend multisets with a partial order, they supply a formalism in which we can interpret trees using both commutative and sequential conjunctive refinements. SP graphs therefore provide a canonical semantics for SAND trees in which multiplicity and ordering of goals and actions are significant. The idea is to interpret an attack tree t as a set of SP graphs. The semantics $[\![t]\!]_{\mathcal{SP}} = \{G_1, \ldots, G_k\}$ of a tree t corresponds to the set of possible attacks G_i, where each attack is described by an SP graph labeled by the basic actions of t.

Definition 3. *The* SP *semantics for* SAND *attack trees is given by the function* $[\![\cdot]\!]_{SP} : \mathbb{T}_{\text{SAND}} \rightarrow \mathcal{P}(\mathbb{G}_{SP})$, *which is defined recursively as follows: for* $b \in \mathbb{B}$, $t_i \in \mathbb{T}_{\text{SAND}}$, $1 \leq i \leq k$,

$$[\![b]\!]_{SP} = \{\xrightarrow{b}\}$$
$$[\![\text{OR}(t_1,\ldots,t_k)]\!]_{SP} = \bigcup_{i=1}^{k} [\![t_i]\!]_{SP}$$
$$[\![\text{AND}(t_1,\ldots,t_k)]\!]_{SP} = \{G_1 \parallel \ldots \parallel G_k \mid (G_1,...,G_k) \in [\![t_1]\!]_{SP} \times \ldots \times [\![t_k]\!]_{SP}\}$$
$$[\![\text{SAND}(t_1,\ldots,t_k)]\!]_{SP} = \{G_1 \cdot \ldots \cdot G_k \mid (G_1,...,G_k) \in [\![t_1]\!]_{SP} \times \ldots \times [\![t_k]\!]_{SP}\}.$$

In the SP semantics, the basic actions of a SAND attack tree are the edges of series-parallel graphs. The semantics of a disjunctive, conjunctive, and sequential conjunctive node are the union, parallel composition, and sequential composition, respectively, of all combinations of SP graphs in the sets that represent the semantics of the node's children.

Example 3. The SP semantics of the attack tree t depicted in Figure 1 is

$$[\![t]\!]_{SP} = \{\xrightarrow{ftp}\xrightarrow{rsh}\xrightarrow{lobf} , \xrightarrow{ssh}\|\xrightarrow{rsa}\}.$$

As shown in Example 3, the SP semantics provides an alternative graph representation for attack trees and therefore contributes a different perspective on an attack scenario. The SAND attack tree emphasizes the refinement of goals, whereas SP graphs highlight the sequential aspect of attacks.

The SP semantics provides a natural partition of $\mathbb{T}_{\text{SAND}}$ into equivalence classes.

Definition 4. *Two* SAND *attack trees* t_1 *and* t_2 *are equivalent with respect to the* SP *semantics if and only if they are interpreted by the same set of SP graphs, i.e.,* $[\![t_1]\!]_{SP} = [\![t_2]\!]_{SP}$.

By Definition 4, if the SP semantics provides accurate assumptions for an attack scenario, then two SAND attack trees represent the same attack scenario if and only if they are equivalent with respect to the SP semantics.

4   Axiomatization of the SP Semantics

In this section we introduce a complete axiomatization of SAND attack trees with respect to the SP semantics. Such an axiomatization provides us with syntactic transformation rules for SAND attack trees that preserve the trees' SP semantics. In other words, it allows us to manipulate SAND attack trees without the need to convert them to SP graphs. Moreover, we derive a term rewriting system from the axiomatization as a means to effectively decide whether two SAND attack trees are equivalent with respect to the SP semantics. As a consequence, we obtain a canonical representation of SAND attack trees which we prove to be isomorphic to sets of SP graphs.

4.1 A Complete Set of Axioms for the SP Semantics

Let $\mathbb{V}$ be a set of variables denoted by capital letters. Following the approach developed in [9], we axiomatize SAND attack trees with equations $l = r$, where l and r are terms over variables in $\mathbb{V}$, constants in $\mathbb{B}$, and the operators AND, OR, and SAND. The equations formalize the intended properties of refinements and provide semantics-preserving transformations of SAND attack trees.

Example 4. Let Sym_ℓ denote the set of all bijections from $\{1, \ldots, \ell\}$ to itself. The axiom $\mathtt{AND}(Y_1, \ldots, Y_\ell) = \mathtt{AND}(Y_{\sigma(1)}, \ldots, Y_{\sigma(\ell)})$, where $\sigma \in \mathrm{Sym}_\ell$, expresses that the order between children refining a parallel conjunctive node is not relevant. In other words, the operator AND is commutative. This implies that any two trees of the form $\mathtt{AND}(t_1, \ldots, t_l)$ and $\mathtt{AND}(t_{\sigma(1)}, \ldots, t_{\sigma(l)})$ represent the same scenario.

Our goal is to define a complete set of axioms, denoted by $E_{\mathcal{SP}}$, for the SP semantics for SAND attack trees. Intuitively, $E_{\mathcal{SP}}$ is a set of equations that can be applied to transform a SAND attack tree into any equivalent SAND attack tree with respect to the SP semantics. Before defining the set $E_{\mathcal{SP}}$, we formalize the notion of a complete set of axioms for a given semantics for (SAND) attack trees, following [9].

Let $T(\mathbb{V}, \Sigma)$ be the free term algebra over the set of variables $\mathbb{V}$ and signature Σ, and let E be a set of equations over $T(\mathbb{V}, \Sigma)$. The equation $t = t'$, where $t, t' \in T(\mathbb{V}, \Sigma)$, is a *syntactic consequence* of E (denoted by $E \vdash t = t'$) if it can be derived from E by application of the following rules. For all $t, t', t'' \in T(\mathbb{V}, \Sigma)$, $\rho \colon \mathbb{V} \to T(\mathbb{V}, \Sigma)$, and $X \in \mathbb{V}$:

- $E \vdash t = t$,
- if $t = t' \in E$, then $E \vdash t = t'$,
- if $E \vdash t = t'$, then $E \vdash t' = t$,
- if $E \vdash t = t'$ and $E \vdash t' = t''$, then $E \vdash t = t''$.
- if $E \vdash t = t'$, then $E \vdash \rho(t) = \rho(t')$,
- if $E \vdash t = t'$, then $E \vdash t''[t/X] = t''[t'/X]$, where $t''[t/X]$ is the term obtained from t'' by replacing all occurrences of the variable X with t.

Let $\mathbb{T}_{\mathsf{SAND}}^{\mathbb{V}}$ denote the set of terms constructed from the set of variables $\mathbb{V}$, the set of basic actions $\mathbb{B}$ (treated as constants), and operators OR, AND and SAND. Let $\mathbb{T}^{\mathbb{V}}$ be the set of terms constructed from the same parts, except for the operator SAND. Using the notion of syntactic consequence, we define a complete set of axioms for a semantics for attack trees.

Definition 5. *Let $\llbracket \cdot \rrbracket$ be a semantics for attack trees (resp. SAND attack trees) and let E be a set of equations over $\mathbb{T}^{\mathbb{V}}$ (resp. $\mathbb{T}_{\mathsf{SAND}}^{\mathbb{V}}$). The set E is a complete set of axioms for $\llbracket \cdot \rrbracket$ if and only if, for all $t, t' \in \mathbb{T}$ (resp. $\mathbb{T}_{\mathsf{SAND}}$)*

$$\llbracket t \rrbracket = \llbracket t' \rrbracket \iff E \vdash t = t'.$$

We are now ready to give a complete set of axioms for the SP semantics for SAND attack trees. These axioms allow us to determine whether two visually distinct trees represent the same security scenario according to the SP semantics.

Theorem 1. *Given $k, m \geq 0$, and $\ell \geq 1$, let $\overline{X} = X_1, \ldots, X_k$, $\overline{Y} = Y_1, \ldots, Y_\ell$, and $\overline{Z} = Z_1, \ldots, Z_m$ be sequences of variables. Let Sym_ℓ be the set of all bijections from $\{1, \ldots, \ell\}$ to itself. The following set of equations over $\mathbb{T}^{\vee}_{\mathsf{SAND}}$, denoted by $E_{\mathcal{SP}}$, is a complete set of axioms[2] for the SP semantics for SAND attack trees.*

$$\mathsf{OR}(Y_1, \ldots, Y_\ell) = \mathsf{OR}(Y_{\sigma(1)}, \ldots, Y_{\sigma(\ell)}), \quad \forall \sigma \in \mathrm{Sym}_\ell \qquad (E_1)$$

$$\mathsf{AND}(Y_1, \ldots, Y_\ell) = \mathsf{AND}(Y_{\sigma(1)}, \ldots, Y_{\sigma(\ell)}), \quad \forall \sigma \in \mathrm{Sym}_\ell \qquad (E_2)$$

$$\mathsf{OR}(\overline{X}, \mathsf{OR}(\overline{Y})) = \mathsf{OR}(\overline{X}, \overline{Y}) \qquad (E_3)$$

$$\mathsf{AND}(\overline{X}, \mathsf{AND}(\overline{Y})) = \mathsf{AND}(\overline{X}, \overline{Y}) \qquad (E_4)$$

$$\mathsf{SAND}(\overline{X}, \mathsf{SAND}(\overline{Y}), \overline{Z}) = \mathsf{SAND}(\overline{X}, \overline{Y}, \overline{Z}) \qquad (E_{4'})$$

$$\mathsf{OR}(A) = A \qquad (E_5)$$

$$\mathsf{AND}(A) = A \qquad (E_6)$$

$$\mathsf{SAND}(A) = A \qquad (E_{6'})$$

$$\mathsf{AND}(\overline{X}, \mathsf{OR}(\overline{Y})) = \mathsf{OR}(\mathsf{AND}(\overline{X}, Y_1), \ldots, \mathsf{AND}(\overline{X}, Y_\ell)) \qquad (E_{10})$$

$$\mathsf{SAND}(\overline{X}, \mathsf{OR}(\overline{Y}), \overline{Z}) = \mathsf{OR}(\mathsf{SAND}(\overline{X}, Y_1, \overline{Z}), \ldots, \mathsf{SAND}(\overline{X}, Y_\ell, \overline{Z})) \qquad (E_{10'})$$

$$\mathsf{OR}(A, A, \overline{X}) = \mathsf{OR}(A, \overline{X}) \qquad (E_{11})$$

The numbering of the axioms in $E_{\mathcal{SP}}$ corresponds to the numbering of the axioms for the multiset semantics for standard attack trees, as presented in [9], while new axioms (involving SAND) are marked with primes.

Proof. The proof of this theorem follows the same line of reasoning as the proofs of Theorems 4.2 and 4.3 of Gischer [5], where series–parallel pomsets are axiomatized. The details can be found in the extended version of this work [6]. □

4.2 SAND Attack Trees in Canonical Form

Let $[\![\cdot]\!]$ be a semantics for (SAND) attack trees. A complete axiomatization of $[\![\cdot]\!]$ can be used to derive a canonical form of trees interpreted with $[\![\cdot]\!]$. Such canonical forms provide the most concise representation for equivalent trees and are the natural representatives of equivalence classes defined by $[\![\cdot]\!]$.

When SAND attack trees are interpreted using the SP semantics, their canonical forms consist of either a single basic action, or of a root node labeled with OR and subtrees with nested, alternating occurrences of AND and SAND nodes. Canonical forms correspond exactly to the sets of SP graphs labeled by $\mathbb{B}$ and they depict all attack alternatives in a straightforward way.

In the full version of this work [6], we show how to obtain canonical forms of SAND attack trees using the complete set of axioms $E_{\mathcal{SP}}$ for the SP semantics. By orienting the equations (E_3), (E_4), $(E_{4'})$, (E_5), (E_6), $(E_{6'})$, (E_{10}), $(E_{10'})$, and (E_{11}) from left to right, we obtain a term rewriting system, denoted by $R_{\mathcal{SP}}$. We show that $R_{\mathcal{SP}}$ is terminating and confluent. The canonical representations

---

[2] Note that the axioms are in fact *axiom schemes*. The operators OR, AND and SAND are *unranked*, representing infinitely many k-ary function symbols ($k \geq 1$).

of SAND attack trees correspond to normal forms with respect to R_{SP}. They are unique modulo commutativity of OR and AND.

Example 5. The canonical form of the SAND attack tree t in Figure 1 is the tree

$$t' = \mathrm{OR}\big(\mathrm{SAND}(\mathit{ftp}, \mathit{rsh}, \mathit{lobf}), \mathrm{AND}(\mathit{ssh}, \mathit{rsa})\big)$$

shown in Figure 3. It is easily seen to be in normal form with respect to R_{SP}.

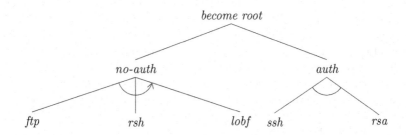

Fig. 3. SAND attack tree t' equivalent to SAND attack tree t from Figure 1

4.3 SP Semantics as a Generalization of the Multiset Semantics

Having a complete set of axioms for the SP semantics allows us to formalize the relation between SAND attack trees under the SP semantics and attack trees under the multiset semantics, denoted by $[\![\cdot]\!]_{\mathcal{M}}$. This is achieved by extracting a complete set of axioms for the multiset semantics for attack trees from the set E_{SP}. Let $E_{\mathcal{M}}$ be the subset of axioms from E_{SP} that do not contain the SAND operator, i.e., $E_{\mathcal{M}} = \{(E_1), (E_2), (E_3), (E_4), (E_5), (E_6), (E_{10}), (E_{11})\}$.

Theorem 2. *The axiom system $E_{\mathcal{M}}$ is a complete set of axioms for the multiset semantics for attack trees.*

The proof can be found in a full version of this paper [6].

By comparing the complete sets of axioms E_{SP} and $E_{\mathcal{M}}$ we obtain that two attack trees are equivalent under the multiset semantics if and only if they are equivalent under the SP semantics. This is formalized in the following theorem.

Theorem 3. SAND *attack trees under the SP semantics are a conservative extension of attack trees under the multiset semantics.*

Proof. We need to prove that, for all standard attack trees t and t', we have $[\![t]\!]_{\mathcal{M}} = [\![t']\!]_{\mathcal{M}}$ if and only if $[\![t]\!]_{SP} = [\![t']\!]_{SP}$. From $E_{\mathcal{M}} \subset E_{SP}$, we conclude that $[\![t]\!]_{\mathcal{M}} = [\![t']\!]_{\mathcal{M}}$ implies $[\![t]\!]_{SP} = [\![t']\!]_{SP}$. Conversely, we remark that the equations belonging to $E_{SP} \setminus E_{\mathcal{M}}$ do not introduce new equalities on standard attack trees. A complete proof of this fact is given in the full version of this work [6].   □

5 Attributes

Attack trees do not only serve to represent security scenarios in a graphical way. They can also be used to quantify such scenarios with respect to a given parameter, called an *attribute*. Typical examples of attributes include the likelihood that the attacker's goal will be met and the minimal time or cost of an attack. Schneier described [19] an intuitive bottom-up algorithm for calculating attribute values of attack trees: attribute values are assigned to the leaf nodes and two functions[3] (one for the OR and one for the AND refinement) are used to propagate the attribute value up to the root node. Mauw and Oostdijk showed [13] that if the binary operations induced by the two functions define a semiring, then the evaluation of the attribute on two attack trees equivalent with respect to the multiset semantics yields the same value. This result has been generalized to any semantics and attribute that satisfy a notion of *compatibility* [9] and we briefly discuss it for SAND attack trees at the end of this section. We start with a demonstration of how the bottom-up evaluation algorithm can naturally be extended to SAND attack trees.

An *attribute domain for an attribute* A_α *on* SAND *attack trees* is a tuple $D_\alpha = (V_\alpha, \nabla_\alpha, \triangle_\alpha, \Diamond_\alpha)$, where V_α is a set of values and $\nabla_\alpha, \triangle_\alpha, \Diamond_\alpha$ are families of k-ary functions of the form $V_\alpha \times \cdots \times V_\alpha \rightarrow V_\alpha$, associated to OR, AND, and SAND refinements, respectively. An *attribute for* SAND *attack trees* is a pair $A_\alpha = (D_\alpha, \beta_\alpha)$ formed by an attribute domain D_α and a function $\beta_\alpha : \mathbb{B} \rightarrow V_\alpha$, called *basic assignment* for A_α, which associates a value from V_α with each $b \in \mathbb{B}$.

Definition 6. *Let* $A_\alpha = ((V_\alpha, \nabla_\alpha, \triangle_\alpha, \Diamond_\alpha), \beta_\alpha)$ *be an attribute. The attribute evaluation function* $\alpha : \mathbb{T}_{\mathsf{SAND}} \rightarrow V_\alpha$, *which calculates the value of attribute* A_α *for every* SAND *attack tree* $t \in \mathbb{T}_{\mathsf{SAND}}$, *is defined recursively as follows.*

$$\alpha(t) = \begin{cases} \beta_\alpha(t) & \text{if } t = b, \ b \in \mathbb{B} \\ \nabla_\alpha\big(\alpha(t_1), \ldots, \alpha(t_k)\big) & \text{if } t = \mathsf{OR}(t_1, \ldots, t_k) \\ \triangle_\alpha\big(\alpha(t_1), \ldots, \alpha(t_k)\big) & \text{if } t = \mathsf{AND}(t_1, \ldots, t_k) \\ \Diamond_\alpha\big(\alpha(t_1), \ldots, \alpha(t_k)\big) & \text{if } t = \mathsf{SAND}(t_1, \ldots, t_k) \end{cases}$$

The following example illustrates the bottom-up evaluation of the attribute *minimal attack time* on the SAND attack tree given in Example 1.

Example 6. Let α denote the minimal time that the attacker needs to achieve her goal in the scenario of Example 1. We make the following assignments to the basic actions: *ftp* $\mapsto$ 3, *rsh* $\mapsto$ 5, *lobf* $\mapsto$ 7, *ssh* $\mapsto$ 8, *rsa* $\mapsto$ 9. Since we are interested in the minimal attack time, the function for an OR node is defined by $\nabla_\alpha(x_1, \ldots, x_k) = \min\{x_1, \ldots, x_k\}$. The function for an AND node is $\triangle_\alpha(x_1, \ldots, x_k) = \max\{x_1, \ldots, x_k\}$, which models that the children of a conjunctively refined node are executed in parallel. Finally, in order to model that the

---

[3] These are actually families of functions representing infinitely many k-ary function symbols, for all $k \geq 2$.

children of a SAND node need to be executed sequentially, we let $\Diamond_\alpha(x_1, \ldots, x_k) = \sum_{i=1}^{k} x_i$. According to Definition 6, the minimal attack time is

$$\nabla_\alpha \left(\Diamond_\alpha (\Diamond_\alpha(3,5), 7), \triangle_\alpha (8,9) \right) = \min \left(\Sigma(\Sigma(3,5), 7), \max(8,9) \right) = 9.$$

In the case of standard attack trees, the bottom-up procedure uses only two functions to propagate the attribute values to the root – one for conjunctive and one for disjunctive nodes. This means that the same function is employed to calculate the value of every conjunctively refined node, independently of whether its children need to be executed sequentially or can be executed simultaneously. Evidently, with SAND attack trees, we can apply different propagation functions for AND and SAND nodes, as in Example 6. Therefore, SAND attack trees can be evaluated over a larger set of attributes, and hence may provide more accurate evaluations of attack scenarios, than standard attack trees.

To guarantee that the evaluation of an attribute on equivalent attack trees yields the same value, the attribute domain must be *compatible* with a considered semantics [9]. Our complete set of axioms is a useful tool to check for compatibility with the SP semantics. Consider an attribute domain $D_\alpha = (V_\alpha, \nabla_\alpha, \triangle_\alpha, \Diamond_\alpha)$, and let σ be a mapping $\sigma = \{\text{OR} \mapsto \nabla_\alpha, \text{AND} \mapsto \triangle_\alpha, \text{SAND} \mapsto \Diamond_\alpha\}$. Guaranteeing that D_α is compatible with a semantics axiomatized by E amounts to verifying that the equality $\sigma(l) = \sigma(r)$ holds in V_α, for every axiom $l = r \in E$. It is an easy exercise to show that the attribute domain for minimal attack time, considered in Example 6, is compatible with the SP semantics for SAND attack trees.

6   Conclusions

We have formalized the extension of attack trees with sequential conjunctive refinement, called SAND, and given a semantics to SAND attack trees in terms of sets of series-parallel graphs. This SP semantics naturally extends the multiset semantics for attack trees from [13]. We have shown that the notion of a complete set of axioms for a semantics and the bottom-up evaluation procedure can be generalized from attack trees to SAND attack trees, and have proposed a complete axiomatization of the SP semantics.

A number of recently proposed solutions focus on extending attack trees with defensive measures [9,18]. These extensions support reasoning about security scenarios involving two players – an attacker and a defender – and the interaction between them. In future work, we intend to add the SAND refinement to such trees. Afterwards, we plan to investigate sequential disjunctive refinement, as used for instance in [2]. Our goal is to propose a complete formalization of trees with attack and defense nodes, that have parallel and sequential, conjunctive and disjunctive refinements. Finally, our results will be used to extend the software application ADTool [8]. In particular, the axiomatization proposed in this paper and its term rewriting system $R_{\mathcal{SP}}$ will be implemented and used to decide on the equivalence of SAND attack trees.

Acknowledgments. The research leading to these results has received funding from the European Union Seventh Framework Programme under grant agreement number 318003 (TREsPASS) and from the Fonds National de la Recherche Luxembourg under grant C13/IS/5809105.

References

1. Ardi, S., Byers, D., Shahmehri, N.: Towards a structured unified process for software security. In: SESS 2006, pp. 3–10. ACM (2006)
2. Arnold, F., Hermanns, H., Pulungan, R., Stoelinga, M.: Time-dependent analysis of attacks. In: Abadi, M., Kremer, S. (eds.) POST 2014 (ETAPS 2014). LNCS, vol. 8414, pp. 285–305. Springer, Heidelberg (2014)
3. Byers, D., Ardi, S., Shahmehri, N., Duma, C.: Modeling software vulnerabilities with vulnerability cause graphs. In: ICSM 2006, pp. 411–422 (2006)
4. Camtepe, S., Yener, B.: Modeling and detection of complex attacks. In: SecureComm 2007, pp. 234–243. IEEE (2007)
5. Gischer, J.L.: The Equational Theory of Pomsets. Theor. C. Sc. **61**, 199–224 (1988)
6. Jhawar, R., Kordy, B., Mauw, S., Radomirović, S., Trujillo-Rasua, R.: Attack Trees with Sequential Conjunction. CoRR abs/1503.02261 (2015). http://arxiv.org/abs/1503.02261
7. Khand, P.A.: System level security modeling using attack trees. In: IC4 2009, pp. 1–6 (2009)
8. Kordy, B., Kordy, P., Mauw, S., Schweitzer, P.: ADTool: security analysis with attack–defense trees. In: Joshi, K., Siegle, M., Stoelinga, M., D'Argenio, P.R. (eds.) QEST 2013. LNCS, vol. 8054, pp. 173–176. Springer, Heidelberg (2013)
9. Kordy, B., Mauw, S., Radomirović, S., Schweitzer, P.: Attack-Defense Trees. Journal of Logic and Computation **24**(1), 55–87 (2014)
10. Kordy, B., Piètre-Cambacédès, L., Schweitzer, P.: DAG-Based Attack and Defense Modeling: Don't Miss the Forest for the Attack Trees. Computer Science Review **13–14**, 1–38 (2014)
11. Kordy, B., Pouly, M., Schweitzer, P.: Computational aspects of attack–defense trees. In: Bouvry, P., Kłopotek, M.A., Leprévost, F., Marciniak, M., Mykowiecka, A., Rybiński, H. (eds.) SIIS 2011. LNCS, vol. 7053, pp. 103–116. Springer, Heidelberg (2012)
12. Kordy, B., Pouly, M., Schweitzer, P.: A probabilistic framework for security scenarios with dependent actions. In: Albert, E., Sekerinski, E. (eds.) IFM 2014. LNCS, vol. 8739, pp. 256–271. Springer, Heidelberg (2014)
13. Mauw, S., Oostdijk, M.: Foundations of attack trees. In: Won, D.H., Kim, S. (eds.) ICISC 2005. LNCS, vol. 3935, pp. 186–198. Springer, Heidelberg (2006)
14. Peine, H., Jawurek, M., Mandel, S.: Security goal indicator trees: a model of software features that supports efficient security inspection. In: HASE 2008, pp. 9–18. IEEE Computer Society (2008)
15. Piètre-Cambacédès, L., Bouissou, M.: Beyond attack trees: dynamic security modeling with boolean logic driven Markov processes (BDMP). In: EDCC 2010, pp. 199–208. IEEE Computer Society, Los Alamitos (2010)
16. Pinchinat, S., Acher, M., Vojtisek, D.: Towards synthesis of attack trees for supporting computer-aided risk analysis. In: Canal, C., Idani, A. (eds.) SEFM 2014 Workshops. LNCS, vol. 8938, pp. 363–375. Springer, Heidelberg (2015)
17. Qin, X., Lee, W.: Attack plan recognition and prediction using causal networks. In: 20th Annual Computer Security Applications Conference, pp. 370–379 (2004)

18. Roy, A., Kim, D.S., Trivedi, K.S.: Attack Countermeasure Trees (ACT): Towards Unifying the Constructs of Attack and Defense Trees. Security and Communication Networks **5**(8), 929–943 (2012)
19. Schneier, B.: Attack Trees: Modeling Security Threats. Dr. Dobb's Journal of Software Tools **24**(12), 21–29 (1999)
20. Wang, J., Whitley, J.N., Phan, R.C.W., Parish, D.J.: Unified Parametrizable Attack Tree. Int. Journal for Information Security Research **1**(1), 20–26 (2011)
21. Wen-ping, L., Wei-min, L.: Space based information system security risk evaluation based on improved attack trees. In: (MINES 2011), pp. 480–483 (2011)
22. Jürgenson, A., Willemson, J.: Serial model for attack tree computations. In: Lee, D., Hong, S. (eds.) ICISC 2009. LNCS, vol. 5984, pp. 118–128. Springer, Heidelberg (2010)

Enhancing the Security of Image CAPTCHAs Through Noise Addition

David Lorenzi[1], Emre Uzun[1], Jaideep Vaidya[1 (✉)],
Shamik Sural[2], and Vijayalakshmi Atluri[1]

[1] Rutgers University, Newark, NJ 07102, USA
{dlorenzi,emreu,jsvaidya,atluri}@cimic.rutgers.edu
[2] Indian Institute of Technology, School of Information Technology,
Kharagpur, India
shamik@sit.iitkgp.ernet.in

Abstract. Text based CAPTCHAs are the de facto method of choice to ensure that humans (rather than automated bots) are interacting with websites. Unfortunately, users often find it inconvenient to read characters and type them in. Image CAPTCHAs provide an alternative that is often preferred to text-based implementations. However, Image CAPTCHAs have their own set of security and usability problems. A key issue is their susceptibility to Reverse Image Search (RIS) and Computer Vision (CV) attacks. In this paper, we present a generalized methodology to transform existing images by applying various noise generation algorithms into variants that are resilient to such attacks. To evaluate the usability/security tradeoff, we conduct a user study to determine if the method can provide "usable" images that meet our security requirements – thus improving the overall security provided by Image CAPTCHAs.

1 Introduction

CAPTCHAs (Completely Automated Public Turing test to tell Computers and Humans Apart) are now ubiquitously found on the web to ensure that the entity interacting with a website is indeed human. While CAPTCHAs ensure that abuse of online forms is reduced, web users are forced to suffer through increasingly convoluted and unfriendly CAPTCHAs that negatively impact their user experience. Text-based CAPTCHAs are the most common implementation in use, due to their scalability, robustness, and ease of implementation. However, given their prevalence, many techniques have been developed to break such CAPTCHAs. As a result, alternative methods of form control and human verification have been sought for by the research community. Among the several different modalities that have been explored, image based CAPTCHAs have emerged as a plausible alternative, more suitable for the smartphone/mobile touch-capable environment. However, image CAPTCHAs come with their own set of problems, particularly in terms of scalability – it is hard to find large quantities of labeled/tagged images; and robustness – there is limited variation in the challenge question and vulnerability to single style of attack. In particular, reverse image search (RIS) has emerged as a particularly insidious type of attack against image CAPTCHAs

H. Federrath and D. Gollmann (Eds.): SEC 2015, IFIP AICT 455, pp. 354–368, 2015.
DOI: 10.1007/978-3-319-18467-8_24

[10]. In this paper, we propose a generalized methodology to transform existing images into more resilient variants. The basic idea is to introduce noise into the images using various noise generation algorithms which make it difficult to automatically retrieve the exact same image from the web, while still allowing humans to extract the key concepts from the image to correctly answer the CAPTCHA. Through this transformation, image CAPTCHAs can again become a viable alternative to text based CAPTCHAs having a similar level of security while providing a superior level of usability.

One interesting aspect of using noise generation algorithms to secure images is that the images produced by the algorithms we selected are very "grainy" or "pixelated" in appearance – very similar to a snowy TV picture. The noise introduced is primarily additive and multiplicative in nature, thus it tends to shift around color values in various pixels based on a threshold of our choosing. The benefit to this noise is demonstrated when the image is viewed as a matrix of numbers (as a computer would "see" the image), the values vary wildly and do not follow the patterns typical of a structured image. However, when viewed by a human eye (along with a human mind behind it), the colors blend into an image that is coherent and cognizable (the "Pointillism effect"). Strangely, this side effect of enhancing security actually does not impact usability negatively (to a point). In general, this effect is easier to achieve the further away your eye is from the image, or if the image is small in dimensions (scaled down). In honor of one of the co-creators of the Pointillism technique, 19th century French neo-impressionist painter Paul Signac, we have named our procedure SIGNAC (Secure Image Generation Noise Algorithms for CAPTCHAs).

Our method is similar to the concept of "emergence" - which refers to the unique human ability to aggregate information from seemingly meaningless pieces, and to perceive a whole that is meaningful [15]. The image CAPTCHA utilization of this idea relies on the absence of meaningful information in local image parts which largely hinders existing computer vision algorithms from recognizing emerging figures [9]. The difference between our proposed SIGNAC method and emergence is that we are using an original image (I) and altering it to a new image (I') through a series of image transformations and alterations. We believe this provides a stronger "concrete" foundation for the images generated by the SIGNAC method than would be created by emerging images without giving away too many clues to segmentation/edge detection algorithms.

The rest of the paper is structured as follows. In Section 2 we review the related work. Section 3 details attacks and defense strategies. Section 4 presents the proposed methodology. Sections 5 and 6 present the experimental evaluation and the usability study respectively. Finally, Section 7 concludes the paper.

2   Related Work

From the first introduction of the CAPTCHA [17], there has been significant work on categorizing and creating different CAPTCHA challenges based on alternate modalities such as images [2]. Usability is often a key challenge – Yan et al. [18] provide a general framework for evaluating usability. In recent years, the complexity of text-based CAPTCHAs has been steadily increasing to provide robustness against attacks, but also hampering their usability. As mentioned above, this has led to alternatives such as image based CAPTCHAs. However, given the continuous improvement in computer vision algorithms, image CAPTCHAs have also become vulnerable to attack from methods such as edge detection, object recognition, or pattern recognition. As demonstrated by several studies [5,6,8,11,19], newly deployed real world CAPTCHAs frequently do not take into account advances in computer vision research literature and make common mistakes that could have been accounted for during their design phase.

Newer CAPTCHAs leverage the power of images to exploit the human-machine gap. For example, image orientation [7] is comparatively easy for humans but difficult for computers. Similarly, "scene tagging" [13] tests the ability to recognize a relationship between multiple objects in an image that is automatically generated via composition of a background image with multiple irregularly shaped object images. IMAGINATION [4] also uses a similar "image composition" method. Image distortion [14] has also been suggested as an alternative. One interesting recent invention is that of the GOTCHA [1], which is essentially a randomized puzzle generation protocol, which produces unique images similar to inkblot tests. While questions about its usability remain, it is a promising emerging avenue of anti-bot security methods research.

The main enemy of modern image CAPTCHAs that attempt to work at scale is the modern Content Based Image Retrieval (CBIR) engine [3]. Most major search engines today offer some CBIR capability with their "image search" feature, usually in the form of image retrieval, which can allow an attacker to find an exact match (Reverse Image Search) or other uses of an image on the web that have been used in a CAPTCHA challenge. One subset of CBIR, Automated Image Annotation, provides an extreme threat to simple naming image CAPTCHAs as it can provide an automated answer in the form of a tag for what is presented in the image. Recently, Lorenzi et al. [10] have shown how CBIR and ALA can be used to break several modern image CAPTCHAs.

3   Attack Methods and Defense Strategies

We now discuss two particular types of attack – Reverse Image Search (RIS) engine attacks and Computer Vision (CV) attacks. These are particularly strong against image CAPTCHAs. We also discuss the general defense strategy of adding noise to the image to make it more robust to these attacks. As with all CAPTCHAs, we are again faced with the challenge of balancing security with usability. Since we are utilizing a noise addition method, the image cannot be altered to the degree that a human observer loses the ability to recognize the content of the image (rendering it useless for our purposes).

3.1   Stopping Image Search Attacks

First, our noise addition algorithms must stop reverse image search engines from finding image matches indexed online (Google image search[1] and Tineye [2]).

---

[1] https://www.google.com/img

[2] https://www.tineye.com/

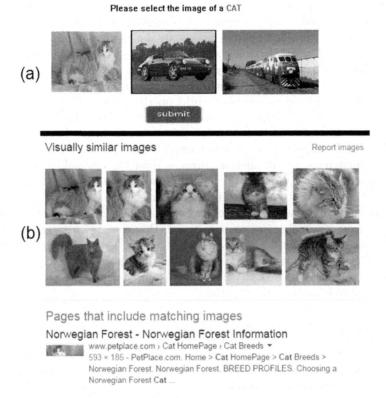

Fig. 1. Reverse image search attack with metadata. (a) depicts the CAPTCHA images without noise, (b) depicts results of a Google image search.

This is an important security enhancement as image CAPTCHAs traditionally have problems in defending against database attacks and tag matching attacks, which can be viewed as a scalability issue (too few unique images). The following scenario is an example of an RIS attack in action: Imagine an image based CAPTCHA challenge asking the user to identify which image out of a set of images depicts a cat as shown in Figure 1. The attacker then: 1) Makes a copy of the images from the CAPTCHA 2) Runs them through an RIS engine to find exact matches 3) Scrapes and stores the metadata from the RIS engine 4) Uses Regular Expressions to match the keyword "cat" to the search that locates a copy of the image used somewhere else online with the filename "cat.jpg", which happened to be found on a website with the URL that contains the word "cat" e.g. http://www.coolcatpics.com.

At this point, the attacker can probabilistically determine which image is most likely the cat image (or eliminate the other image choices through the same process). The bad news for those attempting to develop security measures against RIS engine attacks is that the engines themselves are proprietary (trade secret) and closed source, forcing the CAPTCHA security developer to devise a set of experiments that attempt to probe a "black box" to learn its behavior. The good news is that the RIS engines are available for use by the public with reasonable limits established (50 test images per day, up to 150 per week), and a security expert with access to or knowledge of "image fingerprinting" and image processing literature can use this body of knowledge to provide clues for educated guesses as to the methods that RIS engines are utilizing to identify matches. The noise generation method we propose works on the premise of introducing an amount of noise such that the image used for a CAPTCHA challenge has been altered enough from the original that the various "image fingerprinting" metrics used to determine matches have been "tricked" - that is they no longer see the image as a match as its information diverges from the original image beyond their threshold/similarity metric. Technically speaking, the image returned by the method is a different image, as the noise changes the values of the pixels in the image. A distance metric (change from original) is useful to model the noise alterations from original image to new image. However, the new image (post-noise) is still functionally depicting the same content as the original, albeit in a degraded fashion. Stopping RIS engines from finding matches means indexed images can be used as CAPTCHA challenges again, increasing the sample space of potential usable images significantly.

3.2   Stopping Computer Vision Attacks

Second, the noise algorithms must be able to alter the image enough to hinder or stop altogether, general image/object recognition algorithms that would attempt to solve image recognition challenges.

One popular CV algorithm is SIFT [12], which stands for Scale-Invariant Feature Transform. While it has previously been used in many applications, we are interested only in its ability to perform object recognition tasks. ASIFT [16], which stands for affine-SIFT, is an improvement over SIFT. It considers the lattitude and longitude angles that are ignored by SIFT and then combines that information with SIFT to provide a more complete analysis than SIFT alone. As such, it significantly outperforms SIFT and is more of a challenge to defeat. By adding noise to the image, it should throw off the keypoints calculations so that when it compares two images, the noised image does not have the same keypoints and it fails to return a match. Note that the web application uses grayscales and resizes the images before the CV algorithm is run.

Another important point to consider is that we used an online service to perform the SIFT and ASIFT analysis [16]. The above computation could be completed in approximately 7 seconds through a web form. As more of these services move online, an attacker no longer needs to run local image matching or CV tools, and can script a live attack that pipes the CAPTCHA challenge through the appropriate tools to generate and even submit a correct response.

For example, in our aforementioned cat image scenario, imagine in this case the attacker decides to use image/object recognition with a CV toolkit. The attacker has trained and tested their algorithm of choice (e.g., SIFT) on various images of cats gathered from around the web and can recognize them with a

Fig. 2. CV Attack with SIFT & ASIFT

good degree of accuracy. When he feeds the CAPTCHA challenge image into the algorithm, it returns a high probability of the image being of a cat. Using the noise generation algorithms, the image of the cat can be altered enough so that the CV algorithms return a low probability or cannot determine what the image is depicting, but a human can still determine it is showing a cat. The intention is to use the noise to distort the edges of scenes/objects and alter the patterns within the image enough such that various commonly used CV techniques fail to provide meaningful results for an attacker. Also image filters can be used to distort and move pixel neighborhoods such that detection and mapping algorithms fail to achieve matches and/or detect similarity. Figure 2 shows that both SIFT and ASIFT can overcome scaling issues (mappings are found to a smaller, cropped image of the cat), and ASIFT typically provides more mappings than SIFT.

4   Methodology

Our method is designed to work with existing image CAPTCHAs that rely on a database of images for challenges. After application of SIGNAC, we demonstrate that the same database of images provides better security against RIS and CV based attacks. The MATLAB image processing toolbox is used to generate the new secure images. The function imnoise is used to add noise to the images. The test image set contains 100 images in total, 10 images in each of 10 different categories: airplane, bird, car, cat, doll, fish, flower, monkey, robot, and train. The categories are deliberately made "concrete" instead of abstract, as this makes it easier to create naming and distinguishing image CAPTCHAs that will be straightforward for user/usability testing. This also provides the CV algorithms with an "object" to recognize.The noise functions utilized in the method are the four generalized noise functions available in the MATLAB IPT[3].

4.1   The SIGNAC Approach

As discussed above, SIGNAC is implemented using the MATLAB Image Processing Toolbox. The script below gives an idea of the method in action. X is

---

[3] http://www.mathworks.com/help/images/ref/imnoise.html

the image at the initial starting point when it is read into the IPT. *c1* through *c5* represent the image at various stages of its alteration. Note that this example is a multimethod output, as different noise and filter functions are being used to generate an image at each step. It is important to note that ordinality plays a large factor in the outcome of the image's success or failure in defeating an RIS engine, as discussed in the following section. This script is designed to create the image filter, read in the image file, apply noise, filter the image, then apply noise 3 more times before writing the image to a file.

```
f=fspecial('motion',11,3)
x=imread('1.jpg')
c1=imnoise(x,'salt & pepper',0.35)
c2=imfilter(c1,f)
c3=imnoise(c2,'speckle',0.35)
c4=imnoise(c3,'gaussian',0,0.35)
c5=imnoise(c4,'poisson')
imwrite(c5,'1', 'jpg');
```

This script represents the final script used to create the secure image set used in our experiments. Salt and pepper noise can be considered the most destructive type of noise, as it is the most extreme - changing pixel values to 0's and 1's. The motion filter is then applied to the image with a len of 11 pixels and a theta of 3 degrees counterclockwise, which serves to relocate the pixels that were changed with the addition of the salt and pepper noise to new areas around the image. This aids in obfuscation of clues about pixel values in a particular neighborhood, i.e., multiple pixels will now be distorted with values that differ from the original. After the filter is applied, multiplicative noise in the form of the speckle noise function distributes its noise in a uniform fashion throughout the image, followed by the addition of white Gaussian noise. The final step involves using the Poisson noise function, which does not add artificial noise, instead it generates noise from the image data and then applies it to the image using a Poisson distribution. This serves to further obfuscate the artificial noise that was added during previous steps by shifting the pixel values around.

4.2   RIS Engine Probing

Figure 3 shows an example of a single image test working against the RIS engine Tineye. For the original figure (3a), Tineye provides exact match results.

Single Noise Function, Single Stage. Currently, the initial image returns 16 exact matches from across the web. These results were gathered using a single image noise function in a single step on the original image to produce an image that returns 0 exact matches. Note that these values are unique to this image, and vary based on the image properties.

(a) RIS Probe Test
Image
(b) Gaussian Noise
with 0.2 Mean
(c) Salt & Pepper
Noise with 0.3 Mean
(d) Speckle Noise
with 0.4 Mean

Fig. 3. RIS Engine Probing

Table 1. Results of Ordinality Test

Primary Noise Function	Permutations	# of Results	Primary Noise Function	Permutations	# of Results
Gaussian (G)	GKPS	10	Speckle (K)	KGPS	09
	GKSP	10		KGSP	11
	GPKS	11		KPGS	10
	GPSK	10		KPSG	10
	GSKP	10		KSGP	11
	GSPK	10		KSPG	11
Salt and Pepper (S)	SGKP	11	Poisson (P)	PGKS	10
	SGPK	11		PGSK	09
	SKGP	09		PKGS	10
	SKPG	10		PKSG	10
	SPGK	11		PSGK	10
	SPKG	09		PSKG	09

Ordinality Test. This test demonstrates the ordinality of noise functions. These tests were run with the default settings of each noise generation function to see if the order in which the functions are applied affects the results. Table 1 gives the results with the different orders. Note that these results were obtained using the original cat image, and these results apply only to that image. From these results, it is clear that order makes a difference as the range for matches is +-2 matches, with a high of 11 matches and a low of 9 matches. We then further investigate the chain of methods that produce the least amount of matches.

Threshold Determination. After deciding on an appropriate ordinality for noise methods, it must be determined the minimum threshold at which zero matches are reached - the key to our anti-RIS security criterion. A rough metric is used first, incrementing each mean value by 0.1 until zero matches are found. Then it decrements by 0.05 until a match and then increments or decrements by 0.01 until the minimal value is reached with zero matches. Figure 4 shows two scripts that embody these principles in action. Note that both scripts provide zero matches, however, the second script produces a clearer image because less noise overall is added during the application of additional functions. This is important for usability reasons - as the clearer the image is, the easier the chance a real human will have in recognizing what it depicts.

```
x=imread('cat.jpg')                  x=imread('cat.jpg')
c1=imnoise(x,'salt & pepper',0.11)   c1=imnoise(x,'salt & pepper',0.11)
c2=imnoise(c1,'poisson')             c2=imnoise(c1,'poisson')
c3=imnoise(c2,'speckle',0.11)        c3=imnoise(c2,'speckle',0.05)
c4=imnoise(c3,'gaussian',0,0.11)     c4=imnoise(c3,'gaussian',0,0.05)
imshow(c4)                           imshow(c4)
(a) Minimal Equal Noise via (SPKG)   (b) SPKG Current Working Minimum
```

Fig. 4. SIGNAC MATLAB Scripts

However, the values are extremely sensitive. For example, decrementing the mean in the initial noise function of the previous script by 0.01 to 0.1 produced 5 matches. Decrementing both means c_3 and c_4 by 0.01 each produced 8 matches. It is a painstaking and involved process to tune each image for a working minimum. Unfortunately, this process must be done for each image on an individual basis and cannot be generalized beyond offering a rough threshold for which any series will return zero matches, and this threshold is usually quite high and may impact usability.

As such, this script serves as the endpoint for security against RIS engines, as zero matches are returned with these values. Computer vision based attacks are an entirely different subject, and there are no guarantees that this RIS minimum will have any impact on the ability of CV tools to perform recognition tasks.

4.3 Noise for Anti-computer Vision

While stopping RIS engines was the primary challenge, CV tools are powerful and have been successfully used to defeat image based CAPTCHAs in the past. Thus, we aim to make it as difficult as possible to use them in performing object recognition tasks. One such CV attack case is that of edge detection. This is a key component of object recognition, and being able to foil it will go a long way in stopping any CV attacks from performing this task on an image recognition CAPTCHA challenge.

In Figure 5a, we can see the results of a Sobel edge detection run on the test image. It clearly depicts a cat, while also picking up some of the wrinkles in the sheet behind the cat. Enough detail of the cat comes through that a CV algorithm could make a decision about what is depicted in the image. Note that when edge detection is performed, the image is first converted from RGB to grayscale, and then to binary (hence the black & white) after the edge detection algorithm is run. Figure 5b shows the same Sobel edge detection method run on the image of the cat that has been noised. It can be seen that the cat has completely disappeared - only white dots on a black background appear. No useful information can be gained from this image.

(a) Original Image Edge Detection   (b) Edge Detection after Noising

Fig. 5. Edge detection tests

Fig. 6. SIFT & ASIFT image matching

5 Experimental Results and Analysis

We now describe the experimental evaluation to test image security against both RIS engine attacks and CV attacks using the aforementioned online tools. We have gathered 100 random indexed images from 10 categories and applied the method described in Section 4. Note that the image filter values did not change during the course of the experiments, only the mean values of the noise functions.

5.1 RIS Engine Testing

The goal of this experiment was to establish a baseline for which a set of noise functions can provide zero exact matches against both Google (G) and Tineye's (T) reverse image search engines. As mentioned in the Methodology section, the approach we use is more conservative from the security perspective, in that many of the images are no longer returning matches at much lower levels of noise overall. We consider even 1 match a failure - thus we do not report specific numbers of matches for each image failure. The number following the search engine designation is the number in the set of 10 for that category, e.g., car contains 10 images total, numbered 21-30 - T22 means that image 22 failed to produce zero matches as matches were found on Tineye (but not Google).

Table 2. RIS Engine Testing

CategoryID	Category	Noise Functions at 0.25 Mean		Noise Functions at 0.30 Mean	
		Pass	Fail	Pass	Fail
1	airplane	T,G		T,G	
2	bird	T,G		T,G	
3	car	G	T22	T,G	
4	cat	T	G32	T,G	
5	doll	T,G		T,G	
6	fish	T	G57	T,G	
7	flower	T,G		T,G	
8	monkey	T	G77,G79	T,G	
9	robot		T84,T85,G81,G84,G85		T84,G84
10	train	T,G		T,G	

Table 2 shows that at 0.25 mean noise, we have 8 out of 100 unique images returning matches. Tineye has one unique hit (T22) and Google has five unique hits (G32,G57,G77,G79,G81). There is overlap on image 84 and 85 as both engines returned matches. This means that out of our random sample of 100 indexed images, 92 out of 100 returned zero matches. At 0.30 mean noise, we have 1 out of 100 unique images returning a match. Tineye and Google both return matches for the same image. This means that out of our random sample of 100 indexed images, 99 out of 100 returned zero matches.

5.2 Computer Vision Testing

In this section, we evaluate the effectiveness of SIFT and ASIFT to provide object detection and image matching. The key takeaway is to fool the keypoints calculator into examining incorrect correspondences by inflating the number of keypoints in an image or not finding any matches due to an insignificant matching value. Figure 6 demonstrates failure to find matching keypoints on an exact image match (original clear image vs. noised image).

It may be observed from Figure 7 that SIFT has returned zero matches, but ASIFT has returned 31 matches. However, upon further investigation, we can see that some of the matches are false positives. More specifically, we can see that some of the points provided are incorrect, as it seems the noise has been mistaken for keypoints. However, in both cases, SIFT has returned zero matches, and caused enough doubt in the ASIFT responses, thus discouraging potential attackers. In Figure 8, we can see that ASIFT was fooled by a similarly shaped image. In this case the fish and the hat have a similar shape, and it was enough to return matches, even though clearly the two images are quite different. It is worth noting that in this example, as we scaled the size of the hat image, the ASIFT results dropped to zero. Note that the ASIFT and SIFT engines are sensitive to slight changes in any images (noised or otherwise), and thus generalizing the results to all images will require more study.

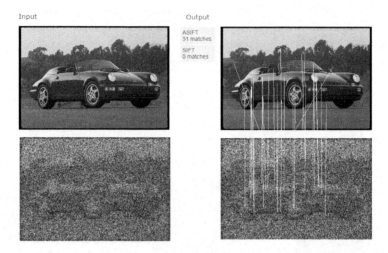

Fig. 7. Exact Match Test: Original Vs. Noise with false positives

Fig. 8. Shape Test: Noised image with similar shape image

5.3 Limitations

As with all noise generation functions, there exists the possibility that their alterations to the image can be significantly decreased with smoothing functions/image filters or reversed entirely by an appropriate function. Sufficiently advanced attackers with image processing experience may be able to reverse some of the distortion effects that come as a result of the noise generation to the degree that the image becomes vulnerable to RIS or CV attacks again. We attempt to minimize this weakness by using randomness in the function when applying the algorithms to the images, as well as using image specific properties to provide alterations within the image. We believe the method has enough merit to be explored further and that the CAPTCHA security community will provide the appropriate level of vetting of our methodology in due time.

Secondly, there exist images that cannot be satisfactorily "noised" – more specifically, the image will either fail to be recognizable by a human due to the excessively high level of noise added to the image to provide the security guarantee, or it will be recognizable to a human but fail to meet the security guarantee because the noise level is too low. This tends to occur when the image

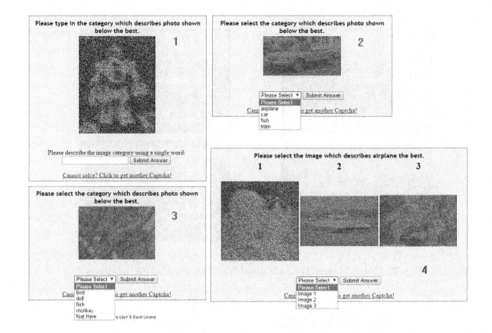

Fig. 9. CAPTCHA Styles

does not have colors (e.g. it is mostly composed of black and white.) We plan to explore this behavior in the future and propose solutions for it.

6   Usability Study

To test the usability of the noise method on human users, we designed 4 different styles of image CAPTCHA with varying degrees of difficulty. Style 1 displays an image and asks the user to describe it by entering a description (freeform response). Style 2 displays an image and provides a dropdown box with 4 responses, with 1 of the 4 choices being the correct answer. Style 3 displays a dropdown box with 5 responses, 4 choices and not here. Style 4 asks the user to select the image from 3 images that best represents X, where X is an image category. The order of difficulty is (1,3,2,4) from most difficult to least difficult. All example of each is depicted in Figure 9. For this experiment, 100 noised images were generated in total, 10 images gathered from a web search in each of 10 different categories. The 10 image categories were chosen to be "concrete", to lower ambiguity for the user (airplane(1), bird(2), car(3), cat(4), doll(5), fish(6), flower(7), monkey(8), robot(9), train(10)). All 4 styles have the option to click a link to serve up a new CAPTCHA if the user cannot understand/decipher/solve the one they have been given. This is tallied as "no response" by our database. The study contained approximately 60 undergraduate students who provided

Table 3. Results for CAPTCHA Style Responses

CAPTCHA Style	% Right	% Wrong	% No Response
1	45%	20%	35%
2	64%	11%	24%
3	67%	21%	13%
4	78%	12%	10%

anonymous responses to a random series of CAPTCHAs served in the various styles of previously described. The results are shown in Table 3. Not surprisingly, style 1 shows the highest percentage of no response (N), which means that the user was unable to decipher the image or felt unable to answer the question. This is followed by style 2 at 24% and 3 and 4 at 13% and 10% respectively. It is important to understand that styles 2(20%), 3(25%), and 4(33%) provide clues for a chance to guess correctly to the user. As such, one can expect a higher level of correct responses as guessing plays a factor in the results. With the case of 3 and 4, the correct response is provided within the framework of the CAPTCHA. From the data we gathered from users, there is an initial period where the users familiarize themselves with the different challenge styles and give more incorrect responses. As they continue to answer questions and become acquainted with various styles, their accuracy and correctness increase significantly. While the number of images used for testing (100) is not very large, the results amply demonstrate that this is a valid method that can be used by humans to a successful degree.

7 Conclusions and Future Work

In this paper we have shown how noise addition can serve as an effective method to solve the scalability problem of image CAPTCHAs and effectively foil Reverse Image Search and Computer Vision attacks. In the future, we plan to test various additional methods of image alterations. We also plan to develop and test multimodal CAPTCHAs, that is, CAPTCHAs that utilize one or more test methods (text based, image based, audio based, etc.) using a combination of protection methods and usability enhancements to provide a comfortable user experience with the maximum level of security possible given those criteria.

References

1. Blocki, J., Blum, M., Datta, A.: Gotcha password hackers!. In: AISec 2013, pp. 25–34 (2013)
2. Chew, M., Tygar, J.D.: Image recognition captchas. In: Zhang, K., Zheng, Y. (eds.) ISC 2004. LNCS, vol. 3225, pp. 268–279. Springer, Heidelberg (2004)
3. Datta, R., Joshi, D., Li, J., Wang, J.Z.: Image Retrieval: Ideas, Influences, and Trends of the New Age. ACM Comput. Surv. 40(2), 5:1–5:60 (2008)

4. Datta, R., Li, J., Wang, J.Z.: Imagination: a robust image-based captcha generation system. In: MULTIMEDIA 2005, pp. 331–334 (2005)
5. El Ahmad, A.S., Yan, J., Marshall, L.: The robustness of a new captcha. In: EUROSEC 2010, pp. 36–41 (2010)
6. Fritsch, C., Netter, M., Reisser, A., Pernul, G.: Attacking image recognition captchas. In: Katsikas, S., Lopez, J., Soriano, M. (eds.) TrustBus 2010. LNCS, vol. 6264, pp. 13–25. Springer, Heidelberg (2010)
7. Gossweiler, R., Kamvar, M., Baluja, S.: What's up captcha?: a captcha based on image orientation. In: WWW 2009, pp. 841–850 (2009)
8. Hernandez-Castro, C.J., Ribagorda, A., Saez, Y.: Side-channel attack on the humanauth captcha. In: SECRYPT 2010, pp. 1–7 (2010)
9. Jian, M.-F., Chu, H.-K., Lee, R.-R., Ku, C.-L., Wang, Y.-S., Yao, C.-Y.: Emerging images synthesis from photographs. In: ACM SIGGRAPH 2013, pp. 97:1–97:1 (2013)
10. Lorenzi, D., Vaidya, J., Sural, S., Atluri, V.: Web services based attacks against image captchas. In: Bagchi, A., Ray, I. (eds.) ICISS 2013. LNCS, vol. 8303, pp. 214–229. Springer, Heidelberg (2013)
11. Lorenzi, D., Vaidya, J., Uzun, E., Sural, S., Atluri, V.: Attacking image based captchas using image recognition techniques. In: Venkatakrishnan, V., Goswami, D. (eds.) ICISS 2012. LNCS, vol. 7671, pp. 327–342. Springer, Heidelberg (2012)
12. Lowe, D.G.: Object recognition from local scale-invariant features. In: ICCV 1999, pp. 1150–1157 (1999)
13. Matthews, P., Mantel, A., Zou, C.C.: Scene tagging: image-based captcha using image composition and object relationships. In: ASIACCS 2010, pp. 345–350 (2010)
14. Mehrnejad, M., Bafghi, A., Harati, A., Toreini, E.: Multiple seimcha: multiple semantic image captcha. In: ICITST 2011, pp. 196–201 (2011)
15. Mitra, N.J., Chu, H.-K., Lee, T.-Y., Wolf, L., Yeshurun, H., Cohen-Or, D.: Emerging images. In: ACM SIGGRAPH Asia 2009, pp. 163:1–163:8 (2009)
16. Morel, J.-M., Yu, G.: Asift: A New Framework for Fully Affine Invariant Image Comparison. SIAM J. Img. Sci. **2**(2), 438–469 (2009)
17. von Ahn, L., Blum, M., Langford, J.: Telling Humans and Computers Apart Automatically. Commun. ACM **47**(2), 56–60 (2004)
18. Yan, J., El Ahmad, A.S.: Usability of captchas or usability issues in captcha design. In: SOUPS 2008, pp. 44–52 (2008)
19. Zhu, B.B., Yan, J., Li, Q., Yang, C., Liu, J., Xu, N., Yi, M., Cai, K.: Attacks and design of image recognition captchas. In: CCS 2010, pp. 187–200 (2010)

Software Security

SHRIFT System-Wide HybRid Information Flow Tracking

Enrico Lovat[1], Alexander Fromm[1], Martin Mohr[2(✉)],
and Alexander Pretschner[1]

[1] Technische Universität München, Garching bei München, Germany
{enrico.lovat,alexander.fromm,alexander.pretschner}@cs.tum.edu
[2] Karlsruhe Institute of Technology, Karlsruhe, Germany
martin.mohr@kit.edu

Abstract. Using data flow tracking technology, one can observe how data flows from inputs (sources) to outputs (sinks) of a software system. It has been proposed [1] to do runtime data flow tracking at various layers simultaneously (operating system, application, data base, window manager, etc.), and connect the monitors' observations to exploit semantic information about the layers to make analyses more precise. This has implications on performance—multiple monitors running in parallel— and on methodology—there needs to be one dedicated monitor per layer. We address both aspects of the problem. We replace a *runtime* monitor at a layer L by its *statically* computed input-output dependencies. At runtime, these relations are used by monitors at other layers to model flows of data through L, thus allowing cross-layer system-wide tracking. We achieve this in three steps: (1) static analysis of the application at layer L, (2) instrumentation of the application's source and sink instructions and (3) runtime execution of the instrumented application in combination with monitors at other layers. The result allows for system-wide tracking of data dissemination, across and through multiple applications. We implement our solution at the Java Bytecode level, and connect it to a runtime OS-level monitor. In terms of precision and performance, we outperform binary-level approaches *and* can exploit high-level semantics.

1 Introduction

Information flow analyses try to answer the question of whether or not data will potentially flow, or has potentially flowed, from inputs (*sources*) to outputs (*sinks*) of a certain system. Different analyses cater to different kind of source-sink dependencies, mainly distinguishing between *explicit* information flows (data-flow dependencies or *data flows*) and *implicit* information flows (like e.g. dependencies caused solely by control-flow). Data flow tracking solutions are generally tailored to one particular level of abstraction, like source code, byte code, machine code, or the operating system level (cf. §5).

Recently, data flow tracking technologies have been augmented by concepts of distributed data usage control [1–5] and performed at *multiple layers of*

© IFIP International Federation for Information Processing 2015
H. Federrath and D. Gollmann (Eds.): SEC 2015, IFIP AICT 455, pp. 371–385, 2015.
DOI: 10.1007/978-3-319-18467-8_25

abstraction, to the end of expressing and enforcing more complex policies (e.g. "any representation of this picture must be deleted after thirty days"). Multi-layer monitoring is important to preserve the *high-level semantics* of objects (e.g. "a mail") and events (e.g. "forward"), which is otherwise hard to capture at lower levels. But this benefit does not come for free: even a small number of monitors running in parallel may seriously compromise the performance of the overall system, and dedicated high-level monitors are not always available for every domain. In this case, the usual solution is to rely on conservative estimations provided by lower layers. For instance, if a dedicated monitor for a process is not available, an OS-level monitor would have to treat the process as a "black box" and assume that every sensitive data it got in touch with is propagated to every future output. This solution likely introduces many false positives and in this sense grossly overapproximates the set of potential information flows.

We propose SHRIFT, an approach to mitigate this issue. The core idea behind SHRIFT is to replace the runtime monitoring of how data flows through a process (or its *black-box* overapproximation) by consultations of a *statically precomputed mapping* between its inputs and outputs.

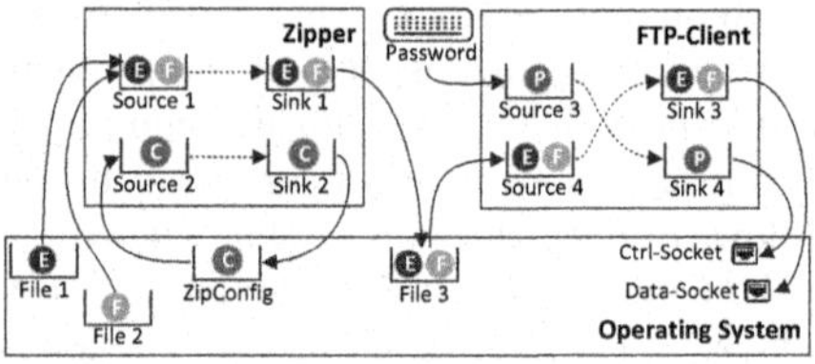

Running Example: *A company enforces the policy* "upon logout, delete every local copy of customer data" *to prevent clerks to work with outdated material. Upon every login, a clerk must download from a central server a fresh version of the customer data he is interested in. In this setting, a clerk uses the* Zipper *application to compress multiple customer data (**E**, **F**) into a single archive file (*`File 3`*), which he then sends to the company server using* Ftp-Client.

In this example, a data-flow tracking system can help tracking down every copy of to-be-deleted customer data in the system. However, if the tracking is imprecise (too many false positives), additional important resources may be accidentally deleted as well. For example, `ZipConfig` (Zipper's configuration file), which is updated during every run of Zipper, could be mistakenly marked as containing data `E` and deleted upon logout, making Zipper unusable in the future. Similar concerns also apply to the Ftp-Client: FTP works with two channels, one for commands, and one for payload. In a black-box monitoring situation, once sensitive data is read, every write to any of the two channels may be possibly carrying sensitive information, and, as such, it should propagate the taint to the socket connection, and possibly to the recipient side. In this case, the credentials (marked as `P` in the figure), sent via the command channel, and the database in which they are stored on the server side would also be marked as "to-be-deleted".

Our approach improves the precision of information-flow tracking *system-wide*, i.e. through and in-between different processes/applications, like the flow of data **E** and **F** through the Zipper application (`Source 1`→ `Sink 1`) into `File 3` and then through the Ftp-Client application (`Source 4` → `Sink 3`) till the payload channel, with lower execution overhead than other dynamic monitors for comparable scenarios (cf. §3).

Problem: Concurrently running multiple monitors at different layers of abstraction allows to exploit high-level semantic information (e.g., "screenshot" or "mail") but is performance-wise expensive and requires dedicated monitoring technologies for every layer/application. On the other hand, relying only on estimates provided by other layers (e.g., the above black-box approach) improves performance but comes at the cost of (possibly significant) precision loss.

Solution: We propose a dynamic monitoring approach for generic processes that replaces runtime intra-process data flow tracking by consultations of a statically computed taint-propagation table. Such a monitor is more performant than equivalent runtime monitors for the same application and more precise than the OS-level overapproximation adopted when such a monitor is not available.

Contribution: To the best of our knowledge, we are the first to combine static and dynamic data-flow tracking for different levels of abstraction and *through multiple different applications*. Our solution improves the precision of OS level data flow tracking with minimal intra-process runtime tracking overhead.

2   Our Approach

We consider a setting with monitors at two levels of abstraction: a dynamic monitor at the OS level, based on system-call interposition [2], and one or more inline reference monitors at the application level. Our goal is to improve tracking precision at the OS level with minimal performance penalties. Although our approach is generic in nature and could be applied to any language or binary code, in this work we focus on an instantiation for the Java Bytecode (JBC) level.

We use standard terminology: a *source* is a method invoked by the application to get input data from the environment. A *sink* performs the dual output invocation. While in some contexts one can find detailed lists of source and sink methods [6], in general the choice is left to the analyst. In our work, a source (sink) is the invocation of a Java standard library method that overrides any overloaded version of InputStream.read (OutputStream.write) or Reader.read (Writer.write), or a method that indirectly invokes one of them, e.g., Properties.load(), which uses an input stream parameter to fill a properties table.

The idea is the following. If a source in an application is executed, the respective input's taint mark is stored. If a sink is executed, all sources (and therefore all taint marks) with potential flows to this sink are determined using a static mapping of potential flows between sources and sinks. There is hence a need to instrument sources and sinks, but *not all the instructions in-between them*.

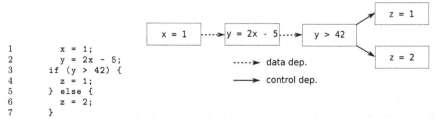

```
1        x = 1;
2        y = 2x - 5;
3        if (y > 42) {
4            z = 1;
5        } else {
6            z = 2;
7        }
```

Fig. 1. A code snippet and its PDG

Our approach consists of three phases:

2.1. Static analysis: An application X is analyzed for possible information flows between sources and sinks. During this phase we generate a report containing a list of all sources and sinks in the application and a mapping between each sink and every source it may depend on.

2.2. Instrumentation: All sinks and sources identified by the static analysis (and those instructions *only*) are instrumented in the bytecode of X, allowing us to monitor their execution.

2.3. Runtime: Every time a source or a sink is executed by the instrumented application, information about the data being read or written is exchanged with the OS-level monitor.

In the remainder of this section, we will describe these phases in details, using Zipper and Ftp-Client as examples. Notice, however, that in principle our work can be applied in a push-button fashion to any Java program.

2.1   Static Analysis

In this phase, we perform a static information flow analysis of the application and generate a list of all sources and sinks in the application and of their respective dependencies. To do so, we use JOANA [7,8], a static information flow analysis tool, but the choice is not binding because our approach is generic in nature and the techniques used by JOANA are also implemented by other tools, e.g. [9].

JOANA operates in two steps: first, it builds a *Program Dependence Graph* (PDG) [10] of the application; second, it applies slicing-based information flow analysis [11] on the PDG to find out which set of the sources influences which sinks. In order to reduce the number of false positives, JOANA leverages several program analysis techniques. In the following, we explain some fundamental concepts behind JOANA.

PDGs and Slicing: A PDG is a language-independent representation of a program. The nodes of a PDG represent statements and expressions, while edges model the syntactic dependencies between them. There exist many kinds of dependencies, among which the most important are *data dependencies*, (a statement using a value produced by another statement) and *control dependencies* (a statement or expression controlling whether another statement is executed or not). The PDG in Figure 1 contains a data dependency between the statements in line 1 and in line 2 because the latter uses the value of x produced by the former, and a control dependency between the **if**-statement in line 3 and the statements in lines 4 and 6 because whether line 4 or 6 is executed depends on the value of the expression in line 3.

PDG-based information flow analysis uses *context-sensitive slicing* [12], a special form of graph reachability: given a node n of the PDG, the *backwards slice* of n contains all nodes from which n is reachable by a path in the PDG that respects calling-contexts. For sequential programs, it has been shown [13] that a node not contained in the backwards slice of n cannot influence n, hence PDG-based slicing on sequential programs guarantees *non-interference* [14]. It is also possible to construct and slice PDGs for concurrent programs [15]. However, in this context, additional kinds of information flows may exist, e.g. probabilistic channels [16]. So the mere slicing is not enough to cover *all* possible information flows between a source and a sink. A PDG- and slicing-based algorithm providing such guarantee has recently been developed and integrated into JOANA [17].

Analysis Options: JOANA is highly configurable and allows to configure different aspects of the analysis, e.g. to ignore all control flow dependencies caused by exceptions, or to specify different types of *points-to analysis* [18]. Points-to-analysis is an analysis technique which aims to answer the question which heap locations a given pointer variable may reference. JOANA uses points-to information during PDG construction to determine possible information flows through the heap and therefore depends heavily on the points-to analysis precision. JOANA supports several points-to analyses, including 0-1-CFA [19], k-CFA [20] and object-sensitive [21] points-to analysis.

The outcome of this phase is a list of the sources and sinks in the code of the application and a table that lists all the sources each sink depends on.

2.2 Instrumentation

In this phase, we take the report generated by the static analysis and instrument each identified source and sink. For each source or sink, the analysis reports the *signature* and the exact *location* (parent method and bytecode offset).

```
1   void zipIt(String file, String srcFolder) {
2     fos = new FileOutputStream(file);
3     zos = new ZipOutputStream(fos);
4     fileList = this.generateFileList(srcFolder);
5     byte[] buffer = new byte[1024];
6     for (String file : fileList) {
7       ze = new ZipEntry(file);
8       zos.putNextEntry(ze);
9       in = new FileInputStream(file);
10      int len;
11      while ((len = in.read(buffer)) > 0)
12        zos.write(buffer, 0, len);
13      in.close();}}
```

Listing 1.1. Java code fragment from Zipper

Consider the code snippet in Listing 1.1, used in our Zipper application: static information flow analysis detects the flow from the source at line 11 (**Source1**), where the files are read, to the sink at line 12 (**Sink1**), where they are written into the archive. Listing 1.2 shows the corresponding analysis report: lines 1 - 9 specify that the return value of the

read method invocation at bytecode offset 191 in method **zipIt** is identified as **Source1**. The same holds for **Sink1** (lines 12-20), but in this case the first parameter (line 19) is a sink, not a source. In the final part, the report also provides information about the dependency between **Sink1** and **Source1** (line 21 - 25), which is then used to model possible flows.

We use the *OW2-ASM* [22] instrumentation tool to wrap each reported source and sink with additional, injected bytecode instructions. We refer to the set of these additional instructions as *inline reference monitor*. The outcome of this phase is an instrumented version of the original application, augmented with a minimal inline reference monitor that interacts with the OS-level monitor when a source or a sink is executed. This way incoming/outgoing flows of data from/to a resource, like files or network sockets, can be properly modeled.

```
1   <source><id>Source1</id>              14       (Ljava/lang/String;Ljava/lang/String
2     <location>JZip.zipIt                            ;)V:185
3       (Ljava/lang/String;Ljava/lang/String  15    </location>
          ;)V:191                          16       <signature>
4     </location>                          17         java.util.zip.ZipOutputStream.
5     <signature>                                       write([BII)V
6       java.io.FileInputStream.read([B)I  18       </signature>
7     </signature>                         19       <param index="1"/>
8     <return/>                            20     </sink>
9   </source><source><id>Source2</id>     21   <flows>
10    ...                                  22     <sink id="Sink1">
11  </source>                              23       <source id="Source1"/>
12  <sink><id>Sink1</id>                   24     </sink>
13    <location>JZip.zipIt                 25   </flows>
```

Listing 1.2. Static analysis report listing sinks, sources and their dependencies

2.3   Runtime

This phase represents the actual runtime data-flow tracking, where we execute the instrumented applications in a dynamically monitored OS. At runtime a single OS-level monitor exchanges information with multiple inlined bytecode-level reference monitors, one per application. We assume that the information to be tracked is initially stored somewhere in the system, e.g. in some files or coming from certain network sockets, and marked as sensitive. In our example in §1 we assume data **E** and **F** to be already stored in **File 1** and **File 2**, respectively.

Once a source instruction is about to be executed, the instrumented code queries the OS-monitor to obtain information about the tainting of the input. It then associates this information to the source id (e.g. **ZipConfig** → **Source2** in our example). When a sink instruction is about to be executed, the instrumented code fetches tainting information from *all the sources the current sink depends on* according to the analysis report (**Source2** → **Sink2**). Such information denotes all the possible inputs the current output may depend on, but, most importantly, it denotes all the inputs the current output does *not* depend on: this is where we reduce false positives, mitigating the overapproximation of potential flows. The tainting information is then propagated to the output.

With this approach, even if the application reads additional data (like data **E**) before generating the output, the tainting associated with the sink (and, consequently, with the output) remains the same, as long as the input does not influence the output. In contrast, in a process treated as a black-box every output is as sensitive as the union of *all* the sources encountered till then. The information about the content being output by the current sink (Sink2 → ZipConfig) is forwarded to the OS monitor, which will carry on the tracking outside the boundaries of the application. Since the process described here applies to every instrumented application, this allows us to track the flows of data between any pair of applications, even through OS artifacts (like files), OS events (like copying a file) and non-instrumented processes (via black-box tracking).

3   Evaluation

Our goal is to improve system-wide, i.e. OS-level, data-flow tracking precision without the extreme overhead of process-level runtime data-flow tracking. We evaluated our work in terms of *precision* (false positives[1].) and *performance*, and addressed the following research questions by means of case studies:

RQ1 How much more precise is this approach with respect to the estimation provided by an OS-level monitor alone?
RQ2 How long does the static analysis phase take?
RQ3 How much slower is the instrumented application, and how do we compare with purely dynamic solutions?

We performed our experiments on the applications described in our running example (cf. §1), Zipper and Ftp-Client. Zipper was written by a student, while Ftp-Client was found online [23]. The code of these applications is intentionally minimal, in order to facilitate manual inspection of the results. Moreover, these applications stress-test our solution because our approach instruments only entry and exit points in the code (sources and sinks), but the vast majority of executed instructions are indeed sources or sinks; for comparison, we also run our solution on an application with little I/O and large amount of computation in-between: the Java Grande Forum Benchmark Suite[2], a benchmark for computationally expensive Java applications. We chose this framework, among others, to compare our results to those of related work [24].

3.1   Settings

Our evaluation was performed on a system with a 2.6 GHz Xeon-E5 CPU and 3GB of RAM. We ran our static analyser on all the applications using the different configurations described in §3.2. We report the median value for 30+ executions of each configuration, to weed out possible environmental noise. As OS

---

[1] We assume the static analysis to be sound: all actual flows are reported, i.e., there are no false negatives. Limitations of our approach are discussed in §4
[2] https://www2.epcc.ed.ac.uk/computing/research_activities/java_grande/index_1. html

monitor, we used an implementation from the literature [25]. All the runtime experiments use the objsens-D (§3.2) configuration for the static analysis phase. We decided for it because of its high precision in our tests; any other analysis, however, would generate statistically indistinguishable runtime performances.

3.2   Precision (RQ1) and Static Analysis Performance (RQ2)

First, by construction, our approach cannot be less precise than treating the processes as black boxes (= every output contains every input read so far), the typical conservative estimation made by OS-level monitors [2]. Second, while dynamic analyses usually rely on explicit flows only, static analyses consider additional kinds of dependencies between instructions (e.g. control-flow dependencies), generating more dependencies between sources and sinks. Third, even if we configure our static analyser to consider explicit-flows only, a static approach considers *every* possible execution at once, meaning that if at least one execution leads to a flow, then the sink statically depends on the source.

```
1   in=input();
2   if (cond) {
3       out=in;
4   }
5   output(out);
```

For instance, for the code on the left static analysis reports that the sink at line 5 depends on the source at line 1, even considering explicit flows only. A runtime monitor would report the dependency only during those runs where condition cond at line 2 is satisfied. Replacing the runtime monitoring with a static dependency table introduces overapproximation by making the sink depending on the source during *every* execution, regardless of cond's value.

We ran experiments on the scenario described in §1. We created the Zipper's configuration file, assigned to data C, and two files with random content (data E and F, respectively). In this scenario, we assumed that the only data read from the standard input is the password, marked as P. We then ran the scenario (i.e. we zipped the files using Zipper and sent them to the server using Ftp-Client) and looked at the sensitivity of the content that reached the sockets.

As expected, the execution using a black-box approach yielded a rather coarse-grained result (all data reached both sockets); in contrast, our solution provided the expected result (data E and F flowed only to the data socket, while P only to the control socket).

Table 1. Static analysis results for different configurations

	Points-To	Time (s)	#Sources/ #Sinks	Precision (DI / D)
Ftp-Client	0-1-CFA	32	9 / 46	38% / 51%
	1-CFA	64	9 / 46	58% / 73%
	2-CFA	153	9 / 46	58% / 73%
	objsens	220	9 / 46	38% / 74%
Zipper	0-1-CFA	53	10 / 56	24% / 43%
	1-CFA	82	10 / 55	25% / 53%
	2-CFA	185	10 / 55	55% / 78%
	objsens	353	10 / 55	57% / 84%
JGFBS	0-1-CFA	211	8 / 84	56% / 59%
	1-CFA	580	8 / 81	71% / 75%
	2-CFA	626	8 / 81	71% / 77%
	objsens	360	8 / 81	73% / 79%

However, it is hard to *quantify* such an improvement in general. Considering that a black-box approach would always be as precise as our approach when every source is connected to every sink, a possible metric for precision improvement could be *the number of source-to-sink connections that we can safely discard*, thanks to static analysis. We let #*flows* denote the number of statically

Table 2. Runtime analysis results. Underlined value taken from the literature, all others measured. Values in italic refer to results of comparable tests (cf. §3.3). $Zipper_{32}$ indicates the archiving of 261MB using internal buffers 32x bigger.

	Size (bytecode) orig.→instr.	Average overhead per sink/source		Overhead in total				
		Intra	Intra+OS	Intra	Intra+OS	[26]	[24]	[27]
Zipper	1611 → 2192	2.06x	22.92x	2.09x	34.28x	220.4x	-	-
Ftp-Client	9191 → 9785	0.16x	4.37x	0.28x	6.75x	25.7x	-	-
Java Grande	29003 → 30123	6.33x	144.65x	0.001x	0.07x	10.5x	*0.25x - 1x*	-
$Zipper_{32}$	1611 → 2192	0.24x	7.11x	0.33x	11.61x	19.7x	-	*15.2x - 28.1x*

computed dependencies between sources and sinks, and measure precision as $1 - (\#flows/(\#sources \times \#sinks))$, where 0 indicates that every source flows to every sink (like in the black-box approach) and 1 indicates that all sinks are independent from the sources, i.e. no data propagation. We are not aware of any better metric to measure precision of static analysis w.r.t dynamic monitoring.

As reported in Table 1, we ran our analysis with various *points-to-analyses* (0-1-CFA [19], 1-CFA, 2-CFA, object-sensitive, cf. §2.1), considering only explicit (D), and additional implicit (DI), information flows. According to the formula above, the improved precision of the instrumented applications varies between 24% and 84% for Zipper, between 38% and 74% for Ftp-Client and between 56% and 79% for Java Grande F.B.S., depending on the configuration. Although some of these analyses are incomparable in theory, object-sensitivity tends to deliver more precision, as was already reported for various client analyses [21]. Note that these numbers are hard to relate to dynamic values, because they depend on the specific application under analysis and they do not take into account how many times a certain source/sink instruction is executed at runtime.

To answer **RQ2**, we also measured the time required to statically analyse our exemplary applications: between 30 and 626 seconds were needed to perform the static analysis (cf. Table 1), of which 80-90% are invested in building the PDG, while the rest is spent on slicing. The choice of the points-to-analysis determines the size of the PDG and thus directly affects the total analysis time; our PDGs have between 10^4 and 10^6 nodes and between 10^5 and 10^7 edges.

3.3   Runtime Performance (RQ3)

We tested our approach with multiple experiments based on our scenario (§1): transfer a 20K file to a remote server using Ftp-Client, and compress it using Zipper. We also ran our tool on the Java Grande F.B.S., the computationally expensive task with limited I/O used in the evaluation of [24]. We evaluated our approach (cf. Table 2) in terms of the bytecode space overhead (column "Size (bytecode)"), the average execution time of a single instrumented source/sink (column "Average overhead per sink/source"), and the total execution time of the instrumented application (column "Overhead in total") compared to its native execution. We measured the execution runtime overhead with both monitors at the application and OS level (columns "Intra+OS"), and with just one inlined reference monitor at the application level observing only sources' and sinks' executions (columns "Intra"). In addition, we compared our work to other approaches, either by running our tool on the same scenario used to evaluate them [24] or, if possible, by running those tools on our tests. The latter is the case for *LibDFT* [26], an intra-process data-flow tracking framework for binaries.

Zipper and Ftp-Client applications are stress-testing our approach because they transfer data in blocks of 1KB at a time. This results in a huge number of read/write events: for comparison, creating a zip file from 261MB of data with our Zipper generated ~122K write and ~256K read events, whereas *gzip*, an equivalent tool used in [27]'s evaluation, only generates 3781 writes and 7969 read system calls for the same input and the same output. Because [27] is a dynamic monitor that connects information flow tracking results for multiple applications across the system, we found a comparison to this work to be particularly relevant. To perform it, we ran a fourth experiment: archiving 261MB of linux source code with our Zipper application after increasing the size of the internal buffers by a factor of 32x; this way, for the same input, Zipper generates the same number of I/O events of the tool used in [27]. We are aware that comparing different applications is always tricky; however, since the number and type of generated events is almost identical, we believe the comparison to be informative and likely fair. Our results are presented in the last row of Table 2. The overhead for archiving 261MB (11.61x) using our Zipper is smaller than the best value for gzip mentioned in [27] (15.2x-28.1x). Similarly, on the Java Grande test, we outperformed [24]'s analysis of one order of magnitude (0.07x vs 0.25x-0.5x).

Note that the static analysis and the instrumentation are executed only once per application. For this reason, we excluded the time to perform them from the computation of the relative runtime overhead (columns Intra and Intra+OS in Overhead, Table 2). Also, the values in Table 2 do not include the time required to boot the Java Virtual Machine, which is independent of our instrumentation and thus irrelevant. It is worth noticing that we tried different configurations of LibDFT but we could only reproduce overheads more than ten times larger than those reported in the original paper [26].

4   Discussion

We now offer a general summary of our experimental results, elaborating on some of the technical and fundamental highlights and limitations of our approach.

By combining static and dynamic data flow technologies, we manage to track system-wide information flows between different programs and across different application layers. Our prototype implementation performs better than existing approaches although we are aware that this strongly depends on the application under analysis. While we have not "tuned" our approach to the examples in the case studies, we need to refrain from generalizing our findings. As we instrument only sources and sinks, on computationally intensive tasks with little I/O, like the Java Grande F.B.S., our tool exhibits a negligible overhead in practice (<0.07x). In more I/O intensive scenarios, our results are comparable or better than existing approaches. Note that while the tracking overhead per source/sink is stable (~0.08ms "Intra", ~2.2ms "Intra+OS"), the time to execute specific sources/sinks (e.g. >7ms for printing a certain string on standard output) can be longer than for others (e.g. ~0.011ms for reading 1KB from a file), resulting in vastly different relative overhead.

We could improve the precision of our approach by leveraging additional information, e.g. the context in which a certain sink/source is executed [19]. However, this requires a) the use of a context-sensitive points-to-analysis, like 1-CFA, usually more costly than a context-insensitve one (cf. §3), and b) additional instrumentation, which is the reason why we decided not to go for it. Other options to improve the precision of static analysis are ignoring certain kinds of flows, like those solely caused by exceptions, or manually adding declassification annotations to the code. While the first idea is acceptable, as long as one is fine with the respective change in the notion of soundness, we decided against manual annotations, envisioning the application of our tool in a scenario where static analysis is performed *automatically* on *unknown* code.

JOANA currently does not support dynamic language features like reflection and callbacks, challenging tasks for any static information flow analysis: dealing with reflection in a meaningful way requires approximating the possible values of strings which are passed as class or method names or to exploit runtime information [28], while callback-based applications (e.g. using Java Swing) require a model that captures the way the callback handlers are invoked. In other words, while JOANA can analyse multi-threaded programs (cf. §2.1), library-supported asynchronous communication between threads is still a limitation.

If we configured the static analysis to ignore all implicit flows (easy to circumvent [29]), the combination of our OS runtime monitor and the application reference monitors would guarantee a property similar to Volpano's *weak secrecy* [30]. On the other hand, a sound and precise system-wide non-interference analysis (including *all* information flows), would require to analyse all applications simultaneously, to also capture flows caused by the concurrent interactions on shared resources [16]. This is unfeasible even for a small number of applications and likely leads to prohibitively imprecise results. Our approach lies somewhere in-between: the static intra-process analysis guarantees non-interference between inputs and outputs of each application, while data flows across applications are captured at runtime. This property is stronger than weak secrecy, which completely ignores implicit flows, but still weaker than system-wide non-interference.

5   Related work

Approaches in the field of Information Flow Analysis can be roughly categorized in static, dynamic and hybrid solutions.

Static approaches analyze application code before it is executed and aim to detect all possible information flows [31,32]. A given program is certified as secure, if no information flow between sensitive sources and public sinks can be found. Such a static certification can for example be used to reduce the need for runtime checks [33]. Various approaches (apart from PDGs) can be found in the literature, usually based on type checking [32] or hoare logic [34]. Because of their nature, static approaches have problems with handling dynamic aspects of applications like callbacks or reflective code (§4), and are confined to the application under analysis, i.e. no system-wide analyses.

Dynamic approaches track data flows during execution and thus can also leverage additional information, like concrete user inputs, available only at runtime. *TaintDroid* [35] is a purely dynamic data flow tracking approach for system-wide real-time privacy monitoring in Android. Despite its relatively small runtime overhead, TaintDroid focuses on explicit data flow tracking only. [36] proposes *ShadowReplica*, a highly optimized data flow tracker that leverages multiple threads to track data through binary files. While performance in general depends on the application under analysis, on I/O-intensive tasks ShadowReplica's runtime overhead is comparable to ours (cf. §3). [26] presents LibDFT, a binary-level solution to track data flows in-between registers and memory addresses. Although LibDFT's reported evaluation mentions little performance overhead, we could not reproduce these numbers: as shown in Table 2, LibDFT imposed a bigger performance overhead than our approach; it is also unable to perform system-wide tracking because, in contrast to our approach, it cannot model flows towards OS resources (e.g. files) or in-between processes.

Whole-system tainting frameworks, on the other hand, can specifically track such kind of flows; among them we find *Panorama* [37], an approach at the hardware and OS levels to detect and identify privacy-breaching malware behaviour, *GARM* [38], a tool to track data provenance across multiple applications and machines, and *Neon*[39], a fine-grained system-wide tracking approach for derived data management. While the performance penalty they induce is comparable to ours, because of their dynamic nature, none of these tools can cope with implicit flows, nor exploit application-level semantics ("screenshot", "mail").

Hybrid approaches aim at combining static and dynamic information flow tracking approaches, usually to mitigate runtime-overhead. [24] presents a hybrid solution for fine-grained information flow analysis of Java applications; in this work, statically computed *security annotations* are used at runtime to track implicit information flows and to enforce security policies by denying the execution of specific method calls. In [40] the authors propose to augment a hybrid tracking approach with declassification rules to downgrade the security levels of specific flows and controlling information flows by allowing, inhibiting, or modifying events. Although both [24,40] show promising results, they do not take into account flows through OS-level abstractions, like files, nor between different applications or abstraction layers, as we do. We did not discuss so far the possibility of enforcing usage control requirements at the Java bytecode level in a *preventive* fashion [41] (i.e. execute a certain source/sink only if the tracker's response is affirmative), because, while requiring only minor changes in the instrumentation, denying method executions at this level may make the system unstable.

Other approaches model inter-application information flows by instrumenting sources and sinks in the monitored applications, relying on pure dynamic tracking [27] or on static analysis results [42] for the intra-application tracking. All of them, however, perform the inter-application flow tracking relying on the "simultaneous" execution of a sink in the sender application and a source in the receiver. None of them can model a flow towards an OS resource, like a file, nor towards a non-monitored application. In these scenarios, these approaches lose track of the data, while ours delegates the tracking to the OS level monitor.

6   Conclusions and Future Work

We described a new, generic approach to perform precise and fast system-wide data-flow tracking. We integrated static information flow analysis results with runtime technologies. In our case studies, our solution could track flows of data through and in-between different applications more precisely than the black-box approach does and faster than comparable dynamic approaches do. At present we cannot substantiate any claim of generalization of these results to other scenarios, but we are optimistic. While our proof-of-concept implementation connects executed Java code to an OS-level runtime monitor, other instantiations are possible. For instance, static approximations for flows in a database could be connected to dynamic measurements in a given application. Also, our general methodology is not restricted to specific programming languages or tools, so instantiations for languages other than Java are possible.

To the best of our knowledge, this is the first system-wide runtime analysis that replaces the internal behavior of applications by their static source/sink dependencies. Although hybrid approaches have already been proposed before, this kind of integration of static and dynamic results is the first of its kind.

Our experiments confirmed the intuition that the improvement in precision and performance depends on the type of information flows considered, and on the amount of I/O instructions executed (w.r.t the total number of instructions). Our solution is more suitable if this ratio is low, i.e. for applications that perform large computations on few inputs to produce a limited number of outputs.

We plan to apply our work to other programming languages, or the x86-binary level, although static analysis tools at this level exhibit bigger limitations. Additionally, we want to better understand the issues described in §4, in particular the exploitation of context-sensitive analysis information.

Acknowledgments. This work was supported by the DFG Priority Programme 1496 "Reliably Secure Software Systems - RS^3" (grants PR-1266/1-2 and Sn11/12-1), and by the *Peer Energy Cloud* project, funded by the German Federal Ministry of Economic Affairs and Energy.

References

1. Pretschner, A., Lovat, E., Büchler, M.: Representation-independent data usage control. In: Garcia-Alfaro, J., Navarro-Arribas, G., Cuppens-Boulahia, N., de Capitani di Vimercati, S. (eds.) DPM 2011 and SETOP 2011. LNCS, vol. 7122, pp. 122–140. Springer, Heidelberg (2012)

2. Harvan, M., Pretschner, A.: State-based usage control enforcement with data flow tracking using system call interposition. In: Proc. Netw. and Sys. Sec. (2009)
3. Kelbert, F., Pretschner, A.: Data usage control enforcement in distributed systems. In: Proc. 3rd ACM CODASPY (2013)
4. Lovat, E., Pretschner, A.: Data-centric multi-layer usage control enforcement: a social network example. In: Proc. 16th SACMAT (2011)
5. Pretschner, A., et al.: Usage control enforcement with data flow tracking for X11. In: Proc. 5th Intl. Worksh. on Sec. and Trust Man. (2009)
6. Rasthofer, S., Arzt, S., Bodden, E.: A machine-learning approach for classifying and categorizing android sources and sinks. In: Proc. NDSS (2014)
7. JOANA. http://joana.ipd.kit.edu
8. Graf, J., Hecker, M., Mohr, M.: Using JOANA for information flow control in java programs - a practical guide. In: Proc. 6th ATPS (2013)
9. Tripp, O., et al.: TAJ: effective taint analysis of web applications. In: Proc. PLDI 2009
10. Ferrante, J., Ottenstein, K.J., Warren, J.D.: The program dependence graph and its use in optimization. ACM Trans. Program. Lang. Syst. (1987)
11. Hammer, C., Snelting, G.: Flow-sensitive, context-sensitive, and object-sensitive information flow control based on program dependence graphs. IJIS (2009)
12. Reps, T., Horwitz, S., Sagiv, M., Rosay, G.: Speeding up slicing. In: FSE (1994)
13. Wasserrab, D., Lohner, D.: Proving information flow noninterference by reusing a machine-checked correctness proof for slicing. In: 6th Int. Verif. Worksh. (2010)
14. Goguen, J., Meseguer, J.: Security policies and security models. In: S & P 1982
15. Giffhorn, D.: Slicing of Concurrent Programs and its Application to Information Flow Control. Ph.D thesis, Karlsruher Institut für Technologie (2012)
16. Sabelfeld, A., Myers, A.C.: Language-based information-flow security. IEEE Journal on Selected Areas in Communications (2003)
17. Giffhorn, D., et al.: A New Algorithm for Low-Deterministic Security. IJIS (2014)
18. Andersen, L.: Program Analysis and Specialization for the C Programming Language. Ph.D thesis, University of Copenhagen (1994)
19. Grove, D., Chambers, C.: A Framework for Call Graph Construction Algorithms. ACM Trans. Program. Lang. Syst. (2001)
20. Shivers, O.: Control flow analysis in scheme. In: Proc. PLDI (1988)
21. Milanova, A., Rountev, A., Ryder, B.G.: Parameterized Object Sensitivity for Points-to Analysis for Java. ACM Trans. Softw. Eng. Methodol. (2005)
22. OW2-ASM instrumentation framework. http://asm.ow2.org/
23. JavaFTP. http://sourceforge.net/projects/javaftp/ (last access: 16 June 2014)
24. Chandra, D., Franz, M.: Fine-grained information flow analysis and enforcement in a java virtual machine. In: ACSAC (2007)
25. Wuchner, T., Pretschner, A.: Data loss prevention based on data-driven usage control. In: IEEE Software Reliability Engineering (ISSRE) (2012)
26. Kemerlis, V., et al.: Libdft: practical dynamic data flow tracking for commodity systems. In: Proc. 8th Conf. on Virtual Execution Environments (2012)
27. Kim, H.C., Keromytis, A.D., Covington, M., Sahita, R.: Capturing information flow with concatenated dynamic taint analysis. In: ARES (2009)
28. Bodden, E., et al.: Taming reflection: aiding static analysis in the presence of reflection and custom class loaders. In: 33rd Int. Conf. on Softw. Eng. (2011)
29. King, D., Hicks, B., Hicks, M.W., Jaeger, T.: Implicit flows: can't live with 'em, can't live without 'em. In: Sekar, R., Pujari, A.K. (eds.) ICISS 2008. LNCS, vol. 5352, pp. 56–70. Springer, Heidelberg (2008)

30. Volpano, D.: Safety versus secrecy. In: Cortesi, A., Filé, G. (eds.) SAS 1999. LNCS, vol. 1694, p. 303. Springer, Heidelberg (1999)
31. Denning, D.E.: A Lattice Model of Secure Information Flow. Comm. ACM (1976)
32. Volpano, D., et al.: A Sound Type System for Secure Flow Analysis. JCS (1996)
33. Denning, D.E., Denning, P.J.: Certification of Programs for Secure Information Flow. Comm. ACM (1977)
34. Banatre, J., Bryce, C., Le Métayer, D.: Compile-Time Detection of Information Flow in Sequential Programs (1994)
35. Enck, W., et al. TaintDroid: an information-flow tracking system for realtime privacy monitoring on smartphones. In: OSDI (2010)
36. Jee, K., et al.: ShadowReplica: efficient parallelization of dynamic data flow tracking. In: Proc. CCS (2013)
37. Yin, H., Song, D., Egele, M., Kruegel, C., Kirda, E.: Panorama: capturing system-wide information flow for malware detection and analysis. In: CCS (2007)
38. Demsky, B.: Cross-application Data Provenance and Policy Enforcement. ACM Trans. Inf. Syst. Secur. (2011)
39. Zhang, Q., et al.: Neon: system support for derived data management. In: SIGPLAN Not. (2010)
40. Rocha, B.P.S., Conti, M., Etalle, S., Crispo, B.: Hybrid Static-Runtime Information Flow and Declassification Enforcement. IEEE Inf. For. and Sec. (2013)
41. Fromm, A., Kelbert, F., Pretschner, A.: Data protection in a cloud-enabled smart grid. In: Cuellar, J. (ed.) SmartGridSec 2012. LNCS, vol. 7823, pp. 96–107. Springer, Heidelberg (2013)
42. Rasthofer, S., Arzt, S., Lovat, E., Bodden, E.: DroidForce: enforcing complex, data-centric. system-wide policies in android. In: Proc. ARES (2014)

ISboxing: An Instruction Substitution Based Data Sandboxing for x86 Untrusted Libraries

Liang Deng$^{(\boxtimes)}$, Qingkai Zeng, and Yao Liu

State Key Laboratory for Novel Software Technology,
Department of Computer Science and Technology, Nanjing University,
Nanjing 210023, China
dengliang1214@smail.nju.edu.cn, zqk@nju.edu.cn

Abstract. Dynamically-linked libraries are widely adopted in application programs to achieve extensibility. However, faults in untrusted libraries could allow an attacker to compromise both integrity and confidentiality of the host system (the main program and trusted libraries), as no protection boundaries are enforced between them. Previous systems address this issue through the technique named data sandboxing that relies on instrumentation to sandbox memory reads and writes in untrusted libraries. However, the instrumentation method causes relatively high overhead due to frequent memory reads in code.

In this paper, we propose an efficient and practical data sandboxing approach (called ISboxing) on contemporary x86 platforms, which sandboxes a memory read/write by directly substituting it with a self-sandboxed and function-equivalent one. Our substitution-based method does not insert any additional instructions into library code and therefore incurs almost no measurable runtime overhead. Our experimental results show that ISboxing incurs only 0.32%/1.54% (average/max) overhead for SPECint2000 and 0.05%/0.24% (average/max) overhead for SFI benchmarks, which indicates a notable performance improvement on prior work.

Keywords: Data sandboxing · Instruction substitution · Untrusted libraries · Instruction prefix

1 Introduction

Applications commonly incorporate with dynamically-linked libraries to achieve extensibility. However, a library, which might be buggy or even come from a malicious source, could be used by attackers to disrupt both integrity and confidentiality of the host system. Even though the host system contains no vulnerabilities, bugs and malicious behaviors in the library can lead to compromise of the entire application since no protection boundaries are enforced.

One major type of protections to address this issue is through software-based fault isolation (SFI) which isolates untrusted libraries from a trusted host system. The original SFI technique named *sandboxing* (including data sandboxing

© IFIP International Federation for Information Processing 2015
H. Federrath and D. Gollmann (Eds.): SEC 2015, IFIP AICT 455, pp. 386–400, 2015.
DOI: 10.1007/978-3-319-18467-8_26

and code sandboxing) was first proposed by Wahbe et al. [1]. Data sandboxing prevents sandboxed libraries from accessing memory outside a designated data region by inserting inline guards before their memory-access instructions (memory writes and memory reads). Thus both integrity and confidentiality of data in the trusted host system are protected. Code sandboxing instruments indirect-jump instructions to restrict the control flows in sandboxed libraries to a designated code region. A carefully designed and validated interface is also required when sandboxed libraries invoke the host system. Additionally, control flow integrity (CFI) [14] is a more restrictive enforcement than code sandboxing, which further guarantees that the control flows must follow a static control flow graph (CFG).

Recent work [9,15] has realized both code sandboxing and CFI with minimal performance overhead, however data sandboxing, despite of its long history(first proposed in 1993 [1]), still suffers from a perception of inefficiency which may hinder practical applications.

For avoiding high overhead, many previous approaches [2,5,10] only sandbox memory writes for integrity, but ignore protecting confidentiality due to the high cost of sandboxing memory reads that appear more frequently in code. However, in security-critical systems (e.g., military or financial systems), confidentiality is of importance as an exploited library would read secrets in the host system. NaCl-x86-32 [3] and Vx32 [4] leverage hardware segmentation to efficiently restrain memory access. However, hardware segmentation is unavailable on contemporary x86-64. As a result, NaCl-x86-64 [5] designed for x86-64 relies on instrumentation to sandbox memory writes only (or both reads and writes with significant performance overhead [12]).

Recent researches [7,8] utilize a series of performance optimizations that remove redundant instrumentation instructions, for the case of protecting both integrity and confidentiality. However, their methods are not so easy to implement correctly. For example, they need considerable efforts, which are complex and error prone, to verify the security of removed checks. Their optimizations also require static analysis (e.g., control flow analysis, register liveness analysis) and compiler-level support, which however are not compatible with existing libraries that are released as pure binaries. Additionally, due to the high frequency of memory reads in code, they incur some overhead even after optimizations, e.g., the reported overhead in Strato [8] is 32%/62%(average/max) for SFI benchmarks, and 17%/45%(average/max) for SPECint2000.

In this paper, we present ISboxing, an approach to sandbox both memory reads and writes in untrusted libraries on contemporary x86-64 platforms. Unlike previous instrumentation-based approaches, ISboxing sandboxes a memory-access instruction by directly substituting it with a *self-sandboxed* and function-equivalent one, which takes advantage of the flexibility offered by the extensive x86 instruction set.

We argue that while recent approaches focus on improving performance, they do not address the issue of practicality and hence are of limited applicability. In addition, their non-trivial overhead may still be an obstacle in some applications.

Instead, ISboxing trades some protection granularity for both practicality and efficiency. We highlight three key features which distinguish ISboxing from prior work:

- **Easy-to-implement.** ISboxing achieves data sandboxing efficiently without complex optimization work. It just needs to identify each memory-access instruction and substitute it, which is easy to implement correctly.
- **Binary-only.** ISboxing is implemented as pure binary transformation requiring no cooperation from source code or debugging symbols, and thus compatible with legacy libraries.
- **Efficient.** ISboxing incurs negligible overhead for sandboxing both memory reads and writes, since the substitution-based method requires no additional instrumentation instructions.

We have implemented ISboxing to sandbox user-space libraries on Windows. The implementation has a clear architecture comprised of a disassembler, a rewriter and a verifier. The disassembler disassembles a given library's binary executable (e.g., a PE file) and identifies memory-access instructions. The rewriter then statically substitutes each memory-access instruction. ISboxing includes a tiny verifier at the end of its workflow to validate the output of the rewriter. In this way, we can remove the disassembler and the rewriter from the TCB.

2   Related Work

SFI. Since SFI was first proposed by Wahbe et al. [1], a main portion of its following work focuses on reducing the runtime overhead of sandboxing especially on popular hardware platforms (e.g., x86). PittSFIeld [2] is the first work that applies SFI to x86 platforms which feature variable-length instructions. NaCl-x86-32 [3] and Vx32 [4] provide efficient data sandboxing relying on x86-32 segmentation. NaCl-x86-64 [5] further adapts SFI to contemporary x86-64 platforms, but it only sandboxes memory writes for performance and requires compiler-level supports. XFI [6] provides a stronger and more comprehensive protection system for executing untrusted code. Besides sandboxing, XFI provides a high-integrity stack protection model for protecting return addresses. The system of Zeng et al. [7], on the other hand, focuses on exploring a more efficient support for data sandboxing by combining CFI and static analysis. Strato [8] explores the building of a re-targetable framework for CFI and data sandboxing on a compiler intermediate representation where many optimizations can be realized without sticking to a certain hardware platform. REINS [9] is the first work that implements SFI through pure binary rewriting with trivial performance overhead, however it actually only implements code sandboxing, without discussing data sandboxing. Additionally, a series of papers [10,11] study how to enforce fine-grained SFI and memory access control. MIP [13] proposes an x86-64 SFI approach similar to ours. However, it still needs to insert additional instructions for data sandboxing, and thus it avoids sandboxing memory reads for performance. Its method also does not address the issue of practicability, e.g., it requires complex compiler-level register liveness analysis to find scratch registers.

CFI. CFI was first introduced by Abadi et al. [14] for enforcing the integrity of a program's CFG constructed by sophisticated pointer analysis. CFI is a generic software methodology, which in theory can be applied to any systems (e.g., smartphones [17,18], and commodity OS kernels [19]). However, the construction of a precise CFG is difficult on pure binaries, and enforcing precise CFG in a program often incurs high performance overhead. For practical applications, researchers have attempted to leverage a relaxed CFI model and apply it to legacy binaries [15,16].

3   Assumptions and Attack Model

As with prior work, we assume the host system and the verifier are correct. We assume code regions and data regions in executables to be separated. The data regions are not executable and the code regions are not writable. This requirement is satisfied due to the wide deployment of W⊕X protection in modern OSes (e.g., DEP in Windows). We assume that the libraries do not self-modify their code or dynamically generate code. This requirement is always satisfied for traditional executables compiled from high-level languages. We assume that the libraries have well defined APIs which specify their parameter types and calling conventions. This is reasonable since it is necessary for the user of a library to understand how to use it. However, source code or debugging information is not required.

Two sources of attacks we consider are libraries designed by malicious authors, and libraries with bugs that could be subverted by attackers. Since untrusted libraries run in the same address space with the host system, when compromised, they would access arbitrary data and execute arbitrary code in memory. Therefore, the data integrity, data confidentiality and control flow integrity of the host system cannot be guaranteed any longer.

4   Instruction Substitution Based Data Sandboxing

4.1   Data Sandboxing Policy

ISboxing divides the address space into a protected domain and a trusted domain. ISboxing runs untrusted libraries in the protected domain to contain faults, while the host system (the main program and trusted libraries) runs in the trusted domain. Hereafter we refer to the libraries running in the protected domain as *sandboxed libraries*. The data sandboxing policy dictates that both memory reads and memory writes in sandboxed libraries must be restricted to a designated continuous data region, so that the integrity and confidentiality of the host system can be guaranteed. Hereafter we refer to this data region as *sandbox region*. In the following, we will detail ISboxing's data sandboxing approach to enforce this policy. For a better understanding, we start with the background.

(a) unsafe memory-read instruction   (b) previous data sandboxing

```
mov  rcx , [rax+0x10]                    push  rflags
    (0x 48 8b 48 10 )                    push  rdx
                                         lea   rdx , [rax+0x10]
                                         and   rdx , $MASK
                                         mov   rcx , [rdx]
(c) ISboxing's data sandboxing           pop   rdx
                                         pop   rflags

mov  rcx , [eax+0x10]
    (0x 67 48 8b 48 10 )
```

Fig. 1. An example to illustrate previous data sandboxing and ISboxing's data sandboxing

4.2 Background: x86 Memory Addressing

We first introduce the memory addressing on x86 platforms [20]. In a memory-access instruction, the address of its memory operand is referenced by means of a segment selector and an offset. In x86-64, segmentation is generally disabled, that is, the effective address of the memory operand is directly the offset. The offset can be specified as a *direct* offset which is a static value encoded in code, or an *indirect* offset through an address computation made up of one or more of the following components: displacement, base register, index register and scale. Rip-relative addressing is also available, which calculates the offset by adding a displacement to the value of current *rip* register. Data sandboxing only needs to sandbox memory-access instructions with indirect offset, because memory-access instructions with direct offset and rip-relative addressing instructions can be statically verified.

Operand Size and Address Size. On x86 platforms, the operand of an instruction has an *operand size* and an *address size* [20]. The operand size selects the size of operand and the address size determines the size of address when the operand accesses memory. In 64-bit mode, the default address size is 64 bits and the default operand size is 32 bits, but defaults can be overridden using instruction prefixes. For example, when an instruction uses the operand-size prefix (0x66) or the REX opcode prefix (0x48), its default operand size (32 bits) will be overwritten to 64 bits. When a memory-access instruction uses the address-size prefix (0x67), its default address size (64 bits) will be overwritten to 32 bits. As a result, it cannot address the memory outside 32 bits. The original motivation of these prefixes is to allow mixed 32/64-bit data and 32/64-bit addresses at instruction granularity.

4.3 Previous Data Sandboxing

In Figure 1(a), we give an example of a memory-access instruction with indirect offset (a memory read) in pseudo assembly syntax. In the example, the instruction loads data from the memory operand (*[rax+0x10]*) to the *rcx* register. The memory operand is referenced by an indirect offset computed from a base register (the *rax* register) and a displacement (*0x10*). We show the x86 binary encoding of the instruction within the parentheses in the figure. We assume this instruction is a memory read in an untrusted library. In the following, we will illustrate how to sandbox it with previous data sandboxing.

For protecting confidentiality, the memory address represented by *[rax+0x10]* should be checked before the memory read. Figure 1(b) presents a sequence of instructions that should be inserted to perform the check. In the sequence, the register *rdx* is used as a scratch register for the check. Since the original value of *rdx* would be needed, the sequence should first save its value on the stack and restore it after the check. The *rflags* register also needs to be saved and restored in case that the *and* instruction would change its value and influence the subsequent computation. In the *and* instruction, the constant *$MASK* denotes the data-region mask that guarantees the memory read is restricted to the sandbox region.

4.4 ISboxing's Data Sandboxing

For comparison, we use the same example to illustrate how ISboxing's data sandboxing works.

Overall Idea. From another perspective, the memory-read instruction (Figure 1(a)) is unsafe because it is an "all-powerful-addressing" instruction whose address size is 64 bits. That is to say, an untrusted library can generate arbitrary value in the *rax* register, and use this instruction to access arbitrary memory in the whole 64-bit address space (the range of $[0,2^{64}]$). This observation inspires us to sandbox the memory-read instruction by changing its address size.

Without inserting any instructions, we only substitute the memory-read instruction. In the new substitute (as shown in Figure 1(c)), we only add the address-size prefix (0x67) which transforms the address size from 64 bits to 32 bits (the upper 32 bits of the address will be zero-extended by the processor). In this way, the new substitute is self-sandboxed by its address-size prefix, as if we implicitly inserted a bitwise *and* instruction whose data-region mask is 0x00000000ffffffff. Therefore, the sandbox region of ISboxing is the range of $[0,2^{32}]$, and using the new substitute to access memory outside the sandbox region becomes impossible.

Most importantly, to guarantee the correctness of the substitution, we must ensure that the new substitute is function-equivalent with the original one. To achieve this, we should ensure that the address of the memory operand is originally within the range of $[0,2^{32}]$ (the sandbox region), so that the new substitute will perform the same computation when ignoring the upper 32 bits. This requires us to relocate all the library's memory to the sandbox region, as detailed in the following sections.

Handling Stack Instructions. In x86, there is one exception that the address size of the stack is always 64 bits when stack instructions (*push, pop, call* and *ret*) are performed to read/write data on the stack. Therefore, an untrusted library may maliciously set the stack pointer (the *rsp* register) to an address outside the sandbox region and use stack instructions to access disallowed memory. In this situation, our data sandboxing relying on address size cannot work.

We address this issue by sandboxing the *rsp* register based on instruction substitution. In x86, the operand size of each instruction determines the number of valid bits in the register (e.g., the *rsp* register): 64-bit operand size generates a 64-bit result in the register, while 32-bit operand size generates a 32-bit result, zero-extended to a 64-bit result in the register [20]. With this, we substitute each instruction modifying *rsp* (hereafter named rsp-modify instruction, e.g., *sub rsp,$0x10*) with an equivalent instruction (*sub esp,$0x10*) whose operand size is changed to 32 bits. The substitution work is easily performed by just removing the REX opcode prefix of the original instruction. Then the new substitute cannot be used to set the *rsp* register to any value outside the sandbox region, because the upper 32 bits of the *rsp* register are always zero-extended by the processor. It seems as if we implicitly inserted a bitwise *and* instruction.

Additionally, in x86, stack instructions (*push*, *pop*, *call* and *ret*) can implicitly modify the *rsp* register. Although they can only increase/decrease the *rsp* register by at most 8 bytes for each time, an attacker would chain a number of stack instructions to manipulate the *rsp* register (e.g., using ROP attacks [24,25]). We prevent this by simply inserting a guard page at the end of the sandbox region. The guard page is mapped as neither readable nor writable in the address space and thus any read/write on it will cause a page fault. Specifically, when an untrusted library uses stack instructions to modify the *rsp* register, the guard page cannot be crossed since the *rsp* register can only be increased by 8 bytes for each time. When the stack pointer reaches the guard page, executing any stack instruction again will cause a page fault and crash the untrusted library.

Constraints and Analysis. Comparing to previous data sandboxing whose sandbox region can be any size and in any position, ISboxing restricts the sandbox region to a fixed size and a fixed position in the address space. However, this is not a problem for sandboxing untrusted libraries in practice. First, the fixed size of ISboxing's sandbox region (4 GB) is large enough to contain quite a few libraries, since the virtual memory consumption of a real-world library is much smaller than 4 GB. In our observation, the virtual memory consumption of even a whole application is usually much smaller than 4 GB. Second, the constraint of the fixed position requires us to relocate libraries' memory to the sandbox region. As discussed in the next section, the memory relocation can be practically realized on libraries' executable binaries without any aids from source code or debug information.

5   Sandboxing Untrusted Libraries

Based on ISboxing's data sandboxing approach above, we further describe how to sandbox untrusted libraries on Windows. The implementation is realized through pure binary transformation on application binaries without any special support from underlying OS.

5.1 Binary Disassembling and Rewriting

We adopt CCFIR's disassembling method [15] which can correctly disassemble an x86 binary without source code or debug information. We take advantage of the fact that ASLR and DEP are widely adopted on Windows, and leverage the relocation information to disassemble binary code recursively and identify all possible instructions. Then we can find and substitute all memory-access instructions and rsp-modify instructions to enforce ISboxing's data sandboxing.

5.2 Memory Relocation

Data sandboxing requires that the memory of sandboxed libraries must reside within the sandbox region and the memory of the host system must reside outside the sandbox region. In this way, sandboxed libraries cannot access the memory of the host system. However, in real-world applications, their memory regions are often overlapped with each other. For example, the libraries and the host system often use the same Window's API *HeapAlloc* to allocate heap memory from the same heap, and their heap memory may be overlapped. In the following, we will detail the memory relocation for sandboxed libraries. The memory relocation for the host system is essentially identical.

Executable Relocation. Due to the ASLR mechanism, a binary executable's load base can be randomized without affecting the execution. To relocate an executable, we simply disable system's ASLR for the executable and modify the *ImageBase* field in the executable's file header which specifies the load base of the executable. In addition, some code and data in the executable should also be adjusted since they are generated based on the original *ImageBase*. Though system's ASLR is disabled, existing practical and more fine-grained randomization techniques [15,26,27] can be added to ISboxing.

Stack Relocation. The host system associates a separate stack with each thread that executes in a sandboxed library. Like XFI [6], our current implementation uses a memory pool from which host-system threads draw stacks when they call the library. The stacks in this pool are all allocated in the sandbox region, and managed by a state array and a single lock. The size of the pool can be adjusted at runtime.

Heap Relocation. On Windows, applications invoke Windows APIs to allocate heap memory from the heap provided by system. The address of the heap memory is determined by system heap manager and is transparent to applications. For heap relocation, ISboxing realizes another heap manager (named ISboxing heap manager) to satisfy heap allocations for both sandboxed libraries and the host system. In our current implementation, ISboxing heap manager is a simplified version of Glibc's heap manager. It wholesales large memory chunks from the sandbox region using Windows API *VirtualAllocEx* and provides small memory blocks for sandboxed libraries. In this way, sandboxed libraries' heap memory will always reside within the sandbox region.

File Mapping Relocation. File mapping is the association of a file's contents with a portion of the virtual memory (file-mapping memory). Fortunately, unlike heap memory, applications can use Windows API (*MapViewOfFileEx*) to specify the base address of file-mapping memory. This facilitates the realization of our file mapping relocation. ISboxing reserves a range of virtual memory in the sandbox region dedicated to file mapping for sandboxed libraries, and redirects libraries' file mapping requests to the API *MapViewOfFileEx*.

5.3   CFI Enforcement

Instead of code sandboxing, we leverage CFI, which is a more restrictive enforcement, to sandbox the control flows of untrusted libraries. The CFI enforcement, which guarantees a single stream of intended instructions, also ensures that ISboxing's data sandboxing cannot be bypassed. While CFI enforcement technique has been practically realized in CCFIR [15] with low performance overhead, we adopt CCFIR's method but use a simplified 1-ID CFI protection model. However, the code sandboxing approach discussed in REINS [9] can also be used as an alternative.

As with CCFIR, we introduce a code section called Springboard. For each legal indirect target in library code, the Springboard has an associated stub containing a *direct* jump to it. Then, we instrument each indirect jump in the library to make sure that any indirect control flow will first jump to the Springboard and then use its stubs (containing direct jumps) to complete the control flow transition. Since the Springboard only contains direct jumps whose targets are legal, the CFI is ensured. In addition, a restrictive and validated host-system interface is enforced when the libraries invoke the host system. The interface only allows three kinds of control flows (which can also be specified and validated by host-system policies): 1) Imported function calls whose targets are referenced by sandboxed libraries' import address table (IAT). 2) Function calls whose targets are resolved at runtime by special API, e.g., *GetProcAddress*. 3) Returns to the host system. The details of how to protect these control flows are well discussed in CCFIR's Section IV-D.

The CFI enforcement also inherits the deficiencies of CCFIR. For example, the relaxed CFI enforcement was shown to be broken in face of new control-flow attacks [21–23]. Nevertheless, it is enough to sandbox untrusted libraries' control flows, and is more restrictive than the code sandboxing approach in previous SFI work.

6   Implementation

In our implementation, we have developed three major tools (a disassembler, a rewriter and a verifier) to transform library binaries (PE executables) for enforcing all ISboxing's protection on them. The implementation of the disassembler is similar to CCFIR and will not be repeated. The rewriter, whose input is the output of the disassembler, mainly performs the following work. First, the rewriter rewrites each memory-access instruction by adding the address-size prefix and each rsp-modify instruction by removing the REX opcode prefix. Second, it instruments each indirect jump and creates the Springboard section for CFI enforcement. Third, it modifies executable's file headers, relocation information and redirects heap allocation APIs to realize memory relocation. A library only needs to be rewritten once, and the rewritten binary can be shared by different applications for code reuse. In our current implementation, the rewriter takes about 3.5k LOC.

We provide a separate verifier to validate the correctness of ISboxing's protection. First, the verifier identifies all possible instructions in the rewritten binary. This is realized by scanning instructions one by one started from all indirect jump targets (in Springboard section), export table entries and the EntryPoint of the binary. For instructions not identified in this way, the CFI enforcement guarantees that they will never be executed in the runtime, because no control flows are allowed to be transferred to them. Then, for each possible instruction, the verifier checks if it conforms to the following rules: 1) If it is an indirect jump, it has been checked and redirected to the Springboard section. 2) If it is a memory-access instruction with indirect offset, its address size has been changed to 32 bits. 3) If it is an rsp-modify instruction, its operand size has been changed to 32 bits. 4) Memory-access instructions with direct offset, direct jumps and rip-relative addressing instructions are also statically validated since the code may come from a malicious source. In our current implementation, the verifier is self-contained and takes about 2.5k LOC, most of which are interpretation for x86 opcode decoding.

We have also developed a tool to transform host-system binaries (the main program and libraries) so that their memory will reside outside the sandbox region in the runtime. The tool also identifies host system's calls to the sandboxed libraries and adds a communication runtime for wrapping them (e.g., by identifying and wrapping imported function pointers and dynamically resolved function pointers). The communication runtime, which runs as a DLL in the host system, completes tasks such as copying arguments and results, switching stack and enforcing host system's policies, before transferring to the sandboxed libraries. In addition, the ISboxing heap manager used for heap relocation is developed as a dynamic library (a DLL in the host system) that satisfies heap allocations for both sandboxed libraries and the host system.

We have successfully applied ISboxing's implementation to SPECint2000, SFI benchmarks and some third-party libraries (e.g., JPEG decoder, 7-ZIP, plugins in Google Chrome), all of which are pure binaries (EXEs or DLLs) on Windows. It is worth noting that all the work is performed offline and does not influence the runtime performance.

Table 1. ISboxing's runtime overhead on SPECint2000

	CFI	RELOC	RELOC+DS	CFI+RELOC+DS
gzip	2.41%	-0.37%	0.72%	3.78%
vpr	0.01%	-0.33%	0.43%	0.33%
gcc	6.12%	-1.55%	-1.83%	5.01%
mcf	0.64%	-0.55%	-0.57%	0.01%
crafty	0.88%	-0.08%	0.12%	0.88%
parser	8.55%	-0.17%	0.14%	7.81%
eon	3.89%	-1.18%	-1.01%	3.14%
perlbmk	9.76%	-2.81%	-2.28%	7.27%
gap	4.81%	0.11%	0.00%	4.87%
vortex	5.72%	-1.70%	-1.23%	5.23%
bzip2	2.31%	-0.59%	0.95%	1.89%
twolf	0.04%	-2.49%	-3.33%	-2.85%
avg	3.76%	-0.98%	-0.66%	3.11%

Table 2. ISboxing's runtime overhead on SFI benchmarks

	CFI	RELOC	RELOC+DS	CFI+RELOC+DS
md5	0.69%	0.01%	-0.08%	0.81%
lld	0.95%	-0.21%	-0.21%	0.57%
hotlist	2.79%	-0.05%	0.19%	3.01%
avg	1.48%	-0.08%	-0.03%	1.46%

7   Evaluation

7.1   Performance Evaluation

To evaluate our implementation, we conducted experiments on a Dell Optiplex 9010 computer configured with an Intel i7-3770 (4 cores) 3.40 GHz processor, 8 GB RAM, an Intel 82579LM Gigabit Ethernet card and a Windows 7 64-bit system. We measured the execution-time overhead of sandboxing a wide range of benchmark binaries on Windows, including SPECint2000 and SFI benchmarks. SFI benchmarks contain three programs (hotlist, lld and md5) which have been widely used by previous SFI work for evaluation [8]. We treat each benchmark as if it were an untrusted library. All experiments were averaged over five runs.

Table 1 presents the execution-time percentage increases of SPECint2000, compared to the unmodified version. The standard deviation is less than 0.8 percent. The *CFI* column shows the results of CFI enforcement. CFI enforcement is necessary for data sandboxing because it ensures a single stream of intended instructions. We are pleased to see that, with CCFIR's method, the overhead (average/max) is only is 3.76%/9.76% for x86-64 binaries. The *RELOC* column reports the overhead of the memory relocation discussed in Section 5.2. As we see, ISboxing gains some performance improvement. Through analysis, this is because ISboxing uses a simplified heap manager for memory relocation in our current implementation. ISboxing's users are free to choose other heap managers

Table 3. Code-size increase on SPECint2000

	gzip	vpr	gcc	mcf	crafty	parser	eon	perlbmk	gap	vortex	bzip2	twolf	avg
increase (%)	5.8%	6.3%	6.5%	5.8%	6.2%	6.2%	7.1%	7.2%	7.7%	7.8%	5.6%	7.6%	6.7%

either for high performance [28] or for high level of security [29]. This performance difference can be mostly eliminated if they use a heap manager similar to Window's. The *RELOC+DS* column gives the results when both memory relocation and data sandboxing(for both memory reads and writes) are enabled, yet CFI enforcement is disabled at this time. As shown in the table, if we ignore the performance improvement of memory relocation(*RELOC+DS* minus *RELOC*), the pure data sandboxing overhead in ISboxing is only **0.32%/1.54%(average/max)** on SPECint2000. This overhead is unsurprising as ISboxing does not insert any additional instructions into the benchmarks to achieve data sandboxing. The *CFI+RELOC+DS* column shows the overhead when all ISboxing's protections are enabled.

Table 2 presents the results of SFI benchmarks. The standard deviation is less than 0.6 percent. The results show that the pure data sandboxing overhead is **0.05%/0.24%(average/max)** for SFI benchmarks.

Performance Comparison with Related Systems. We next compare ISboxing with the system of Zeng et al. [7] and Strato [8], which sandbox memory writes as well as reads with a number of optimizations to reduce runtime overhead. The pure data sandboxing overhead reported in Strato is as large as 17%/45%(average/max) for x86-64 SPECint2000 and 32%/62%(average/max) for SFI benchmarks (without adding CFI and memory relocation overhead). In Zeng et al.'s system, the pure data sandboxing overhead is 19%/42%(average/max) for x86-32 SPECint2000. It does not provide the results for x86-64, and thus the comparison is preliminary. Although other systems [2–5,13] incur low overhead, they either ignore sandboxing memory read or use hardware segmentation not available on contemporary x86 platforms.

7.2 Code-Size Increase

As a side benefit, ISboxing requires very small code-size increase to realize data sandboxing, since no additional instrumentation instructions are added to code. Table 3 presents the text-section size increase comparing to unmodified version for SPECint2000. On average, the text section grows only 6.7% for data sandboxing when CFI is not equipped.

8 Discussion

ISboxing trades some protection granularity for both efficiency and practicability. It only provides a single sandbox (the protected domain) running all untrusted libraries isolated from the host system, but cannot further provide multiple sandboxes. Thus it cannot deal with inter-module data accesses between untrusted libraries. Nevertheless, we believe ISboxing has a wide range of applications such as isolating untrusted third-party libraries or browser plugins from the host system (trusted libraries and the main program), especially when source code is unavailable and confidentiality is of importance.

In addition, an alternative method is to sandbox only memory reads (performance critical) in a single sandbox with ISboxing, while further sandboxing memory writes (less performance critical) in multiple sandboxes using previous instrumentation methods. In this way, we can achieve a better tradeoff between performance and granularity. In real world, security secrets (e.g., secret keys) often reside in the host system, thus a single sandbox for memory reads is enough to protect their confidentiality. If a library contains security secrets, we can choose to run it in the host system.

9 Conclusion

In this paper, we present an instruction substitution based data sandboxing, which is quite different from previous instrumentation based approaches. Unlike pure software approaches, we explore how an x86 feature (instruction prefix) can help build an efficient, practical and validated data sandboxing on contemporary x86-64 platforms. We apply our approach to practically sandboxing untrusted libraries on Windows, and perform a set of experiments to demonstrate the effectiveness and efficiency.

Acknowledgments. This work has been partly supported by National NSF of China under Grant No. 61170070, 61431008, 61321491; National Key Technology R&D Program of China under Grant No. 2012BAK26B01.

References

1. Wahbe, R., Lucco, S., Anderson, T., Guaham, S.: Efficient software-based fault isolation. In: ACM Symposium on Operating Systems Principles (1993)
2. McCamant, S., Morrisett, G.: Evaluating SFI for a CISC architecture. In: USENIX Security Symposium (2006)
3. Yee, B., Sehr, D., Dardyk, G., Chen, J., Muth, R., Orm, T., Okasaka, S., Narula, N., Fullagar, N.: Native client: a sandbox for portable, untrusted x86 native code. In: IEEE Symposium on Security and Privacy (2009)
4. Ford, B., Cox, R.: Vx32: lightweight user-level sandboxing on the x86. In: USENIX Annual Technical Conference (2008)
5. Sehr, D., Muth, R., Biffle, C., Khimenko, V., Pasko, E., Schimpf, K., Yee, B., Chen, B.: Adapting software fault isolation to contemporary CPU architectures. In: Usenix Security Symposium (2010)
6. Erlingsson, U., Abadi, M., Vrable, M., Budiu, M., Necula, G.: XFI: Software guards for system address spaces. In: Symposium on Operating Systems Design and Implementation (2006)

7. Zeng, B., Tan, G., Morrisett, G.: Combining control flow integrity and static analysis for efficient and validated data sandboxing. In: ACM Conference on Computer and Communications Security (2011)
8. Zeng, B., Tan, G., Erlingsson, U.: Strato: a retargetable framework for low-level inlined-reference monitors. In: USENIX Security Symposium (2013)
9. Wartell, R., Mohan, V., Hamlen, K., Lin, Z.: Securing untrusted code via compiler-agnostic binary rewriting. In: 28th Annual Computer Security Applications Conference (2012)
10. Castro, M., Costa, M., Martin, J., Peinado, M., Akritidis, P., Donnelly, A., Barham, P., Black, R.: Fast byte-granularity software fault isolation. In: ACM Symposium on Operating Systems Principles (2009)
11. Akritidis, P., Costa, M., Castro, M., Hand, S.: Baggy bounds checking: an efficient and backwards-compatible defense against out-of-bounds errors. In: Usenix Security Symposium (2009)
12. Ansel, J., Marchenko, P., Erlingsson, U., Taylor, E., Chen, B., Schuff, D., Sehr, D., Biffle, C., Yee, B.: Language-independent sandboxing of just-in-time compilation and self-modifying code. In: ACM SIGPLAN Conference on Programming Language Design and Implementation (2011)
13. Niu, B., Tan, G.: Monitor integrity protection with space efficiency and separate compilation. In: ACM Conference on Computer and Communications Security (2013)
14. Abadi, M., Budiu, M., Erlingsson, U., Ligatti, J.: Control flow integrity. In: ACM Conference on Computer and Communications Security (2005)
15. Zhang, C., Wei, T., Chen, Z., Duan, L., Szekeres, L., McCamant, L., Song, D., Zou, W.: Practical control flow integrity & randomization for binary executables. In: IEEE Symposium on Security and Privacy (2013)
16. Zhang, M., Sekar, R.: Control flow integrity for cots binaries. In: USENIX Security Symposium (2013)
17. Davi, L., Dmitrienko, A., Egele, M., Fischer, T., Holz, T., Hund, R., Nurnberger, S., Sadeghi, A.: MoCFI: a framework to mitigate control-flow attacks on smartphones. In: Annual Network and Distributed System Security Symposium (2012)
18. Pewny, J., Holz, T.: Control-flow restrictor: compiler-based CFI for iOS. In: Annual Computer Security Applications Conference (2013)
19. Criswell, J., Dautenhahn, N., Adve, V.: KCoFI: complete control-flow integrity for commodity operating system kernels. In: IEEE Symposium on Security and Privacy (2014)
20. Intel Corporation: Intel 64 and IA-32 architectures software developer's manual volume 1: Basic architecture (2013)
21. Davi, L., Sadeghi, A., Lehmann, D., Monrose, F.: Stitching the gadgets: on the ineffectiveness of coarse-grained control-flow integrity protection. In: USENIX Security Symposium (2014)
22. Goktas, E., Athanasopoulos, E., Bos, H., Portokalidis, G.: Out of control: overcoming control-flow integrity. In: IEEE Symposium on Security and Privacy (2014)
23. Carlini, N., Wagner, D.: Rop is still dangerous: breaking modern defenses. In: USENIX Security Symposium (2014)
24. Shacham, H.: The geometry of ennocent flesh on the bone: return-into-libc without function calls (on the x86). In: ACM Conference on Computer and Communications Security (2007)
25. Checkoway, S., Davi, L., Dmitrienko, A., Sadeghi, A., Shacham, H., Winandy, M.: Return-oriented programming without returns. In: ACM Conference on Computer and Communications Security (2010)

26. Wartell, R., Mohan, V., Hamlen, K., Lin, Z.: Binary stirring: self-randomizing instruction addresses of legacy x86 binary code. In: ACM Conference on Computer and Communications Security (2012)
27. Hiser, J., Nguyen-Tuong, A., Co, M., Hall, M., Davidson, J.: ILR: whered my gadgets go? In: IEEE Symposium on Security and Privacy (2012)
28. Berger, E., Zorn, B., McKinley, K.: Composing high performance memory allocators. In: ACM SIGPLAN Conference on Programming Language Design and Implementation (2001)
29. Novark, G., Berger, E.: DieHarder: securing the heap. In: ACM Conference on Computer and Communications Security (2010)

Exploit Generation for Information Flow Leaks in Object-Oriented Programs

Quoc Huy Do$^{(\boxtimes)}$, Richard Bubel, and Reiner Hähnle

Department of Computer Science, TU Darmstadt, Darmstadt, Germany
{do,bubel,haehnle}@cs.tu-darmstadt.de

Abstract. We present a method to generate automatically exploits for information flow leaks in object-oriented programs. Our approach combines self-composition and symbolic execution to compose an *insecurity formula* for a given information flow policy and a specification of the security level of the program locations. The insecurity formula gives then rise to a model which is used to generate input data for the exploit.

A prototype tool called KEG implementing the described approach for Java programs has been developed, which generates exploits as executable JUnit tests.

Keywords: Test generation · Symbolic execution · Information flow

1 Introduction

Analyzing programs to ensure that they do not leak secrets is necessary to improve confidence in the ability of a system to not put the security and privacy of its users at stake.

Information flow analysis is concerned with one aspect of this task, namely, to ensure that an outside agent with well-defined properties cannot learn secrets by observing (and initiating) several runs of a program. The nature of the secrets to be protected is specified by an information flow policy. The strongest one is non-interference, which does not allow the attacker to learn *any* kind of information about the secret. This is often too strong, e.g., an authentication program leaks the information whether an entered password is correct, hence, other policies like declassification (see [22] for a survey) exist that allow to specify what kind of information may be released.

Several approaches to analyze programs for secure information flow relative to a given information flow policy exist. Many of these are either type-based [4,15,18,21,26] or logic-based [6,11,23]. In this paper we use a logic-based approach with self-composition (first introduced in [10]; the name self-composition was coined in [6]), but our focus is not to verify that a program has secure information flow; instead we approach the problem from a bug finding point of view.

The work has been funded by the DFG priority program 1496 "Reliably Secure Software Systems".

© IFIP International Federation for Information Processing 2015
H. Federrath and D. Gollmann (Eds.): SEC 2015, IFIP AICT 455, pp. 401–415, 2015.
DOI: 10.1007/978-3-319-18467-8_27

For a given program we try to automatically generate exploits that demonstrate unintended information flows. Exploits are small programs that run the program of interest multiple times and report whether they could observe a leak. The generated exploits are well-structured and support the developer in identifying the origin of the leak and in understanding its nature.

To generate exploits we build on work from test generation [12,16] with symbolic execution. Our implementation outputs the found exploits as JUnit tests such that the test fails if the program is insecure. The exploits can thus easily be added to a regression test suite.

The paper is structured as follows: Sect. 2 introduces basic notions and techniques. Sect. 3 explains the logic formalization of insecurity for noninterference and delimited information release. In Sect. 4 we discuss the analysis of programs containing loops and method invocations. Sect. 5 presents our tool KEG and demonstrates the viability with case studies. We compare our work with others in Sect. 6 and conclude with Sect. 7.

2   Background

2.1   Information Flow Policies

To analyze that a program does not leak confidential information, we need to define the security level of the program locations (program variables and fields) as well as an *information flow policy* which defines whether and what kind of information may flow between program locations of a different security level.

In this subsection we recapture the definitions of two well-known information flow policies which are supported by our approach.

Noninterference. Noninterference [9,26] is the strongest possible information flow policy. It prohibits *any* information flow from program locations containing confidential information (high variables) to publicly observable program locations (low variables); the opposite direction is allowed. As we consider only deterministic programs, noninterference can be easily formalized by comparing two program runs:

A program has secure information flow with respect to noninterference, if any two executions of the program starting in initial states with identical values of the low variables, also end in final states which coincide on the values of the low variables.

Let p denote a program and *Var* the set of all program variables of p.

Definition 1 (Program State). *A program state σ maps each program variable $v \in Var$ of type T to a value of its concrete domain D^T, i.e.,*

$$\sigma : Var \to D$$

with $\sigma(v : T) \in D^T$ and D being the union of all concrete domains. The set of all states for a given program p is denoted as $States_p$.

We define coincidence of program states w.r.t. a set of program variables:

Definition 2 (State Coincidence). *Given a set of program variables V and two states $\sigma^1, \sigma^2 \in States_p$. We write $\sigma^1 \simeq_V \sigma^2$ iff. σ^1 and σ^2 coincide on V, i.e., $\sigma^1(v) = \sigma^2(v)$ for all $v \in V$.*

A *concrete execution trace* τ of a program p is a possibly infinite sequence of program states $\tau = \sigma_0\sigma_1 \ldots$ produced by starting p in state σ_0. In this paper, we are only concerned with terminating programs, and consequently, all of our execution traces are finite. Thus, we represent a concrete execution X of a program p as tuple $\langle \sigma^X, \sigma^X_{out} \rangle$, where $\sigma^X \in States_p$ is the initial program state and $\sigma^X_{out} \in States_p$ is the final program state. The set of all possible concrete executions of p is denoted as Exc_p.

We can now define the noninterference property as follows:

Definition 3 (Noninterference). *Given a noninterference policy $NI = (L, H)$ where $L \ \dot\cup \ H = Var$ s.t. L contains the low variables and H the high variables.*

A program p has secure information flow with respect to NI iff. for all concrete executions $X, Y \in Exc_p$ it holds that if $\sigma^X \simeq_L \sigma^Y$ then $\sigma^X_{out} \simeq_L \sigma^Y_{out}$.

Declassification. For many practical cases noninterference is too strict. E.g., a login program leaks usually the information whether an entered password is correct; or a database may be queried for aggregated information like the average salary of the employees, but not for the income of an individual employee.

Declassification is a class of information flow policies which allows to express that some confidential information may be leaked under specific conditions. The paper [22] provides an extensive survey of declassification approaches.

In this paper we focus on *delimited information release* as introduced in [21]. Delimited information release is a declassification policy which allows to specify what kind of information may be released. To this end so called *escape hatch* expressions are specified in addition to the security level of the program locations. For instance, the escape hatch $\frac{\sum_{e \in Employees} salary(e)}{|Employees|}$ can be used to declassify the average of the income of all employees. The formal definition of delimited information release is similar to Def. 3:

Definition 4 (Delimited Information Release). *Given a delimited information release policy $Decl = (L, H, E)$ with L, H as before and E denoting a set of escape hatch expressions.*

A program p has secure information flow with respect to $Decl$ iff. for all concrete executions $X, Y \in Exc_p$ it holds that if $\sigma^X \simeq_L \sigma^Y$ and for all $e \in E : [\![e]\!]_{\sigma^X} = [\![e]\!]_{\sigma^Y}$ then $\sigma^X_{out} \simeq_L \sigma^Y_{out}$. The expression $[\![e]\!]_\sigma$ denotes the semantic evaluation of e in state σ.

2.2 Logic-Based Information Flow Analysis

Symbolic Execution. Symbolic Execution [16] is a versatile technique used for various static program analyses. Symbolic execution of a program means to run

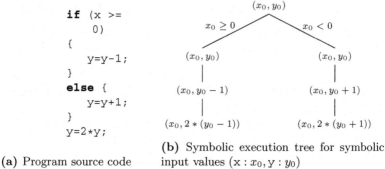

```
if (x >=
    0)
{
    y=y-1;
}
else {
    y=y+1;
}
y=2*y;
```

(a) Program source code

(b) Symbolic execution tree for symbolic input values $(x : x_0, y : y_0)$

Fig. 1. Program and its symbolic execution tree

it with symbolic input values instead of concrete ones. Such a run results in a tree of symbolic execution traces, which covers all possible concrete executions.

Each node in a symbolic execution tree is annotated by its symbolic state. In the example shown in Fig. 1b, the root node is a branching node whose outgoing edges are annotated by their branch conditions. Here the symbolic execution splits into two branches: the left one for the case where the symbolic value x_0 is non-negative and the right one for a negative x_0. Both branches might be possible as we do not have any further information about the value of x_0. The path condition pc_i of a path sp_i is the conjunction of all its branch conditions and characterizes the symbolic execution path uniquely. As long as the program does not contain loops or method invocations, a path condition is a quantifier-free formula in first order logic.

From the above tree we can extract that in case of a non-negative input value for x, the program terminates in a final state in which the final value of x remains unchanged (i.e., x_0) while the final value of y is $2(y_0 - 1)$.

We fix the following notations as convention: Given a path i we refer to its path condition by pc_i and to the final value of a program variable $v \in Var$ by f_i^v. If we want to make explicit that the final value of a program variable v depends on the symbolic input value of a program variable u we pass it as an argument to f_i^v. For instance, $f_0^y(x_0, y_0) := 2(y_0 - 1)$ in case of the final value of y on the left branch.

In case of unbounded loops or unbounded recursive method calls a symbolic execution tree is no longer finite. We overcome this obstacle and achieve a finite representation by making use of specifications as proposed in [14]. This approach uses loop invariants and method contracts to describe the effect of loops and method calls. The basic idea is that loop invariants and method contracts contribute to path conditions and to the representation of the symbolic state. The approach has been implemented as a symbolic execution engine based on the verification system KeY [8], which we use as backend for the exploit generation presented in this paper.

Self-composition. Our exploit generation approach is derived from a logic-based formalization of noninterference using self-composition as introduced in [10,11], based on a direct semantic encoding of noninterference in a program logic. The Hoare triple $\{Pre\}$ p $\{Post\}$ is valid iff. the program p started in any initial state that satisfies formula *Pre* terminates, then formula *Post* must hold in the reached final state. The semantic definition of noninterference as given in Definition 3 requires the comparison of two program runs. The authors of [11] achieve this by copying the analyzed program and replacing all variables with fresh ones, such that the original and the copied program version do not share any memory. In more detail, let p(l,h) be the original program with $l \in L, h \in H$ being the only program variables occurring in program p. Further, let p(l′,h′) represent the copied program constructed from p by renaming variable l to l' and h to h'. Then

$$\{l \doteq l'\}\text{p(l,h); p(l',h')}\{l \doteq l'\}$$

is a direct formalization of noninterference. A major drawback of the formalization is that it requires program p to be analyzed twice. Several refinements have been presented since then to avoid the repeated program execution [5,24]. We make use of an approach based on symbolic execution. The fundamental idea is to execute the program symbolically only once and then to use the path conditions and symbolic states to construct a single first-order formula with the same meaning as the Hoare Triple. To express the noninterference property, we simply copy path conditions and symbolic values, replacing the symbolic input values with fresh copies.

3   Exploit Generation for Insecure Programs

3.1   Logic Characterization of Insecurity

Our objective is to generate an exploit for a given program p which demonstrates that p is insecure with respect to a specified information flow policy. The basic idea is that the exploit runs p twice and throws an exception if an unintended information flow is detected. The problem that needs to be solved is how to find the initial states for both runs such that an information leak can be observed.

To this end we construct a first-order formula which is satisfiable, if the program is insecure. The formula is constructed in such a way that any satisfying model can be directly used to construct the required initial states.

For noninterference, as defined in Def. 3, that formula is constructed as follows: Let $NI = (L, H)$ denote the noninterference policy with low variables L and high variables H. Each path sp_i $(i \in \{0, \dots, n-1\})$ in the symbolic execution tree of p is uniquely characterized by its path condition $pc_i(L, H)$.

To represent two independent program runs, we create a copy of all program variables $Var' = \{v' \mid v \in Var\}$ and obtain the sets L' and H' as copies of L and H, i.e., $L' = \{l' \mid l \in L\}$ (analogously H'). Intuitively, the first run is performed using Var, while the second one uses the copy Var'. Both runs are independent as they do not share any common memory. Then the *NI-insecurity formula*

$$\bigvee_{0\leq i\leq j<n} ((\bigwedge_{l\in L, l'\in L'} l \doteq l') \wedge pc_i(L,H) \wedge pc_j(L',H') \wedge \bigvee_{l\in L} f_i^l(L,H) \neq f_j^l(L',H')) \quad (1)$$

is satisfied iff. there is a model (i.e., state) σ assigning values to the program variables L, L', H, H' such that there exist two paths i, j ($i = j$ possible) with identical low level input, consistent path conditions (i.e., both paths can actually be taken), but for which the final value of at least one low level variable differs. In other words, the model σ assigns concrete values to L, L', H and H' such that p produces different low level output for two runs from initial states with identical low level input. (Formula (1) can be made more succinct by replacing L' with L and omitting the first conjunct, which states $L \doteq L'$.)

Example 1. The insecurity formula (1) for the example program from Fig. 1 and the NI policy $L = \{y\}, H = \{x\}$ becomes

$$x_0 \geq 0 \wedge x_0' \geq 0 \wedge 2(y_0 - 1) \neq 2(y_0 - 1)$$
$$\vee\ x_0 \geq 0 \wedge x_0' < 0 \wedge 2(y_0 - 1) \neq 2(y_0 + 1)$$
$$\vee\ x_0 < 0 \wedge x_0' < 0 \wedge 2(y_0 + 1) \neq 2(y_0 + 1)$$

It is easy to see that the first and third disjunct are unsatisfiable, but the second disjunct is satisfiable, e.g., for the model $x_0 \mapsto 0, x_0' \mapsto -1, y_0 \mapsto 1$.

The NI-insecurity formula (1) can be rewritten into the equivalent formula

$$\bigvee_{l\in L} \bigvee_{0\leq i\leq j<n} \overbrace{((\bigwedge_{v\in L, v'\in L'} v \doteq v') \wedge pc_i(L,H) \wedge pc_j(L',H') \wedge}^{Leak(H,L,l,i,j)}$$

$$f_i^l(L,H) \neq f_j^l(L',H')) \quad (2)$$

which helps us later to incorporate declassification. The formula $Leak(H, L, l, i, j)$ allows to ascribe leaks to a specific target, i.e., it is satisfiable, if some information is leaked from the program variables in H to variable l.

3.2   Target Conditional Delimited Release

We extend the insecurity formula for noninterference (2) to delimited information release (DIR) [21]. In addition to the standard version of DIR, our policy describes not only what information might be released by using escape hatches, but it also allows to express under which condition and to whom (target) the information might be leaked.

Definition 5 (Target Conditional Delimited Release). *Given a program p with Var being the set of all variables occurring in p and a noninterference policy $NI = (L, H)$. A Target Conditional Delimited Release (TCD) policy $(\mathcal{D}, NI)$ is a set of TCD specification triples where each triple $(e, C, T) \in \mathcal{D}$ consists of*

- *an escape hatch expression (i.e., first order term) e over Var,*
- *a declassification condition formula C over Var and*
- *$T \subseteq L$, a set of program variables to which the specified escape hatch is allowed to be leaked.*

A program satisfies a given TCD policy $(\mathcal{D}, NI)$ if there is no information flow from H to L, except for the cases covered by a triple $(e, C, T) \in \mathcal{D}$ which allows the program to release the information captured by the escape hatch expression e to a location in T, if condition C is satisfied in the initial state of a program run.

Given a TCD policy $(\mathcal{D}, NI)$ and a program p. We give the insecurity formula for the case that $\mathcal{D} = \{(e, C, T)\}$ consists of a single TCD specification triple:

$$\bigvee_{l \in L} \left(Leak(H, L, l, i, j) \wedge ((l \in T \wedge C(Var) \wedge C(Var')) \rightarrow e(Var) = e(Var')) \right) \quad (3)$$

The formula coincides for locations $l \in L$ that are not allowed release targets (i.e., $l \notin T$) with the noninterference insecurity formula. Otherwise, the new second conjunct adds

$$C(Var) \wedge C(Var') \rightarrow e(Var) = e(Var')$$

as an additional restriction to the initial states for both runs, namely, that if both initial states satisfy the declassification condition C then they must also coincide on the value of the escape hatch expression. The rationale is that if there are two runs s.t. their respective initial state coincides on the low level input and on the escape hatches and if the final value for an allowed target differs, then more information than just the escape hatch must have been released.

The generalization of the above formula to more than one triple is straightforward and omitted for space reasons.

4   Exploit Generation Using Program Specifications

In this section we discuss how to use program specifications like loop invariants and method contracts to analyze and generate exploits for programs involving unbounded loops or recursive method calls. These specifications need to be user-provided at the moment, but work on automatic generation of specifications is ongoing. We focus on the noninterference analysis case, the extension to declassification is straightforward.

4.1   Loop Specification

The path conditions *pc* for a program p are computed by symbolic execution of p. The problem to solve is how to symbolically execute a loop. In case a fixed bound is known a priori the loop can simply be unwound, but this is impractical if the bound is large and not possible at all for unbounded loops.

In program verification, loops are handled by providing a loop specification. A loop specification $LS = (I, mod)$ consists of a loop invariant formula I and a set of program variables mod which contains all program variables the loop is allowed to modify. In [14] it is shown how to use such a specification for symbolic execution and we can simply reuse that option in our setting.

In the following we describe briefly how a loop specification is reflected in the NI- insecurity formula. Let b be the loop guard and $LS = (I, mod)$ the loop specification. The basic idea in [14] is that the loop specification describes the state after exiting the loop. This means, we can treat the loop as a black-box and continue execution after the loop in a state for which the variables mod that might have been modified by the loop are set to an unknown value. Unknown values are represented by the set of fresh symbolic variables V_{mod}. The only knowledge about the values of these variables is provided by the loop invariant and by the fact the loop guard b must be false (as we exited the loop).

Our insecurity formulas are always expressed as a constraint over the initial state. For instance, the final value f_i^l of variable l is given in terms of the initial symbolic values of the program variables. The same holds for the path conditions. We make this implicit weakest precondition computation here explicit for the loop guard and the invariant, i.e., I^{wp} is the weakest precondition of I computed in the state directly after the loop (similar for the loop guard).

For the sake of simplicity, we only show how to adapt $Leak(H, L, l, i, j)$ for the case that both paths i, j contain the same loop:

$$Leak(H, L, l, i, j) \equiv (\bigwedge_{v \in L} v = v') \wedge pc_i(V_S) \wedge pc_j(V_S')$$

$$\wedge (I^{wp}(V_S) \wedge \neg b^{wp}(V_S)) \wedge (I^{wp}(V_S') \wedge \neg b^{wp}(V_S')) \wedge f_i^l(V_S) \neq f_j^l(V_S') \quad (4)$$

where $b^{wp}(V_S)$ is the symbolic value of the guard after the loop, $V_S = Var \cup V_{mod}$. If one or both of paths i, j do not contain this loop, or have other loops, corresponding conjuncts are omitted or added accordingly.

Example 2. We illustrate formula (4). Consider the loop below with low variable l and high variable h. The loop specification is given as $(I : l \geq 0, mod : \{l\})$

```
1 l = h * h;
2 while (l > 0) { l = l - 1; }
3 l = l + h;
```

Let l_{mod}, l'_{mod} be the fresh values representing the value of l directly after the loop. Computing the weakest precondition of the invariant gives us $l_{mod} \geq 0$ and for the guard $l_{mod} > 0$ for the first run (analog for the second run). The resulting formula is:

$$l = l' \wedge (l_{mod} \geq 0 \wedge \neg(l_{mod} > 0)) \wedge (l'_{mod} \geq 0 \wedge \neg(l'_{mod} > 0)) \wedge l_{mod} + h \neq l'_{mod} + h'$$

The formula is satisfiable for $l = l' = 10$, $l_{mod} = l'_{mod} = 0$, $h = 1$ and $h' = 2$. And actually the program is insecure. Removing the last statement would make it secure and the formula unsatisfiable as the comparison of the final values would change to $1_{mod} \neq 1'_{mod}$ which would be unsatisfiable.

4.2 Method Contracts

Let m denote a method. A contract C_m for m is a triple $(Pre_m, Post_m, Mod_m)$ with precondition Pre_m, postcondition $Post_m$ and modifies (or assignable) clause Mod_m, which enumerates all program variables that m is allowed to change.

A method satisfies its contract, if it ensures that when invoked in a state for which the precondition is satisfied, then in the reached final state the postcondition holds and at most the program variables (locations) listed in the assignable clause have been modified.

Analysing Noninterference w.r.t. to a Precondition. Given a method m with contract C_m. We want to analyze whether m respects its noninterference policy $NI = (L, H)$ under the condition that m is only invoked in states satisfying its precondition Pre_m. Changing the noninterference formula (2) is easy and only requires adding a restriction to the initial states requiring them to satisfy the method's precondition:

$$Leak(H, L, l, i, j) \wedge Pre_m(L, H) \wedge Pre_m(L', H') \tag{5}$$

Analyzing Programs for Noninterference using Method Contracts. A similar problem as for loops manifests itself when symbolically executing a program which invokes one or more methods. One solution is to replace the method invocation by the body of the invoked method. If the methods are small this is a viable solution, but it is impractical if the invoked method is complex and is even impossible for recursive methods without a fixed maximal recursion depth.

This problem is solved in [14] by using method contracts in a similar way loop specifications have been used. Instead of a loop invariant, the pre- and postconditions become parts of the path conditions. The modifies clause gives again rise to fresh variables used to represent the symbolic value of the program variables that might have been changed as side-effect of the method invocation.

Let m be the method that is analyzed for secure information flow and which invokes a method n. The method contract of n is given as $(Pre_n, Post_n, Mod_n)$. For the case that both two paths i, j contain one method call for n we get:

$$Leak(H, L, l, i, j) \equiv (\bigwedge_{v \in L} v = v') \wedge pc_i(V_S) \wedge pc_j(V'_S) \wedge (Pre_n^{wp}(V_S) \wedge Post_n^{wp}(V_S))$$
$$\wedge (Pre_n^{wp}(V'_S) \wedge Post_n^{wp}(V'_S)) \wedge f_i^l(V_S) \neq f_j^l(V'_S) \tag{6}$$

where V_S is the set of program variables extended by the newly introduced variables resulting from the modifies clause of method n and $Pre_n^{wp}, Post_n^{wp}$ are the weakest preconditions of $Pre_n, Post_n$ computed directly before (resp. after) the method invocation. The general case is similar to loops.

Fig. 2. Exploit Generation by KEG

4.3 General Observations and Remarks

Using loop specifications or method contracts has one major drawback, namely, that not all models of a formula give rise to an actual information leak, or even worse, the insecurity formula of a secure program might become satisfiable. This case does not effect the soundness, but triggers false warnings. The reason is that the specifications might be too weak and allow behaviours that are not possible in the actual program. These false warnings can be filtered out by actually running the generated exploit. If the exploit fails to demonstrate the information leak, we know that our model was a spurious one. We can even start a feedback loop with a conflict clause which rules out the previously found model.

On the other side if loop or method specifications are not just too weak, but wrong in the sense that they exclude existing behaviour, leaks might not be detected. This can be avoided by verifying the specifications using a program verification tool. As we are concerned with bug detection and not verification, this case is not too bad as we do not claim to find all bugs.

5 Implementation and Experiments

5.1 The KeY Exploit Generation Tool

We implemented our approach as a tool called *KeY Exploit Generation (KEG)*[1] based on the verification system KeY for Java [8]. KEG uses KeY as symbolic execution (SE) engine, which supports method and loop specifications to achieve a finite SE tree. The SMT solver Z3 is used to find models for the insecurity formulas. KEG is able to deal with object types and arrays (to some extent).

Fig. 2 outlines KEG's work-flow. As starting point it serves a Java method m which is analysed for secure information flow w.r.t. a given information flow specification. First, method m is symbolically executed (using KeY) to obtain the SE tree with the method's path conditions and the final symbolic values of the program locations modified by m. Using this information the insecurity formulas are generated and given to a model finder (in our case the SMT solver Z3). If a model for the insecurity formula has been found, the model is used to determine the initial states of two runs which exhibit a forbidden information flow. The generated exploit sets then up two runs (one for each initial state) and inspects the reached final states to detect a leak. KEG outputs the exploited program as a JUnit test to be included into a regression test suite.

5.2   Exploit Generation Using a Simple Example

We explain KEG using the simple example shown below:

```
1  public class Simple {
2      public int l; private int x, y;
3      /*! l | x y ; !*/
4
5      /*@ escapes (x*y) \to l \if x>-1; @*/
6      public void magic() { if(x>0) { l=x*y; } else { l=0; } }
7  }
```

Class Simple contains three integer typed fields l, x and y as well as a method called magic() which assigns a value to l depending on the sign of field x. The information flow policy is annotated as special comment types. Line 3 is a class level specification and forbids any information flow from x and y to l. Hence, here x and y are high variables and l is a low variable. However, this strict noninterference policy is relaxed in line 5 for method magic() by providing a target conditional release specification consisting of an escape hatch (x*y), the target l and the condition x>-1.

Running KEG on the above example produces a symbolic execution tree consisting of two paths; one for each branch of the conditional statement. KEG generates for each pair of these paths the corresponding insecurity formulas and passes them on to an SMT solver. Of the three generated insecurity formulas only one is satisfiable and Z3 provides a model:

Insecurity Formula	Model
`(let ((a!1 (not (and (> self_x_1 (- 1)) (> self_x_2 (- 1))))))` `(and (>= self_x_1 1)   (<= self_x_2 0)` `    (or (not (= self_x_1 self_x_2)) (not (= self_y_1 self_y_2)))` `    (= self_l_1 self_l_2) (not (= (* self_y_1 self_x_1) 0))` `    (or a!1 (= (* self_x_1 self_y_1) (* self_x_2 self_y_2)))))`	self_x_1 : 1 self_x_2 : -1 self_y_1 : -1 self_y_2 : 1 self_l_1 : 0 self_l_2 : 0

The formula comparing two runs which take different branches of the conditional statement and thus leak the sign of field x. KEG generates exactly one exploit, which is output as a well-structured and human readable JUnit test.

5.3   Experiments

We performed a number of small experiments[2] for a first evaluation of our approach. Table 1 shows the aggregated results. All experiments were done on an Intel Core i7-4702HQ processor with JVM setting -Xmx4096m.

Concerning the runtime performance: A significant amount is spent for parsing the program, this can be reduced by parser optimizations, e.g., by using a hand-coded version instead of a generated parser. Model finding time can be optimized by performing simple techniques like symmetry reduction, learning and caching, all of which have not yet been implemented. Another factor is the programming language Java whose optimizations are performed at runtime and, hence, code run only a few times will not be optimized at all.

---

[2] www.se.tu-darmstadt.de/fileadmin/user_upload/Group_SE/Tools/KEG/
experiments.zip

Table 1. Case studies statistics

File name	Analyzed Method	#L/MI	Policy (NI/D)	S/I	T_L (ms)	T_{SE} (ms)	T_{MF} (ms)	T_{Tot} (ms)	#GE/FW
Mul	product	0 / 0	D	I	4187	847	1188	6266	1 / 0
Mul_StrongLI	product	1 / 0	D	I	4275	1746	1211	7274	1 / 0
Mul_WeakLI	product	1 / 0	D	I	4214	1909	1293	7463	2 / 1
Mul_WrongLI	product	1 / 0	D	I	4397	1678	1169	7285	0 / 0
Comp_StrongMC	doWork	0 / 1	NI	I	4181	1491	2278	7995	3 / 0
Comp_WeakMC	doWork	0 / 1	NI	I	4217	1383	2417	8065	3 / 3
Comp_WrongMC	doWork	0 / 1	NI	I	4182	1395	2275	7887	0 / 0
Company	calculate	1 / 1	NI	I	4283	2496	1990	8816	3 / 0
ExpList	magic	0 / 0	NI	I	4178	1911	2535	8668	1 / 0
ExpLinkedList	magic	0 / 4	NI	I	4229	4690	6564	15526	2 / 0
ExpArrayList	magic	0 / 5	NI	I	4230	8975	11505	24752	3 / 0
ArrMax	findMax	1 / 0	NI	I	4215	3584	963	8804	1 / 0
ArrSearch	search	1 / 0	D	S	4199	2934	2400	9568	0 / 0

#(L/MI/GE/FW): nr of **L**oops/**M**ethod **I**nvocations/**G**enerated **E**xploits/**F**alse **W**arnings
NI/D: **N**on-**I**nterference/**D**eclassification, S/I: **S**ecure/**I**nsecure
T_X: Time for **L**oading/**S**ymbolic **E**xecution/**M**odel **F**inding/**T**otal

A few observations concerning some of the concrete case studies: For the examples *Mul* and *Comp*, we analyzed also the effect of loop specifications resp. method specifications in case of strong, weak and wrong specifications (*filename*_Strong/Weak/Wrong_LI/MC). As expected in case of sufficiently strong specifications, all insecure paths could be identified and corresponding exploits have been generated. Weak specifications over-approximated possible behaviour leading to false warnings, while wrong specifications excluded actual behaviours and missed existings leaks. The analysis of method search in class *ArrSearch* identified the method correctly as secure with respect to the specified declassification policy and generated no exploits.

6   Related Work

Our approach to exploit generation is based on self-composition [6,10,11]. The paper [11] addresses also declassification. Its authors observe that in their formalization it is possible to express and verify that a program is insecure. Our formalization of insecurity uses this observation. Exploit generation (extraction of models) in our paper owes to techniques developed for automatic test generation. In particular, we build upon work presented in [12,16], where symbolic execution is used as a means to generate test cases for functional properties.

Logic-based approaches such as [7,23] are fully precise and at the same time can flexibly express various information flow properties beyond the policies presented in this paper. The verification process is not fully automatic, however, and non-trivial interactions with the theorem prover are required. In [19] higher order logic is used to express information flow properties for object-oriented programs, which is highly expressive, but poses also a high demand on user interaction.

Pairs of symbolic execution paths instead of standard self-composition have been independently used in [20] to check programs for noninterference. However, the author is only concerned with checking noninterference, but does not support declassification. Unbounded loops and recursive methods are not addressed.

In [25], leaks are inferred automatically and expressed in a human-readable security policy language helping programmers to decide whether the program is secure or not, however it can not give concrete counterexamples that could suggest further corrections. Counterexamples can be used not only to generate executable exploits as in our approach, but also to refine declassification policies quantifying the leakage [1,3]. However, both above approaches do not provide a solution for unbounded loops and recursions.

ENCoVer [2] uses epistemic logic and makes use of symbolic execution (concolic testing) to check noninterference for Java programs. In [17], the authors proposed a tool which checks that a C program is secure w.r.t. noninterference. It transforms the original program and makes use of dynamic symbolic execution to analyze the program's information flow. Both tools check loops and recursive method invocations only up to a fixed depth.

Type-based approaches to information flow like [15,18,21,26] or those based on dependency graphs [13] distinguish themselves by their high performance and ability to check large systems. Common drawbacks are lack of precision and resulting false warnings and/or restrictions on the syntactic form of a program.

None of the logic-based and type-based approaches to noninterference analysis mentioned above does generate exploits from a failed proof or analysis. Our work does not intend to replace their approaches, but to be used complementary.

7   Conclusion

We presented a novel approach for automatically detecting information flow leaks in object-oriented imperative programs. Exploits are generated based on satisfying models of *insecurity formulas* and output as tests so that they can easily be integrated into regression test collections. We also showed how program specifications such as loop invariants and method contracts can be used to overcome the obstacle of an infinite symbolic execution tree in case of unbounded program structures. We have built a prototypical tool (KEG) based on our approach that handles sequential Java programs and we applied it to a number of case studies.

We plan to integrate KEG with the abstraction framework presented in [27] which allows us to automatically generate loop invariant and method contracts to avoid the need for user-provided specifications.

References

1. Backes, M., Kopf, B., Rybalchenko, A.: Automatic discovery and quantification of information leaks. In: Proc. of the 30th IEEE Symp. on Security and Privacy, pp. 141–153. SP 2009, IEEE CS (2009)
2. Balliu, M., Dam, M., Le Guernic, G.: ENCoVer: symbolic exploration for information flow security. In: 25th IEEE Computer Security Foundations Symposium, pp. 30–44. IEEE CS (2012)
3. Banerjee, A., Giacobazzi, R., Mastroeni, I.: What you lose is what you leak: Information leakage in declassification policies. ENTCS **173**, 47–66 (2007)
4. Banerjee, A., Naumann, D.A.: Stack-based Access Control and Secure Information Flow. J. Funct. Program. **15**(2), 131–177 (2005)
5. Barthe, G., Crespo, J.M., Kunz, C.: Relational verification using product programs. In: Butler, M., Schulte, W. (eds.) FM 2011. LNCS, vol. 6664, pp. 200–214. Springer, Heidelberg (2011)
6. Barthe, G., D'Argenio, P.R., Rezk, T.: Secure information flow by self-composition. In: Proc. of the 17th IEEE Workshop on Computer Security Foundations, pp. 100–114. CSFW 2004, IEEE CS (2004)
7. Beckert, B., Bruns, D., Klebanov, V., Scheben, C., Schmitt, P.H., Ulbrich, M.: Information flow in object-oriented software. In: Gupta, G., Peña, R. (eds.) LOPSTR 2013, LNCS 8901. LNCS, vol. 8901, pp. 19–37. Springer, Heidelberg (2014)
8. Beckert, B., Hähnle, R., Schmitt, P.H. (eds.): Verification of Object-Oriented Software: The KeY Approach. LNCS (LNAI), vol. 4334. Springer, Heidelberg (2007)
9. Cohen, E.S.: Information Transmission in Sequential Programs. Foundations of Secure Computation, pp. 297–335 (1978)
10. Darvas, A., Hähnle, R., Sands, D.: A theorem proving approach to analysis of secure information flow. In: Gorrieri, R. (ed.) Workshop on Issues in the Theory of Security. IFIP WG 1.7, ACM SIGPLAN and GI FoMSESS (2003)
11. Darvas, A., Hähnle, R., Sands, D.: A theorem proving approach to analysis of secure information flow. In: Hutter, D., Ullmann, M. (eds.) SPC 2005. LNCS, vol. 3450, pp. 193–209. Springer, Heidelberg (2005)
12. Engel, C., Hähnle, R.: Generating unit tests from formal proofs. In: Gurevich, Y., Meyer, B. (eds.) TAP 2007. LNCS, vol. 4454, pp. 169–188. Springer, Heidelberg (2007)
13. Graf, J., Hecker, M., Mohr, M.: Using JOANA for information flow control in java programs - a practical guide. In: Proc. of the 6th Working Conf. on Programming Languages, pp. 123–138. LNI 215, Springer (February 2013)
14. Hentschel, M., Hähnle, R., Bubel, R.: Visualizing unbounded symbolic execution. In: Seidl, M., Tillmann, N. (eds.) TAP 2014. LNCS, vol. 8570, pp. 82–98. Springer, Heidelberg (2014)
15. Hunt, S., Sands, D.: On flow-sensitive security types. In: ACM SIGPLAN Notices, vol. 41, pp. 79–90. ACM (2006)
16. King, J.C.: Symbolic Execution and Program Testing. Commun. ACM **19**(7), 385–394 (1976)
17. Milushev, D., Beck, W., Clarke, D.: Noninterference via symbolic execution. In: Giese, H., Rosu, G. (eds.) FORTE 2012 and FMOODS 2012. LNCS, vol. 7273, pp. 152–168. Springer, Heidelberg (2012)
18. Myers, A.C.: JFlow: practical mostly-static information flow control. In: Proc. of 26th ACM Symp. on Principles of Programming Languages, pp. 228–241 (1999)

19. Nanevski, A., Banerjee, A., Garg, D.: Verification of information flow and access control policies with dependent types. In: Proc. of the 2011 IEEE Symp. on Security and Privacy, pp. 165–179. SP 2011, IEEE CS (2011)
20. Phan, Q.S.: Self-composition by symbolic execution. In: Jones, A.V., Ng, N. (eds.) Imperial College Computing Student Workshop. OASIcs, vol. 35, pp. 95–102. Schloss Dagstuhl (2013)
21. Sabelfeld, A., Myers, A.C.: A model for delimited information release. In: Futatsugi, K., Mizoguchi, F., Yonezaki, N. (eds.) ISSS 2003. LNCS, vol. 3233, pp. 174–191. Springer, Heidelberg (2004)
22. Sabelfeld, A., Sands, D.: Declassification: Dimensions and Principles. Journal of Computer Security **17**(5), 517–548 (2009)
23. Scheben, C., Schmitt, P.H.: Verification of information flow properties of JAVA programs without approximations. In: Beckert, B., Damiani, F., Gurov, D. (eds.) FoVeOOS 2011. LNCS, vol. 7421, pp. 232–249. Springer, Heidelberg (2012)
24. Terauchi, T., Aiken, A.: Secure information flow as a safety problem. In: Hankin, C., Siveroni, I. (eds.) SAS 2005. LNCS, vol. 3672, pp. 352–367. Springer, Heidelberg (2005)
25. Vaughan, J.A., Chong, S.: Inference of expressive declassification policies. In: Proc. of the 2011 IEEE Symp. on Security and Privacy, pp. 180–195. IEEE CS (2011)
26. Volpano, D., Irvine, C., Smith, G.: A Sound Type System for Secure Flow Analysis. Journal of Computer Security **4**(2), 167–187 (1996)
27. Wasser, N., Bubel, R.: A theorem prover backed approach to array abstraction. In: Proc. of VSL 2014 – WING Workshop (2014)

Memoized Semantics-Based Binary Diffing with Application to Malware Lineage Inference

Jiang Ming$^{(\boxtimes)}$, Dongpeng Xu, and Dinghao Wu

The Pennsylvania State University, University Park, PA 16802, USA
{jum310,dux103,dwu}@ist.psu.edu

Abstract. Identifying differences between two executable binaries (binary diffing) has compelling security applications, such as software vulnerability exploration, "1-day" exploit generation and software plagiarism detection. Recently, binary diffing based on symbolic execution and constraint solver has been proposed to look for the code pairs with the same semantics, even though they are ostensibly different in syntactics. Such logical-based method captures intrinsic differences of binary code, making it a natural choice to analyze highly-obfuscated malicious program. However, semantics-based binary diffing suffers from significant performance slowdown, hindering it from analyzing large-scale malware samples. In this paper, we attempt to mitigate the high overhead of semantics-based binary diffing with application to malware lineage inference. We first study the key obstacles that contribute to the performance bottleneck. Then we propose *basic blocks fast matching* to speed up semantics-based binary diffing. We introduce an union-find set structure that records semantically equivalent basic blocks. Managing the union-find structure during successive comparisons allows direct reuse of previously computed results. Moreover, we purpose to concretize symbolic formulas and cache equivalence queries to further cut down the invocation times of constraint solver. We have implemented our technique on top of iBinHunt and evaluated it on 12 malware families with respect to the performance improvement when performing intra-family comparisons. Our experimental results show that our methods can accelerate symbolic execution from 2.8x to 5.3x (with an average 4.0x), and reduce constraint solver invocation by a factor of 3.0x to 6.0x (with an average 4.3x).

1 Introduction

In many tasks of software security, the source code of the program under examination is typically absent. Instead, the executable binary itself is the only available resource to analyze. Therefore, determining the real differences between two executable binaries has a wide variety of applications, such as latent vulnerabilities exploration [16], automatic "1-day" exploit generation [1] and software plagiarism detection [14]. Conventional approaches can quickly locate syntactical differences by measuring instruction sequences [20] or byte N-grams [11]. However, such syntax-based comparison can be easily defeated by various obfuscation techniques, such as instruction substitution [9], binary packing [19] and self-modifying code [2]. The latest binary diffing approaches [8,15] simulate semantics of a snippet of binary code (e.g., basic block) by symbolic execution and

© IFIP International Federation for Information Processing 2015
H. Federrath and D. Gollmann (Eds.): SEC 2015, IFIP AICT 455, pp. 416–430, 2015.
DOI: 10.1007/978-3-319-18467-8_28

represent the input-output relations as a set of symbolic formulas. Then the equivalence of formulas are verified by a constraint solver. Such logic-based comparison, capturing the intrinsic semantic differences, has been applied to finding differences of program versions [8], comparing inter-procedural control flows [15] and identifying code reuse [14, 17].

On the other hand, malware authors frequently update their malicious code to circumvent security countermeasures. According to the latest annual report of Panda Security labs [18], in 2013 alone, there are about 30 million malware samples in circulation and only 20% of them are newly created. Obviously, most of such malware samples are simple update (e.g., apply a new packer) to their previous versions. Therefore, hunting malware similarities is of great necessity. The nature of being resilient to instruction obfuscation makes semantics-based binary diffing an appealing choice to analyze highly obfuscated malware as well. Unfortunately, the significant overhead imposed by the state-of-the-art approach has severely restricted its application in large scale analysis, such as malware lineage inference [10], which normally requires pair-wise comparison to identify relationships among malware variants. In this paper, we first diagnose the two key obstacles leading to the performance bottleneck, namely high invocations of constraint solver and slow symbolic execution.

To address both factors, we propose *basic blocks fast matching* by reusing previously compared results, which consists of three optimization methods to accelerate equivalent basic block matching. Our key insight is that malware variants are likely to share common code [12]; new variant may be just protected with a different packer or incremental updates. As a result, we exploit code similarity by adopting union-find set [6], an efficient tree-based data structure, to record semantically equivalent basic blocks which have already been identified. Essentially, the union-find structure stores the md5 value of each matched basic block after normalization. Maintaining the union-find structure during successive comparisons allows direct reuse of previous results, without the need for re-comparing them. Moreover, to further cut down the high invocation times of constraint solver, we purpose to concretize symbolic formulas and cache equivalence queries. We have implemented these optimizations on top of iBinHunt [15] and evaluated them when performing malware lineage inference on 12 malware families. Our experimental results show that our methods can speed up malware lineage inference, symbolic execution and constraint solver by a factor of 4.4x, 4.0x and 4.3x, respectively. Our proposed solution focuses on accelerating basic blocks matching and therefore can be seamlessly woven into other binary diffing approaches based on equivalent basic blocks. In summary, the contributions of this paper are as follows:

1. We look into the high overhead problem of semantics-based binary diffing and identify cruxes leading to the performance bottleneck.
2. We propose *basic blocks fast matching* to enable more efficient binary comparison, including maintaining a union-find set structure, concretizing symbolic formulas and caching equivalence queries.
3. We implement our approach on a state-of-the-art binary diffing tool and demonstrate its efficacy in malware lineage inference.

The rest of the paper is organized as follows. Section 2 provides the background information. Section 3 studies the performance bottleneck of semantics-based binary diffing. Section 4 describes our optimization methods in detail.

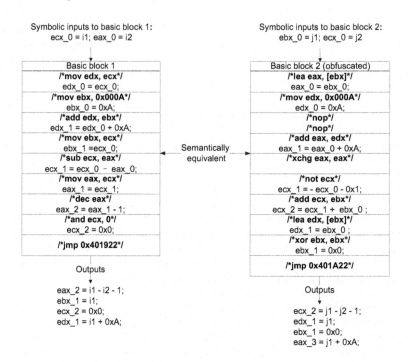

Fig. 1. Basic block symbolic execution

We evaluate our approach in Section 5. Related work are introduced in Section 6. At last, we conclude the paper in Section 7.

2   Background

In this section, we introduce the background information of semantics-based binary diffing. The core method of current approaches [8,14,15] are matching semantically equivalent basic blocks. Basic block is a straight line code with only one entry point and only one exit point, which makes a basic block highly amenable to symbolic execution (e.g., without conjunction of path conditions). Fig. 1 presents a motivating example to illustrate how semantics of a basic block is simulated by symbolic execution. The two basic blocks in Fig. 1 are semantically equivalent, even though they have different x86 instructions (listed in bold). In practice, symbolic execution is performed on a RISC-like intermediate language (IL), which represents complicated x86 instructions as simple Single Static Assignment (SSA) style statements (e.g., ecx_0, edx_1).

Taken the inputs to the basic block as symbols, the output of symbolic execution is a set of formulas that represent input-output relations of the basic block. Now determining whether two basic blocks are equivalent in semantics boils down to find an equivalent mapping between output formulas. Note that due to obfuscation such as register renaming, basic blocks could use different registers or variables to provide the same functionality. Hence current approaches exhaustively try all possible pairs to find if there exists a bijective mapping between

Query result	eax_3	ebx_1	ecx_2	edx_1
eax_2	false		**true**	false
ebx_1	false		false	**true**
ecx_2		**constant (0)**		
edx_1	**true**		false	false

Fig. 2. Output formulas equivalence query results

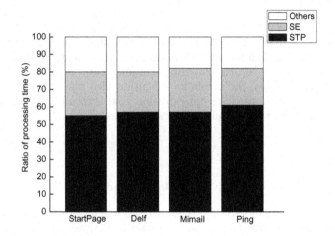

Fig. 3. Ratio of processing time of iBinHunt

output formulas. Fig. 2 shows such formulas mapping attempt for the output formulas shown in Fig. 1. The "true" or "false" indicates the result of equivalence checking, such as whether $edx\_1 = eax\_3$. After 10 times comparisons, we identify a perfect matched permutation and therefore conclude that these two basic blocks are truly equivalent.

Based on the matched basic blocks, BinHunt [8] computes the similarity of control flow graphs of two binaries by graph isomorphism; iBinHunt [15] finds semantic differences between execution traces and Luo et al. [14] detect software plagiarism by matching "longest common subsequence of semantically equivalent basic blocks".

3   Performance Bottleneck

We look into the overhead imposed by semantics-based binary diffing and find that there are two factors dominating the cost. The first is the high number of invocations of constraint solver. Recall that current approaches check all possible permutations of output formulas mapping. The constraint solver will be invoked every time when verifying the equivalence of formulas. For example, two basic blocks in Fig. 1 have 3 symbolic formulas and 1 constant value respectively. As shown in Fig. 2, We have to employ constraint solver at most 9 times to find an equivalent mapping between 3 output formulas. Too frequently calling constraint solver incurs a significant performance penalty. The second is the slow processing speed of symbolic execution. Typically symbolic execution is much slower than native execution, because it simulates each x86 instruction by interpreting a sequence of IL statements.

To quantitatively study such performance bottleneck, we selected 4 malware families from our evaluation dataset (see Section 5.1): 3 families have large number of samples (StartPage, Delf and Mimail) and one family (Ping) has the maximal code size. We applied iBinHunt [15] to compare execution traces of pair-wise samples within each family. The constraint solver we used is STP [7]. Fig. 3 shows the ratio of each stage's processing time on average: constraint solver solving time ("STP" bar), symbolic execution time ("SE" bar) and other operations ("Others" bar). Apparently, STP's processing time accounts for most of running time of iBinHunt (more than 50%). Experiments on EXE [4] and KLEE [3] report similar results, in which running time is dominated by the constraint solving. Besides, the symbolic execution also takes up to about 23% running time. Thus, an immediate optimization goal is to mitigate too frequent invocations of constraint solver and slow symbolic execution.

4   Optimization

4.1   Union-Find Set of Equivalent Basic Blocks

When we compare malware variants to identify their relationships (a.k.a, lineage inference [10]), our key observation is that similar malware variants are likely to share common code [12]. For example, all of the Email-Worm.Win32.NetSky samples in our dataset search for email addresses on the infected computer and use SMTP to send themselves as attachments to these addresses. The net result is we have to re-compare large number of basic blocks that have been previously analyzed. Therefore our first optimization is to utilize union-find set [6], an efficient tree-based data structure, to reuse previous matched equivalent basic blocks. More specifically, we first normalize basic blocks to ignore offsets that may change due to code relocation and some nop instructions. MD5 value of the byte sequence of each basic block is then calculated. Secondly, we dynamically maintain a set of union-find subsets to record semantically equivalent basic blocks, which are represented by their MD5 value. The basic blocks within the same subset are all semantically equivalent to each other. Next we'll discuss these two steps in detail.

Normalization. Binary compiled from the same source code often have different address value caused by memory relocation during compilation. What's more, malware authors may intentionally insert some instruction idioms like nop and xchg eax, eax to mislead calculation of hash value. The purpose of normalization is to ignore such effects and make the hash value more general. Taken the basic block 2 in Fig. 1 as an example, Fig. 4 presents how to normalize a basic block, in which we replace address values with zeros and remove all nop statements. After that, the MD5 value of the basic block's byte sequence is calculated.

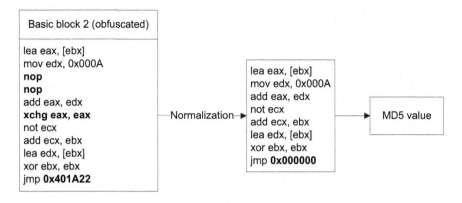

Fig. 4. Basic block normalization

Maintain Union-Find Set. We define the three major operations of union-find set as follows:

1. `MakeSet`: Create an initial subset structure containing one element, which is represented by a basic block's MD5 value. Each element's parent points to itself and has 0 depth.
2. `Find`: Determine which subset a basic block belongs to. `Find` operation can be used to quickly find two basic blocks are equivalent if both of them are within the same subset.
3. `Union`: Unite two subsets into a new single subset. The depth of new set will be updated accordingly.

The elements within a subset build up a tree structure. `Find` operation will always recursively traverse on the tree structure. However the tree structure might degrade to a long list of nodes, which incurs $\mathcal{O}(n)$ time in the worst case for `Find`. To avoid highly unbalanced searching tree, an improved path compression and weighted union algorithm are applied to speed up `Find` operation. Algorithm 1 shows the pseudo-code of `MakeSet`, `Find` and `Union`. `MakeSet` creates an initial set containing only one basic block. Path compression is a way to flatten the structure of the tree when `Find` recursively explores on it. As a result, each node's parent points to the root `Find` returns (Line 7). Weighted `Union` algorithm attaches the tree with smaller depth to the root of taller tree (Line 17, Line 20), which only increases depth when depths are equal (Line 24).

Fig. 5 shows an example of maintaining an union-find set. Given previously matched basic block pairs (as shown in left most block), after initial `MakeSet` and `Union` operations, we get three subsets, that is, $\{a, b\}$, $\{c, d\}$ and $\{e, f, g\}$. Then assuming b and c, two basic blocks coming from different subsets (subset 1 and 2), have the same semantics, that means all of the basic blocks in these two subsets are in fact equivalent. Therefore we perform weighed union and path compression to join the two subsets to a new subset (subset 4). The resulting tree is much flatter with a depth 1. After union, we can immediately determine that b and d are equivalent, even if these two basic blocks were not compared before. In addition to union-fine set, we also maintain a `DiffMap` to record two subsets that have been verified that they are not equivalent. As shown in the

Algorithm 1. MakeSet, Find and Union

```
 1: function MAKESET(a)                                        ▷ a is a basic block
 2:     a.parent ← a
 3:     a.depth ← 0
 4: end function
 5: function FIND(a)                                           ▷ path compression
 6:     if a.parent ≠ a then
 7:         a.parent ← Find(a.parent)
 8:     end if
 9:     return a.parent
10: end function
11: function UNION(a,b)                                        ▷ weighted union
12:     aRoot ← Find(a)
13:     bRoot ← Find(b)
14:     if aRoot = bRoot then
15:         return
16:     end if
17:     if aRoot.depth < bRoot.depth then
18:         aRoot.parent ← bRoot
19:     else
20:         if aRoot.depth > bRoot.depth then
21:             bRoot.parent ← aRoot
22:         else
23:             bRoot.parent ← aRoot
24:             aRoot.depth ← aRoot.depth + 1
25:         end if
26:     end if
27: end function
```

lower right side of Fig. 5, if we find out a and e are different, we can safely conclude that basic blocks in subset 4 are not equivalent to the ones in subset 3, without the need for comparing them anymore.

4.2   Concretizing Symbolic Formulas

Fig. 2 shows a drawback of semantics-based binary diffing: without knowing the mapping of output formulas for equivalence checking, current approaches have to exhaustively try all possible permutations. To ameliorate this issue, we introduce a sound heuristic that *if two symbolic formulas are equivalent, they should generate equal values when substituting symbols with the same concrete value.* Therefore we give preference to the symbolic formulas producing the same value after concretization. Taken the output formulas in Fig. 1 as example, we substitute all the input symbols with a single concrete value 1. In this way, we can quickly identify the possible mapping pairs and then we verify them again with STP. As a result, we only invoke STP 3 times, instead of 9 times as is previously done. Note that using STP for double-check is indispensable, as two symbolic formulas may happen to generate the same value. For example, $i << 1$ is equal to $i * i$ when $i = 2$.

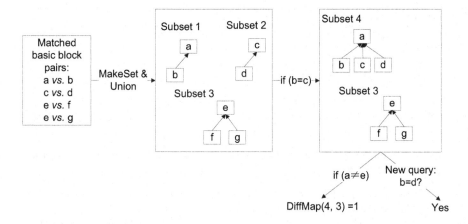

Fig. 5. Example of MakeSet-Union-Find operations

4.3 Caching Equivalence Queries

Besides, in order to further reduce the invocations of STP when possible, we manage a `QueryMap` to cache the result of equivalence queries, which is quite similar to constraints caching adopted by EXE [4] and KLEE [3]. The key of `QueryMap` is MD5 value of an equivalence query, such as whether `edx_1 = eax_3` in Fig. 1; the value of `QueryMap` stores STP query result (true or false). Before calling STP on a query, we first check `QueryMap` to see whether it gets a hit. If not, we'll create a new `(key, value)` entry into QueryMap after we verify this query with STP.

4.4 Basic Blocks Fast Matching

We merge all three optimization methods discussed above together to comprise our *basic blocks fast matching* algorithm (as listed in Algorithm 2). Our basic blocks fast matching exploits syntactical information and previous result for early pruning. When comparing two basic blocks, we first normalize the basic blocks and compare their hash value (Line 4). This step quickly filters out basic blocks with quite similar instructions. If two hash values are not equal, we will identify whether they belong to the same union-find subset (Line 7). Basic blocks within the same subset are semantically equivalent to each other. If they are in the two different subsets, we continue to check DiffMap to find out whether these two subsets have been ensured not equivalent (Line 10). At last, we have to resort to comparing them with symbolic execution and STP, which is accurate but computationally more expensive. At the same time, we leverage heuristic of concretizing symbolic formulas and QueryMap cache to reduce the invocations of STP. After that we update union-find set and DiffMap accordingly (Line 15~22).

Algorithm 2. Basic Block Fast Matching

1: **function** FASTMATCHING(a, b)   ▷ a, b are two basic blocks to be compared
2:     $a' \leftarrow$ Normalize(a)
3:     $b' \leftarrow$ Normalize(b)
4:     **if** Hash(a') = Hash(b') **then**   ▷ a and b have the same instructions
5:         **return** True
6:     **end if**
7:     **if** Find(a') = Find(b') **then**   ▷ within the same subset
8:         **return** True
9:     **end if**
10:     **if** DiffMap(Find(a'), Find(b'))=1 **then**   ▷ semantically different subsets
11:         **return** False
12:     **else**
13:         Perform symbolic execution on a' and b'
14:         Check semantical equivalence of a' and b'
15:         **if** $a' \sim b'$ **then**   ▷ a', b' are semantically equivalent
16:             Union(a', b')
17:             Update DiffMap
18:             **return** True
19:         **else**   ▷ a', b' are not semantically equivalent
20:             Set DiffMap(Find(a'), Find(b'))
21:             **return** False
22:         **end if**
23:     **end if**
24: **end function**

---

5   Experimental Evaluation

5.1   Implementation and Experiment Setup

We have implemented our basic blocks fast matching algorithm on top of iBin-Hunt [15], a binary diffing tool to find semantic differences between execution traces, with about 1,800 Ocaml lines of code. The saving and loading of union-find set, DiffMap and QueryMap are implemented using the Ocaml Marshal API, which encodes arbitrary data structures as sequences of bytes and then stores them in a disk file.

We collected malware samples from VX Heavens[1] and leveraged an online malware scan service, VirusTotal[2], to classify the samples into an initial 12 families. These malware samples range from simple virus to considerably large Trojan horse. The dataset statistics is shown in Table 1. The experimental data are collected during malware lineage inference within each family, that is, we perform pair-wise comparison to determine relationships among malware variants. The forth column of Table 1 lists the number of pair-wise comparison of each family and the total number is 1,008. Our testbed consists of Intel Core i7-3770 processor (Quad Core with 3.40GHz) and 8GB memory. The malware execution traces are collected when running in Temu [22], a whole-system emulator. Since most of malware are packed, we developed a generic unpacking plug-in to monitor

---

[1] http://vxheaven.org/src.php
[2] https://www.virustotal.com/

Table 1. Dataset statistics

Malware Family	Category	#Samples	#Comparison	Size(kb)/Std.Dev.
Dler	Trojan	10	45	28/6
StartPage	Trojan	21	210	10/1
Delf	Trojan	24	276	17/4
Ping	Backdoor	8	28	247/41
SpyBoter	Backdoor	16	120	34/16
Progenic	Backdoor	6	15	88/27
Bube	Virus	10	45	12/7
MyPics	Worm	12	66	31/4
Bagle	Worm	9	36	40/17
Mimail	Worm	17	136	17/6
NetSky	Worm	7	21	41/12
Sasser	Worm	5	10	60/28

malware sample's unpacking and start to record trace only when the execution reaches the original entry point (OEP) [13].

5.2 Performance

Cumulative Effects. We first quantify the effects of the set of optimizations we presented in our basic blocks fast matching algorithm (Algorithm 2). Fig. 6 shows the speedup of malware lineage inference within each family when applying optimizations cumulatively on iBinHunt. Our baseline for this experiment is a conventional iBinHunt without any optimization we proposed. The "O1" bar indicates the effect of normalization, which can quickly identify basic block pairs with the same byte sequences. Such simple normalization only achieve notable improvement on several families such as Ping and Bube, in which instructions are quite similar in syntax. The bar denoted as "O2", captures the effect of the union-find set and DiffMap, which record previously compared results. Optimization O2 brings a significant speedup from 1.4x to 2.9x on average. Especially for some highly obfuscated malware families, such as Delf and Bagle, O2 outperforms O1 by a factor of up to 3.1. The "O3" bar, denoting concretizing symbolic formulas, introduces an improvement by 17% on average. Optimization of QueryMap (O4) offers an enhanced performance improvement by average 30% and with a peak value 46% to the NetSky. Particularly, since StartPage samples adopt different implementation ways to tamper with the startup page of Internet browsers, we observer quit large similarity distances among StartPage variants. In spite of this, our approach still accelerate the binary code diffing greatly.

Furthermore, we study the effect of our basic blocks fast matching over time. We choose Sasser to test because the impact of the optimizations on Sasser is close to the average value. As shown in Fig. 7, as the union-find set is enlarged and QueryMap is filled, our approach becomes more effective over time. The number of executed basic blocks is normalized so that data can be collected across intra-family comparisons.

Alleviate Performance Bottleneck. In Section 3, we identified two factors that dominate the cost of semantics-based binary diffing: namely symbolic

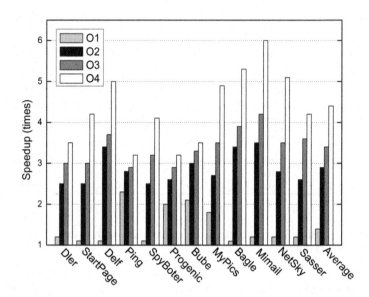

Fig. 6. The impact of basic blocks fast matching on malware lineage inference: O1 (normalization), O2 (O1 + union-find set and DiffMap), O3 (O2 + concretizing symbolic formulas), O4 (O3 + QueryMap)

execution and constraint solver. In this experiment, we study the effect of our optimizations on these two performance bottlenecks. The column 2~4 of Table 2 lists the average symbolic execution time and speedup before/after optimization when comparing two malware variants in each family using iBinHunt. Similarly, the column 5~7 shows the effect to reduce the number of STP invocations. In summary, our approach outperforms conventional iBinHunt in terms of less symbolic execution time by a factor of 4.0x on average, and fewer STP invocations by 4.3x on average.

Optimizations Breakdown. Table 3 presents our optimizations breakdown when performing lineage inference for the four large malware families shown in Fig. 3. The first row shows the ratio of matched basic block pairs with the same byte sequences after normalization (line 4 in Algorithm 2). The low ratio also demonstrates the necessity of semantics-based binary diffing approach. The next two rows list statistics of union-find set, including number of union-find subsets and the maximum number of equivalent basic blocks in one subset. The row 4 and 5 present the hit rate of union-find set (line 7 in Algorithm 2) and DiffMap (line 10 in Algorithm 2). The row 6 shows the time cost incurred by building and managing the union-find set structure and DiffMap. The following two rows lists hit rate and time cost for QueryMap. The saving of concretizing symbolic formulas is shown in row 9, in which we avoid at least more than 50% output variables comparisons. At last, we present the overall memory cost to maintain

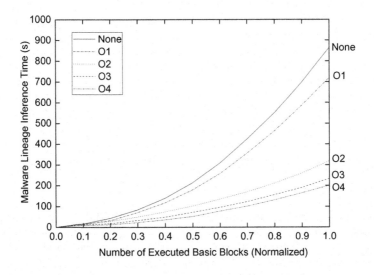

Fig. 7. The effect of our optimizations over time on Sasser family

Table 2. Improvement to performance bottleneck

Malware Family	SE Times (s)			# STP Invocations		
	None	Optimization	Speedup	None	Optimization	Speedup
Dler	10.1	2.5	4.0	1123	346	3.2
StartPage	13.5	3.3	4.1	1350	314	4.3
Delf	8.8	2.0	4.4	1685	324	5.2
Ping	32.2	10.7	3.0	6740	1926	3.5
SpyBoter	16.6	4.4	3.8	2020	493	4.1
Progenic	20.2	6.3	3.2	2566	856	3.0
Bube	5.1	1.8	2.8	847	250	3.4
MyPics	11.4	2.5	4.6	1235	257	4.8
Bagle	24.4	5.1	4.8	5570	1092	5.1
Mimail	9.0	1.7	5.3	2901	484	6.0
NetSky	20.6	4.6	4.5	4958	972	5.1
Sasser	24.2	6.2	3.9	5616	1338	4.2
Average			4.0			4.3

union-find set, DiffMap and QueryMap. Reassuringly, the overhead introduced by our optimizations is small.

6   Related Work

Our efforts attempt to speed up semantics-based binary diffing, which can find equivalent binary pairs that reveal syntactic differences [8,14,15,17]. We have introduced the latest work in this direction in Section 2. In this section, we focus

Table 3. Optimization breakdown

	StartPage	Delf	Mimail	Ping
Normalization ratio	9%	12%	12%	51%
# union-find subsets	125	130	304	546
Max. # basic blocks in one subset	5	6	8	10
union-find hit rate	36%	44%	37%	41%
DiffMap hit rate	47%	53%	44%	54%
Union-find set and DiffMap cost (s)	9.5	14.3	12.0	13.7
QueryMap hit rate	62%	70%	65%	75%
QueryMap cost (s)	8.6	8.8	6.4	7.6
Concretizing saving	60%	65%	55%	52%
Memory cost (MB)	10	12	28	45

on the literature related to our optimization approach. Malware normalization relies on ad-hoc rules to undo the obfuscations applied by malware developers [2,5]. Our approach first performs a simple normalization to eliminate the effect of memory relocation and instruction idioms. Yang et al. [21] proposed Memoise, a trie-based data structure to cache the key elements of symbolic execution, so that successive forward symbolic execution can reuse previously computed results. Our union-find structure is like Memoise in that we both maintain an efficient tree-based data structure to avoid re-computation. However, our approach aims to accelerate basic blocks matching and our symbolic execution is limited in a basic block, which is a straight line code without path conditions. Our optimization of caching equivalence queries is inspired by both EXE [4] and KLEE [3], which cache the result of path constraint solutions to avoid redundant constraint solver calling. Different from the complicated path conditions cached by EXE and KLEE, our equivalence queries are simple and compact. As a result, our QueryMap enjoys a higher cache hit rate.

7   Conclusion

The high performance penalty introduced by the state-of-the-art semantics-based binary diffing approaches restricts their application from large scale application such as analyzing numerous malware samples. In this paper, we first studied the cruxes leading to the performance bottleneck and then proposed memoization optimization to speed up semantics-based binary diffing. The experiment on malware lineage inference demonstrated the efficacy of our optimizations with only minimal overhead. Another possible application of our approach is to study the life cycle of metamorphic malware variants. we plan to explore this direction in our future work.

Acknowledgments. This research is supported in part by the National Science Foundation (NSF) grants CCF-1320605 and CNS-1223710.

References

1. Brumley, D., Poosankam, P., Song, D., Zheng, J.: Automatic patch-based exploit generation is possible: techniques and implications. In: Proceedings of the 2008 IEEE Symposimu on Security and Privacy, SP 2008 (2008)
2. Bruschi, D., Martignoni, L., Monga, M.: Using code normalization for fighting self-mutating malware. In: Proceedings of the International Symposium of Secure Software Engineering (2006)
3. Cadar, C., Dunbar, D., Engler, D.: KLEE: unassisted and automatic generation of high-coverage tests for complex systems programs. In: Proceedings of the 2008 USENIX Symposium on Operating Systems Design and Implementation, OSDI 2008 (2008)
4. Cadar, C., Ganesh, V., Pawlowski, P.M., Dill, D.L., Engler, D.R.: EXE: automatically generating inputs of death. In: Proceedings of the 2006 ACM Conference on Computer and Communications Security, CCS 2006 (2006)
5. Christodorescu, M., Kinder, J., Jha, S., Katzenbeisser, S., Veith, H.: Malware normalization. Technical Report 1539, University of Wisconsin, Madison (November 2005)
6. Cormen, T.H., Leiserson, C.E., Rivest, R.L., Stein, C.: Data structures for disjoint sets, chapter 21. In: Introduction to Algorithms, 2nd edn, pp. 498–524. MIT Press (2001)
7. Ganesh, V., Dill, D.L.: A decision procedure for bit-vectors and arrays. In: Damm, W., Hermanns, H. (eds.) CAV 2007. LNCS, vol. 4590, pp. 519–531. Springer, Heidelberg (2007)
8. Gao, D., Reiter, M.K., Song, D.: BinHunt: automatically finding semantic differences in binary programs. In: Chen, L., Ryan, M.D., Wang, G. (eds.) ICICS 2008. LNCS, vol. 5308, pp. 238–255. Springer, Heidelberg (2008)
9. Jacob, M., Jakubowski, M.H., Naldurg, P., Saw, C.W.N., Venkatesan, R.: The superdiversifier: peephole individualization for software protection. In: Matsuura, K., Fujisaki, E. (eds.) IWSEC 2008. LNCS, vol. 5312, pp. 100–120. Springer, Heidelberg (2008)
10. Jang, J., Woo, M., Brumley, D.: Towards automatic software lineage inference. In: Presented as part of the 22nd USENIX Security Symposium, USENIX Security 2013 (2013)
11. Kolter, J.Z., Maloof, M.A.: Learning to detect malicious executables in the wild. In: Proceedings of the 10th ACM SIGKDD Conference, KDD 2004 (2004)
12. Lindorfer, M., Di Federico, A., Maggi, F., Comparetti, P.M., Zanero, S.: Lines of malicious code: insights into the malicious software industry. In: Proceedings of the 28th Annual Computer Security Applications Conference, ACSAC 2012 (2012)
13. Liu, L., Ming, J., Wang, Z., Gao, D., Jia, C.: Denial-of-service attacks on host-based generic unpackers. In: Qing, S., Mitchell, C.J., Wang, G. (eds.) ICICS 2009. LNCS, vol. 5927, pp. 241–253. Springer, Heidelberg (2009)
14. Luo, L., Ming, J., Wu, D., Liu, P., Zhu, S.: Semantics-based obfuscation-resilient binary code similarity comparison with applications to software plagiarism detection. In: Proceedings of the 22nd ACM SIGSOFT International Symposium on Foundations of Software Engineering, FSE 2014 (2014)
15. Ming, J., Pan, M., Gao, D.: iBinHunt: binary hunting with inter-procedural control flow. In: Proceedings of the 15th Annual International Conference on Information Security and Cryptology, ICISC 2012 (2012)
16. Ng, B.H., Hu, X., Prakash, A.: A study on latent vulnerabilities. In: Proceedings of the 29th IEEE Symposium on Reliable Distributed Systems, SRDS 2010 (2010)
17. Ng, B.H., Prakash, A.: Exposé: discovering potential binary code re-use. In: Proceedings of the 37th IEEE Annual Computer Software and Applications Conference, COMPSAC 2013 (2013)

18. Panda Security. Annual report 2013 summary. http://press.pandasecurity.com/wp-content/uploads/2010/05/PandaLabs-Annual-Report_2013.pdf (last reviewed February 12, 2014)
19. Roundy, K.A., Miller, B.P.: Binary-code obfuscations in prevalent packer tools. ACM Computing Surveys **46**(1) (2013)
20. Sikorski, M., Honig, A.: Practical Malware Analysis: The Hands-On Guide to Dissecting Malicious Software. No Starch Press (February 2012)
21. Yang, G., Păsăreanu, C.S., Khurshid, S.: Memoized symbolic execution. In: Proceedings of the 2012 International Symposium on Software Testing and Analysis, ISSTA 2012 (2012)
22. Yin, H., Song, D.: TEMU: binary code analysis via whole-system layered annotative execution. Technical Report UCB/EECS-2010-3, EECS Department, University of California, Berkeley (January 2010)

Mitigating Code-Reuse Attacks on CISC Architectures in a Hardware Approach

Zhijiao Zhang[1], Yashuai Lü[2(⊠)], Yu Chen[1], Yongqiang Lü[1], and Yuanchun Shi[1]

[1] Department of Computer Science and Technology, Tsinghua University, Beijing, China
nudt_acer@163.com, {luyq,shiyc,yuchen}@mail.tsinghua.edu.cn
[2] Academy of Equipment, Beijing, China
freelancer_lys@163.com

Abstract. Recently, code-reuse attack (CRA) is becoming the most prevalent attack vector which reuses fragments of existing code to make up malicious code. Recent studies show that CRAs especially jump-oriented programming (JOP) attacks are hard and costly to detect and protect from, especially on CISC processors. One reason for this is that the instructions of CISC architecture are of variable-length, and lots of unintended but legal instructions can be exploited by starting from in the middle of a legal instruction. This feature of CISC architectures makes the finding of so called gadgets for CRAs is much easier than that of RISC architectures. Most of previous studies for mitigating CRA on CISC processors rely on software-only means to tackle the unintended instruction problem, which makes their approaches either very costly or can only be applied under restricted conditions. In this paper, we propose two hardware supported techniques. The first, which is the main contribution of this paper, is to eliminate the execution of an unintended instruction. This technique only requires a few modifications to the processor and operating system. Furthermore, the proposed mechanism has little performance impact on the examined SPEC CPU 2006 benchmarks (-0.093% ~2.993%). Second, we propose using hardware control-flow locking as a complementary technique to our protection mechanism. By using the two techniques together, an attacker will have little chance to carry out CRAs on a CISC processor.

Keywords: CISC processor · Unintended instruction · Code-reuse attack · Instruction execution verification

1   Introduction

As the popularity of the Internet increases, so does the number of computer security threats from increasingly sophisticated attackers [1]. One common way to compromise a normal application is exploiting memory corruption vulnerabilities and transferring the normal program execution to a location under the control of the attacker. In these attacks, the first step is trying to overwrite a pointer in memory. Buffer overflow [2] and format string vulnerability exploitation [3] are two well-known techniques to achieve this goal. Once the attacker is able to hijack the control flow of

© IFIP International Federation for Information Processing 2015
H. Federrath and D. Gollmann (Eds.): SEC 2015, IFIP AICT 455, pp. 431–445, 2015.
DOI: 10.1007/978-3-319-18467-8_29

the application, the next step is to take control of the program execution to carry out some malicious activities. One of the typical and early attack techniques is code injection attack, in which a small payload that contains the machine code to perform the desired task is injected into the process memory. A wide range of solutions have been proposed to defend against memory corruption attacks, and to increase the complexity of performing buffer overflow and format string vulnerability exploitation [4-8]. To mitigate the code injection attack, a protection technique called $W \oplus X$ [9] was proposed. Under this protection regime, a memory page is either marked as writable or executable, but may not be both. Thus, an attacker may not inject data into a process's memory and then execute it simply by transfer control flow to that memory. Although the $W \oplus X$ technique is not foolproof [10, 11], it was thought to be a sufficiently strong protection regime that both the processor venders like Intel and AMD and prevalent operating systems like Windows [12], Linux [13], Mac OS X, and OpenBSD [14] now support it.

However, recently, attackers circumvented the $W \oplus X$ protection by employing *code-reuse* attacks (CRAs), which reuse the functionality provided by the exploited application. Using this technique, which was originally called return-to-libc [15], an attacker can compromise the stack and transfer the control to the beginning of an existing libc function. Often the system call system( ) is used to launch a process or mprotect( ) is used to create a writable, executable memory region to bypass $W \oplus X$. In 2007, Shacham showed that $W \oplus X$ protection regime could be entirely evaded by so called return-oriented programming (ROP) [16] technique. In ROP, so called *gadgets* (small snippets of code ending in ret) are weaved together to achieve Turing complete computation without code injection. Since the advent of ROP, several effective defense techniques have been proposed [17-19]. However, a new class of code-reuse attacks called jump-oriented programming (JOP) that does not rely on rets has been proposed [20-22]. In these JOP attacks, the attacker chains the gadgets by using a sequence of indirect jump instructions, rather than **rets**, thus bypassing the defense mechanisms designed for ROP. Until now, there is no efficient technique can prevent both ROP and JOP attacks.

The x86 microprocessors are the most widely used general purpose processor series today. As a typical CISC architecture, instructions on the x86 platforms are of variable-length, and decoding an instruction from any byte offset is allowed. As a consequence, every x86 executable binary contains a vast number of *unintended* code sequences that can be accessed by jumping to an offset not on an original instruction boundary. Both the ROP and JOP take advantage of this feature to discover useful gadgets, which makes CRAs more easily to be carried out on CISC processors than that of RISC processors. Some of the previous studies that target for CRA defense tackle this problem in software-only approaches, which makes the applications of their techniques limited to constrained circumstances.

In this paper, we propose effectively mitigating CRAs on CISC architectures in a hardware supported approach. The main contributions of the work in this paper are:

- The unintended instruction problem of CISC processors is thoroughly resolved with only a few hardware and software modifications, and no application binary modification.
- The techniques are evaluated by cycle-accurate simulations of SPEC CPU 2006 benchmarks. The experimental results show that our proposed techniques have very little performance impact on these benchmarks.
- We further propose using hardware control-flow locking as a complementary technique to our protection mechanism.

The remainder of this paper is organized as follows. Section 2 describes the related work. The methodology and implementation details are presented in Section 3. The experimental evaluation is presented in Section 4. Section 5 offers some concluding remarks.

2   Related Work

The first step of a code reuse attack is to gain control of the program counter to divert program control flow to the first gadget. An attacker then may overwrite either the return address for the calling function or a function pointer with the address of the first gadget to divert the program control flow. Both software and hardware approaches were developed to prevent attackers from exploiting software vulnerabilities [4-8][23-26]. However, either these mechanisms are not adopted by hardware products or they are frequently not turned on as default when programs are compiled. As a result, attackers can always exploit software flaws to gain control of the program counter.

One tricky problem for CRA defense techniques on CISC platforms like x86 is the allowing of unintended instruction execution, which makes these defense techniques face more gadgets on CISC architectures. Before the advent of CRAs, some researchers of prior work [39, 40] realized that the unintended instructions could be a potential security problem, and solved it by imposing alignment in the environment of a sandbox. Since the advent of CRAs, previous CRA defenses rely on dynamic binary instrumentation tools monitoring unintended instructions without the help of hardware [34, 35], which limits their practical use.

Another problem is unintended control flow transfers. To solve this problem, a number of defense techniques have been proposed, and most of them are against ROP attacks. Several approaches use a shadow stack to prevent control flow manipulation that relies on overwritten stack values [27, 28]. Some try to detect gadget execution by monitoring return properties [17, 18], and others proposed monitoring pairs of call and return instructions [29, 30]. Several prevention approaches attempt to eliminate possible gadgets in library code [31, 32], and alternative strategies include creating binaries or kernels that lack necessary characteristics for ROP attacks [19, 33]. Most of these techniques rely on known characteristics of ROP attacks, and some were proved to have flaws that the defense mechanisms can be bypassed. Several approaches require recompilation of the program, library or kernel binaries, which may pose a problem when the source code is not available.

Since JOP is a recently proposed technique, there are only a few proposals that target for JOP defenses. Among these defense techniques, [34], [35] and [36] are pure software approaches. To distinguish normal program execution from CRA attacks, they rely on the software dynamic binary instrumentation. As a result, to apply their techniques, the programs must be executed through a dynamic binary instrumentation tool like Pin [37] or a virtual machine, which limits the practical use of their approaches. [30] and [38] are hardware supported approaches proposed by Kayaalp et al. By using binary rewriting, the branch regulation approach in [30] inserts markers to make jumps stay in a legal function. Branch regulation requires binary rewriting and cannot easily protect legacy binaries. It is also possible that a function may exist that can provide sufficient gadgets to mount an attack, and in this case security is not completely guaranteed. The work in [38] proposes a hardware supported signature-based protection mechanism. While this approach supports legacy software, it needs user to configure thresholds for CRA detection. Again, it is also one type of techniques that rely on known characteristics of CRAs.

3   Methodology

3.1   Elimination of Unintended Instructions

Figure 1 illustrates an example of unintended instruction sequence, which is similar to the one showed in [30]. The x86 assembly language used in this paper is written in Intel syntax. The disassembled code snippet is from the _IO_vfprintf function of libc-2.12-32. This code snippet consists of three instructions if decoded normally. However, if the decoding starts from the third byte of the call instruction, a different instruction sequence can be decoded as shown at the bottom of Figure 1, which contains three entirely different instruction. This unintended instruction sequence could possibly be used as a gadget, as the last jump instruction can be used to direct control flow to other gadgets (the memory location that register ebx points to). It should be noted that finding indirect jump instructions from unintended code sequence is extremely easy on x86 platforms, as byte FF represents the opcode of an indirect jump instruction on x86 [41], and FF is a common byte used in immediate values (bit-masks and sign bits of negative values).

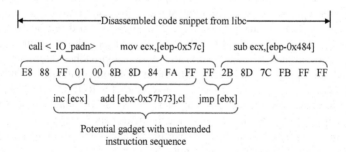

Fig. 1. Example unintended instruction sequence from libc

Problem Analysis.
As well known, the processor pipeline can be roughly divided into five stages (i.e. IF, ID, EX, MEM and WB). Of the five stages, the instruction fetch stage fetches instructions from I-Cache according to the address pointed by program counter (PC), as illustrated in Figure 2. Therefore, it may be the most suitable stage to check whether an instruction is an intended instruction or not.

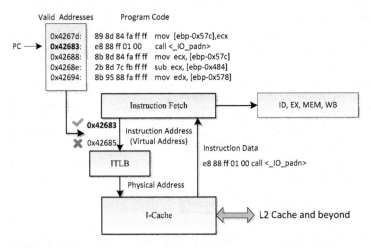

Fig. 2. Process of instruction fetch and instruction address validation

For a variable-length instruction architecture, to know whether the current PC points to an unintended instruction, the processor needs a list of valid instruction addresses to be compared with, as illustrated in Figure 2. One way of acquiring the list of valid instruction addresses is disassembling the executable binary before its execution. When an executable binary has been loaded into memory, OS knows the location of each binary code section in the virtual memory space, and the valid address of each intended instruction can be obtained by sequentially disassembling the instructions from the start of each code section. Now with the list of valid instruction addresses, how to validate the legality of an instruction address? An inefficient preliminary solution is illustrated in Figure 3.

The solution depicted in Figure 3 first uses a recently validated address buffer (RVAB) to validate the current PC. The RVAB can be implemented in processor and functions similar to other LRU buffers in the processor. If the PC is not found in RVAB, then a further lookup will be needed. A program is often composed of several code sections, including the code sections from shared libraries. Instruction addresses within a code section are contiguous, but different code sections may not be contiguous in virtual memory space. Therefore, if a PC is not hit the RVAB, then the solution in Figure 3 first needs to find which code section this PC belongs to from a code section range list which can be derived from section information after the program has been loaded into memory. To save memory consumption, this preliminary solution organizes several contiguous addresses into an address chunk. The size of the chunk can be multiple of a byte. The first four bytes (for a 32-bit system) stores the first address, and each following byte stores an offset from the first address. To find a specific address, the processor must search through the address chunks of a code section. If a binary search algorithm is used, the average time consumption can be O(log n) (n is the number of chunks in a code section), which means a processor may need accessing off-chip memory log n times to validate an address, and at the meantime, the processor pipeline must be stalled in order to wait for the result of the validation. Apparently, the overhead of this solution is too high for a modern processor.

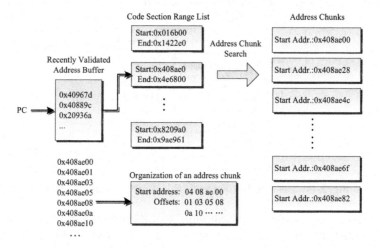

Fig. 3. A preliminary solution for instruction address validation

Proposed Mechanism.
This subsection provides a more practical and efficient solution to the intended instruction validation problem in detail.

Recently Validated Address Buffer.
A proposed hardware implementation of RVAB is depicted in Figure 4. The buffer storage is divided into M sets and N lines. A branch target address to be validated is evaluated with a hash function to determine which set it belongs to. Each set contains N validated addresses or invalid empty entries. The address to be validated is compared with these addresses in parallel to quickly check whether the branch target hits the RVAB or not. For a practical implementation, a pseudo-LRU algorithm is used as the replacement strategy for the addresses within a set. Apparently, the hardware cost of RVAB mainly depends on its storage size. We will evaluate the choices of M and N in the experimental evaluation section.

Validation of Branch Target Address.
Theoretically, to ensure only intended instructions are executed, the addresses of all instructions that are going to be executed should be compared with valid instruction addresses. However, if we assume that the program starts from a valid instruction address, then we only need to validate the branch targets of control transfer instructions, as a CISC processor always decodes out instructions one by one sequentially. As a further optimization measure, if the $W \oplus X$ protection mechanism is present, we can restrict the validations to indirect control transfer instructions. This is based on the fact that the branch target of a direct control transfer instruction is written into the code section which cannot be modified when $W \oplus X$ protection mechanism is applied.

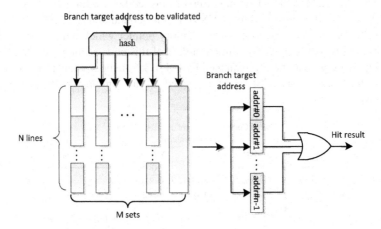

Fig. 4. The structure of recently validated address buffer

Representation of Valid Instruction Addresses.
The solution in Figure 3 requires $\log n$ search times for validating an address that does not hit RVAB, which makes the searching very inefficient. Another way of representing instruction addresses is using one bit to indicate whether an address is the start of a valid instruction, Figure 5 depicts this idea.

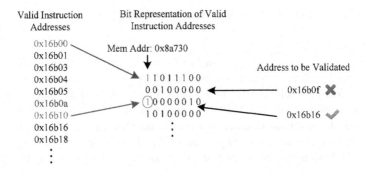

Fig. 5. Using one bit to indicate the validity of instruction address

In Figure 5, suppose the instruction address validation data are stored beginning from 0x8a730 in memory, and the first bit represents the instruction address 0x16b00. If we want to know whether address 0x16b16 is a valid instruction address or not, then we can check the 7th bit of the byte at address 0x8a732 ((0x16b16 - 0x16b00)/8 + 0x8a730). Compared with the solution in Figure 3, this way of representing instruction addresses may consume more memory space (1/8 of the total code binary size), but greatly reduces instruction address validation time.

Code Section Range Lookup Table.
If the address representation in Figure 5 is used, then the code section range list acts more like a lookup table. The function of this code section range lookup table (CSRLT) is described in Figure 6. A CSRLT entry contains three items: the start and the end address of a code section and a memory pointer which points to the memory offset of the instruction address validation data of this code section. A full CSRLT is stored on off-chip memory and managed by OS. Like memory page TLB, some of the recently used entries in CSRLT are cached in an on-chip buffer (denoted by CSRLTB)

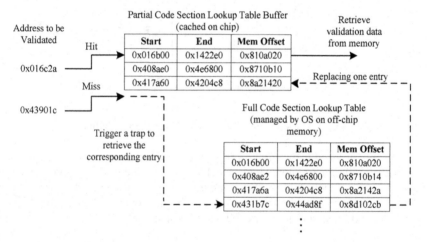

Fig. 6. The function of code section range lookup table

Integration with Processor Pipeline.
Now we explain how to integrate our proposed mechanism with an out-of-order processor pipeline, which is illustrated in Figure 7. As there is no need to validate every fetched instruction's address except for branch target, the validation process is better moved from instruction fetch stage to commit stage. There are two reasons behind this: firstly, the real branch target of a control transfer instruction can only be determined after the EX stage; secondly, some of the control instructions in EX stage may be aborted due to failed speculation and commit stage is where precise exceptions are usually carried out in out-of-order processors. However, validating the branch target address when the instruction is just about to commit will stall the processor pipeline for each validation even if the address hits RVAB. Thus, a better solution is carrying

out the validation when the control instructions are at the front of the ROB committing queue but have not reached the head yet, and using one bit to indicate the branch
target is valid or not.

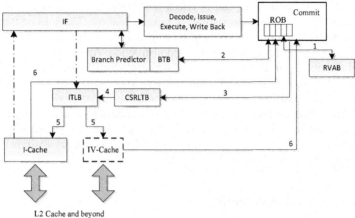

Fig. 7. The integration with an out-of-order pipeline

3.2 Further Protection Measures

Statistical results in [30] shows that limiting the dispatcher gadgets to intended
instructions greatly reduces the number of potential dispatcher candidates. However,
the remaining dispatcher candidates can still be expored for carrying out JOP attacks.
As a result, we propose using *control flow locking* (CFL) as the complementary technique to our mechanism. CFL was proposed by Bletsch et al. in [36].

The idea of CFL is illustrated in Figure 8. This code snippet is from **libssl.a**. The
actual destination of indirect jump in address 0x451 is address 0x4f0. In [36], to implement CFL, a small snippet of *lock* code is inserted before each indirect control
flow transfer. This code asserts the *lock* by simply changing a certain *lock value* in
memory, and each valid destination for that control transfer contains the corresponding unlock code, which will de-assert the *lock* if and only if the current *lock value* is
deemed "valid". In Figure 8, variable k is the *control flow key*, and value 1 means
locked while 0 means unlocked.

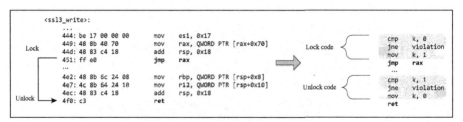

Fig. 8. An illustrative example of CFL

As this paper focuses on hardware supported techniques to mitigate JOP attacks, we propose using hardware to efficiently implement a weaker version of CFL. First, for each committed indirect jump, the processor needs to record that the processor is in a *jump locking* state. Second, we can devise a new instruction or just add a prefix to current instructions to denote an indirect jump destination. The role of the new instruction or prefix is to *unlock* the *jump locking* state, and this *unlocking* instruction must be committed just after an indirect jump instruction. Apparently, this mechanism is not hard to implement in hardware. For the hardware CFL, the compiler is responsible for correctly inserting indirect jump destination instruction or prefix when translating high level language source code into machine binary code. A difference to software CFL is that we omit the *lock value*. We argue that implementing *lock value* will introduce much more hardware and software cost. With the elimination of unintended instructions and the support of hardware CFL, it is already extremely hard to find out enough gadgets to carry a JOP attack.

4   Performance Evaluation

For evaluating the performance of our techniques, we used the gem5 [43] simulator to simulate a 4-core x86 CMP. All our experiments were carried out on a high-end desktop computer which has a 3.4 GHz Core i7-4770 CPU with 16GB memory, and the operating system is CentOS 6.4 x86-64. We selected 21 benchmarks from the SPEC CPU2006 [44] benchmark suit and used test input data set for our experiments. These benchmarks were compiled using CentOS's native GCC compiler (version 4.4.7) with -O3 optimizations. For each benchmark, we ran the simulation for 10 billion instructions or until its completion.

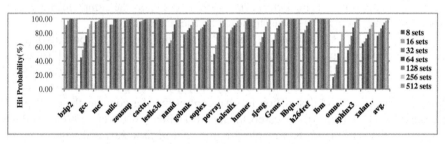

Fig. 9. RVAB hit probability for validations of all control instructions

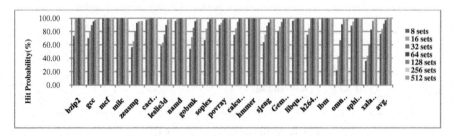

Fig. 10. RVAB hit probability for validations of indirect control instructions

First, we will evaluate the configurations of RVAB. In the work of this paper, we used 4 entries for each set, and pseudo-LRU for replacement strategy. For the hash function, we simply used lower part of the address as set index. Now we only need to investigate how many sets will be enough for a high RVAB hit probability.

Figure 9 illustrates the RVAB hit probability when all control instructions were considered, and Figure 10 illustrates the result when only indirect control instructions were validated. It can be observed that for the same number of set and the same benchmark, the hit probability of Figure 10 is higher than that of Figure 9. An important observation is that when the number of set reaches 128, the hit probability does not change very much, especially for 256 sets and 512 sets. For the benchmarks in Figure 9, the average hit probabilities of 128 sets, 256 sets and 512 sets are 94.68%, 97.35% and 98.84%; and for the benchmarks in Figure 10, the average hit probabilities of 128 sets, 256 sets and 512 sets are 99.11%, 99.61% and 99.70%. Based on this observation, we selected 128 as the set number for the following experiments, and the total number of RVAB entries is 128x4 = 512. As we can see, the hardware cost of RVAB is very small.

We evaluated three configurations for performance impact evaluation. The first configuration is validating all control instructions and using branch predictor as lookup backup (denoted as BP & AC); the second is only validating indirect control instructions and using BP as lookup backup (denoted as BP & IC); the third configuration is only validating indirect control instructions but without using BP as backup. Figure 11a shows the IPC results of the baseline and the three configurations. Here we count x86 micro-ops as instruction counts. To get a clearer view, Figure 11b-11d shows relative performance slowdown of these three configurations.

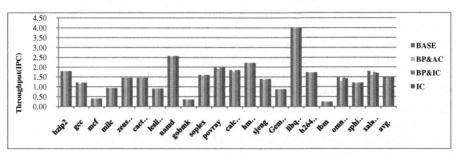

Fig. 11a. Throughput comparison (IPC) of baseline and three different configurations

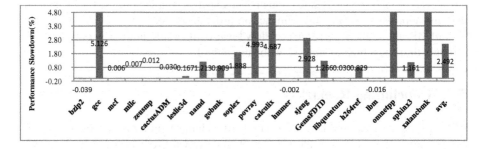

Fig. 11b. Relative performance slowdown of BP&AC configuration.

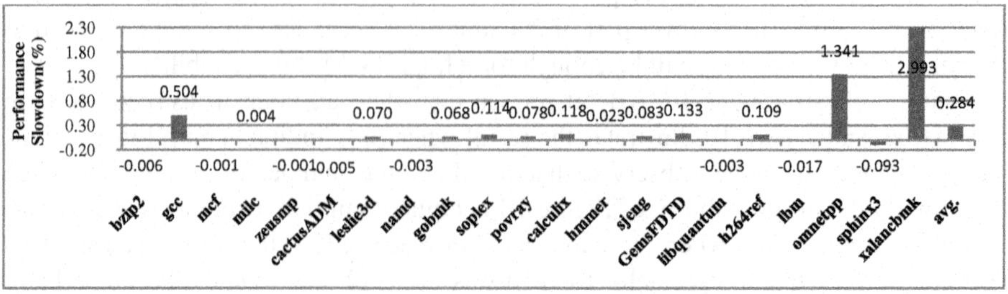

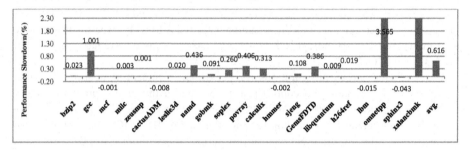

Fig. 11c. Relative performance slowdown of BP&IC configuration

Fig. 12d. Relative performance slowdown of IC configuration

From Figure 11a, we can see that the performance impacts of our proposed methodology are very small for all three configurations. For the BP&AC configuration, the average performance slowdown is 2.492%, the highest performance slowdown is 12.623% (**omnetpp**), the smallest is -0.039%(**bzip2**, which means IPC gets a little increase), and there are 11 benchmarks whose performance slowdowns are below 1%. As we expect, the BP&IC configuration gets the best performance result. Its performance slowdown is between -0.093% and 2.993%, and is 0.284% on average. Only two benchmarks' slowdowns exceed 1%. Without BP as backup, the performance result of the IC configuration is a little worse than the BP&IC configuration, but better than the BP&AC configuration. Its slowdown is between -0.043% and 5.247%, and is 0.616% on average.

Since the W ⊕ X mechanism is widely used in modern systems, only validating indirect control instructions is safe enough. The experimental data in Figure 11 indicate that this approach has very little impact on program performance. Even without the help of BP, the highest performance slowdown of IC configuration is only 5.247%, and only three benchmarks have slowdowns above 1%.

5   Concluding Remarks

In this paper, we proposed hardware supported techniques to mitigate CRAs on CISC architectures. We addressed the CRA problem by two protection mechanisms: (1)

preventing executions of unintended instructions; (2) preventing unintended control flow transfers. The work in this paper mainly focuses on the first problem, as no previous work addressed it by an effective hardware approach. We addressed the second problem by using a hardware version of CFL. We also demonstrated that our approach has a very modest cost on both hardware and software. For the BP&IC configuration, the performance loss is -0.093% ~2.993%.

Acknowledgements. This work is supported in part by the Natural Science Foundation of China under Grant No. 61170050, National Science and Technology Major Project of China （2012ZX01039-004）. The authors would also like to thank anonymous reviewers who have helped us to improve the quality of this paper.

References

1. Symantec: Internet Security Threat Report (2014). http://www.symantec.com/security_response/publications/threatreport.jsp
2. One, A.: Smashing the stack for fun and profit. Phrack Magazine 7(49), 14–16 (1996)
3. Scut, T.T.: Exploiting format string vulnerabilities (2001)
4. Cowan, C., Beattie, S., Johansen, J., Wagle, P.: Pointguard TM: protecting pointers from buffer overflow vulnerabilities. In: Proceedings of the 12th Conference on USENIX Security Symposium, vol. 12, pp. 91–104, August 2003
5. Cowan, C., Pu, C., Maier, D., Walpole, J., Bakke, P., Beattie, S., Hinton, H: StackGuard: automatic adaptive detection and prevention of buffer-overflow attacks. In: Usenix Security, vol. 98, pp. 63–78 (1998)
6. Cowan, C., Wagle, P., Pu, C., Beattie, S., Walpole, J.: Buffer overflows: attacks and defenses for the vulnerability of the decade. In: Proceedings of DARPA Information Survivability Conference and Exposition, DISCEX 2000, vol. 2, pp. 119–129. IEEE (2000)
7. Etoh, H., Yoda, K.: GCC extension for protecting applications from stack-smashing attacks (2014). http://www.research.ibm.com/trl/projects/security/ssp/
8. Shield, S.: A stack smashing technique protection tool for Linux (2014). http://www.angelfire.com/sk/stackshield/
9. Pax Team: Non-executable pages design and implementation. http://paxgrsecurity.net/docs/pageexec.txt
10. Krahmer, S.: x86-64 buffer overflow exploits and the borrowed code chunks exploitation technique (2005). http://www.suse.de/krahmer/no-nx.pdf
11. McDonald, J.: Defeating Solaris/SPARC non-executable stack protection. Bugtraq (1999)
12. Microsoft. KB 875352: A detailed description of the Data Execution Prevention (DEP) feature in Windows XP Service Pack 2, Windows XP Tablet PC Edition 2005, and Windows Server (2003). http://support.microsoft.com/KB/875352 (September 2006)
13. Designer, S.: Linux kernel patch from the Openwall project. http://www.openwall.com/linux
14. OpenBSD Foundation. OpenBSD 3.3 release (2003). http://www.openbsd.org/33.html
15. Solar Designer.: Return-to-libc attack. Technical report, bugtraq (1997)
16. Shacham, H.: The geometry of innocent flesh on the bone: Return-into-libc without function calls (on the x86). In: Proceedings of the 14th ACM Conference on Computer and Communications security, pp. 552–561. ACM (2007)

17. Davi, L., Sadeghi, A.R., Winandy, M.: Dynamic integrity measurement and attestation: towards defense against return-oriented programming attacks.: In: Proceedings of the 2009 ACM Workshop on Scalable Trusted Computing, pp. 49–54 (2009)
18. Chen, P., Xiao, H., Shen, X., Yin, X., Mao, B., Xie, L.: DROP: detecting return-oriented programming malicious code. In: Prakash, A., Sen Gupta, I. (eds.) ICISS 2009. LNCS, vol. 5905, pp. 163–177. Springer, Heidelberg (2009)
19. Li, J., Wang, Z., Jiang, X., Grace, M., Bahram, S.: Defeating return-oriented rootkits with return-less kernels. In: Proceedings of the 5th European Conference on Computer systems, pp. 195–208. ACM (2010)
20. Bletsch, T., Jiang, X., Freeh, V.W., Liang, Z.: Jump-oriented programming: a new class of code-reuse attack. In: Proceedings of the 6th ACM Symposium on Information, Computer and Communications Security, pp. 30–40. ACM (2011)
21. Checkoway, S., Davi, L., Dmitrienko, A., Sadeghi, A.R., Shacham, H., Winandy, M.: Return-oriented programming without returns. In: Proceedings of the 17th ACM Conference on Computer and Communications Security, pp. 559–572. ACM. (2010)
22. Chen, P., Xing, X., Mao, B., Xie, L., Shen, X., Yin, X.: Automatic construction of jump-oriented programming shellcode (on the x86). In: Proceedings of the 6th ACM Symposium on Information, Computer and Communications Security, pp. 20–29. ACM (2011)
23. McGregor, J.P., Karig, D.K., Shi, Z., Lee, R.B.: A processor architecture defense against buffer overflow attacks. In: Proceedings of the IEEE International Conference on Information Technology: Research and Education, ITRE 2003, pp. 243–250 (2003)
24. Lee, R.B., Karig, D.K., McGregor, J.P., Shi, Z.: Enlisting hardware architecture to thwart malicious code injection. In: Hutter, D., Müller, G., Stephan, W., Ullmann, M. (eds.) Security in Pervasive Computing. LNCS, vol. 2802, pp. 237–252. Springer, Heidelberg (2004)
25. Davi, L., Sadeghi, A.R., Winandy, M.: ROPdefender: A detection tool to defend against return-oriented programming attacks. In: Proceedings of the 6th ACM Symposium on Information, Computer and Communications Security, pp. 40–51. ACM (2011)
26. Xu, J., Kalbarczyk, Z., Patel, S., Iyer, R.K.: Architecture support for defending against buffer overflow attacks. In: Workshop on Evaluating and Architecting Systems for Dependability (2002)
27. Davi, L., Sadeghi, A.R., Winandy, M.: ROPdefender: A detection tool to defend against return-oriented programming attacks. In: Proceedings of the 6th ACM Symposium on Information, Computer and Communications Security. pp. 40–51. ACM. (2011)
28. Francillon, A., Perito, D., Castelluccia, C.: Defending embedded systems against control flow attacks. In: Proceedings of the first ACM Workshop on Secure Execution of Untrusted Code, pp. 19–26. ACM (2009)
29. Chen, P., Xing, X., Han, H., Mao, B., Xie, L.: Efficient detection of the return-oriented programming malicious code. In: Jha, S., Mathuria, A. (eds.) ICISS 2010. LNCS, vol. 6503, pp. 140–155. Springer, Heidelberg (2010)
30. Kayaalp, M., Ozsoy, M., Abu-Ghazaleh, N., Ponomarev, D.: Branch regulation: Low-overhead protection from code reuse attacks. In: International Symposium on Computer Architecture (ISCA) (2012)
31. Hiser, J., Nguyen-Tuong, A., Co, M., Hall, M., Davidson, J.W.: ILR: Where'd my gadgets go? In: IEEE Symposium on Security and Privacy, pp. 571–585. IEEE (2012)
32. Pappas, V., Polychronakis, M., Keromytis, A.D.: Smashing the gadgets: Hindering return-oriented programming using in-place code randomization. In: IEEE Symposium on Security and Privacy (SP), pp. 601–615 (2012)

33. Onarlioglu, K., Bilge, L., Lanzi, A., Balzarotti, D., Kirda, E.: G-Free: defeating return-oriented programming through gadget-less binaries. In: Proceedings of the 26th Annual Computer Security Applications Conference (ACSAC), pp. 49–58. ACM (2010)
34. Huang, Z., Zheng, T., Shi, Y., Li, A.: A Dynamic detection method against ROP and JOP. In: International Conference on Systems and Informatics (ICSAI) (2012)
35. Jacobson, E.R., Bernat, A.R., Williams, W.R., Miller, B.P.: Detecting code reuse attacks with a model of conformant program execution. In: Jürjens, J., Piessens, F., Bielova, N. (eds.) ESSoS. LNCS, vol. 8364, pp. 1–18. Springer, Heidelberg (2014)
36. Bletsch, T., Jiang, X., Freeh, V.: Mitigating code-reuse attacks with control-flow locking. In: Proceedings of the 27th Annual Computer Security Applications Conference, pp. 353–362. ACM (2011)
37. University of Virginia, Pin. http://www.cs.virginia.edu/kim/publicity/pin
38. Kayaalp, M., Schmitt, T., Nomani, J., Ponomarev, D., Abu-Ghazaleh, N.: SCRAP: Architecture for signature-based protection from code reuse attacks. In: IEEE 19th International Symposium on High Performance Computer Architecture (HPCA), pp. 258–269, February 23-27, 2013
39. McCamant, S., Morrisett, G.: Efficient, verifiable binary sandboxing for a CISC architecture. In: MIT Technical Report. MIT-CSAIL-TR-2005-030 (2005)
40. Yee, B., Sehr, D., Dardyk, G., Chen, J.B., Muth, R., Ormandy, T., Fullagar, N.: Native client: A sandbox for portable, untrusted x86 native code. In: 30th IEEE Symposium on Security and Privacy, vol. 53(1), pp. 79–93 (2009)
41. Intel Corporation: Intel 64 and IA-32 Architectures Software Developer's Manual, vol. 2 (2013)
42. Udis86 Disassembler Library for x86/x86-64. http://udis86.sourceforgenet/
43. Binkert, N., Beckmann, B., Black, G., Reinhardt, S.K., Saidi, A., Basu, A., Wood, D.A.: The gem5 simulator. Computer Architecture News 39, 1–7 (2011)
44. Henning, J.L.: Spec cpu2006 benchmark descriptions. ACM SIGARCH Computer Architecture News, 1–17 (2006)

Integrity for Approximate Joins
on Untrusted Computational Servers

Sabrina De Capitani di Vimercati[1], Sara Foresti[1], Sushil Jajodia[2],
Stefano Paraboschi[3], and Pierangela Samarati[1] (✉)

[1] Università degli Studi di Milano, 26013 Crema, Italy
{sabrina.decapitani,sara.foresti,pierangela.samarati}@unimi.it
[2] George Mason University, Fairfax, VA 22030-4444, USA
jajodia@gmu.edu
[3] Università di Bergamo, 24044 Dalmine, Italy
parabosc@unibg.it

Abstract. In the last few years, many efforts have been devoted to
the development of solutions aiming at ensuring the confidentiality and
integrity of data and computations in the cloud. In particular, a recent
solution for verifying the integrity of equi-join queries is based on the
insertion of checks (markers and twins) whose presence provides probabilistic guarantees on the integrity of the computation. In this paper,
we propose an approach for verifying the integrity of *approximate join
queries*, which is based on the introduction of a discretized version of the
join attribute and on the translation of the approximate join into an equi-
join defined over the discrete attribute added to the original relations.
The proposed approach guarantees the correctness and completeness of
the join result, while causing a limited overhead for the user.

1 Introduction

Cloud computing has brought enormous benefits in terms of the availability of
a universal access to data as well as of elastic storage and computation services. More and more often users and organizations put their (possibly sensitive) data in the hands of external cloud providers, which become responsible
for the storage and management of such data [5,10,16]. A recent trend in cloud
computing is a distinction between providers of *storage* services and providers of
computational services. This diversification supports the development of efficient
applications that combine the functions offered by different cloud providers. In
this context, users and organizations can therefore decide to store their data at
reliable and well-known storage servers and perform computationally intensive
processes (e.g., join operations) using the computational services offered by a less
expensive and potentially untrusted computational server. Besides performance
considerations, an important advantage of relying on storage and computational
servers is due to the economic advantage of such a choice [3]. While appealing,
this approach brings inherent risks related to the confidentiality and integrity of
data and computations, which are difficult to mitigate since data are not under

© IFIP International Federation for Information Processing 2015
H. Federrath and D. Gollmann (Eds.): SEC 2015, IFIP AICT 455, pp. 446–459, 2015.
DOI: 10.1007/978-3-319-18467-8_30

the direct control of their owners. The research community has dedicated many efforts in developing solutions for these problems, resulting in several approaches to protect the confidentiality and integrity of data at rest (e.g., [5]), as well as of computations over them (e.g., [12,17,18]).

In this paper, we make a step forward and present a solution for verifying the integrity of *approximate join* queries. An approximate join aims at combining tuples with similar (even if not equal) values for the join attribute, and can be needed in several applications (e.g., to detect duplicate entities in different databases or to identify data clusters). The current techniques can verify the integrity of equi-join queries only (e.g., [3]) and then cannot be directly applied to verify the integrity of approximate joins. Moreover, since data are typically encrypted to protect their confidentiality, the evaluation of similarity conditions characterizing an approximate join cannot be efficiently executed on such encrypted data. A client is then not able to delegate the join operation to a computational server without revealing the plaintext values of the join attribute. In the remainder of this paper, after the presentation of some basic concepts and of the problem we aim at addressing (Section 2), we illustrate an approach for verifying the integrity of approximate joins (Section 3). Our solution consists in adding to the original relations a discretized version of the join attribute, translating approximate joins into equi-joins over the discretized attribute. The equi-join is computed as a semi-join, delegating to an external computational server the execution of the join, which is a computationally intensive operation. The techniques in [3] are used to verify the integrity of the computation performed by the computational server (Section 4). Our solution does not impact the correctness and completeness of the join result, and provides limited overhead for the storage servers and for the user (Section 5).

2 Basic Concepts and Problem Statement

We consider a scenario where a client wishes to evaluate an *approximate join* between two relations B_l and B_r stored at two trustworthy storage servers S_l and S_r, respectively. The computation of the approximate join is delegated to an external and potentially unreliable computational server C_s. Intuitively, an approximate join between B_l and B_r matches tuples that are sufficiently similar, meaning that the values of their join attribute are similar. The similarity between the values of the join attribute can be measured by choosing a distance function (the Euclidean distance in our scenario) and a threshold α set by the client. The query formulated by the client is of the form "SELECT A FROM B_l JOIN B_r ON $|B_l.I - B_r.I| < \alpha$ WHERE C_l AND C_r AND C_{lr}," with A a subset of attributes in $B_l \cup B_r$; I the set of join attributes; $|B_l.I - B_r.I| < \alpha$ the similarity condition and α the threshold fixed by the client; and C_l, C_r, and C_{lr} Boolean formulas of conditions over attributes in B_l, B_r, and $B_l \cup B_r$, respectively. The evaluation of conditions C_l and C_r is pushed down to the storage servers.

Current approaches for integrity verification consider only equi-joins that are executed as semi-joins (or regular joins) by a computational server and are based on the combined adoption of *encryption on the fly* (to protect data confidentiality), and of *markers* and *twins* (to provide integrity guarantees) [2,3]. Each storage server first receives from the client the sub-query it should evaluate and the information necessary for the adoption of encryption on the fly, markers, and twins. It then executes the received sub-query (obtaining relations L and R) and projects the join attribute (obtaining relations LI and RI), thus naturally removing duplicate values. Each storage server then duplicates the tuples in its relation that satisfy a twinning condition C_{twin} defined by the client on the join attribute (to guarantee that twins belong to the join result). Twinned tuples are made unrecognizable to the computational server by combining the value of the join attribute with a random salt before encryption. Each storage server also inserts fake tuples (markers), not recognizable as such by the computational server, into the relation before sending it to the computational server. Markers generated by the two storage servers have the same values for the join attribute (to guarantee their presence in the join result), and these values do not appear in real tuples (to avoid spurious tuples). The resulting relations LI^* and $RI^*$are encrypted by the storage servers (obtaining relations LI_k^* and RI_k^*), with a key communicated by the client and that changes at each query, and are sent to the computational server. The computational server evaluates the equi-join between the two relations received from the storage servers and sends the result JI_k^* to the client. The client decrypts JI_k^*, verifies its integrity (i.e., the client checks whether all expected markers are in the result and twinned tuples do not appear solo), and removes markers and twins (obtaining relation JI). The client then sends JI to both the storage servers, which return to the client all the tuples in L and R having a value for the join attribute in JI. Upon receiving these relations (LJ and RJ) the client recombines them with JI obtaining the join result. Figure 1 illustrates an example of execution of an equi-join, assuming to adopt one marker (with value m for the join attribute), and to twin tuples whose join attribute is equal to a or d.

The semi-join approach mentioned above cannot be used for approximate joins. In fact, the computational server should evaluate a similarity condition $|L.I - R.I| < \alpha$ over encrypted attributes, which is possible only if the encryption function supports the evaluation of arithmetic operations. Such encryption functions (e.g., homomorphic encryption) are inefficient and not suitable for all scenarios. Also, the definition of markers and twins should be revised to comply with the similarity condition, without revealing the nature of the tuples in the encrypted relations.

3   Approximate Join Transformation

Our approach for verifying the integrity of an approximate join is based on a discretization process applied on the domain of the join attribute. This discretization allows us to translate an approximate join into an equi-join. For simplicity, we assume that the domain D of the join attribute is the set of real, natural, or integer numbers. We note however that our solution can be extended to operate also over any domain characterized by a total order relationship.

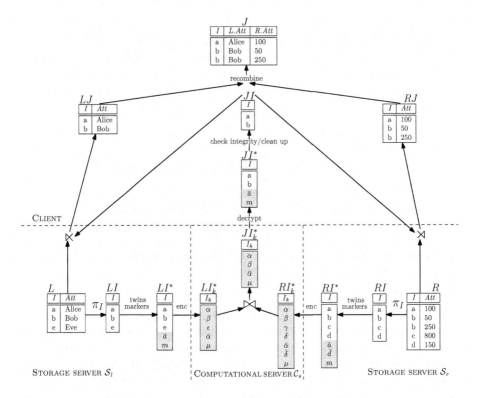

Fig. 1. Equi-join execution as a semi-join

3.1 Discretized Domain

The discretization process redefines the domain of the join attribute, transforming it into a (coarser grained) discrete domain. In this way, the similarity condition $|L.I - R.I| < \alpha$ can be transformed into an equality condition over the discretized join attribute, transforming the approximate join into an equi-join.

The discretization of domain D requires to define a *discrete domain* $\hat{D}$ and a *mapping function* f that maps original values into discrete values. To this aim, we chose a *granularity* γ of the discrete domain, which corresponds to the distance between two consecutive values in $\hat{D}$, and a *reference point* p. The reference point p is a value in the original domain D that belongs also to the discretized domain $\hat{D}$ and that, together with γ, can be used to determine the values in $\hat{D}$. We define the values in $\hat{D}$ to be at a distance multiple of γ from p. Formally, a discretized domain is defined as follows.

Definition 1 (Discretized domain). *Let D be a continuous domain, γ be a granularity, and p be an element in D. A discretized domain $\hat{D}$ of D is defined as the set of values in D whose distance from p is a multiple of γ, that is, $\hat{D} = \{v \in D : v - p = x\gamma, \text{ with } x \in \mathbb{Z}\}$.*

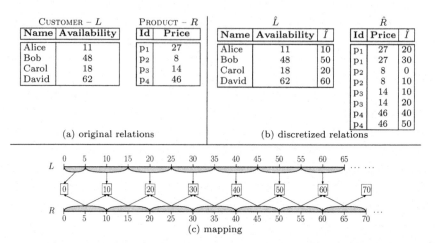

Fig. 2. An example of two relations (a), their discretization with $\alpha = 5$ (b), and the corresponding mapping of the join attribute (c)

For instance, a discretized domain of the natural numbers $\mathbb{N}$, which is the domain of attribute Availability in relation CUSTOMER in Figure 2(a), is domain $\hat{D} = \{0, 10, 20, \ldots\}$, assuming 0 as reference point and 10 as granularity.

The discretized domain of the join attribute should be the same for both the relations involved in the join operation to permit the correct evaluation of the equi-join condition between them. However, the mapping function used to map each tuple in L to a value in $\hat{D}$ (i.e., the partitioning of D into intervals of size γ and their association with discrete values) may be different from the mapping function used for the tuples in R, as discussed in the following.

3.2   Choosing the Correct Granularity

Each relation stored at the two storage servers $\mathcal{S}_l$ and $\mathcal{S}_r$ is complemented with an additional attribute, denoted $\hat{I}$, whose values have been obtained through the discretization of the corresponding join attribute domain. The similarity condition $|L.I - R.I| < \alpha$ is then transformed into an equi-join condition of the form $L.\hat{I} = R.\hat{I}$. The set of tuples returned by the evaluation of this equi-join condition should be *correct*, meaning that all tuples satisfying the original similarity condition should be part of the result, and should include a *limited number of spurious tuples* (i.e., tuples that do not satisfy the similarity condition).

To guarantee the correctness of the join result and to reduce the number of spurious tuples, the granularity γ and the mapping function f should be carefully chosen. In fact, a too coarse granularity may cause the presence of an excessive number of spurious tuples, and a too fine granularity could cause the absence of tuples from the join result. Analogously, a bad mapping function could cause the incompleteness of the join result. (The reference point p influences neither the number of spurious tuples nor the correctness of the join). The correctness of the join result is guaranteed when the values at distance lower than α are mapped to the same discrete value. Suppose to choose $\gamma = \alpha$, and a mapping function $f : D \rightarrow \hat{D}$ that associates with each tuple t in L and R the value v in $\hat{D}$ closest to $t[I]$ (i.e., $f(t[I]) = \{v \in \hat{D} : |v - t[I]| < 0.5\gamma\}$). In this case, the equi-join result would not be correct because some tuples satisfying the original similarity condition would be omitted. For instance, consider relations CUSTOMER and PRODUCT in Figure 2(a) and assume $\alpha = 5$ and $p = 0$. The discrete domain $\hat{D}$ is $\{0, 5, 10, \ldots\}$ and f maps: values in the interval $[0,2.5)$ to 0, values in the interval $[2.5, 7.5)$ to 5, and so on (we assume that the upper bound of each interval is excluded from the interval itself). Value 18 (associated with Carol) and value 14 (associated with p$_4$) would then be mapped to different discrete values (i.e., 20 and 15, respectively), even if the difference between them is 4. Therefore, the pair $\langle$Carol,p$_4\rangle$ satisfies the similarity condition but does not satisfy the equi-join condition over the discrete attributes. This problem happens independently from the granularity chosen. In fact, values at distance lower than α may be associated with different discrete values by function f. Consider, as an example, two values $1.5\gamma + \varepsilon$ and $1.5\gamma - \varepsilon$, with ε an arbitrarily small value, and assume that $\hat{D} = \{0, \gamma, 2\gamma, \ldots\}$. It is easy to see that, independently from the granularity γ, the first value is mapped by f to 2γ, while the second value is mapped by f to γ. Hence, the corresponding tuples will not satisfy the equi-join condition even if the difference between the two original values is $2\varepsilon \leq \alpha$.

Our solution consists in *replicating* the tuples in the original relations and in associating a different discrete value with each replica. The number of copies to be generated for each tuple depends on the granularity γ (i.e., the finer the granularity, the higher the number of necessary replicas). Let us consider $\gamma = \alpha$. In this case, it is necessary to duplicate each tuple in L and each tuple in R, and to associate each tuple t with the two values closest to $t[I]$ in $\hat{D}$. Hence, the mapping function f is defined as $f : D \rightarrow \hat{D} \times \hat{D}$ with $f(t[I]) = \{v_1, v_2 \in \hat{D} : |v_1 - (t[I] - 0.5\gamma)| < 0.5\gamma$ and $|v_2 - (t[I] + 0.5\gamma)| < 0.5\gamma\}$. This approach, although effective, has the drawback of doubling the data transferred from the storage servers to the computational server. If instead $\gamma = 2\alpha$, only the tuples in one of the two relations (say R) should be duplicated. In this case, it is sufficient to associate each tuple l in L with the discrete value nearest to $l[I]$. Each tuple r in R is instead duplicated and associated with the two discrete values nearest to $r[I]$. This approach limits the communication overhead as only one of the two relations (possibly the smallest) is duplicated. Further, increasing γ does not provide advantages and causes a higher number of spurious tuples in the equi-join result. A good balance between the number of spurious tuples in the join result and the number of additional tuples in the relations is then $\gamma = 2\alpha$. Figure 2(c) illustrates how the values of attributes Availability and Price are mapped assuming $\alpha = 5$ and $p = 0$. The mapping function for relation CUSTOMER is $f_L(t[I]) = \{v \in \hat{D} : |v - t[I]| < 5\}$, while the function for relation PRODUCT is $f_R(t[I]) = \{v_1, v_2 \in \hat{D} : |v_1 - (t[I] - 5)| < 5$ and $|v_2 - (t[I] + 5)| < 5\}$. The original domain is then partitioned in a different way for the two relations. In particular, there is a shift of $\alpha = 5$, which guarantees an intersection between the intervals of original values associated with the same discrete values in L and R, guaranteeing the effectiveness of the equi-join condition. As an example, values in $[5,15)$ in CUSTOMER are mapped to 10, as well as the values in $[0,20)$ in PRODUCT (intervals $[0,10)$ and $[10,20)$), with an intersection of width $\gamma=10$. The relations resulting from the discretization are then formally defined as follows.

Definition 2 (Discretized tables). *Let $L(I,\text{Attr})$ and $R(I,\text{Attr})$ be two relations, I be the join attribute defined over domain D, and α be the threshold fixed by the similarity condition. The* discretized *versions $\hat{L}$ of L and $\hat{R}$ of R are two relations defined over schema $(I,\text{Attr},\hat{I})$ where the domain of $\hat{I}$ is the discretized domain $\hat{D}$ of D with $\gamma = 2\alpha$, and:*

- *$\forall l{\in}L$, $\exists \hat{l}{\in}\hat{L}$ s.t. $\hat{l}[I]{=}l[I]$, $\hat{l}[\text{Attr}]{=}l[\text{Attr}]$, and $\hat{l}[\hat{I}]{=}f_L(l[I])$, with $f_L : D \to \hat{D}$ and $f_L(l[I]){=}\{v \in \hat{D} : |v - l[I]| < \alpha\}$;*
- *$\forall r{\in}R$, $\exists \hat{r}_1,\hat{r}_2{\in}\hat{R}$ such that $\hat{r}_1[I]{=}\hat{r}_2[I]{=}r[I]$, $\hat{r}_1[\text{Attr}]{=}\hat{r}_2[\text{Attr}]{=}r[\text{Attr}]$, and $(\hat{r}_1[\hat{I}],\hat{r}_2[\hat{I}]){=}f_R(l[I])$, with $f_R : D \to \hat{D} \times \hat{D}$ and $f_R(r[I]){=}\{v_1, v_2 \in \hat{D}: |v_1 - (r[I] - \alpha)| < \alpha \text{ and } |v_2 - (r[I] + \alpha)| < \alpha\}$.*

Figure 2(b) represents the discretized version of relations CUSTOMER and PRODUCT in Figure 2(a), obtained considering the discretized domain in Figure 2(c). Note that each original tuple in PRODUCT is replaced by two tuples with discrete values representing the end-points of the interval to which the original value belongs. The size of the discretized relation is then twice as the size of the original relation.

4   Join Evaluation and Correctness of the Approach

Like for the execution of an equi-join, the storage and computational servers do not need to coordinate for join execution. The client sends to the storage servers their sub-queries along with the information necessary to encrypt their relations, to generate markers and twins, and to perform the discretization process. The storage servers execute their sub-query and on the resulting relations apply the discretization process illustrated in Section 3. The storage servers then project attribute $\hat{I}$, insert markers and twins, and encrypt the resulting relations. The execution of the join then proceeds according to the semi-join strategy described in Section 2. Due to the discretization process, the relation $\hat{J}$, resulting from the recombination performed by the client and the integrity check and clean up phase, may include spurious tuples. In fact, the maximum distance between two (non discretized) values in D that map to the same discrete value in $\hat{D}$ is 3α (e.g., 6 in L and 19 in R are both mapped to 10). The client will then filter spurious tuples from $\hat{J}$ to obtain the approximate join result J. For instance, with reference to relations CUSTOMER and PRODUCT in Figure 2(a), consider a query that aims to return, for each customer, the products that have a price within a range of 5 with respect to what the customer is willing to spend (which is represented by attribute `Availability`). Figure 3 illustrates the evaluation of such an approximate join query with similarity condition |`Availability`−`Price`|<5,

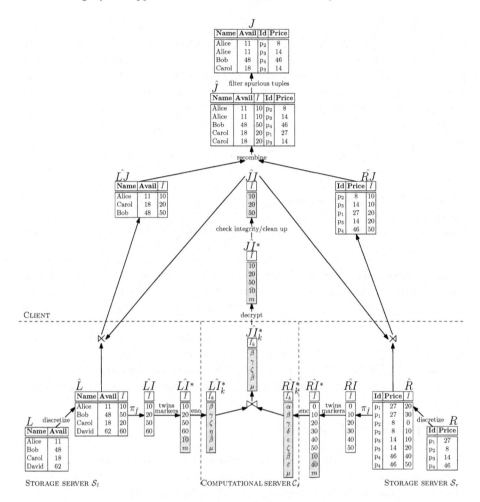

Fig. 3. An example of execution of an approximate join

adopting the discretized domain in Figure 2(c). Relation $\hat{J}$ includes one spurious tuple combining Carol (with value 18 mapped to 20) with p_1 (with value
27 mapped to 20 and 30) even if the difference between their values is 9 (hence
greater than 5). We note that spurious tuples can be filtered from the result only
when the join result has been completely reconstructed. However, this filtering
can be combined with the evaluation of possible selection conditions involving
attributes in both relations (i.e., condition C_{lr}) that only the client can evaluate.

The adoption of encryption on the fly, markers, and twins guarantees the
correctness and completeness of the equi-join result [2]. More precisely, the probability $\wp$ that the omission of d tuples by the computational server go undetected
is equal to $\wp_m \cdot \wp_t$, where $\wp_m = (1 - d/F)^m$ is the probability that no marker
is omitted and $\wp_t = ((1 - d/F)^2 + (d/F)^2)^t$ is the probability of either omitting

or preserving every pair of twins without detection by the client, with F the number of tuples in the join result (including m markers and t twins). We note that, as discussed in [2], a limited number of markers and twins provide strong protection guarantees (e.g., 50 markers and 5% twins reduce to 0.007 the probability that an omission of 50 tuples goes undetected, independently from the number of tuples in the join result). To demonstrate the correctness of our approach, we only need to prove that the discretization process does not discard tuples that satisfy the approximate join condition from the equi-join result, as stated by the following theorem. (The proof has been omitted from the paper for space constraints.)

Theorem 1 (Completeness). *Let L and R be two relations, $\hat{L}$ and $\hat{R}$ be their discretized version (Definition 2). Relation $\hat{J}$ resulting from the equi-join between $\hat{L}$ and $\hat{R}$ includes all the tuples in the result of the approximate join between L and R with similarity condition $|L.I - R.I| < \alpha$.*

If the computational server behaves correctly, the equi-join result includes all the tuples of the approximate join formulated by the client and some additional spurious tuples, which can be easily identified and removed. The discretization process does not compromise data confidentiality. In fact, the computational server only receives the encrypted values of the discretized join attribute. Furthermore, the frequency distribution of discretized join values is not revealed to the computational server, because it operates on relations including the discrete join attribute only where the duplicate values have been removed by projection.

5   Experimental Results

To evaluate the performance of the proposed approach, its effectiveness, and the amount of spurious tuples introduced by the discretization process, we implemented a Java prototype enforcing our protection techniques. We tested the prototype using a machine with Intel Core i5-2400, 3.10GHz CPU and 8.00GB RAM. We randomly generated between $1,000$ and $5,000$ tuples in the two relations. The join attribute values have been generated following a Zipf probability distribution with ζ between 0 and 1 (lower values of ζ correspond to more occurrences of fewer values), and with a domain including between $1,000$ and $2,500$ different values. We fixed the number of markers to 100 and the number of twins to 25% of the tuples in the original relations, which is much more than the values we expect to be used in real-world scenarios. The experimental results are computed as the average of five runs.

Spurious tuples. Figure 4 compares the percentage of spurious tuples obtained with parameter ζ of the Zipf function equal to 0.1, 0.5, and 1, varying the value of threshold α, and with relations of $1,000$ tuples (Figure 4(a)) and $5,000$ tuples (Figure 4(b)). The number of spurious tuples is not influenced by the number of tuples in the original relations but grows with α. In fact, a higher threshold implies a higher number of matching tuples in the approximate join result, but

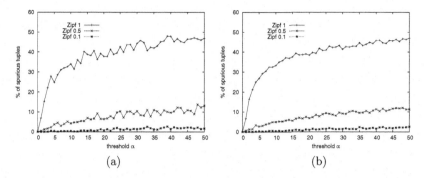

Fig. 4. Percentage of spurious tuples in the equi-join result varying threshold α and the Zipf parameter ζ, with relations including $1,000$ (a) and $5,000$ (b) tuples

also a larger grain of discretization. The number of false positive matches then grows since the values mapped to the same discrete value becomes larger. Also the distribution of the frequency of the join attribute values influences the percentage of spurious tuples. Figure 4 shows that the percentage of spurious tuples is always below 5% when ζ is 0.1, and below 15% when ζ is 0.5. The percentage grows when ζ is 1 and, for high values of α, reaches 45%.

Response time. A second set of experiments was aimed at analyzing the response time of an approximate join query. We focused on the overhead caused by the discretization and filtering processes, which are specific of the translation of an approximate join into an equi-join. We considered configurations characterized by relations of different sizes, generated in such a way that the distribution of the join attribute values follow a Zipf distribution with parameter $\zeta = 0.5$.

Figure 5(a) illustrates the time required for the discretization process, which takes place at the storage servers, varying threshold α. The figure compares the values obtained considering relations of three different sizes. As expected, the discretization time grows with the size of the relations. In fact, the storage server needs to associate one (or two) discrete value(s) with each tuple in its relation. The discretization time is instead not affected by the value of α since the computation of the discrete values does not depend on the granularity of the discretized domain. It is interesting to note that the time necessary for the discretization process is always very low (less than 10ms).

Figure 5(b) reports the time for the client to filter spurious tuples, varying threshold α and comparing three configurations obtained with relations of different sizes. Like for the discretization process, the time necessary for filtering spurious tuples does not depend on α, but it depends on the number of tuples in the relations, and then also in the join result. In fact, the client needs to check every tuple in the join result to discard spurious tuples. The overhead caused by filtering is however limited, remaining below 7s even for relations with $5,000$ tuples (less than 0.05s for relations with $1,000$ tuples).

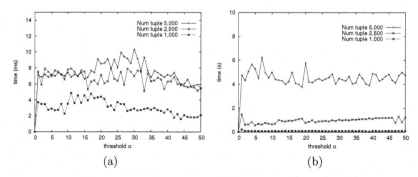

Fig. 5. Time taken by the discretization process (a) and by the filtering process (b) varying α and the number of tuples in the relations

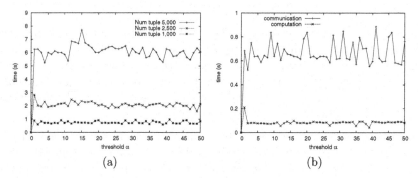

Fig. 6. Time taken by the client to recombine the join result (a) and its computation and communication components (b), varying α and the number of tuples in the relations

The adoption of a semi-join, in contrast to a regular join, strategy for query evaluation implies an additional overhead for the client due to the recombination of the join result computed over the join attribute with the semi-tuples received from the storage servers. Figure 6(a) illustrates the overhead of the recombination phase, obtained summing the communication time of sending the semi-tuples to the client and the computation time for the client to obtain the final result. As expected, the recombination time grows with the size of the join result, but it is not affected by the discretization threshold α. Figure 6(b) illustrates the communication and computation components of the recombination overhead obtained with relations of $1,000$ tuples. As expected, the communication time is higher than the computation time.

Figure 7(a) compares the (total) response time for the computation of an approximate join of configurations obtained varying the number of tuples in the original relations. The response time is higher for relations with a higher number of tuples, and does not depend on α. Figure 7(b) compares the response times obtained joining relations with 1,000 tuples each, but generated with different values for the parameter ζ of the Zipf distribution. We can observe that the response time is not affected by this parameter.

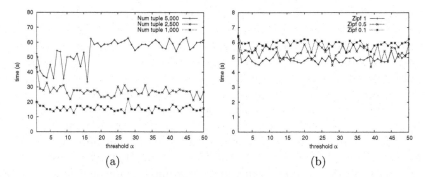

Fig. 7. Overall response time varying the number of tuples in the relations (a) and the parameter ζ of the Zipf distribution (b)

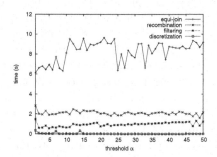

Fig. 8. Components contributing to the response time

To better assess the impact of the discretization process in the computation of an approximate join result, we analyzed the impact of each component of the response time. Figure 8 illustrates the contribution to the total response time due to each phase of the process. The figure shows that the discretization time has a very limited impact (0.27% on average), as well as the filtering phase (nearly 11.20% on average). The time necessary for the recombination is higher (22.52% on average), but it also includes communication costs. However, the most time consuming phase is the evaluation of the equi-join (nearly 66.02% on average of the response time) and is delegated to the computational server. We can then conclude that also approximate joins can benefit from the presence of inexpensive external computational servers (especially if threshold α is low).

6   Related Work

Previous related work has been devoted to protect the confidentiality of data outsourced to *honest-but-curious* servers (e.g., [8,15,16]). Most of these solutions encrypt data before outsourcing and complement them with indexes designed to support different kinds of SQL clauses (e.g., [5,8]).

Other works have considered the problem of guaranteeing integrity when the external server is not trusted. These solutions are based on the adoption of authenticated data structures or on probabilistic approaches. Approaches that rely on authenticated data structures (e.g., Merkle trees [12] and signature-based schemas [13]) return, together with the query result, a verification object that is used by the client to verify the correctness and completeness of the result. Authenticated data structures provide deterministic guarantees but they are defined over a specific attribute and only queries operating on it can be verified. Probabilistic approaches can be adopted with any query, but provide probabilistic guarantees only (e.g., [3,17,18]). The approach in [18] inserts into the original relation a set of fake tuples, generated according to a deterministic function, before outsourcing the relation. Absence of the expected fake tuples in a query result signals its incompleteness. The solution in [17] duplicates a subset of the tuples in the original relation and encrypts them with a different key. Since the external server cannot recognize duplicated tuples, their absence from the query result signals a misbehavior. The use of twins and markers for the join integrity verification has been first introduced in [2–4]. Here, we extend these proposals to the support of approximate joins. Besides correctness and completeness, techniques aimed at providing freshness by periodically changing the verification object have also been proposed (e.g., [19]).

A related, but different, line of work is represented by discretization approaches. The solutions proposed for producing a discrete version of continuous domains have the goal of making data suitable to machine learning and/or data mining applications, of supporting proximity tests, or of anonymizing pseudonyms (e.g., [6,9,11,14]). These solutions are therefore not suited to the scenario considered in this paper. The goal of works studying the evaluation of approximate joins is to limit the performance impact due to the evaluation of conditions based on distance measures (e.g., [1,7]). These solutions cannot then be adopted in our scenario as they do not not operate over encrypted data and hence do not translate approximate into equality conditions.

7   Conclusions

We have presented an approach that enables a user to assess the integrity of the result of an approximate join query, leveraging on the techniques introduced for equi-join queries. We have proposed a discretization of the join attribute to translate an approximate join into an equi-join query. Due to the discretization process, the join result may include additional (spurious) tuples that the client must remove. Also, the experimental evaluation has confirmed the effectiveness of our approach and has demonstrated its limited overhead. Our work leaves space to further investigations, including the consideration of non-Euclidean distance metrics, possibly also operating in multidimensional scenarios.

Acknowledgments. The authors would like to thank Riccardo Moretti for support in the implementation of the system and in the experimental evaluation. This work was supported in part by: the EC within the 7FP under grant agreement 312797 (ABC4EU) and within the H2020 under grant agreement 644579 (ESCUDO-CLOUD), the Italian Ministry of Research within PRIN project "GenData 2020" (2010RTFWBH), and NSF under grant IIP-1266147.

References

1. Das, A., Gehrke, J., Riedewald, M.: Approximate join processing over data streams. In: Proc. of ACM SIGMOD, San Diego, CA (June 2003)
2. De Capitani di Vimercati, S., Foresti, S., Jajodia, S., Livraga, G., Paraboschi, S., Samarati, P.: Integrity for distributed queries. In: Proc. of CNS, San Francisco, CA (October 2014)
3. De Capitani di Vimercati, S., Foresti, S., Jajodia, S., Paraboschi, S., Samarati, P.: Integrity for join queries in the cloud. IEEE TCC **1**(2), 187–200 (2013)
4. De Capitani di Vimercati, S., Foresti, S., Jajodia, S., Paraboschi, S., Samarati, P.: Optimizing integrity checks for join queries in the cloud. In: Atluri, V., Pernul, G. (eds.) DBSec 2014. LNCS, vol. 8566, pp. 33–48. Springer, Heidelberg (2014)
5. De Capitani di Vimercati, S., Foresti, S., Samarati, P.: Managing and accessing data in the cloud: Privacy risks and approaches. In: Proc. of CRiSIS, Cork, Ireland (October 2012)
6. Dougherty, J., Kohavi, R., Sahami, M.: Supervised and unsupervised discretization of continuous features. In: Proc. of ICML, San Francisco, CA (July 1995)
7. Gravano, L., Ipeirotis, P., Jagadish, H., Koudas, N., Muthukrishnan, S., Srivastava, D.: Approximate string joins in a database (almost) for free. In: Proc. of VLDB, Rome, Italy (September 2001)
8. Hacigümüş, H., Iyer, B., Mehrotra, S., Li, C.: Executing SQL over encrypted data in the database-service-provider model. In: Proc. of SIGMOD, Madison, WI (June 2002)
9. Han, J., Kamber, M.: Data Mining, Southeast Asia Edition: Concepts and Techniques. Morgan Kaufmann (2006)
10. Jhawar, R., Piuri, V., Samarati, P.: Supporting security requirements for resource management in cloud computing. In: Proc. of CSE 2012, Paphos, Cyprus (December 2012)
11. Kerschbaum, F.: Distance-preserving pseudonymization for timestamps and spatial data. In: Proc. of WPES, Alexandria, VA (October 2007)
12. Li, F., Hadjieleftheriou, M., Kollios, G., Reyzin, L.: Authenticated index structures for aggregation queries. ACM TISSEC **13**(4), 32:1–32:35 (2010)
13. Mykletun, E., Narasimha, M., Tsudik, G.: Authentication and integrity in outsourced databases. ACM TOS **2**(2), 107–138 (2006)
14. Nielsen, J., Pagter, J., Stausholm, M.: Location privacy via private proximity testing. In: NDSS, San Diego, CA (February 2011)
15. Ren, K., Wang, C., Wang, Q.: Security challenges for the public cloud. IEEE Internet Computing **16**(1), 69–73 (2012)
16. Samarati, P., De Capitani di Vimercati, S.: Data protection in outsourcing scenarios: Issues and directions. In: Proc. of ASIACCS, Beijing, China (April 2010)
17. Wang, H., Yin, J., Perng, C., Yu, P.: Dual encryption for query integrity assurance. In: Proc. of CIKM, Napa Valley, CA (October 2008)
18. Xie, M., Wang, H., Yin, J., Meng, X.: Integrity auditing of outsourced data. In: Proc. of VLDB, Vienna, Austria (September 2007)
19. Xie, M., Wang, H., Yin, J., Meng, X.: Providing freshness guarantees for outsourced databases. In: Proc. of EDBT, Nantes, France (March 2008)

Applied Cryptography

Fast Revocation of Attribute-Based Credentials for Both Users and Verifiers

Wouter Lueks$^{(\boxtimes)}$, Gergely Alpár, Jaap-Henk Hoepman, and Pim Vullers

Radboud University, Nijmegen, The Netherlands
{lueks,gergely,jhh,pim}@cs.ru.nl

Abstract. Attribute-based credentials allow a user to prove properties about herself anonymously. Revoking such credentials, which requires singling them out, is hard because it is at odds with anonymity. All revocation schemes proposed to date either sacrifice anonymity altogether, require the parties to be online, or put high load on the user or the verifier. As a result, these schemes are either too complicated for low-powered devices like smart cards or they do not scale. We propose a new revocation scheme that has a very low computational cost for users and verifiers, and does not require users to process updates. We trade only a limited, but well-defined, amount of anonymity to make the first practical revocation scheme that is efficient at large scales and fast enough for smart cards.

1 Introduction

More and more governments are issuing electronic identity (eID) cards to their citizens [18,23,25]. These eID cards can be used both offline and online for secure authentication with the government and sometimes with other parties, like shops. Attribute-based credentials (ABCs) [9] are an emerging technology for implementing eID cards because of their flexibility and strong privacy guarantees, and because they can be fully implemented on smart cards [29]. Every credential contains attributes that the user can either reveal or keep hidden. Such attributes describe properties of a person, like her name and age. ABCs enable a range of scenarios from fully-identifying to fully-anonymous.[1] When using a credential fully anonymously (i.e., without revealing any identifying attributes),

An extendend version of this paper is available in the Cryptology ePrint Archive [21]. The work described in this paper has been supported under the ICT theme of the Cooperation Programme of the 7th Framework Programme of the European Commission, GA number 318424 (FutureID) and the research program Sentinels (www. sentinels.nl) as project 'Mobile IDM' (10522) and 'Revocable Privacy' (10532). Sentinels is being financed by Technology Foundation STW, the Netherlands Organization for Scientific Research (NWO), and the Dutch Ministry of Economic Affairs. This research is conducted within the Privacy and Identity Lab (PI.lab) and funded by SIDN.nl (http://www.sidn.nl).

[1] This is why we prefer the term 'attribute-based credentials' over the more traditional term 'anonymous credentials'.

© IFIP International Federation for Information Processing 2015
H. Federrath and D. Gollmann (Eds.): SEC 2015, IFIP AICT 455, pp. 463–478, 2015.
DOI: 10.1007/978-3-319-18467-8_31

proper ABC technologies guarantee that the credential is unlinkable: it is not possible to connect multiple uses of the same credential.

When ABCs are applied, the carriers on which the credentials are stored (for example, smart cards) can be lost or stolen. In such cases, it is important that users can revoke these credentials to ensure that they can no longer be (ab)used. This is also necessary when the owner of the credential herself abuses it. Revocation may, in fact, happen often. As an example, the nationwide Belgian eID system's revocation list contains more than 375 000 credentials [8] for just over 10 million citizens. A practical revocation scheme must therefore efficiently deal with such large revocation lists.

Unfortunately, the unlinkability of ABCs precludes the use of standard, identity-based revocation. There exist many privacy-friendly revocation schemes, with different trade-offs in terms of efficiency (both for users and verifiers), connectivity requirements, and anonymity. It turns out to be hard to satisfy all of these simultaneously. In particular, all revocation schemes proposed so far suffer from at least one of the following two problems: (1) they rely on computationally powerful users, making the scheme unsuitable for smart cards, the obvious carrier for a national eID; or (2) they place a high load on verifiers, resulting in long transaction times.

The IRMA Project. This research is part of the ongoing research project "I Reveal My Attributes" (IRMA).[2] The goal of this project is to demonstrate the practicality of attribute-based credentials. We implemented the entire user-side of the credentials on a smart card [29]. In this paper we focus on this setting.

Our Contribution. Our contribution is a new revocation scheme that has very low computational cost for users and verifiers alike; it is efficient even in the smart card setting, and can therefore be used in practice. We introduce the main idea in Section 2, introduce ABCs in Section 3, and describe the full scheme in Section 4. In our scheme, verifiers need only constant time on average to check revocation status, making it as fast as traditional non-anonymous revocation schemes. Furthermore, the users' computational overhead is small (and updates to reflect revocations are *not* necessary). Our scheme is based on *epochs* that divide time in short (configurable) intervals. Our scheme is unlinkable, except if the user uses her credential more than once per epoch at the same verifier. Our revocation scheme works with most credential schemes. As an example, we instantiate it for Idemix [15] in Section 5. We give pointers for implementing our scheme in practice, and give experimental results as evidence of feasibility of our scheme in Section 6. Finally, we review related work in Section 7 and conclude our paper in Section 8.

---

[2] See http://www.irmacard.org.

2   The Idea

Our scheme enables efficient and privacy-friendly revocation of credentials. As it resembles verifier-local revocation (VLR) schemes [1,4,6], we describe those first.

2.1   Verifier-Local Revocation

The setting is a cyclic group G with prime order q. Every credential encodes a random *revocation value* $r \in \mathbb{Z}_q$. If a credential has to be revoked, its revocation value r is added to the global revocation list RL. When the user shows the credential to a verifier, the verifier needs to check whether the user's revocation value r appears on the revocation list RL. To facilitate this check without revealing r itself, the user chooses a random revocation generator $h \in_R G$, calculates the *revocation token* $R = h^r$, and sends

$$(h, R) \tag{1}$$

to the verifier during showing. The user also proves that the revocation value r embedded into R corresponds to credential she is showing. This proof depends on the type of credential—see Section 5 for an example. Each verifier holds a copy of the revocation list $RL = \{r_1, \ldots, r_k\}$. To check whether the credential is still valid, the verifier checks whether $h^{r_j} = R$ for each $r_j \in RL$ and rejects the credential if one of these equalities holds. This form of verifier-local revocation has some problems in practice:

1. Because the user chooses the revocation generator h at random, the work for the verifier increases linearly with the number of items on the revocation list. This quickly causes performance problems.
2. The scheme is not forward-secure. Once the verifier obtains a revocation value r_i, the verifier can link all past and future interactions involving this value, if it stores the tuples (h, R) from (1). Some solutions have been proposed to solve this problem—see Section 7—but they are not efficient enough for our purposes.

Our scheme addresses these two disadvantages.

2.2   Our Scheme

We propose to split time into epochs and to use one generator per epoch and per verifier. This limits the user to one showing per verifier per epoch if she wants to remain unlinkable (which is not a problem when epochs are small) but makes revocation checking very fast for the verifier. The user uses the per-epoch per-verifier generator $g_{\varepsilon,V}$ to create the values in (1). In particular, she sends $R = g_{\varepsilon,V}^r$ to the verifier.

To check whether the credential is revoked the verifier does not need to know the raw revocation values. Instead, a semi-trusted party, the revocation authority (RA), can store these, and provide the verifier with a revocation list:

$$RL_{\varepsilon,V} = \{g_{\varepsilon,V}^{r_1}, \ldots, g_{\varepsilon,V}^{r_k}\}.$$

The credential is revoked if $R \in RL_{\varepsilon,V}$. This operation takes only $O(1)$ time on average using associative arrays. The average time complexity thus decreases from linear to constant in the length of the revocation list $RL_{\varepsilon,V}$. While some computation load shifts to the RA, the RA does no more work creating the list than a verifier in the VLR scheme does for *every* verification. Also, the verifier can no longer link transactions in different epochs since it does not have the bare revocation values.

Epochs and Generators. The length of an epoch must be sufficiently short so that a user normally never shows her credential twice within the same epoch to the same verifier. If the generator is reused, the corresponding activities of the user become linkable.

The generators form an attack vector for a malicious adversary to link users' activities. It is not sufficient for the user to keep track of the generators she used before. A malicious verifier could take one fixed generator $g_{\varepsilon,V}$, and then create a new one by picking a random exponent $x \in_R \mathbb{Z}_q$ and sending $g_{\varepsilon,V}^x$ to the user. All revocation tokens are then easily reduced to the same base $g_{\varepsilon,V}$, without the user ever seeing a similar generator.

To prevent this attack, users should calculate the generators themselves. The easiest method—and the one we propose here—is to use a hash function and let the generator $g_{\varepsilon,V}$ for a verifier V and epoch ε equal $H(\varepsilon \parallel V)$, where H is a hash function from the strings to the group G and the epoch ε is derived from the current time.

3   A Primer on ABCs

Attribute-based credentials are a cryptographic alternative to traditional credentials like driver's licenses and passports. ABCs contain a set of attributes, typically encoded as numbers, that a user can selectively reveal to the verifier. Even when attributes are hidden, the verifier can still assess the validity of the credential.

A typical attribute-based credential scheme comprises the following three parties.

Issuer. The issuer issues credentials to users. It ensures that the correct data are stored in the credential. A typical credential scheme has multiple issuers.
User. The user holds a set of credentials, obtained from one or more issuers. She can disclose a (user defined) selection of attributes from any number of her credentials to a verifier to obtain a service.

Verifier. The verifier, sometimes called relying party or service provider, checks that the credential is valid, the revealed attributes are as required, and the credential is not revoked. Based on the outcome, it may provide a service to the user.

When the credential scheme supports revocation, another party is present.

Revocation Authority. The revocation authority is responsible for revoking credentials. It determines when to revoke, and stores all information necessary to do so. If necessary, it sends revocation information to users and verifiers.

Our scheme is independent of the choice of credential scheme, but we impose three restrictions on it:

1. The credential must be able to encode a revocation value r from a sufficiently large set.[3] This value can identify a credential if it is revoked. We use the notation $C(r)$ to denote a credential that contains the revocation value r. Depending on the type of credential, other attributes may be present.
2. The issuer should be able to issue a credential $C(r)$ without learning the revocation value r. Otherwise, the issuer can use it to trace credentials. Most credential schemes support blind issuing, which makes this possible.
3. The showing protocol must be extendible to provide the verifier with the revocation token $R = g_{\varepsilon,V}^r$ and a proof that R and $C(r)$ contain the same revocation value r. Fortunately, most credential schemes already rely on zero-knowledge proofs, and these can readily be extended to include the required proof of equality.

Furthermore, we assume that the credential scheme authenticates the verifiers. (This is without loss of generality. It is easy to add such a layer if it is missing.)

4 The Full Scheme

We now describe the full scheme. It expands on the intuition described in Section 2 by explicitly stating how the revocation authority (RA) operates and how it deals with verifiers. Section 6 shows how to implement this scheme.

The revocation authority runs the SetupRA algorithm once.

SetupRA(1^ℓ) This algorithm takes as input a security parameter 1^ℓ. It chooses a cyclic group G of prime order q with generator g such that the DDH problem is hard in G and q has ℓ bits. Furthermore, it picks a hash function $H : \{0,1\}^* \to G$ that maps strings onto this group. It outputs (G, g, q, H). These parameters are public and known to all other parties. The RA keeps

---

[3] For simplicity, we focus on attribute-based credentials, but this is not strictly necessary. Any credential scheme that can encode the revocation value and that satisfies the second restriction can be used with our scheme. One example would be to use the user's private key as the revocation value.

track of the current epoch ε, which it initializes to 0, and the initially empty master revocation list MRL containing revoked credentials identified by their revocation values.

Users and verifiers run the algorithms SetupU and SetupV respectively.

SetupU() The user keeps track of the current epoch ε. She also stores sets $\mathcal{T}_C$ of the verifiers that she has shown credential C to in this epoch. Initially, $\mathcal{T}_C = \emptyset$.

SetupV() The verifier calls GetRevocationList to get an initial revocation list from the revocation authority—see below. It also keeps track of the current epoch ε.

At the beginning of a new epoch, all parties increase the current epoch ε by 1. In particular, we assume that all users know the current epoch.[4] At the start of a new epoch, users additionally clear the list $\mathcal{T}_C$ of verifiers that have seen credential C in this epoch. Every verifier V runs the GetRevocationList protocol with the revocation authority to get its revocation list for the current epoch.

GetRevocationList() This protocol is run between a verifier V and the revocation authority. The parties execute the following steps:
1. The verifier V authenticates itself to the revocation authority.[5]
2. The revocation authority
   (a) calculates the generator $g_{\varepsilon,V} = H(\varepsilon \parallel V) \in G$ for verifier V;
   (b) computes the sorted list $RL_{\varepsilon,V} = \mathsf{sort}(\{g_{\varepsilon,V}^r \mid r \in \mathsf{MRL}\})$; and
   (c) sends $RL_{\varepsilon,V}$ to verifier V.

Sorting the revocation lists $RL_{\varepsilon,V}$ ensures that unlinkability is preserved for all previous activities, even for revoked users (if $|\mathsf{MRL}| > 1$).[6]

To revoke a credential, the Revoke protocol is run with the revocation authority.

Revoke(r) When the revocation authority is asked to revoke a credential with revocation value r, it adds r to the master revocation list MRL.

In a deployed system, it is the RA's responsibility to decide whether to grant the revocation request. In Section 6.1 we discuss how a credential can be revoked in practice.

When showing a credential, the user and the verifier follow the ShowCredential protocol. Using this protocol, the user first authenticates the verifier. Then, she gives a revocation token to the verifier and proves that she has a corresponding credential. The verifier checks the validity of the credential and whether it has been revoked.

---
[4] As we explain in Section 6.2, epochs are represented as time intervals. Users test their knowledge of the current time against this interval to make sure the interval is not in the past.
[5] The verifier reuses the authentication mechanism in the credential scheme.
[6] For this purpose, it suffices to sort on the representation of the elements. All that matters is that the order depends only on information in the list itself.

ShowCredential(C, V) This protocol is run between a user holding credential C and a verifier V. It proceeds as follows.

1. The verifier authenticates itself to the user. The user aborts if the authentication is unsuccessful or if $V \in \mathcal{T}_C$.
2. The user calculates the verifier (and epoch) specific generator $g_{\varepsilon, V} = H(\varepsilon \parallel V)$, and adds V to the list of seen verifiers $\mathcal{T}_C$.
3. The user sends its revocation token $R = g_{\varepsilon, V}^r$ to the verifier. Here, r is the revocation value encoded into the user's credential $C(r)$.
4. The user and the verifier run the normal showing protocol for the user's credential $C(r)$, but in addition the user proves that its revocation token R is well-formed, i.e., that the exponent r is the same as the revocation value encoded in the credential. Section 5 shows an example of such a proof for Idemix.
5. The verifier checks the validity of the credential and whether R is well-formed. Finally, it confirms that R is not on its revocation list $RL_{\varepsilon, V}$ for the current epoch. It aborts if any of these checks fail.

The list $\mathcal{T}_C$ and the epoch ε uniquely determine the generators that the user has used for credential C in this epoch. The checks above ensure that the user never reuses a generator. Also, the user always calculates the generators herself. This prevents the verifier from cheating with the generators.

Checking that $R \notin RL_{\varepsilon, V}$ can be done in constant time (on average) if the verifier processes the revocation list $RL_{\varepsilon, V}$ into an associative array. Some tricks help keep the size of the revocation lists manageable—see Section 6.5.

4.1 Sketch of the Security of the Scheme

A good revocation scheme needs to satisfy two properties: (1) non-revoked credentials are still unlinkable, and (2) a revoked credential is no longer usable. Our scheme satisfies these two properties in a reasonable security model.

To model unlinkability, the adversary can interact with credentials in the system as often as it wants, in any epoch and as any verifier. It can also revoke credentials. In the challenge phase, it picks a verifier, an epoch and two credentials i_0 and i_1 that were not revoked in any earlier epoch nor shown to it in the chosen epoch (since our scheme does not guarantee unlinkability when a credential is shown twice in one epoch to to the same verifier). It is shown one of these credentials; it must determine which one. In the full version of this paper, we show that, assuming the random oracle model and the hardness of the Diffie-Hellman problem, it is not possible to make this distinction [21]. Because credentials can be revoked in epochs past the challenge epoch, this implies forward security.

It is also not possible for an adversary to avoid revocation. The proof in step 4 of ShowCredential binds the revocation token to the revocation value in the credential. Since credentials cannot be forged (by assumption on the credential scheme), the adversary cannot change its revocation value, and hence cannot avoid revocation. A full security model and proof is in the full version of this paper [21].

5   Showing Protocol for Idemix

In this section, we give a brief overview of the Idemix [15] attribute-based credential system and how our revocation scheme can be incorporated into it to enable revocation without losing anonymity. We focus on the way our revocation scheme can be incorporated and omit some of the cryptographic details.

In Idemix, a credential is a Camenisch–Lysyanskaya [11] signature (A, e, v) on the block of messages consisting of the user's private key sk_U and the attributes $a_1, \ldots, a_L$. We can easily incorporate an extra attribute containing the revocation value r into the signature:

$$A \equiv \left(\frac{Z}{S^v \cdot R_K^{sk_U} \cdot R_R^r \cdot \prod_{i=1}^{L} R_i^{a_i}} \right)^{1/e} \pmod{n},$$

where the credential issuer's public key consists of the integers Z, S, R_K, R_R, R_1, $\ldots, R_L, n$. Both sk_U and r should be chosen from a large set. The construction of the signature guarantees that the user cannot change any of the values in the exponents. In the issuing protocol, the revocation value r and the private key sk_U should be hidden.

Given a block of messages sk_U, r and $a_1, \ldots, a_L$ the validity of the signature can be verified by checking that

$$Z \stackrel{?}{\equiv} A^e \cdot S^v \cdot R_K^{sk_U} \cdot R_R^r \cdot \prod_{i=1}^{L} R_i^{a_i} \pmod{n}.$$

When the signature is part of a credential scheme, some of these values can never be shown to the verifier as they would make the credential linkable. Instead, during verification the user uses the following two functions to show a credential anonymously. First, the user randomizes the signature to ensure unlinkability. Second, the user selectively discloses only those attributes appropriate for the application (the private key and the revocation value are never revealed).

A user randomizes the value A of a signature (A, e, v) as follows. If (A, e, v) is a valid signature on sk_U, r and $a_1, \ldots, a_L$, then $(\hat{A}, e, \hat{v})$ is also a valid signature where $\hat{A} := A \cdot S^{-\varrho} \pmod{n}$, $\hat{v} := v + e\varrho$ for any randomly chosen ϱ (in some large interval). This does not yet provide unlinkability by itself—e remains unchanged—but the selective disclosure proof described below also hides the value e.

The selective disclosure protocol is a (non-interactive) zero-knowledge proof constructed by the user. Such a proof reveals a subset of the attributes determined by the index set $\mathcal{D}$ and proves that a (randomised) signature contains these attribute values. To make revocation possible, we also include a predicate that demonstrates that (a) the revocation token R was honestly computed using the generator $g_{\varepsilon, V}$ and (b) the revocation value r corresponds to this credential.

The proof is as follows:[7]

$$PK\Big\{(e,\hat{v},sk_U,r,(a_i)_{i\notin\mathcal{D}}): Z\prod_{i\in\mathcal{D}}R_i^{-a_i} \equiv \hat{A}^e S^{\hat{v}} R_K^{sk_U} R_R^r \prod_{i\notin\mathcal{D}}R_i^{a_i} \pmod{n}$$

$$\wedge\ R = g_{\varepsilon,V}^r \text{ in } G\Big\}.$$

In the congruence above, all the exponents on the left-hand side are known to the verifier (selectively disclosed attributes $(a_i)_{i\in\mathcal{D}}$), while the exponents on the right-hand side remain hidden and the user only proves knowledge of them. The above proof realizes the user's side of steps 4 and 5 in the ShowCredential algorithm—see Section 4.

6 Implementation

We now address some implementation challenges when using our revocation scheme.

6.1 Obtaining Revocation Information

To revoke a credential, one needs to know its revocation value. However, this value also introduces a privacy risk: the party that stores it could revoke the credential and hence detect its use. Many revocation schemes suffer from this problem, see Section 7. We discuss three options for storing and using revocation values.

In all cases, the user herself generates the revocation value. The issuer will include this revocation value in the credential without ever learning its value.[8]

Option 1: Only the user knows the revocation value. The privacy of the credential owner is best protected when only she knows the revocation value. When she loses her credential, she reveals the revocation value to the RA, who then uses this to revoke the credential. To get even better privacy, she can calculate the future revocation tokens herself. This is computationally intensive, but lowers the trust in the RA significantly.

When a smart card acts on behalf of the user, there is another difficulty to overcome: how does the user access the revocation values when the card is lost or stolen? We propose to use a trusted terminal to print the (card-generated) revocation values (for example, as a QR code) when the credential is issued. The user can then store the revocation values separately from the card and use them to revoke credentials.

---

[7] We use a simplified version of the Camenisch–Stadler notation [13] for zero-knowledge proofs of knowledge. Only the prover knows the values in front of ':', other values are also known by the verifier. We also omited the range proofs; see the Idemix specification [15] for details.

[8] The method for encoding these attributes is similar to the 'blind' encoding of the user's private key in a credential. Idemix and U-Prove support this.

Option 2: a trusted third party stores revocation information. A second option is for a (possibly distributed) trusted third party (TTP) to store the revocation values. During issuance, the user creates not only a revocation value, but also a verifiable encryption [12] of the revocation value (for example, Idemix supports this). The user proves that the TTP can decrypt its revocation value, and the issuer verifies this proof before issuing the credential to the user. Hence, the user cannot avoid revocation later on.

In theory, this allows the TTP to revoke a credential when it is abused. However, the credentials do still provide anonymity, so it is not easy to pinpoint the abuser. This is where the final option comes in.

Option 3: revocation information is escrowed during showing. For the third option, the user escrows the revocation value during a showing proof using verifiable encryption. When abuse is detected, the ciphertext can be used to recover the revocation value and thus revoke the user.

The latter two solutions do reduce the efficiency of the underlying credential scheme, and introduce a lot of trust in the third party. In practice, one has to weigh whether it is better to accept some abuse or to decrease efficiency and privacy.

6.2   Instantiating Epochs

To keep the protocol description simple, we assumed that all parties are aware of the current epoch. To achieve this, epochs are, in practice, based on time. The revocation authority determines the length of an epoch, by specifying its start time t_s and end time t_e, so the current epoch ε is modelled by the tuple $\varepsilon = (t_s, t_e)$.

In step 2 of the ShowCredential protocol, the user checks that $t_s \leq t \leq t_e$ where t is the current time. If this equation is not correct, the user aborts. In this way, users always use the correct generator.

Embedded Devices. The above description does not suffice for smart cards, our target platform, as they lack a built-in clock, and thus have no notion of time. Nevertheless, an embedded device must also be able to calculate the generators itself, to prevent a verifier from adversarially choosing them.

We propose the following solution, similar to the method used in Machine Readable Travel Documents, like the new European passport [7]. The embedded device keeps track of an estimate t^* of the current time. The estimate is always at or before the current time. Every time the embedded device interacts with a verifier, it

1. receives a description of the current epoch (t_s, t_e) signed by the RA;
2. confirms that the epoch (t_s, t_e) is possible given its time estimate t^* by checking that $t^* \leq t_e$ (this is done in step 1 of the ShowCredential protocol); and
3. updates its estimate $t^* \leftarrow \max(t_s, t^*)$ if the signature is valid.

The signature by the revocation authority on the epoch makes it impossible for verifiers to trick the device into creating a too futuristic estimate t^* of the current time.

6.3 How to Choose the Epochs

Epochs determine during what period a credential is linkable. Ideally, at most one showing happens at each verifier within an epoch. The period between two showings wildly differs among applications. For example, a citizen credential may be used only a couple of times a year for filing tax returns with the government, while it may be used weekly to prove having reached legal drinking age in a pub or a store. A credential for accessing an online newspaper subscription could even be used daily.

At the same time, computing revocation lists for every epoch can become computationally intensive and transferring uses bandwidth. Therefore, we propose not to have a global epoch, but instead create epochs per verifier. The length of the epoch should be chosen in such a way that no credential is normally reused within the epoch for that particular verifier.[9] Using time to instantiate epochs (as described in Section 6.2) allows us to use verifier-specific epochs easily.

6.4 Experiments

We did two experiments to prove the validity of our scheme: we estimated the performance impact on an existing smart card implementation and tested the impact on the revocation authority. As the extra work for the verifier is extremely small, we did not measure its overhead.

Fast Smart Card Implementation. We estimate the efficiency of this scheme based on the work by Vullers and Alpár [29] in the IRMA project. To assess the performance of the implementation, we compare it to its version without revocation. As described in Section 5, we add an extra attribute to every credential to hold the revocation value.

As group G, we use the quadratic residues modulo a 1024-bit safe prime (this is somewhat small, but matches the security level used in the implementation of Vullers and Alpár [29]). This group is cyclic and the DDH problem is hard. Furthermore, hashing onto this group is easy. It takes five 256-bit hash calculations (to get a statically uniformly random element) and a squaring (which can be precomputed as part of the revocation value). Calculating a 256-bit hash takes about 10 milliseconds. We estimate a total extra time of 390 milliseconds for including the revocation value as an attribute, generating the revocation

---

[9] Note that when a user *does* use her credential more often within the same epoch a lot of anonymity remains. The uses within this epoch are linkable, but they are still unlinkable to uses in other epochs or at other verifiers. In particular, this will usually not reveal the user's identity.

token and adding the equality proof [26]. This is very practical. Since showing a credential takes 1.0–1.5 seconds, the overhead is limited too.

We did not implement the verification of the certificate for the epoch yet, but we believe that the cost of doing this to be approximately 150 milliseconds.

Fast Revocation List Calculation. The main remaining burden of the revocation scheme is on the revocation authority, which has to generate revocation lists for all verifiers, and has to do so for each epoch. This can amount to a large number of exponentiations. However, the reader should be aware that the amount of work the revocation authority has to do per generator (i.e., per epoch and per verifier) equals the work that a verifier has to do for *every verification* in the standard VLR setting.

We implemented the calculation of the revocation list to confirm that this approach is valid. The efficiency of this calculation depends on the group. For the Idemix setting, we created a (non-optimized) implementation that calculates about 7 500 revocation tokens per second. However, one can do much better, as is shown by our optimized implementation for the ECC library by Bernstein et al. [2]. This implementation calculates about 50 000 revocations per second. These results show that even for large scale systems revocation lists can be generated sufficiently fast.

6.5   The Size of a Revocation List

At the start of every epoch, verifiers retrieve new revocation lists. It might seem that when the revocation lists are big, the storage and transfer costs become prohibitive. This is not the case. Since our scheme does not do group operations on revocation tokens, it suffices to store their hashes. Furthermore, if one is willing to accept a false positive rate of 10^{-7}, Bloom filters [3] reduce the storage requirements by another order of magnitude. This allows, for example, 250 000 elements to be stored in only 1 MiB.

7   Related Work

Revocation has been widely studied in the literature; we refer to, for example, Lapon et al. [17] for a nice overview of current revocation techniques for attribute-based (Idemix) credentials. Traditional revocation techniques, like CRLs and OCSPs, require credentials to have a unique identifier that is always visible to the verifier. A certificate revocation list (CRL) [14] is a list of revoked credential identifiers, published by the issuer. Alternatively, the verifier can ask the issuer if a credential is still valid using the Online Certificate Status Protocol (OCSP) [27]. Both situations require the credential to be recognizable, which is undesirable for ABCs. However, revocation is fast: there is no extra work required on the side of the user, and the verifier can test validity in constant time.

Domain-specific pseudonyms [5,15,16] only slightly improve the situation: instead of being globally linkable, different uses are only linkable by the same

Table 1. We compare CRLs [14], accumulators [8,10,24], traditional VLR schemes [1, 4,6], VLR schemes with backward unlinkability (VLR-BU) [22], blacklistable anonymous credentials (BLAC) [28], and our scheme. We compare the complexity of the operations and data transfers. A proving time of 1 means that it is constant, while a proving time of $|RL|$ means that it scales linearly with the size of the revocation list. Of all the constant-time proving schemes, the accumulator has the biggest overhead. Our scheme is the only privacy-friendly scheme that has constant-time proving and verification while users do not need to receive updates.

	CRL	Accumulators	VLR	VLR-BU	BLAC	Our scheme
User can be offline	✓	×	✓	✓	✓	✓
Data to verifier						
per epoch	$|RL|$	1	$|RL|$	$|RL|$	$|RL|$	$|RL|$
per update	1	1	1	1	1	1
Proving (time)	1	1	1	1	$|RL|$	1
Verifying (time)	1	1	$|RL|$	$|RL|$	$|RL|$	1
Security	-	+	+/-	+	+	+

verifier, but not across different verifiers. We believe this still weakens the unlinkability too much.

We now focus our attention on solutions that do offer sufficient privacy guarantees for the user. Table 1 compares these schemes with our scheme and the CRL scheme. A digital accumulator is a constant-sized representation of a set of values. Every value in the accumulator comes with a witness, which enables efficient membership checks. Camenisch and Lysyanskaya [10] proposed an updatable accumulator that can be used for revocation. A credential is unrevoked as long as it appears on the whitelist, represented by the accumulator. Another approach is to accumulate revoked credentials to create a blacklist. A credential is unrevoked if it is not on this blacklist [19,24].

Accumulators change. For whitelists, this is after an addition; for blacklists, this is after a revocation. Thus users need to receive updates (for schemes like Camenisch et al. [8], these updates are public and can be provided by the verifier) and process them, inducing extra load on carriers like smart cards. Additionally, the (non-)membership proofs are expensive. Lapon et al. [17] show an overhead of 300% in the showing protocol. Other schemes, like Libert et al. [20] are equally inefficient, making them impractical.

Where accumulators place the load on the users—who need to get new witnesses after revocations or additions—and the revocation authority—who needs to create those witnesses—verifier-local revocation (VLR) [1,4,6] places the majority of the load at the verifier. As we saw in Section 2, the verifier needs to do a check that is linear in the length of the revocation list, however, apart from sending the extra revocation token, the extra work for the user is minimal.

A downside of traditional VLR schemes is that once a user is revoked, all of its transactions (also past ones) become linkable. Nakanishi and Funabiki [22] proposed a VLR scheme that is backward unlinkable, like our scheme. Similar to our scheme, they create different revocation tokens per epoch, so that verifiers cannot use the revocation token for the current epoch and apply it to earlier ones. However, their scheme is still linear in the number of revoked users, and needs to perform a pairing operation per revoked user. This makes it less efficient than previous and our solutions. The security of their scheme hinges on the fact that the per-epoch revocation tokens are maintained by a trusted party. It thus requires the same trusted party as our scheme does.

Finally, blacklistable anonymous credentials (BLAC) [28] take a different approach to revocation: misbehaving users can be blacklisted without requiring a TTP to provide a revocation token. In every transaction, the user provides a ticket, similar to our revocation token, that is bound to the user. To blacklist a user, the verifier places this ticket on the blacklist. In the second step of the authentication, the user proves that her ticket is not on the blacklist. The complexity of this proof is linear in the number of items on the blacklist, so this scheme places a high load on the user. Even if a user's credential is revoked, the verifier does not learn her identity, nor can the verifier trace her.

8   Discussion and Conclusion

Our revocation scheme is fast. It can be combined with ABC showing protocols and can be *fully* implemented on a smart card. It incurs minimal overhead, while at the same time the revocation check can be performed efficiently by the verifier. We created a security model for our scheme and proved that our scheme is forward secure as long as the revocation authority is trusted. The proofs are included in the full version of this paper [21]. We showed that we can remove this trust assumption when the users calculate the revocation tokens themselves.

To obtain this speedup, we traded some traceability, but with an appropriate choice of epoch length this should not be a problem in practice. The fact that this enables us to create a revocation system that is truly practical makes this a worthwhile trade-off.

We believe our scheme is a valuable contribution to making large scale attribute-based credentials possible. It would be interesting to investigate protocols that further reduce the trust assumption on the revocation authority.

References

1. Ateniese, G., Song, D.X., Tsudik, G.: Quasi-Efficient revocation in group signatures. In: Blaze, M. (ed.) FC 2002. LNCS, vol. 2357, pp. 183–197. Springer, Heidelberg (2003)
2. Bernstein, D.J., Duif, N., Lange, T., Schwabe, P., Yang, B.Y.: High-speed high-security signatures. Journal of Cryptographic Engineering 2(2), 77–89 (2012)
3. Bloom, B.H.: Space/Time Trade-offs in Hash Coding with Allowable Errors. Communications of the ACM 13(7), 422–426 (1970)
4. Boneh, D., Shacham, H.: Group signatures with verifier-local revocation. In: CCS 2004, pp. 168–177. ACM (2004)

5. Brands, S., Demuynck, L., De Decker, B.: A practical system for globally revoking the unlinkable pseudonyms of unknown users. In: Pieprzyk, J., Ghodosi, H., Dawson, E. (eds.) ACISP 2007. LNCS, vol. 4586, pp. 400–415. Springer, Heidelberg (2007)
6. Brickell, E., Camenisch, J., Chen, L.: The DAA scheme in context. In: Mitchell, C.J. (ed.) Trusted Computing, Professional Applications of Computing, vol. 6, ch. 5, pp. 143–174. Institution of Electrical Engineers (2005)
7. BSI: Advanced security mechanisms for machine readable travel documents - extended access control (eac). Tech. Rep. TR-03110, Bundesamt für Sicherheit in der Informationstechnik (BSI), Bonn, Germany (2006)
8. Camenisch, J., Kohlweiss, M., Soriente, C.: An accumulator based on bilinear maps and efficient revocation for anonymous credentials. In: Jarecki, S., Tsudik, G. (eds.) PKC 2009. LNCS, vol. 5443, pp. 481–500. Springer, Heidelberg (2009)
9. Camenisch, J., Krontiris, I., Lehmann, A., Neven, G., Paquin, C., Rannenberg, K., Zwingelberg, H.: D2.1 Architecture for Attribute-based Credential Technologies. Tech. rep., ABC4Trust (2011)
10. Camenisch, J., Lysyanskaya, A.: Dynamic accumulators and application to efficient revocation of anonymous credentials. In: Yung, M. (ed.) CRYPTO 2002. LNCS, vol. 2442, pp. 61–76. Springer, Heidelberg (2002)
11. Camenisch, J., Lysyanskaya, A.: A signature scheme with efficient protocols. In: Cimato, S., Galdi, C., Persiano, G. (eds.) SCN 2002. LNCS, vol. 2576, pp. 268–289. Springer, Heidelberg (2003)
12. Camenisch, J., Shoup, V.: Practical verifiable encryption and decryption of discrete logarithms. In: Boneh, D. (ed.) CRYPTO 2003. LNCS, vol. 2729, pp. 126–144. Springer, Heidelberg (2003)
13. Camenisch, J., Stadler, M.: Efficient group signature schemes for large groups. In: Kaliski Jr., B.S. (ed.) CRYPTO 1997. LNCS, vol. 1294, pp. 410–424. Springer, Heidelberg (1997)
14. Cooper, D., Santesson, S., Farrell, S., Boeyen, S., Housley, R., Polk, W.: Internet X.509 Public Key Infrastructure Certificate and Certificate Revocation List (CRL) Profile. RFC 5280 (Proposed Standard), updated by RFC 6818, May 2008
15. IBM Research Zürich Security Team: Specification of the Identity Mixer cryptographic library, version 2.3.4. Tech. rep., IBM Research, Zürich, February 2012
16. Kutyłowski, M., Krzywiecki, Ł., Kubiak, P., Koza, M.: Restricted identification scheme and Diffie-Hellman linking problem. In: Chen, L., Yung, M., Zhu, L. (eds.) INTRUST 2011. LNCS, vol. 7222, pp. 221–238. Springer, Heidelberg (2012)
17. Lapon, J., Kohlweiss, M., De Decker, B., Naessens, V.: Analysis of revocation strategies for anonymous idemix credentials. In: De Decker, B., Lapon, J., Naessens, V., Uhl, A. (eds.) CMS 2011. LNCS, vol. 7025, pp. 3–17. Springer, Heidelberg (2011)
18. Lehmann, A., Bichsel, P., Bichsel, P., Bruegger, B., Camenisch, J., Garcia, A.C., Gross, T., Gutwirth, A., Horsch, M., Houdeau, D., Hühnlein, D., Kamm, F.M., Krenn, S., Neven, G., Rodriguez, C.B., Schmölz, J., Bolliger, C.: Survey and Analysis of Existing eID and Credential Systems. Tech. Rep. Deliverable D32.1, FutureID (2013)
19. Li, J., Li, N., Xue, R.: Universal accumulators with efficient nonmembership proofs. In: Katz, J., Yung, M. (eds.) ACNS 2007. LNCS, vol. 4521, pp. 253–269. Springer, Heidelberg (2007)
20. Libert, B., Peters, T., Yung, M.: Group signatures with almost-for-free revocation. In: Safavi-Naini, R., Canetti, R. (eds.) CRYPTO 2012. LNCS, vol. 7417, pp. 571–589. Springer, Heidelberg (2012)

21. Lueks, W., Alpár, G., Hoepman, J.H., Vullers, P.: Fast revocation of attribute-based credentials for both users and verifiers. Cryptology ePrint Archive, Report 2015/237 (2015). http://eprint.iacr.org/
22. Nakanishi, T., Funabiki, N.: Verifier-local revocation group signature schemes with backward unlinkability from bilinear maps. In: Roy, B. (ed.) ASIACRYPT 2005. LNCS, vol. 3788, pp. 533–548. Springer, Heidelberg (2005)
23. Naumann, I., Hogben, G.: Privacy features of European eID card specifications. Network Security **2008**(8), 9–13 (2008)
24. Nguyen, L., Paquin, C.: U-prove designated-verifier accumulator revocation extension. Tech. Rep. MSR-TR-2014-85, Microsoft Research, June 2014
25. OECD: National Strategies and Policies for Digital Identity Management in OECD Countries (2011)
26. de la Piedra, A., Hoepman, J.-H., Vullers, P.: Towards a full-featured implementation of attribute based credentials on smart cards. In: Gritzalis, D., Kiayias, A., Askoxylakis, I. (eds.) CANS 2014. LNCS, vol. 8813, pp. 270–289. Springer, Heidelberg (2014)
27. Santesson, S., Myers, M., Ankney, R., Malpani, A., Galperin, S., Adams, C.: X.509 Internet Public Key Infrastructure Online Certificate Status Protocol - OCSP. RFC 6960 (Proposed Standard), June 2013
28. Tsang, P.P., Au, M.H., Kapadia, A., Smith, S.W.: Blacklistable Anonymous Credentials: Blocking Misbehaving Users without TTPs. In: CCS 2007, pp. 72–81. ACM (2007)
29. Vullers, P., Alpár, G.: Efficient selective disclosure on smart cards using idemix. In: Fischer-Hübner, S., de Leeuw, E., Mitchell, C. (eds.) IDMAN 2013. IFIP AICT, vol. 396, pp. 53–67. Springer, Heidelberg (2013)

Chaotic Chebyshev Polynomials Based Remote User Authentication Scheme in Client-Server Environment

Toan-Thinh Truong[1]([✉]), Minh-Triet Tran[1],
Anh-Duc Duong[2], and Isao Echizen[3]

[1] University of Science, VNU-HCM, Ho Chi Minh City, Vietnam
{ttthinh,tmtriet}@fit.hcmus.edu.vn
[2] University of Information Technology, VNU-HCM, Ho Chi Minh City, Vietnam
ducda@uit.edu.vn
[3] National Institute of Informatics, Tokyo City, Japan
iechizen@nii.ac.jp

Abstract. Perfect forward secrecy is considered as the most important standard to evaluate a strong authentication scheme. There are many results researched to achieve this property without using hard problems. Recently, the result of Chang et al has some advances such as, the correctness of schemes mutual authentication and session key agreement demonstrated in BAN-logic or the overheads reduction of system implementation. However, in this paper, we prove that their scheme is still vulnerable to impersonation attacks and session key leakage. To overcome those limitations and be practical, we use different notion to propose time efficient scheme conducted in experiment. Our proposed method can be applied for remote user authentication in various scenarios, including systems with user authentication using mobile or wearable devices.

Keywords: Authentication · Anonymity · Impersonation · Session key · Chaotic chebyshev polynomials

1 Introduction

Nowadays, wireless communication is the necessary fundamental. With non-stop growth of handheld and wearable devices, there are many online services widely deployed on the Internet. Customers demand an immediate response, privacy and cryptography in their transactions with service providers. Therefore, incorporating mathematical results into user authentication schemes is an inevitable trend.

User authentication is the first task which any online service needs to perform. It is said that two basic standards a scheme should achieve are the security and time efficiency. However, simultaneously obtaining those goals is a difficult mission. As for security, there are many criteria and one of them is exactly user identification. Basic method [1] is storing a verification table including records

© IFIP International Federation for Information Processing 2015
H. Federrath and D. Gollmann (Eds.): SEC 2015, IFIP AICT 455, pp. 479–494, 2015.
DOI: 10.1007/978-3-319-18467-8_32

(identity/password) on server side. When a user logins, the server checks the existence of identity and password in the table. Although simple, this method is vulnerable to stolen verification attack. Furthermore, providing static identity through common channel is not suitable for some applications, such as mobile pay-TV [2] or online voting. To overcome those limitations, some authors proposed the notion of dynamic identity [3–5], but these results still have some drawbacks such as, symmetric message easy to replay attack or poor design easy to information injection attack. In general, most schemes employ one-way hash function which does not provide scheme with strong security. To enhance security, however, a method of using hard problems is more and more given consideration.

Typically, RSA [6] is one of popular methods incorporated into user authentication scheme, but main disadvantage is using certificates leading to additional computations to its verification. Clearly, this is not suitable for resource-limited handheld or wearable devices. Some authors publish the results [7–9] based on elliptic curve are considered reasonable for time efficiency and security. However, those results use a special kind of hash function, Map-To-Point which has non-negligible cost and is not standardized. Also, Chebysev polynomial is given consideration [10,11] and its semi-group property is widely applied in global mobile networks environment [12] or public key based cryptosystems [13]. There are some algorithms [14] used in public key cryptosystem based on this approach. It is said that authentication scheme using Chebysev polynomial is better way to keep the tradeoff between time efficiency and security.

In 2013, Chang et al proposed the time efficiency scheme [15] with one-way hash assumption about collision resistant. Besides, the correctness of the scheme is proved based on BAN-logic [16]. Their scheme truly has some successes, for example, providing mutual authentication, achieving session key establishment and without using time-synchronized mechanism. However, their basic limitations are that challenge is only derived from server side and distribution of common secret information to all valid members. In this paper, we prove that Chang et al.'s scheme does not resist impersonation attack and fail to protect session key. Furthermore, it does not provide users anonymity in their transactions. Next, we apply semi-group of Chevbysev polynomial for tradeoff balance and session key protection in generic client-server environment in which this approach has not been considered. In addition, our design has challenges derived from two parties, client and server, to make the fairness in transaction. Also, our scheme is proven correct according to BAN-logic. It is said that our result truly is enhanced security and efficiency in practice, including systems with user authentication using handheld or wearable devices to create smart interactive environments.

The remainder of this paper is organized as follows: section 2 quickly reviews Chang et al.'s scheme and discusses its limitations. Then, proposed scheme is presented in section 3, while section 4 discusses the security and efficiency of proposed scheme. Finally, our conclusions are presented in section 5.

2   Review and Cryptanalysis of Chang et al.'s Scheme

In this section, we review Chang et al.'s scheme [15] and show that their scheme is vulnerable to impersonation attack. Besides, it cannot provide user's anonymity.

2.1   Review of Chang et al.'s Scheme

In this subsection, we review Chang et al.'s scheme. Their scheme includes four phases: registration phase, authentication phase, password change phase, and lost card revocation phase. Below are some important notations in this scheme:

- U_i: i^{th} user.
- id_i: U_i's identity.
- pw_i: U_i's password.
- S: Remote server.
- id_s: S's identity.
- x, y: The secret keys of remote server.
- $h(.)$: A cryptographic one-way hash function.
- sn_i: Smart card's serial number.
- SK: Common session key.
- SC: Smart-card.
- $\oplus$: exclusive-or operation.
- $\|$: concatenation operation.

Registration Phase. U_i freely chooses a fixed length id_i and pw_i. Then U_i has to submit his/her id_i, pw_i to S through a secure channel. When receiving U_i's message, S performs following steps.

- S randomizes 128-bit sized integer r_i. Then, S computes $R_1 = h(id_i \parallel x \parallel r_i)$, $R_2 = g^{xy} \bmod p$, where p is a large prime number and g is a primitive element in Z_p^*, and $R_3 = h(id_i \parallel R_2) \oplus h(pw_i)$.
- S issues a SC with a 32-bit sized sn_i, where sn_i has a specific format. Then, S combines sn_i with U_i's id_i as $SID_i = (id_i \parallel sn_i)$.
- Finally, S saves R_1, R_2, R_3, SID_i and $h(.)$ into SC and send it to U_i via a secure channel.

In this registration phase, we see that there are some problems: Because U_i sends plain pw_i to S, S knows user's true password and may try using it in another system. Furthermore, using two secret keys x and y is more security, but we should use only one with high entropy for enough security. Therefore, we will change this in our registration.

Authentication Phase. When U_i accesses S, U_i inserts SC into terminal device and provides id_i and pw_i. Then SC performs following steps.

- SC computes $C_1 = R_3 \oplus h(pw_i)$ and $V_1 = R_1 \oplus C_1$.

- Next, SC randomly generates a 160-bit sized integer n_1, then computes and $DID_i = h(R_2 \parallel n_1) \oplus SID_i$.
- Finally, SC sends $m_1 = \{DID_i, V_1, n_1\}$ to S via common channel.
- Upon receiving m_1 from U_i, S re-computes $SID_i = DID_i \oplus h((g^{xy} \bmod p) \parallel n_1)$. Then, S retrieves id_i and sn_i and checks their format. If they are valid, S continues to compute $R_1^* = V_1 \oplus h(id_i \parallel (g^{xy} \bmod p))$ and randomly generates 160-bit sized integer n_2.
- Next, S computes $V_2 = h(R_1^* \parallel id_s \parallel n_1)$, $V_3 = h(h(h(id_i \parallel (g^{xy} \bmod p)) \parallel n_1) \oplus n_2$ and send $m_2 = \{id_s, V_2, V_3\}$ to U_i via common channel.
- Upon receiving m_2 from S, SC computes $V_2^* = h(R_1 \parallel id_s \parallel n_1)$ and check if $V_2^* ?= V_2$. If it holds, S is successfully authenticated; otherwise, the connection is terminated.
- SC obtains random value $n_2 = V_3 \oplus h(C_1 \parallel n_1)$ and generates $SK = h(n_1 \parallel SID_i \parallel R_2 \parallel n_2)$.
- Finally, SC computes $V_4 = h(SK \parallel (n_2 + 1))$ and send $m_4 = \{V_4\}$ to S via common channel.
- After receiving m_4 from U_i, S computes $SK = h(n_1 \parallel SID_i \parallel (g^{xy} \bmod p) \parallel n_2)$ and $V_4^* = h(SK \parallel (n_2 + 1))$. Next, S check if $V_4^* ?= V_4$. If it holds, U_i is successfully authenticated. Otherwise, the connection is terminated.

In their authentication phase, we see that only S generates random value n_2 to challenge U_i, while U_i's n_1 is opened in a common channel. This design will limit random value's power in scheme. Furthermore, user's identity can be leaked because their scheme distributes $g^{xy} \bmod p$ to all users. We will analyze in next section.

Password Change Phase. When U_i wants to change his/her pw_i, U_i can perform following steps.

- U_i inserts SC into another terminal device, and enters id_i, pw_i.
- SC computes $Q_1 = h(id_i \parallel R_2)$ and $Q_1^* = R_3 \oplus h(pw_i)$ and compares with each other. If $Q_1 = Q_1^*$, SC goes to next step; otherwise, the procedure is terminated.
- SC computes $R_3' = h(id_i \parallel R_2) \oplus h(pw_i) \oplus h(pw_i) \oplus h(pw_i')$ and replace R_3 with R_3'.

In their password change phase, we see that password update is performed without interacting with S. In our scheme, we will inherit this idea from [15].

Lost Card Revocation Phase. When U_i discovers SC's information is leaked, U_i can request S to revoke SC via a secure channel. When receiving revocation request, S validates U_i by checking U_i's secret personal information. After successfully validation, S saves sn_i of revoked SC in the database and issue a new SC with new sn_i' for U_i. Finally, U_i chooses a new pw_i similarly to the steps in registration phase.

2.2   Cryptanalysis of Chang et al.'s Scheme

In this subsection, we present our results on Chang et al.'s scheme. We demonstrate that their scheme is vulnerable to impersonation and session-key stolen attacks. Besides, their scheme does not provide user's anonymity.

Inability to Protect User Anonymity. In Chang et al.'s scheme, we see that another user sends $m_1 = \{DID_i, V_1, n_1\}$. However, important information ($g^{xy} \bmod p$) is distributed to all valid users. Hence, anyone who is legitimate user can steal other users' identity by performing following steps:

- Malicious user captures $m_1 = \{DID_i, V_1, n_1\}$
- Next, he/she obtains $SID_i = DID_i \oplus h((g^{xy} \bmod p) \parallel n_1)$
- Finally, he/she extracts id_i and sn_i from SID_i and knows who is authenticating with S.

Clearly, their scheme does not defend user's anonymity against attackers.

Impersonation Attack. Because of inappropriate design, Chang et al.'s scheme is vulnerable to server and user impersonation attack. First of all, we present the steps which another malicious user employs to masquerade as the server:

- Similarly to above steps, malicious user obtains another user's id_i and sn_i.
- With id_i, he/she computes $R_1^* = V_1 \oplus (id_i \parallel (g^{xy} \bmod p))$ and $V_2^* = h(R_1^* \parallel id_S \parallel n_1)$, which V_1 and n_1 belongs to $m_1 = \{DID_i, V_1, n_1\}$ which is captured by him/her.
- Next, he/she generates a random value n_2^* and computes $V_3^* = h(h(id_i \parallel (g^{xy} \bmod p)) \parallel n_1) \oplus n_2^*$.
- Finally, he/she sends $m_2^* = \{id_S, V_2^*, V_3^*\}$ to user.

Upon receiving m_2^*, U_i re-computes $V_2 = h(R_1 \parallel id_S \parallel n_1)$ and compares it with V_2^*. Clearly, they are equal and malicious user successfully impersonates S. Furthermore, he can impersonate another U_i authenticating with S. Following are some steps to masquerade as legitimate user.

- Malicious user captures $m_1 = \{DID_i, V_1, n_1\}$, he/she extracts SID_i by computing $SID_i = DID_i \oplus h(R_2 \parallel n_1)$, where R_2 is his/her smartcard's information.
- Afterwards, he/she generates a random value n_1^* and re-computes $DID_i^* = h(R_2 \parallel n_1^*) \oplus SID_i$.
- Next, he/she sends $m_1^* = \{DID_i^*, V_1, n_1\}$ to S.
- After receiving m_1^*, S computes and re-sends $m_2 = \{id_S, V_2, V_3\}$ to him/her. In this time, he/she computes $n_2 = V_3 \oplus h(h(id_i \parallel R_2) \parallel n_1^*)$, where id_i is obtained by him/her.
- With n_2, he/she computes $SK^* = h(n_1^* \parallel SID_i \parallel R_2 \parallel n_2)$ and $V_4^* = h(SK^* \parallel (n_2 + 1))$.
- Finally, he/she sends $m_3^* = \{V_4^*\}$ to S.

After receiving m_3^*, S computes V_4 and compares it with V_4^*. Clearly, they are equal and malicious user successfully impersonate another legitimate U_i.

Session Key Attack. Another malicious user can observe outside and compute common session-key SK by performing following steps:

- First of all, he captures three packages m_1, m_2 and m_3 in common channel.
- Next, he computes $SID_i = DID_i \oplus h((g^{xy} \bmod p) \parallel n_1)$ and extracts id_i.
- Afterwards, he obtains n_2 by performing $n_2 = V_3 \oplus h((id_i \parallel R_2) \parallel n_1)$.
- Finally, he computes $SK = h(n_1 \parallel SID_i \parallel R_2 \parallel n_2)$.

Clearly, all data encrypted with session-key will be revealed.

3　Proposed Scheme

At first, we depict Chebysev polynomial [17] which is our scheme's security foundation. Chebysev polynomial has the form: $T_n(x) = cos(n * arccos(x))$, where n is an integer degree and $x \in$ [-1, 1]. Besides, we have its recurrent formulas:

- $T_0(x) = 1$
- $T_1(x) = x$
- ...
- $T_{n+1}(x) = 2x\,T_n(x)$ - $T_{n-1}(x)$ and $n \geq 2$.

Moreover, our scheme utilizes polynomial's semi-group property: $T_q(T_w(x)) = cos(q * arccos(cos(w * arccos(x)))) = cos(qw * arccos(x)) = cos(wq * arccos(x)) = cos(w * arccos(cos(q * arccos(x)))) = T_w(T_q(x))$.

Next, we propose an improved scheme that eliminates aforementioned security problems. Before presenting each phase, we present general ideas in our scheme. In registration phase, our main objective includes providing authentication key $h(X_S \parallel e)$ and storing $h(id_i) \oplus X_S$ in server's database to check identity's validity. Especially, random value e helps to create different keys at different time. In login and authentication phases, we use two random values R_U and R_S combined with Chebysev polynomials for challenge. In addition, we employ three-way challenge-response handshake technique to better resist replay and impersonation attacks [9]. Eventually, it is essential to obtain SK for encrypting data transmitted between user and server after successfully authentication phase. Our scheme is also divided into five phases of registration, login, mutual authentication, password update and lost card revocation.

3.1　Registration Phase

Before presenting this phase, we suggest three conditions which registration phase should satisfy: Firstly, user's password should be concealed from the server. In our scheme, although the server generates user's password, the user will change his/her password after receiving it from the server. Secondly, the server must provide different authentication keys at different time. By using random value, our scheme completely achieves this requirement. Thirdly, the server should store user's identity for later checking in next phases such as login or authentication phase. Our scheme is designed to achieve these fundamentals.

When U_i registers to S, he/she must submit his/her chosen id_i via a secure channel. When receiving this information, S performs following steps:

1. S generates pw_i and random value e.
2. Next, S computes authentication key $K = h(X_S \| e)$, masked key $M = K \oplus h(id_i \| pw_i)$ and confirmation $L = h(K \| id_i \| pw_i)$, where X_S is S's master key.
3. Afterwards, S stores $h(id_i) \oplus X_S$ in S's database for later checking.
4. Finally, S sends $\{pw_i, SC(M, L, e, h(.), T_s(x))\}$ via a secure channel, where $\{x, T_s(x)\}$ is S's public information.

After receiving SC and pw_i, U_i updates pw_i via our password-update phase.

3.2   Login Phase

In login phase, checking user's identity and password must be performed at client side to prevent the attackers from overwhelming the server with a false identity and password in order to busy the server for a long time. Besides, login-message should be dynamic at different time to protect user's information especially identity. Our login phase is also designed to satisfy these requirements.

When U_i inputs his/her id_i and pw_i to login S, then SC performs:

1. SC computes $K = M \oplus h(id_i \| pw_i)$ and $L^* = h(K \| id_i \| pw_i)$.
2. Next, it compares L^* with L. If they are the same, id_i and pw_i are correct and SC goes to next steps; otherwise, it terminates the session.
3. Afterwards, SC generates a random large integer r_U, computes $R_U = T_{r_U}(x)$, $DID_i = id_i \oplus h(R_U \| K)$ and $R_2 = h(K \| id_i \| R_U)$.
4. Finally, it sends $\{e, R_U, R_2, DID_i\}$ to S via common channel.

3.3   Authentication and Session Key Agreement Phase

In authentication phase, both user and server must challenge each other to prove their legitimacy. Additionally, they should obtain common session-key after successful authentication. Our phase has these two important features.

In this session, after receiving U_i's $\{e, R_U, R_2, DID_i\}$ in login phase. S performs the steps to authenticate U_i.

1. S computes $h(X_S \| e)$ and extracts $id_i = DID_i \oplus h(R_U \| h(X_S \| e))$.
2. Next, S check id_i by performing $h(id_i) \oplus X_S$, and searches its existence in S's database. If it exists, id_i is valid; otherwise, S terminates the session.
3. Afterwards, S computes $R_2^* = h(h(X_S \| e) \| id_i \| R_U)$ and compares R_2^* with R_2. If they are the same, S goes to next step; otherwise, S terminates the session.
4. S generates r_S, computes $R_S = T_{r_S}(x)$, $SK = h(T_{r_S}(R_U) \| h(X_S \| e) \| id_i)$ and $R_4 = h(h(X_S \| e) \| id_i \| SK)$.

5. Finally, S sends $\{R_S, R_4\}$ to U_i via common channel.
6. After receiving S's $\{R_S, R_4\}$, U_i re-computes $SK = h(T_{r_U}(R_S) \parallel K \parallel id_i)$, $R_4^* = h(K \parallel id_i \parallel SK)$ and compares R_4^* with R_4. If they are the same, U_i successfully authenticates S.
7. U_i computes $R_5 = h(SK)$ and sends to S via common channel.
8. After receiving U_i's $\{R_5\}$, S re-computes $R_5^* = h(SK)$ and compares it with R_5. If they are the same, S successfully authenticates U_i.

3.4   Password Update Phase

When U_i wants to change pw_i, U_i performs:

1. U_i inserts SC and inputs id_i and pw_i.
2. Next, SC computes $K = M \oplus h(id_i \parallel pw_i)$ and $L^* = h(K \parallel id_i \parallel pw_i)$.
3. Afterwards, SC compares L^* with L stored in it. If they are the same, SC accepts user's request; otherwise, it terminates the session.
4. U_i inserts new password pw_{inew}. Then, SC computes $M_{new} = K \oplus h(id_i \parallel pw_{inew})$ and $L_{new} = h(K \parallel id_i \parallel pw_{inew})$
5. Finally, SC replaces L, M with L_{new}, M_{new}.

3.5   Lost Card Revocation Phase

If U_i losts his/her SC, U_i must notify S. Then, S will re-issue new SC with the old U_i's id_i.

1. U_i re-submits id_i and *request-re-issue-smart-card* to S via a secure channel.
2. After receiving U_i's request, S computes $h(id_i) \oplus X_S$ and searches its existence in S's database. If it exists, S accepts U_i's request; otherwise, S terminates the session.
3. Next, S generates a new random value e_{new} and performs steps which are the same as registration phase's. Finally, S re-issues new SC to U_i via a secure channel.

4   Security and Efficiency Analysis

In this section, we analyze our scheme on two aspects: security and efficiency. Before further analysis, we introduce three basic computational assumptions which proposed scheme employs, that are one-way hash function ([15] for more details), Chebysev discrete logarithm problem (**CDLP**) and Diffie-Hellman problem (**CDHP**)([11,18] for more details).

- Chebysev Discrete Logarithm Problem: Given $x \in [-1, 1]$, $T_n(\mathrm{x})$, where n, $s \in \mathbf{N}$, the discrete logarithm problem is to find unknown degree n.
- Chebysev Diffie-Hellman Problem: Given $x \in [-1, 1]$, $T_q(\mathrm{x})$ and $T_s(\mathrm{x})$, where q, $s \in \mathbf{N}$, the computational Diffie-Hellman problem is to find $T_{q*s}(x)$ or $T_{s*q}(x)$, where $T_{q*s}(x) = T_q(T_s) = T_s(T_q) = T_{s*q}(x) \in [-1, 1]$.

4.1   Correctness Proof

To correct evaluate about authentication scheme, we employ BAN-logic [16] proposed by Burrows. We introduce some basic symbols used in this method as follows: symbols P and Q stand for principals, X and Y range over statements, and K represent the cryptographic key. For more details about the notations and postulates, please refer to Burrows' result. In the following, we use BAN-logic to prove proposed scheme achieves correct mutual authentication and session key agreement. In stead of using P, Q, we let U_i, S stand for user and server participating in the scheme. Furthermore, we formalize our goals denoted as $\boldsymbol{G_j}$, where $j \in [1, 8]$ as follows:

1. $U_i \mid\equiv U_i \overset{id_i}{\leftrightarrow} S$
2. $U_i \mid\equiv S \mid\equiv U_i \overset{id_i}{\leftrightarrow} S$
3. $S \mid\equiv U_i \overset{id_i}{\leftrightarrow} S$
4. $S \mid\equiv U_i \mid\equiv U_i \overset{id_i}{\leftrightarrow} S$
5. $U_i \mid\equiv U_i \overset{SK}{\leftrightarrow} S$
6. $U_i \mid\equiv S \mid\equiv S \overset{SK}{\leftrightarrow} U_i$
7. $S \mid\equiv S \overset{SK}{\leftrightarrow} U_i$
8. $S \mid\equiv U_i \mid\equiv U_i \overset{SK}{\leftrightarrow} S$

Then, we idealize proposed scheme as follows:

- $\boldsymbol{DID_i} = <U_i \overset{id_i}{\leftrightarrow} S, T_{r_U}, U_i \overset{h(X_S\|e)}{\leftrightarrow} S>$
- $\boldsymbol{R_2} = <U_i \overset{id_i}{\leftrightarrow} S, U_i \overset{h(X_S\|e)}{\leftrightarrow} S, T_{r_U}>$
- $\boldsymbol{R_4} = <U_i \overset{h(X_S\|e)}{\leftrightarrow} S, U_i \overset{id_i}{\leftrightarrow} S, U_i \overset{SK}{\leftrightarrow} S>$
- $\boldsymbol{R_5} = <T_{r_S}(R_U), U_i \overset{h(X_S\|e)}{\leftrightarrow} S, U_i \overset{id_i}{\leftrightarrow} S>$

Next, we give some assumptions (denoted as $\boldsymbol{A_t}$, where $t \in [1, 8]$) about proposed scheme's initial states

1. $U_i \mid\equiv U_i \overset{id_i}{\leftrightarrow} S$
2. $U_i \mid\equiv U_i \overset{h(X_S\|e)}{\leftrightarrow} S$
3. $U_i \mid\equiv S \Rightarrow U_i \overset{SK}{\leftrightarrow} S$
4. $S \mid\equiv U_i \Rightarrow U_i \overset{id_i}{\leftrightarrow} S$
5. $S \mid\equiv U_i \Rightarrow U_i \overset{SK}{\leftrightarrow} S$
6. $S \mid\equiv S \overset{h(X_S\|e)}{\leftrightarrow} U_i$
7. $U_i \mid\equiv \#(T_{r_S})$
8. $S \mid\equiv \#(T_{r_U})$

Finally, with $\boldsymbol{A_t}$ and BAN-logic's postulates, we demonstrate our scheme successfully achieves $\boldsymbol{G_j}$.

- U_i registers id_i with S, so we achieve $\mathbf{G_1}$

$$U_i \mid\equiv U_i \overset{id_i}{\leftrightarrow} S$$

- With $\mathbf{A}_6$ and DID_i, applying the message-meaning rule to derive

$$\frac{S\mid\equiv S^{\overset{h(X_S\|e)}{\leftrightarrow}}U_i, S\lhd(U_i\overset{id_i}{\leftrightarrow}S,T_{r_U},U_i\overset{h(X_S\|e)}{\leftrightarrow}S)_{h(X_S\|e)}}{S\mid\equiv U_i\mid\sim U_i\overset{id_i}{\leftrightarrow}S,T_{r_U},U_i\overset{h(X_S\|e)}{\leftrightarrow}S}(1)$$

- With $\mathbf{A}_8$ and applying freshness rule to infer

$$\frac{S\mid\equiv\#(T_{r_U})}{S\mid\equiv\#(U_i\overset{id_i}{\leftrightarrow}S,T_{r_U},U_i\overset{h(X_S\|e)}{\leftrightarrow}S)}(2)$$

- With (1) and (2), applying the nonce - verification rule to derive

$$\frac{(1),(2)}{S\mid\equiv U_i\mid\equiv U_i\overset{id_i}{\leftrightarrow}S,T_{r_U},U_i\overset{h(X_S\|e)}{\leftrightarrow}S}(3)$$

- With (3), applying believe rule to derive

$$\frac{(3)}{S\mid\equiv U_i\mid\equiv U_i\overset{id_i}{\leftrightarrow}S}(G_4)$$

- With $\mathbf{G}_4$ and $\mathbf{A}_4$, applying jurisdiction rule to infer

$$\frac{S\mid\equiv U_i\Rightarrow U_i\overset{id_i}{\leftrightarrow}S, S\mid\equiv U_i\mid\equiv U_i\overset{id_i}{\leftrightarrow}S}{S\mid\equiv U_i\overset{id_i}{\leftrightarrow}S}(G_3)$$

- With $\mathbf{A}_2$ and R_4, applying the message-meaning rule to derive

$$\frac{U_i\mid\equiv U_i\overset{h(X_S\|e)}{\leftrightarrow}S, U_i\lhd(U_i\overset{h(X_S\|e)}{\leftrightarrow}S,U_i\overset{id_i}{\leftrightarrow}S,U_i\overset{SK}{\leftrightarrow}S)_{h(X_S\|e)}}{U_i\mid\equiv S\mid\sim U_i\overset{h(X_S\|e)}{\leftrightarrow}S,U_i\overset{id_i}{\leftrightarrow}S,U_i\overset{SK}{\leftrightarrow}S}(4)$$

- With (4) and $\mathbf{A}_7$, applying the freshness rule to derive

$$\frac{(4),U_i\mid\equiv\#(T_{r_S})}{U_i\mid\equiv\#(U_i\overset{h(X_S\|e)}{\leftrightarrow}S,U_i\overset{id_i}{\leftrightarrow}S,U_i\overset{SK}{\leftrightarrow}S)}(5)$$

- With (4) and (5), applying the nonce - verification rule to derive

$$\frac{(4),(5)}{U_i\mid\equiv S\mid\equiv U_i\overset{h(X_S\|e)}{\leftrightarrow}S,U_i\overset{id_i}{\leftrightarrow}S,U_i\overset{SK}{\leftrightarrow}S}(6)$$

- With (6), applying the believe rule to derive

$$\frac{(6)}{U_i\mid\equiv S\mid\equiv U_i\overset{id_i}{\leftrightarrow}S}(G_2)$$

With $\mathbf{G}_1$, $\mathbf{G}_2$, $\mathbf{G}_3$, and $\mathbf{G}_4$, we prove U_i and S can mutually authenticate with dynamic identity. Next, we demonstrate U_i and S can share SK as follows.

- With R_4 and $\mathbf{A}_2$, applying the message-meaning rule to derive

$$\frac{U_i\mid\equiv U_i\overset{h(X_S\|e)}{\leftrightarrow}S, U_i\lhd(U_i\overset{h(X_S\|e)}{\leftrightarrow}S,U_i\overset{id_i}{\leftrightarrow}S,U_i\overset{SK}{\leftrightarrow}S)_{h(X_S\|e)}}{U_i\mid\equiv S\mid\sim U_i\overset{h(X_S\|e)}{\leftrightarrow}S,U_i\overset{id_i}{\leftrightarrow}S,U_i\overset{SK}{\leftrightarrow}S}(7)$$

- With R_4 and $\mathbf{A}_7$, applying the freshness rule to derive

$$\frac{U_i |\equiv \#(T_{r_S})}{U_i |\equiv \#(U_i \overset{h(X_S \| e)}{\leftrightarrow} S, U_i \overset{id_i}{\leftrightarrow} S, U_i \overset{SK}{\leftrightarrow} S)} (8)$$

– With (7) and (8), applying the nonce - verification rule to derive

$$\frac{(7),(8)}{U_i |\equiv S |\equiv U_i \overset{h(X_S \| e)}{\leftrightarrow} S, U_i \overset{id_i}{\leftrightarrow} S, U_i \overset{SK}{\leftrightarrow} S} (9)$$

– With (9), applying the believe rule to derive

$$\frac{(9)}{U_i |\equiv S |\equiv S \overset{SK}{\leftrightarrow} U_i} (G_6)$$

– With A_3 and G_6, we apply the jurisdiction rule to infer

$$\frac{U_i |\equiv S \Rightarrow U_i \overset{SK}{\leftrightarrow} S, U_i |\equiv S |\equiv U_i \overset{SK}{\leftrightarrow} S}{U_i |\equiv U_i \overset{SK}{\leftrightarrow} S} (G_5)$$

– With R_5 and A_6, applying the message-meaning rule to derive

$$\frac{S |\equiv S \overset{h(X_S \| e)}{\leftrightarrow} U_i, S \lhd (T_{r_U * r_S}, U_i \overset{h(X_S \| e)}{\leftrightarrow} S, U_i \overset{id_i}{\leftrightarrow} S)_{h(X_S \| e)}}{S |\equiv U_i |\sim T_{r_U * r_S}, U_i \overset{h(X_S \| e)}{\leftrightarrow} S, U_i \overset{id_i}{\leftrightarrow} S} (10)$$

– With R_5 and A_8, applying the freshness rule to derive

$$\frac{S |\equiv \#(T_{r_U})}{S |\equiv \#(T_{r_U * r_S}, U_i \overset{h(X_S \| e)}{\leftrightarrow} S, U_i \overset{id_i}{\leftrightarrow} S)} (11)$$

– With (10) and (11), applying the nonce - verification rule to derive

$$\frac{(10),(11)}{S |\equiv U_i |\equiv T_{r_U * r_S}, U_i \overset{h(X_S \| e)}{\leftrightarrow} S, U_i \overset{id_i}{\leftrightarrow} S} (12)$$

– With (12) and A_6, applying the believe rule to infer

$$\frac{(12), S |\equiv S \overset{h(X_S \| e)}{\leftrightarrow} U_i}{S |\equiv U_i |\equiv U_i \overset{SK}{\leftrightarrow} S} (G_8)$$

– With (12) and A_5, applying the message-meaning rule to infer

$$\frac{(12), S |\equiv U_i \Rightarrow U_i \overset{SK}{\leftrightarrow} S}{S |\equiv T_{r_U * r_S}, U_i \overset{h(X_S \| e)}{\leftrightarrow} S, U_i \overset{id_i}{\leftrightarrow} S} (13)$$

– With (13), applying the believe rule to derive

$$\frac{(13)}{S |\equiv S \overset{SK}{\leftrightarrow} U_i} (G_7)$$

With G_5, G_6, G_7 and G_8, we prove both S and U_i believe the other believes SK shared between U_i and S. Below are common kinds of attacks proposed scheme can withstand.

4.2   Resistance to Common Attacks

In this subsection, we prove our scheme can withstand many common kinds of attacks based on above two basic assumptions. Our context is that both server and user are authenticating in open channel. Hence, anyone is capable of intercepting all messages transmitted between them. Besides, we assume anyone can obtain SC's information.

Replay Attack. In this kind of attack, adversary captures the user's old messages for next transaction. It is hard to perform in proposed scheme. For example, when adversary sends package $\{e, R_U, R_2, DID_i\}$ at another session to cheat the server, he/she needs to resend R_5 at the end of the session. Clearly, knowing U_i's r_U, id_i and $h(X_S \parallel e)$ is impossible to adversary. It is said that proposed scheme can withstand replay attack.

User And Server Impersonation Attack. In this kind of attack, adversary has two options, which are user and server impersonation. Firstly, we consider the case of user impersonation. In the users login message, only two messages that adversary can forge are e and $R_U = T_{r_U}(x)$ because they do not include identity information. Consequently, adversary randomly chooses r_U^* to compute $R_U^* = T_{r_U^*}(\mathrm{x})$, where e^* is adversary's own random value. Finally, he/she sends $\{e^*, R_U^*, R_2, DID_i\}$ to server. When receiving, server computes $h(X_S \parallel e^*)$ and extracts id_i by computing $DID_i \oplus h(R_U^* \parallel h(X_S \parallel e^*)) = id_i \oplus h(R_U \parallel h(X_S \parallel e)) \oplus h(R_U^* \parallel h(X_S \parallel e^*))$. Clearly, we see the result of this computation is nonsense. Therefore, server will detect and terminate this session. Secondly, we consider the case of server impersonation. We see that adversary needs to successfully compute $\{R_S, R_4\}$ and this is impossible because $R_4 = h(h(X_S \parallel e) \parallel id_i \parallel SK^*)$, where SK^* is random session key computed from adversary's random value r_S^*. Hence, adversary needs U_i's $h(X_S \parallel e)$ and id_i. In short, proposed scheme can resist two-side impersonation attack.

User Anonymity Protected. In this kind of attack, adversary wants to know whose transaction this is. Therefore, he/she will find the way to extract identity from the message DID_i. We see that user's identity is combined with random value R_U and key $K = h(X_S \parallel e)$. With two values, adversary has no chance to extract true identity. Specially, DID_i is different at each session due to random value R_U. Also, adversary does not know whether or not DID_i and DID_i' belong to the same person. Hence, proposed scheme achieves strong user anonymity.

Perfect forward secrecy (PFS). In this kind of attack, assume that long-term key of the server and all users is leaked, so the system is broken. However, the previously transactions should be secured from the adversary and this means that generated session keys should be secured. In proposed scheme, in case of leakage of server S's X_S and user U_i's $h(X_S \parallel e_i)$, the adversary has $R_U = T_{r_U}(x)$, $R_S = T_{r_S}(x)$ and id_i. Nevertheless, computing $T_{r_S} * r_U(x)$ is the same as computing the **CDHP**. It is said that proposed scheme can achieve **PFS** based on **CDHP**.

Chang et al.'s ideas are inherited by proposed scheme. For example, no using password or state table due to the increase of computational overload, or using random value instead of time-stamp to save time-synchronization mechanism cost. Likewise, using cryptographic hash function allows the users to freely choose their password without worrying about bit-length. In short, those properties

Table 1. The comparison between our scheme and previous ones for security

Items	Das's[19]	Wang's[20]	Chang's[15]	Ours
Mutual authentication	No	Yes	Yes	Yes
Password chosen by users	Yes	No	Yes	Yes
User anonymity	Yes	No	No	Yes
Without registration table	Yes	Yes	Yes	Yes
Withstand impersonation attack	No	No	No	Yes
Without time-synchronized mechanism	No	No	Yes	Yes
Session key establishment	No	No	Yes	Yes
Perfect forward secrecy	No*	No*	No	Yes
* Do not provide session key establishment				

completely exist in proposed scheme. Table 1 is the comparison between our scheme and previous schemes including Chang et al.'s for security.

4.3 Efficiency Analysis

To compare efficiency between our scheme and previous ones, we let H be the hash operation, $\uparrow$ be modular exponentiation operation, $\oplus$ be exclusive-or operation and T be computational operation of polynomial. At registration phase, Das's scheme needs $1\times\oplus$, $2\times H$; Wang's needs $2\times\oplus$, $2\times H$; Chang's needs $1\times\oplus$, $3\times H$, $1\times\uparrow$; Ours needs $2\times\oplus$, $4\times H$. At login and authentication phases, Das's scheme needs $14\times\oplus$, $7\times H$; Wang's needs $14\times\oplus$, $6\times H$; Chang's needs $7\times\oplus$, $10\times H$, $1\times\uparrow$; Ours needs $4\times\oplus$, $14\times H$, $4\times T$. Compared with previous schemes, our scheme's computational cost increases perceptibly. However, this is essential because of enhancement of security. Furthermore, in according to [14], we believe if practical implemented, our scheme will be still efficient enough. The theorical comparison of cost at this phase is presented in Table 2.

Let t_H, $t_\oplus$, t_T, $t_\uparrow$ denote running-time corresponding to each operation H, $\oplus$, T, $\uparrow$. We see that $t_\oplus << t_H << t_\uparrow < t_T$, so we only compare between two algorithms, modular exponentiation and Chebysev polynomial which are used in Chang's scheme and ours. To relatively compare, we re-implement $T_n(g) \bmod p$ using BigInteger class in Java. Also, we re-use 'ModPow' function in Java to stand for $g^n \bmod p$. Our experiment is conducted in personal computer, Intel Core 2 Quad CPU 2.66GHz. By measuring running-time between two algorithms with prime numbers which range from 10 to 400 digits, we propose using 512-bit

Table 2. A comparison of computation costs

Items	Authentication	Login	Registration
Das[19]	$3\times H$, $7\times\oplus$	$4\times H$, $7\times\oplus$	$2\times H$, $1\times\oplus$
Wang[20]	$4\times H$, $10\times\oplus$	$2\times H$, $4\times\oplus$	$2\times H$, $2\times\oplus$
Chang[15]	$8\times H$, $4\times\oplus$, $1\times\uparrow$	$2\times H$, $3\times\oplus$	$3\times H$, $1\times\oplus$, $1\times\uparrow$
Ours	$10\times H$, $2\times\oplus$, $3\times T$	$4\times H$, $2\times\oplus$, $1\times T$	$4\times H$, $2\times\oplus$

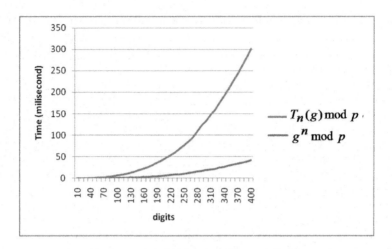

Fig. 1. Comparison of time cost between $T_n(g)\ mod\ p$ and $g^n\ mod\ p$

prime number to guarantee time efficiency ($\approx$ 150ms) and security because of solution space up to 2^{512} when facing **CDLP**. Although running-time between $g^n\ mod\ p$ used by Chang's scheme and $T_n(g)\ mod\ p$ used by ours is a little different, practical running-time of our scheme $\sum_{i=1}^{4} t_T \approx 0.6$s when using prime number with appropriate bit amount. Therefore, it is said that our scheme is still enough efficiency when practically implemented. Experiment's result with different prime numbers is presented in Figure 1.

5   Conclusions

In this paper, we review Chang et al.'s scheme. Although their scheme has some positive characteristics but it is vulnerable to impersonation attack. Furthermore, it cannot provide user's anonymity and does not have the property of perfect forward secrecy. Hence, we suggest a different improved scheme using Chebysev polynomial to overcome such pitfalls. Compared with Chang's scheme schemes, our scheme has the following main advantages; (1) A user need not choose the password at first. (2) It provides user's anonymity. (3) It does not maintain verification table. (4) It provides property of perfect forward secrecy.

From our security evaluation, our proposed method can resist known methods of attacks. As the proposed scheme can be used in various client-server environment for remote user authentication, it can be applied for systems that accept user authentication with mobile or wearable devices to create smart interactive environments. Furthermore we also study to integrate biometric features into Chebyshev polynomial-based authentication scheme.

Acknowledgments. This research is supported by National Institute of Informatics (Japan) and funded by Vietnam National University HoChiMinh City (VNU-HCM) under grant number B2015-18-01.

References

[1] Lamport, L.: Password authentication with insecure communication. Communications of the ACM **24**(11), 770–772 (1981)

[2] Chen, T.H., Chen, Y.C., Shih, W.K., Wei, H.W.: An efficient anonymous authentication protocol for mobile pay-tv. Journal of Network and Computer Applications **34**(4), 1131–1137 (2011)

[3] Shin, S., Kim, K., Kim, K.-H., Yeh, H.: A remote user authentication scheme with anonymity for mobile devices. International Journal of Advanced Robotic Systems **9**(13), 1–7 (2012)

[4] Liao, I.E., Lee, C.C., Hwang, M.S.: Security enhancement for a dynamic id-based remote user authentication scheme. In: International Conference on Next Generation Web Services Practices, vol. 6(2), pp. 517–522 (2005)

[5] Yoon, E.-J., Yoo, K.-Y.: Improving the dynamic ID-based remote mutual authentication scheme. In: Meersman, R., Tari, Z., Herrero, P. (eds.) OTM 2006 Workshops. LNCS, vol. 4277, pp. 499–507. Springer, Heidelberg (2006)

[6] Rivest, R.L., Shamir, A., Adleman, L.: A method for obtaining digital signatures and public key cryptosystems. Communications of the ACM **21**(2), 120–126 (1978)

[7] Yang, J.-H., Chang, C.-C.: An ID-based remote mutual authentication with key agreement scheme for mobile devices on elliptic curve cryptosystem. Computers and Security **28**(3–4), 138–143 (2009)

[8] Yoon, E.-J., Yoo, K.-Y.: Robust ID-based remote mutual authentication with key agreement scheme for mobile devices on ECC. In: IEEE International Conference on Computational Science and Engineering, vol. 2, pp. 633–640 (2009)

[9] Islam, S.H., Biswas, G.P.: A more efficient and secure ID-based remote mutual authentication with key agreement scheme for mobile devices on elliptic curve cryptosystem. Journal of Systems and Software **84**(11), 1892–1898 (2011)

[10] Wang, K., Pei, W.J., Zou, L.H., Cheung, Y.M., He, Z.Y.: Security of public key encryption technique based on multiple chaotic system. Journal of Physics Letters A **360**(2), 259–262 (2006)

[11] Zhang, L.: Cryptanalysis of the public key encryption based on multiple chaotic systems. Journal of Chaos, Solitons & Fractals **37**(3), 669–674 (2008)

[12] Guo, C., Chang, C.-C., Sun, C.-Y.: Chaotic maps-based mutual authentication and key agreement using smartcards for wireless communications. Journal of Information Hiding and Multimedia Signal Processing **4**(2), 99–109 (2013)

[13] Prasadh, K., Ramar, K., Gnanajeyaraman, R.: Public key cryptosystems based on chaotic chebyshev polynomials. Journal of Engineering and Technology Research **1**(7), 122–128 (2009)

[14] Zhi-Hui, L., Yi-Dong, C., Hui-Min, X.: Fast algorithms of public key cryptosystem based on chebyshev polynomials over finite field. The Journal of China Universities of Posts and Telecommunications **18**(2), 86–93 (2010)

[15] Chang, C.-C., Lee, C.-Y.: A smart card-based authentication scheme using user identify cryptography. International Journal of Network Security **15**(2), 139–147 (2013)

[16] Burrows, M., Abadi, M., Needham, R.: A logic of authentication. ACM Transactions on Computer System **8**, 18–36 (1990)

[17] Xiao, D., Liao, X., Wong, K.: An efficient entire chaos-based scheme for deniable authentication. Journal of Chaos, Solitons & Fractals **23**(4), 1327–1331 (2005)

[18] Bergamo, P., Arco, P., Santis, A., Kocarev, L.: Security of public key encryption technique based on multiple chaotic system. IEEE Transactions on Circuits and Systems I **52**(7), 1382–1393 (2005)

[19] Das, M.L., Saxena, A., Gulati, V.P.: A dynamic ID-based remote user authentication scheme. IEEE Transactions on Consumer Electronics **50**(2), 629–631 (2004)

[20] Wang, Y.Y., Kiu, J.Y., Xiao, F.X., Dan, J.: A more efficient and secure dynamic ID-based remote user authentication scheme. Computer Communications **32**(4), 583–585 (2009)

A Secure Exam Protocol Without Trusted Parties

Giampaolo Bella[1], Rosario Giustolisi[2]([envelope]),
Gabriele Lenzini[2]([envelope]), and Peter Y.A. Ryan[2]

[1] Dipartimento di Matematica e Informatica, Università di Catania, Catania, Italy
[2] SnT, University of Luxembourg, Luxembourg, Luxembourg
{rosario.giustolisi,gabriele.lenzini}@uni.lu

Abstract. Relying on a trusted third party (TTP) in the design of a security protocol introduces obvious risks. Although the risks can be mitigated by distributing the trust across several parties, it still requires at least one party to be trustworthy. In the domain of exams this is critical because parties typically have conflicting interests, and it may be hard to find an entity who can play the role of a TTP, as recent exam scandals confirm. This paper proposes a new protocol for paper-based and computer-based exams that guarantees several security properties without the need of a TTP. The protocol combines oblivious transfer and visual cryptography to allow candidate and examiner to jointly generate a pseudonym that anonymises the candidate's test. The pseudonym is revealed only to the candidate when the exam starts. We analyse the protocol formally in ProVerif and prove that it satisfies all the stated security requirements.

1 Introduction

This paper considers written exams and studies how to guarantee secure and fair examination although any participant can cheat.

The security of exam protocols has been brought to the public attention by recent surveys and scandals [11,14,15]. They show that information technology makes cheating easier and that candidates and authorities have interest in frauds. For example, in the Atlanta public school scandal [11], the authorities raised all the markings to improve the school's ranking and get more public funds. In spite of that, previous exam systems still consider candidate's cheating as the sole security threat, while exam authorities and examiners are assumed to be fully trusted. A deeper understanding of the exam's threats would be also useful for similar assessment systems, such as public tenders, personnel selections, and project reviews. As in the case of exams, the security of such systems should not rely on TTP.

Recently a few works argued about the security of exam with corrupted examiners (e.g., [4,16]); however, their designs still assume some trusted parties.

G. Lenzini—Supported by CORE-FNR, project C11/IS/1183245 STAST.

H. Federrath and D. Gollmann (Eds.): SEC 2015, IFIP AICT 455, pp. 495–509, 2015.
DOI: 10.1007/978-3-319-18467-8_33

We propose a new security protocol for exams that requires no trusted party while meeting a set of stringent security properties that extend the requirements for ones defined by Dreier et al. [8,9]. Our protocol relies on oblivious transfer and visual cryptography techniques to generate a pseudonym that anonymises a candidate's test. No participant learns the pseudonyms until the exam starts. Candidates take the exam in a test center, and testing is the only face-to-face phase, while the other phases are remote. Our protocol suits both paper-based and computer-based examination.

Contribution. This paper provides three main contributions. First, it extends a set of security requirements for exams with three new authentication and one accountability property. Second, it proposes a new exam protocol that satisfies the extended requirements without relying on a TTP. Finally, it formalises the protocol in ProVerif and proves the protocol ensures all the properties.[1]

Outline. The paper is organized as follows. Section 2 outlines the related work. Section 3 describes and formalises the desired properties our protocol aims to ensure, and defines the threat model. Section 4 details the protocol. Section 5 describes the formal analysis of our protocol in ProVerif [5], and discusses the results. Section 6 outlines future work and concludes the paper.

2   Related Work

The majority of works on exam protocols describe security requirements only informally (e.g., [3,22]) with a few exceptions. Dreier *et al.* [8] propose a formal framework in the applied π-calculus to define and analyse authentication and privacy requirements for exams. They analyse two existing electronic exam protocols as case studies. Foley *et al.* [12] introduce a formalisation of confidentiality requirements for Computer Supported Collaborative Working. They propose exams as case study with no references to specific exam protocols.

Other works propose secure exam protocols, but argue informally their security. Castella-Roca *et al.* [6] introduce an exam protocol which guarantees a number of authentication and privacy properties in presence of a fully trusted exam manager. Bella *et al.* [4] describe WATA IV, a protocol that also relies on visual cryptography and considers corrupted examiner, but assumes an honest-but-curious anonymiser. Huszti and Pethő [16] propose an exam protocol with minimal trust requirements, but a trusted *registry*. Giustolisi *et al.* [13] describe *Remark!*, an internet-based exam protocol that ensures authentication and conditional anonymity requirements with minimal trust assumption. The protocol generates pseudonyms via an exponentiation mixnet, which assumes at least one honest mix server.

Maffei *et al.* [18] suggest anonymous credential schemes to guarantee privacy in course evaluation systems without relying on a TTP. Their approach seems to be alternative to ours, as we use oblivious transfer and visual cryptography.

---

[1] Our code is available at http://apsia.uni.lu/stast/codes/exams/pv_isec15.tar.gz

Formal approaches have been proposed in the area of conference management systems, a domain close to exams. Arapinis *et al.* [2] propose and formally analyse ConfiChair, a cryptographic protocol that addresses secrecy and privacy risks coming from a malicious cloud. Their work has been recently extended to support any cloud-based system such as public tender management and recruitment process. Kanav *et al.* [17] introduce CoCon, a formally verified implementation of conference management system that guarantees confidentiality. All of the mentioned systems, however, assume trusted managers.

3   Security Requirements and Threat Model

An exam basically involves two main roles: the *candidate*, who takes the test, and the *examiner*, who evaluates it. A typical exam runs in phases: at *preparation*, the exam is set up, for instance, the candidate registers and questions are generated; at *testing* the candidate gets the questions and takes the exam, while the examiner collects the answered test; at *marking* the examiner evaluates the test; at *notification*, the candidate is informed of her mark. Some duties may be assigned to sub-roles. For instance, an administrative office might ensure the registration of candidates, and notify them the marks.

We start considering the security requirements that other works argued to be relevant for exams [4,8], and extend this set with five new requirements, including novel authentication and accountability properties. To express our requirements unambiguously, we use the applied π-calculus [1] as done in [8]. Therefore, we assume that our requirements refer to a model of an exam modelled as applied π-calculus process. The applied π-calculus defines events to formulate correspondence assertions (authentication), and uses observational equivalence to express indistinguishability (privacy).

Authentication. In the applied π-calculus, an event is a message output $e(\vec{a})$: e is the event channel and $\vec{a}$ a, possible empty, list of arguments. The message appears in the trace as soon as the execution of the process reaches the event. To formalise authentication, we use some of the events defined in [8] as follows.

The term id_c is the candidate's identity, *pid* is the form identifier, *ques* indicates the exam questions, *ans* indicates the candidate's answers, *mark* is the mark. The event $reg(id_c)$ denotes a successful registration of the candidate id_c. The event $submitted(id_c, ques, ans, pid)$ is emitted when the candidate submits her answer, while $collected(id_c, ques, ans, pid)$ is emitted by the examiner when he collects the answer. Finally, the event $notified(id_c, mark, pid)$ is emitted when the examiner notifies and registers a mark to the candidate.

We add $requested(id_c, pid)$ to the set of events outlined above. It is emitted by the candidate process at notification, where candidate id_c sends the request to learn her mark using the identifier *form*.

The first requirement we consider is *Answer Authenticity*, which informally says that the examiner collects the answer as submitted by the candidate.

Definition 1 (Answer Authenticity). *An exam protocol ensures Answer Authenticity if the event collected(id_c, ques, ans, pid) is preceded by the event submitted(id_c, ques, ans, pid) in every execution trace of the protocol.*

Answer Origin Authentication says that the examiner only collects answers originated by registered candidates.

Definition 2 (Answer Origin Authentication). *An exam protocol ensures Answer Origin Authentication if the event collected(id_c, ques, ans, pid) is preceded by the event reg(id_c) in every execution trace of the protocol.*

We define three novel authentication requirements: *Mark Authenticity, Candidate Authorisation,* and *Notification Request Authentication.*

Definition 3 (Mark Authenticity). *An exam protocol ensures Mark Authenticity if the event notified(id_c, mark, pid) is preceded by the event submitted(id_c, question, answer, pid) in every execution trace of the protocol*

Mark Authenticity says that the mark is correctly registered to the corresponding candidate. Dreier et al. defines it as "the candidate is notified with the mark delivered by the examiner" [8]. Despite looking similar, our formulation expresses something different: in ours the authenticator is the examiner because he emits the event *notified*, while in Dreier et al. the authenticator is the candidate, since the event is emitted in the candidate process. We think that Def. 3 avoids overlapping definitions because, as we shall see later, Mark Verifiability considers the candidate as authenticator. It describes that a candidate can check if she has been notified with the correct mark despite a corrupted examiner.

The second novel requirement, *Candidate Authorisation*, describes that only registered and authenticated candidates can take the exam.

Definition 4 (Candidate Authorisation). *An exam protocol ensures Candidate Authorisation if the event submitted(id_c, ques, ans, pid) is preceded by the event reg(id_c) in every execution trace of the protocol.*

The last additional requirement is *Notification Request Authentication*. It says that a mark can be associated with the candidate only if she requests to learn her mark. This unusual requirement is useful in the exam scenarios of some universities, where candidates have to skip the next exam session if they get a fail, unless they withdraw from the exam before notification.

Definition 5 (Notification Request Authentication). *An exam protocol ensures Notification Request Authentication if the event notified(id_c, mark) is preceded by the event requested(id_c, pid) in every execution trace of the protocol.*

Privacy. For reason of space, we present only the informal definitions of the privacy requirements. The formal definition in applied π-calculus can be found in [8].

The first relevant privacy requirement is *Anonymous Marking*, which says that no one can learn the author of a test before it is marked. In other words, no one but the author can link the test with the candidate identity until after the marking phase. *Question Indistinguishability* says that no candidate learns the question before the testing phase. A strong requirement is *Mark Privacy*, which describes that no one, besides the examiner and the concerned candidate, learns the marks. It implies that marks cannot be public. The last privacy requirement is *Mark Anonymity*, which says that no one, besides the examiner and the concerned candidate, can learn the mark assigned to a candidate. Note that Mark Privacy is intuitively stronger than Mark Anonymity: a system that publishes the marks cannot guarantee Mark Privacy while may still ensure Mark Anonymity provided no one can link a mark to a candidate identity.

Verifiability and Accountability. We propose two properties, one for verifiability, and one for accountability of exams. Generally speaking, a protocol is verifiable with respect to a specific property if the protocol provides a test for the property, and the test is sound and complete [9]. *Mark Verifiability* says that the candidate can verify she has been notified with the mark assigned to her test. Mark Verifiability subsumes the existence of an algorithm testMV that outputs *true* if the candidate has been notified with the mark assigned to her test, or *false* otherwise. In the applied π-calculus, testMV is a process that emits the event $OK(id_c, pid, mark)$ when it is supposed to output *true* and KO when it supposed to output *false*. The event $published(pid)$ is emitted when a test identified with pid is available. The event $assigned(id_c, pid, mark)$ is emitted by the candidate at end of notification.

We say that testMV is sound if the event $OK(id_c, pid, mark)$ is preceded by the events $assigned(id_c, pid, mark)$ and $published(pid)$ in every execution trace of the protocol. We say that testMV is complete if the event KO is emitted in no execution trace of the protocol when the test fed with correct data.

Definition 6 (Mark Verifiability). *An exam protocol ensures Mark Verifiability if* testMV *is sound and complete.*

Finally, we introduce an accountability requirement, namely *Testing Dispute Resolution*. Accountability allows to identify which party is responsible for a protocol failure. In the case of exam, a candidate should be able to submit a test and receive the corresponding mark. If she fails in any of these, Testing Dispute Resolution describes that the participant who caused such failure can be identified.

We formally model Testing Dispute Resolution similarly to Mark Verifiability, with a difference: we use (non)reachability of the event *Cguilty* or *Eguilty* also to prove soundness. In the applied π-calculus, dispute is a process that emits the event *Cguilty* when the candidate is the culprit and *Eguilty* if the examiner is the culprit. If the protocol executes the process dispute then either the examiner or the candidate is corrupted. Thus, regarding soundness, the idea is to check that `dispute` cannot return an honest party instead of the corrupted one.

We say that `dispute` is sound with respect to a corrupted examiner and honest candidate if the event *Cguilty* is emitted in no execution trace of the protocol. Similarly, we say that `dispute` is sound with respect to a corrupted candidate and honest examiner if the event *Eguilty* is emitted in no execution trace of the protocol. Finally, we say that `dispute` is complete if neither the event *Eguilty* nor *Cguilty* are emitted in any execution trace of the protocol with honest roles.

Definition 7 (Testing Dispute Resolution). *An exam protocol ensures Testing Dispute Resolution if* `dispute` *is sound and complete.*

3.1   Threat Model and Assumptions

According our exam terminology, we consider the threats coming from the three following adversaries. (1) Corrupted candidates, who want to be assigned with a mark higher than an objective evaluation of their answers deserve. They thus may not follow the protocol and collude each other to achieve their goal. (2) A corrupted examiner, who wants to assess a candidate unfairly. (3) An intruder, who wants to get exam's private information or tamper with tests and marks, and may corrupt candidates or the examiner.

We assume that (a) remote communications between examiner and candidate occur via TLS; (b) model answers are kept secret from candidates until after testing; (c) during the testing, invigilators supervise candidates to mitigate cheating, and (d) an authenticated append-only bulletin board is available.

4   The Protocol

In a nutshell, the protocol works as follows. At preparation, candidate and examiner jointly generate the candidate's pseudonym (an alphanumeric *pid*) as a pair of visual cryptography shares, by means of an oblivious transfer scheme. One share is hold by the candidate, who prints it on a paper sheet together with the candidate ID and signatures meant for integrity and accountability purposes. The other share is held by the examiner, who prints it on a transparency printout. Each share alone does not reveal the pseudonym, which is revealed only when the shares are overlapped. This is possible only at testing, when the candidate and the examiner physically meet, and the examiner hands his transparency to the candidate. Any dispute that happens at testing can be solved thanks to the signatures printed with the printouts. The candidate can write the pseudonym down into the answer sheet, and the testing concludes when all answer sheets are returned to the examiner. At marking, the examiner evaluates the answers, and assigns a mark to each pseudonym, which she commits and publishes on a bulletin board. At notification, a candidate can retrieve her mark by proving she owns the share that (re)-reveals the pseudonym. The examiner's share is

1. *Candidate* calculates $y_i = g^{x_i} h^{\gamma_i}$ where:
   - $x_i \in_{\mathcal{R}} \mathbb{Z}_q^*$.
   - $\gamma_i \in_{\mathcal{R}} [1, k]$.
   - $i = 1, 2, \ldots, l$ with $l > n$.
2. *Candidate*$\rightarrow$*Examiner*: $y_1, y_2, \ldots, y_l$.
3. *Examiner* calculates $\beta_{ij} \leftarrow_{\pi_{\mathcal{R}}} (\alpha_i \oplus c_j)$, $\omega_{ij} = \langle a_{ij}, b_{ij} \rangle \leftarrow \langle g^{r_{ij}}, \beta_{ij} \left(\frac{y_i}{h^j} \right)^{r_{ij}} \rangle$,
   $com = h^s \prod_{i=1}^{l} g_i{}^{\alpha_i}$, and $sign1 = Sign_{SSK_E}\{idC, ex, com\}$ where:
   - $\alpha_i \in_{\mathcal{R}} [0, 1]^{t \times u}$.
   - $s, r_{ij} \in_{\mathcal{R}} \mathbb{Z}_q^*$.
   - $g_i \in_{\mathcal{R}} \mathbb{G}_q$.
   - $i = 1, 2, \ldots, l$.
   - $j = 1, 2, \ldots, k$.
   or runs the challenge procedure against $y_1, y_2, \ldots, y_l$.
4. *Examiner*$\rightarrow$*Candidate*: $(\omega_{11}, \ldots, \omega_{1k}), \ldots (\omega_{l1}, \ldots, \omega_{lk})$ and $sign1$.
5. *Candidate* calculates $\chi_i \in [1, l]$ and $\sigma_j \in [1, l]$ where:
   - $i = 1, 2, \ldots, m$.
6. *Candidate*$\rightarrow$*Examiner*: $\chi_1, \chi_2, \ldots, \chi_m$ and $\sigma_1, \sigma_2, \ldots, \sigma_n$.
7. *Examiner* calculates $ev_{\chi_i} = \langle \alpha_{\chi_i}, (\beta_{\chi_i 1}, \beta_{\chi_i 2}, \ldots, \beta_{\chi_i k}), (r_{\chi_i 1}, r_{\chi_i 2}, \ldots, r_{\chi_i k}) \rangle$ and
   $sign2 = Sign_{SSK_E}\{idC, ex, (\sigma_1, \sigma_2, \ldots, \sigma_n)\}$ where
   - $i = 1, 2, \ldots, m$.
   - $j = 1, 2, \ldots, k$.
   and prints $transp = \langle (\alpha_{\sigma_1}, \alpha_{\sigma_2}, \ldots, \alpha_{\sigma_n}), idC, ex, QR3 \rangle$ where
   - $QR3 = idC, ex, (\alpha_1, \alpha_2, \ldots, \alpha_l, s)$.
8. *Examiner*$\rightarrow$*Candidate*: $ev_{\chi_1}, ev_{\chi_2}, \ldots, ev_{\chi_m}$ and $sign2$.
9. *Candidate* checks ev_{χ_i}, calculates $\beta_{\sigma_j} = \frac{b_{\sigma_j \gamma_j}}{(a_{\sigma_j \gamma_j})^{x_{\sigma_j}}}$ where
   - $i = 1, 2, \ldots, m$.
   - $j = 1, 2, \ldots, n$.
   and prints $paper = \langle (\beta_{\sigma_1}, \beta_{\sigma_2}, \ldots, \beta_{\sigma_n}), idC, ex, QR1, QR2 \rangle$ where
   - $QR1 = idC, ex, sign1$.
   - $QR2 = idC, ex, sign2$.

---

10. *Candidate*$\xrightarrow{hands}$*Examiner*: idC'
11. *Examiner* checks if $idC' = idC$
12. *Examiner*$\xrightarrow{hands}$*Candidate*: $transp, test\_question$
13. *Candidate* calculates $pid = (\alpha_1, \alpha_2, \ldots, \alpha_n) \oplus (\beta_1, \beta_2, \ldots, \beta_n)$ and writes $test\_answer = (answers, pid)$
    or runs the Testing Dispute Resolution algorithm if no pseudonym appears.
14. *Candidate*$\xrightarrow{hands}$*Examiner*: $test\_answer$

---

15. *Examiner* calculates $c = g^v h^{mark}$ and $sign3 = Sign_{SSK_E}\{pid, c\}$ where:
    - $v \in_{\mathcal{R}} \mathbb{Z}_q^*$.
    - $mark \in M$.
16. *Examiner*$\rightarrow$$\mathcal{BB}$: $sign3$
17. *Candidate*$\rightarrow$*Examiner*: $(\beta_1, \beta_2, \ldots, \beta_n), sign1, sign2, sign3$
18. *Examiner* calculates $sign4 = Sign_{SSK_E}\{idC, ex, pid, mark, v\}$
19. *Examiner*$\rightarrow$*Candidate*: $sign4$

Fig. 1. Our protocol divided in phases

required for this phase, but there is no need for the candidate and the examiner to meet. The candidate sends her share and the signatures to the examiner, and any dispute happening at notification can be again solved using the signatures associated with the shares.

The protocol combines a few cryptographic primitives, namely visual cryptography, commitment, and oblivious transfer schemes:

Visual Cryptography. It is a secret sharing scheme, first devised by Naor and Shamir [19] that allows a visual decryption of a ciphertext. A secret image is "encrypted" by splitting it into a number of image *shares*. In the 2-out-of-2 version, which is the one adopted in our protocol, the secret image is split into two shares. When the shares are overlapped, they reveal the secret image. Many schemes for visual cryptography have been proposed over the years. We use the Naor and Shamir scheme for our protocol, but we conjecture that any other visual scheme can be used as well.

Commitment Schemes. A commitment scheme is used to bind a committer to a value. The committer publishes a commitment that hides a value, which remains secret until the committer reveals it. Should he reveal a different value, this would be noticed, because two identical commitments hide the same value. Our protocol uses a generalized Pedersen commitment scheme [20], which guarantees unconditional hiding and allows the commitment to many values at once.

Oblivious Transfer. Oblivious transfer schemes allow a chooser to pick some pieces of information from a set a sender offers him, in such a way that (a) the sender does not learn which pieces of information the choosers picks, and (b) the chooser learns no more than the pieces of information he picks. Our protocol adopts Tzeng's oblivious transfer scheme [21]. In Tzeng's scheme, the chooser commits to some elements from a set, and sends the commitments to the sender. This, in turn, obfuscates all the set's elements, and the chooser will be able to de-obfuscate only the elements he has committed to. It guarantees unconditional security for the receiver's choice, and it is efficient since it works with the sender and receiver's exchanging only two messages.

4.1 Description of the Protocol in Detail

We describe our protocol in reference to the four exam phases. In the description we assume a few public parameters, namely:

n	length of the candidate's pseudonym
$C = \{s_1, \ldots, s_k\}$	alphabet of pseudonym's characters
$c_j \in \{0,1\}^{t \times u}, \; j = 1, \ldots, k$	$(t \times u)$-pixel representation of a character
idC	candidate ID
ex	exam code
SPK_E	examiner's public key
M	set of possible marks
$g, h \in_R \mathbb{G}_q$	commitment generators

Preparation. The goal of preparation is to generate a candidate's pseudonym, which is a string of n characters taken from alphabet C, and to encode it into two visual cryptographic shares. Both candidate and examiner cannot know the pseudonym until they meet at testing, when the candidate learns her pseudonym by overlapping the examiner's share with hers. The underlying idea is that the candidate provides a commitment to an index into an array. The examiner fills the array with a secret permutation of the characters, and only when the two secrets are brought together is the selection of a character determined.

This phase is inspired by one of the schemes used to print a secret, proposed by Essex *et al.* [10]. We tailor the scheme in such a way to be able to generate a pseudonym. More specifically, we extend it to support an algorithm to resolve a dispute that may arise when the overlapping of the shares will not reveal any intelligible pseudonym. The main technical differences between our preparation and the original scheme are: (a) a modified oblivious transfer protocol that copes with several secret messages in only one protocol run; (b) the generation of signatures that will be used for accountability in the resolution of disputes.

Figure 1 gives the description of the steps of preparation. The protocol begins with the candidate providing a sequence of l commitments y_i to an index into an array of length k. (steps 1-2).

In detail, the parameter l, is chosen so that the $l - n$ elements can be later used for a cut-and-choose audit. The examiner can challenge the candidate to check whether the committed choices are in fact in the interval $[1, k]$. Otherwise, the examiner generates a sequence of randomly chosen $t \times u$ images, indicated as $\alpha_1, \ldots, \alpha_l$ in Figure 1. A sequence of k images, $(\beta_{i1}, \ldots, \beta_{ik})$, are generated from α_i and each possible character c_j. The sequence is randomly permuted and repeated for all i, resulting in l sequences of $(\beta_{11}, \ldots, \beta_{1k})$, $\ldots$, $(\beta_{l1}, \ldots, \beta_{lk})$. The secret permutation and the commitment allow that the selection of character is determined only when the two secrets are brought together.

The examiner then generates the obfuscation ω_{ij} from each β_{ij} and generates a commitment on each α_i, indicated as *com* (step 3), which is signed and sent with the sequences of obfuscations $(\omega_{11}, \ldots, \omega_{1k}), \ldots, (\omega_{l1}, \ldots, \omega_{lk})$ to the candidate (step 4). The obfuscation allows the candidate to retrieve only the elements whose indexes correspond to the choices she committed in step 1 (y_i).

The candidate performs a cut-and-choose audit, selecting a random set of $l-n$ sequences amongst the ω. Doing so, she can check whether the examiner generated the sequence of images correctly. The remaining substitutions $\sigma_1, \sigma_2, \ldots, \sigma_n$ select the indexes of the images that make the pseudonym. Thus, the visual share of the examiner consists of the concatenated images $(\alpha_{\sigma_1}, \ldots, \alpha_{\sigma_n})$ (step 5-6).

The examiner then generates the proofs for the cut-and-choose audit, and prints the visual share in a transparency printout. This also include all the elements $\alpha_1, \ldots, \alpha_l$ and the value used for their commitment (step 7), which are stored in the form of QR code. The examiner then sends the proofs and the signed substitutions σ to the candidate (step 8). In turn, the candidate checks the proofs, de-obfuscates the elements ω, and retrieves the visual share consisting of the concatenated image $(\beta_{\sigma_1}, \beta_{\sigma_2}, \ldots, \beta_{\sigma_n})$. She finally prints the share, together with the two signatures, on a paper printout (step 9). At this point, both candidate and examiner have a visual share, which once overlapped reveal an intelligible sequence of characters that serves as pseudonym.

The candidate's paper printout includes two QR codes (*QR1*, and *QR2*) while the examiner's transparency only one (*QR3*). All the three QR codes share the same candidate identity idC and exam identifier ex. *QR1* and *QR2* encode the two signatures of the examiner, respectively on commitment of the elements α and on the substitutions σ, while *QR3* encodes the elements α.

Testing. The candidate brings the paper printout, and the examiner the transparencies. The examiner authenticates the identity of the candidate by checking her identity document (step 10-11). He then gives the candidate her corresponding transparency and a copy of the questions (step 12). The candidate overlaps her paper printout with the transparency, and learns her pseudonym, which writes it on the answer sheet (step 13). If no pseudonym appears, then this may happen only if the candidate or the examiner misprinted their printouts, and the Testing Dispute Resolution outlined in Algorithm 1 reveals the party that is accountable for the misbehaviour. At the end of the phase, the candidate returns the answer sheet anywhere in the pile of tests (step 14), and takes both transparency and paper printouts home.

Marking and Notification. At marking the examiner evaluates the anonymous tests; at notification, the candidate to learn her mark, but only if she wants to. The examiner evaluates the answers and generates a commitment on the assigned mark (step 15). Then, he signs both mark and pseudonym found on the answer sheet, and publishes the signature on a bulletin board (step 16).

Notification opens for a fixed time, during which the candidate can remotely request to learn and register her mark. She has to send the ordered sequences of $\beta_1, \ldots, \beta_n$ and all the signatures so far she collected to examiner (step 17). The examiner checks the signatures, overlaps the given sequence with the corresponding sequences of $\alpha_1, \ldots, \alpha_n$, and learns the pseudonym. Again, if no registered pseudonym appears, Dispute Resolution reveals the party who misbehaved. The examiner signs the mark and the secret parameter used to commit the mark (step 18), and sends the signature to the candidate (step 19). In so doing, the candidate can verify the assigned mark against the bulletin board.

Dispute Resolution. A corrupted examiner may misprint the visual share printed on the transparency. Thus, the candidate retrieves no intelligible pseudonym when she overlaps the visual shares, making her answers impossible to be anonymous. On the other hand, a corrupted candidate may misprint her paper printout and charge the examiner for misprinting the transparency. Should, such a dispute would arise, Algorithm 1 provides an efficient way to find the culprit.

We assume that the invigilator has an electronic device with a camera, such as a smart phone or tablet, which stores the public key of the examiner. The input

---

Data: Public parameters: $(C, n, g_i, h, idC, SPK_E)$

- $paper = ((\beta_{\sigma_1}, \beta_{\sigma_2}, \ldots, \beta_{\sigma_n}), idC', ex', sign1, sign2)$ where:
    - $sign1 = Sign_{SSK_E}\{idC'', ex'', com\}$
    - $sign2 = Sign_{SSK_E}\{idC''', ex''', (\sigma_1', \sigma_2', \ldots, \sigma_n')\}$
- $transp = (\alpha_{\sigma_1''}, \alpha_{\sigma_2''}, \ldots, \alpha_{\sigma_n''}), idC', ex', (\alpha_1', \alpha_2', \ldots, \alpha_l', s).$

Result: Corrupted participant
if $sign1$ is verifiable with SPK_E **and** $sign2$ is verifiable with SPK_E **and**
$idC = idC' = idC'' = idC'''$ **and** $ex = ex' = ex'' = ex'''$ **then**

> **if** $com \neq h^s \prod\limits_{i=1}^{l} g_i{}^{\alpha_i'}$ **or** $pid=(\alpha_{\sigma_1'}', \alpha_{\sigma_2'}', \ldots, \alpha_{\sigma_n'}') \oplus (\beta_{\sigma_1}, \beta_{\sigma_2}, \ldots, \beta_{\sigma_n})$ **then**
> > | **return** Examiner
> **else**
> > | **return** Candidate

else
| **return** Candidate

Algorithm 1. Dispute resolution

of the Algorithm are the two QR codes printed on the paper printout (QR1 and QR2) and the QR code printed on the transparency (QR3), which the invigilator scans with the device camera.

First, the algorithm checks the correctness of the signatures encoded in QR1 and QR2. It also checks whether the candidate identity and the exam identifier reported on the paper printout match the ones in QR1 and QR2. If any one of the checks fails then the candidate misprinted her paper printout thus she is the culprit. Otherwise, the algorithm uses the data in QR3 to check the correctness of the examiner's commitment and that no pseudonym appears using the α elements indexed with the σ substitutions encoded in QR3. If any one of these checks fails then the examiner misprinted the transparency and thus he is guilty, otherwise the candidate is the culprit.

5   Analysis

We analyse our protocol in ProVerif, a security protocol verifier that allows the automatic analysis of authentication and privacy properties in the Dolev-Yao model [7]. The input language of ProVerif is a variant of the applied π-calculus.

5.1   Modelling Choices

No private Channels. We model TLS and face-to-face communications among the roles using shared key cryptography rather than private channels. This choice is motivated because the attacker cannot monitor communications via ProVerif's private channels, and even know if any communication happens. We think this is a too strong assumption that may miss attacks. By renouncing to private channels, we achieve stronger security guarantees when analysing our protocol.

Moreover, our choice has a triple advantage: it allows the attacker to learn when a candidate registers for the exam or is notified with a mark; it suffices to share the key with the attacker when either the candidate or the examiner is corrupted; it increases the chance the ProVerif verification terminates. Thus, the attacker has more discretional power because he can observe when a candidate is given the questions and when she submits the answers.

Equational Theory. We use the following equational theory to model the cryptographic primitives needed in our protocol.

Probabilistic symmetric key	$sdec(senc(m, k, r), k) = m$
Signature	$getmess(sign(m, ssk)) = m$
	$checksign(sign(m, ssk), spk(ssk)) = m$
Visual cryptography	$overlap(share, gen\_share(m, share)) = m$
	$overlap(share, share) = share$
Obfuscation	$deobf(obf(r, m, \mathtt{sel}, commit(r', \mathtt{sel})), r') = m$

The theory for probabilistic symmetric key and signature specifications are well-known in ProVerif. We introduce a novel theory to model oblivious transfer and visual cryptography. The function *obf* allows the examiner to obfuscate the elements $\beta_1, \ldots, \beta_i$, while the function *deobf* returns the correct element β_{sel} to the candidate, depending on the choice she committed. We also provide the theory for the Pedersen commitment scheme with the function *commit*. Finally, we model the generation of a visual cryptography share with *gen_share*, and their overlapping with the function *overlap*.

We verify Anonymous Marking in presence of a corrupted examiner. We add the process *collector* that simulates the desk where candidates leave their tests. Question Indistinguishability considers corrupted candidates, while Mark Privacy and Mark Anonymity both consider corrupted eligible candidates. To analyse Mark Verifiability, we define the algorithm testMV for our protocol as depicted in Algorithm 2. We model an honest candidate, corrupted examiner and co-candidates to prove the soundness of testMV. In particular, we use correspondence assertions to verify the soundness of the algorithm in ProVerif, and (non)reachability of the event *KO* to verify completeness. We check the two soundness properties that regard Testing Dispute Resolution considering a corrupted examiner in one, and corrupted candidates in the other.

A limitation of the formal model is the specification of the cut-and-choose audit due to the powerful ProVerif's attacker model. In fact, if the attacker plays the cutter's role, he might cut the set of elements such that the subset audited by the chooser is correct, while the other subset not. Although in reality the probability of success of this attack for a large set of elements is small, it is a valid attack in ProVerif irrespective of the number of elements. In our case, the chooser is the candidate and the cutter the examiner. We thus have a false attack when the examiner is corrupted, namely controlled by the attacker. In this case, we avoid this situation by allowing the candidate to check all the elements of

> **Data**: Public parameters: (g, h, SPK_E)
> - $sign3 = Sign_{SSK_E}\{pid, c\}$
> - $idC, pid', mark, v$.
>
> **Result**: Whether the candidate was notified with the mark assigned to her test.
> **if** $pid = pid'$ **and** $c = g^v h^{mark}$ **then**
> | **return** *true*
> **else**
> | **return** *false*

Algorithm 2. The `testMV` for our protocol

the set. This is sound because the candidate plays the role of the chooser, thus she is honest and follows the protocol although she knows the extra information.

Results. Table 1 outlines the results of our analysis. ProVerif confirms that our protocol guarantees all the authentication properties despite allowing an unbounded number of corrupted eligible co-candidates. Thus, our properties hold although the attacker can register to the exam. Concerning privacy properties, ProVerif proves that our protocol guarantees Anonymous Marking, Question Indistinguishability, Mark Privacy, and Mark Anonymity. Finally, our protocol is Mark Verifiable because `testMV` is sound and complete, and ensures Testing Dispute Resolution: ProVerif shows that our protocol charges the misbehaving party and not the honest, if the `dispute` algorithm is executed (soundness), and the algorithm is not executed when both examiner and candidate roles are honest (completeness).

Table 1. The result of the formal analysis in ProVerif with a machine Intel i7, 8GB

Property	Result	Time
Candidate Authorisation	✓	8s
Answer Authenticity	✓	7s
Answer Origin Auth.	✓	7s
Notification Request Auth.	✓	8s
Mark Authenticity	✓	8s

Property	Result	Time
Anonymous Marking	✓	27s
Question Indist.	✓	<1s
Mark Privacy	✓	28m 41s
Mark Anonymity	✓	52m 12s
Mark Verifiability	✓	<1s
Testing Dispute Res.	✓	<1s

6 Conclusion and Future Work

We propose a new protocol for exams without the requirement of a trusted role. The underlying idea is to combine oblivious transfer and visual cryptography to generate a pseudonym which anonymises the test for the marking. A formal analysis in ProVerif confirms the protocol ensures all the stated properties.

As future work we intend to extend our design to yield a larger set of verifiability properties. Moreover, to extend the application scenarios of our protocol, we intend to modify the notification phase in order to avoid the involvement of the candidate at notification. To achieve this, we envisage a temporal deanonymization solution similar to the one in Remark! [13]. Regarding the formal analysis, we aim to study compositional proofs that integrate computational proofs of the cryptographic primitives used in our protocol with the symbolic ones obtained in ProVerif. Finally, we intend to implement a prototype of the protocol, and verify if different visual cryptography schemes can be used to increase the perceptual security of an examination.

References

1. Abadi, M., Fournet, C.: Mobile values, new names, and secure communication. In: POPL 2001. ACM (2001)
2. Arapinis, M., Bursuc, S., Ryan, M.: Privacy-supporting cloud computing by in-browser key translation. J. of Computer Security **21**(6), 847–880 (2013)
3. Auernheimer, B., Tsai, M.: Biometric authentication for web-based course examinations. In: HICSS 2005, p. 294b. IEEE (2005)
4. Bella, G., Giustolisi, R., Lenzini, G.: Secure exams despite malicious management. In: PST 2014, pp. 274–281. IEEE (2014)
5. Blanchet, B.: An efficient cryptographic protocol verifier based on prolog rules. In: CSFW 2001, pp. 82–96. IEEE (2001)
6. Castella-Roca, J., Herrera-Joancomarti, J., Dorca-Josa, A.: A secure e-exam management system. In: ARES 2006. IEEE (2006)
7. Dolev, D., Yao, A.C.: On the Security of Public Key Protocols. IEEE Trans. on Information Theory **29**(2), 198–208 (1983)
8. Dreier, J., Giustolisi, R., Kassem, A., Lafourcade, P., Lenzini, G., Ryan, P.Y.A.: Formal analysis of electronic exams. In: SECRYPT 2014. SciTePress (2014)
9. Dreier, J., Giustolisi, R., Kassem, A., Lafourcade, P., Lenzini, G.: On the verifiability of (electronic) exams. Tech. Rep. TR-2014-2, Verimag (2014)
10. Essex, A., Clark, J., Hengartner, U., Adams, C.: How to print a secret. In: HotSec 2009. USENIX Association (2009)
11. Flock, E.: APS embroiled in cheating scandal. Washington Post, July 2011
12. Foley, S.N., Jacob, J.L.: Specifying Security for Computer Supported Collaborative Working. J. of Computer Security **3**, 233–253 (1995)
13. Giustolisi, R., Lenzini, G., Ryan, P.Y.A.: Remark!: A secure protocol for remote exams. In: Christianson, B., Malcolm, J., Matyáš, V., Švenda, P., Stajano, F., Anderson, J. (eds.) Security Protocols 2014. LNCS, vol. 8809, pp. 38–48. Springer, Heidelberg (2014)
14. Guénard, F.: La Fabrique des Tricheurs: La fraude aux examens expliquée au ministre, aux parents et aux professeurs. Jean-Claude Gawsewitch (2012)
15. Hallak, J., Poisson, M.: Corrupt Schools, Corrupt Universities: What Can be Done?. Ethics and corruption in education, Education Planning, UNESCO (2007)
16. Huszti, A., Pethö, A.: A secure Electronic Exam System. Publicationes Mathematicae Debrecen **77**(3–4), 299–312 (2010)
17. Kanav, S., Lammich, P., Popescu, A.: A conference management system with verified document confidentiality. In: Biere, A., Bloem, R. (eds.) CAV 2014. LNCS, vol. 8559, pp. 167–183. Springer, Heidelberg (2014)
18. Maffei, M., Pecina, K., Reinert, M.: Security and privacy by declarative design. In: CSF 2013, pp. 81–96. IEEE (2013)

19. Naor, M., Shamir, A.: Visual cryptography. In: De Santis, A. (ed.) EUROCRYPT 1994. LNCS, vol. 950, pp. 1–12. Springer, Heidelberg (1995)
20. Pedersen, T.P.: Non-interactive and information-theoretic secure verifiable secret sharing. In: Feigenbaum, J. (ed.) CRYPTO 1991. LNCS, vol. 576, pp. 129–140. Springer, Heidelberg (1992)
21. Tzeng, W.G.: Efficient 1-out-of-n Oblivious Transfer Schemes with Universally Usable Parameters. IEEE Trans. on Computers **53**(2), 232–240 (2004)
22. Weippl, E.: Security in E-Learning, Advances in Information Security, vol. 16. Springer (2005)

Mobile and Cloud Services Security

ApkCombiner: Combining Multiple Android Apps to Support Inter-App Analysis

Li Li[1]([⊠]), Alexandre Bartel[2], Tegawendé F. Bissyandé[1],
Jacques Klein[1], and Yves Le Traon[1]

[1] Interdisciplinary Centre for Security, Reliability and Trust (SnT),
University of Luxembourg, Luxembourg, Luxembourg
{Li.Li,tegawende.bissyande,Jacques.Klein,Yves.LeTraon}@uni.lu
[2] EC SPRIDE, Technische Universität Darmstadt, Darmstadt, Germany
Alexandre.Bartel@ec-spride.de

Abstract. Android apps are made of components which can leak information between one another using the ICC mechanism. With the growing momentum of Android, a number of research contributions have led to tools for the intra-app analysis of Android apps. Unfortunately, these state-of-the-art approaches, and the associated tools, have long left out the security flaws that arise across the boundaries of single apps, in the interaction between several apps. In this paper, we present a tool called **ApkCombiner** which aims at reducing an inter-app communication problem to an intra-app inter-component communication problem. In practice, **ApkCombiner** combines different apps into a single apk on which existing tools can *indirectly* perform inter-app analysis. We have evaluated **ApkCombiner** on a dataset of 3,000 real-world Android apps, to demonstrate its capability to support static context-aware inter-app analysis scenarios.

1 Introduction

Everyday, millions of users exploit their handheld devices, such as smartphones, for online shopping, social networking, banking, email, etc. At the Google I/O 2014, it was revealed that there are now more than 1 billion active Android users and over 50 billion app downloads so far. Thus, mobile applications are increasingly playing an essential role in our daily life, making the safety guards in mobile operating systems an important concern for researchers and practitioners. Because the Android OS accounts for more than 80% of the global smartphone shipments, it has become a primary target of hackers who are now developing malicious apps at an industrial scale [1]. Kaspersky has even reported in a recent security bulletin that, 98% of mobile malware found target the Android platform.

An Android app is a combination of components that use a special interaction mechanism to perform Inter-Component Communication (ICC). This communication model has been exploited by developers to design rich application scenarios by reusing existing functionality. Unfortunately, because many Android developers have limited expertise in security, the ICC mechanism has

© IFIP International Federation for Information Processing 2015
H. Federrath and D. Gollmann (Eds.): SEC 2015, IFIP AICT 455, pp. 513–527, 2015.
DOI: 10.1007/978-3-319-18467-8_34

brought a number of vulnerabilities [4,18]. Examples of known ICC vulnerabilities [1] include the *Activity Hijacking* vulnerability (where a malicious *Activity* is launched in place of the intended *Activity*) and the *Intent spoofing* vulnerability (where a malicious app sends Intents to an exported component which originally does not expect Intents from that app). In previous work [17], we have shown that Android components can exploit such ICC vulnerabilities to leak private data. More recent works have further demonstrated that Android apps exhibit various privacy leaks that are built around the ICC mechanism [13,16,20].

The privacy leaks in Android are further exacerbated by the fact that several applications can interact and "collaborate" to leak data using the inter-app communication (IAC) mechanism. IAC and ICC are similar in Android, and thus present the same vulnerabilities. Unfortunately, state-of-the-art analysis tools are focused on ICC by analyzing a single app at a time. Consequently, inter-app privacy leaks cannot be identified and managed by existing tools and approaches from the literature.

In this paper we propose to empower existing static analysis tools for Android to work beyond the boundaries of a single app, so as to highlight security flaws in the interactions between two or more apps. To that end we have designed and developed a tool called `ApkCombiner` which takes as input several apps that may cohabit in the same device, and yields a single app package (i.e., apk) combining the different components from the different apps. The resulting package is ensured to be ready for analysis by existing tools. Thus, since the IAC mechanism is the same as the ICC mechanism, by combining apps, `ApkCombiner` reduces an IAC problem to an ICC problem, allowing existing tools to indirectly perform inter-app analysis without any modification.

During the combination of multiple Android apps, some classes may conflict with one another. In this paper, we take into account two types of conflict: 1) the conflicted classes are exactly same (same name and same content), we solve this type of conflicts by simply dropping the duplicated classes and 2) the conflicted classes are different (same name but different content), we solve this type of conflicts by first renaming the conflicted classes, and then ensuring that all dependencies and calls related to those classes are respected throughout the app code.

The contribution of this paper are as follows:

- We discuss the need for tools to support inter-app analysis, and present a non-intrusive approach that can be leveraged by existing tools which are focused on intra-app analysis.
- We provide a prototype implementation of `ApkCombiner`[2], using an effective algorithm to solve different conflicts which may arise during the combination of multiple Android apps into one.
- We propose an evaluation of `ApkCombiner` on both a motivating example and on a dataset of real-world Android apps. The experimental results show

[1] Refer to Section 2.1 for the concept of component, Activity and Intent in Android.
[2] We make available our full implementation, along with the experimental results at: https://github.com/lilicoding/ApkCombiner

that state-of-the-art intra-app analyzers can efficiently leverage our approach to indirectly perform inter-app analyses.

2   Background and Motivation

In this section we first briefly introduce different concepts that are specific to Android (cf. Section 2.1). Then, we motivate our work by highlighting the limitations of state-of-the-art static analysis approaches targeting the Android system (cf. Section 2.2). Finally, we discuss in Section 2.3 an IAC vulnerability through a running example.

2.1   Android IAC Overview

In Android, the inter-component communication (ICC) mechanism allows two components to exchange data and invoke each other. The Android inter-app communication (IAC) mechanism works in the same way and exploits the ICC mechanism to make components from different apps interact. An ICC is typically triggered by one of several specific Android methods which are related to the different components in presence (i.e., either an `Activity, Service, Content Provider, Broadcast Receiver`). Those methods[3] take as parameter a special kind of object, called Intent, which specifies the target component(s), either explicitly, by setting the name of the target component's class, or implicitly, by setting the action, the category and the input data to perform. Since it is hard for developers to predict which other apps will be available at the same time, IAC invocations are almost always performed through implicit Intents. In order to receive implicit Intents, target components in separate apps need to declare their capabilities, through an Intent Filter, in the app manifest file so that the Android system may match them when requested by a given app.

2.2   Static Analysis for Android Apps

Static program analysis has been widely used to address security issues, e.g., related to data integrity and confidentiality of information flow [7], as well as for anomaly detection [11,19]. More recently, static analysis techniques have also been applied for dissecting Android applications [9,12,14]. However, we note that current approaches still present a number of limitations when they are targeted to code from the Android system.

In the most common case, a static analysis of Android is reduced to an intra-app analysis, where the bytecode of an app is extracted, and parsed to produce a control-flow graph (CFG) to further perform specific analysis. For example, FlowDroid [2], a state-of-the-art Android analysis approach, builds CFG for static taint analysis. When the analysis must take into account the interaction between two or more apps, it is referred to as an inter-app analysis and may operate in three different ways as illustrated in Fig. 1.

---

[3] Except `Content Provider` related methods.

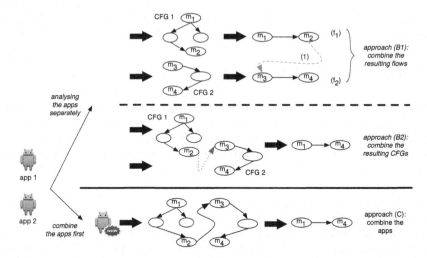

Fig. 1. Different approaches for Enabling Inter-App analysis of Android apps

At a high level, there are two options for enabling inter-app analysis: (1) perform intra-app analysis of each app independently from the others and rely on these analysis results to infer inter-app analysis output; or (2) combine the apps first before performing the analysis.

In scenario (B_1), the results of the intra-app analyses (i.e., flows f_1 and f_2) are combined to yield a potential flow between the apps. However, because the combination is performed after the analysis, no context data (e.g., variable values such as data handled by the Intents) is available, and thus the scenario requires to approximate the flows between the apps (e.g., here line (1)). This scenario may thus lead to a significant number of false positives.

Scenario (B_2) is an improved version of (B_1) where it is no longer the results that are combined but the CFGs instead. This scenario thus supports a context-aware inter-app analysis by operating on a combined CFG and on a data dependence graph (DDG) between the apps. Nevertheless, such an approach cannot be generalized to any instances of CFG. In practice for example, the workload for combining CFGs generated by Soot [15] can not even be applied in the case of CFGs generated by Wala[4]. Thus, specific development effort must be put into each and every static intra-app analyzer to support inter-app analysis.

Scenario (C) considers the caveats of all previous approaches by further improving scenario (B_2) to yield a **general** approach for enabling **context-aware** *inter-app* analysis of Android apps. Thus, instead of combining separate CFGs from different apps as in scenario (B_2), the approach consist in combining the complete apps at the bytecode level. The generated single app package is thus immediately ready for analysis with static intra-app analysis tools. The analysis results will then contain information that could only be obtained through inter-app analysis. This paper presents the design and implementation of a tool for

---

[4] http://wala.sourceforge.net/wiki/index.php

supporting such an approach where no modification of current state-of-the-art tools will be required to perform inter-app analyses.

Table 1 summarizes the fact that most state-of-the-art static analysis approaches for Android only deal with intra-app analysis. DidFail [13], the only approach that considers inter-app analysis, falls under scenario (B_1) described above. Yet, as reminded by the classification in Table 2, this scenario leads to a context-unaware analysis, and thus to many false positives in the results.

Table 1. State-of-the-art approaches

Intra-App(Inter-Comp)	Inter-App
IccTA [16]	DidFail [13]
AmanDroid [20]	
ScanDroid [10]	
SEFA [21]	
CoChecker [5]	

Table 2. Classification of scenarios for static inter-app analysis approaches. (B_1), (B_2) and (C) refer to the scenarios illustrated in Fig. 1.

	Non-General	General
Context-Unaware	(B_1)	
Context-Aware	(B_2)	(C)

2.3   A Running Example

Fig. 2 presents a running example that shows an IAC vulnerability. The example is extracted from a test case of DroidBench[5] referred among its list as *InterApp-Communication_sendBroadcast1*. The example consists of two Android applications, referred to as *sendBroadcast1_source* and *sendBroadcast1_sink*.

App1: sendbroadcast1_source

App2: sendbroadcast1_sink

```
1: class OutFlowActivity extends Activity{
2: protected void onCreate(Bundle b) {
3: //tm = default TelephonyManager;
4: String imei = tm.getDeviceId();
5: Intent i = new Intent();
6: i.setAction("lu.uni.serval.iac_sendbroadcast1.ACTION");
7: i.putExtra("DroidBench", imei);
8: sendBroadcast(i); }}
```

```
11: class InFlowActivity extends Activity
12: {
13: protected void onCreate(Bundle b) {
14: Intent i = getIntent();
15: String imei = i.getStringExtra("DroidBench");
16: Log.i("DroidBench", imei);
17: }}
```

```
21: <activity android:label="@string/app_name" android:name="lu.uni.serval.iac_sendbroadcast1_sink.InFlowReceiver">
22:   <intent-filter>
23:     <action android:name="lu.uni.serval.iac_sendbroadcast1.ACTION" />
24:     <category android:name="android.intent.category.DEFAULT" />
25:   </intent-filter>
26: </activity>
```

App2: AndroidManifest

Fig. 2. A running example that shows an inter-app vulnerability

App *sendBroadcast1_source* contains a simple *Activity* component, named `OutFlowActivity`, which first obtains the device ID (line 4) and then stores

---

[5] DroidBench is a set of hand-crafted Android apps used as a ground truth dataset to evaluate how well static and dynamic security tools find data leaks. https://github.com/secure-software-engineering/DroidBench

it into an Intent (line 7) which is then forwarded to other components (potentially in other applications since the Intent is implicit (line 6)). App *sendBroadcast1_sink* contains a component called `InFlowActivity`, which first extracts data from the received Intent and then logs it onto disk.

In this example, we consider device ID, which is protected by a permission check of the Android system, to be sensitive data. We also consider the *log()* method to be dangerous behavior since it writes data onto disk, therefore leaving it accessible to any applications, including anyone which does not have permission to access the device ID through the Android OS. Thanks to the declarations in the *Manifest* file in the package of *sendBroadcast1_sink*, `OutFlowActivity` is able to communicate with `InFlowActivity` using the *sendBroadcast()* ICC method. Thus, through the interaction between these two apps, a sensitive data can be leaked.

Unfortunately, the current state-of-the-art static analysis tools, including FlowDroid and IccTA, cannot tackle this kind of IAC problem. Since these tools have already proven to be efficient in statically identifying bugs and leaks across components inside a single app, we aim at enabling them to do the same across applications. We further put a constrain on remaining non intrusive, i.e., to avoid applying any modification on them, so as to avoid introducing limitations or new bugs in these tools. We thus propose `ApkCombiner`, which, by combining multiple apps into one, reduces the IAC problem to an ICC problem that state-of-the-art tools can solve in an intra-app analysis.

3   ApkCombiner

We now discuss the design and implementation of `ApkCombiner`. First we present an overview of the approach in Section 3.1 before providing details on how we address the case of conflicting code, typically same-name classes, when combining apps (cf. Section 3.2). Although, for the sake of simplicity, we describe the case of merging two apps, the approach, and the prototype tool, can merge any number of apps.

3.1   Overview

The main objective of our work is to enable Android-targeted state-of-the-art static analysis tools, which have proven to be effective in *intra*-app analyses, to perform as well in *inter*-app analyses. `ApkCombiner` takes a set of Android apps as input and yields a new Android app as output. The newly generated app contains all the features of the input apps except for their IAC features: there is no more IAC but only ICC in the new generated app.

The different steps of how `ApkCombiner` works are shown in Fig. 3. Each app is first disassembled into *smali* files and a Manifest file using a tool for reverse engineering Android apk files, namely android-apktool[6]. Second, all files from

---

[6] https://code.google.com/p/android-apktool/

the apps are checked together for conflicts and integrated (with conflicts solved) into a directory. The Manifest files, one from each app, are merged into a single Manifest file. Finally, ApkCombiner assembles the smali files and the Manifest file along with all other resources, such as image files, into a single apk. Although potential conflicts on such extra-resources may be met, ApkCombiner does not take them into account since the objective is not to produce a runnable apk, but an apk that can be analyzed statically.

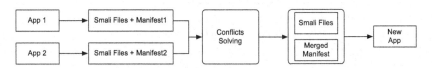

Fig. 3. Working steps of ApkCombiner

3.2 Resolution of Conflicts

Our prototype of ApkCombiner is focused on solving conflicts that may arise in the merging of code from two different apps. Such conflicts occur when two classes have the same name (up to the package level, i.e., the absolutely full qualified name). Thus, given class c_1 in app a_1 and class c_2 in app a_2, if $name(c_1) = name(c_2)$, we consider that there is a conflict between a_1 and a_2.

Fig. 4 illustrates the process of conflict checks we use. ApkCombiner considers that there is no conflict when two classes are named differently. If the name of two classes are the same, ApkCombiner distinguishes two cases according to the content of the classes. In a first type of conflict, the classes share the same name and their content is also the same (after verification of their footprint with the cryptographic hash), In this case, one copy of the class files is simply dropped. In the second type of conflict, i.e., when the content of the conflicting files are different, a thorough refactoring is necessary. This type of conflict occurs when, for example, two classes are actually from two different versions of the same library used in the two apps.

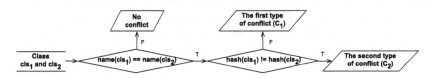

Fig. 4. The conflict checking process of ApkCombiner. Class cls_1 and cls_2 are from different apps.

Algorithm 1 details the described strategy for solving conflicts during merging as implemented by the procedure CheckAndSolveConflicts(). Given two sets (set1 and set2) of class files corresponding to the code of two apps (a_1 and a_2), the algorithm must identify and manage all conflicts.

Algorithm 1. Checking and solving conflicts

```
1: procedure CHECKANDSOLVECONFLICTS(set1, set2)
2:     confliSameMap ← new Map()
3:     confliDiffMap ← new Map()
4:     for all cls1 ∈ set1 do
5:         if set2.contain(cls1) then
6:             cls2 ← set2.get(cls1)
7:             if hash(class(cls1)) == hash(class(cls2)) then
8:                 confliSameMap.put(cls1, cls2)
9:             else
10:                confliDiffMap.put(cls1, cls2)
11:            end if
12:        end if
13:    end for
14:    if empty(confliSameMap, confliDiffMap) then
15:        return
16:    end if
17:    for all cls1, cls2 ∈ confliSameMap do
18:        remove class(cls2)
19:        if isComponent(cls2) then
20:            remove cls2 from Manifest2
21:        end if
22:    end for
23:    for all cls1, cls2 ∈ confliDiffMap do
24:        rename cls2
25:        solvingDependence(cls2, set2)
26:        if isComponent(cls2) then
27:            rename cls2 in Manifest2
28:        end if
29:    end for
30: end procedure
```

First, two maps, referred to as $confliSameMap$ and $confliDiffMap$ are created to keep track of the classes that belong to the two types of conflict (lines 2-3). After identifying the kind of conflict that exists for each pair of classes across the two sets, the algorithm can attempt to solve the eventual conflicts. This resolution is performed in a two-step process. In step 1 (lines 17-22), the algorithm addresses the cases of type 1 conflicts. In step 2, type 2 conflicts are solved by refactoring the code.

Refactoring the code to solve conflicts is not as straightforward as renaming the conflicting classes. Indeed, there is a lot of dependencies to consider within the code of other classes. Procedure solvingDependence(), in line 25, is used to handle these dependencies, where we take into account three types of dependencies: 1) for a given class c we need to rename, another class c_i may use it as one of its attribute, 2) method m_i of class c_i may hold a parameter of c and 3) statement s_i of method m_i may use c as a variable. For the third type of dependency, we deal with statements that instantiate the variable as well as access the variable's attributes and methods because only such statements hold information related to class c.

To combine multiple Android apps to one, we need not only to integrate the different apps' bytecode, but also to merge their Manifest files. In particular the merge of Manifest files must take into account the fact that some classes where dropped while others were renamed. If those classes represent Android components, and not helper code, these changes should be reflected in the final Manifest of the new app (line 20 and 27).

4   Evaluation

To assess the efficiency of our approach, we must evaluate the run time performance of ApkCombiner to ensure that this does not hinder its practical usability (cf. Section 4.1). Then, using a dataset with real-world apps, we check whether our approach is, in the end, capable of enabling state-of-the-art intra-app analyzers to support *inter-app* analysis (cf. Section 4.2).

Hypotheses. To run our experiments, we start with the assumption that the inter-app analysis may reveal significant security issues when a malicious application can exploit a leak in another, or when two apps can collude to leak data. To that end, we select a dataset containing both benign and malicious apps, and assume that, by pairs, they may cohabit on the same device.

Experimental Setup. We select two app sets G and M for our evaluation, where G is a set of apps randomly selected from Google Play store and M is a set of malicious apps. These malicious apps were recognized as such after analysis by VirusTotal antivirus products: we consider that an app is "really" malicious when at least 20 different antivirus flag it as such. Both G and M consist each of 3,000 Android apps. Then, for each app g_i randomly selected from G, we associate an app m_i, also randomly selected from M. This random combination only considers the possibility that two apps in one device may be independently installed by a user on his device. This kind of association provides 3000 opportunities of merging to ApkCombiner.

Our prototype tool succeeded in combining $2,648$ (88.3%) pairs of apps. Most failures were actually due to the limitations of android-apktool[7]. A few failures must however be attributed to the current implementation strategy of the refactoring process in ApkCombiner. These failures however are currently under investigation to improve the tool.

During the process of successful combinations, ApkCombiner solved 1,789 first type conflicts in 322 (12.2%) cases of combining pairs of apps. ApkCombiner also addressed 3,557 second type conflicts in 493 (18.6%) combination cases.

---

[7] Android-apktool often throws `brut.common.BrutException` for some combinations (e.g., *could not exec command* or *Too many open files*).

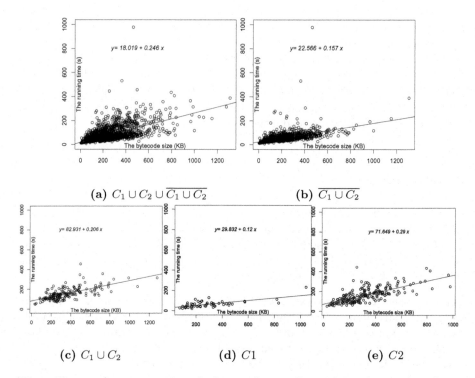

(a) $C_1 \cup C_2 \cup \overline{C_1 \cup C_2}$ **(b)** $\overline{C_1 \cup C_2}$

(c) $C_1 \cup C_2$ **(d)** $C1$ **(e)** $C2$

Fig. 5. Time performance against the byte code size. C_1 represent the set of combinations where first type conflicts were solved, while C_2 represents the set of combinations with second type conflicts.

4.1   Time performance

The evaluation of time performance investigates the scalability of our approach. Indeed, a user may have on its device dozens apps that cohabit together. Thus, the inter-app analysis may require a fast combination of all those apps. Fig. 5 plots the running times[8] of `ApkCombiner` for each combined app. The running time is plotted against the sum size of each pair of apps (we use the bytecode size, as resource files that are not considered in the merging may introduce a bias).

Let C_1 and C_2 represent the successful combinations where conflicts of, respectively, first type and second type were solved. Consequently, $C_1 \cup C_2 \cup \overline{C_1 \cup C_2}$ represents all the successful combinations.

Fig. 5a plots the time performance for all combinations. The linear regression between the plots shows that there is a correlation between the execution time and the bytecode size. Comparing with Fig. 5b, we note that the slope of the regression is lower when we do not consider combinations that lead to conflicts.

---

[8] Note that in this paper we consider the wall clock time (from start to finish of the execution). That means not only the actual CPU time but also the waiting time (e.g., waiting for I/O) are taken into account.

The limited difference in slope values (0.246 against 0.157) indicates that the conflict solving module is not a runtime bottleneck.

The differences between Fig. 5c, Fig. 5d and Fig. 5e further confirm how the resolution of second type conflicts requires more execution time than the resolution of first type conflicts.

4.2   Inter-app analysis

We consider IccTA [16], a state-of-the-art Android intra-app analysis tool, which originally aims at detecting inter-component privacy leaks inside a single Android app. We select IccTA to validate our approach by investigating the effectiveness of ApkCombiner in supporting existing tools for performing inter-app analyses.

With ApkCombiner we build app packages by combining pairs of apps. We then feed IccTA with these newly generated apps and assess its analysis results. We evaluate the use of IccTA in combination with ApkCombiner in two steps. In the first step, we evaluate the impact of ApkCombiner on DroidBench, which includes three test cases related to inter-app communication leaks. We found that IccTA is able to report inter-app privacy leaks for the analyzed apps by analyzing the combined package provided by ApkCombiner. To the best of our knowledge, DidFail is currently the only tool which claims to be able to perform static inter-app analysis for privacy leaks. We therefore compare DidFail with our approach associated to an existing state-of-the-art tool for intra-app analysis. The results in Table 3 based the DroidBench benchmark show that IccTA, while it cannot handle inter-app analysis alone, outperforms DidFail when it is supported by ApkCombiner. The reason why DidFail fails on two test cases is that at the moment DidFail only focuses on Activity-based privacy leaks.

Table 3. Comparison between IccTA, DidFail and ApkCombiner+IccTA

Test Case (from DroidBench)	IccTA	DidFail	ApkCombiner+IccTA
InterAppCommunication_startactivity1	✗	✓	✓
InterAppCommunication_startservice1	✗	✗	✓
InterAppCommunication_sendbroadcast1	✗	✗	✓

In the second step, we evaluate ApkCombiner on 3,000 real Android apps. We first build an IAC graph through the results of our extended Epicc [16,18], where an app stands for a node and an inter-app communication is modeled as an edge. For each of such edges, we launched ApkCombiner on the associated pair of apps and then used IccTA on the generated app.

We were thus able to discover an IAC leak between app *Ibadah Evaluation*[9] and app *ClipStore*[10]. In the Ibadah Evaluation apk code, the source method *find-ViewById* is called in component com.bi.mutabaah.id.activity.Statistic, where the data of a *TextView* is obtained. Then this data is stored into an Intent

---

[9] https://worldapks.com/ibadah-evaluation/, com.bi.mutabaah.id in our dataset.

[10] https://worldapks.com/clipstore/, jp.benishouga.clipstore in our dataset.

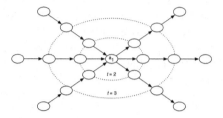

Fig. 6. An example of an IAC graph and a trade-off threshold t

along with two extras, a subject named `android.intent.extra.SUBJECT` and the text referred to as `android.intent.extra.TEXT`. Subsequently, the triggering method *startActivity* is used to transfer the Intent data to the ClipStrore app which extracts the data from the Intent with the same extra names and writes all the data into a file named `clip.txt`. Note that we consider saving sensitive data onto disk as a leak.

5   Discussion

Scalability. As introduced in Section 4.1, `ApkCombiner` scales linearly with the bytecode size. Unfortunately, in practice, when increasing the bytecode size (e.g., increasing the number of apps to combine), the processing time and memory requirement of Android analysis tools (e.g., IccTA or FlowDroid) also grow significantly. Thus such approaches may not be scalable when running on top of `ApkCombiner`. To limit the impact of this scalability issue, a possible approach is to limit the number of Android apps to combine. This is a reasonable limitation, as the number of apps obstructs the work of attackers as well. For example, the more number of apps involved in an attack, the more complex to build such an attack and the less likely that all the involved apps are installed by a single user. Our solution is to build an IAC graph to represent the dependencies among apps, the idea being that if there is no link (edge) between two apps (nodes) there is no need to combine them. Based on the IAC graph, we introduce a threshold t to denote the maximum number of apps `ApkCombiner` may combine together. The trade-off limitation length t enables existing intra-app analyzers to remain scalable when used with `ApkCombiner`.

Let us take Fig. 6 as an example, which shows an IAC graph and the concept of threshold t. For app a_1, if we set $t = 2$, then we only need to run `ApkCombiner` 6 times (the small circle) and most importantly we only need to combine 2 (or t) apps each time. Notice that with the built IAC graph, new apps can be added to the graph in an iterative and incremental manner. When new apps are involved, we only need to add them to the existing IAC graph. We do not need to run the previously computed apps again when adding the new apps. In short, by building an IAC graph and setting up a threshold t, the original set of Android apps is split into multiple small sets that both `ApkCombiner` and the state-of-the-art intra-app analysis tools can analyze.

Limitations. At the moment, we do not offer a guarantee that the newly generated app can be executed. Except from the bytecode and Manifest, we simply combine all the other resources such as native code, layout files without checking whether they are conflicted or not. This may result in errors for analysis tools that rely on such resources.

6   Related Work

To the best of our knowledge, in the Android community, our approach is the first work that attempts to complement existing state-of-the-art intra-app analysis tools to indirectly support inter-app analyses. Our approach is also the first proposal that supports context-aware inter-app analysis. However, research on detecting IAC vulnerabilities is not new.

Privilege escalation attack, an IAC vulnerability, has been studied by a large body of works [3,6,8]. Davi et al. [6] show that a genuine app can be exploited at runtime and a malicious app can escalate granted permissions. Prominent examples of privilege escalation attacks are *confused deputy* and *collusion attacks* [3]. Confused deputy attack is about the possibility for malicious app to exploit another privileged (but confused) app's vulnerable interface. Collusion attack concerns the collusion of apps that combine their permissions to be able to perform actions beyond their individual privileges. Our approach differs from theirs because we are focusing on supporting static inter-app analysis, while they are using dynamic testing to detect such vulnerabilities.

ComDroid [4] analyzed inter-app communication in Android apps and discovered IAC vulnerabilities such as *Broadcast Injection* and *Activity Hijacking*. Epicc [18] is another tool that dedicated to identify IAC vulnerabilities in Android apps. Besides, Epicc records the actual values of IAC objects, which makes it appropriate to build inter-component (or inter-app) links. ContentScope [22] is another tool which detects Content Provider based vulnerabilities. It argues that a Content Provider component can leak sensitive data to other apps and malicious apps can also pollute data maintained by a Content Provider. More recently, PCLeaks [17] was proposed to perform data-flow analysis on the top of IAC vulnerabilities to discover potential component leaks, which may leak private data across Android apps. While the above static approaches are tackling IAC vulnerabilities, they are actually only analyzing one app at a time and their outputs are so-called potential results. Our approach is able to complement them by enabling them to indirectly perform inter-app analysis and give them an opportunity to conform that the aforementioned potential vulnerabilities are exploitable in real-world apps.

To the best of our knowledge, there is only one, recent, static approach, DidFail [13], which is able to perform static inter-app analysis. However, as shown in Section 2.2 (type (B_1)), DidFail simply combines the results of intra-app analyses following an approach which is neither context-aware nor general. In contrast, our approach is able to provide a general context-aware inter-app analysis, and therefore, all intra-app analyzers can benefit from it.

7 Conclusion

We discussed `ApkCombiner`, a tool-based approach for reducing an Inter-App Communication problem into an intra-app Inter-Component Communication problem by combining multiple Android apps into one. After the combination, existing intra-app analysis approaches can be applied on the generated Android app to indirectly report inter-app results. Since we combine apps at code level, our approach is context-aware and general. We evaluate `ApkCombiner` to demonstrate that, despite a conflict resolution algorithm that requires a time-consuming refactoring process, the approach is scalable. We further showed that it can improve the capabilities of existing state-of-the-art tools. For example, we showed that using `ApkCombiner` can enable tools such as IccTA to discover IAC privacy leaks in real-world apps.

Acknowledgments. This work was supported by the Fonds National de la Recherche (FNR), Luxembourg, under the project AndroMap C13/IS/5921289, by the BMBF within EC SPRIDE, by the Hessian LOEWE excellence initiative within CASED and by the DFGs Priority Program 1496 Reliably Secure Software Systems and the project INTERFLOW.

References

1. Allix, K., Jerome, Q., Bissyande, T.F., Klein, J., State, R., Traon, Y.L.: A forensic analysis of android malware-how is malware written and how it could be detected? In: COMPSAC. IEEE (2014)
2. Arzt, S., Rasthofer, S., Bodden, E., Bartel, A., Klein, J., Le Traon, Y., Octeau, D., McDaniel, P.: Flowdroid: Precise context, flow, field, object-sensitive and lifecycle-aware taint analysis for android apps. In: PLDI 2014 (2014)
3. Bugiel, S., Davi, L., Dmitrienko, A., Fischer, T., Sadeghi, A.-R., Shastry., B.: Towards taming privilege-escalation attacks on android. In: NDSS (2012)
4. Chin, E., Felt, A.P., Greenwood, K., Wagner, D.: Analyzing inter-application communication in android. In: MobiSys. ACM, New York (2011)
5. Cui, X., Yu, D., Chan, P., Hui, L.C., Yiu, S., Qing, S.: Cochecker: Detecting capability and sensitive data leaks from component chains in android. In: ACISP 2014 (2014)
6. Davi, L., Dmitrienko, A., Sadeghi, A.-R., Winandy, M.: Privilege escalation attacks on android. In: Burmester, M., Tsudik, G., Magliveras, S., Ilić, I. (eds.) ISC 2010. LNCS, vol. 6531, pp. 346–360. Springer, Heidelberg (2011)
7. Denning, D.E., Denning, P.J.: Certification of programs for secure information flow. Communications of the ACM **20**(7), 504–513 (1977)
8. Enck, W., Gilbert, P., Chun, B.-G., Cox, L.P., Jung, J., McDaniel, P., Sheth, A.: Taintdroid: An information-flow tracking system for realtime privacy monitoring on smartphones. In: OSDI (2010)
9. Enck, W., Octeau, D., McDaniel, P., Chaudhuri, S.: A study of android application security. In: USENIX Security (2011)
10. Fuchs, A.P., Chaudhuri, A., Foster, J.S.: Scandroid: Automated security certification of android applications. Univ. of Maryland, Manuscript (2009)

11. Giffin, J.T., Jha, S., Miller, B.P.: Efficient context-sensitive intrusion detection. In: NDSS (2004)
12. Haris, M., Haddadi, H., Hui, P.: Privacy leakage in mobile computing: Tools, methods, and characteristics (2014). arXiv preprint arXiv:1410.4978
13. Klieber, W., Flynn, L., Bhosale, A., Jia, L., Bauer, L.: Android taint flow analysis for app sets. In: SOAP@PLDI, pp. 1–6. ACM (2014)
14. La Polla, M., Martinelli, F., Sgandurra, D.: A survey on security for mobile devices. IEEE Communications Surveys & Tutorials 15(1) 446–471
15. Lam, P., Bodden, E., Lhoták, O., Hendren, L.: The soot framework for java program analysis: a retrospective. In: CETUS (2011)
16. Li, L., Bartel, A., Bissyandé, T.F., Klein, J., Le Traon, Y., Arzt, S., Rasthofer, S., Bodden, E., Octeau, D., Mcdaniel, P.: IccTA: detecting inter-component privacy leaks in android apps. In: ICSE (2015)
17. Li, L., Bartel, A., Klein, J., Le Traon, Y.: Automatically exploiting potential component leaks in android applications. In: TrustCom. IEEE (2014)
18. Octeau, D., McDaniel, P., Jha, S., Bartel, A., Bodden, E., Klein, J., Le Traon, Y.: Effective inter-component communication mapping in android with epicc: An essential step towards holistic security analysis. In: USENIX Security (2013)
19. Wagner, D., Dean, D.: Intrusion detection via static analysis. In: S&P (2001)
20. Wei, F., Roy, S., Ou, X., et al.: Amandroid: A precise and general inter-component data flow analysis framework for security vetting of android apps. In: CCS (2014)
21. Wu, L., Grace, M., Zhou, Y., Wu, C., Jiang, X.: The impact of vendor customizations on android security. In: CCS, pp. 623–634. ACM (2013)
22. Zhou, Y., Jiang, X.: Detecting passive content leaks and pollution in android applications. In: NDSS (2013)

Assessment of the Susceptibility to Data Manipulation of Android Games with In-app Purchases

Francisco Vigário[✉], Miguel Neto, Diogo Fonseca,
Mário M. Freire, and Pedro R.M. Inácio

Instituto de Telecomunicações, Department of Computer Science, University of Beira
Interior, Rua Marquês d'Ávila e Bolama, 6201-001 Covilhã, Portugal
{fvigario,miguel.neto,diogompaf}@penhas.di.ubi.pt
{mario,inacio}@di.ubi.pt

Abstract. This paper describes a study for assessing how many free
Android games with in-app purchases were susceptible to data manipulation via the backup utility. To perform this study, a data set with
more than 800 games available in the *Google Play* store was defined.
The backup utility, provided by the Android Operating System (OS),
was used to backup the app files into a Personal Computer (PC) in order
to find and manipulate sensitive data. In the cases where sensitive data
was found, the applications were restored and the games tested to assess
if the manipulation was successful and if it could be used to the benefit
of the user. The results included show that a significant percentage of the
analyzed games save the user and app information in plaintext and do
not include mechanisms to detect or prevent data from being modified.

Keywords: Android · Data manipulation · Integrity · Mobile operating
system · Security · storage

1 Introduction

In the last few years we have witnessed an significant growth in the use of mobile
devices [15]. The massive adoption of these devices led several companies, as
Google and Apple, to direct their efforts into the development of mobile Operating Systems (OSs), driven by the needs of users. Along with these OSs, they also
provide app stores, (Google Play [12] and Apple Store [3]), which offer point and
click access to commercial or free applications to their users. Internetworking is
also increasing with the adoption of mobile devices, all contributing to a rich and
heterogeneous environment where sensitive data is sometimes flowing in the network, or stored in mobile devices in an insecure manner. This data is a tempting
target for malicious users or developers, which try to exploit vulnerabilities to
steal it or manipulate it for their own profit.

Similarly, to traditional computer software, games comprise a substantial part
of the revenue of this industry, reflected either in number of existing games or in

© IFIP International Federation for Information Processing 2015
H. Federrath and D. Gollmann (Eds.): SEC 2015, IFIP AICT 455, pp. 528–541, 2015.
DOI: 10.1007/978-3-319-18467-8_35

the effort to develop them. There are several business strategies for such applications and, in the case of mobile applications, some developers prefer to provide their games for free, to then offer the users the possibility to expand the game or add functionalities in return for a payment or several micro-payments. These are nowadays known as *in-app purchases*. Many developers choose to ask for a fee during the installation process. Sometimes, the applications come with the additional functionalities already implemented, but blocked. Some programming logic prevents the user from accessing those parts of the application before the purchase. This programming logic may be based on the values of variables, which are stored as app information in the internal storage of the device. As such, it is often assumed that the internal storage is protected (e.g., by the OS) against manipulation by other applications, and difficult to directly access by the user.

In mobile applications, *in-app purchases* are used to remove advertisements included in the free versions of apps, and add additional advanced or premium functionalities. In the case of Android games, which are addressed in this work, these purchases can also be used to unlock additional levels, get extra points, progress faster in the game and obtain hidden items, apart from the aforementioned ones. This mechanism is, thus, an important block in the business model of developers.

This paper describes a study concerning the possibility of accessing and manipulating internal data storage of Android games with *in-app purchase*, using the backup utility provided by the Android OS. The data set used for this analysis consists of more than 800 free games offering *in-app purchases*, which were downloaded from the *Google Play* store. All games of the data set were subject to human analysis after their installation in a non-rooted smartphone and transfer to a Personal Computer (PC). The procedure includes backing up the applications to a PC, searching for interesting data, changing it, and restoring the application back to the smartphone, to then assess if the behavior of the game changes as a result of the manipulation. The results show that a notable part of the analyzed games are susceptible to data manipulation, which can be easily exploited by users. Sometimes, the procedure applied in the scope of this paper may be applied, by typical users, to enjoy blocked functionalities without paying for them. Results clearly show that developers should pay more attention to data integrity and encryption mechanisms in mobile OSs.

This paper is structured as follows. Related works and the motivation underlying this study are included in section 2. Section 3 discusses the data set used in the scope of this work and elaborates on the type of applications used. The method used to perform the analysis is described in detail on section 4. Section 5 discusses the results of the analysis, as well as the number and type of applications that are susceptible to data manipulation using the described method. The main conclusions and some lines of future work are described in section 6.

2   Related Work

Due to the popularity of the Android OS and also to the personal nature of mobile devices, security involving this OS is nowadays a hot research topic. The sub-topic discussed herein is also receiving a lot of attention lately, as shown by the recent works on this area, discussed below. In 2011, the non-for-profit organization Open Web Application Security Project (OWASP) began a project with focus on threats to the mobile environment. At the end of 2014, the threat occupying the first position of the OWASP Top 10 Mobile Risks was *Weak Server Side Controls*, with *Insecure Data Storage and Insufficient Transport Layer Protection* coming up next in the second position [14], which also motivated this work.

C. Håland, in his Masters thesis entitled *An Application Security Assessment of Popular Free Android Applications* [5], includes a study of 20 popular free applications, testing them for the OWASP Top 10 mobile risks. He found several vulnerabilities of this list in the applications, namely *Insecure Data Storage*, *Weak Server Side Controls*, *Insufficient Transport Layer Protection*, etc. The author states that most of the attacks were only possible in rooted devices. For example, he mentions that, with root privileges, the owner of the device can access any file or folder, which comprises a *Insecure Data Storage* problem. He was able to change the value of the coins used in the 4Pics1Word game, without paying for that feature, by simply searching the files storing the status of the application. Wordfeud Free was another application with a similar problem but, in this case, he was able to retrieve the username and password of the Facebook account that was used to login in the application, because the credentials were stored in plaintext in an Extensible Markup Language (XML) file.

C. Xiao, a researcher in Palo Alto Networks, delivered a talk entitled *Insecure Internal Storage in Android* in the Taiwan Conference (HITCON) [6] regarding the subject at hands. He processed a total of 12,351 applications downloaded from Google Play, having concluded that, from these applications, only 556 were not allowing backup by means of the backup utility, and that only other 156 applications were implementing a BackupAgent to protect the data. In other words, approximately 94,2% of the most popular applications allow transferring the package and all the internal storage files to a computer in a packed format. The authorization to backup applications can be set up by adjusting the `android:allowBackup` property to `true` or `false` in the manifest file. His study was focused on the applications with at least 500,000 downloads. The idea of manipulating data from Android apps via the backup utility was already circulating in specialized forums and its genesis is hard to obtain.

In the Masters thesis entitled *Android Application Security with OWASP Mobile Top 10 2014* [13], James King analyzed the FourGoats Android application, in which he identified several types of vulnerabilities, including *Insecure Data Storage*. The version of the application under analysis was using a local database file to store the credentials of the users in plaintext, and an attacker with physical access to the device could thus obtain them, even without root privileges (e.g., using the method described in section 4). In the Masters thesis, the author also describes problems related with *Insufficient Transport Layer Protection*, stating that the majority of the applications selected for analysis were not using encryption to transmit data over the network, which leaves them vulnerable to Man-In-The-Middle (MITM) attacks. In some cases, the credentials of users could also be obtained from traffic sniffing (because they were sent unencrypted). Other vulnerabilities discussed in this study include *Poor Authorization and Authentication, Broken Cryptography, Improper Session Handling* and *Lack of Binary Protections* related problems.

In [8], Fahl et al. tried to assess how, and to which extent, Secure Sockets Layer (SSL)/Transport Layer Security (TLS) was being used to protect the contents of network communications from Android applications. The inadequate usage or integration of the protocol could be as serious as not using it at all, and both situations lead to MITM related vulnerabilities. In the scope of their work, the authors developed `MalloDroid`, which is a small tool that can be used to find broken SSL certificate validation procedures in Android apps. A total number of 13,500 popular free apps downloaded from Google Play were then analyzed with this tool. They concluded that approximately 8% of the analyzed applications (1,074 apps) were potentially vulnerable to MITM attacks.

This paper is focused on the manipulation of locally stored data (no MITM attacks were performed). Nonetheless, the procedure described herein may be combined with MITM attacks to perhaps obtain an even higher success rate, since it was noticed that some apps were using the network to store values and to detect data modification.

3   Data Set

The analysis described in this paper was performed on a fairly large data set of Android games, which are free to download but have the *in-app purchase* characteristic. Even though simple tasks of this work used automated scripts, most of the analysis was performed manually, meaning that all games were subject to human analysis. The data set was collected between September and November of 2014 and it is consists of 849 games from the 15 different categories defined in *Google Play* for this type of software [12]. Table 1 summarizes the number of games-per-category considered in the analysis. Although some applications without *in-app purchases* were also analyzed in the meantime, they were not considered in the scope of this particular work, because the main objective was to evaluate whether a user could use the method described below to use premium or paid functionalities without purchasing them, i.e., by only modifying internal data.

Prior studies on Android OS security (e.g., [4,7,9,10]) have mainly focused their analysis on the most popular apps available in Google Play (or Android Market, as it was designated previously). This work takes the number of downloads into account in the analysis of the results, but the popularity of the applications was not considered when choosing the games for installation. As such, our approach differs from some of the previously described ones in two ways: (i) all applications were subject to manual analysis, so that minor details concerning the way that data was stored by different applications was not overlooked; (ii) the study is not limited to popular or to a small set of applications.

In order to give an idea of the popularity of the games comprising the data set, Table 2 shows the number of games in the data set for each of the 11 different

Table 1. Number of analyzed games by category

Category														
	Action	Arcade	Puzzle	Casual	Strategy	Sports	Racing	Simulation	Adventure	Role Playing	Card	Word	Family	Trivia	Music
Number of Games	141	138	99	91	91	58	50	39	37	35	34	16	13	6	1

download intervals defined by Google Play. A large slice of the data set was in the 1 to 5 billion download interval (approximately 35%), and approximately 71% had more than 1 billion downloads.

Notice that, not limiting the data set to the most popular games also provided a way to later on assess if there was an obvious relation between popularity and the problems related with *Insecure Data Storage*.

Table 2. Number of games in the data set per number of downloads

Number of Downloads	Number of Games-per-Interval
100 000 000 - 500 000 000	13
50 000 000 - 100 000 000	16
10 000 000 - 50 000 000	111
5 000 000 - 10 000 000	110
1 000 000 - 5 000 000	296
500 000 - 1 000 000	106
100 000 - 500 000	157
50 000 - 100 000	23
10 000 - 50 000	11
5 000 - 10 000	4
1 000 - 5 000	2

4   Method

The method to perform the analysis described in this paper required the usage of a smartphone and a PC with specific software installed. The smartphone was running a non-rooted Android OS (version 4.4.2). Nonetheless, any version of the

(a) RSA Key fingerprint   (b) Backup utility dialog

Fig. 1. Screenshots of important steps of the method used in the scope of this work. (a) Screenshot of the RSA key fingerprint dialog for enabling USB debugging from a given computer; (b) Screenshot of the Backup utility provided by the OS.

OS higher than 4.0.0 would suffice for all purposes of this work, since the backup utility (which is critical for the method) was provided natively from that version on [2]. As further explained below, a snapshot of each analyzed game needs to be copied to the PC. This was done via an Universal Serial Bus (USB) cable and the communications were managed by the Android Debug Bridge (ADB) tool [1], which was installed in the computer. The PC was running a Linux based OS also, with the following tools installed: pax, tar, OpenSSL, dd and grep. Some of these tools (e.g., OpenSSL and grep) come natively with most of the Linux distributions available, while others are very simple to obtain, e.g., via package managers. These tools were used to handle the package transferred from the smartphone. Typically, OpenSSL is used to perform cryptographic tasks but, in this case, it was used to compress and decompress packages resorting to the *zlib* library. pax was used to read and write files and copy directory hierarchies. dd and tar were responsible for converting and extracting files with the .tar format, respectively. Finally, grep was used for searching patterns in the data files of an application.

After the establishment of the initial setup and installation of the tools described above, a set of steps to explore the data storage problems was applied. The method can be divided into 10 different steps. Each step resorts to a set of commands, which are entered in a traditional shell. It should be emphasized that, apart from the already available and aforementioned tools, no particular secondary application needs to be developed to apply this method, and parts of it can be found online in specialized forums (e.g., [11]), which contributes to the severity of this problem. The method explained below presumes that the game to be analyzed was previously installed in the system. The steps are described with more detail as follows:

1. The first step consists of connecting the mobile device to the computer via USB. The debug mode should be active when the connection is performed

(or needs to be activated on the device). The OS normally asks the user to allow the communication in debug mode, exhibiting a dialog with an RSA public key fingerprint, as shown on Figure 1a. The connection needs to be explicitly allowed for the method to work.

2. The app backup to the computer is performed in the second step, by issuing a command similar to the following one in the terminal:

```
adb backup -f data.ab -apk PATH
```

The PATH parameter represents the fully qualified path of the game in the smartphone internal storage. This command will trigger the backup utility in the Android OS, illustrated on Figure 1b, that asks the explicit permission to perform the backup operation for that app. An optional password for encrypting the package may be provided.

Once the command is successfully executed, a compressed and non-encrypted archive (in this case referred to as data.ab), which contains a small header with 24 bytes, and the files composing the app, is transferred to the PC.

3. The third step consists of removing the header and converting the data.ab into a tar file, so as to enable the extraction of the compressed files in the subsequent step. This can be achieved by piping the following commands:

```
dd if=data.ab bs=1 skip=24 | openssl zlib -d > data.tar
```

4. The fourth step consists of obtaining an exact snapshot of the names of the files and directory structure inside of the data.tar archive with:

```
tar -tf data.tar > data.list
```

This will enable packaging the application back perfectly after file manipulation and before restoring.

5. The fifth step is the one were the data.tar archive is decompressed using a command similar to the next one:

```
dd if=data.ab bs=1 skip=24 | openssl zlib -d | tar -xvf -
```

6. The sixth step is where one tries to manipulate the data of the application. This work was just focused on trying to change data that could enable accessing paid functionalities or changing the behavior of the game without paying for them. For example, we were interested in changing the number of coins in a game. To achieve this objective, a simple procedure based on human analysis of the files and resorting to the grep tool was applied with commands similar to:

```
grep -R "xxx" app/PATH/
```

Several strategies were adopted to try to find out the interesting values. Some were based on thorough (human) analysis of the files. Another one, which proved to be very successful, consisted in playing the game in the smartphone for a limited period of time, leaving it with a given number of coins or in a given game level (which are numbers). Afterwards, those numbers were searched in the data files of the application using `grep` and all occurrences were further analyzed and manipulated. For example, we would legitimately play a game until 1234 coins were generated, to then look for and modify that value in this step. Sometimes, the `sqlite3` tool had to be used to perform the modification, as some apps use sqlite3 to store the data. This stage included the modification of XML, sqlite, JavaScript Object Notation (JSON) and text files.

7. The seventh step begins the *app* restore process. First of all, it is necessary to compress all *app* files in the exact same order they were decompressed using the information saved in the *data.list* file:

```
cat data.list | pax -wd > newdata.tar
```

8. The header that was previously stripped out needs to be properly inserted again so that the file has the right format, using:

```
echo -e "ANDROID BACKUP\n1\n1\nnone" > backup.ab
```

9. The application can then be compressed and concatenated to the end of the `backup.ab` file, which already contains the header:

```
openssl zlib -in newdata.tar >> backup.ab
```

The `backup.ab` is an archive compatible the Android OS.

10. The last step consists of issuing the command to restore the archive to the device, which will trigger a dialog similar to the one in Figure 1b.:

```
adb restore backup.ab
```

Notice that, all previous steps were performed on each one of the games included in the data set. After concluding the last step of the method successfully, the game was once again executed in the Android OS and it was assessed if the data modifications were producing the expected results. Sometimes, this procedure was repeated several times, to minimize the possibility of having overlooked some minor artifact. If the behavior of the game was changed without detection (some games detect modifications by storing values in the network) as a consequence of the manipulation, it was considered vulnerable. The results are discussed below.

5   Discussion and Results

The data set used in the scope of this work is constituted by 849 free (to download) games with the *in-app purchase* characteristic. From those 849, a total of 148 were susceptible to data manipulation performed using the method described in section 4, which corresponds to 17,43% of the tested games. This percentage is significant, taking into account that it refers to cases where developers are dependent of that specific income (the game is free to download, only the add-ons are paid). Also, worth of note is the fact that the method does not depend,

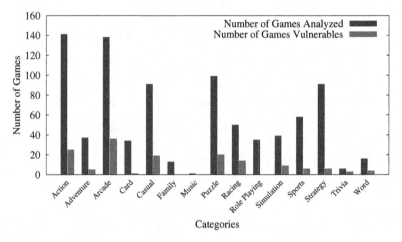

in any way, of having the OS rooted or not and that the tools to perform data modification are readily available. Actually, it would be easy to automate the described method and pack the required tools to construct a program for cracking a given game, based on these findings.

The chart in Figure 2 compares the number of games that were found to be susceptible to data manipulation with the total number of games in the data set for each one of the *Google Play* categories. The results suggest that *Trivia* is the most affected category (with 50% of vulnerable games), but it is also one of the ones containing fewer games (only 6). Some of these games work both online and offline, and the paid add-ons are often aids to which the user may resort to answer questions right. In the vulnerable games, it was noticed that the access to such functionalities was controlled by values stored in plaintext files without any integrity mechanism.

Fig. 2. Total number of games versus the number of games susceptible to data manipulation, per category

After *Trivia*, the two categories with the most expressive results were *Racing* and *Arcade*, where 28% and 26% of the games were susceptible to data manipulation, respectively. In these types of games, the paid add-on or functionality is also normally comprised by means to have more virtual money or faster ways to progress in levels, namely by buying certain virtual items. The results derive from the fact that the money balance of a game is frequently stored in plaintext XML or text files, or in SQLite databases, without integrity or authentication codes, which are easy to find and modify.

The categories of *Role Playing*, *Family* and *Music* had no vulnerable games. These results are mostly due to the fact that, in this type of games, *in-app purchases* are used to remove advertisements or to, for example, buy the whole game or expansions (new levels, weapons or characters). In such cases, the purchase typically requires downloading new files (or a new version of the game) to the system and, therefore, these files were not previously available for manipulation. Purchases requiring the user to interact with a remote server are inherently less susceptible to data manipulation because, in such cases, it is not about changing the flow or status information of the application. *Role Playing* games usually have a higher longevity, and they are updated more times than, e.g., *Arcade* games. Some updates address previously known issues, namely the ones related with *Insecure Data Storage* when *crack* tools leak into the Internet. Probably, the effort in implementing security features in these categories is larger.

The *Cards* and *Strategy* categories had 2.9% and 6.5% of the games suscepti- ble to data manipulation, respectively. These low values are related with the fact that both types of games are typically played online, which means that applica- tion information is either stored remotely or checked frequently against the last known (or normal) snapshot of such values. Some games allowed changing some app related values in the PC, but they were then restored when the connection was again established.

In order to assess if there was a relation between the popularity of a game and its susceptibility to data manipulation, an analysis similar to the previous one was conducted for the same data set segregated by number of downloads. The chart in Figure 3 summarizes this part of the work.

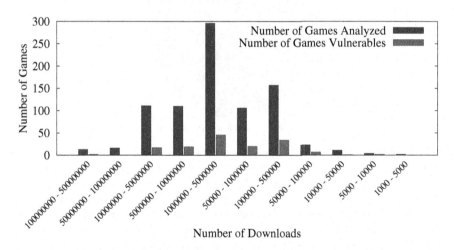

Fig. 3. Total number of games versus the number of games susceptible to data manip- ulation, segregated by popularity

The most vulnerable games are the ones with the number of downloads in the ranges 5000–10000 and 50000–100000, though the first interval only contained 4 games (of which 2 were vulnerable to the method applied herein). In the second interval, 7 games were vulnerable, corresponding to approximately 30% of the total number of games in that range. The results suggest that the number of vulnerable games is not dependent of their popularity, even though no vulnerable games were found in the range 50000000–100000000 (there were only 16 games in this interval). In the range with most of the games (1000000–5000000), 15.4% were vulnerable to data manipulation, which corresponds to 46 games in a total of 296.

Focusing only on the vulnerable games, Figure 4 emphasizes the type of files used to sale application data in the internal storage of the Android OS. As shown in the pie chart, 76% of the vulnerable games resort to XML files, while 9% use SQLite databases and 14% use .txt or JSON files. This distribution was expected since XML comprises a simple and standard format for storing data and, in Android, one of the suggested storage options for saving application related data is known as *Shared Preferences*, which is used to save values from primitive JAVA types in XML format. Nonetheless, these results also show that manipulation is possible in a variety of formats. Data stored within SQLite databases is also stored in ASCII, except if encoded using application logic, which also enables one to easily find patterns in the files.

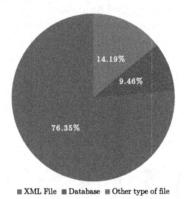

■ XML File ■ Database ■ Other type of file

Fig. 4. Type of file used to save application data in Android internal storage in vulnerable games

Finally, it should be mentioned that only 21 games, corresponding to approximately 2.5% of the data set, had the property android:allowBackup set to false in the AndroidManifest.xml. By default, this property is set to true, which means that, if the developer does not explicitly adjust it to false, the game will be inherently more prone to the method described herein. The possibility to backup an application is a commodity utility for the user and it makes sense to exist. The problem is that it can be easily exploited with different intentions. Setting the aforementioned property to false will solve the problem in non-rooted OSs, but legitimate users may miss the functionality. Apart from that, such setting would not solve the issue in rooted OSs.

Due to the reasons mention in the previous paragraph, integrating data integrity mechanisms into the application may comprise the best means to address this issue or, at least, make the exploitation more difficult. For example, developers may use hash functions, Message Authentication Code (MAC) or digital signature algorithms to calculate and store digests, MACs or signatures for the files where the sensitive data is stored (databases, text or implementation files, etc.). Encrypting the files will have a similar effect. Nonetheless, this imposes some additional computational burden, since the application needs to calculate the aforementioned codes when the contents of the files change and verify them at each execution. If encryption is used, the application needs to decrypt and encrypt the data before accessing or storing it in the files, respectively. Since the cryptographic secrets, used in these mechanisms, need to be available for the application, a specially motivated attacker may still try to manipulate the data by finding the keys and the data integrity mechanisms. If the cryptographic secrets are transferred with the backup, the manipulation is harder to achieve, but still within reach. As such, this topic needs more attention.

Curiously, 3.2% of the games in the data set (corresponding to 27 games) were publicized with the *in-app purchase* characteristic in *Google Play*, but had really nothing to buy in the application. In another 3.9% of the data set (i.e., 27 games), the *in-app purchase* was to remove advertisements or to buy their respective full version, which involves downloading additional files and, as such, they are not vulnerable to data manipulation.

6   Conclusions and Future Work

This paper is focused on the *Insecure Data Storage* threat defined by OWASP for mobile devices. It elaborates on the specific problem of manipulating application data from Android games to get free access to paid add-ons or functionalities. Herein, it was discussed that the backup and restore functionalities, provided natively with recent versions of the Android OS, could be used to transfer games to and from a PC, in which they could be tampered to obtain access to the aforementioned add-ons or functionalities. This procedure does not require the system to be rooted, only the users consent (for allowing the USB connection and for transferring the specific application). This procedure is already used by some tools for cheating some games since it can be easily automated for a specific application.

In order to quantify the problem, a total of 849 games offering *in-app purchases* were downloaded, from Google Play, and then manually analyzed using a method based on searching patterns on the data transferred with the application during the backup. An expressive number of 148 games were found vulnerable to this method, meaning that it was possible to change the application flow or status by searching for ASCII patterns on XML, JSON, txt or SQLite files. Results suggest that the vulnerability is not related with the popularity of the games and we argue that disabling the backup feature for a game should not be seen as a preventive measure against this problem, though it would certainly contribute for its attenuation. The possibility to backup the applications constitutes a commodity utility and it should not be disabled. Data integrity and encryption mechanisms comprise the best mechanisms to prevent *Insecure Data Storage* problems, like the ones discussed herein.

A possible line of future work consist on performing a similar assessment for other mobile OSs. For example, *iOS* provides also a means to transfer applications to a PC, e.g., for the cases when the user wants to switch phones.

Another line of work consists of expanding the data set to other types of applications and broaden the scope of the analysis. During the study described herein, a few other (non-game) applications were analyzed and it was found that many of them were saving user related data in plaintext files. Worst than that, some applications were enabling the access to others users online profiles via data manipulation, because they were storing other users information locally. A more detailed analysis is nonetheless required.

Acknowledgments. Authors acknowledge the financial support from EyeSee, Lda. This work was performed in the scope of the R&D Unit 50008, financed by the applicable financial framework (FCT/MEC through national funds and when applicable co-funded by FEDER – PT2020 partnership agreement).

References

1. Android Developers: Android Debug Bridge (2014). http://developer.android.com/tools/help/adb.html (accessed December 2014)
2. Android Developers: Dashboards — Android Developers (2014). https://developer.android.com/about/dashboards/index.html (accessed December 2014)
3. Apple: Official Apple Store (20). http://store.apple.com/us (accessed January 2015)
4. Barrera, D., Kayacik, H.G., van Oorschot, P.C., Somayaji, A.: A methodology for empirical analysis of permission-based security models and its application to android. In: Proceedings of the 17th ACM Conference on Computer and Communications Security, CCS 2010, pp. 73–84. ACM, New York (2010). http://doi.acm.org/10.1145/1866307.1866317
5. Håland, C.: An Application Security Assessment of Popular Free Android Applications. Master's thesis, Norwegian University of Science and Technology (2013)
6. Xiao, C., Olson, R.: Insecure Internal Storage in Android - Palo Alto Networks BlogPalo Alto Networks Blog (2014). http://researchcenter.paloaltonetworks.com/2014/08/insecure-internal-storage-android/ (accessed December 2014)
7. Enck, W., Ongtang, M., McDaniel, P.: On lightweight mobile phone application certification. In: Proceedings of the 16th ACM Conference on Computer and Communications Security, CCS 2009, pp. 235–245. ACM, New York (2009). http://doi.acm.org/10.1145/1653662.1653691
8. Fahl, S., Harbach, M., Muders, T., Baumgärtner, L., Freisleben, B., Smith, M.: Why eve and mallory love android: An analysis of android ssl (in)security. In: Proceedings of the 2012 ACM Conference on Computer and Communications Security, CCS 2012, pp. 50–61. ACM, New York (2012). http://doi.acm.org/10.1145/2382196.2382205
9. Felt, A.P., Chin, E., Hanna, S., Song, D., Wagner, D.: Android permissions demystified. In: Proceedings of the 18th ACM Conference on Computer and Communications Security, CCS 2011, pp. 627–638. ACM, New York (2011). http://doi.acm.org/10.1145/2046707.2046779

10. Felt, A.P., Greenwood, K., Wagner, D.: The effectiveness of application permissions. In: Proceedings of the 2nd USENIX Conference on Web Application Development, WebApps 2011, p. 7. USENIX Association, Berkeley (2011). http://dl. acm.org/citation.cfm?id=2002168.2002175
11. Forums, X.: GUIDE How to extract, create or edit android adb backups — Android Development and Hacking — XDA Forums (20). http://forum.xda-developers. com/showthread.php?t=2011811 (accessed January 2015)
12. Google: Google Play (2014). https://play.google.com/store (accessed December 2014)
13. King, J: Android Application Security with OWASP Mobile Top 10 2014. Master's thesis, Luleå University of Technology (2014)
14. OWASP: Projects/OWASP Mobile Security Project - Top Ten Mobile Risks - OWASP (2014). https://www.owasp.org/index.php/Projects/OWASP_Mobile_Security_Project_-_Top_Ten_Mobile_Risks (accessed November 2014)
15. Pieterse, H., Olivier, M.: Android botnets on the rise: Trends and characteristics. In: Information Security for South Africa (ISSA 2012), pp. 1–5, August 2012

An Empirical Study on Android for Saving Non-shared Data on Public Storage

Xiangyu Liu[1], Zhe Zhou[1], Wenrui Diao[1], Zhou Li[2], and Kehuan Zhang[1(✉)]

[1] The Chinese University of Hong Kong, Hong Kong, China
khzhang@ie.cuhk.edu.hk
[2] RSA Laboratories, Cambridge, USA

Abstract. With millions of apps provided from official and third-party markets, Android has become one of the most active mobile platforms in recent years. These apps facilitate people's lives in a broad spectrum of ways but at the same time touch numerous users' information, raising huge privacy concerns. To prevent leaks of sensitive information, especially from legitimate apps to malicious ones, developers are encouraged to store users' sensitive data into private folders which are isolated and securely protected. But for non-sensitive data, there is no specific guideline on how to manage them, and in many cases, they are simply stored on public storage which lacks fine-grained access control and is almost open to all apps.

Such storage model appears to be capable of preventing privacy leaks, as long as the sensitive data are correctly identified and kept in private folders by app developers. Unfortunately, this is not true in reality. In this paper, we carry out a thorough study over a number of Android apps to examine how the sensitive data are handled, and the results turn out to be pretty alarming: most of the apps we surveyed fail to handle the data correctly, including extremely popular apps. Among these problematic apps, some directly store the sensitive data into public storage, while others leave non-sensitive data on public storage which could give out users' private information when being combined with data from other sources. An adversary can exploit these leaks to infer users' location, friends and other information without requiring any critical permission. We refer to both types of data as "non-shared" data, and argue that Android's storage model should be refined to protect the non-shared data if they are saved to public storage. In the end, we propose several approaches to mitigate such privacy leaks.

1 Introduction

The last decade has seen the immense evolution of smartphone technologies. Today's smartphones carry much more functionalities than plain phones, including email processing, social networking, online shopping, etc. These emerging

---

All vulnerabilities described in this paper have been reported to corresponding companies. We have got the IRB approval before all experiments related to human subjects.

© IFIP International Federation for Information Processing 2015
H. Federrath and D. Gollmann (Eds.): SEC 2015, IFIP AICT 455, pp. 542–556, 2015.
DOI: 10.1007/978-3-319-18467-8_36

functionalities are largely supported by mobile applications (*apps*). As reported by [1], the number of Android apps on Google Play is hitting 1.55 million.

Most of the apps need to access some kind of users' data, like emails, contacts, photos, service accounts, etc. Among them, some data are to be shared with other apps by nature, like photos from camera apps, while others are not to be shared (which is called "app-private data" in this paper), like temporary files, user account information, etc. To protect these app-private data, Android has provided multiple security mechanisms. A private folder is assigned in internal storage that can only be accessed by the owner app.

App developers tend to further divide app-private data into sensitive and non-sensitive ones (the reasons are discussed in Section 7). The sensitive data, like user authentication information, are saved to internal storage, while the data deemed as non-sensitive are saved to public storage (including external SD card and shared partition in built-in Flash memory) which lacks fine-grained access control and is open to almost all other apps [1]. At first glance, it seems reasonable and secure to differentiate and save those "non-sensitive" data to public storage. However, this is a dangerous practice for two reasons. First, app developers prone to make mistakes on identifying sensitive data, especially when the data are massive and complicated. Second, some data could be turned into sensitive when combined with data from other apps or publicly available information, even though they are non-sensitive when being examined individually.

In this paper, we investigated a large number of apps, and the results show that many app developers indeed have failed to make right decisions and app-private data that are originally thought as "non-sensitive" could actually leak lots of user privacy (more details are described in Section 4). We also demonstrate one concrete attack example on inferring user's location by exploiting those "non-sensitive" information in Section 5, which further proves the seriousness of the problem.

We argue that the problem identified in this paper is distinct from previous works. It reveals the gap between the assumptions of Android security design (i.e., the security relies on the knowledge of app developers and permissions) and the limitations in real-world (i.e., apps always need to be compatible with all Android versions and all devices and app developers are not security experts). Our study suggests a vast number of Android apps fall into the trap due to this gap, which is much more serious than people's thought before and needs to be addressed urgently. However, such problem neither originates from system vulnerability nor is introduced when user is fooled, and the existing protection mechanisms are therefore ineffective. To bridge the gap, we believe that app developers should scrutinize their code and avoid saving any non-shared data to public storage, no matter if they are identified as sensitive or not. In other words, "public storage" can only be used to save data to be publicly shared

---

[1] Although an app needs the corresponding permissions (like READ_EXTERNAL_STORAGE or WRITE_EXTERNAL_STORAGE, READ and WRITE for short) to access public storage, these permissions are very common and are usually granted by users without any hesitation since they are requested by most apps.

with other apps. Another less painful approach requires the update of Android infrastructure by bringing fine-grained access control to current public storage model, which essentially converts shared public storage to non-shared storage.

Our Contributions. We summarize our contributions as follows:

- We revisit Android's public storage model, including its evolution and access control mechanism.
- Our study is the first to examine the privacy leakage on public storage by investigating real-world apps. Some discovered issues are critical and should be fixed as soon as possible. We manually checked the most popular Android apps on whether they store the data correctly, and the results show that most of them (with billions of installations in total) leave user's private information on public storage. Our large-scale automated analysis further indicates that such a problem exists in a large number of apps. We also show it is possible to harvest sensitive information from very popular apps through a showcase.
- We suggest several approaches to protect app-private data on public storage.

2 Adversary Model

The adversary studied in this paper is interested in stealing or inferring device owners' sensitive information by exploiting the app-private data located at public storage. In order to acquire app-private data, it is assumed that a malicious app with the ability to **read** data on public storage (by requiring the READ or WRITE permission) and access the Internet (by requiring INTERNET permission) has been successfully installed on an Android device. The app will read certain app-private folders selectively on public storage, extract data that can be used for privacy attacks, and then upload them to a malicious server where the data are analyzed to infer victim's sensitive information.

The above assumptions are easy to be satisfied. First, the app requires only two very common permissions. A statistical analysis on 34369 apps (crawled by us) shows that about 94% of apps request INTERNET permission, and about 85% of apps request the permission to access public storage, ranking No.1 and No.3 respectively. This malicious app should hardly raise alarm to the device owners during installation. Second, it only uploads data when Wi-Fi is available and therefore it is hard to be detected by looking into data usage statistics. Finally, the app does not exhibit obvious malicious behaviors, like sending out message to premium number or manipulating the device like bot-client, and could easily stay under the radar of anti-virus software.

3 Background of Android Public Storage

Android provides 5 options for an app to store data, including *shared preferences, internal storage, external storage* ("public storage" referred in this paper), *SQLite databases* and *remote storage*. In this paper, we focus on public storage since the protection enforced is weaker than the other options.

Evolution. Before Android 3.0, *external storage* only includes real external SD card. Since the size of built-in Flash memory is limited in the early stage of Android, external storage is a preferable option for app developers, especially to store large files, like audio files and images. In recent years, we have seen a significant growth of the size of built-in Flash memory (e.g., 64GB), and it turns out internal storage can also hold large files. However, app developers still prefer to consider external storage to hold app's data for two reasons: First, the Android devices with limited built-in Flash memory are still popular, especially in less developed countries or areas; second, the external and internal storage run with different model and are operated with different APIs, which forces the developers to make unneglectable changes if switching to internal storage. To maximize the use of its storage without incurring additional overhead to developers, Android adopts FUSE [4] to emulate a sdcard daemon (mounted as */data/media*) inside userdata partition (*/data*). File operations on this partition resembles the ones on external SD card and we consider both as public storage.

Access Control Model on External Storage. Access to external storage is protected by various Android permissions, however, our attack aims to retrieve users' private information and hence we only elaborate the details of read access. Before Android 4.1, there is no permission restricting read operations on public storage. READ permission is added to Android since then, and an app has to be granted with such permission to read files on public storage. This permission is supported through attaching a Linux GID sdcard_r to all the files on public storage and an app (corresponding to a process in Linux) has to be granted with GID sdcard_r as well before visiting any file there. A fundamental issue with this model is that there is no finer-grained control over what files are accessible to one app if sdcard_r is granted, which exposes one app's private data to all other apps. It is worth noting that the permission WRITE_MEDIA_STORAGE introduced from Android 4.4 enforces finer-grained control over write operations, but nothing has been changed for read operations.

4 Survey on Information Leaks from Public Storage

It is true that some app-private data is not sensitive. However, the model of letting apps write their private data to public storage relies on a strong assumption that app developers can make right decisions to tell sensitive data from non-sensitive ones. In this section, we present a survey of the information leaks through app-private data stored on public storage, which shows that such an assumption is problematic. The survey includes two parts: the first is a detailed examination on 17 most popular apps, and the other is a more general and large scale study.

4.1 Investigation on Popular Apps

What Apps Have been Surveyed. According to our adversary model, the attackers are interested in privacy attacks over app-private data, so we have selected 17 most popular apps from three categories: "social networking", "instant messaging" and "online shopping&payment", which are believed to be more likely to touch users' sensitive information. The categories, versions and total users of these apps are shown in Table 1.

How to Check App-Private Data. These apps are installed on three Samsung Galaxy S3 mobile phones. Then we manually simulate three different users on three phones, including account registration, adding good friends, sending message, and etc. Finally, we check the public storage, search sensitive data for each app and classify them.

How the Information is Leaked. By studying the popular apps, we found 10 of them leak various sensitive information through app-private data on public storage, as shown in Table 2. Such information is leaked in different forms which are discussed as below, and the details are elaborated in Appendix A.

Table 1. The categories, versions and total users of the popular apps

Category	App Name	Installed Version	Total Users (Millions)
Social networking	Facebook	13.0.0.13.14	900M
	Instagram	6.2.2	100M
	Twitter	5.18.1	310M
	Linkedin	3.3.5	300M
	Vine	2.1.0	40M
	Weibo	4.4.1	500M
	Renren	7.3.0	194M
	Momo	4.9	100M
Instant messaging	WhatsApp	2.11.186	450M
	Viber	4.3.3.67	300M
	Skype	4.9.0.45564	300M
	Line	4.5.4	350M
	KakaoTalk	4.5.3	100M
	Tencent QQ	4.7.0	816M
	WeChat	5.2.1	450M
	EasyChat	2.1.0	60M
Online shopping &payment	Alipay	8.0.3.0320	300M

Table 2. Sensitive information acquired from the popular apps

Sensitive Information	App Name	Content/Remarks
User Identity	Weibo, Renren	UID
	Linkedin	User's profile photo
Phone Number	Viber, Alipay, EasyChat	User's phone number
Email	Weibo, Renren	Registered email
Account	Tencent QQ,Viber,Renren,Momo,Weibo	UID
	WeChat	QQ UID / Phone number
Connection	EasyChat	Call records
	Linkedin	Profile photos of friends
	KakaoTalk	Chatting buddies
	Renren	Friends' UIDs
	WhatsApp	Phone numbers of friends

Fig. 1. The result of searching a user's Linkedin profile photo

Leak through text files. Some apps store user's profile into a text file. For example, `Viber` directly saves user's name, phone number into a plain text file without any encryption. User's username, email address[2] are stored by `Weibo` in a file named by the user's UID. Some apps also keep text logs which reveal quite rich information, i.e., `EasyChat` keeps call records in a file, so caller's number, callee's number and call duration can be easily recovered by simply parsing each record.

Leak through file names. We found several apps organize data related to the user or her friends into a dedicated file named with sensitive or non-obvious sensitive information. For example, a file created by `Weibo` is named as user's UID, `WhatsApp` stores user's friends photos with that friend's phone number as file name. They seem meaningless but could have significant privacy implications when combined with other public information, i.e., the owners of the phone numbers acquired from `WhatsApp` can be found by comparing these acquired portraits with photos from user's social networks.

Leak through folder names. Some apps use account name as folder name directly, like `Renren` and `Momo`. While `KakaoTalk` will create folders with the same name in both two users' phones if they chat with each other, files (i.e., photos) sent to each other will be saved in the folder and also with the same name. Such a naming convention reveals the connections among people, and even can be leveraged to infer user's chat history.

Leak through photos. The social networking apps usually cache user's profile photos in public storage, like `LinkedIn` in our study. The photo itself is non-sensitive if without knowing who is in the photo, however, our study shows that user's `LinkedIn` profile photo can be linked to her identity by Google image search, as shown in Fig. 1.

---

[2] If the user uses her email to register Weibo account. The user also can use phone number to register an account.

Table 3. Privacy protection level of the 17 popular apps

Privacy Level	App Name	Issues
★★★	Facebook, Twitter, Instagram, Skype	-
★★	Line, Vine, WeChat	Audio files without encryption
★	WhatsApp, Linkedin, Viber, KakaoTalk, Momo Tencent QQ, Alipay, Renren, Weibo, EasyChat	Detailed problems are shown in Appendix A

Leak through specific patterns. We could use the command */system/bin/sh -c grep -r @xxx.com path* to match and extract email addresses from files in public storage. If the files are stored by apps, the corresponding emails are very likely belong to the phone's owner. It is worth noting that the email found by grep command in Table 2 is from a *log.txt* file left by Renren old version (5.9.4).

What Information has been Leaked. As shown in Table 2, there is indeed some important sensitive information leaked through the app-private data. To better understand the privacy implication of such leaks, we use Personal Identifiable Information (PII) [11], a well-known definition for private data, to classify and evaluate the leaked information. We defined two categories of sensitive data, *Obvious sensitive data* and *Non-obvious sensitive data*, by refining the concept of PII as below:

- *Obvious sensitive data.* It contains identifiers in PII related to user's real-world identity, including full name, phone numbers, addresses, date of birth, social security number, driver's license id, credit card numbers, and etc.
- *Non-obvious sensitive data.* It contains identifiers in PII related to user's virtual-world identity and also her friends' information. The virtual-world identifiers include email addresses, account name, profile photos, and etc.

How to Infer User's Identity. As shown in Table 2, attackers can exploit the sensitive data left by several apps to infer user's identity information. For example, A user's identity can be acquired from her personal homepage by using her Renren UID, Weibo Username/UID, Linkedin profile photo. Moreover, We could find someone on Facebook with a high probability by the email addresses extracted from public storage and also the usernames acquired from other apps, since people prefer to use the same username and email address among their various social networking apps [5].

We divided the apps into three categories with privacy protection level from high to low, and shown in Table 3. Apparently, leaking obvious sensitive data should be prohibited and requires immediate actions from the app developers and Android development team. While our study also demonstrates the feasibility to infer obvious sensitive data from non-obvious ones, therefore the latter should also be well protected.

4.2 Investigation on Apps with a Large Scale

Our study on the popular apps indicates that the sensitive information of device owners could be leaked even from very popular apps. To understand the scale of this problem, we launched a large-scale study on more apps through a customized static analysis tool. Specifically, we first decompile app's apk to `smali` code using Apktool [2] and then search for APIs or strings which indicate storing private data to public storage. Our analysis is conducted on `smali` code instead of decompiled Java code (done by [8,10]) since information could be lost during the code transformation of latter approach. Dynamic analysis, though usually producing more accurate results, is not used here, because it takes long time for even one app to reach proper states (e.g., registration, sending messages, etc.). Again, we focus on the categories described in Table 1 and totally select 1648 different apps from our app repository (34369 apps) for analysis.

Ultimately, our tool should be able to classify the information kept on public storage as sensitive or not, which turns out to be very challenging or nearly impossible without intensive efforts from human. Whether a piece of data is truly sensitive to the device owner depends on the context. We therefore simplifies this task and only checks whether an app **intends** to store sensitive information on public storage. Particularly, if the names of the private folders or files on public storage created by an app contain specific keywords, it is considered as suspicious. Our keywords list include `log`, `files`, `file`, `temp`, `tmp`, `account`, `meta`, `uid`, `history`, `tmfs`, `cookie`, `token`, `profile`, `cache`, `data`, and etc., which are learned from the problematic apps and are usually associated with sensitive content. Some keywords (e.g., `cache` and `data`) appear to be unrelated to sensitive information, but they turn out to be good indicators based on our study, as shown in Appendix A.

For each app, we build a control flow graph (CFG) based on its `smali` code to confirm whether the "*sensitive*" data is truly written to public storage. We demonstrate our approach as follows: we start from extracting the method block in `smali` code by finding the texts between keywords *.method* and *.end method*. Next, we select instructions beginning with keywords *invoke-static*, *invoke-direct*, *invoke-virtual* to construct CFG for the method. Then, we check if the methods listed in Table 4 are used to access public storage and whether files or folders are created there (by inspecting methods like `mkdir` and `FileOutputStream`). Finally, we check whether the strings sent to these methods contain keywords in our list. Each function f in the CFG will be marked based on the three criteria. To notice, we do not consider special methods like `touch` as they are also used for other purposes by developers.

We implemented Algorithm 1 on the marked CFG, the depth parameter of the *DFS* procedure was set as 3 empirically, since it resulted in reasonable resources consumption and also yielded high accuracies when examining the known problematic apps. The results show that 497 apps from the 1648 apps being analyzed intend to write some "*sensitive*" app-private data on public storage, which indicate that the privacy leakage problem revealed in this paper is widely exist among apps. However, this method may lead to false positives when an app stores "*sensitive*" data in other places. To have a verification, we randomly chose 30 apps from the suspicious apps, and manually checked them. We found that as large as 27 apps truly wrote "*sensitive*" app-private data on public

Table 4. Methods of accessing public storage

Category	Methods
API Call	*getExternalFilesDir(), getExternalFilesDirs()* *getExternalCacheDir(), getExternalCacheDirs()* *getExternalStorageDirectory(), getExternalStoragePublicDirectory()*
Hardcoded Path	*"/sdcard"*, *"/sdcard0"*, *"/sdcard1"*

storage, suggesting this simple static method is valid. This result also suggests there are common patterns among app developers on dealing with sensitive data.

5   Inferring User's location

In this section, we present an example attack based on the non-obvious sensitive information extracted from app-private data. We begin with a brief introduction to the design of a malicious Android app called SAPD ("Smuggle App-Private Data"), followed by detailed description of the attack.

5.1   Attack Preparation

The weakest part of the malicious app might be the potential outstanding network traffic footprint, especially for users with limited 3G plan. We implemented two optimizations in our app prototype SAPD to get around this limitation. First, try to minimize the uploaded data since it is reasonable to assume that attackers have already studied the vulnerable apps. Another optimization is to upload data only when Wi-Fi network is available. Instead of using `WiFiManager` which needs to require `ACCESS_WIFI_STATE` permission, SAPD is able to know whether a WiFi network is connected or not by reading public files (*procfs*), since Android puts the parameters of ARP in the file `/proc/net/arp` and other wireless activities in `/proc/net/wireless`. In addition, to minimize the possibilities of being caught due to suspicious CPU usage or abnormal battery consumptions, SAPD will only reads and uploads filtered useful data, and it will never perform any kind of intensive computations.

5.2   Attack Framework

Location of a phone user is considered as sensitive from the very beginning and there are already a lot of research works on inference attacks and also protections [15–17]. In recent years, location-based social discovery (LBSD) is becoming popular and widely adopted by mobile apps, i.e., `WeChat` and `Momo` investigated in this paper. Though apps adopt some protection mechanisms, i.e., only distance between the user and the viewer is revealed, such location inference attacks are still feasible. Our attack also aims to infer user's location from LBSD networks, but we make improvements since the profile information is extracted from victim's phone, thus leads to a realistic threat. As a showcase, we demonstrate our attack on `WeChat` app.

Algorithm 1. Detecting suspicious apps

Input: $Class\_set\ C,\ Keyword\_Patterns\_set\ KS,\ Path\_set\ PA,\ Write\_set\ WA$
Output: $bool\ sensitive$
1: **for** $class\ c\ in\ C$ **do**
2:     **for** $function\ f\ in\ c$ **do**   ▷ *Each f has been marked following the rules*
3:         $condition.clear()$;
4:         $DFS(f,\ depth)$;
5:         **if** $condition == Union(KS,\ PA,\ WA)$ **then**   ▷ *All the criteria are met*
6:             **return** $true$;   ▷ *Marked as suspicious app*
7:         **end if**
8:     **end for**
9: **end for**
10: **return** $false$;
11:
12: **procedure** $DFS(function\ f, int\ depth)$
13:     **if** $depth == 0$ **then**
14:         $return$;
15:     **end if**
16:     **for** $all\ element\ e\ in\ f.mark$ **do**
17:         $condition(e) = true$;
18:     **end for**
19:     **for** $all\ callee\ ce\ of\ f$ **do**
20:         $DFS(ce,\ depth - 1)$;
21:     **end for**
22: **end procedure**

The LBSD module in WeChat is called "People Nearby", through which, the user can view information of other users within a certain distance, including nick name, profile photo, posts (called *What's Up*), region (city-level) and gender. Though WeChat UID is not stored on public storage, QQ UID and phone number are stored instead, they are bound to WeChat account and has to be unique for each user. As described in section 4.1, this information has been collected by SAPD and sent to one of our servers (denoted as S_1). These servers are installed with emulated Android environment for running WeChat app. S_1 will first create a database by querying the server of Tencent (the company operating WeChat) for profile information. Then, the attacker needs to instruct another server (denoted as S_2) to run WeChat using fake geolocations, to check People Nearby and to download all the profile information and their corresponding distances. The profile information stored on S_1 is then compared with the grabbed profile information (downloaded by S_2) in another server (denoted as S_3) followed the steps shown in Fig. 2. If a match happens, S_2 will continue to query People Nearby for two more times using different geolocations (faked) to get two new distances. Finally, the target's location can be calculated using the three point positioning method. We elaborate the details of two key steps as below:

Getting Users' Profile Information. The attacker uses QQ userid or phone number to query Tencent server for user's profile information. The returned profile consists of 5 fields: nick name, profile photo, posts (*What's Up*), region and

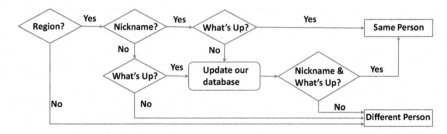

Fig. 2. The diagram of profile information comparison

gender. Our task is to assign the location information for each profile. Unfortunately, this profile is updated according to the user's location. What we do here is to frequently retrieve profiles and distances information by faking to different locations. A challenge here is to extract the profiles and distances from WeChat, as there is no interface exposed from WeChat to export this information. After we decompile its code, we found the app invokes an Android API setText from android.widget.TextView to render the text on screen whenever a profile is viewed. We therefore instrument this API and dump all the texts related to profiles into log files. This helps us to extract three fields of a profile, including *Region, Nickname and What's Up* and also its corresponding distance.

Comparing Process. The comparison processes performed in S_3 are shown in Fig. 2, which is based on such an observation: People can be distinguished from each other by the three fields (*Region, Nickname and What's Up*). Note that we ignore the special case that different people have the same values of the three fields, since such a possibility is very low due to we require that any of the three fields should not be blank. To avoid the situation that people may have changed her *Nickname* or *What's Up* information before our comparison, we will update her profile by querying Tencent server if only one of them is matched with the data stored in our database.

An app called "Fake GPS location" [3] is leveraged to fake server's GPS to different places. For the densely populated places, we added several more anchor points, since People Nearby only display limited amount of users (about 100). In addition, we use a monkeyrunner script to automatically refresh People Nearby. For each point, to load all the people's profile information, the script will scan people's profile one-by-one through triggering event KEYCODE_DPAD_DOWN until loading the last one's information. This process has to request data from Tencent. To avoid raising alarm from Tencent, the script sleeps a while before changing to a new anchor point.

Attack Evaluation. We evaluate our attack on 20 participants. Each participant has installed *WeChat* with People Nearby turned on (so their profiles will be open to view). Our attack successfully revealed the live locations for 17 participants and have been verified by them. Note that some of the inferred locations are not exact where the user stays, but they are all within the acceptable range, i.e., in a specific residential district.

6   Mitigations

We demonstrate the feasibility of our attacks through the examples above. Without probable countermeasures, more devastating consequences would be caused. Hence, we suggest two approaches enforced by app developers and Android system. The details are described below:

Fixing by App Developers. The first suggestion is to ask developers to write *ALL* app-private data to internal storage, which can only be accessed by the folder owner. Though the threat is mitigated, app's functionality could be interrupted when running on devices with limited capacity of internal storage. Moreover, millions of developers are expected to make such change and it is hard to be achieved in the near future.

Patching Android System. On the contrary, modifying the Android system and pushing the upgrades to users' devices would be a more practical way to mitigate the security issues. For this purpose, we propose to augment the existing security framework on public storage by instrumenting the API `checkPermission()`, the framework is described as below:

Architecture. We design a new module named *ownership checker*, which works on Android Middleware layer and can achieve mandatory access control (MAC) for app-private data. Specifically, when the targets are public resources, like music directory, the access is permitted. When the target files are placed under app's private folder, the access is only permitted when the calling app matches the owner. Otherwise, *ownership checker* will return `PERMISSION_DENIED` even if the app has been granted `READ` or `WRITE` permission. To enforce such rule, we create a system file owner_checker.xml storing the mapping between apps and resources, similar to Access Control Lists (ACL) of Ext4 file system. The system code within `checkPermission()` is modified to read the mapping and check the ownership before actual file operations happen. An exception will be thrown if mismatch happens. Alternatively, we could leverage other frameworks like SEAndroid [6] to enforce MAC and protect app-private data.

Ownership Inference. The ownership mappings between apps and resources need to be established. This task turns out be non-trivial, since we have to deal with the case that the public storage has already stored apps' data before our module is installed and the owner of data is not tracked therefore. To fix the missing links, we exploit the naming convention: an app usually saves data to a folder whose name is similar to its package name, which can be acquired from packages.xml under `/data/system`). As a starting point, we initialize the mappings by scanning all the resources. For a given resource, we assign the owner app if the resource location and app package name share a non-trivial portion. To notice, this initialization step could not construct the mapping when an app stores the data in a folder whose name is irrelevant. The access to such resources will be blocked, and we provide an interface for users to manage the ownerships. A new mapping will be added if the ownership is assigned by the user.

To reduce hassles to users, user-driven access control model [13] can be integrated to automatically assign ownership based on user's actions.

7 Discussion

Why does the Problem Persist? In the early stage, Android phone has limited on-board Flash memory (only 256MB for the first android phone, HTC Dream). On the other hand, its storage can be expanded through large volume external SD card, which is usually shipped together. This storage model forces app developers to differentiate sensitive data from non-sensitive data and save the latter (most of the data) to public storage. App developers follow this practice even after recent changes on Android's storage model which offers more flexible storage options (i.e., the sdcard dameon (fused) and userdata */data* share the same partition dynamically).

Limitations of App Study. We built a tool running static analysis on app's `smali` code and use a set of heuristics to determine if the app saves "sensitive" app-private data to unprotected public storage. This simple tool identifies a large number of potentially vulnerable apps and shows reasonable accuracy from our sampling result. However, it is inevitably suffers from false negatives (e.g., the file name does not contain the keywords we used) and false positives (e.g., the information saved is not sensitive). We leave the task of building a more accurate detector as future work.

8 Related Work

Attacks like stealing users' chat history [7] have been proved feasible in the real world. However, these attacks usually depend on certain vulnerabilities identified from the victim apps, while our attacks exploit a more general problem related to Android's storage model. In addition to steal user's sensitive information directly, a lot of research focused on inferring user's location. The authors of [15] showed a set of location traces can be de-anonymized through correlating their contact graph with the graph of a social network in spite of the data has been obfuscated. Based on a large-scale data set of call records, Zang et al. [16] proposed an approach to infer the "top N" locations for each user. A recent work [17] by Zhou et al. targeted to infer information of users from more perspectives, including identities, locations and health information.

To defend against the existing or potential attacks tampering user's privacy, a bunch of defense mechanisms have been proposed. Ongtang et al. proposed a finer-grained access control model (named Saint) over installed apps [12]. FireDroid [14], proposed by Russello et. al., was a policy-based framework for enforcing security policies on Android. Roesner et al. proposed user-driven access control to manage the access to private resources while minimizing user's actions [13]. Besides, efforts have also been paid on code analysis to block the information leakage. Enck et al. developed TaintDroid [9] to prevent users' private data from being abused by third party apps.

9   Conclusion

It is known that public storage on Android is insecure, due to its coarse-grained access model. Therefore, it is highly recommended that the sensitive data should be avoided from saving there. In this paper, we carry out a large-scale study on existing apps on whether app developers follow this rule and the result turns out to be glooming: a significant number of apps save sensitive data into the insecure storage, some of the problematic apps are even ranked top in Android market. By exploiting these leaked data, it is possible to infer a lot of information about the users, drastically violating users' privacy. We urge app developers to fix the vulnerabilities. Besides, we also propose an approach to patch Android system with MAC support and envision it could mitigate the threat in the short term.

Acknowledgments. We would like to thank the anonymous reviewers for their valuable comments. This work was supported by the Direct Grant of The Chinese University of Hong Kong with project number C001-4055006.

A   The Details of User Private Data

Viber. The text file *.userdata* in *.../.viber/* [3] reveals lots of user's information, including real name, phone number, and the path of user's profile photo.

WhatsApp. The user's profile photo is stored in *.../.shared/* with file name *tmpt*. The profile photos of user's friends are saved under *.../Profile pictures/*, and they are named by profile owners' phone numbers without any obfuscation.

Linkedin. This app cache the photos into the directory */Android/-data/.../li_images/*. The user's profile photo can be distinguished by file size and modified time.

KakaoTalk. If user A has chatted with user B, the app will create a content folder with the same name in both users' phones, under the path */Android/-data/.../contents/*. The files, i.e., photos, on the two phones also have the same name, size and the same path.

Tencent QQ. User's account can be got from log files in the path *.../mobileqq/*.

Weibo. A file named as user's UID is saved under the path *.../page*, and we can acquire the user's username and her email address. User's username and UID can be leveraged to access her homepage by constructing specific URLs, i.e., *http://www.weibo.com/UID*.

Alipay. User's phone number can be obtained from the *_meta* file in *.../cache/*, it also points out the other file which discloses the user's phone number.

Renren. A folder named by user' UID is stored in */Android/data/.../cache/*. Even user' visit histories are also stored in this folder, which contains the name, UID of user's friends. The audio files are named as the format *UID+hash value*. We can find the user's personal home page by the URL *http://www.renren.com/UID* in a browser.

---

[3] We use ... to represent part of the full path since sometimes the full path is too long.

Momo. A folder named as user's account is saved in *.../users/*. By the account, we can not only get her profile information, but also infer her location.

EasyChat. The file *pjsip_log.txt* in */Yixin/log/* contains all the call records information.

Audio files. Instant message apps, like WhatsApp, Line, WeChat, Tencent QQ, and KakaoTalk, store the audio files into public storage without encryption.

References

1. Android apps on google play. http://www.appbrain.com/stats/number-of-android-apps
2. Apktool. http://code.google.com/p/android-apktool/
3. Fake gps location. https://play.google.com/store/apps/details?id=com.lexa.fakegps
4. Filesystem in userspace. http://fuse.sourceforge.net/
5. like it or not, sharing tools spur privacy concerns. http://usatoday30.usatoday.com/tech/news/2011-07-05-social-media-privacy-concerns_n.htm
6. Seandroid. http://seandroid.bitbucket.org/
7. Whatsapp user chats on android liable to theft due to file system flaw. http://www.theguardian.com/technology/2014/mar/12/whatsapp-android-users-chats-theft
8. Au, K.W.Y., Zhou, Y.F., Huang, Z., Lie, D.: Pscout: analyzing the android permission specification. In: Proceedings of the 2012 ACM Conference on Computer and Communications Security, pp. 217–228. ACM (2012)
9. Enck, W., Gilbert, P., Chun, B.-G., Cox, L.P., Jung, J., McDaniel, P., Sheth, A.: Taintdroid: An information-flow tracking system for realtime privacy monitoring on smartphones. In: OSDI, vol. 10, pp. 1–6 (2010)
10. Gibler, C., Crussell, J., Erickson, J., Chen, H.: AndroidLeaks: automatically detecting potential privacy leaks in android applications on a large scale (2012)
11. McCallister, E.: Guide to protecting the confidentiality of personally identifiable information. Diane Publishing (2010)
12. Ongtang, M., McLaughlin, S., Enck, W., McDaniel, P.: Semantically rich application-centric security in android. Security and Communication Networks 5(6), 658–673 (2012)
13. Roesner, F., Kohno, T., Moshchuk, A., Parno, B., Wang, H.J., Cowan, C.: User-driven access control: Rethinking permission granting in modern operating systems. In: 2012 IEEE Symposium on Security and Privacy (SP) (2012)
14. Russello, G., et al.: Firedroid: hardening security in almost-stock android. In: Proceedings of the 29th Annual Computer Security Applications Conference, pp. 319–328. ACM (2013)
15. Srivatsa, M., Hicks, M.: Deanonymizing mobility traces: Using social network as a side-channel. In: Proceedings of the 2012 ACM Conference on Computer and Communications Security, pp. 628–637. ACM (2012)
16. Zang, H., Bolot, J.: Anonymization of location data does not work: A large-scale measurement study. In: Proceedings of the 17th Annual International Conference on Mobile Computing and Networking (MobiCom), pp. 145–156. ACM (2011)
17. Zhou, X., Demetriou, S., et al.: Identity, location, disease and more: Inferring your secrets from android public resources. In: Proceedings of the 2013 ACM SIGSAC Conference on Computer & Communications Security, pp. 1017–1028. ACM (2013)

The Dual-Execution-Environment Approach: Analysis and Comparative Evaluation

Mohamed Sabt[1,2]([✉]), Mohammed Achemlal[1,3], and Abdelmadjid Bouabdallah[2]

[1] Orange Labs, 42 rue des coutures, 14066 Caen, France
{mohamed.sabt,mohammed.achemlal}@orange.com
[2] Heudiasyc, Centre de recherche Royallieu, Sorbonne universités,
Université de technologie de Compiègne, 60203 Compiègne, France
{madjid.bouabdallah,mohamed.sabt}@hds.utc.fr
[3] Greyc ENSICAEN, 6 Bd Maréchal Juin, 14050 Caen, France

Abstract. The dual-execution-environment approach (dual-EE) is a trusted model that was defined to allow mobile smart devices to guarantee tamper-resistant execution for highly sensitive applications. Although various solutions implementing dual-EE have been proposed in the literature, this model has not been formalized yet. In this paper, we revisit the dual-EE approach and propose a theoretical framework to systematize the design of dual-EE solutions regarding well-established primitives defined in the Multiple Independent Levels of Security (MILS) architecture. We provide a general classification of the different dual-EE proposals based on their isolation properties. We introduce a comparative framework allowing dual-EE solutions to be evaluated across a common set of criteria. The relevance of our framework is examined by applying it on three technologies, each one represents one category in our classification. Results are consistent and explain some hidden and unexpected properties of each technology. For instance, we find that bare-metal hypervisors are ill-adapted to provide high assurance security even though they might improve the overall security level of the system.

Keywords: Trusted computing · Separation kernel · MILS · TrustZone

1 Introduction

The wide use of modern mobile devices spurs service providers to propose access to their services via smart devices. The growing number of attacks against such devices puts mobile applications under potential security risks. Thus, smart devices are not ideal for services requiring trusted platforms with proved security. Examples include enterprise applications and NFC-based payment solutions. Indeed, the adoption of mobile devices in sensitive business environments has been hindered by the lack of appropriate level of security.

Sensitive-service providers require that their applications run on tamper-resistant execution environment. Such an environment should at least guarantee

© IFIP International Federation for Information Processing 2015
H. Federrath and D. Gollmann (Eds.): SEC 2015, IFIP AICT 455, pp. 557–570, 2015.
DOI: 10.1007/978-3-319-18467-8_37

the following three properties [23]: (1) *authenticity*: the code under execution should not have been changed; (2) *integrity*: runtime states (e.g. CPU registers, memory and sensitive I/O) should not have been tampered with; and (3) *privacy*: code, data and runtime states should not be observable by unauthorized applications or even underlying OS that might have been compromised.

The default protection mechanisms of smart devices are insufficient to provide tamper-resistant environment. This is due to the fact that these protection mechanisms are mainly based on the operating system, and thus as long as the operating system has not been compromised, sensitive applications are considered as protected. Unfortunately, despite continued efforts to improve the security of operating systems of smart devices [9,20], they are still essentially untrustworthy for two reasons. First, they are complex and often developed using unsafe languages. Therefore, they are inherently error prone because design flaws and implementation bugs are unavoidable. Second, they allow poor isolation among applications. Indeed, a process with the root privilege can easily access private data and tamper with the execution of other processes. Meanwhile, using specially tailored operating systems can only have very limited success due to their restricted features and compatibility to existing applications.

To remedy this situation, there have been numerous efforts aimed at providing tamper-resistant execution environments. Generally, those efforts can be classified into three categories. First, architectural enhancements based approach, such as XOMOS [19] and AEGIS [24], allows sensitive applications to run on untrustworthy operating system. This approach requires nontrivial modifications to the core processor architecture. Second, micro-kernel based approach, such as SeL4 [16], tries to reduce the trusted computer base (TCB) by running a limited code in the privileged mode. This approach requires a redesign of operating systems, thereby requiring nontrivial modifications to port existing applications. Third, the dual-execution-environment approach (dual-EE), such as TLR [22], solves the problem by multiplexing the feature-rich OS and a specialized OS with restricted functionalities on the same smart device. It relies on the specialized OS to provide tamper-resistant capabilities. Applications that demand tamper-resistant protection run only on the specialized trustworthy OS.

Compared to other approaches, the dual-EE is considered as a promising approach intended for practical use [10]. The literature is full of proposals [2, 10,13,17,27]. However, proposals differ substantially from each other in their design objectives. Some address very specific environments, while others silently seek generic solutions that fit all environments. Too often, authors claim the superiority of their solutions and their assertion is based on self-defined criteria. To make progress, we believe that knowledge regarding the dual-EE approach must be systematized. There is a need to provide a theoretical framework which defines how best to evaluate dual-EE proposals.

In this paper, we analyze the dual-EE approach in the context of the trusted computing domain and the MILS architecture. We propose a standard benchmark and framework allowing dual-EE solutions to be rated across a common, broad spectrum of criteria. Our work provides insights which prove useful in designing more efficient dual-EE schemes. To the best of our knowledge, this is the first comparative evaluation of the dual-EE solutions available on mobile smart devices. Moreover, we believe that our comparative framework is extendable and sufficiently general to be used to evaluate more fine-grained classifications.

Summary of Contributions: We make the following contributions:

- We construct a compact security model of the dual-EE approach using the *separation kernel* model that provides a relevant abstraction level, thereby contributing to a deeper understanding of the dual-EE approach. We reinterpret well-known security technologies, such as UICC card and TrustZone, in the light of this model.
- We provide a framework to evaluate the dual-EE solutions. Our criteria are divided into three categories: (1) *functional criteria*: schemes are evaluated whether they implement all the requirements of a tamper-resistant environment; (2) *security criteria*: the properties of the separation kernel layer of the scheme are analyzed; and (3) *deployability criteria*: schemes are evaluated whether they could be easily deployed in a real context.
- We provide a classification of the different dual-EE solutions. Nevertheless, our goal is not to provide a comprehensive survey, but to show the relevance and the interest of our abstraction by providing a general classification on which our comparative framework could be applied.

This paper is structured as follows: Section 2 gives a background information on the MILS architecture. In Section 3, we give a general classification of the dual-EE solutions. Section 4 explains our comparison methodology and thoroughly defines our chosen set of criteria. We apply our comparative framework to our classification in Section 5. The resulted comparative evaluation is discussed in Section 6. Section 7 surveys related work, and we end with a brief summary.

2   Background

Building a secure system has traditionally been a cat and mouse game. No sooner are new security mechanisms integrated into systems than hackers find how to bypass them. Research on trusted computing aims to replace this endless game with a methodical process. The domain of trusted computing provides the abstract concepts as well as the theoretical base on which *ideal secure systems* are built [11]. It introduces various security models, called *trusted models*. Each trusted model defines a set of security objectives, a threat model, and security requirements to be satisfied by the component that enforces the security policy. In this paper, we focus on the 'separation kernel' trusted model introduced by John Rushby [21], or more precisely, on MILS [25].

MILS stands for Multiple Independent Levels of Security. This architecture was developed in order to resolve the difficulty to evaluate the assurance level of the widely deployed trusted model 'reference monitor' [18] because of its

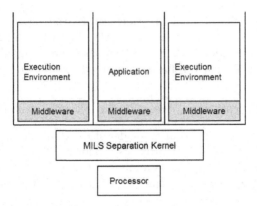

Fig. 1. An Overview of the MILS Architecture

continually growing complexity. MILS adopts a divide-and-conquer approach. It separates a complex system that includes various modules requiring different levels of security into smaller, hence verifiable components. Thus, instead of evaluating the whole complex system, these small components are individually evaluated. An abstract view of the MILS architecture is depicted in figure 1. The primary component of MILS is the separation kernel layer (SK). This layer is responsible for creating a set of isolated functional units called *partitions*. All communication between partitions is monitored by the SK layer. MILS is based on separation technology and secure inter-partition communication.

In order to work properly, the SK layer must satisfy several requirements. The SK should be designed so that it cannot be modified or disabled by rogue partitions. In addition, all inter-partition communication requests must go through it. Furthermore, it must be well-structured and small enough, so that its correctness can be validated. In other words, the SK must be (1) tamper-proof, (2) always invoked, and (3) evaluable. These properties correspond respectively to the three principles: isolation, completeness and verifiability.

The dual-EE approach can be seen as a particular case of the MILS architecture where the separation kernel creates two partitions only. The next section provides more details.

3   Dual-EE Solutions

There is an increasing need to use smart mobile devices for applications requiring high security levels, such as enterprise and payment applications. However, their openness and complexity impose fundamental limitations on the security which these devices are able to provide. The dual-EE approach attempts to resolve these limitations by providing trust and high-assurance security while keeping the rich model of smart devices. It brings the best properties of open and trusted systems to smart devices without any compromise. It partitions the system into two execution environments running side-by-side: general-purpose execution environment (GPEE), and secure execution environment (SEE).The

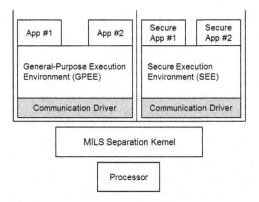

Fig. 2. Representation of the Dual-EE Approach in the MILS Abstraction

GPEE runs the legacy, complex operating system, while the SEE runs a special trusted OS with a selection of applications designed specifically for it. The SEE is designed to be trustworthy to provide tamper-resistant capabilities.

Secure isolation is essential for the dual-EE approach. Generally, the security of a system is reduced to that of its most vulnerable component. In dual-EE, the security level is, by definition, supposed to be that of the GPEE. However, the two execution environments are *strongly isolated* so that the compromise of the GPEE does not impact the SEE. Figure 2 depicts the representation of the dual-EE approach in the MILS architecture. In this paper, we consider MILS as the abstract trusted model of the dual-EE approach in which only two partitions exist and the strong isolation is guaranteed by the SK layer. The main advantage of this representation is to use MILS properties as primitives to better understand and thoroughly analyze the dual-EE approach. For instance, MILS defines a set of design principles for the SK layer. These principles provide an abstract model to define the isolation properties required between the two execution environments. We discuss these principles in the next section.

According to their isolation technology, we classify the dual-EE solutions into three categories:

1. **Isolation based on external hardware module:** this category consists in introducing an additional secure coprocessor or integrated circuit to smart devices. A secure coprocessor is a hardware module containing CPU, bootstrap ROM, and secure non-volatile memory. This hardware module is physically shielded from illegal access, and the I/O interface to the module is the only way to access its internal states. Hardware modules cannot only store cryptographic keys without risk of release, but also they can perform arbitrary computations using their CPU. In dual-EE, the SEE runs inside the secure coprocessor. Tamper-resistant execution is guaranteed, since the GPEE and the SEE run on physically two separated memories. Popular examples are UICC card and baseband processor;

2. **Isolation based on bare-metal hypervisor:** this category consists in executing a hypervisor in the most privilege mode of the processor. A *hypervisor*

is a software layer that implements the same instruction-set architecture as the hardware on which it is executed. Thus, it allows multiple operating systems to coexist on the same hardware. Full-virtualization is not possible on ARM processors, which represents 95% of the market of smart devices [1], since ARM is not a virtualizable architecture [7]. ARM introduced hardware virtualization support with the ARMv7 architecture. However, the use of hardware-supported virtualization on ARM is still limited. Instead, para-virtualization approach is prevalent and a myriad of solutions exists [15]. In para-virtualization, OS needs to be modified in order to run on the underlying hypervisor. In dual-EE, the hypervisor plays the role of the SK layer, and the number of virtual machines is limited to two;

3. **Isolation based on special processor extensions:** this category consists in enhancing general-purpose processors with new hardware extensions. These newly-introduced extensions allow the execution of secure code within a potentially compromised OS. The most prevalent secure extensions targeting smart devices is ARM TrustZone [4]. In this paper, we only consider ARM TrustZone because, to the best of our knowledge, it is the most deployed security extensions in practice. A processor with TrustZone extensions provides a special form of virtualization. It enables two virtual processors with two security domains: the "secure" zone and the "normal" zone. In dual-EE, the GPEE resides in the normal zone and the SEE resides in the secure zone. The isolation of both zones or "worlds" is implemented by a complex mechanism using hardware controllers, a configuration bit and a new execution mode called *monitor mode*.

4   Comparison Methodology

In order to evaluate dual-EE solutions, we define three categories of criteria: functional, security and deployability.

4.1   Functional Criteria

Schemes are evaluated whether they implement all the requirements of a tamper-resistant environment. The SEE should provide the following features [12]:

- *Protected Execution.* The execution of secure applications should be protected from any interference caused by malicious software. Runtime states of the SEE should be protected from being observed or tampered with.
- *Sealed Storage.* The integrity, secrecy and freshness of secure applications' content should be protected. Content includes code as well as data.
- *Protected Input.* The SEE should protect their input data from being sniffed or tampered with by malicious applications, such as key loggers.
- *Protected Output.* The integrity and the confidentiality of the output data are protected. Protected input and output do not only concern user interface.
- *Attestation.* The SEE should provide mechanisms allowing secure applications to authenticate themselves to remote trusted parties.

4.2 Security Criteria

In dual-EE, isolation–an essential task to implement–is provided by the SK layer. Schemes are evaluated whether the design principles of the SK layer [3] are implemented in software or hardware in order to ensure:

- *Data Separation.* Data within one partition, namely execution environment, cannot be read or modified by other partitions.
- *Information Flow Control.* Communication between partitions cannot occur unless explicitly permitted by the SK layer.
- *Sanitization.* Shared resources cannot be used to leak information into other partitions.
- *Damage Limitation.* Security breach in one partition cannot spread to other partitions.

4.3 Deployability Criteria

The dual-EE approach is intended to be implemented in a real context. Thus, we evaluate how easy schemes can be deployed. Deployability criteria are numerous. In our study, we only consider the following properties:

- *Support of Legacy Systems.* We evaluate the amount of modifications needed for the GPEE to run on the underlying SK layer. Ideally, no modification, except for the inter-EE communication driver, is required.
- *Cost.* The addition of any software architecture has a cost. We only evaluate the extra silicon cost that the scheme generates. For instance, the addition of hardware module or internal processor extensions are factors which make schemes costly.
- *Overhead.* Schemes should have minimal impact on applications that do not require tamper-resistant protection. They should not incur too much overhead to the SEE either.
- *SEE Performance.* We evaluate how fast the SEE could execute complex operations.

Throughout the paper, for brevity and consistency, each criterion is referred to with an italicized mnemonic title. In our study, we will rate each solution based on its capability to offer the criteria described above. We emphasize that it would be naive to rank dual-EE solutions simply by counting how many criteria each satisfies. Some criteria clearly deserve more weight than others. In this paper, we do not suggest any weights, since providing appropriate weights depend strongly on the specific goal for which the dual-EE solutions are being compared.

5 Comparative Evaluation

We now use our criteria to evaluate three different solutions of the dual-EE approach. Due to space constraints, we only explain one particular solution for each category. We emphasize that, in selecting a particular solution, we do not necessarily endorse it as better than alternatives–merely that it is reasonably representative, or illuminates in some way what the category can achieve.

5.1   External Hardware Module: Smart Card

A smart card is essentially a minimal computing environment composed of a CPU, ROM, EEPROM, RAM, and I/O port. It is capable of running applications (called applets or cardlets) with a high level of security. In smart devices, smart cards come in several flavors. They could be implemented either by an embedded smart card chip, in an SD card that could be inserted in the device, or in the SIM/UICC which is used by mobile operators to authenticate subscribers to their network. In most cases, the SEE consists of Java Card OS, and the GPEE can be any commodity operating system.

Smart cards physically shield the SEE from all types of software attacks coming from the GPEE. Thus, no interference is possible during the execution of secure applications. Moreover, tamper-resistant hardware prevents protected data from being extracted by hardware attacks like microprobing and fault generation. To sum up, smart cards provide *protected execution* and *sealed storage*. *Attestation* is guaranteed, since only authenticated code can run in the SEE. However, smart cards fail to provide *protected input* and *protected output*. In practice, smart cards are designed in a way that there is no direct communication link with the I/O devices. Smart cards, for instance, cannot control user interface to allow users to securely enter their PIN code.

Regarding the SK layer, it is almost implemented in hardware. Both execution environments, namely the GPEE and the SEE, run in two different CPU with their own memory and I/O devices. As a result, the software part of the SK layer does not need to take care of either *data separation* or *sanitization*. However, *damage limitation* depends on how well the inter-EE communication is controlled. The *information flow control* is implemented in the SEE. In fact, the SEE includes the SK part which is responsible for protecting the SEE from accidental or malicious communication attempts that violate the system policy.

For reasons of silicon *cost*, smart cards are often made with limited resources. An additional CPU increases the power consumption and the global cost of the device. Cost and power consumption constraints lead to design smart cards with limited processing power, slow processing speed and small permanent and temporary memory [27]. Therefore, secure applications have low *performance* and cannot perform complex computations. Clearly, smart cards support *legacy systems* and incurs no *overhead* to the SEE.

5.2   Bare-Metal Hypervisor: KVM/ARM

KVM/ARM is *the* ARM hypervisor in the mainline Linux kernel [7]. It is the first hypervisor to leverage ARM hardware virtualization support to run unmodified operating systems on ARM hardware. It builds on KVM and leverages existing infrastructure in the Linux kernel. KVM/ARM is a hosted bare-metal hypervisor, where the hypervisor is integrated with a host kernel. It runs the hypervisor in normal privileged CPU modes to leverage existing OS mechanisms without modification, while at the same time leveraging ARM hardware virtualization. In contrast to standalone bare-metal hypervisors (e.g. Xen), it supports a wide range of ARM devices despite the fact that there is no standard hardware in the ARM world. In dual-EE, the two execution environments (GPEE and SEE) are two virtual machines running on the underlying hypervisor.

Hypervisors provide isolation properties to prevent potentially malicious VM (GPEE) from attacking another VM (SEE). However, hypervisors only defend against software-based attacks and do not take hardware attacks into account. This isolation property works fine for data centers, but the threat model of mobile smart devices includes hardware attacks. We illustrate the threat by two examples. First, an attacker with physical access to the system can read any data present in memory using the cold boot attack [14]. This attack is based on the fact that RAMs retain their contents for several seconds after power is lost. Second, an attacker with access to the system disk can run a modified version of KVM/ARM that integrates malicious introspection mechanisms to snoop on the runtime states of the SEE. The KVM/ARM hypervisor provides *protected execution*, but not *sealed storage* because encryption keys can be retrieved using, for instance, the cold boot attack. Furthermore, it defines several mechanisms to provide I/O virtualization and interrupt virtualization. Thus, it provides *protected input* and *protected output*. The KVM/ARM alone does not provide *attestation*; trust anchors, such as TPM, are required. It is worth noting that any person who has physical access to the smart device can easily clone the SEE and capture its internal states. This might result in serious attacks, such as rolling back security updates, thus leaving the system vulnerable.

Regarding the SK layer, it is *entirely implemented in software*. All of its design principles are performed by the KVM/ARM hypervisor. Therefore, the hypervisor must be tamper-resistant and evaluable. To the best of our knowledge, KVM/ARM is the smallest bare-metal hypervisor. It is comprised of only 12,883 lines of code. However, it is still too big to be formally verified.

For KVM/ARM, platforms with hardware virtualization capabilities are required. Hardware-based virtualization is not supported on all platforms. Therefore, it presents an additional *cost* to the system. The fact that KVM/ARM leverages hardware virtualization support presents two advantages. First, it can run *legacy systems*, unlike hypervisors based on para-virtualization. Second, the incurred overhead is minimal in comparison with other virtualization solutions. For example, it uses Stage-2 translations to achieve low I/O performance overhead with very little implementation effort. However, KVM/ARM still generates within 10% of *overhead* over a multicore. In some contexts of smart devices, 10% of overhead is not negligible.

5.3 Special Processor Extensions: TrustZone

ARM TrustZone technology can be seen as a special kind of virtualization with hardware support for memory, I/O and interrupt virtualization [4]. This virtualization enables ARM core to provide an abstraction of two virtual cores (VCPUs): secure VCPU and non-secure VCPU. The monitor is seen as a minimal hypervisor whose main role is the control of information flow between the two virtual cores. In dual-EE, the SEE runs on the secure VCPU, while the

GPEE runs on the non-secure VCPU. It is worth mentioning that ARM Trust-Zone was designed and optimized to implement the dual-EE approach. Indeed, it implements all the hardware extensions defined in [3] and which the SK layer requires in order to work properly.

Similar to bare-metal hypervisor, ARM TrustZone provides *protected execution*, *protected input* and *protected output*, but it does not provide *sealed storage* or *attestation*. However, TrustZone is often completed with additional features, such as secure boot and root of trust (RoT) hardware module, which allow TrustZone to satisfy all the requirements of a tamper-resistant environment.

Regarding the SK layer, it is *mainly implemented in hardware*. The software components to be trusted are minimal, hence *evaluable*. For instance, most CPU registers are banked. Thus, saving and restoring CPU registers are performed by the processor. In addition, TrustZone enables the co-existence of cache entries of both SEE and GPEE. Thus, cleaning the cache memory during a context switch is not required. As a result, the *sanitization* process performed during a context switch is both fast and secure, since it is almost done by the hardware. *Data flow* is well controlled. To enter the secure world, only a well-defined set of interfaces exist. Any transition between the two worlds must go through the monitor mode. This allows the SK layer to satisfy the *completeness* engineering principle.

TrustZone incurs a limited execution *overhead*. The performance is nearly native because both execution environments can access their corresponding resources directly without going through an abstraction layer. Moreover, it can run *legacy systems* without modifications, since each world has its own user and privileged modes, and thereby removing the necessity of instruction emulation. It is true that TrustZone presents an additional *cost* as it requires some modifications to the core processor, but these modifications are already extensively deployed and implemented in a wide range of ARM platforms.

6   Discussion

A summary of our comparative evaluation is presented in table 1. We note that the size of the SK layer is directly proportional to the number of the isolation properties implemented in software [11]. A small SK is better for security because the property of verifiability cannot be satisfied when the SK layer is too complex. Therefore, solutions with many isolation properties provided by hardware are considered *better* than those implementing their SK layer in software.

To our surprise, bare-metal hypervisors achieve the lowest score in our framework. We did not expect this result, since the literature is abundant of solutions presenting hypervisors as a promising approach to improve system security [7,13,15]. In this paper, we showed that this approach inherently suffers from three main shortcomings. First, hypervisors come from the world of data centers, and therefore their threat model does not include stolen devices. Even simple physical attacks, like cold boot attacks, can compromise the privacy requirement of tamper-resistant execution. Second, the isolation properties are entirely implemented in software, thereby negatively impacting the verifiability characteristic

Table 1. Summary of our Comparative Evaluation of Dual-EE Solutions

Comparison Category	Comparison Criteria	*Smart Card*	*KVM*	*TrustZone*
Security Requirements	Protected Execution	√	√	√
	Sealed Storage	√	×	√*
	Protected Input	×	√	√
	Protected Output	×	√	√
	Attestation	√	×	√*
Isolation Properties	Data Separation	HW	SW	HW
	Information Flow Control	SW	SW	HW
	Sanitization	HW	SW	HW/SW
	Damage Limitation	HW	SW	HW
Deployability Criteria	Legacy Systems	√	√	√
	Low Overhead	√	×	√
	Low Cost	×	×	√*
	High Performance	×	√	√

√: satisfies the criterion; ×: does not satisfy the criterion;
√*: needs widely available additional hardware modules to satisfy the criterion;
HW: satisfied by hardware module; **SW:** satisfied by software implementation.

of the SK layer. Third, although dedicating the whole virtualization layer to hosting security tools present numerous advantages, it is not practical because it will deprive the system from using other virtualization capabilities. Furthermore, it is true that hardware-based virtualization solutions produce better overhead and fewer modifications to existing systems compared to para-virtualization solutions. However, they require specific extensions that are not supported on all platforms. For example, the widely-used Qualcomm Snapdragon MSM8974 and APQ8084 processors do not implement the hypervisor extension.

On the contrary, external hardware modules achieve the highest score in terms of security. Our results are expected, as these modules provide a confined execution environment which protects the application's authenticity, integrity and privacy against even sophisticated physical attacks. Nevertheless, external hardware modules do not fit to a certain kind of secure applications that need user interaction and better processing speed.

As for ARM TrustZone, it comes close to perfect score. Our results are consistent and expected because TrustZone implements all the hardware extensions that the SK layer requires in order to work properly. TrustZone provides a balanced trade-off between bare-metal hypervisors and external hardware modules. Indeed, it does not resist against some physical attacks and it requires a part of the SK to be implemented in software [4]. In addition, TrustZone does not provide sealed storage and attestation without additional hardware modules. However, it is more secure than solutions based on bare-metal hypervisors and more flexible than those based on external hardware modules. Our framework shows that TrustZone-based solutions are efficient for real contexts. Once again, our results are consistent with existing work. At present, millions of devices integrate TrustZone-based technologies. Examples are ObC in Lumia phones [17], TIMA/TZ-RKP in Samsung smartphones [6], and <t-base of Trustonic [2].

7 Related Work

The two main research directions that our work targets is trustworthy execution and trusted computing in mobile smart devices. Extensive discussion of trusted computing solutions for mobile devices is found in [5]. Authors in [26] evaluate existing hardware security features available on mobile devices for creating tamper-resistant execution. However, these surveys fail to identify dual-EE as a promising model that brings trusted computing for smart devices.

Earlier works focus solely on a particular dual-EE technology discussing the advantages that it presents compared to other existing technologies. For instance, the case of TrustZone is presented in [27] and that of bare-metal hypervisors is presented in [13]. Too often, authors assert the superiority of their solution without explicitly stating their evaluation criteria. As such, consensus is unlikely as objective comparison between different solutions is not possible.

The closest work to ours is [8], both of which propose a standard benchmark and framework allowing dual-EE solutions to be evaluated across a common set of criteria. Authors in [8] construct their comparative framework on security functions which they define to cover the security risks for enterprise mobile applications. On the other hand, we construct our comparative framework on MILS, a well-known trusted model. The main advantage of using MILS is to provide a deeper comprehension of many hidden properties of the dual-EE approach. In addition, some may argue the impartiality of any framework built on self-cooked criteria, while the relevance and the objectivity of our criteria are guaranteed, since they are based on a thoroughly defined trusted model.

8 Conclusions and Future Work

In this paper, we revisited the dual-EE approach, a model that allows mobile smart devices to guarantee a tamper-resistant execution for highly sensitive applications. We introduced the dual-EE approach in the context of trusted computing. The domain of trusted computing gives us convenient abstract models to better represent the characteristics of the dual-EE approach.

In this paper, we also provided a general classification of the dual-EE solutions defined in the literature. The goal of this classification is not to provide an extensive survey, but to examine our framework by applying it on a representative of each class. Results are consistent with related work and sometimes unexpected. They show that TrustZone provides a balanced compromise to implement the dual-EE approach. They also show that systems requiring the maximum level of security should adopt external hardware modules, while hypervisors are ill-adapted to provide high assurance security even though they might improve the overall security level of the system.

We believe that our work can be easily extended to include other comparison criteria. An interesting aspect is the scheduling techniques present on MILS. In some smart devices, it is necessary that malicious allocation of hardware resources (e.g. CPU time) do not impact the SEE execution. Despite their high importance, temporal constraints are rarely taken into account in dual-EE solutions. Our abstract model forms a theoretical basis that systematizes the design of dual-EE solutions regarding primitives defined in the MILS architecture.

Some might think that dual-EE is nothing but a special case of the multi-EE approach in which an arbitrary number of execution environments runs on the SK layer. However, we prove by induction that the opposite is true: all dual-EE solution can construct a multi-EE architecture. Due to space constraint, we do not include our proof in this paper. Future work will focus on extending our model to include more properties related to the SK layer, a comprehensive evaluation of more dual-EE solutions and formal proofs related to our work.

References

1. ARM Holdings plc. Annual report 2013: Strategic report (2013)
2. Trustonic (2014). https://www.trustonic.com (accessed: January 2, 2015)
3. Alves-Foss, J., Oman, P.W., Taylor, C., Harrison, W.S.: The MILS Architecture for High-Assurance Embedded Systems. International Journal of Embedded Systems **2**(3), 239–247 (2006)
4. ARMLtd. ARM Security Technology - Building a Secure System using TrustZone Technology (2009)
5. Asokan, N., Ekberg, J.E., Kostiainen, K., Rajan, A., Rozas, C., Sadeghi, A.R., Schulz, S., Wachsmann, C.: Mobile Trusted Computing. Proceedings of the IEEE **102**(8), 1189–1206 (2014)
6. Azab, A.M., Ning, P., Shah, J., Chen, Q., Bhutkar, R., Ganesh, G., Ma, J., Shen, W.: Hypervision across worlds: real-time kernel protection from the ARM trustzone secure world. In: Proceedings of the 2014 ACM SIGSAC Conference on Computer and Communications Security, CCS 2014, pp. 90–102. ACM, New York (2014)
7. Dall, C., Nieh, J.: KVM/ARM: The Design and Implementation of the Linux ARM Hypervisor. SIGPLAN Not. **49**(4), 333–348 (2014)
8. El-Serngawy, M.A., Talhi, C.: Securing business data on android smartphones. In: Awan, I., Younas, M., Franch, X., Quer, C. (eds.) MobiWIS 2014. LNCS, vol. 8640, pp. 218–232. Springer, Heidelberg (2014)
9. Enck, W., Ongtang, M., McDaniel, P.: Understanding Android Security. IEEE Security and Privacy **7**(1), 50–57 (2009)
10. Garfinkel, T., Pfaff, B., Chow, J., Rosenblum, M., Boneh, D.: Terra: A Virtual Machine-based Platform for Trusted Computing. SIGOPS Oper. Syst. Rev. **37**(5), 193–206 (2003)
11. Gasser, M.: Building a Secure Computer System. Van Nostrand Reinhold Co., New York (1988)
12. Grawrock, D.: The Intel Safer Computing Initiative: Building Blocks for Trusted Computing. Books by engineers, for engineers. Intel Press (2006)
13. Gudeth, K., Pirretti, M., Hoeper, K., Buskey, R.: Delivering secure applications on commercial mobile devices: the case for bare metal hypervisors. In: Proceedings of the 1st ACM Workshop on Security and Privacy in Smartphones and Mobile Devices, SPSM 2011, pp. 33–38. ACM, New York (2011)

14. Halderman, J.A., Schoen, S.D., Heninger, N., Clarkson, W., Paul, W., Calandrino, J.A., Feldman, A.J., Appelbaum, J., Felten, E.W.: Lest We Remember: Cold-boot Attacks on Encryption Keys. Commun. ACM **52**(5), 91–98 (2009)
15. Hwang, J.-Y., Suh, S.-B., Heo, S.-K., Park, C.-J., Ryu, J.-M., Park, S.-Y., Kim, C.-R., Xen, A.R.M.: System virtualization using xen hypervisor for ARM-based secure mobile phones. In: Proceedings of the 5th IEEE International Conference on Consumer Communications and Networking, CCNC 2008, pp. 257–261, January 2008
16. Klein, G., Andronick, J., Elphinstone, K., Murray, T., Sewell, T., Kolanski, R., Heiser, G.: Comprehensive Formal Verification of an OS Microkernel. ACM Trans. Comput. Syst. **32**(1), 2:1–2:70 (2014)
17. Kostiainen, K., Ekberg, J.-E., Asokan, N., Rantala, A.: On-board credentials with open provisioning. In: Proceedings of the 4th International Symposium on Information, Computer, and Communications Security, ASIACCS 2009, pp. 104–115. ACM, New York (2009)
18. Lampson, B.W.: Protection. SIGOPS Oper. Syst. Rev. **8**(1), 18–24 (1974)
19. Lie, D., Thekkath, C.A., Horowitz, M.: Implementing an Untrusted Operating System on Trusted Hardware. SIGOPS Oper. Syst. Rev. **37**(5), 178–192 (2003)
20. Pandya, V.R., Stamp, M.: iPhone Security Analysis. Journal of Information Security **1**(2), 74–87 (2010)
21. Rushby, J.M.: Design and Verification of Secure Systems. SIGOPS Oper. Syst. Rev. **15**(5), 12–21 (1981)
22. Santos, N., Raj, H., Saroiu, S., Wolman, A.: Using ARM Trustzone to Build a Trusted Language Runtime for Mobile Applications. SIGARCH Comput. Archit. News **42**(1), 67–80 (2014)
23. Seshadri, A., Luk, M., Shi, E., Perrig, A., van Doorn, L., Khosla, P.: Pioneer: Verifying Code Integrity and Enforcing Untampered Code Execution on Legacy Systems. SIGOPS Oper. Syst. Rev. **39**(5), 1–16 (2005)
24. Suh, G.E., Clarke, D., Gassend, B., van Dijk, M., Devadas, S.: AEGIS: architecture for tamper-evident and tamper-resistant processing. In: Proceedings of the 17th Annual International Conference on Supercomputing, ICS 2003, pp. 160–171. ACM, New York (2003)
25. Vanfleet, M.W., Luke, J.A., Beckwith, W.R., Taylor, C., Calloni, B., Uchenick, G.: MILS: Architecture for High-Assurance Embedded Computing. CrossTalk: Journal of Defence. Software Engineering **18**(8), 12–16 (2005)
26. Vasudevan, A., Owusu, E., Zhou, Z., Newsome, J., McCune, J.M.: Trustworthy execution on mobile devices: what security properties can my mobile platform give Me? In: Katzenbeisser, S., Weippl, E., Camp, L.J., Volkamer, M., Reiter, M., Zhang, X. (eds.) Trust 2012. LNCS, vol. 7344, pp. 159–178. Springer, Heidelberg (2012)
27. Wilson, P., Frey, A., Mihm, T., Kershaw, D., Alves, T.: Implementing Embedded Security on Dual-Virtual-CPU Systems. IEEE Des. Test **24**(6), 582–591 (2007)

On the Privacy, Security and Safety of Blood Pressure and Diabetes Apps

Konstantin Knorr[1,2]([✉]), David Aspinall[1], and Maria Wolters[1]

[1] University of Edinburgh, Edinburgh, UK
knorr@hochschule-trier.de,
{david.aspinall,maria.wolters}@ed.ac.uk
[2] Trier University of Applied Sciences, Trier, Germany

Abstract. Mobile health (mHealth) apps are an ideal tool for monitoring and tracking long-term health conditions. In this paper, we examine whether mHealth apps succeed in ensuring the privacy, security, and safety of the health data entrusted to them. We investigate 154 apps from Android app stores using both automatic code and metadata analysis and a manual analysis of functionality and data leakage. Our study focuses on hypertension and diabetes, two common health conditions that require careful tracking of personal health data.

We find that many apps do not provide privacy policies or safe communications, are implemented in an insecure fashion, fail basic input validation tests and often have overall low code quality which suggests additional security and safety risks. We conclude with recommendations for App Stores, App developers, and end users.

1 Introduction

Mobile health (mHealth) applications cover all areas of health IT, from health information databases to personal electronic medical records. They are very popular—according to appbrain.com, in December 2014, Google Play had 21,457 apps in the medical category and 3% of these have been downloaded more than 50,000 times. mHealth apps for Android and iOS are currently largely unregulated [17]. Many of these apps are written by individuals or small companies who see a market niche, or by pharma and drugstore companies that seek to provide added value and collect information about their customer base [23].

Around 20% of medical apps cost money, on average US $9.78, making them the most expensive category. This suggests that users attach a high value to mHealth apps. But does this buy data protection?

Many mHealth apps handle highly sensitive data that require particular privacy and security precautions [13]. For example, insurers demand full disclosure of pre-existing conditions. If insurers find mHealth data that suggest an unreported condition, the applicant may be denied coverage or their policy may be downgraded.

In this paper, we examine how far a representative sample of 154 mHealth Android apps for two common long-term conditions, diabetes and hypertension,

© IFIP International Federation for Information Processing 2015
H. Federrath and D. Gollmann (Eds.): SEC 2015, IFIP AICT 455, pp. 571–584, 2015.
DOI: 10.1007/978-3-319-18467-8_38

succeed in ensuring the privacy, security, and safety of the health data entrusted to them. While previous work has considered relatively diverse samples of 40–50 mHealth apps at once [3, 6, 9, 10], we focus on a the management of long-term conditions which require users to regularly track key health indicators. Such conditions are an ideal mHealth use case. Well-designed apps allow users to enter data when and where they choose, to communicate with carers and health care professionals, and to discover trends and patterns in their own medical data.

Contributions. We introduce a novel method that takes into account the files contained in the APK (i.e., the downloaded package of the app), the dynamic behaviour of the installed app, and the app's privacy policy. We also consider input validation and source code quality. This comprehensive evaluation goes beyond previous studies, which mainly examined permissions and network traffic. In addition, our clear focus on long-term conditions allows an in-depth discussion of the specific privacy concerns.

The rest of the paper is structured as follows: Sect. 2 introduces mHealth apps and the categories we examine in detail; we explain the high-level functionality they provide, and discuss potential privacy threats. Sect. 3 describes the proposed methodology, while Sect. 4 gives the corresponding results and its discussion following the structure of the methodology. Suggestions for improving the current privacy issues of mHealth apps and future work conclude the paper in Sect. 5.

2   Hypertension and Diabetes

We focus on two long-term health conditions, hypertension and diabetes. People with hypertension suffer from chronically elevated blood pressure, which increases the risk of many serious illnesses including cardiovascular disease, stroke, and chronic kidney disease. Diabetes is a group of diseases that are characterised by elevated blood sugar levels. Controlling blood sugar is therefore the main aim of treatment.

Both conditions can be tracked using a simple numerical indicator, blood pressure (hypertension) and blood glucose level (diabetes), both are highly prevalent in the population[1], and for both conditions, self-monitoring is an important part of clinical management [14, 19].

The key function of a monitoring app is to capture a reading of the indicator measure at a given point in time. Fig. 1 shows a sample user interface for manual input of hypertension with a basic set of fields. Fields may not have a clearly defined use, such as "My Item" in our example, and others can contain free text, such as "Note".

Typical additional functionality includes providing reminders; data analysis and reporting; and backup, sharing, and export of recorded data. Some

---

[1] Hypertension affects 25%–55% of the population depending on the country and the definition, while diabetes affects 8.5% of Europeans.

apps support several user profiles, while others include functionality for emergency texts and telephone calls. The main menu screen of *Diabetes Journal* (`com.suderman.diabeteslog`, Fig. 2) shows how this functionality is typically implemented. "Averages" and "Charts" cover the data analysis and reporting function, the "Calendar" supports reminders, "Entries" leads to an entry screen for blood glucose values, and "Profiles" allows users to switch profiles.

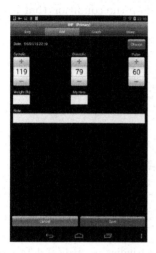

Fig. 1. Input in *iBP Blood Pressure*   **Fig. 2.** Functions of *Diabetes Journal*

For both blood pressure and blood glucose levels, there are well documented clinical guidelines that govern their interpretation, such as those issued by the UK National Institute for Clinical Excellence (NICE). But integrating values collected using mHealth apps into clinical management is difficult. As long as most apps rely on manual data entry [7], data quality is questionable, especially given that, as we will see in Sect. 4, apps may fail to perform basic validity checks on the health data they receive from the user.

2.1 Privacy Threats and Relevant Regulation

In the US, the Health Insurance Portability and Accountability Act (HIPAA) sets legal security and privacy standards for electronically transmitted health information; in the EU, there are diverse country-specific laws that need to be respected [5]. Devices that collect measurements which are used for monitoring, treatment, or diagnosis of health conditions are medical devices and these are regulated by the Food and Drug Administration in the US. The key medical device directive in the EU is Directive 93/42/EEC, which was updated in 2007.

Smartphone apps for monitoring diabetes and hypertension, in particular those that do not directly receive data from a validated blood pressure or blood glucose meter, fall into a grey area that is not adequately covered by current standards [11,17], and finding a good balance between encouraging innovation and ensuring privacy is challenging [22].

Several frameworks have been proposed for classifying the threat that mHealth applications pose to the privacy of health information (e.g. [13]). Most of these focus on information that would make the patient identifiable, in particular ID or social security numbers. While many self-management apps do not collect those data, they do often store name, gender, and date of birth. Privacy threats also depend on the type of mHealth app [11], and on the condition that is being managed.

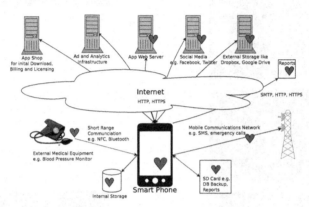

Fig. 3. An mHealth app in context. The heart indicates medical data.

2.2   Threat Scenarios for mHealth Apps in Use

Fig. 3 shows a smart phone with mHealth apps installed. Medical data like blood pressure or glucose values can be input by the user or, less commonly, received from external medical devices via Bluetooth or NFC. The smartphone stores the app's data internally either in a database or the internal file structure. The SD card is used for database backups and restores, and to export reports or selected medical data. Mobile networks are used for emergency SMS and calls.

Five types of servers are potentially connected to the smartphone and app. The *App Shop* is used to initially download and possibly pay for the app. Subsequently, connections for licensing and billing e.g. for in-app purchases or upgrades of the app are maintained. Many of the apps display ads, which are provided by *Ad Servers*, most prominently *Admob* by Google. App developers also use *Analytics* such as Google Analytics to track user behaviour. Many apps allow to upload, backup or synchronize the data to *Social Media*, *Storage Services* or a dedicated external *App Web Server* provided by the app developer or cooperating third parties. This server may provide interfaces to other parties like insurance companies, doctors, or hospitals. Most apps allow sending *e-mails with medical data*. This is typically done via an Android e-mail "intent" which connects to a (implicitly trusted) email app on the phone. Overall, the complexity in this picture emphasises the privacy challenges faced by a user trying to keep control over his/her medical data.

3   Methodology

We selected mHealth apps for diabetes and blood pressure which: (1) had an English or German user interface; (2) would run on a Google Nexus 7 test device with Android 4.4.2 installed; (3) had over 10,000 downloads (for free apps) or over 1,000 (for paid). Most apps came from the medical category and were specifically developed for diabetes and blood pressure monitoring. We ended up with 154 apps in the final test set (55% diabetes, 35% blood pressure, 10% both) that were installed on the Nexus 7. The most popular apps are My Heart (com.szyk.myheart) and BP Watch (com.boxeelab.healthlete.bpwatch) which each have between one and five million downloads.[2]

3.1   Our Method

The investigation has four parts: (A) static analysis; (B) dynamic analysis; (C) web server security and (D) privacy policy inspection. Fig. 4 shows a picture of the method. The results were gathered in a database. Static analysis was applied to the full set of 154 apps; other analysis stages were applied to subsets.

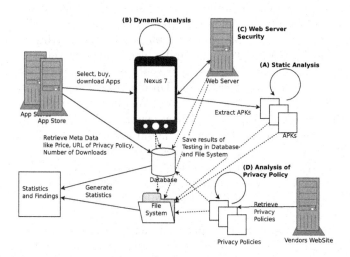

Fig. 4. Analysis method

(A) Static Analysis. The static analysis is based on the information contained in the APK file, including the manifest and the compiled code (in the file classes.dex). Results for the top 10 apps are shown in Table 1. We used Mal-loDroid [8] to identify *faulty SSL usage*, such as the failure to check certificate chains; this would allow man-in-the-middle attacks which enable an attacker to

---

[2] The full details of the apps analysed, along with a database of our results and details about the tools used can be found at the URL http://tinyurl.com/mhealthapps. A more comprehensive description of the method can be found in [12].

access all medical data transmitted. OpenSSL was used to extract certificate information and find certificates with poorly chosen cryptologic parameters [4].

We checked Android *content providers* and debugging flags using Drozer. The ContentProvider class allows sharing data between applications, with its own access control model. A careful implementation will prevent unauthorized access to sensitive data. When the *debug flag* for Android is set, the application can be debugged, even when running on a device in user mode, thereby possibly revealing medical information.

Addons Detector was used to identify and classify the add-on libraries used by the apps. Health apps were scanned for *malicious code*, security vulnerabilities and privacy failings using Snoopwall Privacy App, Clueful, AVG Antivirus Security, AVAST, McAfee, and the Recap vulnerability scanner.

We assessed *code quality* by using FindBugs to count the number of likely-bug patterns occurring in apps; high numbers indicate a likely poor code quality, which suggests possible unreliable behaviour, giving additional security and safety risks.

(B) Dynamic Analysis. We analysed the 72 most frequently downloaded apps, including all those with web interfaces to external servers. We set up Facebook, Twitter, Dropbox, and Gmail accounts for a patient for whom some values were out of the physiologically normal range. The patient was 170 cm tall, weighed 99 kg, had dangerously high blood pressure (200 mmHg/120 mmHg), a physiologically improbable heart rate (333 bpm) and a blood glucose level of 111 mmol/L, which is lethal and indicates that the user confused mg/dL with mmol/L.

We generated Facebook, Twitter and Dropbox accounts for the patient and tested all available export routes for the data. We investigated whether abnormal and illegal inputs were accepted, and how exported data was stored or transmitted. Using the Android debugger command `adb pull` and the `adb logcat` command, we tested whether the backups or log data contained unencrypted medical data. We also established whether the app included a feature to erase all stored medical data, whether there was a privacy policy for the app, and whether the permissions required by the app were reasonable.

(C) Web Server Connection. For apps that can interface with a dedicated web server (n=20) using a user account for uploading data, we checked whether a sensible *password policy* was enforced on the web site and tested the *Web Server connection*. We recorded the URLs used for connections and noted if they used a secure transport (`https:`). We recorded traffic to see if passwords or medical data in textual or graphical form could be sniffed in clear text.

(D) Inspection of Privacy Policies. Only 19% of apps in (A) have a privacy policies. This is far lower than the proportion found by Sunyaev et al. [18] in their survey of the 600 most commonly used apps, where 30% of all apps had some form of privacy policy. Since storage of medical data on an external server further stresses privacy concerns, we limited the test to the same apps as in (C).

We assessed privacy policies on *basic information* provided (URL to privacy policy, length in words, version, and country of origin), *completeness* (information about the OECD criteria accountability, security safeguards, openness, purpose, individual participation [2]), and *invasiveness* (possible use for other purposes, storage by third party, potential to be passed on to third parties) by asking basic questions and trying to find answers in the documents.

4   Results and Discussion

Table 1. Analysis results for the top 20 downloaded apps. Columns: lack of a privacy policy, existence of MalloDroid errors, debug flag enabled, missing access protection of content provider, poor certificate parameters, usage of ad and analytics addons, more than 300 FindBugs errors, usage of more than 5 Android permissions, lack of input validation for input data, absence of a wipe feature.

Package	Downloads	Type	lacks pripol	bad SSL	debug set	c'provider	poor cert pars	analytics?	ads?	FindBugs >300	>5 perms	fail safety BP	fail safety GL	no wipe	Score
com.boxeelab.healthl	1000000	BP	×				×		×	×	×	×		×	7
com.szyk.myheart....	1000000	BP			×		×		×	×		×			4
com.ptashek.bplog...	500000	BP					×		×		×			×	4
com.gexperts.ontrack	500000	DIAB					×		×		×	×	×		5
com.fourtechnologies	100000	BP		×			×			×	×		×	×	6
com.orangekit.bpress	100000	BP	×						×	×				×	4
com.szyk.diabetes...	100000	DIAB					×	×	×	×					4
net.klier.blutdruck.	100000	BP		×			×			×	×	×		×	6
com.skyhealth.glucos	100000	DIAB			×		×	×						×	4
org.fruct.yar.bloodp	100000	BP	×				×	×	×	×	×	×			7
com.freshware.bloodp	100000	BP	×				×	×	×		×		×		6
com.jucdejeb.bloodpr	100000	BP	×				×		×	×			×	×	7
com.suderman.diabete	50000	DIAB					×	×	×	×		×	×	×	8
com.zlamanit.blood.p	50000	BP	×					×	×		×		×		5
com.freshware.dbees.	50000	DIAB	×				×			×			×	×	5
com.squaredmed...typ1	50000	DIAB	×				×			×			×		4
com.squaredmed...andr	50000	DIAB	×				×			×	×	×	×	×	7
com.mydiabetes......	50000	DIAB	×				×	×	×	×		×			6
kr.co.openit.bpdiary	50000	BP					×			×	×	×		×	5
com.sidiary.app.....	50000	DIAB					×		×	×	×	×		×	6

Tables 1 and 2 give an overview of our results. In both Tables, × is used to indicate a problem, and the score is the number of problems found.

We found that paid apps tend to use fewer ads (even though some keep the ad libraries code) and offer more functionality (like e-mail or SD card export). Concerning the other tests, we could not find major differences. Especially comparing "twin apps" (free and paid version of same app) produced similar results.

Static Analysis. The number of permissions used ranges from 0 (28 apps) to 17 with an average of 4.35. The most frequently requested Android permissions are INTERNET (126 times), followed by WRITE_EXTERNAL_STORAGE (117), and ACCESS_NETWORK_STATE (109). The permission BLUETOOTH is used 18 times, NFC 3 times. Of the 126 apps using the INTERNET permission, 15 do not correctly verify certificates or certificate paths, allowing for MITM attacks. Six apps had the debuggable flag set to "true" in their manifest, possibly allowing debug connections to inspect medical data. 17 apps use content providers that were accessible to other apps on the device, and four revealed medical data to all other apps on the device.

Apps are infested by ad and analytic addons on a large scale. The addons in the Advertising (74 apps, *Admob* being dominant) and Analytics (27 apps, *Google Analytics* dominant) category have been identified as a major privacy problems transferring device IDs and other data. Eight apps use Facebook or Twitter addons.

All apps used self-signed certificates, although using an acknowledged CA could establish additional trust. Certificates of 4 apps have a life time of ~1,000 years, another 6 of ~100 years. Most of them are valid for ~30 years. The majority use SHA1, and only 17% the more secure SHA256. Only 40 certificates give more information than the name of the developer, thereby not establishing additional trust by adding more detailed information.

The Clueful tool gave a privacy score of 56 out of 100 for the apps on the test device and identified no high risk app and 57 moderate risk apps. The ranking is purely based on permissions. Snoopwall also just lists permissions for each app. Recap is a vulnerability scanner based on 1,800 CVE numbers. All its findings were OS related. We additionally checked if the apps in our test set in its current or earlier version are listed in the National Vulnerability Database http://www.nvd.org (NVD) and found no entries. AVG classified com.stevenmz.BloodPressureDiary as malware and MMSL.BGGlucoDiary as "Potentially Unwanted Program" without giving a detailed explanation[3]. Avast and McAfee did not find any malware, privacy or security issue.

Dynamic Analysis. 43 of 50 blood pressure apps allow users to enter alarmingly high blood pressure values of 200 / 120 mmHg with the current time, some marking this (e.g. colouring the values read), some not. 20 of 50 blood glucose monitoring apps allow the meaningless reading of 111 mmol/L, and 24 of 46 apps that monitor pulse allow a value of 333 bpm (s. Figs. 5 and 6). Some of the apps even allowed to input letters instead of numerical values. This raises serious safety concerns. Lacking input validation stands for poor code quality and is a precondition for attacks like SQL injection, XSS, and XSRF.

The majority of apps do not protect the medical data when stored in the internal storage. An attacker gaining physical access to the device can thereby access or manipulate these data. This attack can be impeded but not entirely

---

[3] We did not find any suspicious network traffic caused by these two apps during the dynamic analysis.

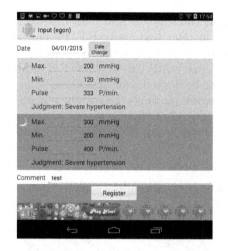

Fig. 5. *BloodPressure Record Lite* allows to enter lethal blood pressure values

Fig. 6. *Diabetes Journal (Suderman)* allows to enter lethal blood sugar values

prevented by using the phone's security mechanisms like PIN protection and device encryption. In contrast to [9,10] we did not find any sensitive data in Android's main and event log. Only 4 apps allowed to protect the app with an extra password.

49 of 72 apps export medical data to SD card. All but one of these do not protect the data when doing so. The one exception is MyLists, which is not a specific health app. Thus, an attacker with physical access to the device can steal the SD card and gain thereby access to the medical data. This finding is surprising as some of the developer tools included in the apps like PDFTron would allow encryption. This also indicates *dead code* in the APKs. Only 32% of the apps provide a "wipe" feature to delete all medical data entered. Unfortunately, the SD card is often omitted from this wipe.

68% of the apps allowed to send e-mails. None of these allowed for sending encrypted messages or attachments. This could allow attackers with access to the network infrastructure (e.g. in WLANs) to sniff or even manipulate e-mails in transit. Besides export to 20 different web servers, we successfully exported data to Facebook (2 apps), Twitter (2), Google Drive (6), and Dropbox (8) without receiving a privacy warning by the app.

Several ad networks transmit the app's package name plus other device and app specific data in clear text which allows a passive eavesdropper to gather the information which device is using which app. This can often traced back to individual users thereby laying open that a user has diabetes or is tracking their blood pressure. We found this among others in HTTP traffic related to doubleclick.net, googleapis.com, gstatic.com, applovin.com. Similar findings (albeit not for mHealth) have been reported in [21].

Web Applications. 35% of all analysed apps transmit medical data in textual or other forms (like pictures, charts, files) in clear text using HTTP. This is not limited to blood pressure or glucose values but also includes weight, BMI, and pulse (Fig. 7). The same percentage of passwords can be sniffed in cleartext. The password policies also leave much to be desired. One app allows empty passwords, 5 are fine with one character passwords, and only 3 ask for or generate passwords of 8 characters or more. Additionally, 17 of 20 apps accept password consisting just of numbers in a chronological order which allows easy brute force and dictionary attacks.

Table 2. Results of the privacy policy and web security analysis

Package	Downloads	HTTP?	password len <7	cleartext password	cleartext medical	accountability	safeguards	openness	purpose specified	individual participation	data for other purposes	3rd party storage	sell with company	share with 3rd parties
air.com.softbycloud.glico	1000					-	-	-	-	-	-	-	-	-
androidhive.diabetes.....	1000	×		×		-	-	-	-	-	-	-	-	-
com.diabetesstudio.client	500	×	×	×	×	×	×	×	×		×	-	×	-
com.fourtechnologies.myne	100000	×	×		×	×	×	×	×	×	×	×	×	
com.freshware.dbees......	50000			×		×	×			×	×	-	-	×
com.glooko.logbook.......	5000					×	×	×	×	×	×	-	×	×
com.kiwihealthcare.glubud	5000	×	×	×	×	-	-	-	-	-	-	-	-	-
com.leadingedgeapps.ibp..	5000	×	×	×	×	×	×	×	×		×	-	-	-
com.mysugr.android.compan	50000	×				×	×	×		×	×	-	-	
com.nabdacare.diabetes...	1000	×				-	-	-	-	-	-	-	-	-
com.oxygenhealthcom.lsmea	1000	×	×	×	×	×	×	×	×		-	-	×	×
com.sidiary.app.......	50000	×				-	-	-	-	-	-	-	-	×
com.socialdiabetes.androi	10000	×	×	×	×	×	×	×	×	×	×	-	-	
com.squaremed.diabetescon	50000	×				×	×	×	×	×	×	-	-	
com.squaremed.diabetesplu	50000	×				-	-	-	-	-	-	-	-	-
de.davidfroehlich.diabete	500					×	×				-	-	-	-
it.bytewave.glucowave....	500	×	×	×	×		×	×			×	-	-	-
net.klier.blutdruck......	100000	×				×	×		×		-			
org.fruct.yar.bloodpressu	100000	×				-	-	-	-	-	-	-	-	-

Privacy Policy. Only 19% of all 154 refer to a privacy policy in the app stores, but this number increases to 67% for apps which allow users to sync data with web servers. On average, the policies are 632 words long. Only 6 policies stem from 2014, the others being older, 4 give no date. mHealth is a global business with a trend towards USA and Germany. While the majority of the policies cover the OECD privacy principles of accountability, security safeguards, openness, and purpose at least partly, over half of the policies do not address the rights of the individual like the right of data deletion. None of the policies denies using the data internally e.g., for marketing or research. 9 policies explicitly say that they

```
UserID=2455&MobileLogID=2&LogDate=2015-01-07&LogTime=15%
3A23&Slot=Fasting&ReadingType=BP&Reading1=200&Reading2=120&Reading3=0&Reading4=0&Reading5
=0&Remarks=&tag=ts-measure-addLogHTTP/1.1 200 OK
Cache-Control: private
Content-Length: 46
Content-Type: text/html
Server: Microsoft-IIS/7.5
Set-Cookie: ASPSESSIONIDSQQACCBC=AECHJEECEEBKJCLGFFOOHAMJ; path=/
X-Powered-By: ASP.NET
X-Powered-By-Plesk: PleskWin
Date: Wed, 07 Jan 2015 15:23:45 GMT

{"status":"1","msg":"Log added successfully!"}
```

Fig. 7. Clear text blood pressure reading (`com.oxygenhealthcom.lsmeasure`)

do so. All policies addressing mergers note that medical data may be transferred or even sold. 50% of the apps (that address this issue) say that medical data can be passed on to other 3rd parties (other than required by law).

5   Conclusions

Through our in-depth analysis, we found clear evidence of privacy, safety, and security concerns for the majority of the apps we analysed. Current health policy strongly encourages people to manage chronic conditions themselves, and mHealth is seen as a key tool for effective self management. But the apps people use should not leave them vulnerable to cyberattacks. While the consequences of such attacks may be relatively mild for the conditions we studied, hypertension and diabetes, they may be more severe for stigmatised conditions such as HIV+ or mental illness.

Some of the issues, such as the pervasive lack of encryption, indicate security is not a priority for developers. Reports, charts, and tables of medical data are often stored without any protection, giving thieves and eavesdroppers easy access. Another important threat is advertising. Of the 154 apps tested, 74 include advertisement addons. These addons often transmit the app's package name in clear text in the HTTP header which discloses the usage of this app (which is, per se, sensitive) to eavesdroppers. We also pointed out that current malware and privacy scanners fail to identify privacy issues in mHealth apps.

On the user interface side, we found that input data was often not validated or badly validated. This is a major concern when users want to share their self-curated data with health care professionals. The problems that arise from badly validated and designed data input forms have been studied extensively, and design guidelines have been formulated, but many app developers (and many medical device manufacturers) still fail to adhere to them [20].

App developers also rarely provide privacy policies. Although most users are unlikely to read such policies [15], we would still expect that privacy policies offer a reasonably complete summary of all major privacy issues for people who do read them. Most of the policies we analysed fell far short of this goal. Quote[4]: "Sinovo endeavours to use on the data minimally. The customer expressly agrees to the use of data in this context."

Recommendations. Due to the manifold concerns over the privacy and security of health data that users enter into mHealth apps in good faith, we suggest that *app shops* should mandate and enforce the existence of a privacy policy for apps that would like to be listed in the Health section. They could provide a template which systematically addresses the major principles and encourage automated security checking of apps with tools like MalloDroid or Drozer.

Such a step would automatically encourage *developers* to invest time and effort in ensuring users' privacy. Secure coding guidelines like [1] are a good start. Developers should leverage existing tools to encrypt all data stored both on the device and on external servers. Finally, developers should also ensure that the privacy policy is up to date, follows the OECD principles, and informs end users about use of their data and data protection.

Ad Networks, an important revenue source for free medical apps, are also a major source of privacy leaks. Here, many concerns could be addressed by mandating the usage of SSL to protect the HTTP traffic.

Looking at the *Android operating system*, the `INTERNET` permission seems too coarse. Currently it is not possible to differentiate whether a mHealth app wants to communicate with a health care provider or if an ad server is contacted. A possible solution could be the inclusion of firewall features in future Android versions, but this might conflict with Google's ad driven business model.

The recommendation to *end users* is to perform due diligence, including reading the description, privacy policy, and commenting on security issues, trying to take advantage of scores for privacy measures such as ours and those given by others [3,6]. But the information currently available prior to installation is not enough for users to make these informed decisions. Therefore, a privacy aware user needs to use additional mechanisms like Android's phone encryption, ad block apps, or encryption apps. This is only feasible for technically savvy users.

Related Work. Work closest to our contribution stems from [3,6,9,10]. Njie [6] analyses 43 popular iOS and Android health and fitness apps based on a spreadsheet with the focus on network analysis and mentions the need to restrict future studies to a more specific category of apps. He et al. [9,10] analyse 47 randomly selected iOS and Android mHealth apps in a series of two studies regarding Internet usage, logging, content provider, SD cards, and usage of cloud services and Bluetooth. Adhikari et al. [3] examine the 40 most popular iOS and Android mHealth apps by answering 9 privacy questions yielding a privacy score.

In contrast these studies, our work focuses (1) on apps for specific purposes, rather than selecting randomly from the broad category of mHealth apps and (2) only on Android apps. This gives us a more homogeneous population which can be closely tested and compared, in particular, it allowed us to check input

---

[4] http://www.sinovo.org/?id=144

validation for specific blood pressure and glucose reading ranges. Our testing also goes further than previous work: while permissions and network traffic have been considered, we additionally analyse the APKs and the underlying code and privacy policies, and source code quality.

Future Work. Our methodology is sensitive enough to uncover many privacy and security concerns, and it can be easily extended to apps for conditions that are more stigmatised than diabetes and hypertension, such as mental health [16].

We propose to extend our technical work in three ways. First, we want to extend static analysis to more of the 27 topics in [1], integrating formal usability assessment, and developing automatic tools that might be used to screen new candidate apps for mHealth. Given the prevalence of web servers associated with apps, assessing web application security is an integral part of a full analysis; we'd like to extend this to consider vulnerability to attacks like SQL injection, XSS, and XSRF. Finally, apps that use communication links like Bluetooth and NFC to regulated measurement devices deserve to be examined in detail too, especially in a "wearable scenario".

In order to link our results to the eHealth field, we plan to investigate the motivations of users of mHealth apps and their attitude to the safety, security, and privacy problems we found. We also plan to investigate reasons why developers create insecure apps through a questionnaire study.

References

1. CERT secure coding standards for Android. https://www.securecoding.cert.org (accessed December 28, 2014)
2. OECD guidelines on the protection of privacy and transborder flows of personal data. http://www.oecd.org/internet/ieconomy/ oecdguidelinesontheprotectionofprivacyandtransborderflowsofpersonaldata.htm. (accessed December 29, 2014)
3. Adhikari, R., Richards, D., Scott, K.: Security and privacy issues related to the use of mobile health apps. ACIS (2014)
4. Allix, K., Jerome, Q., Bissyande, T.F., Klein, J., State, R., Traon, Y.L.: A Forensic Analysis of Android Malware: How is Malware Written and How It Could Be Detected?. In: Proc. of the 38th COMPSAC, pp. 384–393. IEEE (2014)
5. Avancha, S., Baxi, A., Kotz, D.: Privacy in mobile technology for personal healthcare. ACM Computing Surveys 45(1), 1–54 (2012)
6. Njie, C.M.L.: Technical analysis of the data practices and privacy risks of 43 popular mobile health and fitness applications. Technical report, PrivacyRights Clearinghouse (2013)
7. Eng, D.S., Lee, J.M.: The promise and peril of mobile health applications for diabetes and endocrinology. Pediatric Diabetes 14(4), 231–238 (2013)
8. Fahl, S., Harbach, M., Muders, T., Baumgärtner, L., Freisleben, B., Smith, M.: Why eve and mallory love Android: An analysis of Android SSL (in) security. In: Proceedings of the 2012 ACM Conference on Computer and Communications Security, pp. 50–61. ACM (2012)
9. He, D.: Security threats to Android apps. Master's thesis, University of Illinois at Urbana-Champaign (2014)

10. He, D., Naveed, M., Gunter, C.A., Nahrstedt, K.: Security concerns in Android mHealth apps. In: Proceedings of the AMIA 2014 (2014)
11. Helm, A.M., Georgatos, D.: Privacy and mHealth: How Mobile Health 'Apps' Fit into a Privacy Framework Not Limited to HIPAA. Syracuse Law Review **64**, (May 2014)
12. Knorr, K., Aspinall, D.: Security Testing for Android mHealth Apps. In: Proceedings of the 6th International Workshop on Security Testing SECTEST, Graz, Austria, April 13, 2015
13. Kotz, D.: A threat taxonomy for mHealth privacy. In: 3rd International Conference on Communication Systems and Networks, COMSNETS 2011 (2011)
14. Labeit, A., et al.: Changes in the prevalence, treatment and control of hypertension in Germany? A clinical-epidemiological study of 50.000 primary care patients. PloS One **7**(12), e52229 (2012)
15. Nissenbaum, H.: A Contextual Approach to Privacy Online. Daedalus 140(4) (2011)
16. Roeloffs, C., Sherbourne, C., Unützer, J., Fink, A., Tang, L., Wells, K.B.: Stigma and depression among primary care patients. General Hospital Psychiatry 25(5), 311–315
17. Schulke, D.F.: Regulatory arms race: Mobile-health applications and agency posturing, the. BUL Rev. **93**, 1699 (2013)
18. Sunyaev, A., Dehling, T., Taylor, P.L., Mandl, K.D.: Availability and quality of mobile health app privacy policies. Journal of the American Medical Informatics Association (2014)
19. Tamayo, T., Rosenbauer, J., Wild, S.H., Spijkerman, A.M.W., Baan, C., Forouhi, N.G., Herder, C., Rathmann, W.: Diabetes in Europe: an update. Diabetes research and clinical practice **103**(2), 206–217 (2014)
20. Thimbleby, H.: Improving safety in medical devices and systems. In: Proceedings IEEE International Conference on Healthcare Informatics (2013)
21. Vallina-Rodriguez, N., Shah, J., Finamore, A., Grunenberger, Y., Haddadi, H., Papagiannaki, K., Crowcroft, J.: Breaking for commercials: characterizing mobile advertising. In: Proceedings of the 2012 ACM Conference on Internet Measurement Conference, pp. 343–356. ACM (2012)
22. Jason, C.: Wang and Delphine J Huang. The HIPAA conundrum in the era of mobile health and communications. JAMA **310**(11), 1121–1122 (2013)
23. Wolters, M.: The minimal effective dose of reminder technology. In: CHI 2014 Extended Abstracts (2014)

A Cloud-Based eHealth Architecture
for Privacy Preserving Data Integration

Alevtina Dubovitskaya[1,2]($\boxtimes$), Visara Urovi[1], Matteo Vasirani[2],
Karl Aberer[2], and Michael I. Schumacher[1]

[1] AISLab, HES-SO VS, Sierre, Switzerland
{alevtina.dubovitskaya,visara.urovi,michael.schumacher}@hevs.ch
[2] LSIR, EPFL, Lausanne, Switzerland
{matteo.vasirani,karl.aberer}@epfl.ch

Abstract. In this paper, we address the problem of building an anonymized medical database from multiple sources. Our proposed solution defines how to achieve data integration in a heterogeneous network of many clinical institutions, while preserving data utility and patients' privacy. The contribution of the paper is twofold: Firstly, we propose a secure and scalable cloud eHealth architecture to store and exchange patients' data for the treatment. Secondly, we present an algorithm for efficient aggregation of the health data for the research purposes from multiple sources independently.

Keywords: Access control · Interoperability · Point-of-care system

1 Introduction

While building an anonymized database from multiple sources of individuals' sensitive data the privacy of a person may be violated. Even if the data are locally anonymized, their aggregation can still reveal sensitive information, especially if the data about an individual are distributed between different local databases [2,3]. Several models in the area of distributed privacy-preserving data publishing have already been proposed (i.e., pseudonymization [9,26], secure multi-party computations (SMC) [6], microaggregation [22], cloning [2]). However, those models significantly affect the utility of the data, and, therefore, an efficient independent release of the data from multiple sources and their aggregation without violation of privacy remains an open problem [10].

This problem is of great interest especially in the case of secondary use of medical data. This includes the analysis of patients healthcare data in order to enhance their health care experiences and the expansion of knowledge about different diseases and appropriate treatment. Datasets containing health related information about an individual are increasingly becoming "open". In this paper, we focus on the medical data to address the following question: How is it possible to share and aggregate medical data for research purposes?

© IFIP International Federation for Information Processing 2015
H. Federrath and D. Gollmann (Eds.): SEC 2015, IFIP AICT 455, pp. 585–598, 2015.
DOI: 10.1007/978-3-319-18467-8_39

Collecting medical data raises privacy concerns as these data are of a personal nature to the patient. Additionally, in medical settings, the following requirements have to be considered: the ability to update the data about a patient (without creating multiple entries corresponding to the same person), and the possibility to recontact the patient through the caregiver that uploaded the data.

Our aim is to create an infrastructure for medical data management that allows the healthcare professionals to release patients' data for research purposes while insuring patients' privacy. To achieve this we employ generalization and pseudonymization techniques. We use binary trees to represent the data generalization and multi-key searchable encryption for generating pseudonyms.

The contribution of this paper is the following: we propose a secure framework for independently and asynchronously sharing, aggregating and searching health data in the cloud, therefore without trust to the server that stores the health data. We have chosen the cloud-based approach because it allows patients and caregivers to access aggregated healthcare data from everywhere anytime (according to the access control policy specified by the patient). Moreover, it facilitates the aggregation of the data and the creation of the database for the research purposes (*RSDB*).

The rest of the paper is organized as follows. In Section 2 we present a use case scenario, in Section 3 we provide the knowledge about encryption scheme and anonymity approach that we use in our work, and we compare our solution with the existing approaches. In Section 4 we describe the architecture of our proposed eHealth system, the protocol for sharing and accessing patients' data in the cloud, and our algorithm for constructing research database. In Section 5 we discuss privacy threats and countermeasures. We present the conclusion and future work in Section 6 of the paper.

2   Use Case Scenario

The treatment of certain diseases, such as cancer, HIV, or other serious medical conditions, relies on the administration of critical drugs used to keep those life-threatening diseases under control. Those drugs (e.g. *Efavirenzum, Imatinib*) have a narrow therapeutic range and a poorly predictable relationship between the dose and the drug concentration in the blood, which may greatly vary among individuals. Therapeutic Drug Monitoring (TDM) aims at improving patient care by monitoring drug levels in the blood and adjust a dosage individually.

In order to ensure a better prediction of the relationship between dose and drug concentration a Bayesian TDM approach [12] has been developed. This approach requires population health data to be collected and analyzed by researchers, therefore, building databases for medical research is of a high importance [8]. We consider a patient, *P*, who visits several caregivers during the treatment (e.g., when there is a need for a consultation from particular specialists, in case of traveling, or if patient has moved). We expect that the patient *P* is able to access his healthcare information and to decide with whom to share it. Storing data in the cloud allows an access from anywhere anytime. However, the question of privacy has to be addressed.

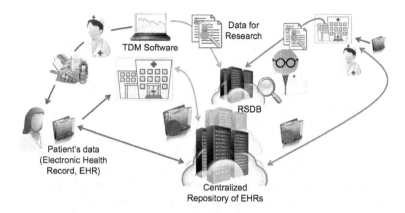

Fig. 1. Use case scenario

A widespread use of the the electronic identity cards and the cards provided by the insurance companies shows that having a smartcard is not a burden in everyday life. Therefore, we assume that a patient could use a smartcard to store a set of cryptographic keys for encryption/decryption of the sensitive data (contained in *EHR*) in order to prevent an un-authorised access.

For example, as it is shown on Figure 1, a set of the Electronic Health Records (*EHRs*) may belong to the same patient but could be generated by different caregivers. Each *EHR* then will be encrypted with the key shared between the patient and the caregiver that generated this *EHR*. The access control policy can be based on sharing the keys with the caregivers to allow access to the data for the treatment. Patients' data can also be collected for the secondary use. Anonymization algorithms are required to preserve patient privacy.

3   Related Work

In this section, first, we recall the details of multi-key searchable encryption scheme [20] that we employ in our solution to generate pseudonyms and annotate *EHRs*. Second, we describe $(k, k^m) - anonymity$ property [21] that we impose on the research database and preserve while updating *RSDB* in the distributed environment. Finally, we present an overview of the related work and specify how they differ from our approach.

3.1   Multi-key Searchable Encryption

Without loss of generality we can assume that the server stores documents (a set of *EHRs*) encrypted with m different keys $k_1, ...k_m$, and a user (patient, or caregiver) that possesses n keys ($n \leq m$) wants to search for T words (e.g., diagnosis, date of visit, etc.) $w_1, ...w_T$ in the documents.

According to the prior work [5,23], in order to perform the search of a word over the documents encrypted using different keys a user has to compute a token

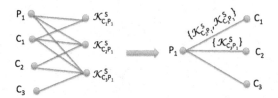

Fig. 2. An example of the access graph

for each word under every key. In this case the complexity of the search will be $\mathcal{O}\ (nT)$. However, with an approach proposed in [20] the complexity of the multi-key search over encrypted data does not exceed $\mathcal{O}\ (n+T)$. The multi-key searchable scheme is constructed using bilinear maps on elliptic curves [4]. The pseudocode for the multi-key searchable encryption scheme and its implementation can be found in [13].

According to the scheme if a user has an access to the keys $k_1, ...k_m$ in order to search for a word w he needs to compute only a single search token for this word: $tk_w^{k_i}$ using the key k_i, and deltas, $\{\Delta_{k_i \to k_j}\}$, an additional information that allows to adjust the token $(tk_w^{k_i})$, computed with the key k_i, to the tokens corresponding to the keys $k_1, ...k_m$ ($\{tk_w^{k_j} : j \neq i, j \in \{1...m\}\}$). These deltas represent the user's access to the documents, and, most important, these deltas can be reused for every search, so the user needs to generate them only once. Efficiency of the scheme has been evaluated and it was shown that performance overheads of using multi-key searchable encryption scheme are modest [13].

In the paper [20] the authors use graphs to represent an access to the shared key. We modify the structure of the access graph by using the labeled graph instead. This allows us to reduce the complexity of the graph. For p patients and c caregivers access graph according to the approach used in [20] will contain at most $p+c+p*c$ nodes and $p*(1+c)$ edges, while in case of using labeled graph it will take as most $p+c$ nodes and $p*c$ edges for the complete access graph. This makes access control policy easier to interpret and manage. Each node of the graph represents a patient or a caregiver. Figure 2 shows an example of access graph. The edge (between P_i and C_j) shows that P_i visited C_j (e.g., P_1 visited caregivers C_1, C_2 and C_3), therefore patient P_i and caregiver C_j connected with the edge share the key that C_j will use to create a pseudonym and encrypt the data about P_i. Labels on the edge shows the keys P_i shared with the caregiver C_j, (e.g., P_1 shares with C_1 the keys P_1 generated together with C_2 and C_3, therefore allowing C_1 access the data about P_1 generated by C_2 and and C_3,), however no label on the edge between P_1 and C_3 indicates that the only data about P_1 that C_3 can access are the data generated by C_3.

3.2 Anonymity of Medical Data

A variety of models, (e.g., ϵ–differential privacy, $k - anonymity$ [24], $(k^m) - anonymity$, $l - diversity$, etc. [11]) can be used for privacy preserving data publishing. However, Poulis et al. show that all these methods are not appropriate for the anonymization of the datasets containing both relational (i.e., single-valued) and transaction (i.e., set-valued) attributes, such as medical datasets that contain patient demographics and diagnosis information together [21].

$(k, k^m) - anonymity$ proposed in [21] ensures that for any record r in the dataset and any set of m or less items in transaction attribute of r, there should be at least $(k-1)$ records that are indistinguishable from record r. However, $k - anonymity$ for relational attributes (i.e., existence of at least $(k-1)$ records that are indistinguishable from record r with respect to relational attributes of the record r) and $(k^m) - anonymity$ for transaction attribute do not imply $(k, k^m) - anonymity$. Poulis et al. developed two frameworks that produce $(k, k^m) - anonymous$ datasets with bounded information loss in one attribute type (relational or transaction) and minimal information loss in the other (transaction or relational). Our algorithmic solution (presented in the Section 4) addresses the problem of maintaining $(k, k^m) - anonymization$ property in a distributed environment.

3.3 Existing Approaches

Using encryption combined with pseudonymization techniques [9,17,26] has been proposed recently for building eHealth system in the cloud. There exists also a number of architectures that employ Attribute-Based encryption (ABE) scheme [14–16,19,27]. However, these approaches have several limitations. ABE still can leak information from the access control policy. Encryption, in general, may affect the system performance especially when there is a need to search over encrypted data for a particular information. In our work we use multi-key searchable encryption scheme [20], for which it was shown that performance overheads of using this scheme are modest [13]. In [17,26] the authors suggest a patient-centric architecture and propose to use the smartcards for the key management. If the smartcard is lost it is very difficult to recover the keys. However, in our solution the keys can be recovered through the caregivers.

Urovi et al. in [25] proposed a secure mechanism for *EHR* exchange over a Peer to Peer (P2P) agent based coordination framework. In this approach the encrypted heterogeneous data are exposed over a P2P network. The authors provide the algorithms for searching and for publishing the *EHRs* in the untrusted P2P network without compromising the privacy, integrity and the authenticity of the shared data. This work, however, does not cover the aggregation of the data for the research purposes, as we propose here.

Using unambiguous pseudonym for the patient [18] allows one to infer additional information about a patient by linking the data from different sources. In case of using multiple pseudonyms, as in [26], their efficient management is problematic. To solve these issues we generate patients' pseudonyms with the means of the multi-key searchable encryption scheme proposed in [20]. We also use this scheme to enable efficient search over the EHRs.

In [6] the authors describe privacy-preserving distributed $k - anonymity$ algorithm that allows merging two local $k - anonymous$ datasets while preserving $k - anonymity$ property in the resulting dataset. However, the solution is not

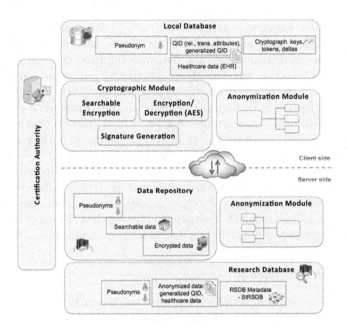

Fig. 3. Architecture overview

scalable and requires using SMC, sharing data is not independent among different sources contributing to the *RSDB*. Baig et al. [2] suggest a model called ϵ-cloning for privacy protection in multiple independent data publications. However, it cannot be applied in our settings because it significantly affects the utility of the data. In [3] the authors proposed an architecture that allows collecting the patients consents for sharing their data for the research in an anonymous way. However, the authors assume that the data are already anonymized.

4   Proposed e-Health Architecture

In this section, we describe our proposed eHealth system. Figure 3 shows an architecture that consists of the following entities: Databases (Local Database, on the client side, Data Repository, and Research Database, both hosted on the cloud server); Cryptographic Module on the side of the client; Anonymization Module (on both sides); and standalone Certification Authority. Local Database, *LDB*, belongs to the caregiver and contains healthcare data about the patients that receive treatment from this caregiver. Data Repository, *DR*, is hosted on the untrusted cloud server and stores *EHR* generated in different medical institutions. Anonymized patients data for the research purposes are stored on the cloud server in Research Database, *RSDB*. Cryptographic Module consists of three parts and its functionalities are the following: to perform multi-key searchable encryption; to encrypt *EHR* before uploading to the cloud server in order to share with the other caregivers, as well as to decrypt when accessing *EHR* according to the access control policy specified by the patient; and, to generate the signature to ensure the authenticity of the data. Anonymization Module is a realization of the algorithm for medical data anonymization presented further in this paper. Certification Authority, CA, is a service that is responsible for issuing certificates of public keys and smartcads for storing private keys that are protected with the PIN known only to the owner of the smartcard.

4.1   Data Structure

Hereafter we describe the structure of the data that are stored in the databases.

- *Pseudonym(s)* – a set of uniquely identifiable patient data, ID_P, (such as combination of date of birth, place of birth and the name) that is encrypted using multi-key searchable encryption scheme proposed in [20], stored in all databases: DR, LDB and $RSDB$.
- *QID* – quasi-identifiers – a set of the attributes ($\{qid\}$) that in combination can uniquely identify the person (e.g., single-valued qid, such as age, gender, address (i.e., ZIP code) and set-valued qid, such as diagnosis codes), $gnrlQID$ – a combination of generalized qid (in a form of a binary string), with which the data about P have been uploaded to the $RSDB$.
- *Healthcare data* – drug intakes (time, dosage, drug name), co-medications, concentration measurements (time, measurement) – multiple attributes, that can be set-, or single-valued)).
- *Cryprographic keys* and *deltas* – a set of the deltas for the keys ($\mathcal{K}^S_{P,C_j}, j \in \overline{1,\mathcal{N}}, i \neq j$) related to the patient and shared with C_i (see Subection 3.1 for more details).
- *Encrypted data* – health data, or, *EHR*, encrypted with symmetric cipher (e.g., AES).
- *Searchable data* – *EHR* or a list of the attributes that describe the content of the *EHR* (encrypted using multi-key searchable encryption scheme).
- *Anonymized data* – consist of generalized QID ($gnrlQID$) and a subset of *healthcare data* from LDB.

$StRSDB$ – is a table that characterizes the current state of the (k, k^m) – *anonymous RSDB*. For each combination of qid that are presented in $RSDB$, $StRSDB$ stores the following information: *PsNumber* – a number of different *pseudonyms* from $RSDB$ associated with the same QID set and the sources of data (C_i that uploaded the data, and $PsNumber^i$, a number of *pseudonyms* associated with this QID). One has to notice that as $RSDB$ is (k, k^m) – *anonymous*, $PsNumber \geq k$ and $\sum_{i \in \overline{1,\mathcal{N}}} PsNumber^i = PsNumber$. Figure 4(c) presents an example of $StRSDB$.

We also assume that each database stores date/time of inserting a record; in DR and $RSDB$ the signature of every record is stored together with $\mathcal{PK}_C$, public key of a caregiver that uploaded the data and sigh them. Figure 4 shows the examples of LDB (a), $RSDB$ (b) and the representation of the metadata of $RSDB$, $StRSDB$, on Figure 4(c). The data from this particular example show the dosage of the drug and its actual concentration in the blood for a group of patients.

PS_P	QID		gnrlQID		healthcareData			$\mathcal{K}^S_{C,P}$	deltas
	age	gender	age	gender	analyte	dose, mg	concentr., mg/l		
Pseudo1	39	f	[38-50)	f	Efavirenzum	600	321	F498...	{A54..., 345...}
Pseudo2	26	m	[25-38)	m	Efavirenzum	550	257	4252...	{779..., 7B2...}
Pseudo3	30	m	[25-38)	m	Efavirenzum	600	354	76B1...	{57C..., 7FA...}
Pseudo4	12	m	[0-25)	m	Efavirenzum	450	214	32C4...	{7B3..., 48A...}
Pseudo5	45	f	[38-50)	f	Efavirenzum	600	319	6812...	{242..., DA4...}
Pseudo6	5	m	[0-25)	m	Efavirenzum	450	214	AB45...	{72F..., 36D...}
...	...	...	...	...	...	...	...	...	...

(a)

prevPS_P	PS_P	gnrlQID		healthcareData		
		age	gender	analyte	dose, mg	concentr., mg/l
	Pseudo1	[38-50)	f	Efavirenzum	600	321
	Pseudo2	[25-38)	m	Efavirenzum	550	257
	Pseudo3	[25-38)	m	Efavirenzum	600	354
	Pseudo4	[0-25)	m	Efavirenzum	450	214
Pseudo15	Pseudo5	[38-50)	f	Efavirenzum	600	319
	Pseudo6	[0-25)	m	Efavirenzum	450	214
Pseudo17	Pseudo7	[38-50)	f	Efavirenzum	650	320
	Pseudo8	[25-38)	m	Efavirenzum	600	210
	Pseudo9	[25-38)	m	Efavirenzum	600	315
	Pseudo10	[0-25)	m	Efavirenzum	450	201
	Pseudo11	[25-38)	m	Efavirenzum	550	270
	Pseudo12	[0-25)	m	Efavirenzum	500	300
...	...	...	...	...	...	...

(b)

gnrlQID	PsNumber	data source $\{(C_n, \text{PsNumber}_n)\}$
{00; 0}	4	$(C_1, 2); (C_1, 2)$
{010; 0}	5	$(C_1, 2); (C_1, 1); (C_1, 2)$
{011; 1}	3	$(C_1, 2); (C_1, 1)$
...	...	...

(c)

Fig. 4. Example of data representation in LDB (a) $RSDB$ (b) and $StRSDB$ (c)

4.2 Sharing and Accessing Patient's Data for the Treatment

Hereafter we present a protocol for storing and accessing patients' data in DR.

- **Step 1.** Patient generates a shared key (using a hash-function H and a random number $r_{1'}$) with Caregiver (C_1) he visits, this key will to be used for multi-key searchable encryption scheme: $\mathcal{K}^S_{P,C_1} = \text{H}(\mathcal{SK}_P \parallel r_{1'})$.

  Since this scheme does not support decryption, the data need to be encrypted twice: once for searching, and once with a traditional encryption scheme like AES, for decryption. Unique AES encryption key $(\mathcal{K}^D_{P,C_1})$ also has to be generated for the caregiver visited by the patient.

  The keys are generated from the Patient's secret key with the use of a smartcard or a mobile device.

- **Step 2.** At the Caregiver's office Patient has to transmit the keys to Caregiver's machine using card-reader device in the Caregiver's office or through a secured channel in the encrypted form: $CT_1 = Enc\left(\mathcal{K}^S_{P,C_1}, \mathcal{K}^D_{P,C_1}\right)_{\mathcal{PK}_{C_1}}$.
  To ensure integrity Patient's signature $(Sign(CT_1)_{\mathcal{SK}_P})$ and Patient's public key $(\mathcal{PK}_P)$ for verification are also required.

- **Step 3.** When the EHR is generated the content is encrypted with the shared keys (CT_2) and signed with the secret key of Caregiver ($Sign(CT_2)_{\mathcal{SK}_{C_1}}$),
  $$CT_2 = \langle Enc^S(EHR)_{\mathcal{K}^S_{P,C_1}}, Enc(EHR)_{\mathcal{K}^D_{P,C_1}} \rangle.$$

To improve efficiency the *indexable* version of the encryption scheme proposed in [13] can be used. One can also apply encryption algorithm for searching only to

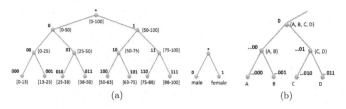

Fig. 5. Binary trees for *qids*: age and gender (a), and any set-valued *qid* (b)

the list of the keywords that describes the content of the *EHR*, such as patient's *ID* (*ID_P*), caregiver's qualification, date of the visit, symptoms, etc. Pseudonym, with which *EHR* can be associated in *LDB* of C_1: $PS_P^1 = (Enc^S (ID_P)_{\mathcal{K}_{P,C_1}^S})$ is generated using patient's set of uniquely identifiable patient data encrypted with the shared key for search. Therefore, a Caregiver will be able to find and update the data about Patient in an efficient way.

Visiting a caregiver Patient can decide *what data* stored at *DR* he wants to share. For instance, to provide Caregiver 1 an access to the *EHR* generated by Caregiver 2, he only needs to share with Caregiver 1 the keys shared between Caregiver 2 and Patient: $\left(\mathcal{K}_{P,C_2}^S, \mathcal{K}_{P,C_2}^D\right)$. To be able to retrieve Patient's *EHR(s)* based on the pseudonyms (or an attribute of *EHR*) a caregiver has to submit to Cloud Platform, *CP*, a token generated for the *ID_P* (or an attribute), as well as the deltas for other keys related to the patient, in order to let *CP* adjust the token. Token and deltas are to be computed according to the scheme described in [20].

4.3 Anonymization of Patients' Data for Research Purposes

In this subsection we present a description of the algorithm that allows to release medical data for the research purposes from different *LDBs* independently, while preserving the anonymity property of *RSDB*. We ensure that given the consent of the patient caregivers will be able to update *RSDB* with the data about the patient without creating multiple entries that correspond to the same person. Our solution also provides a possibility to recontact the patient through a caregiver that uploads the data.

We consider $\mathcal{N}$ Caregivers that may upload the data to *RSDB*. We assume that *RSDB* is initialized as $(k, k^m) - anonymous$, i.e., an algorithm to achieve $(k, k^m) - anonymity$ proposed in [21] had been applied to the local dataset to build the initial version of *RSDB*. For each *qid* there exist a binary tree, according to which generalization is performed. Figure 5 presents an example of binary trees that are constructed for the single-valued *QID*: age and gender (Figure 5(a)) and also shows an example of representing a set-valued attribute (Figure 5(b)). Our algorithm scales for any number of *qids*.

Figure 6 shows the pseudocode of the *RSDB* update algorithm and the generalization procedure used in the algorithm. The algorithm for *RSDB* update has to be executed every time a caregiver C_i wants to update *RSDB* with the data about patient *P*. First, C_i has to check whether he already uploaded the

1: $PS_P \leftarrow LDB^{PS_P}_{PS_P}$

2: $helthcareData \leftarrow LDB^{helthcareData}_{PS_P^i}$

3: if $LDB^{gnrlQID}_{PS_P^i}$ is not empty then

4:     $gnrlQID = LDB^{gnrlQID}_{PS_P^i}$

5: else

6:     $tempPS \leftarrow$ SEARCHOVER$(PS_P, \{\Delta_{\mathcal{K}^S_{P,C_i} \to \mathcal{K}^S_{P,C_j}}\})$

7:     if $tempPS \neq \emptyset$ then

8:         if $\| tempPS \| = 1$ then

9:             $gnrlQID \leftarrow tempPS.\text{LEAST}gnrlQID()$

10:             $PS_P \leftarrow tempPS.PS_P$

11:         else

12:             $gnrlQID \leftarrow$ MERGEPSEUD$(k, tempPS)$

13:         end if

14:     else

15:         $gnrlQID \leftarrow$ GENER(QID)

16:     end if

17: end if

18: insert$(PS_P, gnrlQID, helthcareData)$

(a)

```
procedure GENER(QID)
    VIEW ← StRSDB
    for  i = 0;  i < (|| QID || −1);  i + + do
        d_i = 0
        depth_i = qid.length()
        newTqid = ε
        newFqid = ε
        while (d_i ≠
```
$depth_i \vee (\exists gnrlqid_T, \; gnrlqid_F : (gnrlqid_T = VIEW.QID[i]) \vee (gnrlqid_F = VIEW.QID[i]) \vee (newTqid$ is a prefix of $gnrlqid_T) \vee (newFqid$ is a prefix of $gnrlqid_F))$ do
$$newFqid = newTqid + \neg QID[i].substring(d, d+1)$$
$$newTqid = newTqid + QID[i].substring(d, d+1)$$
$$d_i = d_i + 1$$
```
        end while
        VIEW ← VIEW ∨ (VIEW.QID[i] =
```
$newFqid.substring(0, (d-1)))$
```
    end for
    return VIEW.QID
end procedure
```

(b)

Fig. 6. Pseudocode of the RSDB Update Algorithm (a) and Generalization (b)

data about P to the $RSDB$. He can query his LDB with the patient pseudonym PS_P^i, generated using the shared between P and C_i key $\mathcal{K}^S_{P,C_i}$. If the value in a column $gnrlQID$ in a raw that corresponds to the PS_P^i is not empty, then some data about P are already presented in $RSDB$ with a combination of generalized QID that is described by the vector of binary strings, each represents $gnrlqid$. In this case C_i associates the data of P with these $gnrlQID$ that corresponds to PS_P^i (*lines 3,4* of the algorithm presented in Figure 6(a)). Otherwise, C_i has to perform a SEARCHOVER procedure to check whether there are some data about P that had been upload to $RSDB$ by another caregiver $C_j, j \neq i$ (*line 6*). However, this is only possible if P trusts C_i to check this (i.e., if P gave C_i an access to the $\mathcal{K}^S_{P,C_j}$ – key shared between P and C_j).

If SEARCHOVER procedure returns a single pseudonym, C_i will update $RSDB$ with the P' data with $gnrlQID$ that corresponds to PS_P^j (*lines 8-10*). If the result of SEARCHOVER contains more than one pseudonym, C_i checks whether there is a possibility to merge the pseudonyms related to P by applying MERGEPSEUD procedure (*line 12*). Afterwards, C_i will update $RSDB$ by uploading the data of P with (the least generalized) $gnrlQID$ that corresponds to PS_P^j. If SEARCHOVER procedure returns empty set, then the GENER procedure is performed (*line 15*), and as its output, a combination of the least generalized $gnrlQID$ is generated based on the $StRSDB$ and the P's QID.

SEARCHOVER$(PS_P, \{\Delta_{\mathcal{K}^S_{P,C_i} \to \mathcal{K}^S_{P,C_j}}\})$ procedure takes as an input the following data: patient's pseudonym (PS_P) generated with the key shared between the patient and caregiver C_i $(\mathcal{K}^S_{P,C_i})$; and a set of the deltas $(\{\Delta_{\mathcal{K}^S_{P,C_i} \to \mathcal{K}^S_{P,C_j}}\})$ – values generated for the keys $(\{\mathcal{K}^S_{P,C_j}, j \in \overline{1,N}, i \neq j\})$ related to the patient and shared with the caregiver C_i. Then, according to the schema proposed in [20], a server, which hosts $RSDB$, can perform a search for all the pseudonyms $(\{PS_P\})$ generated by different caregivers with their keys $(\mathcal{K}^S_{P,C_j}, j \in \overline{1,N})$ (adjusting a pseudonym generated by the caregiver C_i with key $(\mathcal{K}_{P,C_i}^S)$ to the one generated by the caregiver C_j with key ($\mathcal{K}_{P,C_j}^S$) without learning neither identity of P, nor the key $\mathcal{K}_{P,C}^S$) over the column that stores pseudonyms in $RSDB$. As a result a set of pseudonyms together with $gnrlQID$ that corresponds to each pseudonym are being returned.

MERGEPSEUD($k, tempPS$) allows to check whether it is possible to merge pseudonyms that correspond to the same patient but generated by different caregivers. It returns the least generalized $gnrlQID$ and merges pseudonyms if does not violate anonymity property of $RSDB$. The input is a parameter k and a set of pseudonyms discovered at the previous step.

Figure 6(b) shows the pseudocode for GENER(QID) procedure that is performed to create the least generalized $gnrlQID$ for the QID of the patient whose data have not been yet upload to $RSDB$ (or the data about the patient P might have been uploaded by the caregiver C_j, but a caregiver C_i that wants to upload the data about patient P for the first time does not possess the key $\mathcal{K}_{P,C_j}^S$). Input of the procedure is QID – an array of binary strings, each corresponds to one qid. Binary strings are constructed according to the representation of the QID using binary trees. During the execution each qid is considered one after another (the order is based on the importance of the qid) and generalized qid is formed by querying first $gnrlQID$ column of $StRSDB$, and then a view created based on the previously generalized qid. The goal is to find the least generalized set $gnrlQID$ for a QID of the patient such that $StRSDB$ already contains at least k entries with this set $gnrlQID$ without disclosing the QID.

5 Discussion

In this section we analyze the limitations of our model and possible privacy threats. We also suggest the countermeasures against the threats.

5.1 Limitations

We assume that caregiver is trusted, meaning that he respects the medical ethic and will share the data about his patient (including the data produced by other caregivers for the treatment of this patient) only according to the access control policy specified by the patient. However, if (by any reason) the patient does not want the caregiver to be able to access patients' data that are stored in the cloud, a new key has to be created, the data have to be re-encrypted on the server side, e.g., with the means of a proxy re-encryption scheme [1]. We also require an existence of a certification authority that provides the certificates for public keys and is able to check the identity of a caregiver to ensure that the data aggregated in $RSDB$ have been uploaded by a real doctor. However, CA does not have an access to the patients healthcare data.

A caregiver C can perform a MERGEPSEUD procedure only before he makes the first update of $RSDB$. Therefore, in order to merge pseudonyms the following strategy can be applied. According to the access control policy specified by the patient a caregiver that possesses the largest number of the keys may perform SEARCHOVER and MERGEPSEUD procedures every time after de-generalization protocol is executed. This will decrease the number of pseudonyms, with which the information about the patient had been uploaded by different caregivers.

With the proposed algorithm we only *preserve* the utility of the *RSDB*. However, *to improve* utility of the data from *RSDB*, the possibility to de-generalize the data from *RSDB* without violation of patients' privacy (during bounded time interval) need to be considered. To define the requirements and selection criteria for *gnrlqid* to be de-generalized are the next steps in our future work.

Generalization step (procedure GENER of the algorithm) requires going through all the *qid* one by one. However, we assume that the number of *qids* stored in the *RSDB* is not high and *qids* are ordered based on their importance with respect to the requirements to the *RSDB*.

5.2   Possible Threats and Countermeasures

If a patient loses his smart card, all the keys can be recovered from the *LDB*s of the caregivers that treat the patient. If the smartcard was stolen it is still difficult access the data or to modify the access control policy for anybody except the patient, because the card is protected with PIN code that is known only to the owner of the card. The limit of attempts to insert a valid PIN code can be set up to prevent brute-force attack.

We assume that the cloud server, where *RSDB* and *DR* are hosted, is honest but curious (it executes protocols and the algorithm correctly but tries to learn about the patient as much as possible). For example, some additional location information can be inferred from the IP address of the device that transmits the data from *LDB*, and these data could be more precise then *gnrlqid* that stands for the patient address. Therefore, this can violate (k, k^m) − *anonymity*. A straightforward countermeasure is to hide the IP address from the cloud server, e.g., using HTTP proxies or anonymous communication service like Tor [7].

Caregivers could potentially link pseudonyms related to the same patient using the column *PrevPS* in case of pseudonyms merging. To prevent this during the procedure of merging the pseudonyms, the previous pseudonym has to be encrypted together with the information about the caregiver that had created this pseudonym. The cipher text and a parameter that will indicate how many times the pseudonym had been updated will be stored in the column *PrevPS*. Then, it will be possible to find the caregiver that initially uploaded the data (i.g., in case of legal issues), through the caregiver(s) that merged pseudonyms.

6   Conclusion and Future Work

In this paper, we proposed an architecture of a secure and scalable privacy-preserving eHealth cloud system (that allows to store and efficiently search over patient data used for the treatment), and an algorithm that allows to build a database with patients' data for the research purposes.

In future work we will focus on the implementation of the architecture proposed in this paper and on its evaluation using a synthetic dataset (http://omop. org/OSIM2), and real patient data from our medical partners in the framework of ISyPeM2 project (www.nano-tera.ch/projects/368.php). We will also work towards de-generalization of *RSDB* to improve utility of the data. Finally, we will focus on improving efficiency of proposed solution by extending representation of the *QID* (from binary trees to n-ary trees) and employing agent based coordination model for the construction of *RSDB*.

Acknowledgments. This work was supported by the Nano-Tera initiative, in the framework of an RTD project ISyPeM2: developing therapeutic drug monitoring by designing a point-of-care system to measure drug concentration in blood samples and adjust dosage accordingly.

References

1. Ateniese, G., Fu, K., Green, M., Hohenberger, S.: Improved proxy re-encryption schemes with applications to secure distributed storage. ACM Trans. Inf. Syst. Secur. **9**(1), 1–30 (2006)
2. Baig, M.M., Li, J., Liu, J., Wang, H.: Cloning for privacy protection in multiple independent data publications. In: Proceedings of the 20th ACM International Conference on Information and knowledge Management, CIKM 2011, p. 885 (2011)
3. Benoist, E., Sliwa, J.: How to Collect Consent for an Anonymous Medical Database. HEALTHINF (2014)
4. Blake, I., Seroussi, G., Smart, N., Cassels, J.W.S.: Advances in Elliptic Curve Cryptography. Cambridge University Press, New York (2005)
5. Boneh, D., Di Crescenzo, G., Ostrovsky, R., Persiano, G.: Public Key Encryption with Keyword Search. In: Cachin, C., Camenisch, J.L. (eds.) EUROCRYPT 2004. LNCS, vol. 3027, pp. 506–522. Springer, Heidelberg (2004)
6. Clifton, C., Jiang, W.: CERIAS Tech Report 2005-134 Information Assurance and Security Privacy-Preserving Distributed k -Anonymity (2005)
7. Dingledine, R., Mathewson, N., Syverson, P.F.: Tor: The second-generation onion router. In: Proceedings of the 13th USENIX Security Symposium (2004)
8. Dubovitskaya, A., Urovi, V., Vasirani, M., Aberer, K., Fuchs, A., Buclin, T., Thoma, Y., Schumacher, M.: Privacy preserving interoperability for personalized medicine. Swiss Medical Informatics (September 2014)
9. Elger, B.S., Iavindrasana, J., Lo Lacono, L., Müller, H., Roduit, N., Summers, P., Wright, J.: Strategies for health data exchange for secondary, cross-institutional clinical research. Computer Methods and Programs in Biomedicine **99**, 230–251 (2010)
10. Gkoulalas-Divanis, A., Loukides, G.: Anonymization of Electronic Medical Records to Support Clinical Analysis. Springer Briefs in Electrical and Computer Engineering (2013)
11. Gkoulalas-Divanis, A., Loukides, G., Sun, J.: Publishing data from electronic health records while preserving privacy: A survey of algorithms. Journal of Biomedical Informatics **50**, 4–19 (2014)
12. Gotta, V., Widmer, N., Montemurro, M., Leyvraz, S., Haouala, A., Decosterd, L.A., Csajka, C., Buclin, T.: Therapeutic drug monitoring of imatinib. Clinical Pharmacokinetics **51**(3), 187–201 (2012)

13. Helfer, J., Valdez, S., Popa, R.A., Stark, E., Zeldovich, N., Frans Kaashoek, M., Balakrishnan, H.: Building web applications on top of encrypted data using Mylar. In: Proceedings of the 11th USENIX Conference on Networked Systems Design and Implementation, pp. 157–172 (2014)

14. Ibraimi, L., Asim, M., Petko, M.: Secure Management of Personal Health Records by Applying Attribute-Based Encryption. In: 6th International Workshop on Wearable Micro and Nano Technologies for Personalized Health (pHealth) (2009)

15. Li, M., Yu, S., Ren, K., Lou, W.: Securing Personal Health Records in Cloud Computing: Patient-Centric and Fine-Grained Data Access Control in Multi-owner Settings. In: Jajodia, S., Zhou, J. (eds.) SecureComm 2010. LNICST, vol. 50, pp. 89–106. Springer, Heidelberg (2010)

16. Li, M., Yu, S., Zheng, Y.: Scalable and Secure Sharing of Personal Health Records in Cloud Computing Using Attribute-Based Encryption. IEEE Tranyactions on Parallel and Distributed Systems 24(1), 131–143 (2013)

17. Li, Z.-R., Chang, E.-C., Huang, K.-H., Lai, F.: A secure electronic medical record sharing mechanism in the cloud computing platform. In: 2011 IEEE 15th International Symposium on Consumer Electronics (ISCE), pp. 98–103, June 2011

18. Lo Iacono, L.: Multi-centric universal pseudonymisation for secondary use of the EHR. Studies in Health Technology and Informatics 126, 239–247 (2007)

19. Lounis, A., Hadjidj, A., Bouabdallah, A., Challal, Y.: Secure Medical Architecture on the Cloud Using Wireless Sensor Networks for Emergency Management. In: Eighth International Conference on Broadband and Wireless Computing, Communication and Applications, pp. 248–252 (2013)

20. Popa, R.A., Zeldovich, N.: Multi-key searchable encryption. Cryptology ePrint Archive, Report 2013/508 (2013)

21. Poulis, G., Loukides, G., Gkoulalas-Divanis, A., Skiadopoulos, S.: Anonymizing Data with Relational and Transaction Attributes. In: Blockeel, H., Kersting, K., Nijssen, S., Železný, F. (eds.) ECML PKDD 2013, Part III. LNCS, vol. 8190, pp. 353–369. Springer, Heidelberg (2013)

22. Solanas, A., Martinez-Balleste, A., Mateo-Sanz, J.: Distributed architecture with double-phase microaggregation for the private sharing of biomedical data in mobile health. IEEE Transactions onInformation Forensics and Security (2013)

23. Song, D.X., Wagner, D., Perrig, A.: Practical techniques for searches on encrypted data. In: Proceedings of the 2000 IEEE Symposium on Security and Privacy (2000)

24. Sweeney, L.: K-anonymity: A model for protecting privacy. Int. J. Uncertain. Fuzziness Knowl.-Based Syst. 10(5), 557–570 (2002)

25. Urovi, V., Olivieri, A.C., Brugués de la Torre, A., Bromuri, S., Fornara, N., Schumacher, M.: Secure P2P cross-community health record exchange in IHE compatible systems. International Journal on Artificial Intelligence Tools 23(1) (2014)

26. Xu, L., Cremers, A.B.: A Decentralized Pseudonym Scheme for Cloud-based eHealth Systems. HEALTHINF (2014)

27. Yu, S., Wang, C., Ren, K., Lou, W.: Achieving Secure, Scalable, and Fine-grained Data Access Control in Cloud Computing. In: INFOCOM. IEEE (2010)

Cyber-physical Systems and Critical Infrastructures Security

Application of a Game Theoretic Approach in Smart Sensor Data Trustworthiness Problems

Konstantinos Maraslis[(✉)], Theodoros Spyridopoulos, George Oikonomou,
Theo Tryfonas, and Mo Haghighi

Cryptography Group, University of Bristol, Bristol, UK
{k.maraslis,th.spyridopoulos,g.oikonomou,
theo.tryfonas,m.haghighi}@bristol.ac.uk

Abstract. In this work we present an Intrusion Detection (ID) and an Intrusion Prevention (IP) model for Wireless Sensor Networks (WSNs). The attacker's goal is to compromise the deployment by causing nodes to report faulty sensory information. The defender, who is the WSN's operator, aims to detect the presence of faulty sensor measurements (ID) and to subsequently recover compromised nodes (IP). In order to address the conflicting interests involved, we adopt a Game Theoretic approach that takes into consideration the strategies of both players and we attempt to identify the presence of Nash Equilibria in the two games. The results are then verified in two simulation contexts: Firstly, we evaluate the model in a middleware-based WSN which uses clustering over a bespoke network stack. Subsequently, we test the model in a simulated IPv6-based sensor deployment. According to the findings, the results of both simulation models confirm the results of the theoretic one.

1 Introduction

Wireless Sensor Networks (WSNs) have been playing a major role in the field of monitoring and controlling complex processes remotely. Their application on industry has facilitated the automation of large, complex and distributed industrial control processes. However, the plethora of applications that they can be used for, including their utilisation in sensitive fields such as military and medical applications, or the Critical National Infrastructure (CNI), renders WSNs an attractive target for a variety of cyber-attacks. Therefore, protecting such networks is of topmost importance. In order to maintain their security, WSNs require a set of policies effectively implemented in an automated fashion, so that faster and more efficient security-related decisions can be made.

   Much research has been conducted into the security aspect of WSNs in an attempt to address the aforementioned issue [1,2]. However, due to the significant

---

The research leading to these results has received funding from the European Union's Seventh Framework Programme (FP7/2007-2013) under grant agreement n° 609094. This work has also been supported by Bristol's Systems Centre and Fraser-Nash Consultancy.

H. Federrath and D. Gollmann (Eds.): SEC 2015, IFIP AICT 455, pp. 601–615, 2015.
DOI: 10.1007/978-3-319-18467-8_40

resource constraints in WSNs' hardware and long unsupervised operations, key challenge in the protection of WSNs is the development of lightweight methods that will be able to efficiently detect and confront attacks under constrained computational resources.

In this work, we utilise the principles of Game Theory to develop two discrete models for the protection of WSNs; an Intrusion Detection System (IDS) and an Intrusion Prevention System (IPS). Our models provide optimal cost-efficient strategies for the detection of an intrusion (IDS model) and the protection of the system (IPS model). Additionally, their ability to take into account all related costs (sensor price, cost of recovery, attack cost etc.) along with the ability to apply their results as a security policy in the WSN without constantly updating the network, renders them an energy-efficient protection solution. Our models provide automated procedures based on which, network operators can either disregard bogus data from compromised sensors or find the optimal way to recover the compromised sensors depending on their capabilities.

To validate our findings, we run two sets of simulations. Initially, we simulate a middleware-based WSN that uses network clustering and a bespoke network stack using Sensomax [3], an agent-based WSN middleware, which supports executing multiple applications with regards to their operational paradigms. Subsequently, we use the Cooja simulator, which is distributed as part of the Contiki[1] open source Operating System for the Internet of Things.

The next section offers some basic background knowledge in the area of WSN protection and Section 3 discusses the key related work in this field. Section 4 presents the models for both the IDS and the IPS, including the results of their simulations. The validation of our models in a cluster-based deployment is provided in Section 5, while Section 6 presents a validation of our models utilising an IPv6-based Deployment. Finally, Section 7 provides the conclusions of our work and some paths for further work.

2   Basic Background

Wireless Sensor Networks (WSNs) are typically composed of self-powered sensors (nodes) that communicate with each other and/or with a base station. The topology of a WSN varies from a simple star-shaped network to more advanced multi-hop wireless mesh networks, while the number of sensors that comprise them can fluctuate between different deployments. Sensors have inherent limitations in terms of storage capacity, processing power, energy availability and network bandwidth. Thus, implementing encryption-based security mechanisms is a challenging task [4].

Various threats like eavesdropping, lack of physical protection of the sensors, Denial of Service (DoS) attacks and injection of malicious data necessitate their protection [5]. This is a challenging task, especially when users and/or nodes take autonomous decisions, which in turn raise non-cooperative behaviours and conflicting interests [6].

---

[1] http://www.contiki-os.org

Conventional WSN security systems mainly use Rule/Signature-based detection mechanisms, which can effectively detect known attacks based on predefined rules, or anomaly-based mechanisms that can detect new attacks by comparing patterns or resource utilization [1]. However, the application of such methods should be driven by security policies that take into account the related resource constrains.

In solving decision making problems of this kind, *Game Theory* seems to be a suitable approach as it suits situations where adversarial interests are included. Every participant can choose an action within a set of predefined actions and for every possible combination of those there is a reward/utility that occurs for each participant. These situations are called *games*, the participants are called *players* and the actions are called *strategies*. The notion of "solution" that a game theoretic approach can offer can have many forms, most of which require that the players are rational, meaning that they *only* seek the maximisation of their personal reward/utility. In addition, there are many kinds of games, depending generally on the piece of information that is disclosed to the players, their relationship and the type of their communication, if any. In this work we only deal with two-player games where every player's loss is equal to the other's reward (zero-sum game). The concept of game solution adopted here is the detection, at the beginning of the (static) game, of strategies such that every player's chosen strategy is the best response to the other player's chosen strategy. In other words, when both players follow their computed optimal strategies, none of them would be tempted to unilaterally change it, because that would only lead to a reduced individual reward, compared to the existing. The concept described, is known as *Nash Equilibrium* of the game [7–9].

3 Related Work

Game Theory has been used in the past for simulating and solving security-related problems in WSNs. For example, the authors of [2] investigate the case where a clustered WSN is under attack. In this project, the attacker targets the cluster heads in an attempt to crowd the data flow or drop it. The underlying IDS monitors the data transfers and attempts to keep the WSN functioning by detecting malicious nodes in the forward path. This situation is modelled as a two-player, non-cooperative, zero-sum game and it is proved that the game has no pure Nash Equilibria. This means that the game is unstable, and therefore does not provide a state at which we would expect the game to be stabilised after a large number of iterations. In the resource-constraint environment of WSNs this instability is translated into increased power demands.

In [10] the behaviour of a system under a Distributed Denial of Service (DDoS) attack is under investigation based on previous work of [11]. The target environment there is a network, however the model is generic and based on the same networking principles that apply to WSNs. The attacker aims to perform a DDoS attack at a system that has implemented a firewall. The attacker's strategy is defined by the number of occupied nodes and the distribution according to which they transmit malicious traffic. The defender on the other hand can control the settings of the system's firewall. This situation was modelled as a two-player, static, non-cooperative, zero-sum game. The research concludes with suggestions for the strategy of the defender which maximize the minimum payoff of the defender regardless of attacker's decision and behaviour.

Authors in [12] try to improve the security and energy efficiency of a WSN by applying a reputation system on its nodes where low-reputed ones are shut down. Every node can improve its reputation by forwarding incoming packages. However, this forwarding causes draining of their batteries. Since conflicting interests are present, a game theoretic model is adopted in order for the maximum possible battery life of the nodes to be assured while sustaining an unproblematic operation. In addition, there are malicious nodes that can cause package drops, making the proper flow of data even more difficult. On all scenarios of the WSN games of this work, the authors solve the problem by finding the network's Nash Equilibrium. Under the assumption that the involved players are rational, the authors find the optimal strategies for both the defender and the attacker that ensure an upper limit for the expected losses when they are followed. As far as the security and power conservation are concerned, the network improves significantly in all three cases, comparing to the scenario were the model was not applied.

Compared to those works, our is about a different scenario. Additionally, the aforementioned works do not address cases where more than one parameters affect each player's strategy simultaneously. Our IPS and IDS models incorporate this capability making the problem multi-dimensional, which not only adds to its complexity but, most importantly, offers the ability to describe a far wider range of problems. A method similar to the one of this work, can be used for even more parameters. However, the complexity and computational workload will increase considerably.

4   Examining Smart Sensor Data Trustworthiness

In our models, the attacker modifies compromised nodes in order to make them report erroneous values. We make the following assumptions about the deployment: 1) All network traffic is encrypted, 2) all sensor measurements are signed and 3) the deployment's topology is not publicly available, which is a reasonable assumption since the logical network topology (e.g. routing topology or cluster membership) is created and maintained at runtime by an algorithm that relies on criteria which can change over time and are not known a-priori, such as the quality of radio links.

For the attacker, we make the following assumptions: 1) S/he is external to the system and highly motivated. 2) S/he can actively initiate attacks against nodes (the firmware running on nodes is susceptible to bugs already discovered by the attacker and therefore, an attack against a node is always successful). 3) S/he has high time availability, but not enough to break cryptography and signature schemes. 4) Due to the inability to break signatures, the attacker can introduce neither her/his own traffic nor malicious nodes. Therefore, the only option is to compromise existing, legitimate nodes. 5) Due to her/his inability to break cryptography, the attacker can passively overhear traffic but cannot understand the contents of network packets. As such, s/he cannot synthesise the deployment's topology from passive eavesdropping. 6) Lastly, the attacker has high, yet not unlimited financial resources. Thus, s/he can choose to attack the entire network, but the criterion is to optimise the financial benefit of an attack. 7) The attacker can choose the number of nodes to attack, but being oblivious about the network topology has no way of identifying which nodes would maximise damage to the network.

4.1   Modification Detection Model

In this model a game between the defender who wants to monitor a specific area and the attacker who randomly chooses which sensors to attack and tries to make the network transmit as much incorrect information as possible, is deployed. The first question that rises for the defender is what should be the density of sensors (i.e. number of sensors per area unit) that should be chosen, as this affects directly the strategy of the attacker. Since the area under investigation is predefined, it is only the number of sensors that can affect the density. Hence, the number of sensors is part of defender's strategy and in the game s/he tries to find the most beneficial value within a set of possible choices.

In addition, every sensor has a coefficient of significance. This coefficient is proportional to the level of trust that is related to the information transmitted by this particular sensor and echoes the probability that the measurements provided by the sensor are true. The reasons that this coefficient differs from sensor to sensor vary from the type of measurements that are taken, to the structural features of the sensing elements.

Tolerance is another strategy of the defender and it is a property of the whole network. Having defined untrusted / trusted / total information as the sum of significance coefficients of untrusted / trusted / all sensors respectively, tolerance denotes the minimum portion of the total information that the untrusted information should be, in order for the latter to be believed by the defender. In other words, it denotes the minimum value that the following fraction can have in order for the incorrect information that has been injected into the network to be treated as correct. We call this fraction Attack Coefficient: $AC = Untrusted\ Information/Total\ Information$. This is part of the defender's strategy since s/he is the one to decide which piece of information is treated as valid. The choice of tolerance can directly affect players' tactics due to formula (1).

At this point it is essential that some basic assumptions of the model are presented: 1) Players are rational. 2) Full area coverage is desired. 3) Two sensors of the same network with identical specifications, operating under identical conditions can still report slightly different values. 4) A compromised sensor cannot affect the information that other sensors transmit. 5) The attacker's goal

is to make a sensor transmit faulty data that demonstrate noteworthy deviation from the data that uncompromised sensors transmit (otherwise the attack
is pointless). 6) Compromised network is the network into which the injected
faulty information is believed by the defender.

Under those assumptions, the network operators try to take into account only
the non-compromised data without knowing in advance which piece of data is
compromised. Therefore, if the attack coefficient is greater than *tolerance* then
the incorrect information is considered to be accurate, correct data is disposed
and the attempt for compromising the network is considered successful, which
in turn increases attacker's payoff. Otherwise, the network is not considered
compromised, which implies a lower payoff for the attacker. Thus, the algorithm
and, in turn, the defender can judge whether the network is under attack by
the percentage of the believed information out of the total information which
justifies its inclusion in the IDM category. Intuitively, tolerance should only be a
value greater than 0.5 (50%) and of course less or equal to 1 (100%). In this way,
the weighted information that will be ultimately "believed" by the defender will
correspond to at least half of the total weight. Our goal is to help the defender
choose the best options (i.e. options that will lead to the highest possible payoff)
about the number of sensors that will constitute the network and the tolerance
adopted.

The attacker can only affect the number of sensors attacked considering that
each one of these attacks bears a cost. Therefore, the optimal strategies are not
obvious and a game theoretic approach would be suitable. The payoff function
(1), with the help of which a payoff matrix will be populated, is affected by the
aforementioned parameters.

$$AP = (\frac{is}{ts} \geq t) \times rcn + s \times cps - a \times cpa + t \times tc \qquad (1)$$

where, AP = Attacker's Payoff, is = incorrect sum (i.e. the sum of significance
coefficients of the actually compromised sensors), ts = total sum (i.e. the sum of
significance coefficients of all sensors), t = tolerance, rcn = reward for compromising the network, s = number of sensors, cps = cost per sensor, a = attacks,
cpa = cost per attack, tc = tolerance cost and:

$$(\frac{is}{ts} \geq t) = \begin{cases} 1 & \text{if inequality holds} \\ 0 & \text{if inequality does not hold} \end{cases} \qquad (2)$$

As the formula denotes, the attacker will only be rewarded with rcn if
s/he manages to compromise the network ($is/ts \geq t$) which is equivalent to
$[(is/ts \geq t) = 1]$, whereas s/he bears the cost of attacks, regardless their impact.
Since the players are antagonistic, the attacker takes advantage of the defender's
expenses. Thus, everything that has a cost for the defender, like the total cost
of sensors ($s \times cps$) or the total tolerance cost ($t \times tc$), is added to the attacker's
reward in formula 1. The necessity of tolerance cost lies in the fact that the
greater the tolerance is, the greater part of the whole information, should be
faulty in order for it to be "believed". That motivates the attacker for a more

comprehensive attack and therefore a less possible recovery by the operators of the network. Under this perspective, it could be preferable for the network to suffer a mild assault that will compromise the network temporarily, than risk suffering a massive one that will render it totally useless or unaffordable to be fixed. It should be noted that the payoff function has no units of measurement. It is just a necessary quantification of the advantage derived for each player due to the actions taken so that the problem can be solved and resembles the role of a utility function.

It is worth noting that although the defender is not aware of which piece of information is compromised, it is still possible to use the outcome of formula 1. In other words, although the defender cannot distinguish between correct and faulty data, s/he is aware of the payoff that s/he receives when both players choose specific strategies. Furthermore, there is a chance that $(cs/ts) < (is/ts) < t$, where cs = correct sum. In this case, the compromised information will not be believed although it is greater portion of the total information than the correct information is and therefore no reward for compromised network is given to the attacker. This is only possible for $t > 0.5$ (50%).

Since every strategy of the defender consists of a pair (m, n) where m is the number of sensors used and n is the acceptable tolerance, we have two-dimensional strategy sets. One way for this to be tackled and thus for the optimal strategies to be found, is the procedure we outline here. The algorithm is described by the following piece of pseudo-code along with Fig. 1. In this figure, green denotes the parameters that are chosen by the defender and constitute their strategy (*Number of Sensors* and *Tolerance*) while orange is used for the parameter that is chosen by the attacker and constitute their strategy (*Attacks* which is the number of attacks performed). *Sensor weights* are the aforementioned significance coefficients of the sensors which can shape defender's strategy, but their value is not chosen by the defender and therefore it is in grey colour. These parameters shape the values of *Attacker's Payoff* (formula (1)) which populate *Attacker's Payoff Matrix* that is seen in Fig. 1. This is the matrix of the game, based on which we will later look for Nash Equilibria. Its pseudo-code is:

```
for  s = Smin to Smax
    SC(all sensors) = 1/follow Uniform/follow Normal
    given the strategy sets for number of attacks and tolerance level
        −populate APMs based on formula(1)
        −calculate ne(APMs) and AR(ne(APMs))
    end for
NE = {ne(APMs), ∀ s}
NEG = {ne(APMs) ∈ NE : AR(ne(APMs)) = min{AR(NE)}}
find which strategies lead to NEG
```

where s is the number of sensors in the network, S_{min} and S_{max} are the minimum and maximum possible number of sensors, respectively, $SC()$ denotes the significant coefficient of deployed sensors, APM_s is the Attacker's Payoff Matrix (Fig. 1) that occurred for *number of sensors* = s, $ne()$ is the Nash

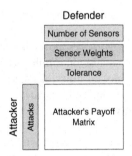

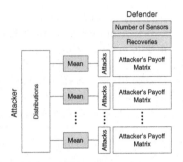

Fig. 1. Schematic description of the IDS model

Fig. 2. Schematic description of the IPS model

Equilibrium/a of a sub-game, $AR(ne())$ is the attacker's reward that corresponds to $ne()$ and NEG is the Nash Equilibrium/a of the whole game.

4.2 Modification Correction Model

In this model's use case there is an attacker who attacks sensors and a defender that protects them, but there are three key differences from the detection instance. Firstly, the defender in this game knows which sensors are compromised and has the ability to recover them. Secondly, there are now two parameters that affect the attacker's strategies, instead of one and thirdly, the game now is repeated for many rounds. However all decisions are made at the beginning and remain unchanged for the whole game, which makes the game static although in a repeated form. Attacker's goal is once more to compromise the network with the least possible cost while defender's is to keep the network uncompromised with the least possible cost. Our scope is to help the defender choose the best options regarding the number of sensors that will constitute the network and the number of recoveries that will be required. Again, the best choices for the attacker are considered the ones that will lead to the highest possible payoff.

The schematic representation of this model is shown in Fig. 2. The logic of the colours is the same as in Fig. 1, therefore the attacker's strategies are defined by *Distributions* (i.e. the distribution that the number of attacks follow) and their *Mean* (i.e. the mean value of the distribution) while defender's strategies are defined by the *Number of Sensors* that constitute the WSN and *Recoveries* which denotes the maximum number of recoveries performed in each round and remains the same for all rounds. *Attacks* occur as a result of the choice of *Distributions* and their *Mean* values (as in the pseudo-code that follows) and affect formula (3) based on which *Attacker's Payoff Matrix* is populated. We then seek for Nash Equilibria on that matrix. At any round of the game the attacker can only make as many attacks as the uncompromised sensors in the network and the defender can only make as many recoveries as the compromised sensors in the network. The payoff this time is computed as the function:

$$AP = ta \times (rcs - ac) + tr \times (rcps - rcs) + s \times sc + (\frac{cse}{tns} \geq t) \times rcn \quad (3)$$

where, AP = Attacker's Payoff, ta = total attacks, rcs = reward for compromising a sensor, ac = attack cost, tr = total recoveries, $rcps$ = recovery cost per sensor, rcs = reward for compromised sensor, sc = sensor cost, cse = compromised sensor at the end, tns = total number of sensors and for n number of rounds:

$$total\ attacks\ (or\ recoveries) = \sum_{i=1}^{n} attacks\ (or\ recoveries)\ at\ round\ i \quad (4)$$

$$\left(\frac{cse}{tns} \geq t\right) = \begin{cases} 1 & \text{if inequality holds} \\ 0 & \text{if inequality does not hold} \end{cases} \quad (5)$$

Again, as a zero-sum game, everything costly for the defender rewards the attacker. For example, an attack has a cost ac for the attacker but as a result a compromised sensor occurs which rewards the attacker (rcs) since it is harmful for the defender. Thus, the total number of attacks (ta) is multiplied by ($rcs - ac$). The same logic explains the terms $tr \times (rcps - rcs)$ and $s \times sc$ while the term $(cse/tns \geq t) \times rcn$ is equivalent to the term $(is/ts \geq t) \times rcn$ in formula (1). In this case the algorithm may choose to intentionally allow mild attacks since that will save the defender of the recovery costs and will still bear a cost for the attacker although the latter will not be rewarded with the rcn, causing an overall small damage. Additionally, there should be $rcs < ac$ and $rcps < rcs$. The first inequality ensures that the attacker will seek the additional reward for compromising the network (rcn) and that his optimal strategy is not necessarily to attack as many sensors as possible. The second inequality ensures that the defender will not overspend his resources protecting more sensors than necessary. As in the previous model, if $[(cse/tns) \geq t] = 1$, then the network is considered compromised and the corresponding reward is given to the attacker. The pseudo-code for this model is:

```
for  s = S_min to S_max
   for  every  D ∈ Distributions = {Normal, Poisson, Exponential}
      for  every  m ∈ MeanValues
         −Generate  attacks(i), i = 1,...,5  that  follow  D(m)
         −Let  attacks(i), i = 1,...,5  be  possible  number  of  attacks
         Given  the  strategy  sets  of  attacks  and  recoveries
            −populate  APM_s  based  on  formula(3)
            −calculate  ne(APM_s)  and  AR(ne(APM_s))
      end  for
   end  for
end  for
NE = {ne(APM_s), ∀ s}
NEG = {ne(APM_s) ∈ NE : AR(ne(APM_s)) = min{AR(NE)}}
find  which  strategies  lead  to  NEG
```

where, $MeanValues$ is the set of all possible mean values and is described later on. By $D(m)$ we mean that the variable follows distribution D with mean m. In the case of Normal distribution, there is also variance (σ^2) needed but is omitted from the pseudocode for simplicity. However, it is taken into account in the execution of the real code. That variance remains unchanged through the model and has been chosen in a way such that all the values that are generated and follow $N(m, \sigma^2)$ lie within the defined range. In addition, the procedure of generating attacks has been designed in a way such that $\{attacks\ that\ follow\ D(m_i)\} \cap \{attacks\ that\ follow\ D(m_j)\} = \emptyset$, for $i \neq j$, $\forall\ D \in Distributions$.

4.3   Model Results

In this section we present our models' simulation results visualized as a threefold graph. The distributions used to describe attacker's behaviour and significance coefficients, are commonly used to describe various elements of network activity [13,14].

For the IDS model, the sample values that were used for formula (1) are: Sensors: [500, 600], t: [0.55, 0.9], Attacks: [500, 600], Significance coefficients: All equal to 1, follow Uniform(1,4) and Normal(2.5, 0.25), $rcn = 10$, $cpa = 1.2$, $cps = 2.3$, $tc = 10$. Conclusions can be extracted by Fig. 3. We interpret the figure, bearing in mind that we help defender to take the best possible decision regarding the maximization of his payoff. In Fig. 3, we can see the Nash Equilibria of all the sub-games that occurred. The horizontal axis in all sub-graphs of the figure is the number of Sensors. A Nash Equilibrium can be seen, as a vertical line that goes through all three sub-figures. If (x, y_1), (x, y_2) and (x, y_3) are the points that this line cuts the blue lines of sub-figures 1, 2 and 3 (starting from the upper one) respectively, that means that the best option for the defender would be to deploy x sensors and tolerance equal to y_3 for the WSN. The best response to that for the attacker is to perform y_2 attacks. That strategy would lead to a payoff for the attacker equal to y_1. The pair (x, y_3) represents the best strategy that the defender can choose in order to respond to attacker's y_2 strategy and vice versa. Since every vertical line that goes through all sub-figures is a Nash Equilibrium (for the values of x that the graphs exist), we want the one that leads to the least payoff for the attacker which is represented by y axis in the top sub-figure. Fig. 3 depicts the outcome of the game for the scenario where all significance coefficients are equal to 1 and from that we see that the the least possible attacker's payoff is 703.3 which is achieved when the defender deploys 511 sensors (x axis) in a WSN with tolerance equal to 0.8 (bottom sub-figure) and the attacker performs 400 attacks (middle sub-figure). Thus, the defender's optimal strategy is $(x, y_3) = (511, 0.8)$ and the optimal strategy for the attacker is $y_2 = 400$. This leads attacker's payoff equal to 703.3.

The gaps of Fig. 3 are observed close to the values that correspond to combinations of strategies that would make the equality $is/ts = t$ from formula (1) to hold. Graphs for the other two scenarios of significance coefficients' distribution, Uniform(1,4) and Normal(2.5, 0.25), are not demonstrated due to their similarity. However, they would be interpreted the same way. The results for all distributions are included in Table 1.

For the IPS model, values for the involved parameters in formula (3) are: Sensors: [200, 400], Recoveries: [1, 70], Distribution of number of attacks: Normal, Poisson, Exponential, $rcs = 1.5$, $ac = 3$, Mean values created per distribution

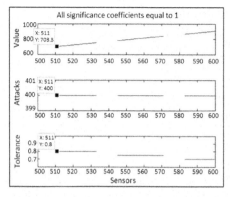

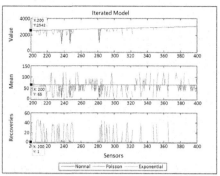

Fig. 3. Attackers Payoff, Number of Attacks and Tolerance for the Nash Equilibrium that occurs for different num. of Sensors when all significance coefficients are equal to 1

Fig. 4. Attacker's Payoff (Value), Mean values and Number of Recoveries of the Nash Equilibria found in the Iterated model

$= 5$, $rcps = 5$, $sc = 4$, $rcn = 2000$, $t = 0.5$, Attacks: $[10, 120]$. Interpretation of Fig. 4 is almost identical to the one of Fig. 3. The only difference is that there are now all three distributions in the same figure. Therefore, the Nash Equilibrium of this game will be the one that leads to the minimax price (i.e. the minimum price out of the highest possible ones) of Value. Given that every vertical line that goes through all sub-figures is a Nash Equilibrium of the game and (x, y_1^i), (x, y_2^i), (x, y_3^i), $i \in \{Normal, Poisson, Exponential\}$ are the 9 points that this line cuts all graphs of all sub-figures then if the defender chooses a specific number of sensors x, the attacker will choose as a response, out of points $\{(x, y_1^i), i \in \{Normal, Poisson, Exponential\}\}$ the distribution i for which $max\{y_1^i, i \in \{Normal, Poisson, Exponential\}\}$ is achieved. Thus, assuming that (x, y_1^i) are the points that the vertical line that goes through x cuts all graphs of the first sub-figure, the defender should choose x for which $min\{max\{ordinate(x, y_1^i)\}\}$ is achieved. The strategies that correspond to the points found that way are Nash Equilibria since they follow the definition of Nash Equilibrium mentioned earlier.

5   Validation in a Cluster-Based Deployment

In this section we conduct a number of experiments to validate both the IPS and the IDS utilising the clustering facilities offered by Sensomax which allows us to validate our simulation with a hardware-in-the-loop approach. In all our experiments, both models were programmed as two separate applications in every sensor node. Those two applications can be executed concurrently in order to detect and prevent attacks, whilst sensor nodes are carrying out their normal

Table 1. Aggregated Results

Intrusion Detection Model			
Significance Coefficients	Optimal # of Sensors	Optimal Tolerance	Optimal # of Attacks
All equal to 1	511	0.8	400
Uniform(1,4)	503	0.85	400
Normal(2.5, 0.25)	500	0.85	400
Intrusion Prevention Model			
Type	Optimal # of Sensors	Optimal # of Recoveries	Optimal # of Attacks
Non-Iterated	200	1	Expon.(mean: 92.5)
Iterated	200	1	Poisson (mean: 65)

operation and meeting the requirements of their given task. The application itself resides in a single node, known as the cluster-head, where all the top-level executions happen. The IDS and IPS applications (i.e. model logic) are present in every sensor node, whilst being executed only in the cluster-heads.

For the first phase of our experiment a network of 600 virtual nodes was created in SensomaX Companion Simulator (SXCS) [15], incorporating 30 clusters, each containing 20 nodes. As a way of a sensing application, all nodes were programmed to constantly report Temperature readings at 1-second intervals. A second network containing 600 nodes without any clustering mechanism was also created to report false temperature readings. Each experiment reported in this section was repeated 100 times to gain the average values. Fig. 5a demonstrates the average number of attacks required before detection. For a 510-node network, the average number of attacks is 398. This result is on par with the results reported in Fig. 3, given the standard deviation, which covers the 400 attacks reported earlier. Fig. 5b depicts the number of nodes required for the IPS model to operate successfully based on a variable number of attacks. The results reported in this figure are also relatively on par with the results reported in Fig. 4, given the standard deviation around the mean values. The impact on the energy consumption of the network is depicted at Fig.5c.

6   Validation in an IPv6-Based Deployment

In this Section we make use of Cooja [16], the network simulator distributed with the Contiki Operating System for the Internet of Things. Within Cooja, we simulate an IPv6-based wireless sensor network. Network nodes use IPv6 over Low-Power Wireless Personal Area Networks (6LoWPAN) [17] and the Routing Protocol for Low Power and Lossy Networks (RPL) [18]. We simulate a network with 1 traffic sink and 40 traffic sources, distributed in a 200x200 grid. Node distribution is entirely random, with the only limitation being that all sources must have a network path to the sink. We choose to simulate a network of 40 nodes in order to achieve full area coverage, as is the assumption in the model. We use 10 different random topologies and for each topology we repeat the experiment 10 times using a new random seed for each iteration.

In the remainder of the section, we use the following notation: n is the index of a node, $N = \{n : n \in \mathbb{Z}^+ \land n \leq 40\}$, $C = \{n : n \in N \land \text{node } n \text{ is compromised}\}$,

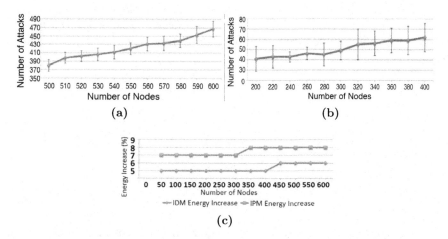

Fig. 5. (a), (b) IDS's & IPS's required number of nodes vs. number of attacks, respectively (c) Impact of IDM & IPM on energy consumption

t is the defender's chosen tolerance, $D_n : n \in N$ is the degree of node n discussed below, $S_n : n \in N$ is the significance of node n, also discussed below. In the model, the choice of node significance is based on a random distribution. In our simulations we model node significance as a function of network density. We first calculate the node degree D_n for each each network device, which is calculated as the number of other network nodes within communication range. The significance S_n for node n is subsequently calculated as $S_n = max(\{D_i : i \in N\})/D_n$.

Thus, S_n corresponds to the maximum node degree observed in the network, divided by the node's own degree. Since, all nodes in the network have a path to the sink, they have at least one other node within communication range. Hence, $D_n > 0$ and the significance calculation's denominator is always nonzero. This way, nodes in dense areas will have lower significance, while nodes in sparse areas will have a high one. That is because the network is used to gather sensory information about an environmental parameter in a geographical region. Even between two identical devices, measurements are likely to be slightly different due to manufacturing inaccuracies and slight fluctuations of environmental parameters even within the same area. Thus, in an area where multiple nodes are reporting, each node's measurement will be of lower significance, whereas in a sparse area where only a few nodes are reporting, it will bear more weight.

According to the model, the optimal attacker strategy is to compromise 78.27% of the total number of nodes in the network (400 out of 511). With this in mind, in each experiment the attacker compromises a random set of 31 nodes ($|C| = 31$). Furthermore, defender's optimal strategy is to select tolerance level $T = 0.85$. An attack is successful if the defender believes the erroneous value to be accurate and this is only true if Attack's Coefficient $(AC) = \sum_{j \in C} S_j / \sum_{i \in N} S_i > T$.

Fig. 6 illustrates the densities of the ten network deployments under investigation. For all deployments, the minimum node degree D_n was between 1 and 3, whereas maximum node degree was between 7 (topology 1) and 13 (topologies 3 and 5).

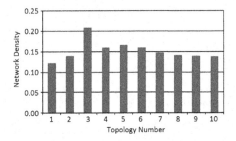

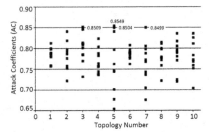

Fig. 6. Topology densities   **Fig. 7.** Attack Coefficients per experiment

Fig. 7 illustrates attack coefficients for each iteration. Across the entire experiment set the attacker was successful only three times. For all other iterations detection was possible. The three successful attacks were observed in topologies 3 and 5, i.e. the ones with the highest network density. This suggests there may be a relation between the model's accuracy and the network density. We shall investigate this in the future.

7   Conclusions

In this paper we show how Game Theory can be used to detect and prevent intrusions in WSNs. These models are applicable to a wide range of use cases, including applications of the Internet of Things, smart metering etc. We demonstrated the effectiveness of the models by two methods of validation. Firstly, with Sensomax where its results matched the ones of the analytical models. Secondly, by using Cooja we investigated the effectiveness of the detection model in an IPv6-connected network of smart objects.

As future work, we aim to extend the model to include quantitative estimation (forecasting), which could be applied on the results of the iterated game with multiple rounds. By fixating the parameters and running the aforementioned game for many different numbers of rounds, one could apply forecasting methods in order to make an approximation of a player's payoff, given the number of iterations. Additionally, we aim to conduct further validation of the prevention model and investigate its applicability in networks of varying densities as well as its scalability with increasing network size.

References

1. Alrajeh, N.A., Khan, S., Shams, B.: Intrusion detection systems in wireless sensor networks: a review. International Journal of Distributed Sensor Networks 2013 (2013)

2. Reddy, Y.B.: A game theory approach to detect malicious nodes in wireless sensor networks. In: Third International Conference on Sensor Technologies and Applications, SENSORCOMM 2009, pp. 462–468. IEEE (2009)
3. Haghighi, M., Cliff, D.: Sensomax: An agent-based middleware for decentralized dynamic data-gathering in wireless sensor networks. In: 2013 International Conference on Collaboration Technologies and Systems (CTS), pp. 107–114, May 2013
4. Ilia, P., Oikonomou, G., Tryfonas, T.: Cryptographic Key Exchange in IPv6-Based Low Power, Lossy Networks. In: Cavallaro, L., Gollmann, D. (eds.) WISTP 2013. LNCS, vol. 7886, pp. 34–49. Springer, Heidelberg (2013)
5. Walters, J.P., Liang, Z., Shi, W., Chaudhary, V.: Wireless sensor network security: A survey, in book chapter of security. In: Xiao, Y. (ed.) Distributed, Grid, and Pervasive Computing, pp. 0–849. CRC Press (2007)
6. Omic, J., Orda, A., Van Mieghem, P.: Protecting against network infections: A game theoretic perspective. In: INFOCOM 2009, pp. 1485–1493. IEEE (2009)
7. Spyridopoulos, T., Oikonomou, G., Tryfonas, T., Ge, M.: Game Theoretic Approach for Cost-Benefit Analysis of Malware Proliferation Prevention. In: Janczewski, L.J., Wolfe, H.B., Shenoi, S. (eds.) SEC 2013. IFIP AICT, vol. 405, pp. 28–41. Springer, Heidelberg (2013)
8. Tambe, M., An, B.: Game theory for security: A real-world challenge problem for multiagent systems and beyond. In: AAAI Spring Symposium: Game Theory for Security, Sustainability, and Health (2012)
9. Roy, S., Ellis, C., Shiva, S., Dasgupta, D., Shandilya, V., Wu, Q.: A survey of game theory as applied to network security. In: 2010 43rd Hawaii International Conference on System Sciences (HICSS), pp. 1–10. IEEE (2010)
10. Spyridopoulos, T., Karanikas, G., Tryfonas, T., Oikonomou, G.: A game theoretic defence framework against dos/ddos cyber attacks. Computers & Security 38, 39–50 (2013)
11. Wu, Q., Shiva, S., Roy, S., Ellis, C., Datla, V.: On modeling and simulation of game theory-based defense mechanisms against dos and ddos attacks. In: Proceedings of the 2010 Spring Simulation Multiconference, Society for Computer Simulation International, 159 (2010)
12. Asadi, M., Zimmerman, C., Agah, A.: A game-theoretic approach to security and power conservation in wireless sensor networks. IJ Network Security 15(1), 50–58 (2013)
13. Chandrasekaran, B.: Survey of network traffic models. Waschington University in St. Louis CSE 567 (2009)
14. Bedi, H.S., Roy, S., Shiva, S.: Game theory-based defense mechanisms against ddos attacks on tcp/tcp-friendly flows. In: 2011 IEEE Symposium on Computational Intelligence in Cyber Security (CICS), pp. 129–136. IEEE (2011)
15. Haghighi, M.: An agent-based multi-model tool for simulating multiple concurrent applications in wsns. In: Journal of Advances in Computer Networks (JACN), 5th International Conference on Communication Software and Networks (2013)
16. Österlind, F.: A sensor network simulator for the contiki os. SICS Research Report (2006)
17. Montenegro, G., Kushalnagar, N., Hui, J., Culler, D.: Transmission of ipv6 packets over ieee 802.15. 4 networks. Internet proposed standard RFC 4944 (2007)
18. Winter, T.: Rpl: Ipv6 routing protocol for low-power and lossy networks (2012)

Securing BACnet's Pitfalls

Jaspreet Kaur[✉], Jernej Tonejc, Steffen Wendzel, and Michael Meier

Fraunhofer FKIE, Bonn, Germany
{jaspreet.kaur,jernej.tonejc,
steffen.wendzel,michael.meier}@fkie.fraunhofer.de

Abstract. Building Automation Systems (BAS) are crucial for monitoring and controlling buildings, ranging from small homes to critical
infrastructure, such as airports or military facilities. A major concern in
this context is the security of BAS communication protocols and devices.
The *building automation and control networking* protocol (BACnet) is
integrated into products of more than 800 vendors worldwide. However,
BACnet devices are vulnerable to attacks. We present a novel solution
for the two most important BACnet layers, i.e. those independent of the
data link layer technology, namely the network and the application layer.
We provide the first implementation and evaluation of traffic normalization for BAS traffic. Our proof of concept code is based on the open
source software Snort.

Keywords: BACnet · Network · Security · Attack · Intrusion detection · Traffic normalization · Building automation · Snort

1 Introduction

BACnet (*Building Automation and Control Networking Protocol*) is an open data
communication protocol developed by ASHRAE (*American Society of Heating,
Refrigerating and Air Conditioning Engineers*), standardized by ISO 16484-5 [1]
and used for building automation systems (BAS). In general, BAS are integrated
in and capable of controlling and monitoring buildings. Moreover, BAS form
networks which can be interconnected with other buildings and the Internet (e.g.,
for remote monitoring purposes). In order to support interoperability, BACnet
can use different lower level network protocols to perform its functions [2]. In
addition to BACnet, the *European Installation Bus* (EIB)/*Konnex* (KNX), and
the *Local Operating Network* (LON) are the most common BAS protocols used in
practice. The main goals of BAS are to improve the energy efficiency of buildings,
to increase the comfort and safety of the people living or working in a building,
and to decrease a building's operational costs.

Because of the immense growth of BAS, especially BACnet, the need for
secure interconnection between BAS devices is increasing. Currently, there are
neither intrusion detection nor intrusion prevention systems which are capable
of detecting or preventing various network and application layer based attacks

© IFIP International Federation for Information Processing 2015
H. Federrath and D. Gollmann (Eds.): SEC 2015, IFIP AICT 455, pp. 616–629, 2015.
DOI: 10.1007/978-3-319-18467-8_41

on BACnet devices. Although security features for BAS protocols are specified in their standards and have improved over time, they are, as highlighted in discussions with our industry partners, usually neither integrated in devices nor used in practice. Due to the Internet connectivity of BACnet systems and the fact that BACnet devices can be found using the SHODAN search engine (cf. www.shodanhq.com), remote attacks on BACnet devices can also be performed. Such attacks can, for instance, compromise smoke detectors or other critical BAS equipment. According to [3], there were more than 100,000 Internet-connected smart devices (including media players, smart televisions and at least one refrigerator) interconnected to a network of computers, which were able to send 750,000 spam emails between December 23, 2013 and January 6, 2014. In addition, the so-called *smart building botnets* could extend the capabilities of today's botnets by taking advantage of a building's physical capabilities (sensors and actuators) [4].

In this paper, we show how to prevent the exploitation of vulnerabilities at the BACnet network and application layers. In particular, devices which interact with humans have to be both secure and safe; otherwise they can threaten and compromise human life. We improve network and application reliability and security with *traffic normalizers* (also known as *protocol scrubbers* [5] from TCP/IP networks). In TCP/IP networks, traffic normalization is capable of preventing various attacks on TCP/IP stack implementations [7]. So far, there is *no* BAS protocol for which traffic normalization has been applied. The building automation devices usually remain in buildings for decades, possess limited processing power and insecure firmware, and often cannot cope with malformed or malicious packets, hence there is an increased need for such normalizers.

We analyze the BACnet network and the application layer with its potential vulnerabilities and its potential non-compliant behavior, with the goal of ensuring that BACnet devices receive correctly formed messages. In addition, we study the well-known attacks from TCP/IP and adapt them to the corresponding BACnet network and application layer, in order to design effective countermeasures. Based on the discovered vulnerabilities, we present the first implementation of traffic normalization for building automation systems in the form of a Snort [6] extension. Additionally, our normalization rules provide a means to counter fuzzing attacks and protect BACnet devices which are are not usually updated because patching is a challenging task for BAS. We design our system to normalize traffic between BAS subnets (e.g., between different floors of a building or between separate buildings). Our normalizer implementation ensures that the transferred packets reach the receiver well-formed according to the protocol standard, without protocol vulnerabilities. The Snort extension is implemented in a way that gives us an opportunity to either limit or prevent the initiated intrusions mentioned in this paper.

The rest of the paper is structured as follows. We summarize the related work in the area of BACnet security in Sect. 2. In order to make our method of protecting vulnerabilities in the BACnet network and application layer understandable, we provide a short overview on the relevant parts of the BACnet protocol in Sect. 3. Section 4 lists several vulnerabilities that were found by looking at the specifications of the standard, together with the adaptations of the TCP/IP attacks. Our normalization rules are presented in Sect. 5. The overview of the testing environment is presented in Sect. 6. In Sect. 7, we evaluate and summarize our results and discuss future work.

2   Related Work

Earlier installations of BAS were designed to work as isolated standalone systems with minimal security features. As the BAS functionality requirements increased, interconnectivity, interoperability, and especially Internet access for BAS became significant features. However, the interconnectivity of BAS enables remote attacks. Attacks on BAS can focus on gaining physical access to a building [8] (e.g., by exploiting window or door actuators), on gaining access to an organizational intranet [9], on terrorist attacks [8] (e.g., turning off fire alarms before a fire is placed), on monitoring inhabitants [10], or on disabling a building's functionality via denial-of-service (DoS) attacks [11]. Celeda et al. [12] and Szlósarczyk et al. [13] showed that different types of DoS attacks exist for BAS. As pointed out by Bowers [14], *BACnet devices are not robust enough to deal with abnormal traffic*, since protocol implementations are vulnerable to malformed packets and various forms of attacks. The *BACnet Attack Framework* (BAF) [14] introduces attack techniques, namely attacks on the BACnet routing, network mapping, DoS and spoofing. The existing work provides a good estimate of the current attack surface for BAS networks.

In terms of defense against (some of) the attacks mentioned above, the *BACnet Firewall Router* (BFR) [15] is the first approach integrating simple firewall functionality in BACnet. BFR is an open source project that implements filters for BACnet messages and is capable of performing NAT, software-side network switching, and routing. However, the BFR does not possess any normalization capabilities. In comparison to the previous work, we present the first traffic normalization for BAS capable of

- countering typical attacks known from TCP/IP networks,
- ensuring compliance, and
- increasing robustness against vulnerability tests and fuzzing attacks.

3   Structure of BACnet NPDU and APDU

BACnet's purpose is to handle a number of application areas such as lighting, fire alarms, and heating, ventilation, and air-conditioning (HVAC) in a cost effective, interoperable, and reliable manner [16]. BACnet defines four layers (physical, data link, network, and application layer), similar to the particular functions of the OSI layers (shown in Fig. 1) and is designed to adapt to different data link and physical layer technologies to achieve data link layer-independent communication. BACnet network layer messages can be encapsulated in UDP (referred to as BACnet/IP), the BACnet-specific protocol MS/TP (RS485) or

LonTalk ZigBee. The BACnet model differs from the OSI layer model in that the BACnet application layer is additionally responsible for performing and handling the message segmentation and reassembly, a feature usually accomplished by the transport layer.

OSI Layer	BACnet Stack Protocol						
Application	BACnet Application Layer						
Network	BACnet Network Layer						
Data Link	BACnet/IP over ISO 8802-2 LLC	MS/TP	LONTalk	PTP	BVLL	BZLL	
Physical	Ethernet	ARCNET	RS485		RS232	UDP/IP	ZigBee

Fig. 1. BACnet OSI Layers, from [1]

Our work focuses on the network and application layers. Therefore, we need to introduce the addressing scheme and the structure of the BACnet *Network Protocol Data Unit* (NPDU) and the *Application Protocol Data Unit* (APDU).

Each BACnet device has a medium access control (MAC) address which is combined with the BACnet (sub)net number to form the network level address. An essential feature in BACnet is *broadcasting*. Due to the nature of BACnet topology, three types of broadcasts are supported: local, global, and remote.

	Octets	Description
NPCI	1	Version
	1	NPCI Control Octet (CO)
	2	Destination Network (DNET)
	1	Destination Address Length (DLEN)
	Variable	Destination Address (DADR)
	2	Source Network (SNET)
	1	Source Address Length (SLEN)
	Variable	Source Address (SADR)
	1	Hop Count
NSDU	Variable	Network Layer Message or Application Layer Protocol Data Unit (APDU)

Bit	Description
7	Indication
6	Reserved
5	Dest. Specifier
4	Reserved
3	Source Specifier
2	Expecting Reply
1	Priority
0	

Fig. 2. BACnet NPDU format (*left*) and NPCI control octet (*right*). In NPCI control octet, Bit 7 indicates whether the NSDU contains a network layer message (bit is set) or an APDU (bit is unset). Based on [1].

3.1   Network Layer

Even if the BACnet network layer is embedded into various data link layer protocols, the NPDU structure remains unchanged. We will focus on BACnet/IP, i.e. BACnet encapsulated in UDP sent over IPv4 [1], for which we define our normalization rules. The structure of the BACnet NPDU is shown in Fig. 2.

3.2 Application Layer

An application program which uses the BACnet protocol interacts with a BACnet peer device. The purpose of the interaction itself is mainly to invoke device-specific behavior, e.g. switching on/off a lighting device or ringing an alarm bell of an alarm device. To realize application-specific behavior, so-called objects are specified for functional behavior and services are specified for the interaction with the devices. The application layer then defines all required objects and services for a device's interaction with an application program. Notice that the application itself is independent of the application layer and is outside the scope of the BACnet ISO standard. In particular, the standard does not specify the Application Programming Interface (API).

For normalization, the relevant part of the APDU is the first region, called the Application Protocol Control Information (APCI), which is always present and whose length varies from 2 to 6 bytes depending on the PDU type. An example of a Confirmed Request PDU is shown in Fig. 3.

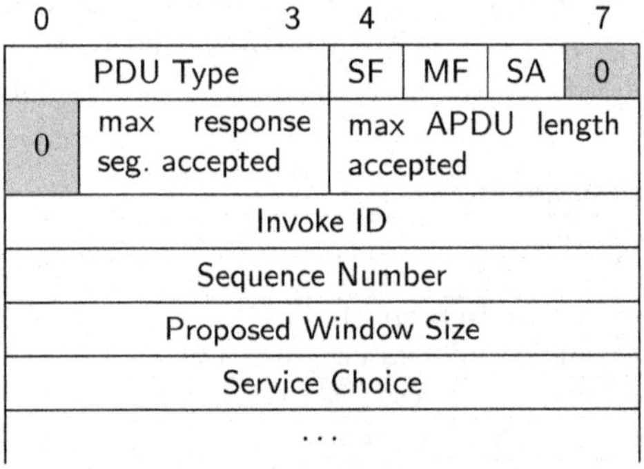

0		3	4			7
PDU Type			SF	MF	SA	0
0	max response seg. accepted		max APDU length accepted			
Invoke ID						
Sequence Number						
Proposed Window Size						
Service Choice						
. . .						

Fig. 3. BACnet APCI for Confirmed Request PDU (PDU Type = 0). From [1, p. 538].

4 Exploiting the BACnet Network and Application Layer

We base our normalization rules and the need for traffic normalization by looking at the potential security deficits in BACnet. We group our attacks on BACnet/IP into two main categories: attacks adapted from TCP/IP, and attacks specific to BACnet. Each category represents the possible vulnerabilities allowing the exploitation of BACnet devices by taking advantage of primitive vulnerabilities in the network or application layer. We give a brief overview of the general attacker model. In this model, the attacker is outside the BACnet network with a goal to exploit a BACnet device. He is sending packets remotely to a BACnet device (e.g. fire alarm, HVAC or a simple door) through a BACnet Broadcast

Management Device (BBMD), which forwards all the packets to the corresponding device. This scenario can be considered as the standard approach to attack BACnet environments remotely as BBMDs are always present to handle broadcasts between BACnet devices. The model is graphically depicted in Fig. 4 *left*.

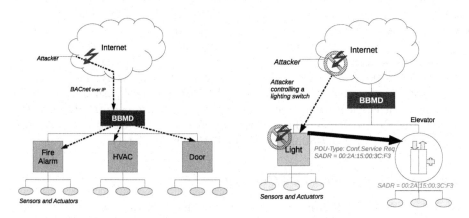

Fig. 4. General Attacker model (*left*) and an attack through a controlled BACnet device (*right*)

4.1 Attacks Adapted from TCP/IP

Covert Channels. As shown in [10], BACnet allows for creating network covert channels, i.e. the policy-breaking communication channels capable of transferring data in a stealthy manner which can enable hidden command and control communication for botnets. Disguised as BACnet traffic, malware could use BACnet covert channels to hide illegitimate or confidential data within unobtrusive Internet-based traffic.

Many hiding techniques for network covert channels are based on the idea of embedding hidden information in the unused NPDU and APDU fields. In the case of BACnet, all reserved bits can serve the purpose of embedding hidden information. Moreover, the use of particular BACnet message types and timing variations between BACnet messages can signal hidden information [10].

Abnormal Behavior Leading to Botnets in BAS. Referring to the example of a refrigerator sending spam mails (cf. Sect. 1), we extended our research to examine the compromised BACnet devices, including BBMDs. Our concern is to provide security measures for the BACnet protocol against the abnormal behavior. Celeda et al. [12] introduced two examples of attacks that can serve as a backdoor for an attacker in a BACnet network. The *WriteProperty* attack can cause a BBMD or a BACnet device to switch on/off, resulting in an opportunity for an attacker gaining access to the restricted BACnet network. In general, the *WriteProperty* attack and disabling of network connection are possible by changing values in BACnet's object properties, respectively misusing BACnet services, i.e. in application layer [12].

In addition, after successfully attacking a BACnet device, an attacker has an opportunity to use the device's communication channel within the subnet. One of the possible examples of such a scenario is shown in Fig. 4 *right*. We assume the attacker has determined the details of both BACnet devices in the subnet with the help of probing. If he takes over the lighting device, as shown in Fig. 4 *right*, then he gains the ability to transfer any kind of message he wants.

For instance, he can send a packet with an APDU containing a *BACnet-Confirmed-Request* to the elevator device in which the service-related data indicates the elevator should stop immediately. Because the lighting device is in the subnet, it is trusted whenever authenticity checks are performed, hence the attacker is able to bypass this security mechanism. The elevator accepts the request, sends a *BACnet-Simple-ACK*, and stops immediately.

4.2   Attacks Specific to BACnet/IP

Standard Non-conformance. We start by simply listing the vulnerabilities which are tolerated by the standard. We distinguish the following terms, related to the packets: *compliant traffic* fulfill the requirements given by the standard and *non-compliant traffic* contain packets that do not conform to the standard, e.g. malformed packets. *Malicious packets* are defined as packets designed to exploit a threat. Malicious packets can either be compliant or not. We present the following two examples to illustrate:

1. *Network Mapping*: An attacker is able to map the network with standard-compliant messages like *Who-is* requests. Additionally, he is able to send NPDUs containing application-specific APDU messages to probe the network. The messages with reachable destination addresses are always forwarded by the BBMD to the corresponding BACnet devices [17]. If a device understands the service-related data contained in the payload, it gives a valid response, otherwise the device returns an error. On getting a response, the attacker knows which kind of devices can be addressed, e.g. fire alarm, HVAC or a door. As all BACnet devices send responses, he is additionally able to infer where (i.e. in which subnet) a device is located since the requests and responses contain the destination and source addresses.
2. *Flooding Attack*: In this case, we consider the malformed packets, i.e. each packet must possess at least one incorrect bit, according to the standard, either in NPDU or APDU. Since BACnet devices do not drop the packets but instead try to accept and process any request, the incorrectly set bits in NPCI and APCI pose a threat to them.

   Thus, an attacker can break a device by sending a flood of identical or different packets, making the number of packets received by the device far higher than normal. As a consequence, this can cause a denial-of-service, or force unintentional behavior by the device.

Vulnerable Protocol Design. By analyzing the protocol structure of BACnet and behavior of devices during communication procedure of certain messages, we categorize the following attacks.

1. *Smurf Attack*: In BACnet, if an attacker is able to modify the source (SADR and SNET) at the network layer, he will be able to spoof the address of broadcast requests and can cause a denial-of-service for selected BACnet devices. A smurf attack on BACnet is feasible as many BACnet devices are either old (BAS hardware is seldom altered over decades) or possess substantially lower processing capabilities than today's desktop computers and smart phones.

2. *Router Advertisement Flooding*: A similar attack is possible if an attacker is able to spoof a target device's source address and source network (SADR and SNET) to send a *Who-is-Router-to-Network* message (requesting a router advertisement for a given network). The result is that the target will receive router advertisements from all the routers in the local network. If the attacker repeats this procedure and sends too many repeated messages, the target is likely to receive more responses in a time window than it can normally handle, causing a denial-of-service.

3. *Traffic Redirection*: An attacker can spoof *I-Am-Router-to-Network* [12] or *Router-Available-to-Network* messages, i.e. messages indicating the availability of a router, with the goal to redirect selected traffic over itself to gain confidential monitoring data (e.g., presence sensor data of a given room to plan a physical break-in [13]).

4. *Re-Routing DoS, Type 1*: To cause a message flood on a router R or a BBMD, an attacker can broadcast spoofed *I-Am-Router-To-Network* messages to the network using the source address of R. Therefore, all possible destination network addresses can be used as a parameter for the router advertisement. This attack forces R to handle all responses to the *I-Am-Router-To-Network* message and, moreover, forces R to handle all remote traffic.

5. *Re-Routing DoS, Type 2*: If the target device of the Type 1 attack is not a router, an attacker can redirect all the traffic for remote networks to a device incapable of forwarding messages, thus, isolating the communication of a subnet. The scenario is similar to the one where the victim's address can be spoofed in a *Router-Available-to-Network* message. It is important to mention that broadcast floods in BACnet networks can also be caused by devices which are not configured properly. At least three examples from practice are known [13]: i) the wrong setup of layer two switches that can lead to loops; ii) the use of multiple broadcasting BBMDs in a chain without a broadcast-limiting router device in the chain; iii) the combination of BACnet/Ethernet ISO 8802-3 and BACnet/IP routers within the same infrastructure configured to use the same UDP port (leads to permanent broadcast exchanges between the two layers).

5   A Snort-Based BACnet Normalizer

We implemented a Snort-based normalizer extension capable of normalizing BACnet/IP traffic based on a configuration file. Supporting BACnet/IP allows extending our work to non-IP-based data link-layer protocols used by BACnet. The Snort extension includes countermeasures for each discussed attack vectors. The rules serve to remove ambiguities within the traffic in order to achieve compliant traffic.

5.1   Standard Conformity

Ensuring robustness for the protocol stacks of BACnet devices is essential as firmware is seldom updated. Therefore, malformed packets violating the rules of the BACnet standard must be modified or discarded to achieve specificity. We list countermeasures in the form of normalization rules for the variants of malformed packets which succeed in compromising a BACnet device or the whole network, as mentioned in Sect. 4. The rules are split into five categories: NPCI field, BACnet non-security message types, BACnet security message types, APCI field, and the handling of BACnet priority messages.

NPCI Field. Being an ever present component of a BACnet NPDU, the NPCI field including the NPCI control octet (CO) can always be normalized. Reasons to **DROP** messages:

1. Protocol Version Number != 0x01
2. DNET = 0, or SNET = 0, or SNET = 0xFFFF
3. Multicasts and local broadcasts with DNET=0xFFFFFFFFFFFF using ISO 8802-3, DNET=0x00 using ARCNET or LonTalk, DNET=0xFF using MS/TP
4. Bit 3 of CO is 1 and SLEN = 0
5. Unicast message with DNET = 0xFFFF

Reasons to **MODIFY** messages:

1. Set DLEN = 0 and DADR=0 if the message is a remote broadcast
2. Set bits 6 and 4 of CO to 0

BACnet Non-Security Message Types. As explained in Sect. 3, bit 7 of the NPCI control octet indicates whether a BACnet message represents a network layer message or an APDU. Table 1 shows the possible network layer message types. We determined the following normalization rules for non-security network layer message types. We **DROP** the message, if the message type is any of the following:

1. 0x02, 0x03, 0x08 or 0x13, and 4 or more bytes follow the type field
2. 0x01, 0x04 or 0x05, and an odd number of bytes follows the type field
3. 0x06 or 0x07, and more than 4× NUMBER_OF_PORTS + Sum of all PORT_INFO_LENGTHs bytes follow the type field
4. 0x00 or 0x09, and more than 2 bytes follow after message type field

Table 1. BACnet Network Layer Message Types. Security message types are marked with *.

Type	Description
0x00	Who-Is-Router-To-Network
0x01	I-Am-Router-To-Network
0x02	I-Could-Be-Router-To-Network
0x03	Reject-Message-To-Network
0x04	Router-Busy-To-Network
0x05	Router-Available-To-Network
0x06	Initialize-Routing-Table
0x07	Initialize-Routing-Table-Ack
0x08	Establish-Connection-To-Network
0x09	Disconnect-Connection-To-Network
0x0A*	Challenge-Request

Type	Description
0x0B*	Security-Payload
0x0C*	Security-Response
0x0D*	Request-Key-Update
0x0E*	Update-Key-Set
0x0F*	Update-Distribution-Key
0x10*	Request-Master-Key
0x11*	Set-Master-Key
0x12	What-Is-Network-Number
0x13	Network-Number-Is
0x14-0x7F	Reserved for use by ASHRAE
0x80-0xFF	Available for vendor proprietary messages

5. 0x00: Limit the number of messages to m per second
6. 0x01 and the message is not transmitted with a broadcast MAC
7. 0x12 and the message is not transmitted with a local address, or if Hop-Count > 0, or if SADR is the same during n minutes
8. 0x13 and SNET/SADR or DNET/DADR is set or the message is sent to a local unicast address

Parameters m and n are configurable and depend on the particular hardware used (for example, in collaboration with industry partners we determined $m = 180$ as a reasonable value).

BACnet Security Message Types. We define rules for security messages as stated in [17]. Error messages in each case should always be sent signed-trusted. We **DROP** the message, if the message type is any of the following:

1. 0x0A, 0x0E, 0x0F or 0x11, and the message is broadcast
2. 0x0A and more than 9 bytes follow the type field
3. 0x0B and more payload is transferred than specified
4. 0x0C and
   (a) the RESPONSE_CODE (RC) is 0x06 and the length ℓ of RESPONSE_SPECIFIC_PARAMETERS is > 4, or
   (b) RC=0x07 and $\ell > 2$, or
   (c) RC=0x0E and ℓ is even and the first byte is not 0x00, or
   (d) RC=0x0F and $\ell > 2$, or
   (e) RC=0x15 and $\ell > 1$, or
   (f) RC=0x16 and $\ell > 3$, or
   (g) RC=0x17 and $\ell > 2$, or
   (h) RC=0x18 and $\ell > 1$
5. 0x0D and more than 19 bytes follow the type field
6. 0x0E and more than 21 bytes + bytes of keys follow the type field
7. 0x0F and more than 1 byte + bytes of keys follow the type field

We **MODIFY** the messages as follows:

1. Set bit 2 of CO to 1 if the type is 0x0A, 0x0D, 0x0E, 0x0F or 0x11
2. Set bit 2 of CO to 0 if the type is 0x0C or 0x10

APCI Field. Whenever bit 7 of the NPCI control octet is 0, the content of the NSDU is an APDU, in which case the APCI field is present and can thus be normalized. Therefore, we implemented additional normalization rules. We **MODIFY** the messages as follows (cf. Fig. 3):

1. Set the first bit in PDU Type to 0
2. Set bits 7 and 8 of APCI to 0 if PDU Type is 0
3. Set bits 4 – 7 of APCI to 0 if PDU Type is 1, 2, 5 or 6
4. Set bits 6 and 7 of APCI to 0 if PDU Type is 3
5. Set bits 4 and 5 of APCI to 0 if PDU Type is 4
6. Set bits 4 – 6 of APCI to 0 if PDU Type is 7

Handling of BACnet Priority Messages. BACnet allows assigning each message a *priority* [1, pp. 68]. The priority is indicated by bits 1 and 0 within the NPCI control octet (11=*Life Safety*, 10=*Critical Equip*, 01=*Urgent*, 00=*Normal*). The highest possible priority of a packet is the life safety message and can be handled in a prioritized way by the receiving devices. However, in practice this feature is rarely used. We aim to introduce normalization for packets of all priority levels if they are not well-formed according to the ISO standard [1]. Nevertheless, we must take into account that not all malformed packets are caused by an attacker, and that dropping a life safety message can result in significant side-effects if the message is not delivered but contains life-essential information. Therefore, we require that life safety messages must be modified (in order to match compliant NPDUs according to the standard as closely as possible) and always forwarded, and should never be dropped. We are aware of the fact that an attacker could explicitly take advantage of such a rule. In order to mitigate such attacks, one could require that BACnet messages sent with life-safety priority MUST always have a trusted level, i.e. they must be either encrypted or physically secured according to [17], so that the receiving device is aware of the sending device. Life safety messages not encoded this way would be dropped. This approach, however, requires the support in the devices, which is not always possible.

5.2   Prevention of Network Covert Channels

The covert storage channels that an attacker could embed in the reserved bits of the BACnet NPDU and APDU are disabled, as the normalizer clears these bits. It is important to mention that other covert channels (especially timing channels) cannot be eliminated with this approach and that many additional hiding techniques for network covert channels are available. To counter additional covert channels, extensions for caching packets before forwarding them would be required, in order to limit the capacity of covert timing channels.

5.3   Closing Protocol Security Flaws

Unconstrained broadcasting in BACnet networks is a problem and allows for a wide spectrum of attacks, as outlined in Sect. 4. In order to prevent flooding and spoofing attacks, the appropriate limits for broadcast messages per time interval must be defined. These limits depend on the particular BACnet devices and are thus vendor-specific. In one empirical study, performed in co-operation with a vendor of BACnet products, we measured that most tested BACnet devices cannot process more than 180 messages per second.

6 BACnet Testbed

Our test environment is implemented using the open source BACnet stack (available at http://bacnet.sourceforge.net) and the virtual machines, each representing multiple BACnet devices (see Fig. 5).

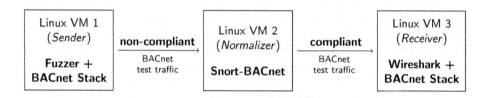

Fig. 5. BACnet testbed for evaluating the Snort extension [13]

We setup the testing environment using three virtual machines (VMs). VM 1 represents the *attacker* who sends non-compliant BACnet traffic using the *fuzzer*. The messages are first examined by the *normalizer* (VM 2) before they are forwarded to the *virtual BACnet device* (VM 3). The destination host VM 3 monitors the received packets using Wireshark.

The fuzzer is implemented using the Scapy packet manipulation tool [19]. It sends invalid and malformed packets to our test system in order to measure the behavior and the performance of the test system. The fuzzer follows the rules related to the structure of the messages as described in the ISO standard. To simulate the denial-of-service scenarios we implemented the packet sending in C, thus achieving very high packet send rates (upwards of 800,000 packets per second).

The normalizer is created as an extension of the existing Snort [6] code with our normalization rules for BACnet messages. Our extension is able to recognize BACnet messages which are sent through UDP over IPv4. Each byte of the NPDU and APDU can be analyzed in order to decide whether to forward, drop or modify each packet according to a predefined rule set.

7 Evaluation and Future Work

The purpose of implementing the testbed is to verify the correctness and the performance of the *Snort-based normalizer* by testing the prevention of attacks (described in Sect. 4). To achieve this, we divided the BACnet/IP packets into two sets, for each normalization rule (rules described in Sect. 5). The first set contained non-compliant and malformed packets and the second set contained compliant and legitimate packets. We created at least one malformed packet for each normalization rule individually. Each set was further subdivided into various subsets of different *message types*. We created different unit and generic test cases to examine the behavior of packets from both sets.

As per the test environment setup, the messages were sent from VM 1 to VM 3. For generic testing, we transmitted the messages using a fuzzer which has the capability to send thousands of messages of a particular message type at a time. This helps to evaluate the performance of the system in handling flooding of messages. We tested scenarios with between 10,000 and 100,000 messages. By using Wireshark on the destination VM (VM 3), we observed that the non-compliant messages were either dropped/blocked or modified correctly, and compliant messages were transmitted to the destination without any interruptions, so that all the received packets were handled as stated in Sect. 5. We carried out this scenario (as stress-testing) to measure performance of the destination, VM 3 – the virtual machine representing the attacked BACnet – with and without a preceding normalizer. We flooded the device with a various numbers of malformed packets. Without the normalizer, the target device was unable to cope with the traffic. When the normalizer was enabled, none of the malformed packets reached the device. During the test, the CPU load on the normalizer VM (VM 2) was below 65% at all times.

For unit testing, we created 48 non-compliant test messages for different message types. Each packet was created to test the normalization rules laid down in Sect. 5. We also created 45 compliant test messages. These test messages were sent individually to test the behavior of the normalizer VM 2. Our tests showed that the normalizer was clearly able to differentiate between compliant and non-compliant traffic and performed necessary actions whenever required before forwarding packets to the destination VM 3.

Our future work will focus on the problem of detecting abnormal behavior of infected or exploited BACnet devices. Celeda et al. [12] introduced a network flow-based detection tool and provided a theoretical comparison to determine anomalies in BACnet control flows using their network monitor tool. The authors were able to record key information in order to detect a flood. Prevention techniques, however, were not implemented in the tool. We plan to expand our Snort normalizer extension to include detection and prevention of abnormal traffic. By analyzing data collected from actual BACnet networks we will develop application-specific rules and create a state machine that can distinguish abnormal states from compliant ones. Furthermore, we plan to expand the normalizer to handle segmentation-based attacks by performing packet reassembly and caching within the normalizer.

References

1. ISO 16484–5:2012 Building automation and control systems - Part 5: Data communication protocol
2. Merz, H., Hansemann, T., Hübner, C.: Building Automation: Communication systems with EIB/KNX, LON and BACnet. Signals and Communication Technology. Springer (2009)
3. Proofpoint Inc.: Proofpoint Uncovers Internet of Things (IoT) Cyberattack. Report (January 2014). http://goo.gl/ENgpTR
4. Wendzel, S., Zwanger, V., Meier, M., Szlósarczyk, S.: Envisioning Smart Building Botnets. In: GI Sicherheit. LNI, vol. 228, pp. 319–329 (2014)
5. Malan, G.R., Watson, D., Jahanian F. and Howell, P.: Transport and application protocol scrubbing. In: Proc. IEEE Conf. Computer Communications (INFOCOM), pp. 1381–1390 (2000)
6. Snort - open source network intrusion prevention system and network intrusion detection system. https://www.snort.org/
7. Handley, M., Paxson, V., Kreibich, C.: Network Intrusion Detection: Evasion, Traffic Normalization, and End-to-End Protocol Semantics. In: Proc. USENIX Security Symposium, Berkeley (2001)
8. Holmberg, D.G.: Enemies at the gates. BACnet Today, B24–B28, November 2003
9. Soucek, S., Zucker, G.: Current developments and challenges in building automation. e&i (Elektrotechnik und Informationstechnik) 129(4), 278–285 (2012)
10. Wendzel, S., Kahler, B., Rist, T.: Covert Channels and their Prevention in Building Automation Protocols - A Prototype Exemplified Using BACnet. In: Proc. 2nd Workshop on Security of Systems and Software Resiliency, pp. 731–736. IEEE (2012)
11. Granzer, W., Kastner, W., Neugschwandtner, G., Praus, F.: Security in networked building automation systems. In: Proc. 2006 IEEE International Workshop on Factory Communication Systems, pp. 283–292 (2006)
12. Čeleda, P., Krejčí, R., Krmíček, V.: Flow-Based Security Issue Detection in Building Automation and Control Networks. In: Szabó, R., Vidács, A. (eds.) EUNICE 2012. LNCS, vol. 7479, pp. 64–75. Springer, Heidelberg (2012)
13. Szlósarczyk, S., Wendzel, S., Kaur, J., Meier, M., Schubert, F.: Towards Suppressing Attacks on and Improving Resilience of Building Automation Systems - an Approach Exemplified Using BACnet. In: GI Sicherheit. LNI vol. 228, pp. 407–418 (2014)
14. Bowers, B.: How to Own a Building: Exploiting the Physical World with BacNET and the BACnet Attack Framework, Shmoocon (2013). http://goo.gl/Ea1LZu
15. Holmberg, D.G., Bender, J., Galler, M.: Using the BACnet firewall router. BACnet Today, B10–B14, November 2006
16. Tom, S.: BACnet for a City - Saving Energy one Small Building at a Time; BACnet Today and the Smart Grid, B4–B9, November 2012
17. ASHRAE: Proposed Addendum ai to Standard 135–2012, BACnet - A Data Communication Protocol for Building Automation and Control Networks (2014)
18. Wendzel, S.: The Problem of Traffic Normalization in a Covert Channel's Network Environment Learning Phase. In: Sicherheit 2012. LNI, vol. 195, pp. 149–161. GI (2012)
19. Biondi, P.: The Scapy community: Scapy Documentation, Release 2.1.1 (2010). http://goo.gl/nPEUFx

On the Secure Distribution of Vendor-Specific Keys in Deployment Scenarios

Nicolai Kuntze, Andreas Fuchs, and Carsten Rudolph[(✉)]

Fraunhofer Institute for Secure Information Technology,
Rheinstraße 75, 64295 Darmstadt, Germany
{kuntze,andreas.fuchs,rudolphc}@sit.fraunhofer.de

Abstract. Product counterfeit is a tremendous challenge for vendors in many areas. Particularly important is a prevention of product counterfeit where products like telecommunication devices interact with other systems and thus a malfunctioning of a single device can jeopardize the complete system. This can also deteriorate the reputation of the vendor. Furthermore, violation of intellectual properties can cause financial losses. Detection of product counterfeit can be based on tracking back each device to the production process of the vendor to ensure the product origin. Devices without a verified source can then be considered counterfeit with a high potential to be malicious or of low quality. Vendors already apply vendor-specific security technologies protecting the distribution. These often employ special hardware-based security mechanisms specifically designed for a particular range of products.

This publication shows the usage of the already available Trusted Platform Module to allow for distribution channel protection and to leverage overall security by allowing the secure identification of a specific device. It also explains a few additional Trusted Platform Module functionalities that can be used.

1 Introduction

Today's international collaboration and outsourcing of production processes results in a separation of device design and device production. One example is the production of network equipment such as routers or switches. The vendor controls the design but other companies (the manufacturers) are subcontracted to actually produce and assemble the devices. Thus, device blueprints and production is not under the direct control of the vendor, but controlled by the manufacturer. One core concern of the vendor is to be able to control that no additional devices are produced and sold bypassing the vendor. The manufacturer could in principle produce more devices and directly bring them to the market. Thus, the manufacturer would diminish the revenue of the vendor. Even worse, clients might believe they buy original products and request support and maintenance from the vendor. This creates additional costs.

Furthermore, outsourcing the production and other steps in the actual creation of the final product results in perils to the vendor's business and to the

An erratum to this chapter is available at 10.1007/978-3-319-18467-8_43

© IFIP International Federation for Information Processing 2015
H. Federrath and D. Gollmann (Eds.): SEC 2015, IFIP AICT 455, pp. 630–644, 2015.
DOI: 10.1007/978-3-319-18467-8_42

end users [1]. The manufacturerers have the knowledge and technology to also build counterfeit products that cannot be easily distinguished from the original devices, but may have less quality, do not comply to the specification, or have back-doors and other malicious software installed. Counterfeit devices with low quality or malicious behaviour also cause a loss of reputation and endanger the brand experience if they cannot be reliably recognized.

The vendor is in a paradoxical situation. All information on how to build the device needs to be given to the manufacturer, while at the same time the vendor wants to keep control on the number and properties of devices being built and sold under the vendor's name. One possible approach to this catch-22 situation is to create individual registrations of each single device and track devices from manufacturer to the customer.

The identification of each single device can be based on individual vendor-specific keys to be inserted into device or on a subsequent registration process using a vendor key not known to the manufacturer. Such a key needs to be protected against duplication. One aspect hereby is that a vendor specific key is only issued to devices after production and final tests to restrict keys to devices being sold. However this would require each device to be inspected by the vendor in a controlled environment, which adds a lot of additional costs.

The state of the art is based on vendor-specific or commercial off-the-shelf hardware tokens providing random-number generation and asymmetric cryptography. These tokens are developed by security hardware vendors and included by the contracted manufacturer into the devices. Tokens can be pre-equipped with unique keys, keys can be generated within the token or the vendor can directly inject a device identity into this hardware token. Through this process each device can be uniquely identified and the vendor can track these devices without requiring direct access to the complete final device in a controlled environment.

By controlling the hardware tokens, the vendor also keeps control over the number and identity of devices being shipped or getting into the market. This approach can provide some protection against counterfeit products, but it also has some disadvantages. First, an additional piece of hardware needs to be included that has no other benefit in the product. These hardware tokens are in many cases single purpose chips and in comparison to a multi-purpose commercial off the shelf chip relatively expensive due to smaller production numbers and additional overhead for logistics. Further, the process for establishing keys creates additional overhead, because the used security hardware does not support protocols suitable for a zero-touch registration and initialization. Another option is to use radio frequency identification (RFID) tags to create unique device identities (see [2]). The drawback with a RFID based solution is that any kind of (remote) enforcement is not applicable and that it requires RFID readers at various places in the value creation chain. It might be more efficient to use general purpose security hardware in the devices that also provides more generic security functionality useful for all other parts of the device's life-cycle.

Security industry has developed various approaches for hardware security anchors. Examples include TrustZone, SmartCards or the Trusted Platform

Module (TPM) as specified by the TCG. The value of TrustZone strongly depends on additional security functions provided by the platform, while Smart-Cards are usually not integrated into a platform but considered to be removable devices suitable e.g. for user authentication or digital signatures. In contrast to this, the Trusted Platform Module is a self-contained chip integrated into the device which offers an interesting basis to implement protection schemes suitable for industry. It provides a hardware-protected identity, various security functionalities and the possibility to establish device-specific keys that cannot be extracted or migrated to other devices. The goal of this paper is to present an approach to use one type of such generic commercial of the shelf security hardware, namely the TPM, to satisfy the industry demand for IP protection and control on logistic processes. Further, this publication will show additional benefits when using the TPM for authentication-only approaches.

This paper presents a concept for the establishment of vendor specific cryptographic keys using the Trusted Platform Module. In the remainder of the paper a more detailed scenario and first requirements towards the distribution process are defined in Section 2. Section 3 presents necessary basic concepts of the TPM for the context of this use case. Based on the requirements and TPM concepts a solution architecture is detailed in Section 4, followed by an analysis in Section 5. The publication concludes in Section 6 showing advanced uses for strengthening the customer's experience as an additional use of the security functionality.

2   Scenario

Given the setting of a vendor (i.e. the equipment manufacturer) outsourcing production to the actual manufacturer (i.e. the assembler) as described above, this section provides a structured and more detailed analysis of the addressed scenario. To counter product counterfeit an understanding of the involved stake-holders and their interactions in the course of the production of equipment is required.

Stake-holders. The value creation chain of a product involves mainly Original Equipment Manufacturer (*OEM*), *Device Assembler*, *Distribution Partner* and *End User*. The role of the *OEM* differs in various business cases which impacts the counterfeit techniques suitable. In more detail, the workflow of producing a device can involve the following stake-holders:

OEM represents the publicly know vendor of the device. The *OEM* often creates the design, owns the intellectual property, and provides product liability and device support to the *End User*. Actual production of the equipment is very often outsourced to contractors to allow the *OEM* to concentrate on development and marketing and to reduce production costs.

Device Assembler represents the contractor of the *OEM* that produces and/or assembles the hardware device. This may actually be several companies not even in the same country (and not under the same jurisdiction) as the *OEM*.

Distribution Partner receives the devices directly from the *Device Assembler* in the name of the *OEM* and sells the device to the *End User*. Devices in stock are not handled by the *OEM* but by subcontractors.

End User buys and uses the device which is perceived as a product of *OEM*.

In addition to these stake-holders, the secure distribution of devices introduces additional security-critical stake-holders to the described scenario. For the proposed solution, the *TPM Supplier* is a vendor that produces and sells TPM hardware modules. The TPM can come with a security certification and pre-established key so-called Endorsement Key that also should be certified by the *TPM Supplier*. Given the security critical focus of these hardware chips, these vendors need to be trustworthy to the *OEM* and usually already have implemented secure production arrangements.

Functional Production Workflow. Ignoring the steps for anti-counterfeit solutions, the following workflow describes the production of a device from a functional perspective. The *OEM* designs a new device using its resources and intellectual property. Then the *OEM* contracts a *Device Assembler* to actually build a larger number of devices. This includes committing the blueprints of the new design and giving all information necessary to build the device to the *Device Assembler*. The *Device Assembler* produces devices according to the blueprints of the *OEM*'s design and might provide evidence, test results, production logs, etc. to the *OEM*. The devices are delivered from the *Device Assembler*'s site directly to the *Distribution Partner*. The *Distribution Partner* sell and ship the final device to the *End User* who then can register the device with the *OEM*.

Security Analysis. Given the above work flow, obviously, by contracting of the *Device Assembler*, the *OEM* loses control of the production process. In this step, the *OEM* provides the *Device Assembler* with all blueprints necessary to produce the device. After this step, the *OEM* has no direct control over the amount of devices produced or sold. It completely relies upon the *Device Assembler*'s and/or *Distribution Partner*' accounting of devices shipped. The *Device Assembler* possibly colluding with one of the *Distribution Partner* has various options to cheat in this process.

Threats. The *Device Assembler* possesses the required blueprints and capabilities to manufacture devices. It might sell these to counterfeit producers or itself produce and sell more devices than it accounts for with the *OEM*. An involvement of *Distribution Partner* and the requirement for call for bids further increase potential for counterfeits purchases by *End User*. Neither *End User* nor *OEM* would be able to reliably recognize counterfeits (beyond potential alterations in production blueprints). Thus, several types of malicious actions by the *Device Assembler* can be distinguished. (i) *Device Assembler* builds a higher number of devices in accordance with the blueprint of the *OEM*. These devices cannot be distinguished from original devices. The only difference is, that the *OEM* does not get any revenue from these devices and the *Device Assembler* gets a much bigger share. Clearly, the *OEM* loses revenue and at the same time is responsible for maintenance, warranty, etc. (ii) *Device Assembler* builds a higher number of the same devices, but sells them under a different brand name, stealing the *OEM*'s IPR. (iii) *Device Assembler* builds devices that are of lower quality, use cheaper hardware elements or have other (possibly intentionally malicious) changes to increase its revenue. This decreases the *OEM*'s revenue and also creates additional risks for the *End User* using the devices.

Security Requirements. The threats described above yield the following security requirements. (i) The *OEM* needs to be able to identify non-counterfeit products and to track all devices sold with the *OEM*'s brand. (ii) Counterfeit devices must be distinguishable to the *OEM* and (depending on the type of device), remote detection of deployed counterfeit products can be necessary. (iii) *End User* need to be able to distinguish counterfeits from original products. This might require the help of the *OEM*. (iv) The *End User* should to be able to recognize counterfeits using an offline scheme without active work of the *OEM*.

3   Trusted Computing Basics

According to the mission statement of the Trusted Computing Group (TCG), Trusted Computing based on hardware roots of trust has been developed by industry to protect computing infrastructure and end points. The TPM provides the core security functions and serves as a root of trust for each individual device.

TCG defines the currently used and market available TPM in version 1.2 but also provides a specification for the next generation of TPMs in form of the version 2.0. Both versions of the TPM design share underlying principles regarding the functionality and functions provided. The TPM is regarded as a trust anchor bound to an individual system. Trust is defined within the TCG to convey an expectation of behaviour. Hereby it needs to be emphasized that a predictable behaviour does not constitute behaviour that is secure or worth to be trusted. However, various security properties for platforms can be satisfied and controlled based on the TPM. For example, to determine the trust in a certain platform, it is required to identify the identity of the platform. The TPM provides a unique identity for a platform which can either used to directly identify a specific platform or provide for pseudonymous identification. The next sections give a more detailed presentation of how a TPM is used to implement its dedicated role as a root of trust. Specifically, it is shown how different roots of trust in a system design complement each other to build platforms with particular security properties. A more detailed description and also explanation of the TPM commands used can be found in the book by Chris Mitchell [3].

3.1   Roots of Trust

The high level concept of Trusted Computing as defined by the TCG introduces different roots of trust in the system design providing complementary security functions (see also [4]). To attest on the health of a system each software component needs to be measured beginning from the initialization of the device. In the reference design according to TCG, the initial start of a system begins with the **Root of Trust for Measurement (RTM)**. A RTM measures itself and is implemented using platform features to ensure the tamper resistance of the RTM. The RTM measures the next stage in the boot process and transfers control to it. By this, the RTM already behaves according to the *measure before execute approach* underpinning the overall measurement of the boot process and of software subsequently started on the system. The second component is the **Root of Trust for Storage (RTS)**, which is usually implemented by protected non-volatile storage within the TPM hardware. The RTS mainly has three roles. First it needs to provide secure storage for the cryptographic identity of the TPM. Second, it also provides secure storage for the keys that are used to encrypt data to be securely stored on (insecure) storage media on the platform or outside the platform (e.g. symmetric keys for bulk encryption). Finally, the third role includes particular protected registers used to store the measurement information as hash-values (i.e. chains of hash values represented by the final value in the chain.). These registers are called Platform Configuration Registers (PCR). The final root of trust is a securely stored cryptographic key (Endorsement Key EK), the **Root of Trust for Reporting (RTR)**. This key is used to create so called Attestation Identity Keys (AIKs) that are then used to digitally sign PCR content in a TPM_Quote and to certify non-migrateable keys generated by the TPM. AIKs can be used to identify a platform with different levels of pseudonymity [5].

3.2 Basic Trusted Platform Features

The TPM provides a large set of security functionalities. The secure distribution of vendor-specific keys in deployment scenarios builds on and uses authentication, attestation and protected location functionalities. **Authentication** can be easily based on the Endorsement Key (EK) that is either established in the TPM by the producer of the TPM or implanted to the TPM in a later stage of the production process. Together with a certificate for the EK, this key is used to build subsequent authentication processes. **Attestation** in this context describes the process of reliably reporting the platform status. The TPM provides the functionality for secure remote attestation. Thus, remote entities can get digitally signed information on the current content of PCRs. Protocols for remote attestation are defined in the TCG standards. **Protected Location** for keys and other data transferred to the platform is provided by the TPM. In the TPM context, the process of encrypting data with a key protected by the TPM and binding this encrypted data to a particular state of the platform (i.e. particular PCR values) is called *Sealing*. Thus, sealed data can only be decrypted when two conditions are satisfied. First, the same TPM needs to be used with the correct key loaded to the TPM (and optional the correct authentication value/password for the key is given) and second, the platform is in the correct state that the PCR values match.

4 Vendor Specific Key Establishment

As described in the previous section, TPMs provide a different kind of unique identities. These identities allow to establish secure channels to the TPMs or respectively a given device. These unique identities are implemented as cryptographic keys that are protected by hardware inside the TPMs. This ensures a higher protection level compared to solely software based solutions.

Based on the concepts of the TPM, there are several ways to establish vendor and end user specific identification keys. These keys may be generated externally and injected into the TPM, where they are stored securely, or the TPM's internal Random Number Generator and Key Generator can be used to create keys and their binding to a certain TPM can be validated. Both of these schemes are presented in this section using different characteristics. The logistics processes involved with each of these approaches are also outlined.

4.1   TPM Generated versus Vendor Injected Keys

The usage of the Endorsement Key is restricted to only very few operations. In particular, it cannot be used for digital signatures at all and for decryption only during a very constrained set of operations. These restrictions are in place, in order to use the TPM in scenarios (such as Consumer Electronics) where a unique identification of devices is not desired. However, TPMs provide additional means to establish context related identities that can be used for the given scenario of counterfeit protection. Generally, vendor established keys can be based on either of two approaches – Generated externally and injected into a device / TPM or generated by the TPM and recorded / certified in a secure way.

Key Injection. In the case of key injection, the *OEM* or *End User* create keys to be used as (context related) identification externally and inject them into the TPM. After the key injection, the keys are protected by the TPM and can be utilized as a primary identity credential for a given device. Based on these keys, the device can proof its origin and identity. This can also be utilized in other technical as well as organizational processes. To ease the process, the *OEM* or *End User* may issue certificates for these injected keys.

TPM Created Keys. The TPM has the ability to create keys on its own, using a strong random number generator. These keys are then protected by the TPM chip, such that the private portion is never known or usable outside of the specific TPM that generated it. In order to achieve an authentication against the *OEM* or *End User*, the public portions of these keys may be read out in a protected environment and stored in a database or the *OEM* or *End User* may issue corresponding certificates. Furthermore, it is possible to certify the origin of these keys using the TPM's functionalities themselves based upon previously established identity keys. An establishment of TPM generated keys is even possible remotely without a protected environment or channel, given that an identity relation has been established before using another key.

4.2   Local Establishment of a TPM 1.2

The workflow for the local establishment of vendor specific key material with a certain TPM works similarly to the deployment of custom security tokens.

The *OEM* or *TPM Supplier* generates key material and injects it into the security chip (in this case the TPM) in a protected environment. The public portion is stored for identification and the private portion is usually deleted, such that it only exists inside the TPM.

Logistics. The logistics process of physical objects (focused on the TPM chip) in this approach acts are as follows. (i) The *TPM Supplier* produces a TPM (optionally without an Endorsement Key (EK) and EK certificate). (ii) The TPM chip is delivered to a protected environment at the *TPM Supplier* or the *OEM* facilities. (iii) Local, in the protected environment, keys are created by or injected into the TPM and their public portions recorded in the *OEM*'s database. (iv) The TPM chip is delivered to the *Device Assembler*. (v) The TPM chip is assembled into the target device. (vi) The target device is shipped and distributed. (vii) Remotely, at any time after assembly (from testing at the *Device Assembler* to the *End User*), additional keys can be created by the TPM or injected into the TPM using the previously established keys.

Identity Establishment. In this usage scenario an establishment of the TPM provided identity means is not necessary, since it is used in a protected environment. The logistics process and trustworthiness between the *TPM Supplier* and the *OEM* need to ensure that a specification conform TPM is used. The TPM needs to be owned (using TPM_TakeOwnership) in order to enable its Root of Trust for Storage, which also activates the ownership of the EK for identity reporting. The *End User* may change the credentials for identity usage after deployment without invalidating the keys. The only constraint is that the ownership may not be cleared, since this would invalidate the vendor supplied keys.

Local Injection of Key. Whilst the TPM is in the protected environment at the *TPM Supplier* or *OEM* facilities, it is possible to inject vendor specific keys (for storage, signing and binding; not for identity) into the TPM key hierarchy. To do so, the *TPM Supplier* or *OEM* generate a new key-pair and construct a MigrationBlob that is targeted at the TPM's Storage Root Key (SRK) using TPM_ConvertMigrationBlob for importing. In order to do so, the TPM must have been taken into ownership before (the SRK's authorization value can be set to the "well-known secret" as defined by the TCG). This process can be repeated several times. Also, if one of the newly created keys is a storage key, this may be used for further key injections as parent. The public portions of these keys (or their fingerprint) are securely saved in the *OEM*'s database for established keys, such that they can be validated in the future. Alternatively, the *TPM Supplier* or *OEM* may issue according certificates to be shipped with the TPM and later stored on the assembled device. The private portions can be deleted, as they are wrapped in TPM bound key blobs. These wrapped key blobs must be shipped with the TPM to the *Device Assembler* to be accessible inside the assembled device (the (limited) TPM non-volatile storage area can be used for this).

Local TPM-based Key Creation. Whilst the TPM is in the protected environment, it is possible to let the TPM generate new keys using its internal Random Number Generator (using TPM_CreateWrapKey or TPM_MakeIdentity) for use as vendor specific keys (for storage, signing, binding as well as identity and sealing). To do so, the TPM must have been taken into ownership before. The SRK is one of these TPM generated keys and can be used as vendor specific storage key itself (without having to be stored in an additional wrap key blob). The public portions of these TPM generated keys can be read (from the public portion of the KeyStorageBlobs) and must be stored in the *OEM*'s database for established keys or an according certificate must be shipped. The private portions are only known to this TPM and are wrapped in TPM bound key blobs. These wrapped key blobs must be shipped with the TPM to the *Device Assembler* (except for the SRK; the TPM's NV storage area can be used for the other keys).

Remote TPM-based Key Generation or Injection after Assembly. If one of the keys that were created in the protected environment is a signing key, it is possible to remotely create new keys and use these vendor specific signing keys to certify (using TPM_CertifyKey) that the newly created keys were generated inside the same TPM and the signing key. This is similar to the Remote Establishment of a TPM 1.2. If one of the keys that were created in the protected environment is a storage key, it is possible to remotely inject new keys and use the vendor specific storage key as target for a MigrationBlob containing this newly created key via the TPM_ConvertMigrationBlob. (This is similar to the Remote Establishment of a TPM 1.2) Both of these processes can happen while the device is at the *Device Assembler*, *Distribution Partner* or even *End User*.

4.3   Remote Establishment of a TPM 1.2

The workflow for the Remote Establishment of vendor specific key material in a TPM 1.2 does not require the existence of a protected environment under the control of the *OEM*. Instead, TPM chips are shipped directly to the *Device Assembler* and the key material is established after device assembly (potentially during a testing and registration phase). It does however require and active network session from the newly assembled device to the *OEM*.

Logistics. The logistics process of physical objects (focused on the TPM chip) in this approach acts are as follows. (i) The *TPM Supplier* produces a TPM (typically shipped with an Endorsement Key (EK) and EK certificate). (ii) The TPM chip is directly delivered to the *Device Assembler*. (iii) The TPM chip is assembled into the target device. (iv) Remotely, keys are created by or injected into the TPM by the *OEM* and their public portions recorded in the *OEM*'s database. (v) The target device is shipped and distributed. (vi) Remotely, at any time after assembly (from testing at the *Device Assembler* to the *End User*), additional keys can be created by the TPM or injected into the TPM using the previously established keys.

Identity Establishment. The approach requires an establishment of a (pseudonym) identity inside the TPM. This can be done with standard TPMs that provide an EK certificate via several approaches (such as [6]) or the *OEM* may have requested certain custom identity establishment from the *TPM Supplier*. This identity only needs to account that it actually belongs to a TPM and is free of collisions. The counting of TPM identities is used to cross check the *Device Assembler*'s production accountings. As a result of this step, there exists an Attestation Identity Key with the TPM that can be used for further operations.

TPM-based Key Creation. It is now possible to remotely use the TPM to generate key pairs (via TPM_CreateWrapKey and TPM_MakeIdentity) using the TPM's internal Random Number Generator (for storage, signing, binding, identity and sealing). Then the Identity Key can be used to certify (via TPM_CertifyKey) that the newly generated key was actually generated by the same TPM that the Identity Key is bound to. From the certificate, the *OEM* may store the public portion (or the fingerprint) of the certified key in the database for established vendor keys or issue a certificate to be shipped with the device. This process may also be performed again after sales of the device at the *End User*, even with newly created identity keys instead of the previously established Identity Key. The original Identity Key can even be deleted.

Injection of Key. It is also possible to remotely inject keys generated by the *OEM* (for storage, signing and binding; not for identity). To do so, the *OEM* generates a key pair and creates a MigrationBlob using one of the certified TPM residing key. This may also include using the Storage Root Key directly. These MigrationBlobs can be imported into the TPM key hierarchy using TPM_ConvertMigrationsBlob and serve as additional vendor specific keys. The *OEM* would save the public portions of these key pairs in its database and delete the private portions, that would be saved in wrapped key blobs on the device. This process may also be performed again after sales of the device at the *End User*, even with newly created identity keys (must be TPM-based Created) instead of the previously established Identity Key. The original Identity Key can even be deleted.

4.4   Local Establishment of a TPM 2.0

With the specification of TPM 2.0 an additional key hierarchy has been introduced that can be used by *OEM*s without interfering with *End User*' use of the TPM. This key hierarchy is called platform hierarchy. With the *OEM* being the designer and administrator of the platform, this key hierarchy is exclusively used by him. The presented approach again requires a protected environment for secure establishment of some keys. Additional keys may be introduced in the future. We do not provide a remote establishment here as the necessary identity establishment is out of scope for this contribution.

Logistics. The logistics process of physical objects (focused on the TPM chip) in this approach acts are as follows. (i) The *TPM Supplier* produces a TPM 2.0 (optionally without an Endorsement Key (EK) and EK certificate). (ii) The TPM chip is delivered to a protected environment at the *TPM Supplier* or the *OEM* facilities. (iii) Local, in the protected environment, a Platform Hierarchy primary key is generated in the TPM the public portion recorded in the *OEM*'s database. (iv) Local, in the protected environment, any number of additional keys in the Platform Hierarchy can be created and their public portions recorded in the *OEM*'s database. (v) The TPM chip is delivered to the *Device Assembler*. (vi) The TPM chip is assembled into the target device. (vii) The target device is shipped and distributed. (viii) Remotely, at any time after assembly (from testing at the *Device Assembler* to the *End User*), additional keys can be created by the TPM or injected into the TPM using the previously established keys.

Identity Establishment. In this scenario, an establishment of TPM identity is not necessary, since it is operated in a protected environment. In the protected environment at the site of the *TPM Supplier* or *OEM* the primary key for the Platform Hierarchy is created using TPM2_CreatePrimary. This key serves as a root key for this hierarchy and protects all subsequently created *OEM* keys. The *OEM* reads and stored the public portion of this key in its database via TPM2_ReadPublic. This can be used for the remote key creation in the future.

Injection of Key. Under the Platform Hierarchy the *OEM* can import any number of keys for different purposes using TPM2_LoadExternal and TPM2_Import. In contrast to TPM 1.2 it is possible to also assign advanced usage policies to these keys. It is now possible to import symmetric keys into the TPM.

TPM-based Key Creation. Under the Platform Hierarchy, the *OEM* can create any number of keys for different purposes using TPM2_Create. It can then read out the public keys inside the TPM and store it in the database for vendor keys.

Injection of Keys Remotely. Using TPM2_LoadExternal and TPM2_Import of the TPM 2.0, it is possible to encrypt a new key with an established key. This way, it is possible to ensure that only the TPM that was targeted can decrypt and use a newly generated key. This allows the *OEM* to inject additional keys into the TPM even after assembly, when the TPM is not in the protected environment.

TPM-based Key Creation Remotely. The TPMs Key Generation capabilities can be used remotelyusing TPM2_Create. The TPM is instructed to generate a new key under the Platform Hierarchy. Then an established storage key is used with the concept of TPM2_ActivateCredential to attest that the newly created key belongs to the same TPM as the previously established key.

5   Analysis

The *OEM* now has the ability to establish vendor specific keys with its devices that can be used for many applications. This section revisits the requirements and analyses their fulfilment. Further, it discusses additional functionalities of TPMs that can be utilized and analyses potential residual threats in this approach.

5.1   Requirement Fulfillment

Given the requirements from Section 2 we come to the following analysis of requirement fulfilment. First, the *OEM* needs to be able to identify non-counterfeit products and can track all devices sold with the *OEM*'s brand name. The *OEM* is able to establish an identity key with the TPMs that allows it to identify an original device and track them. Second, counterfeit devices must be distinguishable to the *OEM* and (depending on the type of device) remote detection of deployed counterfeit products can be necessary. The *OEM* is able to distinguish counterfeit devices from original ones even remotely. Note the potential for Relay Attacks on this. Third, *End User* need to be able to distinguish counterfeits from original products. This might require the help of the *OEM*. Similar to the above requirements, the *End User* can request a device validation by the *OEM*, e.g. via a device management platform. *End User* help via e.g. a management platform helps in the detection of Relay Attacks. Fourth, the *End User* should to be able to recognize counterfeits using an offline scheme without active contribution of the *OEM*. If the *OEM* provides certificates for the public portions of the TPM established identity keys, then the *End User* can validate the originality of a given device without active contribution of the *OEM*.

5.2   Additional TPM Functionalities

Given the installation of a TPM there are additional functionalities that can be leveraged by the *OEM* as well as *End User*. As described in Section 3, one of the most valuable features of the TPM are the *RTM* and the *RTR*. These features allow the *OEM* and the *End User* to assert that a given version of the firmware or configuration is booted on a given device. These may be utilized for reporting but also in order to protect credentials that the device possesses against disclosure or misuse. Note that these depend on the integrity of the RTM as discussed in the section on Residual Attacks below. Furthermore, the TPM offers a certain amount of secure storage space (Non-Volatile memory). This memory can be used for arbitrary data and protected via several means, including passwords, software configuration and advanced policies in case of the TPM 2.0. Finally, there exist slight differences between the possibilities of TPM ownership between TPM 1.2 and TPM 2.0.

TPM 1.2 Ownership. In the case of a TPM 1.2 deployment, the *OEM* is required to take ownership of the TPM in order to deploy its keys. Though this still allows *End User* to change the authentication values and use the TPM for their own purposes additionally, it means that a clearing of the ownership is not possible. This may pose a problem for resale of used devices, since a clearing of ownership is the only way to protect all TPM-bound resources from reuse by the future new device owner. However, the scheme for Remote Establishment of TPM1.2 as described above could be reenacted for a resale scenario. The *OEM* would need to employ an according functionality in its management software.

TPM 2.0 Ownership. With the introduction of the Platform Hierarchy in TPM 2.0, it is now possible to completely separate the ownerships between *OEM* and *End User.* Accordingly, the *End User* may clear their ownership for resale and a new device owner make claim ownership of the TPM again without gaining access to the previous owner's secret material. Given the standard scheme for TPMs in consumer electronics, the *End User* and *OEM* interactions with the different platforms are distributed between OS and firmware. For devices as discussed in this scenario however these distributions may be realized differently, since there is no actual general purpose OS installation planned.

5.3   Residual Threats

Given the presented solutions, the following residual attacks still pose a (minor) threat. These threats are now discussed and their practical relevance evaluated.

Root of Trust for Measurement Manipulation. The integrity of the RTM is under the direct responsibility of the *Device Assembler.* Since the *Device Assembler* acts as one of the potential attackers in this scenario, it seems contradictory to entrust it with this integrity requirement. However, the given scenario in which the *Device Assembler* is a potential attacker was solved without the use of the RTM. The RTM is intended for leveraging the additional TPM functionalities as described above. For these scenarios, a potential mistrust in the *Device Assembler* cannot be technically solved anyways, since the *Device Assembler* may always add additional components into a given device that provide so-called "backdoors". This can create a majour risk for devices in critical infrastructures and cannot be prevented by a TPM. However, the identification of the device based on the TPM will not be affected and, accordingly, the risk potential for successful attacks on the mechanism introduced in teh paper is not as high, but should of course be assessed.

Relay Attacks. A relay attack could be performed from counterfeit products in such a way that devices are assembled without a TPM and any TPM-related request to this device if forwarded to an original device. In this case, however the counterfeiter would require one original device per counterfeited device, which would increase the attack costs beyond the counterfeiter's gain, and could be detected by the *End User* by the additional communication channel from the counterfeited device to the original device. If the counterfeiter would attempt to relay several counterfeited devices to the same original device (which would be profitable), then the *End User* could still detect the additional communication and the *OEM* would recognize the n-to-1 mapping between devices and TPMs, since e.g. a firmware update would be applied n times for only one device.

6   Conclusion and Outlook

TPM chips in the current version 1.2 as well as in the upcoming generation 2.0 provides a large set of hardware-based security functionality. It is a generic mass-market product and billions of devices are estimated to be currently equipped with a TPM. Many of these TPMs are installed in PCs, where they are mostly not used. The counterfeit scenario concentrates on other types of devices, such as routers, embedded systems and other special purpose devices, where hardware-based security functionalities are are often not readily available. The TPM-based approach to counterfeit protection describes a new use-case for this security chip. The process shows that the security functionality provided by the TPM is suitable to establish counterfeit prevention and detection for outsourcing scenarios.

It should be noted that the integration of a TPM as well as the implementation of the initial key enrollment process as part of the anti-counterfeit scheme can be the basis for the efficient and cost-effective realisation of various additional security processes. One example is the remote attestation of software actually running on the system by feeding measurement information into the TPM through a Integrity Measurement Architecture (IMA) [7] and using TPM_Quote to generate securely report these measurements. This information can then be validated by comparing it to the expected status available through current remote software management systems that only know about software installed through the regular process. Changes due to attacks to the device will be recognized by changed hash values for the software that is loaded. into memory and reported by the TPM. Protocols like Trusted Network Connect or trusted mobile ad-hoc networks [8] use this feature to continuously or regularly determine the health by checking the software running with reference values.

Another example of an efficient management process based on the TPM results from the ability to automatically distribute initial configurations to the device without the need to touch it. This zero touch configuration protocol [6] only requires network access and can be implemented without any pre-configuration for particular clients. Also credentials for user authentication can be protected using the TPM. In the context of future production environments and cross-organization processes, a multi purpose trust anchor like the TPM can also be used to implement strong concepts for intellectual property protection.

References

1. Stradley, J., Karraker, D.: The electronic part supply chain and risks of counterfeit parts in defense applications. IEEE Transactions on Components and Packaging Technologies **29**(3), 703–705 (2006)
2. Devadas, S., Suh, E., Paral, S., Sowell, R., Ziola, T., Khandelwal, V.: Design and implementation of puf-based "unclonable" rfid ics for anti-counterfeiting and security applications. In: 2008 IEEE International Conference on RFID. IEEE (2008)
3. Mitchell, C., Mitchell, C., Mitchell, C.: Trusted computing. Springer (2005)

4. Parno, B., McCune, J.M., Perrig, A.: Bootstrapping trust in commodity computers. In: 2010 IEEE Symposium on Security and Privacy (SP). IEEE (2010)
5. Brickell, E., Camenisch, J., Chen, L.: Direct anonymous attestation. In: Proceedings of the 11th ACM Conference on Computer and Communications Security. ACM (2004)
6. Kuntze, N., Rudolph, C.: On the automatic establishment of security relations for devices. In: Proceedings of the IFIP/IEEE International Symposium on Integrated Network Management. IFIP/IEEE (2013)
7. Sailer, R., Zhang, X., Jaeger, T., Van Doorn, L.: Design and implementation of a tcg-based integrity measurement architecture. In: Proceedings of the 13th Conference on USENIX Security Symposium, vol. 13, pp. 16–16 (2004)
8. Oberle, A., Rein, A., Kuntze, N., Carsten, R., Paatero, J., Andrew, L., Racz, P.: Integrating Trust Establishment into Routing Protocols of Today's MANETs. In: 2013 IEEE Wireless Communications and Networking Conference (WCNC 2013), Shanghai, China, pp. 1403–1408, April 2013

Erratum to: On the Secure Distribution of Vendor-Specific Keys in Deployment Scenarios

Nicolai Kuntze and Carsten Rudolph[✉]

Fraunhofer Institute for Secure Information Technology,
Rheinstraße 75, 64295 Darmstadt, Germany
{kuntze,rudolphc}@sit.fraunhofer.de

Erratum to: Chapter 42 in:
H. Federrath and D. Gollmann (Eds.)
ICT Systems Security and Privacy Protection
DOI: 10.1007/978-3-319-18467-8_42

By mistake in the initial version of the paper the author Andreas Fuchs was not included in the author list. Therefore an updated version of the contribution with the authors "Nicolai Kuntze, Andreas Fuchs, and Carsten Rudolph" has been published.

The online version of the updated chapter can be found under
DOI: 10.1007/978-3-319-18467-8_42

© IFIP International Federation for Information Processing 2015
H. Federrath and D. Gollmann (Eds.): SEC 2015, IFIP AICT 455, p. E1, 2015.
DOI: 10.1007/978-3-319-18467-8_43

Author Index

Printed in the United States
By Bookmasters